DATE DUE

10-10-06			
2-24-10			
02/22/17			
10/1/18			

Medical Anthropology

A Handbook of Theory and Method

Edited by THOMAS M. JOHNSON
and
CAROLYN F. SARGENT

GREENWOOD PRESS
New York • Westport, Connecticut • London

Library of Congress Cataloging-in-Publication Data

Medical anthropology : a handbook of theory and method / edited by
  Thomas M. Johnson and Carolyn F. Sargent.
    p. cm.
  Includes bibliographical references.
  ISBN 0–313–25947–X (lib. bdg. : alk. paper)
  1. Medical anthropology. I. Johnson, Thomas M. (Thomas Malcolm),
  1947– . II. Sargent, Carolyn Fishel, 1947–
  GN296.M423   1990
  306.4'61—dc20   89-25733

British Library Cataloguing in Publication Data is available.

Copyright © 1990 by Thomas M. Johnson and Carolyn F. Sargent

All rights reserved. No portion of this book may be
reproduced, by any process or technique, without the
express written consent of the publisher.

A paperback edition of this book, entitled
Medical Anthropology: Contemporary Theory and Method,
is available from Praeger Publishers; ISBN 0–275–93753–4.

Library of Congress Catalog Card Number: 89-25733
ISBN: 0–313–25947–X

First published in 1990

Greenwood Press, 88 Post Road West, Westport, Connecticut 06881
An imprint of Greenwood Publishing Group, Inc.

Printed in the United States of America

The paper used in this book complies with the
Permanent Paper Standard issued by the National
Information Standards Organization (Z39.48–1984).

10 9 8 7 6 5 4 3 2 1

Copyright Acknowledgment

Grateful acknowledgment is made for permission to use "The Mindful Body" by Nancy Scheper-Hughes and Margaret Lock from the *Medical Anthropology Quarterly*, vol. 1, no. 1 (1989). Reproduced by permission of the American Anthropological Association.

CONTENTS

Introduction
Thomas M. Johnson and Carolyn F. Sargent   1

Section 1. Theoretical Perspectives

1. The Therapeutic Process
   Thomas J. Csordas and Arthur Kleinman   11

2. Political Economy in Medical Anthropology
   Soheir Morsy   26

3. A Critical-Interpretive Approach in Medical Anthropology: Rituals and Routines of Discipline and Dissent
   Margaret Lock and Nancy Scheper-Hughes   47

4. Psychoanalytic Perspectives
   Howard F. Stein   73

5. Clinically Applied Anthropology
   Noel J. Chrisman and Thomas M. Johnson   93

Section 2. Medical Systems

6. Ethnomedicine
   Arthur J. Rubel and Michael R. Hass   115

7. Ethnopsychiatry
   Charles C. Hughes   132

8. Ethnopharmacology: Biological and Behavioral
Perspectives in the Study of Indigenous Medicines
Nina L. Etkin 149

9. Studying Biomedicine as a Cultural System
Lorna Amarasingham Rhodes 159

10. Nursing and Anthropology
Molly Dougherty and Toni Tripp-Reimer 174

Section 3. Health Issues in Human Populations

11. Disease, Ecology, and Human Behavior
Peter J. Brown and Marcia C. Inhorn 187

12. Anthropology and Studies of Human Reproduction
Carole H. Browner and Carolyn F. Sargent 215

13. Drug Studies
Linda A. Bennett and Paul W. Cook, Jr. 230

14. Culture, Stress, and Disease
William W. Dressler 248

Section 4. Methods in Medical Anthropology

15. Field Methods in Medical Anthropology
Pertti J. Pelto and Gretel H. Pelto 269

16. Epidemiology and Medical Anthropology
William R. True 298

17. Demography
W. Penn Handwerker 319

Section 5. Policy and Advocacy

18. Professionalization of Indigenous Healers
Murray Last 349

19. International Health and Development
Robert A. Rubinstein and Sandra D. Lane 367

REFERENCES 391

INDEX 463

THE CONTRIBUTORS 475

THE EDITORS 481

INTRODUCTION

Thomas M. Johnson and Carolyn F. Sargent

Medical anthropology has progressed beyond its roots in early ethnographic studies of ritual and religion, the culture and personality school in ethnology, the post–World War II international public health movement, and physical anthropology to claim an identity as a flourishing subfield within anthropology. Courses in medical anthropology currently are offered in most anthropology graduate programs, and the influence of the field extends to such other disciplines as nursing, medicine, and public health. Over the past ten years, there has been a proliferation of research interests such that the field now encompasses a range of concerns, from the historically predominant cross-cultural study of local health beliefs and practices to the cultural construction of biomedicine. Paralleling the diversification of research interests has been an elaboration of research methods. While many medical anthropologists continue to rely on standard ethnographic methodologies for fieldwork, there is a growing reliance on specialized techniques generated by the increasingly interdisciplinary nature of much medical anthropological research.

Accordingly the purpose of this book is to present the state of the art in medical anthropology, capturing the range of theoretical orientations, research findings, and methods characterizing the discipline today. Although each chapter references key historical antecedents to the subject being discussed, the chapters are not intended to be exhaustive reviews. Rather, each chapter is designed to trace the developments in a major subarea of medical anthropology and to speculate about directions for future research and theoretical exploration. Together these chapters represent the essence of medical anthropology: in one book providing an introduction for those not trained in medical anthropology and defining the current parameters and future directions of the field.

The book is organized into five sections. The first is a collection of five chapters addressing core theoretical issues in the discipline in order to present the breadth of current theoretical concerns in medical anthropology. First, Thomas J. Csordas and Arthur Kleinman discuss the therapeutic process, clearly a fundamental theme for any cultural investigation of health and healing. They define the domain of active response to the universal realities of disease and distress and attempt to identify common elements of healing in diverse medical systems, from shamanism to surgery. In discussing the popular subject of symbolic healing, they observe the unfortunate connotation that some therapeutic interventions, particularly biomedical, are not symbolic. They suggest that we examine both the symbolic and nonsymbolic dimensions of different healing systems. Their approach to understanding health and healing focuses on the personal illness experience and the local ideological control inherent in healing. On the other hand, Csordas and Kleinman also advocate for more macrosocial analysis that demands attention to the role of broader economic and social dynamics in the therapeutic process.

Adopting just such a macrosocial orientation, Soheir Morsy discusses the political economy orientation in medical anthropology, which she describes as an expression of a more general, politically informed, historical development in the parent discipline. Morsy explains that, in sharing this approach with anthropology as a whole, medical anthropologists have brought into focus how global power relations pertain to local health systems. She argues that the systemic orientation of political economy, with its attendant blurring of disciplinary boundaries, does not deny cultural specificity. Rather, it promises to reinterpret the concept of culture. The chapter reviews works addressing highly abstracted macroscopic and programmatic issues, as well as those focusing on the cultural expression of sickness in relation to political economic development. In concluding, Morsy considers both the status of political economy–oriented studies within medical anthropology and prospects for future research.

The past decade has witnessed a growing polemicism between the culturological and political-economic perspectives within medical anthropology. Acknowledging the validity of both approaches, Nancy Scheper-Hughes and Margaret Lock offer a unified paradigm that challenges the discipline to reconcile these polarities. They propose a "critical-interpretive" approach, which recognizes the necessity of addressing experiences of illness and broader socioeconomic dynamics. From their perspective, medical anthropology should focus on the way in which all knowledge relating to the body, health, and illness is a cultural product undergoing constant renegotiation. Thus, medical anthropology is no longer only the study of alternative medical systems; biomedicine is itself subject to anthropological analysis as a product of particular historical and cultural processes. They reject the idea of a positivist social science, which seeks to discover "objective laws" of human behavior, asserting that the "culture of science" structures the kinds of questions being asked. They assert that medical anthropology should consider the extent to which the human body is a cultural construction in order to avoid uncritically accepting some of the assumptions of biomedicine.

Much as these authors insist that health and healing cannot be understood

Introduction

without attention to individual experience, cultural meanings, and the structure of society, Howard F. Stein urges attention to unconscious processes as they affect health beliefs and practices—and the anthropologists who study them. He suggests that psychoanalytic anthropology offers greater opportunity to understand belief and behavior by investigating the interplay between conscious and unconscious motivation. He offers a provocative prescription when he suggests that medical anthropologists must examine their own unconscious motivation because of their tendency to idealize non-Western medical systems while devaluing biomedicine.

Whereas these theoretical perspectives provide directions for analyzing medical systems, Noel J. Chrisman and Thomas M. Johnson describe the work of a growing number of applied medical anthropologists working in clinical settings. In contrast to those anthropologists Stein mentioned who condemn biomedicine reflexively, clinically applied medical anthropologists more often are accused of being apologists for the excesses of biomedicine. Chrisman and Johnson, however, describe how difficult it is to translate traditional anthropological knowledge into clinically useful data. The perils of the position of conceptual translator are also discussed; the authors highlight the necessity of studying biomedicine as another ethnomedicine in order to intervene effectively in clinical work. Similarly Chrisman and Johnson respond to the criticism that clinically applied medical anthropologists neglect analysis of macrolevel concerns, essentially collaborating with those interested in maintaining the political and economic status quo, by discussing recent attempts to define a critical clinical anthropology.

Section 2 contains five chapters covering aspects of medical systems. The first three chapters consider various dimensions of ethnomedicine, a term that has connoted non-Western medical systems in a discipline that has traditionally dichotomized medical systems (traditional-modern, local-cosmopolitan, non-Western–Western, and so on). These first chapters, including ethnomedicine, ethnopsychiatry, and ethnopharmacology, hold great interest for medical anthropologists and focus on the most recent trends in the cross-cultural study of health and healing. The final two chapters in the section deal with biomedicine, and their inclusion in the same section with chapters on ethnomedicine is a conscious decision, reflecting the recent emphasis within medical anthropology not to consider biomedicine as separate but rather to subject it to the same scrutiny as other medical systems: that is, to study biomedicine as yet another ethnomedicine.

Arthur J. Rubel and Michael R. Hass provide a historical overview of ethnomedical studies in anthropology, looking at such issues as sickness etiology, healing and social control, and the recruitment and training of healers. Ultimately their goal is to show how ethnomedical studies can contribute to the development of theory and methodology in sociocultural anthropology. They also offer a provocative prescription for future anthropological research in health care: anchoring exploration in the interface between biology and culture. They suggest that the human body and its functioning, as a species-wide phenomenon, be used as the basis for comparative research on cultural practices.

Consistent with a biocultural approach, Charles C. Hughes's chapter on ethnopsychiatry briefly summarizes previous anthropological work that encompasses biological, social, and cultural levels of analysis. He then asks us to reexamine the semantics of the term *ethnopsychiatry*, warning that the cultural structuring of all knowledge and experience that the term implies is at risk of being "dulled through overuse and cursory familiarity." He deals with the cultural construction of normality and abnormality, discussing the culture-bound syndromes and extending his analysis to include the DSM III-R (the official diagnostic system of the American Psychiatric Association) as an ethnopsychiatric artifact. Underlying his chapter is the theme that any distinction between ethnomedicine and ethnopsychiatry is artificial and that by using such terms medical anthropology is unwisely recapitulating the pervasive, institutionalized Western distinction between medicine and psychiatry.

Nina L. Etkin's chapter on ethnopharmacology also is rooted in a biocultural perspective, covering topics from plant taxonomy and phytochemistry to the sociocultural dimensions of plant use. Like Rubel and Hass, Etkin raises the controversial issue of using a biomedical paradigm for analyzing ethnomedical data when she discusses the merits of studying medicinal plant use based on biomedical parameters. She also points out related areas in the literature not readily accessible to anthropologists, such as botany, pharmacology, nutrition, dietetics, and agriculture. For Etkin, ethnopharmacology promises to help us better understand the biological and behavioral dimensions of health and therefore to facilitate more cogent comparative health research.

Following on the theme that biomedicine can be studied as a cultural system, Lorna Rhodes, like Scheper-Hughes and Lock, notes how biomedicine, with its characteristic biological reductionism, presents its own culture-specific assumptions about what it means to know the body. While the biomedical view has tended to be accepted as scientific, and hence the correct view of human existence (and of sickness, as an element of that existence), there is increasing public and anthropological awareness of the limitations of this cultural construction of health and sickness. Rhodes challenges medical anthropologists who work within biomedicine not to be blinded by its aura of factuality. She suggests instead that they analyze the construction of biomedical knowledge and the functions of that construction for its practitioners. She argues that the development of a critical medical anthropology can be facilitated by studying biomedicine while working within it but only by remaining essentially bicultural in orientation.

One group of medical anthropologists who have a unique insider view of biomedicine is the cadre of nurse-anthropologists who have used perspectives from medical anthropology, in part, to define themselves relative to physicians as well as to other medical anthropologists. Molly Dougherty and Toni Tripp-Reimer describe how nurses operate with two models: the biomedical emphasis on disease and the anthropological concept of illness. Nurses integrate the social and biological sciences just as they mediate physician and patient orientations. Training in medical anthropology gives nurses greater facility to be more effective by being more "bicultural," in the sense Rhodes proposed. Finally, Dougherty and Tripp-Reimer echo Rubel and Hass by asserting that a rigorous approach to physiology

Introduction

and an understanding of the ways cultures modify physiological regularities provide a useful anthropological approach to cross-cultural research. Because of their knowledge of applied physiology, nurses can contribute to the development of more effective cross-cultural models for medical anthropological research.

All human populations exist in states of dynamic interaction with their natural and cultural environments. Section 3 contains four chapters, each addressing some aspect of this interaction that has been extensively studied by medical anthropologists. This section also takes a biocultural perspective, including the relationship between diseases and human behavior, cultural responses to human physiological processes throughout the life cycle, and the ways that people put themselves at risk for health problems through cultural practices and patterns such as drug use and urbanization.

Peter J. Brown and Marcia C. Inhorn propose that the study of disease and human behavior from an ecological perspective is a fundamental but heretofore underdeveloped area of research in medical anthropology. They suggest an approach that illuminates the interaction of biology and culture in human evolution, aids in understanding the causes and distribution of diseases worldwide, and assists in anticipating the health consequences of technological change. They discuss basic concepts and methods in the study of disease ecology, illustrating how human behavior plays a role in every major type of disease, including infectious, genetic, nutritional, environmental, psychogenic, and iatrogenic. They suggest that research strategies should address both sides of the ecological equation: the influence of disease on human biology and culture and the implications of human behavior and culture for the distribution of disease.

Carole H. Browner and Carolyn F. Sargent next argue that the domain of reproduction also bridges biology and culture, articulating with gender role issues and larger sociopolitical dynamics. They suggest that all human physiological processes are experienced through cultural filters and that anthropological studies of human reproduction should investigate linkages between a society's structural relationships and symbolic meanings and its paradigms of maternity, the products of sociocultural forces shaping maternal roles and reproductive activities such as menstruation, childbirth, abortion, and menopause. They employ case studies describing the ways societies manage obstetrical events to show how such analyses of reproduction can enhance anthropological understandings of broader cultural and social principles.

Certain cultural practices put people at risk for health problems and yet are ubiquitious cross-culturally. One such practice is the use of psychoactive substances, which has been studied with purposeful relativism as a by-product of ethnographic studies in Latin America, Africa, and Oceania and among North American Indian and Eskimo societies. With the exception of these ethnic enclaves, drug use has either been a neglected research topic or studied as drug-specific examples of deviant, albeit culturally conditioned, behavior. Linda A. Bennett and Paul W. Cook use this as a point of departure, discussing how many more anthropologists are studying substance abuse in interdisciplinary teams, with attention being given to problems associated with drug use (and development of solutions to drug abuse) rather than to only the "normal" use of substances in particular cultural settings. They suggest that there is an embryonic biocultural approach in the field, drawing upon multiple areas of expertise, which is necessary to understand the complex etiology of drug abuse and to design intervention strategies.

William Dressler continues the theme that certain cultural practices put people at risk, focusing on the more general topics of stress, social support, and disease. These issues, which have been controversial in social medicine, are particularly important for medical anthropologists who are interested in studying the health effects of social changes such as migration, industrialization, and acculturation. The chapter examines research that elucidates the sociocultural and psychological factors relating to both acute and chronic disease outcomes, following the recognition that many disease processes, including depression, hypertension, and coronary heart disease, are influenced by such factors. He challenges medical anthropologists to contribute to the identification of those variables most relevant and predictive of disease and demonstrates how social and cultural contexts modify disease processes.

The fourth section of the book contains three chapters on methodology. The topics of preceding chapters clearly suggest that, increasingly, medical anthropologists need to have firm grounding in traditional anthropological techniques and understanding of specialized methodological approaches. This is particularly true as the politics of research funding have influenced anthropologists to participate in interdisciplinary research teams. Clearly the perspectives of funding agencies have had considerable influence in shaping the directions of research methods in medical anthropology. Although not all medical anthropologists will, or should, become experts in methodological specialties like epidemiology or demography, successful involvement on research teams demands an ability to frame research questions, to conduct research, and to present conclusions in ways that are congruent with the expectations of other disciplines. At the very least, medical anthropologists can contribute to interdisciplinary research teams through their willingness to recognize the validity of multiple perspectives and to mediate interaction between the various specialists on such teams.

Pertti J. Pelto and Gretel H. Pelto contribute a chapter that is noteworthy for its rigorous delineation of current research questions, concepts, and methods in medical anthropology. While other chapters have emphasized the contributions that medical anthropology can make to theory in anthropology, Pelto and Pelto assert that medical anthropology is primarily an applied subdiscipline in that health problems throughout the world constitute a domain of research that leads directly to intervention. This research is, by definition, interdisciplinary, employing data from biological and social sciences, as well as clinical medicine. It demands refinement of conventional anthropological methods, including rapid ethnographic assessment procedures, specialized sampling techniques, use of microcomputers, and interdisciplinary team development strategies. They openly address an issue that is frequently left unstated in discussions of methodology: choice of method is strongly affected by national and international agencies sponsoring research, where proposals are often judged by interdisciplinary review panels dominated by biomedical scientists.

William R. True is an example of a medical anthropologist who has utilized postdoctoral training in epidemiology in his work. His chapter on epidemiology is designed to contrast the logic of epidemiologic thinking with that of more traditional anthropological perspectives. In demonstrating how medical anthropologists can learn to think epidemiologically, True contends that we have not recognized that epidemiology shares with anthropology an interest in understanding how human health is directly affected by physical, social, and cultural environments. He asks medical anthropologists to specify research questions more precisely in terms of independent and dependent variables, to consider the advantages of methodologies designed to test directly associations between variables, and to enhance the replicability (and hence the acceptability to other scientists) of anthropological research. The benefits of such methodologies include a greater ability to work with professionals from other disciplines characterized by quantitative rigor, which can be complemented by rich ethnographic description.

A second example of a specialized approach that asks that medical anthropologists become more quantitative in their work is demography, discussed by W. Penn Handwerker. He defines demography as the study of the causes and consequences of population growth and decline and suggests that most medical anthropological research requires more overt attention to demographic conditions through greater facility with demographic methods. Handwerker extends the ecological approach of Brown and Millar and the epidemiological approach of True by arguing that any research examining disease in human communities must inevitably consider demographic factors such as population size, structure, density, and mobility; his chapter provides an introduction to the mathematical formulas necessary for such an analysis. Handwerker offers a provocative synthesis of several areas of anthropology, including theories of human cultural evolution, cultural materialism, and demographic analysis, insisting that demographic conditions merit special attention because throughout human history they have both shaped and reflected the environments in which health issues take on meaning.

Many medical anthropologists join several of the contributors to this book in recognizing that the discipline has a strong applied tradition; one direction that this applied focus has taken is the area of policy and advocacy, the subject of Section 5. There is growing assertion that responsible researchers in medical anthropology must consider the implications of their research for the people and institutions they study and, further, that medical anthropologists can serve a useful role in translating research findings into policy statements. Many may even go further, adopting advocacy roles reflecting certain political orientations or policy objectives. Medical anthropologists who take such positions assert that their work is not only significant academically but has important implications for the delivery of health services and the health status of populations worldwide.

For example, the enduring medical anthropological interest in indigenous healers, and specifically in their recruitment and training, is reflected in Murray Last's chapter, but he also discusses the health care delivery implications of the policy of professionalizing healers in Third World countries. Last defines the meaning of the term *profession* and traces the history of professionalism in medicine. He argues that professionalization is one solution to the dilemmas healers face in confronting competition from alternative medical systems, particularly from biomedicine. His argument links the profession of medicine to the structure of the state and to cultural ideologies. Thus, national medical cultures are the products of dominant political philosophies, as well as cultural responses to health care needs. Competition from biomedicine represents a serious threat to the existence of flourishing systems of indigenous medicine, and there is danger that intellectual insights into how societies function and their inner meanings and rituals may be forever lost with the disappearance of individual healers. Last argues that no country can afford to lose the insight and creative abilities of its indigenous practitioners; organizing healers professionally is one policy alternative for maintaining their viability in health care delivery systems increasingly dominated by biomedicine.

While Last focuses on the policy of professionalization and the fate of indigenous healers, Robert A. Rubinstein and Sandra D. Lane expand the discussion to include other aspects of international health policy. They review the major health problems in the Third World, prior to describing specific international health projects and the roles of medical anthropologists in them. In discussing the potential for international health work by anthropologists, they state that such work is personally challenging and intellectually engaging but potentially frustrating. Frustration is generated by the fact that local health problems and programs are inexorably linked to broader political and economic contexts, as well as to the culture of the international public health community. They discuss a broad range of public health issues, from clean water and sanitation to the health consequences of political repression, violence, and war. Significantly, they discuss the social, cultural, and health consequences of nuclear war; they also take the position that many of the health problems of the developing world result from inequality and that the greatest improvement in health will come through public health measures rather than technological elaboration in health care. Historically, medical anthropologists have been both participants in, and critics of, public health programs. In defining future roles, Rubinstein and Lane urge medical anthropologists to work to eliminate the ethnocentrism involved in exporting health systems and to emphasize the critical role that political processes play in determining the health status of the world's population.

The chapters in this book demonstrate the creative expansion and diversity in medical anthopology over the past decade. The subdiscipline no longer merely draws on the broader field of anthropology for theoretical inspiration but is generating conceptual and methodological advances in its own right. Medical anthropology is increasingly characterized by interdisciplinary interaction, moving the field closer to achieving the type of biocultural synthesis that has long been among the major goals of anthropology as a discipline. The chapters also reaffirm a strong applied focus in the subdiscipline, illustrating how medical anthropologists continue to work at multiple levels—from individual involvement in clinical settings to team participation in international public health efforts. Crosscutting applied and theoretical research in medical anthropology are recent efforts to link microdomains and macrodomains of analysis: to be able to examine individual experiences in the contexts of both local communities and global political and economic dynamics.

These issues and perspectives imply an array of challenges for future work in medical anthropology. This book is intended to provide us with the perspectives and methods needed if we are to continue to expand our abilities in cross-disciplinary collaboration. Clearly some of the responsibility for collaboration rests with medical anthropologists. Significantly the growing diversity of interests also demands even more attention to intradisciplinary cross-fertilization. Applied medical anthropologists face the added burden of competing with credentialed professionals from other recognized clinical fields, who claim greater legitimacy in clinically applied work. This dilemma requires our continued resolve to identify and assuage credibility issues in applied medical anthropology. One fact is clear: global efforts to eradicate disease and promote health present abundant opportunities, both applied and theoretical, for the continued development of medical anthropology and for medical anthropologists to confront problems of fundamental human import.

We would like to acknowledge the generous assistance of David Freidel in the preparation of the reference section and the index.

SECTION 1
THEORETICAL PERSPECTIVES

CHAPTER ONE

THE THERAPEUTIC PROCESS

Thomas J. Csordas and Arthur Kleinman

Therapy, treatment, and *healing* are terms that define the domain of active response to illness, disease, and distress. At the broadest, they are a response to general conditions of life, as for the person who identifies the substance of her religious healing as a letting go of concerns and turning them over to God. At the narrowest, they are the application of a specific remedy to a specific and limited problem, as for the person who takes two aspirin for the relief of a headache. In this chapter we examine the domain of active response, with a view to how we can develop a comparative understanding that encompasses the global repertoire of folk and religious therapies alongside those of psychiatry and biomedicine.

The discussion will be pitched at a level more general than usual in anthropological discussions of symbolic healing. While this concept has been useful in the past, it has the unfortunate connotation that there are other forms of healing that are not symbolic. In fact, even conventional medical treatment has its symbolic component (Kleinman 1973). For this reason, rather than delineating symbolic healing as an abstract category, it would be better to examine symbolic and nonsymbolic aspects of concrete categories such as shamanism, faith healing, herbalism, New Age healing, Ayurvedic medicine, Chinese medicine, Western biomedicine, or psychotherapy.

Our strategy is to define the conceptual terrain on which we can develop a comprehensive understanding of therapeutic process, sketching out the most common distinctions and presuppositions that characterize this area of research. Next we distinguish the concepts of therapeutic process, procedure, and outcome and summarize the variety of ways in which therapeutic process has been defined and conceptualized in the scholarly literature. From there, we provide an account of four approaches to understanding therapeutic efficacy put forward by anthropologists and discuss two dimensions of process that crosscut these approaches. Finally, we offer suggestions for future research on therapeutic process.

CONCEPTUAL DISTINCTIONS AND CONVENTIONS

In introducing the topic of therapeutic process, we immediately encounter a set of conventional distinctions that we as anthropologists cannot take for granted because they encode some of our own cultural presuppositions about the nature of healing. First is the distinction between diagnosis and treatment, which separates identification of a problem from attempts to resolve it. This distinction, borrowed from clinical medical practice, breaks down almost as soon as it is applied in comparative studies of therapeutic systems. Not only is the search for diagnosis itself a form of active response, but it is widely recognized that naming a problem offers the sufferer and his or her family a degree of control through certainty that must itself be considered therapeutic. In some medical systems, diagnosis is so highly elaborated that it can be considered not just a gateway to therapy but part of the therapeutic process itself. In traditional Chinese medicine and homeopathic medicine, for example, diagnostic study of subtle variations in the patient's pulse and the description of symptoms are a central part of the therapeutic process. Clinical encounters in Chinese medicine are rarely private; the interaction with the doctor and other patients in the consulting room during the diagnostic session is also likely to play a therapeutic role. In other systems, diagnosis is either unimportant or dispensed with entirely, and the healer is required neither to ask patients to describe their problems (Finkler 1985) nor to identify the problem through examination.

In addition, some forms of healing appear to have the diagnostic function as their central concern. Contemporary North American astrologers serve a healing function by describing a person's life in terms of a celestial rationale. The treatment is the diagnosis, formulated as the elaborated statement, "This is what you are like and what your life is like." The Navaho who consults a hand trembler, crystal gazer, or other traditional diagnostician feels that he or she has done something about the illness through identification of its cause and the proper healing ceremonies needed to correct it. This is the case even if lack of money for the ceremony precludes holding the ceremony for extended periods of time. Meanwhile, the extensive diagnostic tests he or she receives at the Indian Health Service hospital remain unsatisfying because, while they may tell what is wrong with his or her body (such as cancer), they do not reveal the cause (such as killing a sacred animal or exposure to lightning).

To go beyond the issue of diagnosis in the strict sense to the cultural definition of illness, disease, and distress, it must be recognized that what counts as therapy depends first upon what is defined as a problem. Historically, new problems can emerge, recede, be discovered, or even be created. In North American society, premenstrual syndrome, chronic Epstein-Barr virus infection, and hypoglycemia are medical reformulations of complaints that in other historical epochs may have been otherwise defined or may not have been defined as requiring active response. The chronic fatigue syndrome characteristic of the Epstein-Barr infection is strikingly similar to that associated with neurasthenia in the nineteenth century but carries a different cultural meaning insofar as it is conceived as a viral infection instead of a nervous disorder. Bulemia, or binge-purge syndrome, is now identified as a pathological behavior, whereas it was a refined aristocratic practice in the Roman Empire. The definition of specific psychiatric diseases in the American Psychiatric Association's *Diagnostic and Statistical Manual* (DSM-IIIR) (1987) is a constant subject of debate and revision, with unavoidable implications for the therapeutic process.

Cross-culturally, the same objective condition may be perceived as one of distress or as one to be taken for granted. Some contemporary Christians define the experience of having an abortion as a trauma that requires healing, and some regard the habit of masturbation as a problem equally in need of healing. Chronic parasitic infections in some parts of the world are so common that they are not regarded as in need of treatment. *Latah*, long regarded by scholars as a culture-bound psychotic syndrome unique to Malaysia (Kenny 1978), is on closer inspection a condition not always thought to require treatment by people in the region of its prevalence, and in fact it has been proposed to be essentially a variant of the common startle response (Simons 1985a).

A second conventional distinction is that between medical and nonmedical healing. Encoded in this distinction are several presuppositions, not least of which is that medical healing is scientific while nonmedical healing is nonscientific. We will not take issue with medicine's claim that it is scientific, although medical research might be said in the strict sense to be more scientific than medical treatment. A more salient point is that by extension, nonmedical, nonscientific healing is considered to be nonempirical. That is, it is thought to be based on pure imagination or superstition and to be efficacious only as a placebo. One need only read Sudhi Kakar's (1982) account of how an Indian Muslim *pir* described the empirical evidence for demonic possession or Erik Erikson's (1950) description of the intrapsychic forces dealt with by a shaman of his acquaintance to realize that nonmedical healing is empirical in the sense that it is often based on systematic observation and interpretation of symptoms, suffering, cause, effect, and response to treatment. It is this empirical basis that establishes the ground for comparative study of healing systems.

Another embedded distinction related to that between scientific and nonscientific is that between technological and nontechnological. Although it is only recently that medicine has become "high tech," it is important to include cultural attitudes toward technology and the tendency of technology to dictate or encourage particular practices as an influence on the therapeutic process (Eisenberg 1988). For example, the introduction of elaborate technology for fetal monitoring has not only contributed to the medicalization of pregnancy and childbirth by subjecting women to an intensified clinical gaze; it has also created a more vivid cultural image of the fetus as a being independent of its mother, thereby contributing to the ethical debate over abortion (Kenneth Bassett, personal communication). At the opposite end of the life course, the therapeutic process encounters new illness problems as technology prolongs the life span. The role of technology in the therapeutic process must therefore be considered independently of its popular association with science, from which it obtains much of its prestige.

Yet another distinction taken for granted is that medical treatment is Western, while nonmedical treatment is non-Western. Are there such things as non-Western medical systems? The answer is yes, and one can point as examples to the Ayurvedic medicine of India and the traditional medicine of China. Part of why they are considered "medical," however, is based on yet another implicit distinction—that between professional and nonprofessional treatment. The Indian and Chinese systems have institutionalized formal training, their practitioners are full-time specialists, and they are organized in a way that sociologically qualifies them as true professions (Freidson 1970). The surprise that one feels at first learning that non-Western treatment can count as professional medicine has its counterpart in the realization that Western treatment includes far more than professional medicine. Physicians themselves are likely to be unaware of the wide range of alternative treatments sought by their patients; one study documented over 130 forms of alternative and religious healing in a single suburban New Jersey county (McGuire 1987). Lack of physician interest, often combined with active prejudice against such treatments, is perceived by patients. The patients then refrain from discussing the alternatives with their physicians, who comfortably conclude that nonmedical treatment is not so common after all.

On the other hand, "professional" in the sense we have just used it is not the same as full-time or even fee-for-service practice. Nonmedical healers often practice full time, and some make a living as healers. In the United States, medical doctors are typically paid; religious healers are not. The situation is reversed among Navaho Indians, where one pays quite dearly for the services of a traditional medicine man but receives professional medical services free at the Indian Health Services clinic. Among participants in the contemporary charismatic renewal movement, Christian counselors and clinicians who combine psychotherapy and faith healing are sometimes caught in a conflict between the roles of healer operating for free and therapist charging a fee.

When we turn to the domain of nonmedical treatment, we find that it too is defined in ways that implicitly distinguish it from medical treatment. Foremost among assumptions about nonmedical treatment is that it is essentially religious, whereas medical treatment is nonreligious. If religion is defined in terms of encounter with the sacred, this assumption is problematic since nonmedical practitioners such as herbalists or bonesetters may operate in a very instrumental, purely technical idiom. It is equally in error to read religious meaning into forms of healing that are not religious or to reduce the religious meaning of sacred healing to its medical or clinical significance. The latter error is by far more common. In fact, a paradoxical situation has come about in medical anthropology in which nonmedical forms of healing are explicitly acknowledged as religious but analysis then abandons the explicitly religious to focus on "therapeutic aspects of" healing. Moreover, this is more true of Anglo-American than of French anthropology (Csordas 1987), indicating that the empirical question of religion in healing is clouded by methodological predispositions of varying schools. A valuable corrective would be development of a theory of religion in relation to health.

Another categorical presupposition is that nonmedical forms of healing are more characteristic of stable, traditional societies than of complex industrial societies. Recent advances in the study of complex health care systems that stress the relations among professional, folk, and popular forms of healing (Kleinman 1980) and analyses of medical pluralism (Janzen 1987b; Mullings 1984) appear to transcend this simplistic view. Yet the shaman operating in a "pristine" tribal ambience remains the prototype for scholars writing on these forms of healing. An important consequence for the study of therapeutic process is failure to distinguish clearly between traditional forms of healing such as shamanism and healing movements such as faith healing. The latter are not exclusive to industrialized, developed societies but are distinct from traditional healing in that they recruit adult participants. Unlike the prototypic case of a small-scale society where people take for granted and are familiar from birth with the shaman as healer (although they may be ignorant of the shaman's specialized knowledge), adult recruits to healing movements may never before have considered the possibility of divine healing, requiring secondary socialization to establish a predisposition toward such healing. In addition, unlike healing in traditional societies, such movements typically attract two quite distinct groups, one consisting of committed disciples and the other of marginal participants seeking relief for particular complaints.

PROCEDURE, PROCESS, OUTCOME

Having introduced the topic in terms of a broad network of concepts, we will begin to narrow the focus of our discussion by distinguishing therapeutic process from therapeutic procedure on the one hand and from therapeutic outcome on the other. Procedure (actions taken) and outcome (results obtained) are relatively easy to define and will be dealt with first. We then turn to the concept of process, inherently more complex and used in a variety of ways. We will review four common conceptions of therapeutic process as (1) the course of a treatment event, (2) a sequence of experiential or intrapsychic phenomena, (3) the course of an illness episode, and (4) social and ideological control exercised through healing practice.

Therapeutic procedure can be defined in terms of who does what to whom with respect to medicines administered, physical techniques or operations carried out, prayers recited, symbolic objects manipulated, altered states of consciousness induced or invoked. It is the organized application of techniques with some goal in mind. The shaman may go into trance and take a mystic journey to retrieve the soul of the afflicted or suck on an afflicted part of the patient's body in order to remove an intrusive spiritual object. The native American patient may be treated with a combination of sweat emetic, herbal teas, and ritual chants in order to achieve purification. The psychoanalytic patient is instructed to say whatever comes to mind, and this free association is expected to bring important repressed contents of the unconscious into the scrutiny of the clinical gaze. The surgeon grafts a portion of a vein from the leg into a patient's aorta and coronary arteries, and this coronary bypass is expected to renew the restricted blood flow to the patient's heart. The patient at the temple of Asclepius in ancient Greece offered sacrifices and fell into a sleep during which the god appeared, and this "incubation" was expected to heal the person spontaneously or reveal instructions to follow for a healing. The anthropological literature is replete with descriptions of therapeutic procedures, and in fact such descriptions are much more common than are descriptions of what we shall define as therapeutic process in a strict sense. Familiarity with the ethnographic inventory of therapeutic procedures is essential, but a comprehensive survey of such procedures is beyond the scope of this chapter.

Therapeutic outcome refers to the disposition of participants at a designated endpoint of the therapeutic process, with respect to both their expressed (high or low) satisfaction and to change (positive or negative) in symptoms, pathology, or functioning. It is a remarkably complex phenomenon to study due to the immense number of factors to be taken into account and the difficulty of controlling observer effects. Models for such studies from clinical research include double-blind clinical trials of drugs and comparative studies of psychotherapy, but these are only marginally appropriate for the forms of healing and kind of contexts typically studied by anthropologists. The methodological problems are evident in a study that attempted to determine the therapeutic outcome of healing by prayer by means of a double-blind clinical trial (Joyce and Welldon 1965). For the sake of controlling the effect of suggestion, the researchers eliminated direct contact between the prayer group and their patient, thereby fundamentally altering the natural context of therapy in a way unacceptable to anthropological research. The results were inconclusive.

Psychotherapy researchers have executed systematic comparative outcome studies on different forms of psychotherapy (Luborsky et al. 1985, 1986). Anthropologists' analyses of efficacy in ritual healing paint a much broader picture, ranging from the conclusion that healing is invariably and necessarily effective due to the manner in which its problems are defined (Kleinman and Sung 1979) to the conclusion that it fails to fulfill its claims insofar as it is more a treatment of life-style than of symptoms (Pattison et al. 1973). Anthropologists have only recently and very tentatively attempted systematic studies of outcome, and these are based on patient reports of symptom improvement (Finkler 1985) or expression of their degree of satisfaction with treatment (Kleinman and Sung 1979; Kleinman and Gale 1982). The finding that those treated sometimes maintain their symptoms while at the same time claiming satisfaction bespeaks fundamental conceptual difficulties in the very definition of outcome. Thus it is necessary to take a step backward from assessment of outcome to more systematic descriptive analysis of therapeutic process. In this way anthropologists may come to a more systematic understanding of what might count as efficacy across diverse forms of healing.

Having defined therapeutic procedure and outcome, we can identify at least four distinct senses in which the concept of therapeutic process has been used. The first is process as the unfolding of a specific treatment event. For anthropologists this has typically been a ritual event, and much anthropological literature on healing can be seen as a subset of the literature on ritual. In this genre, the idea of therapeutic process is analogous to the idea of ritual process, the prototype of which is the rite of passage (Turner 1969). Process is understood as the sequence of actions, phases, or stages undergone by the participants. For most contemporary researchers on psychotherapy, on the other hand, process within therapeutic events is constituted by elements of verbal interaction (Labov and Fanshel 1977) and interpersonal relationship between therapist and client (Rogers et al. 1967). Psychotherapy researchers have argued that the relationship between therapist and client is critical for success (Gelso and Canter 1985; Rogers et al. 1967), while some anthropologists point out that the relationship between ritual healers and their clients is frequently superficial (Finkler 1985).

A second conceptualization is in terms of experiential or intrapsychic process, with a focus on the sequence of mental states, the emergence of insight, interpretation of religious experience, and endogenous symbolic or somatic processes. To date, most work from this perspective by anthropologists has focused on the experience of the healer (Noll 1983; Peters and Price-Williams 1980; Peters 1981), although the experience of the patient is beginning to be addressed (Csordas 1988a). While some work in this perspective remains event based, it is more disposed to recognize that therapeutic process often extends beyond the event itself. This is certainly the case in insight-oriented therapies where the significance of some part of the event may become clear only later and in any therapy where change is dependent on the response of others in the social milieu of the afflicted. In Chinese medicine, practitioners have resisted the introduction of herbal remedies in pill form since it is recognized that ritual preparation of teas and infusions is part of the therapeutic process, with the smell of brewing medicine alerting neighbors to the presence of illness and thus attracting community support for the afflicted person.

In the work of Janzen (1978b, 1987) and others, therapeutic process is taken in a third sense—that of progression or course of an illness episode, defined by a sequence of decisions leading to diagnosis and treatment. This work broadens the notion of process to include not only the patient and therapist but the network of people who may be engaged with varying degrees of responsibility in the decision-making process, termed the therapy management group. This work also places therapeutic process squarely in the context of medical pluralism, emphasizing the way therapy management groups negotiate about the use of multiple health resources and, by extension, the interaction or complementarity among those resources. Along with other work on "hierarchies of resort" (Romanucci-Ross 1969) to various sources of healing, it represents the actors' perspective on navigating through a sea of therapeutic choices. The complementary perspective of social organization is represented by analyses of health care systems as complexes of health care resources in a society that may interact in ways that are complementary or contradictory (Fabrega 1976; Field 1976; Kleinman 1980; Leslie 1976). Arthur Kleinman has described the typical structure of health care systems in complex societies in terms of the relation among sectors composed of professionalized healing forms, folk or traditional specialties, and popular health care, including the knowledge and practices of communities, families, and individuals.

A final sense of process that we shall consider is political, that is, the sense in which therapy and healing articulate with broader social issues and concerns. The role of therapy management groups is not only one of support and assistance for the afflicted but one of social control of the patient and ideological control of the values implicit in therapy and illness behavior. This is worked out in the process of deciding which treatments to use and in which order, as well as which are inappropriate and to be ruled out. Victor Turner's (1964) early work on Ndembu healing also emphasized that the process was one of intervention in community relationships as much as attention of the problems of a specific afflicted individual.

A more macrosocial understanding of therapeutic process as political begins when one recognizes the existence of broader economic and social regulatory constraints on the structure of a therapeutic system. These constraints become most evident in situations of radical restructuring of a health care system, such as in the changes in Nicaragua following the 1979 overthrow of the dictator Somoza (Donahue 1986a). In other situations, sociopolitical constraints may not be explicit and may even be invisible on the level of specific therapeutic action. Hence they constitute an important challenge to cultural analysis and critique, which often focus on interpersonal interaction in discrete events.

The opposite possibility is that a reaction to and commentary on the human world in which affliction arises can be built into the structure of therapy itself. Such a perspective is offered in Michael Taussig's (1987) analysis of shamanistic healing in Colombia and Jean Comaroff's (1985) of evangelistic healing in South Africa. Both vividly set against the background of colonial oppression, these works show the inevitable reflection of ambient social conflict and power relations in practices ostensibly directed at individual suffering. Just as the therapeutic process extends beyond specific events into the broader social world of the participants, so also the world is embedded in the therapeutic process.

MODELS OF THERAPEUTIC EFFICACY

Anthropological studies of therapeutic outcome are in a very early stage of development. Lack of progress in determining the degree of success of traditional therapies, however, has not precluded analyses of how those therapies might work. Indeed, despite the inability of researchers to determine definitive outcomes, the very fact that people continue to have recourse to such forms of treatment suggests that they produce some kind of effect, and it remains relevant to search for definitions of that efficacy. In this section we outline the principal anthropological approaches to this problem. One or more of these approaches underlies virtually any anthropological analysis of healing. They should be seen not as mutually exclusive alternatives but as emphases that have appeared in various combinations in the literature.

The *structural* emphasis posits the existence of interrelated analytic levels such as body-emotion-cognition or person-society-culture. The classic example of this approach is Claude Levi-Strauss's (1963c) discussion of how a Cuna pregnancy chant recapitulates on a symbolic level the physiological process of childbirth. The chant includes a narration in which the characters represent reproductive organs, and their actions represent the progression of the fetus through the birth canal. The principle of efficacy in this interpretation is the inherent power of a correspondence or homology between symbolic acts and objects, metaphors, or cosmological structure, and the thoughts, emotions, or behavior of those treated. Researchers in this tradition are often successful in demonstrating the existence of a homology but not in establishing why or whether the homology has an effect.

In a variant of this model, efficacy is said to derive from a transaction of symbol, meaning or emotion between structural levels. In James Dow's (1986) influential formulation, therapeutic process begins with the particularization of mythic symbols to the level of the person, which is to say in effect that healing makes sense of individual distress in terms of broader cultural meanings. The critical therapeutic transaction that ensues is an abstract transaction of emotions between self and somatic levels of the structural hierarchy (cf. Kleinman 1988a). Note that while usually the term *transaction* pertains to exchange between actors, in this context transaction is a form of internal communication. This internal communication is predicated on a tendency in the structural approach to reify the social, self, and somatic conceptually such that one must then specify mechanisms of bridging and transacting between them. The consequence of separating self and body is to preclude conceptualizing a nondualistic body-self (Scheper-Hughes and Lock 1987, Kleinman 1988a), for if all processes are already body-self processes, it becomes moot to specify distinct parties to the transaction.

This abstract character creates a difficulty with the structural emphasis when it is not combined with any of the others we shall be discussing. It appears better suited to explain the efficacy of types of ritual such as rites of passage, where what the rite brings about is either a social fait accompli (such as marriage) or a biological inevitability (such as puberty). Using the structural approach, data can be collected primarily from observation of rituals and interviews with ritual specialists, ignoring the concrete experience of the person in distress and his or her therapy management group. To claim that establishing a homology or carrying out a symbolic transaction is inherently efficacious does not go far beyond the indigenous explanation of healing based solely on the inherent spiritual or supernatural forces mobilized by the healing process.

The *clinical* emphasis is based on the analogy between the traditional healer and a doctor treating an individual patient for a specific illness with a specific treatment in expectation of a definitive outcome. A paradigmatic example is Raymond Prince's (1964) analysis of indigenous Yoruba psychiatry as practiced by ritual specialists in which the analogy to psychiatry is tightly drawn, in terms of specific techniques and elements of efficacy. In a broader cross-cultural survey of ritual therapeutic procedures and their variations, Prince (1980) includes sleep, rest, isolation, dreams, meditation and mystical states, dissociation, and shamanic ecstasy. Despite the existence of such a broad repertoire of techniques, however, arguments about efficacy typically fall back on properties of nonspecific mechanisms such as suggestion (Calestro 1972), catharsis (Scheff 1979), or placebo effect. This inability to identify specific effect in clinical terms begs the question of whether traditional healing has its own forms of specificity.

Except in situations where ethnopharmacological treatment is used, definitive outcomes are rarely observed. Yet rather than being nonspecific, it may better be said that the results of ritual healing are often incremental and inconclusive. That is, quite specific but small and step-by-step effects may be documented, with the result remaining open-ended and characterized by some change but no definitive "cure" (Csordas 1988a). This kind of change is easily overlooked if the focus is on "therapeutic aspects of" ritual healing (Murphy 1964; Messing 1958; Kennedy 1967), following a clinical model in which distress is systematically medicalized as sickness, while the essential character of ritual healing as religious experience is deemphasized (Csordas 1987). If indeed there is a specificity to ritual healing, it may be discovered precisely in its religious rather than its clinical "therapeutic" dimension.

Another interpretation, or group of interpretations, are those which attribute therapeutic efficacy to *social support*. The classic example is V. Turner's (1964) analysis of Ndembu healing in which he shows that therapeutic efforts are directed at conflictual social relationships that have engendered symptomatic manifestations. In this analysis it can be said that the social group, not the individual, is the "patient." The mirror image of this argument is Vincent Crapanzano's (1973) demonstration that a distressed individual is cured by the Moroccan Hamadsha cult by being absorbed into a new social group. Here, healing is a form of social support so encompassing as to constitute a symbiotic relationship among participants and between the afflicted person and a possessing spirit or demon.

Beyond these paradigmatic statements, a substantial body of work examines the proposition that participation in the religious milieu itself has a beneficial effect on health (Levin and Vanderpool 1987). Since many of these studies ask nonspecific questions, they often come up with broadly general conclusions, such as that ritual healing is a treatment of life-style rather than of organic pathology (Pattison et al. 1973) or that religious practices in general have a therapeutic effect on a globally defined existential demoralization (Ness 1980). Studies of religious healing among immigrant groups in the United States, particularly Hispanic Americans, examine the circumstances of resort to and the range of illnesses treated by religious healing (Koss 1975; Harwood 1977a, 1977b; Garrison 1977a; Halifax and Weidman 1973; Sandoval 1979). While the religious dimension of these healing forms is explicitly recognized, there is typically an implicit functionalist orientation so that religion is seen almost exclusively in terms of its promotion of community solidarity and social support of suffering individuals.

The *persuasive* emphasis owes much to Jerome Frank's (1973) formulations concerning the cultivation of expectant faith through the personal influence of a healer or the ideology of the healing form and the rhetorical devices that bring about a shift in the person's "assumptive world," or set of assumptions about the nature of the world that allow a person to predict both the behavior of others and the outcome of his or her own actions. In this approach, the primary effect of therapeutic process is to transform the meaning of an illness for the sufferer (Bourguignon 1976). Healing ritual is understood not as liturgical repetition but as intentional social action directed toward the quality and content of experience.

Continuous with Frank's insight is the work in interpretive anthropology that analyzes rituals not as text but as performance (Csordas 1983; Kapferer 1979a, 1979b; 1983; Schieffelin 1985; Tambiah 1981). These works raise issues of subjective experience among ritual participants, impacts of utterance and action carried out within specific ritual genres, and performative transformation of context as well as of meaning. The form of healing ritual is understood in terms of rhetoric and language, and its content is understood in terms of image and symbol. While this approach has allowed researchers to highlight changes in assumptive worlds, it is generally less attuned to clinical issues and the analogy between ritual healing and psychotherapy.

These methodological approaches are by no means mutually exclusive. For example, in the article by Levi-Strauss (1963c) cited above as paradigmatic of the structural approach, we also find the clinical interpretation invoked in his identification of the psychological defense mechanism of abreaction. Levi-Strauss argues that the patient relives fundamental intrapsychic conflicts evoked in ritual performance, thereby resolving them. Stanley Tambiah's (1977) interpretation of a Thai Buddhist healing cult invokes the homology between personal aspects of illness and an "enduring cosmic paradigm of theodicy and tranquillity" (1977:123) yet at the same time acknowledges the persuasive experience of mystical power among participants. Prince (1982) searches for the biomedical, or more precisely psychophysiological, sources of shamanistic healing in the release of endogenous opiates but in his discussion of endogenous processes also suggests links among physiological, intrapsychic, and cultural domains (Prince 1976). New permutations continue to appear based not only on the methodological predispositions of ethnographers but on the actual diversity among healing forms that invites a diversity of analytic emphases.

DIMENSIONS OF THERAPEUTIC PROCESS

In this section we examine two dimensions of process that crosscut the framework of structural, clinical, social, and persuasive approaches to therapeutic efficacy. The first we shall define as that of discursive-presentational form, referring to the manner in which participants become engaged in therapeutic process. The second we define as specificity-generality in effect, referring to the manner in which therapy formulates and addresses problems or illnesses.

The distinction between discursive and presentational form stems from the work of Suzanne Langer (1957). Discursive form is that of language, understood as a succession of interrelated concepts with consistent internal logic and rationality. Presentational form is characteristic of symbol and metaphor, wherein the meanings are simultaneous and integral and of that kind of intuitive knowledge "which the mind reads in a flash, and preserves in a disposition or an attitude" (1957:98). Therapeutic process can be conceived along a continuum between these forms, with, for example, the "talking cure" of psychoanalysis occupying the discursive pole and healing based on a symbolic gesture such as "laying on of hands" occupying the presentational pole.

A closely related issue Jerome Neu (1977) raised is the degree and nature in which different forms of therapy engage thought processes of the participants. Neu contrasts psychoanalysis with electroconvulsive shock therapy in this respect, but it is not enough to understand the thought-nonthought continuum as simply one between verbal or cognitive modes and nonverbal or somatic modes. Psychoanalysis and behaviorist therapies also contrast in these terms insofar as the former attributes therapeutic efficacy to insight and the latter to conditioning. In addition, it is not enough to focus on the engagement of thought processes alone to the exclusion of emotional and self processes. Indeed the critical question about engagement in therapeutic process may be the way in which thought, emotion, self, and other are integrated.

It must also be acknowledged that any particular type of healing may make use of both forms in succession or combination, as in Sinhalese exorcism rites that alternate discursive narrations and conversational sequences with presentation of demonic characters and symbolic objects (Kapferer 1979a, 1979b, 1983). In Catholic Pentecostal religious healing, methods range from purely discursive sequences of counseling, to narrative unfolding of affectively rich sensory imagery, to the nondiscursive motor dissociation and submergence in the healing sense of divine presence known as "Resting in the Spirit" (Csordas 1983, 1988a). In traditional Navaho medicine, healing ceremonies or "signs" require the patient's participation in as many as nine consecutive nights of chants, prayers, and the rich symbolism of sacred sand paintings, while in the relatively nondiscursive "sucking cure," the medicine man removes a piece of bone or flint allegedly inserted to do harm by a witch who typically remains anonymous (Sandner 1979; Kunitz and Levy 1981). To determine the precise role of thought and emotion in any of these healing forms is an important task of research in therapeutic process, since it is no more the case that insight, for example, is any more inherently effective than the homology between structural levels.

The dimension of specificity and generality in therapeutic process has been cogently presented by Daniel Moerman (1979b). The prototype of specific treatment is, of course, the pharmacologic agent that reverses an organic condition or destroys a pathogen. Moerman defines general treatment empirically in terms of a patient perceiving a field of symbols created by a healer, whether shaman or psychiatrist, and theoretically in terms of the relationship between mind and body, symbol and substance. He cites research on psychosomatic illness, biofeedback, and immunology, as well as links among the body's neural, endocrine, and autonomic systems, to suggest not only the existence of pathways linking body and mind but that these pathways are the locus for broad-based influence of metaphor and symbol on biological processes.

The prototypes for identification of nonspecific dimensions of therapeutic process are voodoo death and the placebo effect. W. B. Cannon (1942) explained death by witchcraft as a generalized reaction of the central nervous system ("fight or flight response") to the severe trauma provoked in someone who believed that he or she was bewitched. This analysis was strengthened by Hans Selye's (1956) definition of the body's response to stress ("General Adaptation Syndrome") and refined in subsequent analyses of the destructive interaction in such cases between sympathetic and parasympathetic nervous systems (Lex 1974). The inverse of voodoo death as a nonspecific response is the placebo effect. A placebo is typically defined as an inert substance or practice that has a general effect, although in fact it is general not for lack of a detectable or measurable therapeutic impact but in that there is no definite causal link between the treatment and its effect. The placebo effect can be understood as an effect of interpersonal communication, activating endogenous healing processes inherent in all human beings (Prince 1980; Hahn and Kleinman 1983; Moerman 1983b). Among these endogenous processes, one that has been singled out in both medical studies of placebo analgesia (Levine, Gordon, and Fields 1978) and anthropological studies or religious healing (Prince 1982) is the release of endorphins or endogenous opiate substances by the body itself. Nevertheless, as Howard Brody (1980) has argued, the placebo effect remains an anomaly of a magnitude that has in the history of science led to serious challenges to basic presuppositions and assumptions.

Daniel Moerman (1979b) has shown that even surgery, commonly regarded as a highly specific medical treatment, has a great deal of metaphoric meaning and that in some instances its effectiveness appears due in part to a generalized placebo effect. His observation that the surgical "laying on of steel" is in some ways parallel to the ritual laying on of hands requires us to acknowledge that contemporary biomedicine has a symbolic dimension (cf. also Kleinman 1973). However, it is less frequently acknowledged that religious healing and even psychotherapy may have their own forms of specificity. When the issue is broached, the terms remain ambiguous. With regard to psychotherapy, for instance, C. H. Patterson (1985) has argued that while the therapist variables of perceived expertness, attractiveness, and trustworthiness are essentially placebos, empathic understanding, warmth or respect, and genuineness have quite specific effects. With regard to religious healing, discussion of therapeutic specificity remains limited to certain kinds of transformations in meaning (Bourguignon 1976; Csordas 1988a; Kapferer 1983) and resolutions of social conflict (Turner 1964, 1968).

Catharsis, or the discharge of negative emotional energy, is another widely reported psychological process that can be understood as specific or nonspecific. While it is most often described as nonspecific, this may be due more to lack of detailed data about therapeutic process in the kinds of healing typically described by anthropologists. Thomas Scheff (1979) has attempted to formulate catharsis more concretely as contingent on the creation in the therapeutic process of an aesthetic distance between the person and the problematic emotion, such that he or she is neither overinvolved nor detached from that emotion. Such a precondition for successful catharsis implies specificity about the relation between emotion and life situation, but this relation is in turn dependent on the relation of thought and emotion in therapeutic process.

Do some forms of general treatment only appear to be so because our research methods are not sophisticated enough to capture their specificity? Are we hopelessly muddled about our own definitions of what counts as a specific effect? Or are some treatments irreducibly general because they treat a problem that is itself generalized and diffuse? The last answer is given for both psychotherapy and religious healing in J. Frank's (1978) formulation of the demoralization hypothesis. Demoralization is understood to characterize all persons who come to the therapeutic process and is characterized by the inability to cope with a life situation, leading to constriction of the life space and preoccupation with threat, depression, self-blame, guilt, and shame. Frank argues that all forms of healing contain elements that counteract this condition, as well as elements that address specific symptoms. Even so, it remains to specify those elements and precisely how they counter particular aspects of the demoralization syndrome.

DIRECTIONS FOR RESEARCH

Perhaps the most frequently encountered assertion in the literature on therapeutic process is that there exists an analogy between psychotherapy and religious or folk healing. In contemporary medical anthropology, this analogy can be traced back at least as far as Simon Messing's (1958) analysis of the Ethiopian *zar* cult as an equivalent of the group therapy then achieving popularity in the United States. The touchstone work for authors invoking the psychotherapy analogy in the 1960s and 1970s was Frank's analysis of the role of assumptive worlds, expectant faith, placebo effect, and demoralization. The seminal work for the 1980s became Scheff's (1979) analysis of catharsis in ritual and therapy. While these works offer valuable theoretical formulations, most studies make use of them only to invoke the psychotherapy analogy. To our knowledge, there has been no direct examination of this analogy through empirical comparison of psychotherapy and religious healing.

This is clearly a critical area for future research in the field. Such research must include comparison of institutional settings, characteristics of interpersonal interaction among participants, characteristics of practitioners and patients, idioms of therapeutic communication, definitions of clinical reality, and therapeutic stages or mechanisms (see Kleinman 1988a for an elaboration of this comparative analytical framework). In this domain of cross-cultural comparison, an area that has been virtually neglected is the adaptation and evolution of Western psychotherapy when transplanted to culturally divergent Third World settings.

The issue of specificity in therapeutic process should also be addressed. Often anthropological arguments about efficacy are based primarily on observation and interviews with healers, extrapolating from these data while lacking detailed data on patients' or supplicants' experience of transformation. This approach results in conclusions that healing is globally effective or ineffective, without allowing for the possibility of incremental or significant but inconclusive effects (Csordas 1988a). Especially important is the need to include the explicitly religious dimension of ritual therapies as a domain in which a particular kind of therapeutic specificity may be elaborated. Such a careful analysis of process is a necessary prelude to comparative outcome studies for different kinds of life problems and disorders.

The therapeutic process does not begin and end with the discrete therapeutic event, and to study it in that way diminishes its character and significance as a social process. This is true first in the sense that the goals of a therapeutic system exist within a historical and social context of values and necessarily have an orientation to that context. The culturally presupposed goal of therapy may be to facilitate a person's adaptation to society or, on the other hand, to criticize societal demands and motivate the person toward creative personal change and social reform. In a second sense, the therapeutic process cannot be understood as bounded by the therapeutic event precisely because it is directed at life beyond the event. If therapeutic transformation is to occur, it must occur not only in the event but in a person's life between events, as a social and experiential process.

CHAPTER 2

POLITICAL ECONOMY IN MEDICAL ANTHROPOLOGY

Soheir Morsy

> In my view the necessity of having to embed political-economic analysis in the terminology of cultural anthropology could have led to positive results. ... On the one hand a focus on "culture"—hence on traditions, values, and attitudes—rather than on class relations can be and is widely used to mask and distort the brutal realities of power and exploitation. On the other hand, however, a focus on culture in the context of political economy discourages superficial and mechanistic interpretations of group behavior, because it requires attention to the role of consciousness and ideology in social process.
> (Leacock 1982:257)

Medical anthropology's current interest in political economy represents a specific expression of a more general, politically informed development in the parent discipline. As postcolonial conditions restricted access to anthropology's substantive focus, the discipline's distinctiveness became primarily institutional rather than theoretical. More "historical" and "sociological" interests now enjoy legitimacy in academic circles (Stocking 1982:176; see also, for example, Asad 1979:608; Frank 1975; Gluckman 1964; Leacock 1982; Worsley 1966). Focus on world historical political economy in anthropological analysis has been accompanied by interest in social contextualization beyond local communities (for example, DeWalt and Pelto 1985; Finkler 1986; Hale 1981; Smith C. 1983). This has directed our views beyond empiricist preoccupations (Marcus and Fischer 1986:77–81). Transcending conventional "emic" accounts, the political economy perspective has brought into focus global power relations that touch the lives of the traditional "other."

While recognizing the principle of cultural specificity, the political economic orientation forces anthropology to redefine its field of inquiry in global processual and relational terms (Wolf 1982:387, 425; Amin 1981; Asad 1987; Worsley 1966, 1984; Hopkins and Wallerstein 1967; Koptiuch 1985). In addition, this perspective provides a corrective for the disciplinary fragmentation of social science that obscures the relationship of economic, political, social, and cultural forces (O'Laughlin 1975:341). Political economy concentrates on the structural relationship among economic systems, political power, and ideologies (Keesing 1981:516). Far from rendering ethnographic detail and the study of individual human experience obsolete, this perspective regards culturally informed interactions between social actors and political economic relationships as dialectically related (Worsley 1984:179–80; Fields 1988).

Although political economy is concerned with systemic relations, it is not a simple expansion of eclectic holism or a particular micro-macro mix (compare Starr 1982; Waitzkin 1983). Distinguished by its materialist emphasis, transcending academic disciplines, dialectical political economy provides researchers with methodological principles that guide the study of historically specific social phenomena, including health. It is a working scientific tradition, "not a . . . dogmatic grid" (O'Laughlin 1975: 341). Although the label *critical medical anthropology* (which has been used synonymously with political economy in medical anthropology) may convey the illusion of distinctiveness, medical anthropologists whose works address political economy are indebted to antecedent intellectual traditions that call into question anthropology's ahistorical, apolitical, and cultural relativistic stance (Morsy 1989).

In short, as an experimental ideal, political economy in anthropology involves attempts to integrate analysis of global processes with ethnographic detail, utilizing the discipline's characteristic comparative method to test the validity of general world-system propositions (for example, Adams 1988; Bassett 1988:2; Whiteford and Montgomery 1985). In rendering the anthropological conception of the "primitive isolate" obsolete, political economic analysis also has directed our view to global power relations and their health consequences. Moreover, by demystifying anthropological ideology, this analytical tradition brings into focus the social foundations of all intellectual developments, including the incorporation of political economic analysis into medical anthropology (compare Estroff 1988:421–22; Kuhn 1970; Mafeje 1976; Navarro 1981, 1985; O'Laughlin 1975:341).

Beyond variant emphases in the political economy of health (Morgan 1987:132), this chapter focuses on academic anthropological works that partake of this evolving analytical orientation. Following a note on methodology, which calls into question the anthropological concept of holism, discussion centers on the incorporation of political economic analysis in medical anthropology. This is addressed as a politically informed development rooted in trends beyond the boundaries of the parent discipline and not simply as a matter of intellectual creativity. I then survey the wide variety of political economic research in medical anthropology over the past decade, including the social production of sickness as it relates to ecological considerations, the labor process, and Third World underdevelopment. This review also includes studies of medicine in advanced capitalist societies and in the context of socialist transformation. I conclude with prospects for future developments in political economic medical anthropology.[1]

HOLISM RECONSIDERED: A NOTE ON METHODOLOGY

Interest in the articulation of community-level social processes with national and international political economies has prompted anthropologists to partake of developments beyond the artificial boundaries of the discipline. While anthropology continues to be differentiated by certain analytical skills and detailed knowledge of local societies, there is increasing appreciation of the contributions of other academic fields (Bennett 1985). It is recognized that academic disciplines are themselves the reified products of sociopolitical processes (see, for example, Leacock 1982; Lee 1978; O'Laughlin 1975). Moreover, it is clear that the anthropological ideal of holism, in which each investigator studies every facet of a social phenomenon, is unattainable in practice. Contrary to the obsession with holism as completeness and the culture-specific orientation of "doing it all," it has become necessary for individual researchers to specify the scope and linkages of their studies and to consider the commensurability and compatibility of related paradigms and research emphases (DeWalt and Pelto 1985:11, 17; Young 1982:279; Lett 1987; Comaroff 1985).

Anthropological studies of political economy vary from highly abstracted programmatic statements to concrete case studies (Lee 1978; Frankenberg 1978; Gough and Sharma 1975; Magubane 1979; Morsy 1988a; Nash 1979; Schneider 1978; Taussig 1980a). Despite some variation, these studies are characterized by historical specificity and a dialectical orientation. Thus, they contrast with conventional anthropology, which renders all societies temporally equal by placing them in an imaginary, timeless space (Saa 1986; Worsley 1966:5) and which is based on integrative rather than conflict models of society (Firth 1975:30).

Political economy studies also contrast with the traditional anthropological preoccupation with systems of "authentic meaning" presumed to be shared by ideologically defined communities, without regard to historical variations in political activity and economic conditions (Asad 1979:614). The political economy perspective, far from ignoring ideology, considers it to be a type of socially constituted knowledge—the product of evolving social forces relating to modes of production. This perspective seeks to analyze the historically specific social conditions or structures of society that are associated with certain types of ideologies. For recent human history, the structures of society extend inevitably to global economy and power relations.

When extended to the discourse on sickness and healing, the trend of broadening the scope of anthropological analysis by taking account of world historical political economy is manifested in the growing concern with "political economy of health" (PEH) (see, for example, Baer 1982; Baer, Singer, and Johnsen 1986; Frankenberg 1974; Morsy 1981; Onoge 1975; Singer 1986a). Identified as the "missing link in medical anthropology" (Morsy 1979; and see Frankenberg 1980:250), this materialist, historically specific, and dialectical perspective emphasizes the social relations of sickness and healing. It illuminates the relatively neglected, although locally influential, effects of national and international power relations (Janzen 1978a; Morgan 1987; Onoge 1975).

In examining the material correlates of health and sickness, political economic medical anthropology (PEMA) is distinguished from antecedent holistic emphases not by singular variables but by the analytical scheme within which variables are integrated. For example, the concept of social class has been addressed in both conventional and political economic studies in medical anthropology. However, whereas a conventional, meaning-centered study might focus on how interclass differences relate to understanding a medical concept (Foster and Anderson 1978:231), the PEH perspective accords social class (in the form of class-linked power differentials) a central role in the study of social relations of sickness and healing (see, for example, Ferguson 1986; Navarro 1986).

PEMA transcends traditional disciplinary boundaries, making possible, for example, "sociological [and anthropological, or political science] contributions to the political economy of health" (Baer 1986b) rather than confining medical anthropologists to "cultural contexts" or sociologists to "social contexts" (Foster 1974:4–5). Additionally, the emphasis in PEH research on explicitly designated macroscopic focuses of inquiry departs from medical anthropology's conventional methodology—informant-focused knowledge production—freeing us to address such nontraditional concerns as the effects of national revolutionary transformation on health services (Donahue 1986a), the impact of regional political and economic developments on the incidence of spirit possession (Morsy 1988c), and the issue of industrial health in advanced capitalist society (Nash and Kirsch 1988). In short, in PEMA, the purposeful divergence from established modes of anthropological investigation enables researchers to expose fundamental social processes that are hidden from easy view in locally grounded, empiricist social analysis (Leacock 1972:60–61).

Epistemologically, PEMA controverts any claims of scientific objectivity and ethical neutrality by explicitly acknowledging the fact that both anthropological and medical knowledge are socially informed (products of particular historical and cultural contexts) (see Mafeje 1976; Martin 1988; Taussig 1980b; Young 1980). Indeed, from the perspective of "political economy of knowledge" (Keesing 1981), PEMA is itself a politically inspired reconsideration of the epistemological premises of the subdiscipline.

BETWEEN SOCIOCULTURALISM AND POLITICAL ECONOMY OF HEALTH

Medical anthropology is rooted in applied research designed to facilitate the introduction of Western biomedical health care into impoverished communities of the allegedly developing world. Following the post–World War II modernist tendency of studying the condition of underdevelopment apart from its processual attributes, medical anthropology tended to emphasize indigenous beliefs and practices. Accordingly, the anthropological approach "defined the problem of resistance [to modern health care] . . . as lying largely with the recipient people" (Foster and Anderson 1978:8). Although the "problem" of "acceptability" was later redefined as "resistances in scientific medical bureaucracies" (Foster and Anderson 1978:233), the historically derived global structural determinants of sickness in "developing" societies remained unscrutinized (see Cameron 1960; Darity 1965; Gould 1965; Polgar 1962; Shiloh 1968).

Over the past decade, medical anthropology's conventional analytical orientation has been subjected to critical evaluation, bringing into question the field's "explicit attention . . . to the role played by cultural influences" (Fabrega 1979:566), its emphasis on "perception . . . as the critical variable" (Foster and Anderson 1978:215), concern with "cognitive dissonance" (Kunstadter 1975), and functionalist "fit" (Foster 1958:7; compare Frankenberg 1974). The "doctrine of the maintenance function of ideology" (Asad 1979:621) clearly applies to medical anthropology:

Historically specific discourses are typically reduced to the status of determinate parts of an integrated social mechanism, and an epistemological paradigm which purports to define the problem of objective knowledge is passed off as a sociological model of analyzing ideology . . . [As for] materially founded authoritative discourse which seeks continually to preempt the space of radically opposed utterances, this has generally remained beyond the concerns of meaning-focused medical anthropology.

The African anthropologist Omafume Onoge rejected the field's emphasis on cultural determinism and its microanalytic focus, describing this orientation as "socioculturalism": a restricted perspective that has tended to elevate narrowly defined, local "culture" into an "omnibus explanation" while "[global] capitalism [remained] . . . a neglected theme in medical anthropology" (Onoge 1975). Others, using different terminology, also criticized anthropology for shunning what Janzen (1978a) has termed the " macrolevel of analysis," which extends beyond the family or the local community. Adoption of socioculturalism has meant that "phenomena other than those covered by the model are ruled out of the court of specialized discourse" (Wolf 1982:10). In the field as a whole, this has resulted in the neglect of the historical, political, economic context of the development of health systems.

In short, synchronic emphasis on the cognitive, affective, and behavioral dimensions of local health systems in medical anthropology is analytically restrictive, ignoring the relationships between local and global power relations that produce and shape sickness (Hopper 1975; Singer and Baer n.d.; Susser 1985:562; Taussig 1980a:12–13; Young 1982:269). Traditional analytical emphasis in medical anthropology undermines the idea that power—a central concept in the study of health systems (Glick 1967; see Morsy 1978)—originates and resides in arrangements between social groups that are not defined simply by local boundaries.

The incorporation of global power relations into medical anthropology cannot be understood apart from the "social epistemology" surrounding this development (see, for example, Goonatilake 1984). The current interest in a world systems paradigm and other variants of the political economy tradition has not been simply the result of anthropologists' intellectual creativity or skill as "disciplinary brokers" (Baer 1986). Recognition of the profound impact of capitalist development on local people and practices (Whiteford and Montgomery 1985:147) is an outcome of the protracted struggles of local populations (the "other") studied by medical anthropologists essentially forcing the " reinvention" of the discipline. A historical review reveals that, during the 1960s, a vocal anti-imperialist movement touched academic circles, prompting reconsideration of the positivist orientation in social research (Leacock 1982; Mafeje 1976; Schoepf 1979).

As former "primitives" challenged the very colonial structures that brought participant observation to their doorsteps, such subjugated peoples started to "talk back at the social scientist" (Scholte 1983:235). Voices were raised from within anthropology to demystify the ideological character of the discipline and expose the power asymmetry underlying anthropological knowledge production (Nader 1969). Among natives-turned-anthropologists, there was a call for "decolonializing anthropology" (Stavenhagen 1971; see, for example, Asad 1973; Banaji 1970; Magubane 1971). In some cases, this call went so far as to suggest the idea of "indigenous anthropology" (Fahim 1982, 1987), thereby threatening to replace one form of essentialism with another (Abaza and Stauth 1988; Morsy 1986a; Morsy et al. 1986). Nevertheless, questioning of anthropological empiricist methodology and "emic" productions by Third World scholars has contributed to shifting anthropological obsession with what is inside peoples' heads to a scrutiny of what is on their backs.

Movements of national liberation abroad, expressed in the United States in the antiwar movement of the 1960s (Sider 1974), were the ferment in which political economic analysis took root as a legitimate, but not uncontested, anthropological orientation. The legitimization of political economic inquiry within medical anthropology is understandable in the light of exposure of the ideological character of anthropology as a whole, including "its support for imperialist domination abroad, and racism and exploitation at home" (Leacock 1982:257). Not unlike socioculturalism, political economy in anthropology is politically informed. Unlike the former, however, any claim to objectivity by its proponents not only is easily betrayed by the explicit labeling of this orientation but also readily negated by associated analyses.

In medical anthropology, the political economy posture has challenged the discipline's focus on "what the natives really mean" and how they perceive themselves. It is now clear that, in our preoccupation with understanding the "soul" of the "cultural Other" (Abaza and Stauth 1988:344), medical anthropologists neglected the social mechanisms by which local power relations and global forces impinge on the body. Beyond the pioneering work of Omafume Onoge, which suggests that medical anthropology must transcend lay conceptions, emphasizing instead social relations and global historical processes, more recent studies have addressed these relations and processes in increasing detail (Frankenberg 1980; Mullings 1984; Scheper-Hughes 1984; Young 1982).

As we have come to acknowledge both the adverse effects of "development" and the political character of biomedicine, our own political orientations have come into sharper focus. Sometimes this promotes disciplinary gatekeeping in the form of sarcastic commentaries on the "whining" and "ideological roars" of political economy theorists. We are said to assume "accusatory," "blaming," and "culprit-seeking" postures vis-à-vis the global hegemony of capitalism and biomedicine (Estroff 1988:421-23, 426; compare, for example, George 1979, 1981; Navarro 1985:11-12). Nevertheless, over the past several years, political economic medical anthropology has included evaluations of health-focused research in Latin America (Bonfil-Batalla 1966), India (Banerji 1984), and the Middle East (Morsy 1981). As a group, these works sensitize anthropologists working around the world to the material determinants of health status (see, for example, Laurell 1989; Asad 1987:596), as well as the social character of medical anthropological knowledge and its often mystified role in legitimizing the status quo (Banerji, 1984; compare, for example, Bannoune 1984; Wulf and Fiske 1987).

While developments in the anthropological periphery continue to provide raw material for theory (see, for example, Nzimiro 1977; Peiris 1969; Shukri 1985), the declaration of "the coming of age of critical medical anthropology" (Singer 1989) also rests on studies of the "dominative medical system" (Baer 1989; see, for example, Frankenberg 1988a; Lazarus 1988a,b; Singer et al. 1984). Some medical anthropologists have begun to extend explicit attention to the connectedness of "Western" and "non-Western" health issues within the framework of global political economy. Allan Young, for example, has described Western medicine as consisting of a "head" in the developed nations and a "tail" in the underdeveloped world, connected by the "economic, political, and social relations that constitute the world political-economy" (Young as cited in Baer 1982:16; compare, for example, Martin 1988:19-20; McDonald 1981).

POLITICAL ECONOMIC MEDICAL ANTHROPOLOGY: BEYOND DISCIPLINARY BOUNDARIES

While it is possible to trace the current popularity of PEMA within "the world order of anthropology" (Stocking 1982), consideration of its specific intellectual constitution and origins takes us back to the wisdom of ancient medical traditions. For example, the early Egyptians identified the "conditions of life" as the major determinants of health status, and Al-Suuyti's medieval treatise on the Medicine of the Prophet (Tibbu-ul-Nabi) recognizes want as a cause of poor health (Elgood 1962). More recently, PEMA clearly relates to Rudolf Virchow's nineteenth-century work, which, in addition to demonstrating the social etiology of compromised health, including powerlessness, insists on the understanding of contradictory social forces that obstruct reform (Taylor and Rieger 1985).

The inspiration for the PEMA approach also comes from Marxist and world system variants of political economy. In addition, the approach is a scholarly expression of the current concern with issues of power and control within popular political movements, notably the international struggle aimed at the liberation of women (Fee 1983). While recognizing class power as the cornerstone of social relations (Navarro 1986:250), medical anthropologists have addressed health issues pertaining to gender power relations (Browner 1989b; Lazarus 1987; Morsy 1982).

The Marxist Tradition

Political economic medical anthropology is indebted to Friedrich Engels's classic account of the conditions of the working class in England, which analyzed health issues in the context of capitalist development (Baer 1982; Morgan 1987). Medical anthropology has also been influenced by contemporary Marxist theorists in other academic fields (see, for example, Navarro 1977; 1985, 1986; Waitzkin 1979, 1983, 1989). In addition to stressing historical context and the centrality of class relations in their analysis of health systems, these Marxist scholars direct attention to the role of the state, the commodification of health care, illness-generating social conditions, and the ideological nature of medical knowledge. Some Marxist scholarship moves beyond macroanalytic concerns to examine the micropolitics of medicine (Waitzkin 1986).

In addition to the influence of Marxist concerns with the political economic determinants of health-related phenomena, medical anthropology has also been informed by Marxist cultural theorizing, notably that of Lukacs (see Taussig 1980a), Gramsci (see Frankenberg 1988c), and E. P. Thompson (see Adams 1988). Humanist Marxism, which focuses on experience as mediating social structure and the individual, has been incorporated into medical anthropology (Scheper-Hughes and Lock 1986; also in this volume). In addition, under the label "critical medical anthropology," researchers have made explicit their indebtedness to Marx's critical theory and the work of the Frankfurt school. Lazarus and Pappas (1986:136), for example, define the goal of critical theory in medical anthropology as "understand[ing] the way in which medical science and medical practice take shape, and the way that possibilities for change and improvement are limited and circumscribed" (see also Baer 1986b, Schroyer 1970).

As Marxism has inspired theoretical reconsideration within medical anthropology, it brings the issue of praxis into the purview of the field. Although academic analysis may well inform political struggles that aim to bring about meaningful reforms, analysis is not equivalent to action (Petrovic 1988; compare Berliner 1977:122–23; Stark 1982:85; Singer 1989a:1201). Aside from the political activism of individual advocates (Hopper 1988; Taussig 1980a:xiii), the theme of praxis has been a relatively neglected theme within PEMA. This is not a minor matter, particularly in view of the popularity of the unfortunately depoliticized, sanitized, and anthropologically assisted international development lobby's efforts to "empower" the peoples of "developing" societies (Werner 1988; compare, for example, Wulff and Fiske 1987).

Dependency Theory and Medical Anthropology: Substitute or Complement?

Many medical anthropologists who advocate political economic analysis have been influenced by the "dependency" or "world system" perspective (Morgan 1987; see also Baer 1982; Leeson 1974; Morsy 1981; Turshen 1984). Accordingly, it is recognized that the world system that emerged from the sixteenth century now encompasses the entire globe. The dependency orientation therefore holds that one cannot undertake analysis of "developing" or "socialist" societies apart from their relation to the world capitalist system. Furthermore, the development of the world system is revealed to be based on conflict between oppressed and controlling social groups (Kennedy 1988:37).

One of the earliest dependency-informed commentaries on health and socioeconomic development (Navarro 1974) links the maldistribution of health resources in Latin America to "the same determinants that cause the underdevelopment of most of that continent"—specifically, the technological-economic dependency of less developed countries and the political economic dominance of national lumpen-bourgeoisie and their foreign counterparts. Extended to the concerns of medical anthropology, this analytical orientation suggests that health problems in underdeveloped countries are not simply culture-specific expressions of ecological or socioeconomic constraints but are "interwoven with . . . the functioning of the capitalist political-economic world system" (Elling 1981:21).

Rooted in struggles for national liberation and postcolonial programs of decolonization, the dependency perspective illuminates the connectedness between "us" and "other"—a dialectical relationship that has been effectively obscured in anthropological discourse by models that juxtapose the West to the non-West, emic to etic, and traditional to modern (Wolf 1982:6; see also Abdel Malek 1963; Naim 1978; Said 1979). Informed by a similar tendency toward reification, medical anthropology differentiates between "Western" and "non-Western" medical systems—"biomedicine" and "ethnomedicine," respectively (Fabrega 1974; Foster and Anderson 1978; Logan and Hunt 1978; Worsley 1982). It is the dependency variant of political economy that extends primary consideration to the very relationship that has been consistently deemphasized in conventional anthropological studies of conceptually isolated "non-Western medical systems." This analytical orientation connects the West (medical anthropologist-biomedicine) to the non-West (native-ethnomedicine) in a dialectical relationship.

Although the dependency orientation has been important in bringing into focus the impact of global economic and power relations, some of its original formulations have been challenged in the light of empirical research (Bratton 1982) and changing world conditions (Kennedy 1988). This has prompted acknowledgment of certain conceptual limitations of this analytical orientation by some of its own advocates (Frank 1977; see also Clawson 1978; El-Sayed 1986; Morsy 1980). While the analytical limitations of the dependency perspective are worthy of serious consideration by medical anthropologists (Morgan 1987), it should be noted that these limitations are not automatically applicable to our studies.

One criticism of the dependency variant or political economy of health is that it neglects social dynamism and cultural specificity. The fact that medical anthropologists are turning to political economy after years of neglect of the perspective does not preclude concern with the cultural, social, and experiential particularities of sickness and healing, although there are differences with regard to selective emphasis of domain and level of analysis. In fact, this type of variation is evident in studies by the same authors. Anne Ferguson (1981) stresses international structural relations of dependency in her study of pharmaceuticals in Latin America but not to the exclusion of local analysis of the process of medicalization, including its relation to "cultural, social, and clinical forms of commerciogenesis." Another political economy–informed study by the same author focuses on local class differences in women's roles as health care managers (Ferguson 1986). Ferguson calls attention to social factors related to women's work patterns and household organization and the implications of class differences for perceptions of illness. Similarly, I have focused on Arab regional political economy in addressing an Islamist expression of biomedical hegemony in one article (Morsy 1988b), and in another I emphasize cultural expression of political economic transformation in a comparative study of spirit possession in two Nile Delta villages (Morsy 1988c).

To conclude this account of the major intellectual elements constituting political economic medical anthropology, it should be stressed that the very identification of political economy as the missing link in medical anthropology (Morsy 1978, 1981) was undertaken in conjunction with the study of social dynamics and cultural specificity. Far from denying the importance of microanalytic studies of the existential particularities of sickness and healing—in essence, discarding the anthropological baby with the bath water—political economic medical anthropology promotes an analytical strategy whereby "the medical anthropologist has to situate his/her work in the context of three processes—development, the making social of disease, and in the more general concepts of anthropological analysis" (Frankenberg 1980:197). The current proliferation of studies that attempt to put this advice into practice suggests that political economy is no longer a neglected theme in medical anthropology, a development at least partly attributable to the dependency perspective.

MEDICAL ANTHROPOLOGY'S EXPERIMENTAL IDEAL: A DECADE OF RESEARCH

Clearly the past decade has witnessed a proliferation of studies indebted to the political economy perspective (see, for example, Baer 1982; Singer 1989a). Some studies declare a definite commitment to political economy, some adopt the designation of "critical medical anthropology," and others avoid explicit labeling (compare Kaufert 1988; Morsy 1979; Singer 1986b). Research in PEMA spans such topics as health care within the framework of colonial and neocolonial relations, as well as socialist transformation (Taussig 1987; Gruenbaum 1981; and New 1975, respectively). Additional concerns include the social production of illness in relation to class-based power asymmetry in industrial settings (Nash and Kirsh 1988; Siskind 1988; Susser 1985) and professional appropriation of control over women's reproductive functions (Lazarus 1987; Morgen 1986; Morsy 1986d). Far from exhibiting a fixed micro-macro "ratio," PEMA studies emphasize different levels, from the consciousness of the patient (Taussig 1980b), to community organization (Susser 1985), regional political economy (Morsy 1988b), and international corporate power (Ferguson 1981).

PEMA studies of the social production of sickness also have been undertaken in conventional anthropological research settings—impoverished and underdeveloped parts of world. These range from consideration of the health consequences of the marginalization of Andean populations (Leatherman et al. 1986) to the health effects of human rights violations in a South African bantustan (Turshen 1986). Political economy methodology has even extended to the study of so-called culture-bound syndromes: reproductive illness behavior in Haiti (Singer, Davison and Gerdes 1988), the production of possession illness in Malaysia (Ong 1988), and the incidence of spirit possession in rural Egypt (Morsy 1978, 1988c). While such studies are grounded in conventional ethnographic research and address culture-specific expressions of resistance, they stand in contrast to socioculturalism by transcending the disciplinary boundaries of this conventional orientation. In her study of the relationship between "school refusal syndrome" and capitalism in Japan, Margaret Lock notes that her analysis, although informed by the traditional ethnomedical approach, "cannot be undertaken satisfactorily without recourse to theories and knowledge acquired within the disciplines of history, economics, and political science, in addition to those of sociology and anthropology" (Lock 1986a:110).

PEMA, Level of Analysis, and Explanatory Priority: Illustrations from Ecology

PEMA's concern with the social relations of sickness and healing contrasts sharply with the individual focus of the biomedical model of disease. It also underscores the analytical limitations of medical ecology. This is illustrated in Nancy Scheper-Hughes's (1984b) study of infant care in northeast Brazil. Beyond the multiple factors that are detrimental to child survival in this part of the world, including ecological, Scheper-Hughes identifies "the macroparasitism of class exploitation" as the mechanism whereby morbidity and mortality are generated. By illustrating how local health problems are locally anchored manifestations of international processes of social production of disease and death, Scheper-Hughes also salvages psychocultural factors that are often neglected in ecological approaches. While this study shows that PEMA is capable of accommodating microlevel variables, it demonstrates that the distinctiveness of this orientation pertains to its explanatory priority.

In a study relying on secondary sources, Merrill Singer (1989b) also demonstrates the priority of social over macro ecological determinants of ill health. Singer suggests that most medical ecologists ignore the "social relations in the origins of health and illness." However, he goes on to explain that, excluding those who "pay lip service" to social relations and political economic forces, many medical ecologists "pay considerable attention to determinant social phenomena without seeming to recognize that they have moved far beyond the basic assumptions of their ecological framework" (Singer 1989b:226). This suggests that "critical" orientations may appear apart from explicit labeling (see Chasin and Franke 1979; Diener et al. 1980; Lewis 1983).

The Labor Process: Disease, Morbidity, and Medical Discourse

PEMA research addressing the social production of morbidity and mortality extends well beyond traditional anthropological field settings to the heartland of industrial development. In PEMA studies influenced by the Marxist variant of PEH and the "rediscovery of the relationship between work and health" (Navarro 1985:535), analysis transcends the important but limiting concern with the exposure of individual workers to harmful physical, chemical, and psychological agents. Instead of the individual-environmental dichotomy implicit in this focus, researchers address "the social relations that determine both the individual worker and the environment" (Navarro 1985:535). From this perspective, the workplace is but a microcosm of social contradictions expressed in the labor process.

The concept of the labor process is based on the differentiation between work as an individual activity and labor as a social phenomenon. Analysis of the labor process, then, involves the social relations that govern the deployment of labor and the allocation of its product (Wolf 1982:74). Within this framework of analysis, health is not simply a correlate of an individual's work. Scrutiny extends to the underlying power relations between producers and others, thereby transcending the harmful effects of the occupational environment. It is power relations and associated ideological orientations extending from the level of management to the level of the state that constitute the focus of political economy methodology.

Traditional Marxist concerns with worker consciousness and the role of the state are expressed in two studies by anthropologists that appeared in a special issue of *Medical Anthropology Quarterly* (Susser 1988). Transcending disciplinary boundaries and informant-based anthropological research methods, Janet Siskind (1988) analyzed historical documents to show that management and worker perceptions of, and reactions to, silicosis in a nineteenth-century U.S. factory were structured by class relations. In another study, Carol MacLennan (1988) addressed state power and the politics of public health. In analyzing the regulation of auto safety, she argues that although the role of the state is significant, the market ideology of U.S. political culture is worthy of scrutiny. Thus, "Though lifesaving and injury-control policies emerged from the noneconomic belief that the human toll from auto accidents and other hazards was unacceptable, safety policies have been increasingly cast in economic terms" (MacLennan 1988:248).

MacLennan's conclusion calls into question David Michael's (1988) recommendation of more governmental regulation of workplace health and safety.

Nevertheless, Michaels's study of the hazards of potent bladder carcinogens in the U.S. dye industry is worthy of the attention of praxis-oriented medical anthropologists who are willing to confront dominant power structures in the struggle for health. This account of health hazards in the dye industry illustrates how definitions of "scientific" evidence are socially mediated. Just as there is ongoing dumping of substances causing sickness and death in the Third World despite the fact that their harmful effects are known, Michaels documents how corporate management permitted worker exposure to potent carcinogens until the body count could no longer be ignored. Scientific knowledge does not necessarily result in action to safeguard human well-being.

Political economy in medical anthropology also includes research on the social production of sickness in agricultural environments. In a study that explicitly addresses the concern with "interweaving macro and micro levels," Jo Scheder (1988) examines Type II diabetes mellitus among Mexican-American farmworkers. Her analysis of the social issues fundamental to the etiology of the disease demonstrates the relationship between stressful life events and life change, social inequality and psychological stress (inherent in the migrant lifestyle), and physiological responses culminating in hyperglycemia. Scheder's analysis is presented as a corrective to dependency analysts' tendency to deemphasize biological disease etiology and associated blocked access "to the tools or ... knowledge to influence the system whose effects we often bemoan" (Scheder 1988:277).

Beyond the specific motivation for incorporating biomedical data in sociomedical studies (see, for example, Browner et al. 1988; Fabrega 1972:213; Morsy 1978:12), the power relations surrounding the discourse of medical science itself have been scrutinized by medical anthropologists (for example, Martin 1988; Morsy 1989b; Rapp 1988a). This is illustrated in June Nash and Max Kirsch's (1988) study of U.S. corporate attempts to suppress epidemiological data supporting opposition to the production and use of polychlorinated biphenyls (PCBs). Inspired by Allan Young's (1980) analysis of the reproduction of conventional knowledge, Nash and Kirsch utilize discourse analysis and contrast their work to Mary Douglas and Aaron Wildavsky's (1982) meaning-focused study of risk and culture. Whereas the latter assign a determinate role to ideology, a priori, Nash and Kirsch address historically specific social conditions. Like other anthropological studies of political economy, their work brings into focus "the materially founded (*authoritative*) discourse which seeks continually to preempt the space of radically opposed (public interest) utterances" (Asad 1979:621; compare Alexander 1988).

Third World Development, Health, and Medicine

In PEMA research on the social production of morbidity and relations of medicine in the Third World, underdevelopment and its resultant health problems are defined as structural rather than conjunctural (Navarro 1985:537). In this reformulation, focus is shifted to world capitalism and imperialism, which heretofore have not been perceived as problematic in conventional medical anthropology (DeWalt and Van Willigen 1984; Foster 1984b; compare Banerji 1984; Sell and Kunitz 1986). As a result of this methodological shift, it is development and dependency, rather than ecology, population pressures, economic underdevelopment, and technological backwardness, that is accorded primary consideration in the study of morbidity and mortality (Borrini 1987; see, for example, Lane 1988; Low 1985b; Stebbins 1986).

From the perspective of the dependency variant of political economic analysis, biomedicine is conceptualized as global and hegemonic (Elling 1981). In terms of colonial "cultural" contact, biomedicine is seen as an effective mechanism for the pacification of dominated populations. By placing her work on the role of health services in the colonial Ivory Coast "within a larger societal analysis" and "link[ing] medical care to the structures of power," Judith Lasker (1977) explains "inequities in health care delivery" and shows how "health systems ... serve nonmedical goals of a society's dominant groups." While acknowledging the humanitarian motivations of individual health service workers, Lasker's study reveals that French colonizers utilized the health system to further their economic and political aims.

In a rare political economy–informed study of health in an Arab society, Ellen Gruenbaum (1981) lends support to Lasker's interpretations of the social functions of colonial medical systems. She shows that aside from the fact that the provision of medical treatment by colonial authorities served important political functions, modern medical services were very limited and most of the population continued to rely primarily on traditional forms of healing (see Gran 1979). As Lasker, and also Pearce (1980), have shown for the Ivory Coast and Nigeria, respectively, Gruenbaum's study in the Sudan documents how political and economic structures of the postindependence period are conducive to disease. She explains, "Post-independence governments have continued the same development policy ... thereby ... play[ing] a role in the maintenance of international power structures and the continued domination of metropolitan capitalist classes" (Gruenbaum 1981:60).

The theme of the colonial legacy in health care receives elaboration in Ogoh Alubo's (1987) study of postcolonial Nigeria. In contrast to constitutional declarations and official health policy, which purports a commitment to "health for all," in practice access to biomedical health care remains highly skewed in favor of the privileged, very much like the situation in colonial days (see also Frankenberg 1980). This is attributed to the reproduction of "the basic ingredients of power, privileges, and hence, domination which sustain class societies like Nigeria" (Alubo 1987:461).

PEMA research reveals that colonial and subsequent neocolonial development proceeded with simultaneous introduction of biomedical care and disease-conducive political and economic strategies. While the major communicable diseases were often brought under control by public health programs, social conditions of underdevelopment lead directly to a variety of other forms of morbidity. For example, Meredith Turshen (1977) addresses the adverse health consequences of colonial agricultural policies in Tanzania, which emphasized export cash crop production. Focusing on "capitalist underdevelopment of the Tanzanian economy," she explains that the neglect of food production for local consumption and subsequent malnutrition in women and children left behind were caused by the system of labor migration imposed by colonial authorities. Regarding more recent developments in health and nutrition, Michael Taussig presents anthropologists with tough questions about food and development policies: "Would not anthropologists and other professionals be more useful to the cause of humanity and truth if they worked for a new structure of inquiry in which the practices and culture of the wealthy and powerful, and not those of the starving, were the subject of investigation?" (Taussig 1979:1).

In a study of nutrition, development, and foreign aid, Taussig evidently practiced what he preaches to others. His study in the Cauca Valley of Colombia (Taussig 1978) focused on peasant development, nutrition, and health programs funded by the Rockefeller Foundation and the U.S. Agency for International Development. Through a historical analysis of the political economy of agricultural development and nutrition, he demonstrates that U.S. efforts in the region were in fact conducive to the maintenance of many of the basic causes of malnutrition and disease. Promoting a strategy of agricultural development based on large-scale farming has led to a majority of peasants being driven off the land. Monopolistic control of the land, essential for the burgeoning agribusinesses, caused formerly independent peasants to lose control over crop acreage and food production. Supposed experts saw the solution in improved diet and controlled birthrate among the proletarianized peasants (see also Dewey 1989; Morsy 1986:367, 370–71; Omvedt 1975; Schuftan 1985).

In another Latin American setting, Asa Laurell and collaborators (1977) compared two Mexican villages "at different degrees of development," revealing that economic development does not automatically lead to improved health. In fact, they attribute a higher general morbidity rate to "a higher degree of capitalist development," placing agricultural capitalist relations of production and exchange "at the center of the problem." Key elements in their analysis include differential access to high-quality land, control over the products of labor, the extent of wage labor, and the commercialization of agriculture.

In addition to the social production of ill health, PEMA research extends to allocation of health resources within the framework of Third World underdevelopment. Gruenbaum's (1981) study of health policy and the state in the Sudan, for example, reveals that international organizations' recommendations of intensive, high-cost health programs coupled with low-cost primary health programs that utilize minimally trained local people do not challenge existing social relations or threaten the political priorities of the state. In fact, the health development strategies of international organizations are judged as significant in reinforcing the role of the state in relation to the production of primary products for the world market, thereby perpetuating international relations of dominance and dependency.

I have analyzed the relationship between state policies and health in another part of the Arab world (Morsy 1988), focusing on health services in Egypt within the framework of the "open door" economic policies. These policies coincide with the recent more complete reintegration of the country into the global political economy, the flow of international medical aid, and the spread of high-technology medicine. While undermining former state-subsidized social welfare programs, the open door orientation has contributed to the privatization of health services, the medical brain drain, the deprofessionalization of physicians—in short, to the generally acknowledged crisis in health care (see, for example, Gish and Godfrey 1979; Horn 1985; Mejia 1980; Price 1988). This study's macroanalytic focus on regional political economic developments surrounding the proliferation of Islamic clinics is complemented by Iman Hammady's (1989) current ethnographic research on this form of medical service.

The complementarity of political economy and ethnographic levels of analysis is the focus of Sjaak Van der Geest's (1987a) plea for more "contextuality" in health care research, particularly in relation to the distribution and use of pharmaceuticals. In a methodological note that has relevance well beyond his specific concern with unequal access to pharmaceuticals in southern Cameroon, Van der Geest presents an explicit delineation of the multidimensional scope of his analytical framework and of his research problem. He explains that "because it is virtually impossible to deal with the whole gamut of relevant contexts, I will restrict myself to considering contextual forces which seem of particular political and economic importance in the rapidly modernizing state of Cameroon" (p. 142). This selective emphasis on the part of the researcher necessarily leaves out "further linkages with the social, domestic, and individual cognitive domain of drug consumers [which although] not discussed are [recognized as] equally important" (p. 155). In another publication devoted to the local perspective in studies of pharmaceuticals in the Third World, Van der Geest urges researchers to consider these "cognitive and domestic factors" (Van der Geest 1987b; see, for example, Alubo 1987; Ferguson 1981; Stock 1987).

PEMA research on the utilization of medical resources in the Third World extends, albeit minimally, to the traditional anthropological concern with medical pluralism. Beyond the general proposition that the "mix of traditional and modern medicine" is a function of "political economy [and] cultural hegemony" (Elling 1981), the work of Allan Young and Ronald Frankenberg is noteworthy. It provides a conceptual scheme for analyzing the process whereby ill health is socialized—to use Frankenberg's terminology, "the making social of disease" (1980:199). In pluralistic medical systems, a set of signs is subject to multiple interpretations, and different sickness labels. As Young (1982:270) explains, "Social forces help to determine which people get which sickness.... Symbols of healing are simultaneously symbols of power ... and medical practices are simultaneously ideological practices."

A study of hegemony and healing in rural North Yemen by Cynthia Myntti (1988) illustrates Frankenberg and Young's idea of the socialization of ill health, defining medical pluralism as "a dynamic process [which is] understood by considering the political and economic context of health and healing" (Myntti 1988:520). Using illness episodes as illustrations, she concludes that, of the multiple healing forms available, Yemenis have come to prefer "a wholly imported medical system, modern Western medicine" (p. 520). The Muslim *ulama* (learned religious figures) do not tap their Arabic Islamic heritage when they fall ill but flaunt the use of modern medicine, thereby setting an example to be emulated. Besides their moral authority, the *ulama* wield economic power based on their role as wealthy urban entrepreneurs. As a dominant group, their utilization of modern medical care is an additional symbol of their privileged status. As in the case of Egypt's contemporary "Islamic" clinics, this Yemeni study suggests that the hegemony of modern Western medicine may well be upheld within the framework of traditional repositories of power.

PEMA, Advanced Capitalism, and Socialist Transformation

In studying global political economy, medical anthropologists have inevitably directed their efforts to studying the industrial center of the world system, thereby trespassing on the territory of sociology. The discipline's tradition of studying the "distinctive-other," and its related concern with the "non-West," has been compromised in favor of research on the hegemonic medical tradition of the West (for example, Baer 1989; Hopper 1988; Lock 1986b; Martin 1987; Scheper-Hughes and Lovell 1986). Studies of the North American medical system have redirected medical anthropology's comparative gaze to the very medical system about which researchers hold "emic" views. The intellectual consequence of this new direction has been positive, undermining the assumption of "a monolithic and inflexible organization... [bringing] into view 'peripheral specialties,' the subcultures of biomedicine,... and the tensions within American medicine over issues such as power and control, different types of knowledge, and dependency and autonomy" (Lock 1986b:931; see also, Lock 1988a: 2–10).

As medical anthropologists directed their attention to the once-sacrosanct terrain of biomedicine, they addressed the field's initial, and yet to be abandoned, concern with patient compliance. Following Brooke Schoepf's seminal study of doctor-patient communication in the United States (Schoepf 1975), Michael Taussig set a precedent for critical analysis of this domain. In a study that partakes of Marxist cultural theorizing, he illuminates the ideological nature of medicine and addresses the mechanisms whereby it contributes to the reproduction of social power relations in capitalist society (Taussig 1980a; see also Leslie and Taylor 1973; Waitzkin 1983; Young 1980).

Following the disciplinary trend of studying your own society (for example, Altorki and El-Solh 1988; Easley 1982; Hahn and Gaines 1985; Messerschmidt 1981), and apart from concern with the issue of "clinical relevance" (Barnett et al. 1985), Hans Baer and Merrill Singer have been active contributors to the study of medicine in the United States (and also, in the case of Baer, in the United Kingdom) in both its "dominative" and "heterodox" forms (Baer 1984, 1989; Singer et al. 1984; Singer 1986b). In a recent study, Baer suggests that the "dominative" medical system of the United States reflects class, racial-ethnic, and gender relations (Baer 1989; and see Campell 1988; Chavez 1986;

Morgan 1986). He explains the demise of medical pluralism as related to the shift in U.S. political economy from competitive capitalism to a monopoly form. As the dominative system, biomedicine has "co-opt[ed] the techniques of specific heterodox medical systems while discarding their theoretical or metaphysical premises" (Baer 1989:110).

Concern with medicine as a social system is also illustrated in Singer's research in the United States, which emphasizes the social production of disease, thereby demystifying social etiology. Singer, like Baer and Taussig, demonstrates that anthropology's traditional idea of fit ("dialectics" in PEMA) between medicine and society in non-Western settings is equally valid for the heartland of scientific medicine (compare, for example, Foster 1958:7; Singer 1984, 1986). Singer reminds us that physicians and patients alike are "but two layers in a larger social dynamic" (Singer 1987).

The theme of social dynamics receives elaboration in PEMA research related to industrial production and health, which documents community-based resistance to corporate action. In a study of PCBs in the U.S. electrical machinery industry, June Nash and Max Kirsch (1986) "extend the political economy of health into the ethnologic domain of community research." Like Ida Susser's account of community action in a Puerto Rican industrial community (Susser 1985) and Rayna Rapp's study of the discourse of genetic counseling in New York City (Rapp 1988a), Nash and Kirsch's work illuminates "not only medical information but also structural power arrangements, social knowledge, and popular meanings about medically defined disability" (Rapp 1988a:143).

In short, as a result of PEMA research over the past decade, Onoge's observation that capitalism is a neglected theme in medical anthropology is less valid today. In fact, it is socialism, the often-proposed alternative for better health, that remains to be studied by medical anthropologists. Social movements that strive to circumvent the allegedly adverse impact of capitalism provide researchers with rare opportunities to test the validity of such assumptions about socialism, capitalism, and health. In this regard, the establishment of a national unified health system in Nicaragua following the Sandinista revolution in 1979 "offers medical anthropologists a unique opportunity to study the dynamics of political economy, decision-making structures, class conflict, and health care delivery" (Ripp 1984:68).

As anthropologists have demonstrated for socialist-oriented Cuba (Guttmacher and Garcia 1975) and the Indian state of Kerala (Rosenfield 1985), John Donahue shows that, in Nicaragua, socialist development is correlated with more equitable allocation of health resources (Donahue 1983, 1984, 1986a, 1986b). Beyond this general observation, Donahue advises against the "ideal type" approach that classifies health systems as capitalistic or socialistic apart from historical analysis, which considers the concrete conditions of the political economy. Alternatively, he proposes "emic analysis," which allows researchers to observe how specific health strategies are negotiated among several interest groups within the same political economy and how the outcome conforms to the stated goals of the political system (Donahue 1984:70). In contrast to modernist analytic frameworks that identify the impetus for change as external, Donahue studies the process of structural transformation from within, addressing the struggle between those who support professionalization of health care and those who advocate popular participation in primary health care programs. At the same time, Nicaragua's health programs are clearly susceptible to U.S. political and military influences in Central America, demonstrating that "taking account of world historical political economy" is equally important in socialist-oriented societies as in any other.

Donahue's study of health in the context of socialist transformation in Nicaragua brings into focus the relationship between political development and health care, a neglected linkage in conventional medical anthropology, including its praxis variant (see, for example, Frank 1975). Within the socialist political agenda, health care development is not a matter of projects, selective health strategies, medical technology transfer, or international medical aid. Instead health care becomes part of a global strategy that aims to increase people's access to the means of production, increase health consciousness through educational campaigns, and encourage popular participation in the delivery of health care. Beyond strategic orientations, Donahue's work in Nicaragua illustrates Vicente Navarro's contention that the road to socialist medicine requires changes in social relations (Navarro 1985).

CONCLUSION

Mirroring the general anthropological interest in political economy, the elaboration of historical and materialist conceptions of health systems now constitutes an established, if evolving, orientation in medical anthropology. Distanced from the problem of cognitive dissonance that once constituted the raison d'être of the field and from the issue of clinical relevance associated with the explanatory model approach, research in PEMA has drawn attention to historically specific social forces, relations, and processes surrounding sickness and health care. Informed by the transdisciplinary orientation of political economy of health, medical anthropologists have gained an understanding of collective health conditions as they relate to social, economic, political, and ideological processes (see, for example, Laurell 1989). Thus informed, medical anthropological studies have brought into focus global structures and power relations, as well as hegemonic ideologies that transcend geographic boundaries.

In the light of this survey of PEMA research, it is evident that political-economic medical anthropology represents a significant epistemological development that promises to address the field's acknowledged theoretical sterility (see, for example, Browner et al. 1988). Indeed, this orientation may constitute the most important paradigm shift in medical anthropology to date. Political economic considerations are no longer automatically excluded from phenomenological studies of health systems. Even medical anthropologists whose work has generally been identified with the explanatory model approach have begun to utilize the conceptual tool kit of PEMA (for example, Good and Good 1988;

Kleinman 1986). Ultimately questions raised in PEMA research are important not just to medical anthropology but to anthropology in general (Susser 1988:198).

Consideration of the evolution of PEMA takes us well beyond matters of intellectual creativity to expose the ideological character of anthropological knowledge itself. Anti-imperialist struggles of anthropology's traditional research subjects have forced the discipline to rediscover the theoretics of confrontation now evident in PEMA's dialectical orientation (see Firth 1975:30–31). Past struggles have imposed upon anthropology recognition of "the fact that imperialist powers [have] been systematically *underdeveloping* Third World nations" (Leacock 1982:258, emphasis in original), although this did not occur without resistance (Owusu 1979). Politically explicit ideological roars in PEMA continue to be considered inappropriate for "scientific" anthropological discourse, as gatekeeping proceeds in the guise of concern for standards of scientific rigor (Estroff 1988).

Despite significant developments in PEMA, and resistance to them, it must be stressed that the political economy perspectives in medical anthropology remain an experimental ideal, achieved only incompletely to date. The research agenda of proponents of PEMA constitutes an implicit acknowledgment of this proposition.

In a recent review of critical medical anthropology/PEMA, Singer (1989a) outlines a number of issues to be addressed in future research. These include evaluation of reciprocal impact of local-level developments on national and international social processes, as well as further consideration of biomedicine in terms of its variable cross-cultural expression, political-economic functions, role in reproduction of social relations, and location in pluralistic healing systems. Additionally, Singer suggests further study of the relation of biomedicine and capitalism, investigations of socialist health care, and the issue of praxis. Carole Browner (1989b) suggests additional research on women's roles as health care providers in the home and as allocators of household resources for health care needs. Regarding research in industrial settings, Ira Susser suggests that "the next step will be to integrate [anthropological] approaches into historical analysis of relations among workers, corporate management, state regulatory activities, and health outcomes in a variety of different industrial situations" (Susser 1988:198).

Beyond specific research agendas, an important epistemological issue involving levels of analysis remains to be addressed in PEMA. While the repeated call for connecting microlevel and macrolevel phenomena is a serious general methodological concern, PEMA is not reducible to micro-macro linkages. Although macro analysis is associated with political economy, it does not define this analytical tradition. As a focus of proposals of analytical rigor, the persistent concern with micro-macro linkages threatens PEMA with confused formulation of the problematic.

In short, PEMA is distinguished from anthropological holism not simply by its scope of analysis but more fundamentally by its priority of embedding culture in long-neglected political-economic variables. Accordingly, the relevance of culture is not restricted to ethnomedical conceptions but extends to issues of power, control, resistance, and defiance.

Critics of PEMA note that this approach depersonalizes and renders the people's voices muted. The combining of phenomenology and political economy has been proposed as a solution to this perceived shortcoming, yet rigor in research does not necessarily imply that every research project take into account all relations pertaining to a phenomenon being studied. A recent critique of conventional conceptions of rigor in health-related research is worthy of consideration:

The research process is more than merely a set of methods for gathering and treating data; when it is viewed as a *whole system* of inquiry, it becomes clear that the process in fact consists of a whole series of interconnected and interactive decision points, each of which requires a subjective, value-laden choice by the researcher among several possible alternatives. Therefore the primary issues about rigor are not technical, but instead, the moral, political, and ideological value-commitments underlying the choices made by those who control the research process. (Ratcliffe and Gonzalez-del-Valle 1988:388)

In the light of this conceptualization of rigor in research, concern with direct expressions of individual experience in health-related research is but one among alternative choices. For medical anthropology, it is this emphasis that has long been the hallmark of informant-focused methodology. In fact, it is in relation to this emphasis—and particularly the concern with giving equal time to parties in fundamentally unequal relationships—that PEMA developed as a corrective, to bring into focus the structural determinants of dehumanization among anthropology's traditional informants. Now that anthropological productions are recognized as artificial researcher-constructed inventions and partial truths, it should not be difficult to acknowledge that in "emic" analysis, informants' voices are selectively muted or magnified.

NOTE

1. The explicit concern with women formed an important element in the development of political economic medical anthropology. In an earlier draft, this chapter addressed this relatively neglected area of research. Since this subject is addressed in Chapter 12 by Browner and Sargent, the editors chose not to retain it here.

CHAPTER 3

A CRITICAL-INTERPRETIVE APPROACH IN MEDICAL ANTHROPOLOGY: RITUALS AND ROUTINES OF DISCIPLINE AND DISSENT

Margaret Lock and Nancy Scheper-Hughes

Medical anthropology has been recognized officially as a subdiscipline of anthropology for over thirty years. The human body in health and illness is the point of departure for research in this field, which includes both historical and cross-cultural studies of representations in connection with the body and also analyses of the universal attempt to explain, classify, and relieve ill health and the effects of aging.

Many of the earlier monographs in which health and illness are discussed were not written with medical anthropology in mind. The authors were ostensibly studying religion, ritual, witchcraft, comparative modes of thinking, and so on, but because the body is "good to think with" and a prime object with which to make symbolic associations in any society, it inevitably loomed large in these works, which rightly have become classics in medical anthropology. The best-known examples are undoubtedly E. E. Evans-Pritchard's *Witchcraft, Oracles and Magic among the Azande* (1937), Victor Turner's *Forest of Symbols* (1967) and *Drums of Affliction* (1968), and *Purity and Danger* by Mary Douglas (1966). None of these authors was explicit as to whether they believed their methods of data collection and analysis were "scientific"; nevertheless, it is probably safe to say that they assumed they were uncovering facts about the respective societies under study. In other words, these authors were working within the tradition of anthropology in which an objective portrayal of other cultures was believed possible.

In retrospect it is evident that a major division in theoretical approach crystallized over the past twenty years or more within the social sciences, including anthropology, around the question of whether "facts" about the world are uncovered or whether, on the other hand, they are produced as the result of the interaction between researcher with the subject of research. Much of the work in contemporary medical anthropology, along with the classical monographs just mentioned, falls into the first of these two camps; that is, it is assumed that rigorous empirical research will lead to a truthful representation of the objects or events under study. The research is for the most part culturally sensitive, cast to show how beliefs and practices in connection with health and illness make sense when analyzed in cultural context and often in addition designed to show that "primitive man," immigrants, refugees, and so on are rational beings. However, there is a striking lack of sensitivity in this type of medical anthropology to the way in which the culture of science structures the kind of questions asked. As Allan Young has pointed out, "epistemological scrutiny is suspended for Western social science and Western medicine" (1982:260). Whereas one can undertake a cultural analysis of "traditional" medical systems, biomedicine ("scientific" medicine) by its very nature is believed to be privileged and exempt from such an analysis.

When such an approach is taken, several assumptions usually follow: that it is theoretically possible to understand the natural world, logically and rationally, through the application of science. Moreover, mastery will eventually be obtained over nature, including the human body, by technological means. At the level of health and illness, it is often assumed that the entire paraphernalia of explanations and behavior ranging from concern about the evil eye to the chanting of sutras in a temple, while understandable as psychological security mechanisms, will not be necessary once universal education in Western biology is commonplace. At such time there will be a general acceptance of the idea that measurable physical changes within the body are "real," whereas all other phenomena are extraneous. We will then find ourselves in agreement with Susan Sontag when she says that "the most truthful way of regarding illness—and the healthiest way of being ill—is one most purified of, most resistant to metaphoric thinking" (1978:3).

TOWARD A CRITICAL-INTERPRETIVE PERSPECTIVE IN MEDICAL ANTHROPOLOGY

The other side of the current theoretical divide in the social sciences is concerned less with orderly explanations and focuses instead on the way in which social life "must fundamentally be conceived as the negotiation of meanings" (Marcus and Fischer 1986:26). The hegemony of positivist social science is explicitly rejected in this critical-interpretive stance, to which phenomenologists, cultural constructionists, and neo-Marxists have contributed. This approach is part of a much broader movement in which reductionistic science as a whole has been subject to a reappraisal, including an examination of the way in which the Western scientific endeavor is a product of specific historical and cultural contexts (Lock and Gordon 1988; Mulkay 1979; Toulmin 1982). This recognition is of special importance to medical anthropology because the world of biomedicine itself thus becomes subject to anthropological analyses.

Medical anthropology is no longer the study of alternative medical systems, beliefs, and practices when a critical-interpretive approach is used. It becomes, instead, a much more radical undertaking. The focus is shifted to the way in which all knowledge relating to the body, health, and illness is culturally constructed, negotiated, and renegotiated in a dynamic process through time and space. Every attempt is made to avoid a conversion of the dialogue that takes place between informants and the anthropologist into categories that originate in Western medical thought, although ultimately a great effort is usually made to go beyond a position of extreme cultural relativism. Moreover, the anthropologist is highly sensitive to the way in which her or his final representation of the other is, in effect, a fiction, a document created out of an ongoing dialogue. Rabinow sums up this approach in the following way: "The ethical is the guiding value. This is an oppositional position, one suspicious of sovereign powers, universal truths, overly relativized preciousness, local authenticity, moralisms high and low. Understanding is its second value, but an understanding suspicious of its own imperial tendencies. It attempts to be highly attentive to (and respectful of) difference, but is also wary of the tendency to essentialize difference" (1986:258). To this extent, medical anthropology is no different from the general field of critical-interpretive anthropology. But one ever-present constraining, and irreducible, fact is rather special to medical anthropology: that of the sentient human body.

Metaphorical flights of fancy come crashing down in the face of the anguish and pain that often surround birth, illness, and death. The relationship between theory and practice takes on special meaning in such a context. The medical anthropologist is repeatedly studying situations where drama is commonplace and where action is deemed imperative. Hence the work of the medical anthropologist rarely stops at an ethnographic description of medical theories and practice but extends willy-nilly into the world of decision making. Because of the scientific endeavor, medical technology (some of it equal or superior to traditional therapies) is available to some extent in most parts of the world. Clearly everyone has a right to benefit from this technology. One of the biggest challenges for medical anthropology is to come to terms with biomedicine, to acknowledge its efficacy when appropriate while retaining a constructively critical stance. At the same time it is necessary to be critical at times of the cultural values and tradition of the societies under study. The webs of culture that people spin and have spun about them are essential for the functioning of humankind in social groups. We cannot strip all metaphor away, as Sontag suggests. However, wherever inequalities and hierarchy are institutionalized, they will of necessity be imposed by means of a dominant cultural ideology, which is likely to inflict a negative self-image, distress, and often ill health on the underprivileged and disenfranchised. Today we have the intellectual freedom and impetus to sort out harmful discourse from that indispensable to the continuity of cooperative social groups. The medical anthropologist must tread lightly between the poles of cultural interpreter and cultural critic, defender of tradition and broker for change.

The task of a critical-interpretive medical anthropology is, first, to describe the variety of metaphorical conceptions (conscious and unconscious) about the body and associated narratives and then to show the social, political, and individual uses to which these conceptions are applied in practice. When using such an approach, medical knowledge is not conceived of as an autonomous body but as rooted in and continually modified by practice and social and political change. Medical knowledge is, of course, also constrained (but not determined) by the structure and functioning of the human body. A medical anthropologist therefore attempts to explore the notion of "embodied personhood" (Turner 1986:2): the relationship of cultural beliefs in connection with health and illness to the sentient human body.

In this chapter we will set out a critical-interpretive perspective in which we draw for inspiration upon some facets of general anthropological discourse about the body. We believe that insofar as medical anthropology fails to consider the way in which the human body itself is culturally constructed, it is destined to fall prey to certain assumptions characteristic of biomedicine. Foremost among these assumptions is the much-noted Cartesian dualism that separates mind from body, spirit from matter, and real (that is, measurable) from unreal. Since this epistemological tradition is a cultural and historical construction and not one that is universally shared, it is essential that we begin by examining this assumption.[1]

THE THREE BODIES

> The body is the first and most natural tool of man.
> —Marcel Mauss (1979 [1950]).

Essential to our task is a consideration of the relations among what we will refer to here as the "three bodies."[2] At the first and perhaps most self-evident level is the individual body, understood in the phenomenological sense of the lived experience of the body-self. We may reasonably assume that all people share at least some intuitive sense of the embodied self as existing apart from other individual bodies (Mauss 1985[1938]). However, the constituent parts of the body—mind, matter, psyche, soul, self—and their relations to each other and the ways in which the body is experienced in health and sickness are highly variable.

At the second level of analysis is the social body, referring to the representational uses of the body as a natural symbol with which to think about nature, society, and culture (Douglas 1970). Here our discussion follows the well-trodden path of social, symbolic, and structuralist anthropologists who have demonstrated a constant exchange of meanings between the natural and the social worlds. The body in health offers a model of organic wholeness; the body in sickness offers a model of social disharmony, conflict, and disintegration. Reciprocally, society in "sickness" and in "health" offers a model for understanding the body.

At the third level of analysis is the body politic, referring to the regulation, surveillance, and control of bodies (individual and collective) in reproduction and sexuality, work, leisure, and sickness. There are many types of polity, ranging from the acephalous groupings of "simple" foraging societies, in which deviants may be simply ignored or else punished by total social ostracism and consequently by death (see Briggs 1970; Turnbull 1962), through to chieftainships, monarchies, oligarchies, democracies, and modern totalitarian states. In each of these polities the stability of the body politic rests on its ability to regulate populations (the social body) and to discipline individual bodies. A great deal has been written about the regulation and control of individual and social bodies in complex, industrialized societies. Michel Foucault's work is exemplary in this regard (1973, 1975, 1979, 1980a). Less has been written about the ways in which preindustrial societies control their populations and institutionalize means for producing docile bodies and pliant minds in the service of some definition of collective stability, health, and social well-being.

The following analysis will move back and forth between a discussion of "the bodies" as a useful heuristic concept for understanding cultures and societies, on the one hand, and for increasing knowledge of the cultural sources and meanings of health and illness, on the other.

THE INDIVIDUAL BODY

How Real Is Real? The Cartesian Legacy

A singular premise guiding Western science and clinical medicine (and one, we hasten to add, that is responsible for its awesome efficacy) is its commitment to a fundamental opposition between spirit and matter, mind and body, and (underlying this) real and unreal. We are reminded of a presentation that concerned the case of a middle-aged woman suffering from chronic and debilitating headaches. In halting sentences the patient explained before the large class of first-year medical students that her husband was an alcoholic who occasionally beat her, that she had been virtually housebound for the past five years looking after her senile and incontinent mother-in-law, and that she worried constantly about her teenage son, who was flunking out of high school. Although the woman's story elicited considerable sympathy from the students, one young woman finally interrupted the professor to demand, "But what is the real cause of the headaches?"

The medical student, like many of her classmates, interpreted the stream of social information as extraneous and irrelevant to the real biomedical diagnosis. She wanted information on the neurochemical changes, which she understood as constituting the true causal explanation. This kind of radically materialist thinking is the product of a Western epistemology extending as far back as Aristotle's starkly biological view of the human soul in *De Anima*. As a basis for clinical practice, it can be found in the Hippocratic corpus (ca. 400 B.C.).[3] Hippocrates and his students were determined to eradicate the vestiges of magico-religious thinking about the human body and to introduce a rational basis for clinical practice that would challenge the power of the ancient folk healers or "charlatans" and "magi," as Hippocrates labeled his medical competitors. In a passage from his treatise on epilepsy, ironically entitled "On the Sacred Disease," Hippocrates (Adams 1939:355–56) cautioned physicians to treat only what was observable and palpable to the senses: "I do not believe that the so-called Sacred Disease is any more divine or sacred than any other disease, but that on the contrary, just as other diseases have a nature and a definite cause, so does this one, too, have a nature and a cause.... It is my opinion that those who first called this disease sacred were the sort of people that we now call 'magi.'"

The natural-supernatural, real-unreal dichotomy has taken many forms over the course of Western history and civilization, but it was the philosopher-mathematician René Descartes (1596–1650) who most clearly formulated the ideas that are the immediate precursors of contemporary biomedical conceptions about the human organism. Descartes was determined to hold nothing as true until he had established the grounds of evidence for accepting it as such. The single category to be taken on faith was the existence of the thinking being, expressed in Descartes' dictum: "Cogito, ergo sum" ("I think, therefore I am"). He then used the concept of the thinking being to establish "proof" for the existence of God whom, Descartes believed, had created the physical world. Descartes, a devout Catholic, stated that one should not question that which God had created; however, by creating a concept of mind, Descartes was able to reconcile his religious beliefs with his scientific curiosity. The higher "essence" of man, the rational mind, was thus extracted from nature, allowing a rigorous objective examination of nature, including the human body, for the first time in Western history. This separation of mind and body, the so-called Cartesian dualism, freed biology to pursue the kind of radically materialist thinking expressed by the medical student, an approach that has permitted the development of the natural and clinical sciences as we know them today.

The Cartesian legacy to clinical medicine and to the natural and social sciences is a rather mechanistic conception of the body and its functions and a failure to conceptualize a "mindful" causation of somatic states. It would take a struggling psychoanalytic psychiatry and the gradual development of psychosomatic medicine in the early twentieth century to begin the task of reuniting mind and body in clinical theory and practice. Yet even in psychoanalytically informed psychiatry and in psychosomatic medicine, there is a tendency to categorize and treat human afflictions as if they were either wholly organic or wholly psychological in origin: "it" is in the body or "it" is in the mind (Kirmayer 1988). In her analysis of multidisciplinary case conferences on chronic pain patients, for example, Kitty Corbett (1986) discovered the intractability of Cartesian thinking among sophisticated clinicians. These physicians, psychiatrists, and clinical social workers "knew" that pain was "real," whether or not the source of it could be verified by diagnostic tests. Nonetheless, they could not help but express evident relief when a "true" (single, generally organic) cause could be discovered. Moreover, when diagnostic tests indicated some organic explanation, the psychological and social aspects of the pain tended to be all but forgotten, and when severe psychopathology could be diagnosed, the organic complications and indices tended to be ignored. Pain, it seems, was either physical or mental, biological or psychosocial—never both or something not quite either.

As both medical anthropologists and clinicians struggle to view humans and the experience of illness and suffering from an integrated perspective, they often find themselves trapped by the Cartesian legacy. We lack a precise vocabulary with which to deal with mind-body-society interactions and so are left suspended in hyphens, testifying to the disconnectedness of our thoughts. We are forced to resort to such fragmented concepts as the "biosocial" or the "psychosomatic" as altogether feeble ways of expressing the many forms in which the mind speaks through the body and the ways in which society is inscribed on the expectant canvas of human flesh. As Milan Kundera (1984:15) recently observed: "The rise of science propelled man into tunnels of specialized knowledge. With every step forward in scientific knowledge, the less clearly he could see the world as a whole or his own self." Ironically, conscious attempts to temper the materialism and reductionism of biomedical science often end up inadvertently recreating the mind-body opposition in a new form. For example, a distinction between disease and illness was elaborated in an effort to distinguish the biomedical conception of "abnormalities in the structure and/or function of organs and organ systems" (disease) from the patients' subjective experience of malaise (illness). (Eisenberg 1977). While this paradigm has certainly helped to sensitize both clinicians and social scientists to the social origins of sickness, one unanticipated effect has been that physicians now often claim both aspects of the sickness experience for the medical domain. As a result, the illness dimension of human distress is being medicalized and individualized rather than politicized and collectivized (see Scheper-Hughes and Lock 1986; Lock 1988b). Medicalization inevitably entails a missed identification between the individual and the social bodies and a tendency to transform the social into the biological.

Mind-body dualism is related to other conceptual oppositions in Western epistemology, such as those between nature and culture, passion and reason, individual and society—dichotomies that social thinkers as different as Emile Durkheim, Marcel Mauss, Karl Marx, and Sigmund Freud understood as inevitable and often unresolvable contradictions and as natural and universal categories. Although Durkheim was primarily concerned with the relationship of the individual to society, he devoted some attention to the mind-body, nature-society dichotomies. In *The Elementary Forms of the Religious Life* Durkheim wrote that "man is double" (1961[1915]:29), referring to the biological and the social. The physical body provided for the reproduction of society through sexuality and socialization. For Durkheim society represented the "highest reality in the intellectual and moral order." The body was the storehouse of emotions that were the raw materials, the stuff, out of which mechanical solidarity was forged in the interests of the collectivity. Building on Durkheim, Mauss wrote of the "dominion of the conscious [will] over emotion and unconsciousness" (1979[1950]:122). The degree to which the random and chaotic impulses of the body were disciplined by social institutions revealed the stamp of higher civilizations.

Freud introduced yet another interpretation of the mind-body, nature-culture, individual-society set of oppositions with his theory of dynamic psychology: the individual at war within himself. Freud proposed a human drama in which natural, biological drives locked horns with the domesticating requirements of the social and moral order. The resulting repressions of the libido through a largely painful process of socialization produced the many neuroses of modern life. Psychiatry was called on to diagnose and treat the disease of wounded psyches whose egos were not in control of the rest of their minds. *Civilization and Its Discontents* may be read as a psychoanalytic parable concerning the mind-body, nature-culture, and individual-society oppositions in Western epistemology.

For Marx and his associates the natural world existed as an external, objective reality that was transformed by human labor. Humans distinguish themselves from animals, Marx and Engels wrote, "as soon as they begin to produce their means of subsistence" (1970:42). In *Capital* Marx wrote that labor humanizes and domesticates nature. It gives life to inanimate objects, and it pushes back the natural frontier, leaving a human stamp on all that it touches.

Although the nature-culture opposition has been interpreted as the "very matrix of Western metaphysics" (Benoist 1978:59) and has "penetrated so deeply . . . that we have come to regard it as natural and inevitable" (Goody 1977:64), there have always been alternative ontologies. One of these is surely the view that culture is rooted in (rather than against) nature, imitating it and emanating directly from it. Cultural materialists, for example, have tended to view social institutions as adaptive responses to certain fixed, biological foundations. M. Harris (1974, 1979) refers to culture as a "banal" or "vulgar" solution to the human condition insofar as it "rests on the ground and is built up out of guts, sex, energy" (1974:3). Mind collapses into body in these formulations.

Similarly, some human biologists and psychologists have suggested that the mind-body, nature-culture, and individual-society oppositions are natural (and presumed universal) categories of thinking insofar as they are a cognitive and symbolic manifestation of human biology. R. E. Ornstein (1973), for example, understands mind-body dualism as an overly determined expression of human brain lateralization. According to this view, the uniquely human specialization of the brain's left hemisphere for cognitive, rational, and analytic functions and of the right hemisphere for intuitive, expressive, and artistic functions within the context of left hemisphere dominance sets the stage for the symbolic and cultural dominance of reason over passion, mind over body, culture over nature, and male over female. This kind of biological reductionism is, however, rejected by most contemporary social anthropologists, who stress instead the cultural sources of these oppositions in Western thought.

We should bear in mind that our epistemology is but one among many systems of knowledge regarding the relations held to obtain among mind, body, culture, nature, and society. For example, some non-Western civilizations have developed alternative epistemologies that tend to conceive of relations among similar entities in monistic rather than in dualistic terms. Representations of holism in non-Western epistemologies in defining relationships between any set of concepts or principles of exclusion and inclusion come into play. Representations of holism and monism tend toward inclusiveness. Two representations of holistic thought are particularly common. The first is a conception of harmonious wholes in which everything from the cosmos down to the individual organs of the human body is understood as a single unit. This is often expressed as the relationship of microcosm to macrocosm in which the relationship of parts to the whole is emphasized. A second representation of holistic thinking is that of complementary (not opposing) dualities in which contrasts are made between paired entities within the whole. One of the better-known representations of balanced complementarity is the ancient Chinese yin-yang cosmology, which first appears in the *I Ching* somewhat before the third century B.C. In this view, the entire cosmos, including the human body, is understood as poised in a state of dynamic equilibrium, oscillating between the poles of yin and yang, masculine and feminine, light and dark, hot and cold. The tradition of ancient Chinese medicine acquired the yin-yang cosmology from the Taoists and from Confucianism a concern with social ethics, moral conduct, and the importance of maintaining harmonious relations among individuals, family, community, and state. Conceptions of the healthy body were patterned after the healthy state. In both there is an emphasis on order, harmony, balance, and hierarchy within the context of mutual interdependencies. The health of individuals depends on a balance in the natural world, and the health of each organ depends on its relationship to all other organs. Nothing can change without changing the whole (Unschuld 1985).

Islamic cosmology, a synthesis of early Greek philosophy, Judeo-Christian concepts, and prophetic revelations set down in the Qur'an, depicts humans as having dominance over nature, but this potential opposition is tempered by a sacred worldview that stresses the complementarity of all phenomena (Jachimowicz 1975; Shariati 1979). At the core of Islamic belief lies the unifying concept of Towhid, which Shariati argues should be understood as going beyond the strictly religious meaning of "God is one, no more than one" to encompass a worldview that represents all existence as essentially monistic. Guided by the principle of Towhid, humans are responsible to one power, answerable to a single judge, and guided by one principle: the achievement of unity through the complementarities of spirit and body, this world and the hereafter, substance and meaning, natural and supernatural, and so on.

The concept in Western philosophical traditions of an observing and reflexive "I," a mindful self that stands outside the body and apart from nature, is another heritage of Cartesian dualism that contrasts sharply with a Buddhist form of subjectivity and relation to the natural world. In writing about the Buddhist Sherpas of Nepal, Robert Paul suggests that they do not perceive their interiority or their subjectivity as "hopelessly cut off and excluded from the rest of nature, but [rather as] . . . connected to, indeed identical with, the entire essential being of the cosmos" (1976:131). In Buddhist traditions the natural world (the world of appearances) is a product of mind, in the sense that the entire cosmos is essentially "mind." Through meditation, individual minds can merge with the universal mind. Understanding is reached not through analytic methods but rather through an intuitive synthesis, achieved in moments of transcendence that are beyond speech, language, and the written word.

The Buddhist philosopher Suzuki (1960) contrasted Eastern and Western aesthetics and attitudes toward nature by comparing two poems, a seventeenth-century Japanese haiku and a nineteenth-century poem by Alfred Tennyson. The Japanese poet wrote:

> When I look carefully
> I see the nazuna blooming
> By the hedge!

In contrast, Tennyson wrote:

> Flower in the crannied wall,
> I pluck you out of the crannies,
> I hold you here, root and all, in my hand,
> Little flower—but if I could understand
> What you are, root and all, and all in all,
> I should know what God and man is.

Suzuki observes that the Japanese poet, Basho, does not pluck the nazuna but is content to admire it from a respectful distance; his feelings are "too full, too deep, and he has no desire to conceptualize it" (1960:3). Tennyson, in contrast, is active and analytical. He rips the plant by its roots, destroying it in the very act of admiring it. "He does not apparently care for its destiny. His curiosity must be satisfied. As some medical scientists do, he would vivisect the flower" (Suzuki 1960:3). Tennyson's violent imagery is reminiscent of Francis Bacon's description of the natural scientist as one who must "torture nature's secrets from her" and make her a "slave" to mankind (Merchant 1980:169). Principles of monism, holism, and balanced complementarity in nature, which can temper perceptions of opposition and conflict, have largely given way to the analytic urge in the recent history of Western culture.

Person, Self, and Individual

The relation of individual to society, which has occupied so much of contemporary social theory, is based on a perceived "natural" opposition between the demands of the social and moral order and egocentric drives, impulses, wishes, and needs. The individual-society opposition, while fundamental to Western epistemology, is also rather unique to it. Clifford Geertz has argued that the Western conception of the person "as a bounded, unique . . . integrated motivational and cognitive universe, a dynamic center of awareness, emotion, judgment, and action . . . is a rather peculiar idea within the context of the world's cultures" (1984:126). In fact, the modern conception of the individual self is of recent historical origin, even in the West. It was only with the publication in 1690 of John Locke's *Essay Concerning Human Understanding* that we have a detailed theory of the person that identifies the I or the self with a state of permanent consciousness that is unique to the individual and stable through the life span until death (Webel 1983:399).

Though not as detailed perhaps, it would nonetheless be difficult to imagine a people completely devoid of some intuitive perception of the independent self. We think it reasonable to assume that all humans are endowed with a self-consciousness of mind and body, with an internal body image, and with what neurologists have identified as the proprioceptive or sixth sense, our sense of body self-awareness, of mind-body integration, and of being-in-the-world as separate and apart from other human beings. David Winnicot regards the intuitive perception of the body-self as "naturally" placed in the body, a precultural given (1971:48). While this seems a reasonable assumption, it is important to distinguish this universal awareness of the individual body-self from the social conception of the individual as "person," a construct of jural rights and moral accountability (LaFontaine 1985:124). *La personne morale*, as Mauss (1985[1938]) phrased it, is the uniquely Western notion of the individual as a quasi-sacred, legal, moral, and psychological entity whose rights are limited only by the rights of other equally autonomous individuals.

Modern psychologists and psychoanalysts (Winnicot among them) have tended to interpret the process of individuation, defined as a gradual estrangement from parents and other family members, as a necessary stage in the human maturation process (see also Johnson 1985; DeVos, Marsella, and Hsu 1985:3–5). This is, however, a culture-bound notion of human development and one that conforms to fairly recent conceptions of the relation of the individual to society.

In Japan, although the concept of individualism has been debated vigorously since the end of the last century, the Confucian heritage is still evident today in that it is the family that is considered the most natural, fundamental unit of society, not the individual. Consequently, the greatest tension in Japan for at least the past four hundred years has been between one's obligations to the state and one's obligations to the family.

The philosophical traditions of Shintoism and Buddhism have also militated against Japanese conceptions of individualism. The animism of Shinto fosters feelings of identification with nature, and many of the techniques of Buddhist contemplation encourage detachment from earthly desires. Neither tradition encourages the development of a highly individuated self.

Japan has been repeatedly described as a culture of social relativism, in which the person is understood as acting within the context of a social relationship, never simply autonomously (Lebra 1976; Smith 1983). One's self-identity changes with the social context, particularly within the hierarchy of social relations at any time. The child's identity is established through the responses of others; conformity and dependency, even in adulthood, are not understood as signs of weakness but rather as the result of inner strength (Reischauer 1977:152). But one fear haunts may contemporary Japanese: that of losing oneself completely, of becoming totally immersed in social obligations. One protective device is a distinction made between the external self (*tatemae*)—the persona, the mask, the social self that one presents to others—and a more private (*honne*), that "natural" hidden self. Clifford Geertz has described a similar phenomenon among the Javanese and Balinese (1984:127–28).

Kenneth Read argues that the Gahuku-Gama of New Guinea lack a concept of the person altogether: "Individual identity and social identity are two sides of the same coin" (1955:276). He maintains that there is no awareness of the individual apart from structured social roles and no concept of friendship, that is, a relationship between two unique individuals that is not defined by kinship, neighborhood, or other social claims. Gahuku-Gama seem to define the self, insofar as they do so at all, in terms of the body's constituent parts: limbs, facial features, hair, bodily secretions, and excretions. Of particular significance is the Gahuku-Gama conception of the social skin, which includes both the covering of the body and the person's social and character traits. References to one's "good" or "bad" skin indicate a person's moral character or even a person's temperament or mood. Gahuku-Gama seem to experience themselves most intensely when in contact with others and through their skins (see also LaFontaine 1985:129–30).

Such sociocentric conceptions of the self have been widely documented for many parts of the world (see Shweder and Bourne 1982; Devisch 1985; Fortes 1959; Harris 1978) and have relevance to ethnomedical understanding. In cultures and societies lacking a highly individualized or articulated conception of the body-self, it should not be surprising that sickness is often explained or attributed to malevolent social relations (that is, sorcery), to the breaking of social and moral codes, or to disharmony within the family or the village community. In such societies therapy, too, tends to be collectivized. The !Kung of Botswana engage in weekly healing trance-dance rituals that are viewed as both curative and preventive (Katz 1982). Lorna Marshall has described the dance as "one concerted religious act of the !Kung [that] brings people into such union that they become like one organic being" (1965:270).

In contrast to societies in which the individual body-self tends to be fused with or absorbed by the social body, there are societies that view the individual as comprised of a multiplicity of selves. The Bororo (like the Gahuku-Gama) understand the individual only as reflected in relationship to other people. Hence, the person consists of many selves: the self as perceived by parents, by other kinsmen, by enemies, and so forth. The Cuna Indians of Panama say they have eight selves, each associated with a different part of the body. A Cuna individual's temperament is the result of domination by one of these aspects or parts of the body. An intellectual is one who is governed by the head, a thief governed by the hand, a romantic by the heart, and so forth.

Finally, the Zinacanteco soul has thirteen divisible parts. Each time a person "loses" one or more parts, he or she becomes ill, and a curing ceremony is held to retrieve the missing pieces. At death the soul leaves the body and returns to whence it came—a soul "depository" kept by the ancestral gods. This soul pool is used for the creation of new human beings, each of whose own soul is made up of 13 parts from the life force of other previous humans. A person's soul force and his or her self is therefore a composite, a synthesis "borrowed" from many other humans. There is no sense that each Zinacanteco is a "brand-new" or totally unique individual; rather, each person is a fraction of the whole Zinacanteco social world. Moreover, the healthy Zinacanteco is one who is in touch with the divisible parts of himself or herself (Vogt 1969:396–374).

While in the industrialized West there are only pathologized explanations of dissociative states in which one experiences more than one self, in many non-Western cultures, individuals can experience multiple selves through the practice of spirit possession and other altered states of consciousness. Such ritualized and controlled experiences of possession are sought after throughout the world as valued forms of religious experience and therapeutic behavior. To date, however, psychological anthropologists have tended to "pathologize" these altered states as manifestations of unstable or psychotic personalities. The Western conception of one individual, one self effectively disallows ethnopsychologies that recognize as normative a multiplicity of selves.

Body Imagery

Closely related to conceptions of self (perhaps central to them) is what psychiatrists have labeled body image (Schilder 1970 [1950]; Horowitz 1966). Body image refers to the collective and idiosyncratic representations an individual entertains about the body in its relationship to the environment, including internal and external perceptions, memories, affects, cognitions, and actions. The existing literature on body imagery (although largely psychiatric) has been virtually untapped by medical anthropologists, who could benefit from attention to body boundary conceptions, distortions in body perception, and so on.

Some of the earliest and best work on body image was contained in clinical studies of individuals suffering from extremely distorted body perceptions that arose from neurological, organic, or psychiatric disorders (Head 1920; Schilder 1970[1950]; Luria 1972). The inability of some so-called schizophrenics to distinguish self from other or self from inanimate objects has been analyzed from psychoanalytic and phenomenological perspectives (Minkowski 1958; Binswanger 1958; Laing 1965; Basaglia 1964). Oliver Sacks (1973[1970], 1985) also has written about rare neurological disorders that wreak havoc with the individual's body image, producing deficits and excesses, as well as metaphysical transports in mind-body experiences. Sacks's message throughout his poignant medical case histories is that humanness is not dependent on rationality or intelligence—that is, an intact mind. There is, he suggests, something intangible, a soul force or mind-self that produces humans even under the most devastating assaults on the brain, nervous system, and sense of bodily or mindful integrity.

While profound distortions in body imagery are rare, neurotic anxieties about the body, its orifices, boundaries, and fluids are quite common. S. Fisher and S. Cleveland (1958) demonstrated the relationship between patients' "choice" of symptoms and body image conceptions. The skin, for example, can be experienced as a protective hide and a defensive armor protecting the softer and more vulnerable internal organs. In the task of protecting the inside, however, the outside can take quite a beating, manifested in skin rashes and hives. Conversely, the skin can be imagined as a permeable screen, leaving the internal organs defenseless and prone to attacks of ulcers and colitis.

Particular organs, body fluids, and functions may also have special significance to a group of people. The liver, for example, absorbs a great deal of blame for many different ailments among the French, Spanish, Portuguese, and Brazilians, but to our knowledge only the Pueblo Indians of the Southwest suffer from "flipped liver" (Leeman 1986). The English and the Germans are, by comparison, far more obsessed with the condition and health of their bowels. Allan Dundes takes the Germanic fixation with the bowels, cleanliness, and anality as a fundamental constellation underlying German national character (1984), while Jonathon Miller writes that "when an Englishman complains about constipation, you never know whether he is talking about his regularity, his lassitude, or his depression" (1978:45).

Blood is a nearly universal symbol of human life, and some people, both ancient and contemporary, have taken the quality of the blood, pulse, and circulation as the primary diagnostic sign of health or illness. The traditional Chinese doctor, for example, often made his diagnosis by feeling the pulse in both of the patient's wrists and comparing them with his own, an elaborate ritual that could take several hours. Loudell Snow (1974) has described the rich constellation of ethnomedical properties attached to the quality of the blood by poor black Americans, who suffer from "high" or "low," fast and slow, thick and thin, bitter and sweet blood. Uli Linke (1986) has analyzed the concept of blood as a predominant metaphor in European culture, especially its uses in political ideologies, such as during the Nazi era. Similarly, the multiple stigmas suffered by North American AIDS patients include a preoccupation with the "bad blood" of diseased homosexuals (Lancaster 1983).

Hispanic mothers from southern Mexico to northern New Mexico focus some of their body organ anxieties on the infant's fontanel. Open, it exposes the newborn to the evil influences of night airs, as well as the envious looks and wishes of neighbors. Until it closes over, there is always the threat of mollera caida, "fallen fontanel," a life-threatening pediatric disorder (Scheper-Hughes and Stewart 1983).

In short, ethnoanatomical perceptions, including body image, offer a rich source of data on both the social and cultural meanings of being human and on the various threats to health, well-being, and social integration that humans are believed to experience.

THE SOCIAL BODY

The Body as Symbol

Symbolic and structuralist anthropologists have demonstrated the extent to which humans find the body "good to think with." The human organism and its natural products of blood, milk, tears, semen, and excreta may be used as a cognitive map to represent other natural, supernatural, social, and even spatial relations. The body, as Mary Douglas observed, is a natural symbol supplying some of our richest sources of metaphor (1970:65). Cultural constructions of and about the body are useful in sustaining particular views of society and social relations.

Rodney Needham, for example, pointed out some of the frequently occurring associations between the left and that which is inferior, dark, dirty, and female, and the right and that which is superior, holy, light, dominant, and male. He called attention to such uses of the body as the convenient means of justifying particular social values and social arrangements, such as the "natural" dominance of males over females (1973:109). His point is that these common symbolic equations are not so much natural as they are useful, at least to those on the top and to the right.

Ethnobiological theories of reproduction usually reflect the character of their associated kinship system, as anthropologists have long observed. In societies with unilineal descent, it is common to encounter folk theories that emphasize the reproductive contributions of females in matrilineal and of males in patrilineal societies. The matrilineal Ashanti make the distinction between flesh and blood that is inherited through women and spirit that is inherited through males. The Brazilian Shavante, among whom patrilineages form the core of political factions, believe that the father fashions the infant through many acts of coitus, during which the mother is only passive and receptive. The fetus is "fully made," and conception is completed only in the fifth month of pregnancy. As one Shavante explained the process to David Maybury-Lewis, while ticking the months off with his fingers: "Copulate. Copulate, copulate, copulate, copulate a lot. Pregnant. Copulate, copulate, copulate. Born" (1967:63).

Similarly, the Western theory of equal male and female contributions to conception that spans the reproductive biologies from Galen to Theodore Dobzhansky (1970) probably owes more to the theory's compatibility with the European extended and stem bilateral kinship system than to scientific evidence, which was lacking until relatively recently. The principle of one father, one mother, one act of copulation leading to each pregnancy was part of the Western tradition for more than a thousand years before the discovery of spermatozoa (in 1677) and the female ova (in 1828) and before the actual process of human fertilization was fully understood and described (in 1875) (Barnes 1973:66). For centuries the theory of equal male and female contributions to conception was supported by the erroneous belief that females had the same reproductive organs and functions as males, except that, as one sixth-century bishop put it, "theirs are inside the body and not outside it" (Laquer 1986:3). To a great extent, talk about the body and about sexuality tends to be talk about the nature of society.

Of particular relevance to medical anthropologists are the frequently encountered symbolic equations between conceptions of the healthy body and the healthy society, as well as the diseased body and the malfunctioning society. John Janzen (1981) has noted that every society possesses a utopian conception of health that can be applied metaphorically from society to body and vice versa. One of the most enduring ideologies of individual and social health is that of a vital balance and harmony such as are found in the ancient medical systems of China, Greece,

India, and Persia, in contemporary Native American cultures of the Southwest (Shutler 1979), and also the holistic health movement of the twentieth century (Grossinger 1980). Conversely, illness and death can be attributed to social tensions, contradictions, and hostilities, as manifested in Mexican peasants' image of the limited good (Foster 1965), in the hot-cold syndrome and symbolic imbalance in Mexican folk medicine (Currier 1969), and in such folk idioms as witchcraft, evil eye, or "stress" (Scheper-Hughes and Lock 1986; Young 1980). Each of these beliefs exemplifies links between the health or illness of the individual body and the social body.

The Embodied World

One of the most common and richly detailed symbolic uses of the human body in the non-Western world is the personification of the spaces in which humans reside. The Qollahuayas live at the foot of Mt. Kaata in Bolivia and are known as powerful healers, the "lords of the medicine bag." They "understand their own bodies in terms of the mountain, and they consider the mountain in terms of their own anatomy" (Bastien 1985:598). The human body and the mountain consist of interrelated parts: head, chest and heart, stomach and viscera, breast and nipple. The mountain, like the body, must be fed blood and fat to keep it strong and healthy. Individual sickness is understood as a disintegration of the body, likened to a mountain landslide or an earthquake. Sickness is caused by disruptions between people and the land, specifically between residents of different sections of the mountain: the head (mountain top), heart (center village), or feet (the base of the mountain). Healers cure by gathering the various residents together to feed the mountain and to restore the wholeness and wellness that was compromised. Bastien concludes that Qollahuaya body concepts are fundamentally holistic rather than dualistic. He suggests that "the whole is greater than the sum of the parts... Wholeness (health) of the body is a process in which centripetal and centrifugal forces pull together and disperse fluids that provide emotions, thoughts, nutrients, and lubricants for members of the body" (p. 598).

Possibly the most elaborate use of the body in native cosmology comes from the Dogon of the western Sudan, as explained by Ogotemmeli to Marcel Griaule (1965) in his description of the ground plan of the Dogon community. The village must extend from north to south like the body of a man lying on his back. The head is the council house, built in the center square. To the east and west are the menstrual huts, which are "round like wombs and represent the hands of the village" (1965:97). The body metaphor also informs the interior of the Dogon house:

> The vestibule, which belongs to the master of the house, represents the male part of the couple, the outside door being his sexual organ. The big central room is the domain and the symbol of the woman; the store-rooms each side are her arms, and the communicating door her sexual parts. The central room and the store rooms together represent the woman lying on her back with outstretched arms, the door open, and the woman ready for intercourse. (1965:94–95)

Other well-known examples of the symbolic use of the human body in cosmological classification include the western Apache (Basso 1969), the Indonesian Atoni (Cunningham 1973), the Desana Indians of the Colombian-Brazilian border (Reichel-Dolmatoff 1971), the Pira-Pirana of the Amazon (Hugh-Jones 1979), the Zinacantecos of Chiapas (Vogt 1970), and the Fali of northern Cameroon (Zahan 1979).

Peter Manning and Horatio Fabrega (1973) have summarized some of the major differences between non-Western ethnomedical systems and modern biomedicine. In the latter, body and self are understood as distinct and separable entities; illness resides in either the body or the mind. Social relations are seen as partitioned, segmented, and situational—generally as discontinuous with health or sickness. By contrast, many ethnomedical systems do not logically distinguish body, mind, and self, and therefore illness cannot be situated in mind or body alone. Social relations are also understood as a key contributor to individual health and illness. In short, the body is seen as a unitary, integrated aspect of self and social relations. It is dependent on, and vulnerable to, the feelings, wishes, and actions of others, including spirits and dead ancestors. The body is not understood as a complex machine but rather as microcosm of the universe.

As Manning and Fabrega note, what is perhaps most significant about the symbolic and metaphorical extension of the body into the natural, social, and supernatural realms is that it demonstrates a unique kind of human autonomy that seems to have all but disappeared in the modern, industrialized world. The confident uses of the body in speaking about the external world convey a sense that humans are in control. It is doubtful that the Colombian Qollahuayas or the Desana or the Dogon experience anything to the degree of body alienation, so common to Western civilization, as expressed in the schizophrenias, anorexias, and bulemias or the addictions, obsessions, and fetishisms of life in the postindustrialized world.

The mind-body dichotomy and body alienation characteristic of contemporary society may be linked not simply to reductionistic post-Cartesian thinking but also to capitalist modes of production in which manual and mental labors are divided and ordered into a hierarchy. Human labor, thus divided and fragmented, is by Marxist definition "alienated." E. P. Thompson discusses the subversion of natural, body time to the clock-work regimentation and work discipline required by industrialization. He juxtaposes the factory worker, whose labor is extracted in minute, recorded segments, with the Nuer pastoralist, for whom "the daily timepiece is the cattle clock" (Evans-Pritchard 1940:100), or the Aran Islander, whose work is managed by the amount of time left before twilight (Thompson 1967:59).

Similarly, Pierre Bourdieu describes the "regulated improvisations" of Algerian peasants, whose movements roughly correspond to diurnal and seasonal rhythms. "At the return of the Azal (dry season)," he writes, "everything without exception, in the activities of men, women and children is abruptly altered by the adoption of a new rhythm" (1977:159). Everything from men's work to the domestic activities of women, to rest periods, and ceremonies, prayers, and public meetings is set in terms of the natural transition from the wet to the dry season. Doing one's duty in the village context means "respecting rhythms, keeping pace, not falling out of line" (1977:161) with one's fellow villagers. Although, as Bourdieu suggests, these peasants may suffer from a species of false consciousness (or "bad faith") that allows them to misrepresent to themselves their social world as the only possible way to think and to behave and to perceive as "natural" what are, in fact, self-imposed cultural rules, there is little doubt that these Algerian villagers live in a social and a natural world that has a decidedly human shape and feel to it. We might refer to their world as embodied.

In contrast, the world in which most of us live is lacking a comfortable and familiar human shape. At least one source of body alienation in advanced industrial societies is the symbolic equation of humans and machines, originating in our industrial modes and relations of production and in the commodity fetishism of modern life, in which even the human body has been transformed into a commodity. Again, Manning and Fabrega capture this well: "In primitive society the body of man is the paradigm for the derivation of the parts and meanings of other significant objects; in modern society man has adopted the language of the machine to describe his body. This reversal, wherein man sees himself in terms of the external world, as a reflection of himself, is the representative formula for expressing the present situation of modern man" (1973:283).

We rely on the body-as-machine metaphor each time we describe our somatic or psychological states in mechanistic terms, saying that we are "worn out" or "wound up" or when we say that we are "rundown" and that our "batteries need recharging." In recent years the metaphors have moved from a mechanical to an electrical mode (we are "turned off," "tuned in," we "get a charge" out of something), while the computer age has lent us a host of new expressions, including the all-too-familiar complaint: "my energy is down." Our point is that the structure of individual and collective sentiments down to the "feel" of one's body and the naturalness of one's position and role in the technical order is a social construct. Thomas Belmonte described the body rhythms of the factory worker: "The work of factory workers is a stiff military drill, a regiment of arms welded to metal bars and wheels. Marx, Veblen and Charlie Chaplin have powerfully made the point that, on the assembly line, man neither makes nor uses tools, but is continuous with tool as a minute, final attachment to the massive industrial machine" (1979:130). The machines have changed since those early days of the assembly line. One thinks today not of the brutality of huge grinding gears and wheels but rather of the sterile silence and sanitized pollution of the microelectronics industries to which the nimble fingers, strained eyes, and docile bodies of a new, largely female and Asian labor force are now melded. What has not changed to any appreciable degree is the relationship of human bodies to the machines under twentieth-century forms of industrial capitalism.

Non-Western and nonindustrialized people are "called upon to think the world with their bodies" (O'Neill 1985:151). Like Adam and Eve in the Garden, they exercise their autonomy, their power, by naming the phenomena and creatures of the world in their own image and likeness. By contrast, we live in a world in which the human shape of things (and even the human shape of humans with their mechanical hearts and plastic hips) is in retreat. While the cosmologies of nonindustrialized people speak to a constant exchange of metaphors from body to nature and back to body again, our metaphors speak of machine-to-body symbolic equations. O'Neill suggests that we have been "put on the machine" of biotechnology, some of us transformed by radical surgery and genetic engineering into "spare parts" or prosthetic humans (1985:153–54). Lives are saved, or at least deaths are postponed, but it is possible that our humanity is being compromised in the process.

THE BODY POLITIC

The relationships between individual and social bodies concern more than metaphors and collective representations of the natural and the cultural. They are also about power and control. Mary Douglas (1966) contends, for example, that when a community experiences itself as threatened, it will respond by expanding the number of social controls regulating the group's boundaries. Points where outside threats may infiltrate and pollute the inside become the focus of regulation and surveillance. The three bodies—individual, social, and body politic—may be closed off, protected by a nervous vigilance about exits and entrances. Douglas had in mind witchcraft crazes, including the Salem trials, contemporary African societies, and even recent witch-hunts in the United States. In each of these instances the body politic is likened to the human body in which what is "inside" is good and all that is "outside" is evil. The body politic under threat of attack is cast as vulnerable, leading to purges of traitors and social deviants, while individual hygiene may focus on the maintenance of ritual purity or on fears of losing blood, semen, tears, or milk.

Threats to the continued existence of the social group may be real or imaginary. Even when the threats are real, however, the true aggressors may not be known, and witchcraft or sorcery can become the metaphor or the cultural idiom for distress. Shirley Lindenbaum (1979) has shown, for example, how an epidemic of kuru among the South Fore of New Guinea led to sorcery accusations and counteraccusatons and attempts to purify both the individual and collective bodies of their impurities and contaminants. Leith Mullings suggests that witchraft and sorcery were widely used in contemporary West Africa as "metaphors for social relations" (1984:164). In the context of a rapidly industrializing market town in Ghana, witchcraft accusations can express anxieties over social contradictions introduced by capitalism. Hence, accusations were directed at individuals and families who, in the pursuit of economic success, appeared most competitive, greedy, and individualistic in their social relations. Mullings argues that witchcraft accusations are an inchoate expression of resistance to the erosion of traditional social values based on reciprocity, sharing, and family and community loyalty. She suggests that in the context of increasing commoditization of human life, witchcraft accusations point to social distortions and disease in the body politic generated by capitalism.

When the sense of social order is threatened, boundaries between the individual and political bodies become blurred, and there is a strong concern with matters of ritual and sexual purity, often expressed in vigilance over social and bodily boundaries.

For example, in Ballybran, rural Ireland, villagers were equally guarded about what they took into the body (as in sex and food) as they were about being "taken in" (as in "codding," flattery, and blarney) by outsiders, especially those with a social advantage over them. Concern with the penetration and violation of bodily exits, entrances, and boundaries extended to material symbols of the body—the home, with its doors, gates, fences, and stone boundaries, around which many protective rituals, prayers, and social customs served to create social distance and a sense of personal control and security (Scheper-Hughes 1979).

In addition to controlling bodies in a time of crisis, societies regularly reproduce and socialize the kind of bodies that they need. Body decoration is a means through which social self-identities are constructed and expressed (Strathern and Strathern 1971). T. Turner developed the concept of the "social skin" to express the imprinting of social categories on the body-self (1980). For Turner, the surface of the body represents a "kind of common frontier of society which becomes the symbolic stage upon which the drama of socialization is enacted" (1980:112). Clothing and other forms of bodily adornment become the language through which cultural identity is expressed.

In our own increasingly "healthist" and body-conscious culture, the politically correct body for both sexes is the lean, strong, androgenous, and physically fit form through which the core cultural values of autonomy, toughness, competitiveness, youth, and self-control are readily manifest (Pollitt 1982). Health is increasingly viewed in the United States as an achieved rather than an ascribed status, and each individual is expected to "work hard" at being strong, fit, and healthy. Conversely, ill health is no longer viewed as accidental, a mere quirk of nature, but rather is attributed to the individual's failure to live right, to eat well, to exercise, and so forth. We might ask what it is our society wants from this kind of body. Lloyd DeMause (1984) has speculated that the fitness-toughness craze is a reflection of an international preparation for war. A hardening and toughening of the national fiber corresponds to a toughening of individual bodies. In attitude and ideology the self-help and fitness movements articulate both a militarist and a social Darwinist ethos: the fast and fit win; the fat and flabby lose and drop out of the human race (Scheper-Hughes and Stein 1987). Robert Crawford (1980, 1984), however, has suggested that the fitness movement may reflect, instead, a pathetic and individualized (also wholly inadequate) defense against the threat of nuclear holocaust.

Rather than strong and fit, the politically (and economically) correct body can entail grotesque distortions of human anatomy, including in various times and places the bound feet of Chinese women (Daly 1978), the 16-inch waists of antebellum Southern socialites (Kunzle 1981), and the tuberculin wanness of nineteenth-century romantics (Sontag 1978). Crawford (1984) has interpreted the eating disorders and distortions in body image expressed in obsessional jogging, anorexia, and bulimia as a symbolic mediation of the contradictory demands of postindustrial American society. The double-binding injunction to be self-controlled, fit, and productive workers and to be at the same time self-indulgent, pleasure-seeking consumers is especially destructive to the self-image of the American woman. Expected to be fun loving and sensual, she must also remain thin, lovely, and self-disciplined. Since one cannot be hedonistic and controlled simultaneously, one can alternate phases of binge eating, drinking, and drugging with phases of jogging, purging, and vomiting. Out of this cyclical resolution of the injunction to consume and to conserve is born, according to Crawford, the current epidemic of eating disorders (especially bulimia) among young women, some of whom literally eat and diet to death.

Cultures are disciplines that provide codes and social scripts for the domestication of the individual body in conformity to the needs of the social and political order. Certainly the use of physical torture by the modern state provides the most graphic illustration of the subordination of the individual body to the body politic (Foucault 1979). The history of colonialism contains some of the most brutal instances of the political uses of torture and the "culture of terror" in the interests of economic hegemony (Taussig 1984, 1987; Peters 1985). Elaine Scarry suggests that torture is increasingly resorted to today by unstable regimes in an attempt to assert the "incontestable reality" of their control over the populace (1985:27).

The body politic can, of course, exert its control over individual bodies in less dramatic ways. Foucault's (1973, 1975, 1979, 1980b) analyses of the role of medicine, criminal justice, psychiatry, and the various social sciences in producing new forms of power-knowledge over bodies are illustrative in this regard. The proliferation of disease categories and labels in medicine and psychiatry, resulting in ever more restricted definitions of the normal, has created a sick and deviant majority, a problem that medical and psychiatric anthropologists have been slow to explore. Radical changes in the organization of social and public life in advanced industrial societies, including the disappearance of traditional cultural idioms for the expression of individual and collective discontent (such as witchcraft, sorcery, rituals of reversal and travesty), have allowed medicine and psychiatry to assume a hegemonic role in shaping and responding to human distress. Apart from anarchic forms of random street violence and other forms of direct assault and confrontation, illness somatization has become a dominant metaphor for expressing individual and social complaint. Negative and hostile feelings can be shaped and transformed by doctors and psychiatrists into symptoms of new diseases such as PMS (premenstrual syndrome), depression, or attention deficit disorder (Martin 1987; Lock 1986a; Lock and Dunk 1987; Rubinstein and Brown 1984). In this way such negative social sentiments as female rage and school phobias can be recast as individual pathologies and "symptoms" rather than as socially significant signs (Lock 1988b, 1988c). This funneling of diffuse but real complaints into the idiom of sickness has led to the problem of medicalization and to the overproduction of illness in contemporary advanced industrial societies. In this process, the role of doctors, social workers, psychiatrists, and criminologists as agents of social consensus is pivotal. As Kim Hopper (1982) has suggested, health professions are predisposed to "fail to see the secret indignation of the sick." The medical gaze is, then, a controlling gaze, through which active (although furtive) forms of protest are transformed into passive acts of "breakdown."

While the medicalization of life (and its political and social control functions) is understood by critical medical social scientists (Freidson 1972; Zola 1972; Roth 1972; Illich 1976; deVries 1982) as a fairly permanent feature of industrialized societies, few medical anthropologists have yet explored the immediate effects of medicalization in those areas of the world where the process is occurring for the first time. In the following passage, recorded by Bourdieu (1977:166), an old Kabyle woman explains what it meant to be sick before and after medicalization was a feature of Algerian peasant life:

In the old days, folk didn't know what illness was. They went to bed and they died. It's only nowadays that we're learning words like liver, lung . . . intestines, stomach . . . , and I don't know what! People only used to know [pain in] the belly; that's what everyone who died died of, unless it was the fever. . . . Now everyone's sick, everyone's complaining of something. . . . Who's ill nowadays? Who's well? Everyone complains, but no one stays in bed: they all run to the doctor. Everyone knows what's wrong with him now.

An anthropology of relations between the body and the body politic inevitably leads to a consideration of the regulation and control not only of individuals but of populations and therefore of sexuality, gender, and reproduction—what Foucault (1980a) refers to as a biopower. Prior to the publication of Malthus's *An Essay on the Principle of Population* in 1798, there existed a two-millennia-old tradition of interpreting the health, strength, and reproductive vigor of individual bodies as a sign of the health and well-being of the state (Gallagher 1986:83). Following Malthus, however, the equation of a healthy body with a healthy body politic was recast; the unfettered fertility of individuals became a sign of an enfeebled social organism. The power of the state now depended on the ability to control physical potency and fertility: "the healthy and, consequently reproducing body [became] . . . the harbinger of the disordered society full of starving bodies" (Gallagher 1986:85).

B. Turner (1984:91) writing about Europe suggests that the government and regulation of female sexuality involves, at the institutional level, a system of patriarchal households for controlling fertility; and at the individual level, ideologies of sexual puritanism were a structural requirement of European societies until the mid-nineteenth century (Imhof 1985) and of rural Ireland through the late twentieth century (Scheper-Hughes 1979).

EMOTION: MEDIATRIX OF THE THREE BODIES

An anthropology of the body necessarily entails a theory of emotions. Emotions affect the way in which the body, illness, and pain are experienced and are projected in images of the well or poorly functioning social body and body politic. To date, social anthropologists have tended to restrict their interest in emotions to occasions when they are formal, public, ritualized, and "distanced," such as the highly stylized mourning of the Basques (W. Douglas 1969) or the deep play of a Balinese cockfight (Geertz 1973a). The more private and idiosyncratic emotions and passions of individuals have tended to be left to psychoanalytic and psychobiological anthropologists, who have reduced them to a discourse on innate drives, impulses, and instincts. This division of labor, based on a false dichotomy between cultural sentiments and natural passions, leads us right back to the mind-body, nature-culture, individual-society epistemological muddle. We would join with Geertz (1980) in questioning whether any expression of human emotion and feeling—public or private, individual or collective, repressed or explosively expressed—is ever free of cultural shaping and cultural meaning.

Insofar as emotions entail both feelings and cognitive orientations, public morality, and cultural ideology, we suggest that they provide an important missing link capable of bridging mind and body, individual, society, and body politic. As John Blacking (1977:5) has stated, emotions are the catalyst that transforms knowledge into human understanding and brings intensity and commitment to human action. Renato Rosaldo (1984) has recently charged anthropologists to pay more attention to the force and intensity of emotions in motivating human action. This challenge has been taken up by several researchers (see, for example, Schieffelin 1976, 1979; M. Rosaldo 1980, 1984; Kleinman 1982b, 1986; Lutz 1982, 1985; Levy and Rosaldo 1983; Kleinman and Good 1985), and the results have provided a major impetus to the development of a critical-interpretive approach in medical anthropology.

In closing this essay, we briefly turn from a description of the cultural construction of the body to its counterpart, the use of the body as a metaphor for the expression of distress.

RITUALS OF RESISTANCE

When illness and distress are conceptualized as conditions that occur to real people as they live out their lives in the context of specific social and cultural milieus, it becomes easier to envision distress as just one of the numerous everyday forms of resistance to what, for many, is the oppressive and monotonous daily round of labor and service. James Scott has pointed out that most subordinate classes throughout history have rarely been afforded the "luxury of open, organized political activity" (1985:xv). This argument can, of course, readily be extended to the situation of the majority of women. Political activity is in fact positively dangerous for most people; nevertheless those who are relatively powerless put up a remarkable assortment of resistances, including "foot dragging, dissimulation, desertion, false compliance, pilfering, feigned ignorance, slander, arson, sabotage, and so on" (Scott 1985:xvi; see also Martin 1987 with reference to women in medical settings)—to which we would add those types of institutionalized behavior that appear with great frequency in medical anthropological writings: accusations of witchcraft, sorcery, or the evil eye, gossip, the use of trance or organized rituals of reversal and fantasy play. Physical distress and illness can also be thought of as acts of refusal or of mockery, a form of protest (albeit often unconscious) against oppressive social roles and ideologies. Of all the cultural options for the expression of dissent, the use of trance or illness is perhaps the safest way to portray opposition—an institutionalized space from which to communicate fear, anxiety, and anger because in neither case are individuals under normal circumstances held fully accountable for their condition (Lewis 1971; Comaroff 1985).

Of course, not all illness episodes are recognized as having political significance; mere ailments thought to be of no significance are recognized everywhere. Gilbert Lewis tells us, for example, that the Gnau of New Guinea say of some illnesses: "They just come," "he is sick nothingly," "he died by no purpose or intent" (Lewis 1975:179). The reductionistic, mechanistic explanations characteristic of mainstream biomedicine routinely ignore the social origins of illness problems (Taussig 1980a), and so too do the explanations often made use of in the traditional medical systems of East Asia where a hypothesized imbalance of the body is said to originate in a lack of personal vigilance (Lock 1980).

If, however, one starts with a notion of "embodied personhood," of someone living out and reacting to his or her assigned place in the social order, then the social origins of many illnesses and much distress and the "sickening" social order itself come into sharp focus. It is then possible to interpret incidents of spirit possession in multinational factories in Malaysia, for example, as part of a complex negotiation of reality in which women factory workers are reacting to both the violation of their traditional identity and demeaning work conditions by bringing production to a halt through the use of possession (Ong 1988). Or again, a traditional interpretive approach would perhaps lead one to believe that Japanese adolescents who refuse to go to school, who lie mute and immobile in their bed all day and often medicated, are reacting against the pressures of the Japanese school system or the aspirations of their parents. A critical-interpretive analysis, in contrast, indicates that this situation is part of a much larger national concern about modernization and cultural identity of which the school system, parental values, and the culturally constructed form of resistance of the children is only one small part (Lock 1988b). Similarly, the large body of research on nerves-nevra-nervios in medical anthropology can be interpreted not merely as a culturally constituted idiom for the expression of distress but also as a dominant, widely distributed, and flexible metaphor for expressing severe distress and for negotiating relations of power (Lock in press; Van Shaik 1989; Scheper-Hughes 1988a). The experiences of women in connection with menstruation, childbirth, and menopause and the variety of ways in which they either embrace, equivocate about, or downright reject dominant American ideology in connection with these life-cycle events (Martin 1987) provide yet another telling example of the dynamic, contested relationship between the three bodies, as does participation in the reflexive discourse of the Zar cult by infertile Sudanese women (Boddy 1988).

The debate as to how cultural categories can best be subsumed under biomedical categories of disease becomes a red herring in a critical-interpretive approach. The transformation of a culturally rich form of communication into the individualizing language of physiology, psychology, or psychiatry is inappropriate. What is crucially important for the medical anthropologist is to demonstrate the way in which polysemic terms such as *nevra, solidao, hara,* and *stress,* and the language of trance, ritual, dreams, carnival, and so on can be made use of in order to facilitate the bringing to consciousness of links between the political and social orders and physical distress. If this form of communication that keeps body metaphorically linked to both mind and society is reduced to the "truthful" language of science, then one of the most impressive "weapons of the weak" (Scott 1985) is made unavailable in the struggle for relief from oppression. Similarly, a culturally relativistic approach that relies exclusively on local explanations or narratives is inadequate because involved actors are often unable to distance themselves and take a reflexive stance about their own condition. Not only oppressors but the oppressed are likely to accept their lot as natural and inevitable even when human social relations are grossly distorted and unjust. A critical-interpretive approach seeks to go beyond a culturally sensitive presentation to reveal the contingency of power and knowledge in both their creation of and relationship to the culturally constructed individual body.

We would like to think of medical anthropology as providing the key to the development of a new epistemology and metaphysics of the body and of the emotional, social, and political sources of illness and healing. If and when we tend to think reductionistically about the mind-body, it is because it is "good for us to think" in this way. To do otherwise, that is, employing a radically different metaphysics, would imply the "unmaking" of our own assumptive world and its culture-bound definitions of reality. To admit the "as-ifness" of our ethnoepistemology is to court a Cartesian anxiety—the fear that in the absence of a sure, objective foundation for knowledge, we would fall into the void, into the chaos of absolute relativism and subjectivity (see Geertz 1973a:28–30).

We have tried to show the interaction among the mind-body and the individual, social, and body politic in the production and expression of health and illness. Sickness is not just an isolated event or an unfortunate brush with nature. It is a form of communication—the language of the organs—through which nature, society, and culture speak simultaneously. The individual body should be seen as the most immediate, the proximate terrain where social truths and social contradictions are played out, as well as a locus of personal and social resistance, creativity, and struggle.

NOTES

1. This chapter is not intended to be a review of the field of medical anthropology. We refer interested readers to a few excellent reviews of this type: Worsley 1982; Young 1982; Landy 1983a. With particular regard to the ideas expressed in this chapter, however, see also Taussing 1980a, 1984; Estroff 1981; Good and Good 1981; Nichter 1981; Obeyesekere 1981; Laderman 1983, 1984; Comaroff 1985; Devisch 1985; Hahn 1985b; Helman 1985; Low 1985.

2. Mary Douglas refers to "The Two Bodies," the physical and social bodies, in *Natural Symbols* (1970). More recently John O'Neill has written *Five Bodies: The Human Shape of Modern Society* (1985), in which he discusses the physical body, the communicative body, the world's body, the social body, the body politic, consumer bodies, and medical bodies. We are indebted to both Douglas and O'Neill and also to Bryan Turner's *The Body and Society: Explorations in Social Theory* (1984) for helping us to define and delimit the tripartite domain we have mapped out here.

3. We do not wish to suggest that Hippocrates' understanding of the body was analogous to that of Descartes or of modern biomedical practitioners. Hippocrates' approach to medicine and healing can only be described as organic and holistic. Nonetheless, Hippocrates was, as the quotation from his work demonstrates, especially concerned to introduce elements of rational science (observation, palpation, diagnosis, and prognosis) into clinical practice and to discredit all the "irrational" and magical practices of traditional folk healers.

CHAPTER 4

PSYCHOANALYTIC PERSPECTIVES

Howard F. Stein

The goal of this chapter is twofold: to introduce readers (1) to psychoanalytic anthropology and (2) to the value of bringing such perspectives to research, teaching, and clinical work in medical anthropology. I argue that a psychoanalytic, or depth-psychological, viewpoint offers the final piece of the puzzle in the interpretation of cultural systems—that it is not a mere epiphenomenon of culture or icing on the cake but part of the very recipe or design of culture and its medical systems.

Over the century of intellectual history beginning with Sigmund Freud (1856–1939), psychoanalytic anthropology has worn two faces: as a theory and study of the universal factors that make us human and how culture gives expression and form to these underlying universal factors. To an extent, this can be characterized as "etic" theory building: the study of human nature and its symbolic forms. The second face is the theory and study of the specific processes that make humans distinctively cultural as members of particular societies (groups) during particular times (history), whether through socialization as a child or through adult learning. This can be characterized as "emic" study of cultural particularism, "thick description," inquiry into "cultural personality" (Hippler 1974). However, within a group's own symbols, rituals, and folklore lies the basis for "etic" inferences (Dundes 1985). Thus, the two faces are not necessarily opposed (Spiro 1986).

A psychoanalytic view of the human condition and of medical institutions and practices turns conventional views of culture upside down. It is as disorienting, unsettling, and disturbing a feeling for the natives of medical and general anthropology as migration and rapid culture change are for many of those whom we study. If culture is not securely "there," a point of adaptive reference to which all can turn, if culture is "really" more of a product of fantasy, wish, anxiety, and defense, one that humans create and then clutch in the darkness, then we medical anthropologists who study others, and those being studied, are more in the same existential boat than we are inclined to realize. A psychoanalytic anthropological approach to all cultural materials—our own as well—is an inquiry into the purpose of culture for those who create, maintain, and constantly reshape "it."

Seymour Parker asserts that "despite disavowals and premature notices of its demise, the use of psychological meanings that link institutionalized to individual behavior remains vital in anthropology" (1988:373). The same is true for the use of depth psychological explanation in anthropology. Daniel Lagache (1973:vii) wrote that "the shocking thing about psycho-analysis is less its emphasis on sexuality than its introduction of unconscious phantasy into the theory of the mental functioning of man in his struggle with the world and with himself." Similarly, Robert A. Paul (1978:67) wrote a decade ago that "it is clear that anthropologists don't like the idea of instincts or innate ideas, but no one can show in a logical, empirical, or sensible way why the idea is not very plausible."

In all groups, professional ones included, stereotyping makes adversaries into far more monolithic menaces than they in fact are. This is certainly the case with many anthropologists' disdainful view of psychoanalysis, one I wish to qualify if I cannot entirely dispel it. While analysts and analytically oriented social scientists are united in their search for depth-psychology accounts of human behavior, they are as faction ridden and divided by clinical-theoretical ideologies as are Marxist (materialist) and symbolic anthropologists. Several decades ago, the most distinctive moiety was that between ego psychology and id or instinct psychology. Today the most visible split is between the Otto Kernberg (1975) school of object relations and the Heinz Kohut (1971, 1977) school of self-psychology. While disciplinary chauvinism (not unlike ethnocentrism) is useful in shoring up precarious personal and group boundaries, it is antithetical to the cause of advancing scientific knowledge and clinical method. In this introduction to psychoanalytic anthropology, I identify multiple points of view, as well as emphasize common themes.

One controversy about the identity of psychoanalytic anthropology, held by those within and outside it, concerns where it should be located in the intellectual great chain of being. Some classify it as one specie of the 1930s and 1940s culture and personality school—and some who classify it this way believe that, like its intellectual genus, it is either extinct or should be. Others locate it as a subdiscipline of cultural anthropology, genealogically parallel to political symbolic, or economic anthropology. Still others, among whom I number myself, regard its concepts and insights and theories about human nature as part of the very foundation of all human sciences.

At least four types of psychoanalytic anthropologists can be identified: (1) anthropologists with some degree of psychoanalytic interest and formal training (Caudill 1962; Dundes 1984; La Barre 1972; Paul 1978); (2) psychiatrist-psychoanalysts and lay analysts with some degree of anthropological interest, formal training, and fieldwork (Boyer 1979; Volkan 1988; Parin 1988; Muensterberger 1969); (3) researchers who are both trained anthropologists and psychoanalysts (Devereux 1980a; Gehrie 1976; Spiro 1986; LeVine 1973); and (4) researchers from closely allied disciplines—such as clinical psychology, political psychology, and sociology—who are interested in and have training in anthropological and analytic theory and conduct fieldwork (De Vos 1973; Endleman 1981).

Whether we are discussing the individual's experience of symptoms, or group concerns such as malevolent ghosts, toxic wastes, environmental pollutants, or infectious disease from plague to AIDS, psychodynamic processes are never absent from the ethnographic picture. As medical anthropologists, whether we are studying such processes, intervening in them, or both, it is important to be able to have access to this level of data and not automatically rule it out because biomedical, political, cognitive, or economic factors initially seem more compelling.

A psychoanalytic approach to human behavior—in any cultural institution and in culture itself—rests upon a difficulty inherent not only in being a member of the culture studied or in conducting cultural research but in being human: unconscious resistance to, and defense against, the very knowledge of the intrapsychic functions culture serves. Whatever else culture is relative to, it is also relative to the observer. It is for this simultaneously theoretical, methodological and clinical reason that George Devereux (1967, 1978), Weston La Barre (1978), William Davidson (1986), and Howard Stein (1985b, 1985f) located researcher subjectivity or "countertransference" as the central issue, the fulcrum of knowledge and ignorance, in all human science. "What I cannot tolerate to know about myself" translates into "what I cannot tolerate to know about those whom I observe (or treat)." Self-reflexivity, and resistance to it, is the foundation of all human inquiry.

SOME KEY CONCEPTS

La Barre draws attention to four distinctive features of psychoanalytic thinking: (1) "Psychoanalysis is the first psychology to take seriously the whole human body as a place to live in" (1968:65); (2) "Psychoanalysis is the first psychology to preoccupy itself with the *purpose* (as opposed to the process) of thinking" (1968:65–66); (3) "[Psychoanalysis is] the first psychology to pay significant attention to the *symbolic content* of thought" (1968:69); (4) "A fourth characteristic of psychoanalysis involves a profound irony. . . . It consists in an unacknowledged understanding of what a man [Freud] said, with clever purpose distorting it, and using it to demolish a straw man of one's own devising ('Freud thinks everything is sex, ha, ha!, and you and I know this isn't so')" (1968:70–71).

A number of concepts can be regarded as foundation blocks of psychoanalytic theory, research, and therapy (see Brenner 1974; Rycroft 1968; LaPlanche and Pontalis 1973). The psyche and all mental functioning are hierarchically or topographically organized (as in the metaphor of an archaeological excavation: deeper means earlier) in terms of conscious, preconscious and unconscious. The relationship between these is dynamic and not merely descriptive (Freud 1923). That is, unconscious ideas, fantasies, wishes, and feelings are not directly felt or experienced by the wakeful person but are revised, edited, and displaced onto symbols, behaviors, and more acceptable thoughts.

The idiom or language of the unconscious is termed primary process and is distinguished from the language of conscious awareness, which is called secondary process. Primary process thinking, surfacing most clearly in dreams and psychoses, is based on wish fulfillment, the negation of time and constraints of reality. By contrast, secondary process is characterized as rational, oriented to reality, open to critical feedback, and adaptive. However, primary process finds countless ways to gain expression in conscious thought, which is never entirely reality dominated. Whereas primary process thinking is governed by the pleasure principle, secondary process is ruled by the reality principle.

In analytically oriented research and in therapy, psychoanalysts rely upon the patient's or informant's free associations of uncensored thoughts and feelings to understand the relationship between the manifest content of dreams or of culture and its unconscious latent content or underlying meanings. Analytically oriented ethnographer and therapist alike listen keenly for the patient's or informant's highly charged cathexis, the emotional valence or charge, associated with certain people, ideas, rituals, and the like. For instance, the shaman or physician is often invested by the patient with qualities of a parent, and the nation serves as a mother symbol.

Mediating between the primal unconscious and the functioning mental system of consciousness is a set of defense mechanisms, the purpose of which is to keep painful or incompatible thoughts, feelings, and wishes from becoming conscious. Prior to becoming conscious, or instead of becoming such, these intolerable wishes and feelings are transformed into something else, becoming a compromise between desire and prohibition (for instance, powerful aggressive impulses are sublimated into the surgeon's wish to heal through cutting or are being reversed into the opposite by reaction formation as in a pacifist's zeal for the antinuclear movement, or are being banished through repression from awareness by the "difficult" patient who protests to the physician that he or she is not noncompliant). These various defense mechanisms operate unconsciously to reduce anxiety, guilt, and shame.

In clinical relationships (physician-patient, shaman-client), indeed in virtually any role relationships, participants often unwittingly perceive and respond to the role partner as if the other were an important person from one's childhood, directing feelings toward the current person as if he or she were that parental figure or were some aspect (part) of an earlier nurturant or punitive figure (breast, penis, face) or some aspect of one's own infantile past (angry, dependent, abandoned, envious). In short, one transfers feelings derived from a childhood relationship onto an adult relationship. When the patient does this, it is termed transference; when the practitioner does this, it is termed countertransference. For purposes of this chapter, let us say that the process or dynamics is the same for both, although initially countertransference denoted only the clinician's inappropriate emotional response to the patient's transference. Transference-type social phenomena, such as occur in clinical relationships and fieldwork, are examples of what Freud (1920) called "the compulsion to repeat." Among the functions of the repetition compulsion is to reexperience and master in the present a repressed traumatic experience or conflict from the past. Both pleasant and unpleasant early experiences are restaged but disguised in the symbols and relationships of the present.

Two related concepts emphasize the fact that the world of the psychoanalytic psyche is rich and complex. The principle of overdeterminism (as in the image of two or several converging straight lines overdetermining, and thereby defining, a single point) directs us to the fact that there is no such thing as the "real" meaning of a dream, a ritual, or a symbol. Instead, meanings and feelings from numerous developmental conflicts and hurts meet or are condensed in that symbol or ritual (as in a curing ceremony or national flag). Psychic determinism thus does not belong to the world of Newtonian cause and effect, of simple, linear plots. Rather, it finds expression through complexly textured story lines. Roy Schafer (1983:8) writes that "the fact that one has discerned further meaning, weightier meaning, more disturbed meaning, more archaic meaning, or more carefully disguised meaning . . . does not justify the claim that one has discovered the ultimate truth that lies behind the world of appearances—the 'real' world."

A parallel concept is the principle of multiple function, according to which symbols, rites, ideas, and so forth can be seen variously to function as implementing ego defenses, as mental representations of early familial relationships (object relations), as conscious or unconscious fantasies and wishes, and as modes of communication between individuals (see, for instance, Apprey 1986). While all these functions occur concurrently, some predominate at particular times; moreover, the observer's or clinician's interests affect which functions are emphasized.

Not only is the mind organized vertically (from conscious to unconscious but horizontally as well. Various horizontal structures appear and developmentally meld into later ones. For instance, the structural model (Freud 1923) consists of the id (embodying the drives, wishes, instincts), the superego (embodying ideals and conscience based on identification with early parent-figures), and the ego (the "executive branch" of the mind, mediating among id, superego, and reality). According to classical psychoanalytic theory (Freud 1923), this mental model comes into being through the resolution of the oedipus complex, which is in turn based on the triangular structure of father-mother-child.

In the view of many theorists, the structural model, however, rests upon an even earlier horizontal model that dominates the infant's mind and its dyadic (mother-infant) interpersonal situation in its earliest months and years. This model is called an object relations model of mental organization (Kernberg 1975; Volkan 1976; Fairbairn 1954; Klein 1955), according to which developmentally early splitting of images or representations of oneself and of important nurturing figures (objects) into "good" (pleasurable) and "bad" (unpleasurable) components to ward off anxiety optimally heals or integrates into a single, relatively unified image of oneself and one's loved ones who can be seen as both nurturant and frustrating.

KEY BACKGROUND LITERATURE

The foundation for gaining a solid foothold in the psychoanalytic anthropology literature remains Sigmund Freud's twenty-four-volume *Standard Edition* of his work.[1] Special emphasis should be given to his extensive clinical cases (such as Little Hans, Rat Man, and Wolf Man), to his interpretations of society (in *Group Psychology and the Analysis of the Ego, Civilization and Its Discontents, The Future of an Illusion, Totem and Taboo*), and his theoretical papers ("Three Essays on the Theory of Sexuality," "Mourning and Melancholia," "The Ego and the Id").

For the student of medical anthropology, two books could serve as a point of departure for a study of the literature in psychoanalytic anthropology. Philip K. Bock's *Rethinking Psychological Anthropology: Continuity and Change in the Study of Human Action* (1988) is a scholarly, even-handed, and prodigiously documented work that locates psychoanalytic thinking and thinkers within the context of psychological anthropology and anthropologists. Richly descriptive of the various currents, fads, and controversies in psychological anthropology, it is an outstanding critical, interpretive account.

A work that splendidly complements Bock's is George Spindler's 1978 edited volume, *The Making of Psychological Anthropology*, in which editorial introductions by Spindler are followed by methodological, theoretical, and ethnographic chapters written by some of the most prominent figures in the psychoanalytic anthropology of 1978, including Victor Barnouw, Melford Spiro, George De Vos, Weston La Barre, George and Louise Spindler, and George Devereux.[2]

CLINICAL IDEOLOGY AND DEPTH PSYCHOLOGY

The medical anthropology literature has established the links in many cultures among clinical assessment, diagnostic labeling, etiological accounting, and formulation of treatment plan. Culturally how a problem is treated is an extension of how that problem is understood. Leon Eisenberg (1977:10) says, for instance, writing of biomedical decision making, "Working models of the disease process determine the data that physicians gather, inform the ways in which 'facts' are integrated into a diagnosis, and circumscribe the boundaries of interventions designated as therapeutic." Furthermore, the ethnographic record has established that the "medical" component or system of a culture is enmeshed in or intertwined with the ethos of that culture, which pervades all institutions. Christie Kiefer (1976:11), for example, writing of Morita therapy in Japan, observes that "Morita Therapy is . . . a kind of cultural institution, subject to the same influences that shape other institutions in this society. One sees characteristic Japanese patterns. . . . One begins at once also to see the fit between Morita Therapy and the prevailing social attitudes of the Japanese.... In short, the study of a treatment modality tells us a surprising amount about the society in which it is practiced."

Richard Lieban writes that "an anthropological study of health and the occurrence and means of coping with disease can involve one deeply in the manner in which people perceive their world, in the characteristics of human social systems, and in social values" (1973:1033). Moreover, an ethnomedical system can readily disclose the core psychodynamic conflicts and defenses characteristic of a given society (Hippler 1977: 18–19; see also Stein and Kayzakian-Rowe 1978 for a discussion of the role of aggression and of isolating and depersonalizing defenses in the biofeedback treatment model for hypertension). Paul Parin and Goldy Parin-Matthey (1978:162) argue that "ethnopsychoanalysis is capable of providing insights into internal conflicts in terms of their relationship to contradictions and tensions in the social structure, conflicts which cannot be elucidated by the analysis of individuals only."

Medical anthropologists have contributed much to the understanding of the interplay between patients' and healers' health-related beliefs, values, decision-making strategies, actions, powers, and statuses. Psychoanalysis offers an additional understanding of the interplay of conscious, preconscious, and unconscious factors in all realms of mental operations and action. It helps, for example, to account for the nature of beliefs and for the choice of, and investment in, specific health-related beliefs. Addressing the issue of the function of culture, and hence its locus, Erik Erikson (1974:91) writes that "each individual, being stamped with such early experiences in space and time, and at first sharing them with a small circle of familiar individuals, must seek an (eventually political) association with wider circles who share a basic world view. Their ideological space-time perspectives... must alleviate for all what anxiety remains from the bodily ontogeny of each." This is true no less of clinical institutions, ideologies, and movements within a culture. Like all other institutions, symbols, rituals, and cultural meaning systems, the clinical domain must—whatever else it also does—address and symbolically-ritually attempt to contain the emotional unfinished business of childhood.

CULTURE AND PERSONALITY: ITS RELATION TO PSYCHOANALYTIC ANTHROPOLOGY

In their account of early culture and personality studies, George Foster and Barbara Anderson (1978:6) describe the context of much of psychoanalytic anthropology during that period:

Except for ethnomedical studies, done largely as a part of tribal studies, most health related publications by anthropologists prior to 1950 deal with psychological and psychiatric phenomena. Beginning in the mid–1930s, anthropologists, psychiatrists, and other behavioral scientists began to ask questions about adult personality, or character, and the sociocultural environment in which this character was displayed. Were adults what they were largely because of the infant's plasticity and its receptivity to the childhood conditioning that it received, as well as later life experiences? Or is there an inherent psychic constitution based on biological factors that plays a major role in determining culture and hence personality? These questions were triggered by a variety of observations about human behavior in different parts of the world.

Although psychoanalytic anthropology's ancestry can be traced in part to the culture and personality movement, it is in at least some respects a false genealogy. Melford Spiro (1978:337–38) writes that

although influenced by psychoanalytic thought, the main thrust of the culture-personality school was precisely the reverse of psychoanalysis. While the latter postulated invariant stages and processes (and even invariant symbol formations and symbolic meanings) in the formation, structure, and functioning of personality, culture-personality (with some important exceptions) was primarily concerned to demonstrate their [developmental stages, symbol formation] cultural variability. Since, according to this school, personality was determined by, and constituted the internalization of, culture, the range of personality variability across groups could hardly be smaller than the range of cultural variability. Indeed, since personality characteristics and personality configurations, respectively, were viewed as isomorphic with cultural characteristics and cultural patterns, the notion of a pan-cultural human nature was viewed as highly unlikely.

In their classic paper, "Some Psychoanalytic Comments on 'Culture and Personality,'" Heinz Hartmann, Ernest Kris, and Rudolph Lowenstein (1969) introduced a distinction between "institutionalized" and "noninstitutionalized" behavior, the former denoting behavioral practices, patterns, and routines and the latter denoting private motivations, unconscious fantasies and affects, and personal attitudes. Although they rightly caution against inferring motivation from behavior (such as sickness ideologies and ethnomedical customs), it is also often the case that group customs, practices, and official ideologies implement and symbolize widely shared childhood-familial experiences, internal conflicts, fantasies, and feelings. Anthropologists tend to overemphasize the developmental significance of specific child-rearing practices and neglect the affective parent-child relationship or ambience.

Moreover, the psychic purpose of official cultural explanations is often dynamically identical to that of secondary elaboration in dreams: simultaneously to give disguised expression to the latent content and to displace attention from it. Among Slovaks and Slovak-Americans, for example, the manifest purpose of swaddling (physical or emotional) was to protect an infant perceived as terribly fragile, vulnerable, and weak. However, the protection was at least partly due to maternal and familial ambivalence and unacceptable infanticidal wishes toward the infant. Such wishes were disavowed and externalized, becoming frightening attributes of the child, who was in turn "treated" through such defense mechanisms as "reaction formation," conscious behavior acting the opposite of the unconscious wish, in this case, highly worried, solicitous, care of the infant (see Stein 1974, 1978; deMause 1982). Throughout culture, the manifest, official, institutionalized, conscious layer symbolizes, expresses, and defends against the latent, unofficial, noninstitutionalized, unconscious. The question then perhaps becomes, To what shall the term *culture* be applied: only the former or the whole that subsumes manifest and latent aspects of group experience?

According to an early culture and personality causal chain proposed by A. Kardiner (1939) and John Whiting (1961), the economic-political system was a given that set the stage for child-rearing practices. In a compromise between wishes or needs and social reality, inevitable frustrations were channeled into what Kardiner called "projective systems." Bodily needs and childhood wishes that could not be satisfied because imperatives of the economic and political systems were unconsciously exteriorized became embodied through symbolization in ghosts, spirits, and deities of such institutions as religion and folklore. Feelings and fantasies that one could not consciously harbor toward the living or expect from them, one invested in those symbolic creations who were projective products of the unconscious imagination. This largely compensatory view of "projective systems" is not far from Karl Marx's characterization of religion as the heart of a heartless world.

Many later writers have come to see not only all "adult" institutions as at least to some degree projective in nature (including economics and politics) but also to see infants, children, and adolescents themselves as projective targets or screens for parents' and other elders' disavowed impulses and conflicts (Devereux 1980b; deMause 1982; Johnson and Szurek 1952). If early culture and personality studies tended to view socialization, and especially projection, in terms of unidirectional causality, many contemporary psychoanalytically oriented anthropologists and anthropologically oriented analysts tend to view much of cultural life as consisting of a constant ebb and flow between projection and introjection (externalization and internalization).

Over the decades, a number of psychoanalytically oriented anthropologists and analysts have used projective techniques (Rorschach inkblots, Thematic Apperception Test, and others), supplementing ethnographic fieldwork and psychoanalytic interviews, to elicit unconscious themes and mental structure (L. Bryce Boyer, George De Vos, Melford Spiro, and A. I. Hallowell, among others). The *Journal of Projective Techniques and Personality Assessment* is devoted to these types of studies. In 1955, the *American Anthropologist* published a symposium, "Projective Testing in Ethnography," featuring a paper by Jules Henry, with commentaries by S. F. Nadel, William Caudill, John J. Honigmann, Melford E. Spiro, Donald W. Fiske, and A. I. Hallowell, all of whom addressed the promises and limitations of projective tests in cultural interpretation. From that same period, Jules Henry and Melford Spiro's paper on projective techniques in fieldwork (1953) remains a useful overview. A Rorschach and field study by Boyer, De Vos, Borders, and Tani-Borders (1978) of Eskimos demonstrated the continued vitality of projective tests in understanding the intrapsychic structure of nonliterate peoples and the relationship of this structure to group symbols and interpersonal relations. Recently De Vos and Boyer (1988) published *Symbolic Analysis Crossculturally: The Rorschach Test*.

CULTURE, FANTASY, AND REALITY

Psychoanalytically oriented anthropologists inquire into the part people play in each other's fantasies and the part the shared fantasy of the group (culture) plays in all members' lives. This viewpoint takes seriously the reality and consequences of unconscious motivation for thought and action (including medical choices). Further, within psychoanalytically oriented anthropological thinking, as throughout medical (and general) anthropology, there is a wide spectrum of viewpoints as to the contribution of, say, human nature, parental behavior (such as child abuse and incest), and parental and children's fantasies in personality organization and subsequent culture. Stating the controversy differently: to what extent are people parts of the circumstances they in part create, and to what extent are they products, if not victims, of these circumstances? The debate over infantile fantasy versus child abuse-incest (Niederland 1974; Schatzman 1973; Masson 1984; deMause 1974, 1982, 1987, 1988; Paul 1985), the interpretation of the relationship between poverty and child abuse and neglect (poverty as lack of opportunity versus cultural ethos) (Scheper-Hughes and Stein 1987; Nations and Rebhun 1988), and the debate over whether aggression is innate or culturally learned (Paul 1978, 1988; Robarchek and Dentan 1987; Dentan 1988) illustrates the vitality of this issue within and beyond psychoanalytic circles.

Many psychoanalytic anthropologists tend to conceptualize stress, acculturation, culture change, poverty, abuse, migration, and the like less as things or entities and more as processes that become imbued with meanings and feelings. La Barre (1971b:23), for instance, writes that "simple theories of stress fail to predict anything about the quality of the response. *It is not stress* [the external stimulus or challenge] *as such but the psychic style of reaction to it that is important* . . . simple stress theory as a single cause cannot predict the nature of the response also because it concentrates too largely on 'outer' realities'' [emphasis in original]. It is not that the outer world is irrelevant (for example abusive, brutal parenting conducted by adults acting out in child care what they dare not feel or remember) but that it always interacts with the inner world and developmental stages that influence emotion, perception, and mental structure. (For a recent masterful synthesis of family process and intrapsychic development, see Dervin 1987, 1988.)

Early in the twentieth century, the Boas-Kroeber school of the "superorganic" argued that culture could be studied and interpreted as a force that operated independently of individual meanings and lives (Kroeber 1917). It was linguist and anthropologist Edward Sapir, Weston La Barre's teacher and mentor at Yale, who reaffirmed the individual as transmitter and active creator of culture (Sapir 1917; see also Mandelbaum 1966). Interestingly, however, Kroeber (1948:848), who had briefly been a psychoanalyst early in his career, concluded his volume *Anthropology* with a clarion call that anthropology's foundation—like that of culture itself—should be the individual human organism: "While psychosomatic individuals do and must precede societies of individuals and the cultures of human societies—must precede them conceptually and evolutionistically—and while psychology is therefore in one sense a science that underlies both sociology and anthropology, nevertheless, in this mid-twentieth century, we have the curious situation that sociologists and anthropologists perhaps explain their proper phenomena less often in terms of the underlying psychic factors than psychologists are cognizant of the overlying sociocultural ones."

Isomorphisms between Ernst Kris's concept of personal myth (1956), Antonio Ferreira's concept of family myth (1963), and Helm Stierlin's (1973) and Lloyd deMause's (1974) concept of group fantasy promise a dynamic bridge joining representations of the self, the family, and the group ("culture"). Kris wrote of the dynamics of the personal myth that "the autobiographical self-image serves a defensive function in the psychic economy, warding off early anxieties and preventing the intensity of traumatic experiences and of aggressive and libidinal impulses from reaching consciousness" (1956:361). Commonly, fantasies in the personal myth were "variations on the theme of the family romance—a distortion of the patient's origins in which he represents himself as not really the child of his own father and mother but of some other, frequently more illustrious, parents" (1956:361–62). The personal myth derives its emotional force of conviction from the repressed unconscious fantasy it replaces but that sustains it from beneath. Compare Kris's concept with Ferreira's (1963:60) formulation that the family myth

refers to a series of fairly well-integrated beliefs shared by all family members, concerning each other and their mutual position in the family life, beliefs that go unchallenged by everyone involved in spite of the reality distortions which they may conspicuously imply. ... The family myth is ... a part of *the inner image* of the group, an image to which all family members contribute and, apparently, strive to preserve.... The family myth "explains" the behavior of the individuals in the family while it hides its motives.... The family myth modifies the perceptual context of family behavior, as it provides ready-made explanations of the directives and rules that are to govern the relationship.... *The family myth is to the relationship what the defense is to the individual.* The myth, like the defense, protects the system against the threat of disintegration and chaos.... Thus, to maintain oneself within a given myth, a certain amount of insightlessness is necessary. The struggle to maintain the myth is part of the struggle to maintain the relationship. (pp. 55, 56, 58; emphasis in original)

Finally, deMause (1977:11), borrowing the concept of group fantasy from small-group dynamics, writes that "an historical group-fantasy is a set of shared unconscious assumptions, quite unrelated to any 'objective' reality, about the way it *feels* to be a member of a historical group at a particular time in history. Group-fantasies are what national opinion polls attempt to capture when they periodically try to determine the 'mood' of America, and ask people whether they feel their leader is strong or weakening, whether they feel the country is safe or in a state of turmoil, whether the enemy is strong or threatening, what they feel the future may bring, and so on."

Kris's concept of the personal myth, Ferreira's formulation of the family myth, Stierlin (1973) and deMause's concept of the group fantasy, and L. Bryce Boyer's

(1979) psychoanalytic interpretation of Apache folklore point to how intraindividual, familial, group, and cultural levels can be dynamically linked. At each level an elaboration can be found that serves as a compromise between the expression of an impulse or feeling and the defense against it; a means for the creation of homeostasis in the face of conflict; a means of preserving the cohesion of a self and/or of a relationship; and a means of reducing guilt, anxiety, shame, and other dysphoric feelings.

The classical psychoanalytic drive theory–based concept of defense emphasized the intrapsychic equilibration of id-ego-superego structures. However, this model has been subsequently expanded to include how other people—based upon mental representations of these "significant others"—help perform this internal function. Fred Sander (1979:129), a psychoanalyst and family therapist, writes that

defenses by definition, defend against unacceptable unconscious impulses, affects, wishes, or fantasies. They protect the ego against instinctual demands and for the most part are intrapsychic in their operation, though they all have some interpersonal consequences. One defense mechanism, that of projection, as A. Freud notes, "disturbs our human relations [as] when we project our own jealousy and attribute to other people our own aggressive acts" (1936:133). She goes on to describe a complex variation of this defense, "altruistic surrender," which permits a person to find *in others* a "proxy in the outside world to serve as a repository for the self's own wishes" (p. 136). In this way gratification of a projected impulse is achieved. As drive theory becomes more integrated with object-relations theory, the concept of defense needs expansion to include its interpersonal ramifications. Perhaps it would be more accurate to speak of such ego activities as serving (1) defensive functions for the individual and (2) equilibrating, adaptive, or maladaptive functions for a family or group.

LEADER AND GROUP

Explorations into the fit between leader and group have suggested that a psychological complementarity is crucial to the dynamics, including that between the clinical shaman and his or her individual, family, or community clientele. As Devereux, La Barre, and others have argued, the shaman-leader is like everyone else but more so. Whatever unilateral power such a shaman leader or healer might possess, he or she also embodies the group fantasy, acts it out, is its container and cleanser. Thus, the leader is as much unconsciously led by the group as he or she consciously leads the group. Viewed this way, the shaman-leader can take the client, family, or group, only where it already is inclined to go. The use and abuse of power, authority, status, and the like occur at least in part through the suggestibility of social transference and countertransference. In contemporary American society, for instance, the popular belief in technological solutions ("fix") for all problems, including health, acting in concert with the wish for bodily immortality and youthfulness, has unconsciously empowered physicians of various biomedical subspecialties, physicians who in turn overrely on technological interventions in patient care (Stein and Hill 1988).

In a study of leadership in an Amazonian society, Waud Kracke (1978:252) writes that " a fundamentally social phenomenon, at the core of social organization, leadership yet has its roots in the inner motives of the psyche of each individual, leader and follower... It fulfills individual needs and strivings as much as it realizes and energizes social forms." Whatever we call or label these various abstractions (such as levels from micro- to macroanalysis, individual and group), we never leave the realm of human beings making choices and decisions, influenced by unconscious forces. In *Dimensions of a New Identity*, Erikson (1974:96) similarly writes:

Nowhere does the quality of leadership become more apparent than in the interplay of the inner deals the leader makes with himself and the inner deals he thinks he can count on in those he leads. For this will decide what kind of political deals he thinks he can offer to his constituents. And... the most sensitive question in this joint arena of inner worlds is the double role of conscience as a benevolent and experienced guide and as a punitive, condemning inner tyrant. What, in the name of all that is holy, we are ready to repress in ourselves and whom, in the name of what we have killed in ourselves, we are ready to annihilate in the world at large—that is the most fateful human question.

Erikson thus proposes that "we study in great detail the relationship of those simplest inner deals which we make with ourselves, and the political deals which we acquiesce in or feel inspired by" (1974:97). It requires little imagination to transpose Erikson's insights from political to medical institutions and their dynamics, for healer-client and healer-community relationships abound in unconscious deals (called "transference" and "countertransference") that become as coercively binding as any real coerciveness of power.

George Devereux's *From Anxiety to Method in the Behavioral Sciences* (1967), a work filled with ethnographic and clinical vignettes, establishes that the researcher-subject or the clinician-patient relationship, and the subjectivity of the observer, are the intellectual and emotional fulcrum on which all human research and clinical work pivots (a point emphasized by La Barre in this chapter, "The Clinic and the Field," in Spindler 1978).

As an example of the countertransference distortions medical anthropologists are capable of unwittingly introducing into research, I have written (Stein 1980a) of our tendency to idealize the medical belief systems and healers of alien, non-Western societies and to devalue, if not condemn, as untherapeutic the Western system of biomedicine and its physician-practitioners. Implicit, unconsciously founded ideologies such as this render ethnographic descriptions and ethnological interpretations suspect. Such an ideological dichotomy as "good shaman"/"bad doctor" derives at least in part from the developmentally early splitting of images of the self and of other persons (in psychoanalytic terms, "objects") into parts, each linked with an affect or emotion, as a means of managing overwhelming anxiety. As I have discussed at length in an article on the psychodynamics of the doctrine of cultural relativism (Stein 1986a), such a compartmentalization is part of a virtually discipline-wide inverted ethnocentrism. According to it, our culture is evil, while their culture is good (inside is bad, while outside is good, suggesting that personal-familial issues are being played out on the projective screen of one's anthropological career).

In the past several years, medical anthropologists have increasingly turned clinical and critical attention toward the complex system of biomedicine and are now investigating it as an ethnomedical system. It behooves us to become more self-conscious of how we see biomedicine—to recognize those conscious and unconscious fantasies we impose on the cultural screen of medicine—as we begin to observe biomedicine more carefully.

BODY, SELF, AND CULTURE

A psychoanalytically oriented human science is founded on—and any human science that ignores this foundation founders on—the species-specific biology of Homo sapiens (La Barre 1954, 1971a). What distinguishes this approach from sociobiology (but see Badcock 1986) is that most sociobiological writers leap from biology to culture without considering the mediation of the unconscious or of early developmental experiences of growing up in a body. Many psychoanalytic anthropologists also question the adaptiveness of many facets of culture rather than assume that, because it derives directly from biology, culture must be adaptive. Such facts of human nature as neoteny (retention of juvenile features into adulthood), familiality, sexual dimorphism, long dependency in childhood, nonseasonal sexuality, and the mediation of adaptation by symbolization all underlie the thesis that the kind of animal we are determines the kind of culture we have and its function and dysfunctions.

One's group(s) is thus an extension of one's conscious and unconscious fantasies about one's body and about others' bodies early in one's development (Stein 1987a, 1987b; Stein and Niederland 1989). The group becomes one's protective membrane. People become bound in societies by shared and mutually constructed "group fantasies" (deMause 1982). This emotional-cognitive reality often becomes more compelling than external reality. People stabilize themselves and one another through the process of constantly trying to put parts or aspects of themselves into others (projection) while making their own what others are attributing to them (introjection). Given the biological body-fantasy of culture ("group"), it is little wonder that the issue of borders and boundaries is universally paramount, especially during periods of stress and regression. What is culturally inside or outside? Where do I begin or end? Who are "we," and where do "they" leave off and "we" begin? Issues of body integrity, violation, fragmentation, annihilation, and restoration are commonly dealt with in cultural responses to disease and variously constructed social problems.

Because that which is unconsciously dissociated from the perception and definition of us is consciously disavowed as being part of us, and is projected or externalized into enemy or adversary groups ("them"), it is plausible to conclude that group boundaries are in fact powerful delusions held by their members (Volkan 1988; Stein 1987b; GAP 1987). Unconscious characteristics of "us" that cannot be incorporated into the self are embodied by enemies (devalued) or allies (idealized). Thus, despite conscious rituals of boundary maintenance, distancing, and war, at the unconscious level, the enemy is an inseparable part of the self. Thus, cultural distinctiveness at the level of content often serves the group mental function of differentiating between "me" and "not me."

The ideological importance of such distinctiveness can be seen as much in Western scientific medicine as in any "primitive" society. Consider how family doctors, internists, pediatricians, psychiatrists, and surgeons each claim the superiority of their own profession's clinical methods and theories over those of colleagues across the nearby border, disassociating from themselves methods and concepts not syntonic with (acceptable to) their own group sense of self. What the other side does and possesses is often envied as much as it is despised.

CULTURE, PSYCHOPATHOLOGY, AND DIAGNOSIS

According to standard psychoanalytic thinking, in neurosis, the ego is in conflict with the id, to the impoverishment of the ego; the result is a symptom. In psychosis, reality is at war with the ego, again to the impoverishment of the ego; the result is a symptom, the loss of reality, and its substitution by a delusion or hallucination. While both neurosis and psychosis are " individual," can entire groups be regarded as pathological when much of their way of life rests upon unconsciously based flawed premises about oneself, others, and the world (Devereux 1980c)? La Barre (1962:67) writes that "it is true that group fantasy confines and delimits our private psychoses, but if the culture of the group comes to resemble a psychosis itself, by a kind of *folie a deux* to the *n*th degree, then the group is worse off than when it started. In this unconscious and unwitting way, all social groups are in the long run either adaptive to a real world, or anti-adaptive. Man is like an existentialist spider who spreads a moral net of symbolism over the void of his own substance—and then walks upon it. But the final safety of the net depends always upon the integrity and the soundness of the postulated points of reference to a real physical world."

Following Casper Schmidt (in La Barre 1984:139), La Barre (1984:130-31) offers the term *archosis* to designate collective, indeed prescribed, pathologies that take the form of beliefs, attitudes, rituals, symbol systems, and the like that are normative (and thereby reassuring) rather than deviant (and thereby anxiety evoking, even if they are accorded a social role): "To the *neurosis* and the *psychosis* as ways of misrepresenting current reality in the processing of new experience, we must now add the archosis. An 'archosis' is a massive and fundamental misapprehension of reality, often of incalculable antiquity culturally, yet which has been inherited from human predecessors, in the normal fashion of any cultural bequest." "Archoses" are transmitted generation to generation with the conviction that the social and natural world must be as they are felt and perceived to be. La Barre writes that "in the reverberant nature of the social animal it is impossible to see where culture ends and character begins. For they are in origin the same: the formative influence of others upon us" (1984:9).

Cultural consensus is identity and safety but often at the expense of reality and truth about oneself. One thus wonders: Can ego-syntonic character organization be regarded as pathognomonic (that is, an identifying characteristic of pathology) and symptomatic even though the individual and his or her reference group use them as their measure of sanity, reality, normality, legality, and coherence (Freud 1927; La Barre 1972; Devereux 1980a)? C. R. Badcock (1980:240), for instance, argue that *"from the point of view of latent content, there is no way of distinguishing between individual psychopathology and its collective equivalents, such as religion"* (emphasis in original). He continues (1980:241), "Those who in recent years have criticized the notion of mental illness as being an arbitrary category of social definition have entirely missed the point. It is not madness, but sanity which is the arbitrary social category, as is proved by the fact that paranoid delusions, like anti-Semitism, can be regarded as perfectly sane if enough of the population believes in them."

Directly challenging the Whorfian equation of language with thought, psychoanalytically oriented anthropological investigation discovers the sinuous texture of language. The work of thinking, like that of dreaming and mythmaking, is to make certain (manifest, conscious, secondary process) ideas stand for or represent certain others (latent, unconscious, primary process fantasies). The process of language serves the mental function of transforming primal fantasies and effects into a form acceptable to the ego. Ella Freeman Sharpe, for instance, wrote an early paper on the psychodynamics of metaphor in human thought (1948), tracing metaphors to various expressed yet disguised bodily functions. More recently R. H. Hook (1979) wrote a masterful overview article on the psychoanalytic view of symbolism and symbol formation.

Further challenging the equation of language with thought, Devereux " sought to define criteria of normality and abnormality [Devereux 1980c] in pan-human terms, such that cultural values could then be understood in a larger context of human nature" (Kilborne 1988:xv). He inquired into the unconscious significance of diagnosis, discovering that its principal purpose is not so much to name as to differentiate between the person (and his or her reference group) performing the diagnosis and the person (and his or her group) who is diagnosed, that is, to distinguish sharply between who is and who is not labeled sick, deviant, criminal, or polluted (Devereux 1980c). Moreover, meditating on the extent of human destructiveness, he noted that not all such widespread and massive destructiveness is conducted by those labeled or diagnosed as "sick," "criminal," "crazy," "antisocial," or otherwise "deviant". It is far too anxiety arousing for most observers and clinicians to recognize the extent of pathology in normative behavior.

An ongoing lively controversy among psychoanalytic anthropologists and other anthropologists as well concerns the relationship between the cause or etiology of psychopathology and culture. Margaret Mead (1947), Paul Barrabee and

Otto von Mering (1953), Jules Henry (1963), Marvin Opler (1957), Stein (1973) and others have argued that psychopathology, like other forms of distress, including organ or tissue disease, is the outcome of culture-wide problems and conflicts, that the relationship between health and illness, the healthy and the sick, is a continuum of efforts to solve shared problems rather than, as is widely imagined (for defensive reasons), two distinct piles of people, the "healthy" and the "sick". Devereux (1980a:94), for instance, gives the spectrum of surgeon-anatomist-butcher-assassin-homicidal maniac as cultural models by which aggression is embodied. A group's heroes, villains, fools, and engaged spectators are all participants in the same unconscious drama. A number of writers about so-called culture-bound syndromes write within this perspective: thus TKS (*taijin kyofusho* or fear of dealing with others) is unimaginable outside Japan (Lock 1987); PMS (premenstrual syndrome) (Johnson 1987), anorexia nervosa, and bulimia are unthinkable outside the modern Western world; ghost sickness is specific to the Apache; and so forth. Devereux (1980d) proposed schizophrenia as the outcome of the impersonalism and complexity of modern society. According to this view, each pathology is relative to, circumscribed by, and the outcome of the society that is its host and medium. An elegant psychodynamic exposition of this holistic approach to pathology was offered by La Barre in his concept of the "social cynosure," that is, categories of people to whom extraordinary attention is paid, categories that capture and articulate an entire cultural ethos: "we must consider more deeply the problem of the *dynamics* of the 'abnormal' milieu, in which the abnormal individual is at home" (1956:545).

In the contemporary United States, cardiovascular disease, cancer, AIDS, alcoholism, chemical dependency, obesity, anorexia nervosa, bulimia (the last three being eating disorders)—both as diagnostic "entities" and the people who "have" them—serve as clinical cynosures. Just as there is often a profound individual emotional transference between practitioner and patient, so also is there a pervasive social transference onto the categories of deviants. That is, often "individual" pathology manifests itself through a symptom bearer (Stein 1985b, 1985d, 1988a), whose pathology bears much familial and cultural freight, an unconscious as well as conscious burden that prevents it from being better understood, if not cured. Thus the dynamics that play a role in conflict and disease formation and perpetuation often involve an unconcious complementarity (Stein 1986b) between the one who is officially sick or acting out and the family and/or cultural system who need the symptom bearer to be symptomatic for them, to embody their own disavowed wishes, fantasies, anxieties, and conflicts. The cultural mainstream thus requires the continuous availability of officially pathological types whom that same mainstream appoints or delegates practitioners or specialists to treat.

But are these dynamics to be construed as exclusively local and different for every society? *Psychotherapy and Culture* by Theodora Abel, Rhoda Metraux, and Samuel Roll (1987) rests cultural variation in symbolism, ritual, and psychopathological expression upon a universal Freudian, developmental base. This is one way to attempt to reconcile cultural holism (understanding pathology within its cultural context), psychobiological universalism, and cross-cultural comparison. The "'abnormal' milieu" becomes both the local configuration and the pan-human condition, on which recurrent themes the local group is a variation.

In an essay on cultural relativism, Melford Spiro (1986: 267–68) approaches the local-universal issue from the viewpoint of psychocultural functionalism:

Given [the] limited and limiting perspective [of epistemological relativism] how could it be denied, for example, that the doctrine of karma is unique to the religious tradition of India? Or that, even within that tradition, its meaning in Buddhism may be different from that in Hinduism. Or, for that matter, that even within Buddhism (Spiro 1982a) and within Hinduism (Keyes and Daniel 1983) it again has different meanings.

If, however, the concept of karma is understood in the context of Hindu and Buddhist praxis—that is, functionally—it is then apparent that, at only a slightly more abstract level, it bears a striking family resemblance to concepts found in many other cultural traditions. Consider, for example, such concepts as luck, fate, predestination, God's will, kismet, fortune, destiny, or, for that matter, cultural determinism! Although formally and semiotically different from each other, and they in turn from karma, all of those concepts, just like karma, provide an explanation for the vagaries of an actor's "life chances" (as Weber called it) without recourse to the agency (and therefore the responsibility) of the actor himself.

From the viewpoint of many writers in psychoanalytic anthropology, saying that a given form or expression of psychopathology (or some other cultural feature) is relative to a specific culture is not incompatible with also saying that it is simultaneously relative to the human condition, since members of all groups are wrestling with the same types of issues characteristic of the human condition. Over three decades ago, for example, Devereux suggested in an argument similar to that of Spiro that a psychological trait "can appear as a *custom* in tribe A, as a *myth* in tribe B and as a *neurotic fantasy* in members of tribe C" (1955:111: emphasis in original). Psychopathology, no less than any other facet of human culture, is a symbol and symptom of the universal conflict and compromise between impulse and defense. Our capacity to understand culturally alien pathological forms, if not the capacity to treat them as well, requires a degree of identification whereby one says from the conviction of experience: "That could be me."

NOTES

1. A number of other outstanding books introduce readers to the principles of psychoanalytic theory, their rationale, and the history of their development: Herman Nunberg's *Principles of Psychoanalysis* (1955); Charles Rycroft's *A Critical Dictionary of Psychoanalysis* (1968); Charles Brenner's *An Elementary Textbook of Psychoanalysis* (1974); J. Laplanche and J.-B. Pontalis's *The Language of Psycho-Analysis* (1973); *Psychoanalytic Pioneers*, edited by Franz Alexander, Samuel Eisenstein, and Martin Grotjahn (1966), a work that includes the intellectual biographies and summaries of the

contributions of many of Freud's closest coworkers in the psychoanalytic movement; *New Directions in Psycho-Analysis*, edited by Melanie Klein, Paula Heimann, and Roger Money-Kyrle (1955); *Experiences in Groups*, by W. R. Bion (1959), which describes the shared unconscious fantasies and agendas (dependency, fight-flight, rebirth through pairing) that are unleashed in avowedly task-oriented groups; and Vamık D. Volkan's *Primitive Internalized Object Relations* (1976), a work that proposes a model of the preoedipal substratum of the classical analytic structural model. Caudill's paper " Anthropology and Psychoanalysis" (1962), La Barre's paper, "Personality from a Psychoanalytic Viewpoint" (1968), and Devereux's "Normal and Abnormal" (1980c) offer excellent overview summaries of key concepts.

2. In the periodical literature (mostly quarterlies), works taking a psychoanalytic anthropological approach appear regularly in the following journals: *Ethos, Journal of Psychoanalytic Anthropology* (1978–1988), *Medical Anthropology Quarterly, Medical Anthropology, Psychiatry, American Journal of Orthopsychiatry, Transcultural Psychiatric Research Review* (which features overview articles, abstracts and commentaries on a wide range of journal articles and books), *Psychoanalytic Review, Journal of American Folklore, Psychoanalytic Quarterly, American Imago, Social Science and Medicine, Journal of the American Psychoanalytic Association, Journal of Projective Techniques and Personality Assessment, British Journal of Medical Psychology*, and *Psyche*.

Two recent special journal issues of interest to those seeking the current state-of-the-art theories, methods, and controversies are: *Ethos* 15(1) (March 1987), an issue devoted to the problem of interpretation in psychoanalytic anthropology; and *Journal of Psychoanalytic Anthropology*, 9(3) (Summer 1986), a double issue dedicated to Weston La Barre that focused on insight into cultural symbolism. Peter Morley (1988) wrote a masterful essay, first summarizing the contents of both issues and then evaluating them in the context of hermeneutics.

The Psychoanalytic Study of Society is a series of volumes now into its thirteenth number, currently edited by L. Bryce Boyer and Simon Grolnick. The series was successor to the series of volumes titled *Psychoanalysis and the Social Sciences*, founded by Geza Roheim in 1950 and later edited by the indefatigable Werner Muensterberger. A paper published by La Barre thirty years ago, "The Influence of Freud on Anthropology" (1958), is of current as well as historic value.

Several journals outside the medical anthropology and psychoanalytic anthropology mainstream regularly publish psychoanalytically informed cultural and historical analysis pertinent to medical anthropologists. These include *Political Psychology, Mentalities: An Interdisciplinary Journal, Psychohistory Review, Journal of American Culture, Journal of Popular Culture*, and *Family Systems Medicine*. *Journal of Psychoanalytic Anthropology*, a quarterly published in 1978 and 1988 (its first two and one-half years as the *Journal of Psychological Anthropology*), ceased existence as a separate publication in 1988 and merged into the *Journal of Psychohistory*, a quarterly whose editorial purview encompasses the primitive-modern, sacred-secular, simple-complex spectrum of societies. Another way of putting this is that important contributions to the substance of psychoanalytic anthropology come from outside the borders of psychoanalysis and anthropology, especially from psychohistory, political psychology, studies in American popular culture, and studies in the family therapy and family systems medicine literature.

3. What might be called a genre of volumes link human biology, individual psychological structure, culture, and history. Building on classical Freudian psychoanalysis but emphasizing the preoedipal situation of the child and its influence upon the experience and meaning of culture, Geza Roheim's 1943 book, *The Origin and Function of Culture*,

is the locus classicus for a statement of the relationship between culture and the human condition of prolonged early dependency and helplessness. Weston La Barre's (1954) book *The Human Animal*, and his later work *The Ghost Dance: The Origins of Religion* (1972), develop this biological-developmental argument according to which the experience of growing up in a sexually dimorphous, gendered body, within the context of a family, and in the further biological context of neoteny (prolonged physical and emotional immaturity, retained into adolescence and adulthood), prefigures, underlies, and shapes the form and significance of culture. For La Barre, as for Roheim and Freud, culture (and the creation and revision of culture) performs the function of not-always-adaptive response to the problem of anxiety.

Erik Erikson's classic *Childhood and Society* (1950) remains an outstanding attempt at synthesizing biological zone and interpersonal mode, the cogwheeling of soma, psyche, culture, and history. Melford E. Spiro's (1982b) *Oedipus in the Trobriands* argues that the oedipus complex is universal rather than culture and era bound to the Victorian West. In Trobriand religion and folklore Spiro finds abundant evidence for oedipal-level conflict and symbolization. Bert Kaplan's *Studying Personality Cross-Culturally* (1961), Douglas Haring's *Personal Character and Cultural Milieu* (1956), and Melford Spiro's *Context and Meaning in Cultural Anthropology* (1965) remain useful anthologies containing many classic papers. Perhaps the most consistently psychoanalytic anthology is Werner Muensterberger's *Man and His Culture* (1969).

Excellent psychoanalytically informed interpretations of religion and social movements are Weston La Barre's *They Shall Take Up Serpents: Psychology of the Southern Snake-Handling Cult* (1969) and *The Ghost Dance: Origins of Religion* (1972), Jay Y. Gonen's *A Psychohistory of Zionism* (1975), Richard A. Koenigsberg's *Hitler's Ideology: A Study in Psychoanalytic Sociology* (1975), and C. R. Badcock's *The Psychoanalysis of Culture* (1980).

L. Bryce Boyer's *Childhood and Folklore* (1979) is a nuanced study of the Apache, with whom Bryce and Ruth Boyer have worked for twenty-five years. Vamık Volkan's *The Need to Have Enemies and Allies* (1988) takes an object-relations approach to the formation of people's group affiliations and to how such identities are bound up with the emotionally bipolar notions of allies and adversaries, an approach taken in *Us and Them* (GAP 1987) published by the Group for the Advancement of Psychiatry, and one I have also taken in studies on intergroup relations and "psychogeography" (Stein 1982, 1984, 1987b).

CHAPTER 5

CLINICALLY APPLIED ANTHROPOLOGY

Noel J. Chrisman and Thomas M. Johnson

More than 35 years ago, William Caudill noted in the first review paper encompassing medical anthropology that "social anthropologists and other social scientists have recently been doing some unusual things" (1953:771). He went on to examine a number of these behaviors: working closely with physicians, teaching in medical schools, collaborating with the public health service, studying hospitals and patients, and conducting psychotherapy with American Indians. Since that time the unusual things have continued, but until 1979 little explicit was said about them. Anthropology was expanding dramatically during the sixties and seventies, and although anthropologists were working in clinical settings, more attention was focused on theoretical concerns within the discipline and on the expansion of such academic subfields as urban, psychological, and medical anthropology. Little was being written about collaboration between anthropologists and health practitioners.

In the preface to *Clinically Applied Anthropology*, Noel Chrisman and Thomas Maretzki (1982b) noted that it was time for a systematic examination of these unusual behaviors—to move beyond the informal dinner conversations among colleagues at professional meetings and to write about what these anthropologists had been doing for more than a decade. That volume became one of a number of published discussions about what some heralded as a new subfield of anthropology. This chapter attempts to provide an overview of how anthropologists have approached working with health practitioners. After examining the debate about what the subfield is called, we discuss how anthropologists currently fit into health science settings, their reliance on holism and system advocacy, the need for theoretical approaches, and the anthropological knowledge frequently used in clinical settings.

THE SCOPE AND NATURE OF CLINICAL INVOLVEMENT

There have been difficulties deciding what to name what anthropologists do in health science centers. Certainly when Caudill wrote, anthropological attention to matters of health and to health care systems was sporadic. There was no need to distinguish the cross-cultural study of health-related phenomena from the activities of anthropologists in medical schools because so few engaged in the latter. Recently, however, the twin pressures of increasing numbers of anthropologists and a shrinking academic job market have made this differentiation meaningful. Anthropologists' current desires to become visible and marketable for new types of professional positions in clinical settings seem to have been a major impetus for naming a new and different kind of anthropological endeavor and discussing how to do it.

In Caudill's time and up until the mid-1970s, it made sense to include anthropological activities in clinical settings as part of medical anthropology. In fact, in Norman Scotch's 1963 review, much of medical anthropology was involved with Western medicine and its introduction in cross-cultural settings (Scotch 1963). Now, however, there are more medical anthropologists, and those who work in clinical settings are able to document their unique contributions to Western medicine and to anthropology. With this emerging anthropological role differentiation, a kind of basic-versus-applied distinction within medical anthropology has emerged.

We see medical anthropology as the study of health-related phenomena. These phenomena range from individual-level biological studies, such as those examining cultural influences on hypertension and malnutrition, to microlevel studies of health care choices and illness beliefs, to macrolevel research on health care systems and their political and economic contexts. In short, medical anthropology is anthropological theory and research devoted to the topics of health, illness, and health care.

The type of anthropology found in health science centers is clearly part of a growing applied arm of the discipline: anthropology devoted to helping health practitioners better do what they do. One medical educator has noted that such a clinical anthropology is "properly distinguished and distinguishable from medical anthropology and other social sciences by virtue of this focus on using the concepts of anthropology to explain and suggest changes for the health care system and patients within the systems" (Swartz 1983:21). Some refer to this practice as "applied medical anthropology" (Hill 1984; Shiloh 1980). Our experience and that of others, however, is that what anthropologists do in clinical settings is to apply all of anthropology to the problems presented (Chrisman and Maretzki 1982a).

The scope of anthropology applied in clinical settings is as much determined by health practitioner expectations as it is by the topics of the field itself (Ablon 1980). As nursing found in its history, however, it is problematic for one field to define itself primarily in terms of its relation to another. In the case of medical anthropologists in clinical settings, the methods and theories they bring to clinical settings are very much those of the parent discipline of anthropology. In fact, the utility of our presence among health practitioners is based on this different perspective. In addition, many anthropologists in clinical settings continue their involvement in anthropological research and rely on peers in the discipline for intellectual response. The advantage of this situation for anthropology has been the development of new areas of research stimulated by actual clinical problems and work with clinicians (Weidman 1983), creating unique opportunities to make contributions to both anthropology and patient care.

Explicit attention to anthropology within health science centers gradually has ameliorated earlier problems with identity and role definition. We hope the discipline has moved beyond the internecine uncertainties alluded to by Scotch (1963:33): "On the other hand, there are those anthropologists who, in working in a medical setting, like to get overinvolved; like to play the role of the doctor or psychiatrist; prefer to play an active role rather than the role of the detached scientist. Their publications suffer accordingly." We argue against anthropologists being detached scientists, for this may inhibit understanding of health science professionals and opportunities for making anthropological knowledge relevant to clinical concerns.

Thus, while anthropologists need to be involved, they also must be wary of allowing system demands to determine their roles. For example, Thomas Johnson (1987b) pointed out the importance of passing the "tests" that clinicians may pose for the anthropologist in order to build rapport but cautions against being seen primarily as a clinician. Such "going native" in clinical settings may reduce objectivity and preclude some potentially unique and powerful contributions. Mark Nichter and colleagues (1985), Linda Alexander (1979), Atwood Gaines (1982), and Johnson (1987a) are good examples of anthropologists who are involved yet maintain their identities as anthropologists.

A MATTER OF TERMINOLOGY

Up to this point, we have been relatively careful to avoid naming the anthropology carried out in health care settings because there is still debate about what to call it. The two most popular alternatives are "clinical anthropology" (Golde and Shimkin 1980; Shimkin and Golde 1983) and "clinically applied anthropology" (Chrisman and Maretzki 1982a). The former has the advantage of being shorter and snappier and has the same connotations as clinical psychology, which claims its own independent clinical mandate. The difficulty with the "clinical anthropology" appellation is that it may not accurately describe the activities of the anthropologist and may imply a more extensive therapeutic role than is desirable or can be accomplished following traditional anthropological training (Ablon 1980).

Both because of the analogy with clinical psychology and the tenor of some of the early writing associated with the term, "clinical anthropology" implies that medical anthropologists are using anthropology to solve clinical problems: for example, to cure or care for somebody (Todd and Clark 1985). Peggy Golde

(1983a, 1983b), a major early writer on the subject who is trained in both anthropology and counseling describes herself as a clinical anthropologist. Hazel Weidman (1980, 1982b) would describe such colleagues with dual training as anthropologist clinicians. Some anthropologists do take care of patients, but this activity occurs primarily because they also have clinical training as a physician, nurse, or counselor (Tripp-Reimer 1983b; Dougherty 1985). All contend that although anthropologist-clinicians bring to their work more than traditional clinicians without training in anthropology, their clinical practices are based primarily on their other profession, not on anthropology.

A number of writers, usually health practitioners themselves (Swartz 1983), have been strongly supportive of the move of anthropology into clinical settings but have warned against attempting to become clinicians based solely on anthropological training. One argument is that anthropology is a research, not a clinical, discipline. We study culture and, although our research insights into the nature of a culture might help understand a patient, conducting research does not prepare us to take care of individuals. A second problem is that anthropology is a discipline without a therapeutic mandate (Chrisman and Maretzki 1982b): not possessing interventions, ethical standards, or societal sanction to treat people.

Chrisman and Maretzki (1982b) argued that anthropologists in health care settings teach, do research, and consult with clinical colleagues. Anthropologists in clinical settings, like anthropologists in any other applied setting, help analyze and resolve problems facing specialists (Weidman 1983). Clinically applied anthropologists direct their attention toward health care much as other applied anthropologists might direct their efforts toward economic development or agrarian change. *Clinically applied anthropology* is more cumbersome than *clinical anthropology* but does not carry the connotation of clinical practice and its implicit threat to the many more traditional clinicians who constitute the medical care system. When we are not directly involved with the care of patients, clinicians need not worry about our presumed lack of clinical skills—or our potential effectiveness—in working with patients (cf. Johnson 1987b). In addition, we are removed in large measure from competition for increasingly difficult-to-obtain health care dollars (Barnett 1980).

A second concern in defining clinically applied anthropology is whether to include the topic of applied anthropology in public health. There is much to recommend its inclusion, especially given the long history and central position that anthropology in public health has had in medical anthropology. The earliest text easily identifiable as medical anthropology was Benjamin Paul's *Health, Culture, and Community*, a series of case studies of the application of anthropology in public health projects (Paul 1955). Nonetheless, most of the writers about clinically applied anthropology have discussed their roles in health care institutions and/or working with clinicians (Kaufman 1980). Although these two traits are true to some extent in applied anthropology in public health, much of the writing in this field is not explicit about collaboration with health practitioners. There is also a matter of emphasis. The Mississippi Project discussed by Shimkin and others in *Clinical Anthropology* is a public health project, but parts of the discussion refer to relationships with clinicians (Shimkin et al. 1983).

Clinically applied anthropology is seen here as the application of anthropological data, research methods, and theory to clinical matters. Weidman and others who have discussed the word *clinical* refer to care of patients in some fashion. This does not mean that the clinically applied anthropologist must be seeing patients, though a number of these specialists do. It refers to the involvement of anthropologists with the everyday tasks of formal health practitioners—seeing patients, teaching students, carrying out research with and on health practitioners, and the like.

ALTERNATIVE CONCEPTIONS AND CRITIQUES

There have been two notable alternative views of clinically applied anthropology. The first was termed therapeutic anthropology by its major proponent, Ailon Shiloh (1977, 1980). Shiloh, commenting primarily about mental health care, asserted that most clients seeking help from community mental health centers do not have problems with either their neurochemistry or their intrapsychic functioning but rather simply have "problems of living." In other words, because many patients cannot cope with the demands of life in modern society, mental health professionals need to be experts on culture rather than on psychology. Shiloh went on to advocate for special training in interpersonal skills for anthropologists, followed by prescribed steps to licensure and certification similar to psychologists and social workers, although it is not clear exactly what such therapeutic anthropologists might do differently from the more traditionally recognized mental health practitioners.

A second alternative vision of clinically applied anthropology has come from a more recent emphasis in medical anthropology, critical medical anthropology. This perspective has never been thought of as explicitly clinical but rather as theoretical: understanding health issues in "light of the larger political and economic forces that pattern human relationships, shape social behavior, and condition collective experience, including forces of institutional, national, and global scale" (Singer 1986a:128). The principal assertions of advocates of this position are that critical medical anthropology promotes a concern for the relationship between microlevels and macrolevels of analysis and that the qualities of class, race, ethnicity, and gender are fundamental to understanding health, illness, and health care (Baer 1988). This important analytic approach has been successful in promoting a much stronger consideration of the ways in which macrolevel political and economic forces affect health in all societies. That is, critical anthropology is influencing theory and research in medical anthropology.

Devotees of the critical approach have soundly criticized clinically applied anthropology on the grounds that it does not consider the inherent power and class differentials between patients and practitioners. Perhaps the initial and most direct challenge came from Michael Taussig (1980a:12), a physician-anthropologist who charged that, by helping physicians to understand patients better, anthropologists who work directly in patient care activities are unwittingly perpetuating the existing class structure and exploitation by helping to "make the science of human management all the more powerful and coercive." Although both Taussig's and Shiloh's approaches are theoretically compelling, their practical nonspecificity makes questionable their individual-level efficacy for resolving patient problems, medical as well as social.

A CRITICAL CLINICALLY APPLIED ALTERNATIVE?

Other more recent proponents of a critical approach, however, have a more encompassing vision that recognizes the need for clinical strategies: "Ultimately a truly critical medical anthropology will need to combine theory *and praxis* into a unified endeavor that aims to liberate human beings in all societies from political-economic structures that exploit and oppress them" (Baer 1988:2; emphasis added). The first approach to praxis has been a suggestion that clinical anthropologists

shift from the individualistic approach advocated by Padgett and Johnson (1987) to a collective one which forms an alliance with other progressive medical social scientists, physicians, patients, and even administrators who seek to create a health care system which places human needs above profit-making and empire-building. *Critical clinical anthropologists will need to inform patients that their health problems are not unique but are shared by others of their class, race, ethnicity, and gender and that social action can serve as a form of therapy.* (Baer 1988:13; emphasis added)

Baer and others recognize that clinically applied anthropologists see themselves as translators of cultural knowledge for clinicians so that the medical care system can become more responsive to patient and societal needs. However, they see this as being trapped in a restricted role and that "clinical anthropologists may be forced to downplay the social origins and reification of illness, the increasing medicalization of social problems, and inequities in the availability and quality of health care" (Baer 1988:5). For the clinically applied anthropologist, two issues are central to this debate: the theoretical stance of the anthropologist and the professional role of the clinically applied anthropologist.

The central theoretical propositions of critical anthropology have been important, but not always salient, in social science analyses for more than a century. How critical theory is constructed, and its utility for analyzing culture and society, including the health care system, continues to be debated in the literature (see, e.g., Morgan 1987; and Morsy in this volume). Critical anthropological analyses of health care systems are illuminating the importance of political and economic processes in health status and health care. In this way, these analyses will affect the body of knowledge on which the clinically applied anthropologist must draw for working with clinicians. Although many clinically applied anthropologists do not sound like critical anthropologists, they are grappling with the issues (see Kleinman 1985:69; and the Johnson and Wright session on "Toward a Critical

Clinically Applied Anthropology'' organized for the 1987 meeting of the American Anthropological Association).

The key concern for critically informed clinically applied anthropology is not so much the validity of a macrolevel political and economic approach; that will be decided on the basis of its utility for understanding society. Rather, it is the particular sort of advocacy position that the critical anthropologists expect clinically applied anthropologists to take (to advocate for patients in their dealings with clinicians and to advocate for social action as a form of therapy). Regarding the latter, social action therapy, we have already argued that anthropologists are not trained as therapists and need to leave those decisions to people who are, such as the physicians Waitzkin (1986) or Taussing (1980a) or the nurse Thompson (1981). For the former, patient advocacy, this chapter stresses the notion of clinical anthropologists as system advocates: helping to resolve the problems of patient and practitioner alike.

Critical medical anthropologists point out that patients are caught in an inferior position, that practitioners' treatment decisions promote an undesirable status quo, and that the health care system is one element in an oppressive capitalist economic system. When the clinically applied anthropologist can introduce this knowledge into the conduct of a clinical case or set of cases so that all participants have an opportunity for a better outcome, the critical approach will have served its useful function. This kind of approach is not absent now, however. For example, Ellen Lazarus's (1988a) analysis of a prenatal clinic provides strong evidence of the need for restructuring simply on humanitarian grounds. Pointing out to residents that they can do little in the clinic for their poor and minority patients not only may restrain them from trying to do too much (such as a massive injection of penicillin rather than a course of pills, sometimes out of compassion, but sometimes punitively as a result of displaced anger) but also may open up opportunities for social welfare interventions. We recognize that these fall short of the agenda of the critical medical anthropologists, but they may move clinician viewpoints beyond the narrow confines of the clinic to consider health care system effects on all participants.

RATIONALE AND METHODS FOR CLINICALLY APPLIED MEDICAL ANTHROPOLOGY

Perhaps the key question for clinically applied anthropology is: What can anthropologists do with and for health practitioners? There has been some agreement about what is needed from anthropologists, who have a long association with health science schools (Leighton 1983) related to the set of topics discussed here. In addition, anthropologists and clinicians have been jointly committed to improving the quality and efficacy of care. Patients have been dissatisfied with high cost, low personal attention, and the related problems of class, race, and cultural differences. For example, Harold Swartz (1983:17) feels that practitioners "need to develop better understanding of the factors that affect an individual's perception and response to health, illness, and therapy. . . .

[Anthropologists] can increase the understanding and use of anthropological concepts in the activities of traditional providers of health care." Practitioners also have been dissatisfied with difficulties in providing care that meets patient needs (and just as important, their own needs) and have noticed that many of their difficulties are related to patients' cultural backgrounds. This recognition has been conditioned strongly by the civil rights and consumer movements of the 1960s, which called attention to group demands for more culturally sensitive care. In addition, some cities have experienced an influx of Southeast Asian refugees whose special needs are visible enough to heighten sensitivity to cultural issues in patient care.

Thus, a key issue in medical care has become the cultures of particular groups and the relationship of culture to the care of patients (Weidman 1983). Anthropologists have been the logical professionals to turn to for help on such problems, and they have been available because of their presence on or near the faculties of medical schools for decades. A number of topics have drawn anthropologists and health practitioners together over the years: defining which behaviors are normal and which are abnormal among humans using cross-cultural research; delineating specialized cultural diagnoses such as the culture-bound syndromes; contributing ethnographic research on health care settings to expand clinician understanding of their own environments; exploring the cultural dimension in human relationships; participation in public health projects overseas; and collaboration in community psychiatry (Chrisman and Maretzki 1982a). Through these years, anthropological contributions have been seen as important, but anthropologists only infrequently were involved in the daily functioning of medical schools.

Medical faculties are accustomed to using basic scientists to provide the specialized information used by medicine to carry out its mission (Hughes and Kennedy 1983; Hasan 1975). For example, physiologists, microbiologists, anatomists, and physical anthropologists are on these faculties to teach about the body, and psychologists (usually called behavioral scientists) are present to teach human behavior. Cultural anthropologists have been present (as another kind of behavioral scientist) to accomplish these same ends (Polgar 1962). For example, Robert Ness (1982) teaches short courses encompassing single topics, such as child abuse or alcoholism, as electives for medical students.

Many anthropologists, however, find it difficult to assume the limited and specialized role of providing information narrowly: to package their information to fit the time demands of clinical settings and to be congruent with the dominant information-processing style of their clinician colleagues (Johnson 1981). Howard Stein (1985a), for example, has complained about the "ethnic cookbook" approach that clinicians frequently seem to demand from anthropologists, in which they want to learn only a series of clinically relevant cultural characteristics of particular ethnic groups. Discussions among clinically applied anthropologists suggest that they prefer a broader mandate, teaching about cultural processes. Conflict can be illustrated by the reciprocal dissatisfactions of a hypothetical anthropologist and physician: the physician asks the anthropologist during hospital rounds to explain about the manifestations of grief among Ethiopians, and the anthropologist provides a 50-minute lecture on Ethiopian culture; the clinician is frustrated by such "information overload" (vowing never to ask a question like that again), and the anthropologist complains in frustration that all physicians want is a "cookbook."

An important dynamic in the relationship between clinicians and anthropologists has to do with the paradigm into which information concerning the care of patients will be put (Friedman 1983; Phillips 1985). Physicians, and to a lesser extent nurses, possess a biological and reductionist way of thinking about health and illness that is satisfying to them. The scheme they use to interpret information usually is successful in the care of patients and, like other belief systems, not easily susceptible to challenge. Although most anthropologists are able to provide ethnic lore for clinical use, they are uncomfortable with its use as immutable fact. We know that these "facts" are subject to wide variation among members of ethnic groups because of diversity of context.

Nevertheless, anthropologists are invited to many health care institutions to provide the information necessary to help physicians and others deal with cultural issues as clinicians see them emerging (Poland 1985). Thus a key issue in clinically applied anthropology is how to formulate anthropological theory and data in ways that will be responsive to the imperatives of clinical settings: time-consciousness and direct relevance to patient care. This is difficult, for while social scientists are trained to elaborate complexity and tolerate ambiguity in data (von Mering 1985), effective clinicians must strive to achieve a state of "optimal ignorance" (knowing enough to be effective but not so much that they become paralyzed by ambiguities and uncertainties).

Like clinicians who must always make decisions based on inadequate data, clinically applied anthropologists are often expected to deliver anthropological information when they have too few data for their own comfort (von Mering 1985). Their primary challenges, then, are translation of anthropology into something usable for clinical practice (Chrisman and Marctzki 1982b) and being comfortable with that style. Arthur Kleinman (1985:70) says, "We need to make ourselves useful in order to make ourselves heard." What this requires of the anthropologist is that he or she know anthropology well enough to transform it into something it was not necessarily designed for and, simultaneously, to know one or another of the health sciences well enough as a cultural system to phrase this information so it will be accepted and incorporated into clinical practice. It is a process very much like culture brokering, especially since mutual goodwill and respect become significant in the process (Weidman 1982b).

There are broader or narrower ways for the anthropologist to conceive of this task, depending on the degree of commitment to the clinical setting. A narrow construction of the translation need might be offered by anthropologists who only occasionally consult about one ethnic group and its behavior and who are likely to learn over time which information is most useful and the ways in which it can best be presented. A broader translation is more likely to arise among anthropologists who spend a significant segment of time with clinicians and feel the necessity for more integrated approaches that might encourage more actual change in the practice of that group of clinicians.

THE ROLE OF HOLISM AND A SYSTEMS PERSPECTIVE

There is debate about the kind of role that a clinically applied anthropologist should have in a health science setting. Actual roles range from that of clinician or researcher, with somewhat singular responsibilities; through roles as teacher or consultant, with broader responsibilities ; to roles that may encompass the former and even include patient advocacy. Linda Alexander (1979) points out that clinical anthropologists must be extremely wary of the tendency to be advocates for patients, families, or specific ethnic groups in a fashion analogous to their predisposition to be "on the side of the natives." They tend to focus on the power differential between doctors and patients and may cheer for the patient as the underdog. In addition, they tend to introduce cultural information to the clinician from the patient's perspective, as is their practice in ethnographies. As logical as this inclination seems to anthropologists, it contradicts another strongly held position within anthropology: holism. Alexander argues that anthropologists should not lose track of this central theoretical perspective simply because they are working in a nontraditional setting.

For Alexander, the advantage of holism is that it forces clinically applied anthropologists to take a systems perspective. When they are able to stand back and analyze the entire system, both clients and clinicians stand to gain. To a large degree, anthropologists are better prepared to use a systems perspective than are their psychology colleagues, and thus they have an additional skill to offer in clinical settings. Psychology shares with biomedicine a relatively narrow focus on the individual. Frequently the anthropologist's introduction of knowledge from a systems level can create many new options for treatment.

A holistic perspective has the practical advantage of reducing the chances of alienating clinical colleagues by appearing to favor one side or the other. Cultivating a reputation for working effectively with all participants is essential in clinical settings (Johnson 1987a). As much as clinicians may want or need patient information, they do not need to have their authority or expertise undermined by a patient advocate who is seemingly working against them. Nichter and colleagues (1985), Johnson (1987b) and Alexander (1979), who have described their "clinical" practices in some detail, mention the need to maintain positive relationships with clinicians while working closely, and frequently confidentially, with their patients. Practitioners are tremendously protective of their control over patients and are reluctant to let outsiders in. Once in, clinically applied anthropologists have a better chance of staying in if they can be seen as systems therapists rather than as patient advocates.

Howard Stein has provided a number of good examples of how the systems perspective works. In an article written for family physicians, Stein (1985c) directs them to distinguish between patient wants and needs; needs are seen as the patient's medical requirements as judged by practitioners. Stein's stance is clearly sympathetic with physicians. He mentions the logical ways in which family doctors can become drawn into meeting patient demands even when they are not the most helpful for the patient. In another paper (1982), he explains how he was able to discern patient meaning regarding an X-ray and thus facilitate communication between doctor and patient. In this example, Stein is behaving much more like a patient advocate, but he sees his actions as facilitating the system. In a third article (1985c), Stein suggests that the clinicians' focus on the culture of patients may be a red herring. First, not all problems of ethnic patients are the result of cultural background. Second, the clinician may call upon the anthropologist to give lengthy explanations of why the person's culture leads him or her to act a particular way when, in fact, difficulties in the doctor-patient relationship or other personally threatening matters are the real issues.

THE IMPORTANCE OF ETHNOGRAPHY

Contributing to anthropologists' holistic view of the world is their central interest in ethnography, which also must be an important aspect of anthropologists' work in clinical settings. For example, their naturalistic descriptions can be the delight of clinicians as long as these are not perceived as overly negative. The early work of William Caudill (1958b) and the more recent work of Robert Edgerton (1967) can be of great value to clinicians. However, as in teaching other aspects of anthropology, clinically applied anthropologists need to do more than simply carry out ethnographies and hand them to clinicians.

An important advantage of anthropology's ethnographic approach for work with clinicians is attention to context (Johnson 1987a; Press 1985). Anthropologists are unlikely to view the patient, or even the patient's immediate family, in isolation. Hospital social organization profoundly influences patient behavior, as well as the behavior of practitioners. Moving beyond the walls of the hospital, community economic and political issues are extremely important to the delivery of health care, and anthropology can expand clinicians' understanding of these. S. Galazka and J. K. Eckert (1986) show how such contextual features can be taught and can make a difference in medical primary care.

Ethnography is also a valuable tool for understanding clinicians and the clinical setting. Some have reasoned (Johnson 1987b; Stein 1982) that anthropologists are accustomed to moving in with the natives to learn their culture. Given the importance of knowing clinician culture well enough to avoid mistakes and to become accepted, it makes sense to use ethnographic skills for this task (Weidman 1983). The benefits of thinking in an ethnographic way about one's job are manifold. (We are not suggesting carrying out a formal ethnography, though our colleagues frequently ask us whether we are doing so.) As all of us learned in field situations, the process of asking purposefully naive or empathic questions about any setting aids in creating rapport with those who work in the setting. This is especially true of hospitals or other health care facilities, where clinicians can be sensitive to criticisms by adversarial social scientists. Moreover, explicit examination of the environment can produce understandings that may not emerge with a less methodologically explicit approach. For example, subtle status differences between types of colleagues may be discovered.

Finally, ethnography might be used as the basis for a process of reconciling different cultural systems, as between practitioners and patients. Michael Agar (1986) sees ethnography as an encounter among different traditions. Perhaps a clinically applied anthropologist can accomplish this reconciliation through carrying out good ethnography (which includes establishing rapport and maintaining status and role ambiguity), communicating its results to patients and practitioners, and acting as an advocate for the entire system.

Clifford Barnett (1985) has suggested that anthropological research is the best avenue for influencing clinicians. Yet such research cannot be reported as it would be to anthropologist colleagues. It is necessary to use a culturally sensitive approach in communicating the results of research to practitioners. In short, ethnography is a legacy of traditional anthropology that must not be abandoned simply because we assume we are working in our own culture.

DEVELOPMENT OF PRESCRIPTIVE THEORY

One of the most significant issues facing clinically applied anthropologists is the matter of theory. Theory may be considered in two ways: as anthropological concepts and their relationships that constitute the core of our discipline (Galazka and Eckert 1986) and as perspectives on how to use these concepts in clinical settings (Friedman 1983). We are able to take the first for granted since anthropological concepts and theories, along with methodology, define much of what anthropologists do. The second, how to apply the discipline, is undeveloped and requires much more thought and practice among clinically applied anthropologists.

Anthropologists must be able to contribute a theoretical perspective to health practitioners since we argue, implicitly or explicitly, that new approaches are needed in medicine. This means that we need to have an explicit rationale for how to provide culturally sensitive care. S. Donaldson and D. Crowley (1978) refer to this as "prescriptive theory." One aspect of prescriptive theory relates to the clinician question: "Under what circumstances should this anthropological approach be used?" Implicit here is the assumption that anthropological approaches are somehow akin to carrying out a medical procedure, such as a patient history or an ophthalmoscopic examination. In medicine, there are some indications for carrying out one procedure and others that suggest a different one. What are some of these indicators to which the clinician should respond with an anthropological approach?

One indicator is simply the presence of patients identified as ethnically different. Health practitioners, who tend to view anthropology as a basic science to provide background data for their practices, are stimulated to think about the need for cultural knowledge when they have ethnically distinct patients. We receive calls two to three times a year asking for information about specific ethnic groups. Frequently the inquirer says that he or she is treating more people from that group and wants to know about their culture so as not to offend them or treat them improperly. This is a positive step for a practitioner to take. From an anthropological viewpoint, however, it is too narrow. Rather than ethnicity as the key to culturally sensitive care, we hope that this type of care would be used more broadly.

The second indicator that motivates practitioners to seek specific cultural information is a particular patient complaint that can be tied to ethnicity. When there is a problem with an ethnic patient, anthropological knowledge makes sense, particularly to clinicians who have had prior positive experiences with anthropology in patient care. It is interesting, and quite unfortunate, that for the same complaint in a "nonethnic" patient, practitioners usually turn to a psychologist for behavioral information or a biological scientist for biological data. One of the major battles for clinically applied anthropologists is continually to assert that cultural data and a culturally sensitive approach are relevant to all patients and not just those whose ethnic background happens to be different.

Although clinically applied anthropologists argue that a culturally sensitive approach is always necessary in health care (Tripp-Reimer 1983b), we have not always been clear or in agreement with each other about what that approach should be. If clinically applied anthropology is to have some validity as a field, development of an anthropological approach to patient care and its dissemination to health practitioners is essential. In other words, we need to develop a prescriptive theory. There are certainly consistencies in what clinically applied anthropologists do in clinical settings. Here we outline what medical anthropologists see as core information for use by clinicians.

Topics that are frequently considered by clinically applied anthropologists include a focus on ethnocentrism, eliciting patient perspectives, the illness-disease distinction, holism, the importance of context when understanding behavior, and the concepts of culture, values, beliefs, customs, ethnic group, and the like. Perhaps what they add up to is a statement of a theoretical view in clinically applied anthropology. How these concepts are used may be the basis for prescriptive theory.

RELEVANT KNOWLEDGE

There are two general bundles of information that clinically applied anthropologists use in their dealings with clinicians. On the one hand, in response to clinicians' felt needs for culture-specific information, anthropologists provide data on a variety of subjects about various ethnic groups—the "ethnic cookbook"—and there are some excellent ones (Harwood 1981; Spector 1985). On the other hand, there also is a set of topics that would be presented in any introductory course in cultural anthropology (Weidman 1983). This latter information is not necessarily well received in undigested form by practitioners, but it is an important part of developing a culturally sensitive approach to health care. Interestingly, some nonanthropologists who write about ethnic health care for clinician audiences include these same topics (Louie 1985).

Culture is an essential concept for anthropologists to introduce because it is so central to the discipline and because a concern with problems evidently caused or exacerbated by culture is a major reason that anthropologists are consulted by health practitioners. Definitions of culture utilized clinically are those traditionally used in anthropology. For example, Toni Tripp-Reimer (a nurse and an anthropologist) defined culture in a chapter for undergraduate nursing students as "the total lifeways of a human group. It consists of learned patterns of values, beliefs, customs, and behaviors that are shared by a group of interacting individuals. More than material objects, culture is a set of rules or standards for behavior" (1984:226). Chrisman uses a shortened version in which culture is defined as "a learned, shared, symbolically transmitted design for living" (Chrisman 1986:62). Rather than transmitting strict definitions, however, clinically applied anthropologists must convey a number of key qualities about culture. The most important of these is that culture supplies a way of perceiving the world, creating different realities across cultures, and thereby provides guidelines for action.

Explicit discussions of culture as an approach to life and its variability across members of the same culture are critical for health practitioners (Isaacs 1983). Practitioners clearly carry around their own versions of reality—tacit understandings of the world, built on a foundation of biomedical knowledge that are concrete in many ways. Certainly physiological processes and anatomy are "real" and observable for them, and even abstractions like diseases are similarly real (Taussig 1980a). Culture can also be seen as concrete, implying to practitioners that knowledge about the cultural pattern of a group will be valid for each individual in the group. This may lead to stereotyping, a problem that clinically applied anthropologists aim to reduce. In fact, clinicians sometimes criticize anthropologists for stereotyping when we talk about patterns of group behavior because their tendency is to "hear" us talking about individual behaviors.

The features of culture as learned and shared are significant aspects of the concept for practitioners. The first, that culture is learned, is clinically important in at least two ways. First, the anthropologist can make the point that not all members of an ethnic group, for example, will share the same culture because of variations in enculturation or acculturation processes. This may reduce problems such as the difficulty created by one clinician who knew about Hispanic health beliefs. He complained that his patient did not know her own culture when she failed to explain her illness in hot and cold terms. Second, if culture can be learned, new perspectives can also be learned from the health practitioner. In fact, we discuss patient teaching with our students as a process of presenting new cultural patterns as options for patients rather than a matter of "truth" divulged by the clinician.

The notion that culture is shared is also clinically relevant. One of the most difficult problems for both clinicians and anthropologists is deciding whether culture is playing a role in a health problem or in its presentation to a practitioner (Stein 1985c). This is most striking in psychiatry and is one reason that anthropologists have been associated with psychiatry for so long. More clinicians now easily entertain the possibility that cultural differences may help explain seemingly bizarre behavior when it occurs, and this may stimulate a telephone call requesting a consultation. A typical call might concern an Asian man who had attempted suicide, stating that his action was part of his religion. That is, he had hoped to speed up the process of achieving higher spiritual status by living his lives quickly. One response would be to say that although we may not have personal knowledge about that as part of Buddhism, the psychiatrist should call a Buddhist priest and ask. Clinicians should use a different approach when a behavior can be located toward the culturally prescribed and shared end of a theoretical continuum than when a behavior can be placed on the idiosyncratic and pathological end of it.

A second important anthropological concept is custom: those observable behaviors exhibited by members of a culture. Discussions of such culturally patterned behaviors are easy for clinicians to appreciate, especially if our own customs are contrasted with similar customs from other groups. Clinicians want information about customs since they include such behaviors as dietary practices, communication patterns, religious behaviors, and health and illness practices. Specific guidelines for altering these behaviors may be given to practitioners. Learning pragmatic techniques constitutes an important portion of health practitioner training so this activity on the part of anthropologists fits with the educational expectations of most medical students and clinicians; in fact, such guidance may be demanded of anthropologists. For example, practitioners find it useful to learn how to adapt ethnic dietary practices to biomedical requirements for diabetes or hypertension. Similarly, religious practices can be respected and promoted in hospital situations as when folk healers are invited to practice in a Western hospital. At the very least, it can be helpful to remind clinicians of the relative imperviousness of customs to change so that they will not view noncompliant patients as purposefully defying them and resort to punitive or neglectful treatment strategies.

Another important concept is value, referring to societal evaluative standards. The idea of value constitutes an important concept for health practitioner use since value differences affect patient and family relations with practitioners. Specifically, varying value orientations (like varying health beliefs) influence care seeking, the style of practitioner interaction preferred by patients, the degree to which practitioner suggestions will be followed, and the kinds of self-care that the patient and family will carry out. It is useful to introduce values to practitioners in terms of how they influence the practitioners' own lives. In fact, the clinician's ability to know his or her own values and beliefs is a critical portion of culturally sensitive care. One approach used by a number of writers (Tripp-Reimer 1984a; Hartog and Hartog 1983; Fong 1985) is to discuss the value orientations Clyde Kluckhohn and Fred Strodtbeck delineated. These broad orientations present ways that societies organize a variety of values that relate to situations of daily life. One orientation popular during the culture of poverty discussions of the 1960s referred to time orientation: past, present, and future. Although there are problems with ethnocentric bias in applying the orientations to specific cases (see Liebow 1967 for a critical evaluation of the misuse of a "present time orientation"), these global perspectives are useful in helping clinicians to comprehend how values pervade everyday life. For example, groups with a future orientation can be seen as more likely to engage in disease prevention.

Beliefs constitute another core concept useful to practitioners. Goodenough's definition—beliefs are propositions accepted as true (1963)—is succinct. However, like culture, beliefs are invisible and thus difficult for clinicians to deal with. The anthropologist must emphasize that patient beliefs need constant attention by clinicians. Most practitioners recognize the possibility that patients may have beliefs that differ from theirs, whether health related or not. It is useful to discuss a variety of beliefs—not only health beliefs—with clinicians so they can begin to recognize the general utility of the term. Case examples about how beliefs can strongly affect behavior are helpful in getting the point across. Experienced clinically applied anthropologists collect a repertoire of cases in which beliefs have affected patients' illness behavior and practitioner care (Kleinman et al. 1978) and transmit them in a way that is culturally accepted in medicine—the war story, almost mythological accounts of particularly difficult patients or disastrous outcomes that reveal "truths" and are passed on as part of the informal socialization process in medicine.

Discussions of health beliefs identified with particular populations (such as ethnic groups) seem to be enjoyable for health practitioners just as they are for anthropology students. Beliefs form part of the esoteric lore that anthropologists are famous for repeating. The literature in anthropology is replete with detailed analyses of such interesting beliefs as spiritual sickness, witchcraft, hot and cold imbalances, vital energy, and the like (Snow 1974; Harwood 1971; Kleinman et al. 1975; Harwood 1981 is a particularly good source for a large number of ethnic groups). It is valuable for practitioners to be acquainted with folk beliefs characteristic of the ethnic groups with which they work so that patients are not referred for psychiatric help when such beliefs are communicated to the practitioner. In addition, these data may help practitioners learn to work with beliefs and behaviors that seem deviant to them. This ability constitutes the kind of challenge that health practitioners sometimes need in order to maintain interest in their work. We have been surprised on occasions when the residents have already engaged the use of indigenous healers to help care for their patients.

The anthropological love affair with esoteric beliefs also needs to be tempered in clinical settings. A culturally sensitive approach to health care requires that all patient beliefs should be attended to, and in primary care settings the types of health beliefs that will arise are not typically exotic. Clinically applied anthropologists need to discuss everyday beliefs about colds, flu, or appendicitis with the same enthusiasm as spirit illness. Clinicians can learn from this approach that popular culture health beliefs are as important as the more esoteric beliefs for understanding patients. In fact laypeople's use of biomedical terminology may be more misleading to clinicians than folk beliefs.

It is not surprising that ethnocentrism and allied ideas such as cultural relativism should be a routine part of the clinically applied anthropologist's repertoire. Their centrality within anthropology is related to the need to understand peoples' diverse beliefs and behaviors without imposing judgments from one's own culture. Their relativist implications, however, contrast strongly with the universalist and action orientations in biomedicine and may threaten some clinicians. Nonetheless, they are the fundamental lessons that anthropologists have to contribute.

One of the difficulties that clinically applied anthropologists must face is that a relativist perspective is in itself relative: that is, a relativist posture may increase the anxiety level of clinicians, who are asked to make decisions based on inadequate data, and therefore reflexively strive to reduce, rather than increase, ambiguity and relativity. Practitioners are often uncomfortable with a relativist position because inquiry in clinical settings must lead to action, but relativism easily can cause doubt and promote inaction bound up with reflection.

One way around this problem when working with practitioners is to point out circumstances under which ethnocentrism is and is not appropriate in practice. For example, ethnocentrism may impede taking an accurate history because significant information will be dismissed because it is "wrong." Patients likely will refuse to divulge important information if their revelations about folk beliefs or practices have previously stimulated negative reactions from practitioners. Practitioners do not like to think of themselves as less than thorough in gathering data, particularly when those data might be "cultural" and thus interesting. Anthropologists can take advantage of this aspect of clinical culture to introduce the necessity of a more relativist approach during the history taking or assessment portion of a clinical encounter (Tripp-Reimer 1983b).

Treatment, on the other hand, requires the confidence, risk taking, and rejection of uncertainty that are requirements of clinical practice. For this element of clinical care, ethnocentrism, with its accompanying confidence in the "rightness" of a particular cultural world, is essential. Thus, a kind of ethnocentrism can be promoted for this set of tasks. Anthropological recognition of differences in the diagnosis and treatment activities of clinicians can ease the insertion of a new perspective into a traditional behavior.

A useful way to operationalize the concept of cultural relativism (or the avoidance of ethnocentrism) is the notion of eliciting patient perspectives. Cultural relativity manifested at the individual level is more closely allied to the way clinicians think than is cultural relativism at a societal level. In addition, practitioners are accustomed to listening to their patients. Unfortunately, much of what the patient says is considered to be subjective, with the connotation of "not real" or not as important as "objective" data such as findings from the physical examination or laboratory tests. Demonstrating that eliciting patients' perspectives on their symptoms can provide equally valuable data makes sense to most clinicians and is usually accepted.

An important related construct for many clinically applied anthropologists is the illness-disease distinction (Fabrega 1972). This seminal idea is related to a relativist point of view and is crucial for the anthropologist who is trying to demonstrate how elicitation of patient perspectives is critical to culturally sensitive care. The last decade has seen more agreement on how to describe the distinction. Illness is identified with the perspective of the popular or folk sectors of the health care system (Kleinman 1980), and thus to the patient; disease is tied to the perspective of the professional sector and its practitioners. In the Western world, disease is a perspective of sickness that refers to some biophysiological abnormality that can be objectively demonstrated by Western scientific means (Chrisman 1986:60). We teach illness as a view of sickness that refers to subjective distress as experienced, described, and explained by the patient and/or the family.

The illness-disease distinction is taught to clinicians so they will be able to recognize multiple ways of experiencing and explaining sickness and the implications of this for care, to recognize that their way of seeing sickness is not necessarily the only way. For clinicians, neither the words nor the idea of such a contrast is new. As is true for many laypeople as well, disease and illness are seen as different. In addition, the meaning of the contrast seems to be similar: for most Americans, disease refers to the biological process, and illness refers to the experience of the disease. The anthropological contribution is not to restate the contrast in different words but to be able to point to differences in beliefs about sickness as a fundamental property of culture. In addition, anthropologists point out that these belief sets influence the behavior of patients and providers alike.

The concept of an explanatory model (Kleinman, Eisenberg, and Good 1978) aids in concretizing the illness-disease distinction for clinicians. Although there is a great deal of debate within anthropology about what an explanatory model (EM) is and how it should be used (Young 1982), the set of questions used to elicit an EM and the idea that it constitutes important data to gather from a patient are easy to transmit to health practitioners. This should not be surprising; Kleinman and Eisenberg are physicians, and the questions strongly resemble questions used in normal primary care encounters. In brief, eliciting an EM involves asking open-ended questions about the patient's notions of symptom etiology, pathophysiology, severity, course, and appropriate treatment.

We try to use the similarity of EM questions and primary care questions as the means to introduce the value of eliciting a patient's EM. We argue that good clinicians obtain most of this information anyway. The requirement for higher cultural sensitivity is to elicit and process the information, the patient's cultural perspective, as an essential step in patient care and not merely as an oddity. In addition, as Kleinman (1988b:chap. 15) points out, these questions and others about family, occupation, and the like promote a fuller view of the patient in ways that may not be obvious on the first encounter but may be crucial later in the practitioner-patient relationship. Medical and nursing students have a difficult time recognizing that when they are in practice, their relationships with patients will often last for long periods of time, in stark contrast to experiences during their training.

Like other anthropological ideas, the notion of an EM has become modified in its usage among health practitioners (Like and Steiner 1986). For example, the family practice residents with whom we work seem to refer only to an

Clinically Applied Anthropology

explanation of cause(s) for symptoms when they use the term. By ignoring the richness of EM information—for example, the range of treatments already used, whether the health problem is chronic, and the fears associated with the sickness—much of the point that illness is embedded in social life can be lost. Graduate students in nursing are susceptible to attending to the model aspect of the concept and use the term to refer to a model of thinking about patients in which culture is taken into account.

The degree to which anthropological ideas and terminology can be tuned to serve the needs of clinicians is nicely illustrated in a paper by Robert Like and R. P. Steiner, "Medical Anthropology and the Family Physician" (1986; see also Galazka and Eckert 1986). Both of these physicians are sophisticated in the clinical applications of anthropology and the other behavioral sciences. They make a similar distinction to the one we made earlier in this chapter between medical and clinically applied anthropology: "The anthropology of family medicine can be considered to represent a subdiscipline within family medicine, and will be defined here as the academic field which specializes in the study of the cultural dimensions of family health and illness in the context of primary care medical practice. The anthropology of family practice, or clinically applied anthropology, focuses on the ways in which family practitioners employ anthropological knowledge and techniques in the everyday care of patients and their families" (Like and Steiner 1986:88). They go on to state the basics of a culturally sensitive approach to patient care. Other authors have reported similar success with culturally sensitive care (Capers 1985; Fong 1985), and their work should encourage clinically applied anthropologists to formulate our roles with clinicians so that they reflect the broad strength of anthropology, including its unique perspectives on the world.

SUMMARY AND CONCLUSIONS

We use the same set of ideas in single lectures to clinicians, to structure whole classes, or to organize our thoughts when collaborating on clinical cases. Having this conceptual framework in mind aids in being consistent over time and with a variety of practitioners. For example, we teach nurses at graduate and undergraduate levels; physicians during medical school, residencies, and as fellows; and other health practitioners such as social workers and occupational therapists; and we work with epidemiologists and biostatisticians in public health settings. We think of what we have to contribute as culture-sensitive care (Chrisman 1986, in press a, in press b). It is based on the notion of culture as a way of imputing meaning to the world. Values and beliefs are analytically distinct aspects of culture that are useful in understanding health-related behavior. Legitimate variation in perception is the fundamental message. Closely linked to these ideas is a discussion of ethnocentrism and cultural relativism, phrased as cautions about losing data or misunderstanding the patient. We see a narrow construction of the health care system and a restriction in understanding of sickness simply to disease as strong contributors to medical ethnocentrism. To counteract this, we introduce Kleinman's more complex view of the health care system with folk, popular, and professional sectors (Kleinman 1980) and the illness-disease distinction.

We use the health-seeking process (Chrisman 1977; Chrisman and Kleinman 1983) as the means to introduce a broad perspective of an illness episode. The idea of an EM and how to elicit one is introduced as part of the patient's perception of the health care problem and is seen as part of the symptom definition element of health seeking. Moreover, for clinicians who work in heterogeneous urban settings, we talk about illness belief systems (Chrisman 1986). These are four types of illness beliefs (equilibrium [hot-cold] beliefs or germ theory beliefs, for example). These identify major illness beliefs in a variety of cultures and serve to acquaint clinicians with beliefs in a way that is usable. We relate the various beliefs with treatments in a discussion of the treatment action element. A key approach is to provide enough information about a variety of healers, including Western practitioners, so that the clinician will recognize strengths as well as weaknesses. This is particularly important with clinicians who worry about quacks (see Chrisman in press a).

We also attempt to include the patient's immediate social environment—seen in terms of family, social network, and community—in a discussion of lay consultation and referral. Finally, we examine the concept of sick role and make two major points. One is that clinicians tend to focus on only one aspect of the sick role—release from normal social obligations—without attending to other aspects such as feelings of responsibility. This approach stresses the negotiation that occurs between patients and their social environment. The second aspect of sick role refers to the chronic sick role. American culture has not yet adopted a cultural definition of chronic illness, and this hampers both practitioners and patients as they work together (see Kleinman 1988b). In a short presentation, we may conclude with the negotiation process (Katon and Kleinman 1980); in other situations, this approach is discussed more or less continuously.

We see negotiation as the culmination of skills and attitudes that are strongly promoted with an anthropological approach: cultural relativism or valuing the patient perspective as a major attitude and open-ended questioning to achieve a native view as a major skill. In addition, we consider the overall approach of valuing alternative realities, expanding the clinical view to encompass much of the social environment, and being willing to negotiate as essential parts of culture-sensitive care.

Clinically applied anthropology emerged from the ongoing activities of anthropologists working in clinical settings. In the beginning, each may have felt somewhat isolated since there was little discussion. Over the past ten to fifteen years, however, discussions of these activities have been published, and clinically applied anthropologists have discovered that we do have some things in common, and we can enunciate a set of skills and perspectives for successful clinical work. Now, however, there is a need for these specialists to go beyond the scope of this chapter and formulate the prescriptive theory. Categorizing such theories will greatly simplify training for clinically applied anthropology. More important, however, is the opportunity to design clinical trials of culture-sensitive care to test systematically what many of us assume to be true based on rewarding clinical experiences: that an anthropological approach changes health care delivery in a positive way.

SECTION 2
MEDICAL SYSTEMS

CHAPTER 6

ETHNOMEDICINE

Arthur J. Rubel and Michael R. Hass

In this chapter we discuss some of the more salient approaches taken by anthropologists in their analyses of illness, healing, and those who provide assistance when sickness strikes. We discuss an anthropological interest that has evolved from curiosity about exotic beliefs and customs related to health and illness into a robust, rapidly growing, anthropological specialization. We will emphasize the evolving approach to attributions of sickness, the social use of sickness and healing for purposes of social control, and the recruitment and training of healers. We hope to demonstrate how these studies have contributed to the development of general theory and methodology in sociocultural anthropology, in addition to the emergence of the subfield of ethnomedicine. The chapter concludes with recommendations for the kinds of research necessary for the continued healthy growth of ethnomedicine.

HISTORICAL OVERVIEW OF ETHNOMEDICAL APPROACHES

Healing, shamanism, and the relationship between illness and supernatural forces have captured the interest of ethnologists and the public from anthropology's earliest days (Tylor 1871; Seligmann 1911; Frazer 1911). The early classics reported from the far corners of the earth seemingly bizarre notions of the causes of illness and described diagnostic procedures that invoked supernatural spirits, machinating spouses, or neighbors. Accounts of the recruitment of diviners and counterwitchcraft specialists to discover the causes of illness had strong appeal for turn-of-the-century readers, whose own beliefs about health had been radically altered by the industrial and scientific revolutions (Osherson and Amarasingham 1981; Starr 1982; Freidson 1970).

By the 1930s research on the origins and provenance of the cultural components of medical systems was a prominent dimension of American cultural anthropology (Clements 1932). Since ideas and behavior related to sickness and healing were considered a significant part of culture, efforts to reconstruct the processes of culture building included close study of the tools and other paraphernalia of healers. In this effort, the distribution of culture traits related to health and the control of sickness were mapped and analyzed by Forrest E. Clements, resulting in identification of five major causes of disease in the nonindustrial world: sorcery, soul loss, breach of a taboo, intrusion by a disease object, and intrusion by a spirit. He concluded that any society can be characterized by the disease cause most prominently reported for it (for example, as a spirit-intrusion society or a soul-loss society), and he sought to infer from the spatial distribution of these traits how long they had been part of a particular culture under study (cf. Kroeber 1947).

Clements's work was roundly criticized by researchers who saw more promise in the configurationist approach being advanced by Ruth Benedict in her *Patterns of Culture* (1934). A major argument, forcefully pursued (Ackerknecht 1971:31), contended that a configurationist approach placed medicine in its cultural context: "What counts are not the forms but the place medicine occupies in the life of a tribe or people, the spirit which pervades its practice, the way in which it merges with other traits from different fields of experience." Ackerknecht's critique was a harbinger of a radical shift from a historical approach to health phenomena to a theoretical orientation. The emerging functional theory viewed society as comprising interrelated parts, with concepts of disease and its cause(s) and the characteristics of healers being interdependent (Ackerknecht 1971:31, 54, 55; Wellin 1977:50–51; Beals 1980:289–291).

One of the earliest (Rivers 1924) and most prominent ways in which ethnomedicine contributed to the development of theory and method in sociocultural anthropology was to show the functional integration of the components of health care institutions within society's cultural matrix, its social organization, or political system. The functional integration approach, together with what have become known as the cognitive and the symbolic approaches, have become the dominant theoretical approaches to institutions of health care in the approximately half-century since Clements published his major work.

As anthropology became more systematic and research more sophisticated, ethnomedicine became one of the essential dimensions of culture to be investigated. As the community study method became more popular, especially in studies of Mexico and Guatemala (Chambers and Young 1979), greater prominence was given a society's conceptualizations of illness, its causes and cures, the role of healers, and the relationship between concepts of disease and cosmology. Links were identified between what had appeared to be bizarre health beliefs and practices and other aspects of the culture or social organization (Cassel 1955; Rubel 1960, 1966a; Marwick 1965; Lieban 1967; O'Nell and Selby 1968; Garrison 1977a,b; Lindenbaum 1979). These findings contributed to a more culturally relativistic attitude toward other peoples' health practices and understandings (Lewis 1975:201). The most exotic health beliefs and behaviors are made understandable, and their contribution to the viability of social forms is made manifest, when viewed in the cultural context in which they are found.

For example, the notion that people become ill because they have been victimized by neighbors transformed into animals was rendered more accessible by the reports of Villa Rojas (1947) and others (e.g., Dillon-Malone 1988; Vogt 1969; Stratmeyer and Stratmeyer 1977; Holland 1963a; Adams and Rubel 1967) that in some societies transgressions of social norms are believed to be sanctioned by illness visited on the transgressor. Anthropology's interest in attribution of sickness as punishment for departures from social norms dates from at least as far back as 1915 (Rivers 1924; see also Ackerknecht 1958:4–5). That theoretical approach was applied to good advantage (Villa Rojas 1947) in an analysis of the causes of sickness among Tzeltals of southern Mexico. The analysis preceded a number of later important works in which associations were drawn between the social norms governing behavior and the attribution of sickness to supernatural forces charged with maintenance of those norms (Dillon-Malone 1988; Vogt 1969; Stratmeyer and Stratmeyer 1977:135–36; Holland 1963; Adams and Rubel 1967). Sometimes those who punish with illness because of failure to follow social norms are those holding official positions; sometimes it is the deceased or supernatural figures who play this role (Vogt 1969; Turner 1967:282; Rubel 1960; Bahr et al. 1974; Evans-Pritchard, cited in Lewis 1975:200; Marwick 1964:263–68; Nadel 1952).

The connection is elegantly developed in a study (Whiting 1950) of a small society of native Americans, the Harney Valley Paiute. These Paiute have few formal mechanisms of social control (police, army, courts, or judges) but a well-developed fear of sorcery. Sickness attributed to sorcery is hypothesized as representing a societal sanction of unacceptable behavior rather than interpersonal enmity. This explanation seems plausible and does elucidate the fear of sorcery as a mechanism for maintenance of social order among the people of Harney Valley. But the vital contribution this study makes about the contribution of beliefs concerning the cause of illness to successful functioning of a society is to test the hypothesis on a worldwide sample of societies. As a result, we now know that in societies in which formal institutions of social control are absent or weak, sorcery attributions are more frequent. In societies where institutions like a police force, courts, or an army are prominent, attributions of sickness to sorcery are less frequent.

A subsequent examination of that hypothesis in connection with a Filipino Christian group under the hierarchical control of the modern Philippine Republic found that sorcery allegations were rampant (Lieban 1967). These allegations prove, however, to be associated with social discord, which is not clearly assigned to a formal social control agency (such as police or an army). Competition for a lover, conflict between spouses, broken verbal agreements, and arguments over ownership of land in which title is not unequivocally vested fall between the cracks, being neither clearly in the domain of a provincial or federal court nor clearly under familial control. In these cases, sickness is a form of punishment presumed exacted by means of sorcery. In other words, sorcery fills the void when responsibility for the resolution of conflict has not been clearly assigned (cf. Gluckman 1965:viii; Marwick 1965; Lindenbaum 1979).

In 1968, the term *ethnomedicine* was applied (Hughes 1968; cf. Ackerknecht 1971:11) to "those beliefs and practices relating to disease which are the products of indigenous cultural development and are not explicitly derived from the conceptual framework of modern medicine." Subsequently (Fabrega 1974:39–43) the term was applied more broadly to refer to "culturally oriented studies of illness." It was argued that the concern of the ethnomedical investigator was to explain "an illness—its genesis, mechanism, descriptive features, treatment, and resolution—as an event having cultural significance." One year later, ethnomedicine was defined (Fabrega 1975:969) as "the study of how members of different cultures think about disease and organize themselves toward medical treatment and the social organization of treatment itself." Shortly after that, a more open-ended definition (Foster and Anderson 1978:51) was suggested: "the vast body of knowledge which has resulted from the curiosity of anthropologists about the medical beliefs and practices of members of traditional societies."

Consideration of ethnomedical matters in the holistic investigation of the cultural life of communities is particularly characteristic of the extensive community study research in Mexico and Guatemala (Chambers and Young 1979). Reports of these investigations give prominence to the group's conceptualizations of illness, its causes and cures, the role of healers, and the relationship between concepts of disease and cosmology. During the same period, a great many other studies more narrowly analyzed specific ethnomedical issues (Cooper 1933, 1934; Hallowell 1934; Honigmann 1947; Teicher 1960; Aberle 1952; Gussow 1960; Wallace 1960). That large amount of attention paid ethnomedical observations in the first half of this century contrasts with a view (Landy 1977) that anthropologists had paid little attention to medical matters in the early twentieth century.[1]

ETHNOMEDICAL SYSTEMS IN COMPARATIVE PERSPECTIVE

The effort to contrast and oppose "other" kinds of medicine with the increasingly dominant allopathy as practiced by medical physicians represents a serious problem, long impeding comparative medical studies. The difficulty contributes to a befuddlement as to the appropriate way to refer to allopathy, much less how to refer to those "other" systems, so as to avoid invidious comparisons. It has been essential to find a nonpejorative term with which to describe biomedicine—the ethnomedicine in which physicians are trained—so as to be able to compare and contrast that ethnomedical system with others without making a priori value judgments. We will refer to the former as cosmopolitan medicine to distinguish it from other ethnomedicines (Dunn 1976:135–37). To do otherwise is to fall prey to absurdities (Leslie 1975). For example, to describe the widespread practices of curing among American, Mexican, or German laypersons in the 1970s and 1980s as not modern when they are widely practiced in the year this is written is foolish. Similarly problematic is to label as non-Western those diagnoses or healing procedures so extensively practiced today in suburban New Jersey or in the neighborhoods of Detroit or Los Angeles (McGuire 1988). To refer to allopathy as the uniquely university-based medicine is to fail to account for the tens of thousands of physicians in India or Sri Lanka trained in the many university medical schools in which Ayurvedic medicine is the subject of lectures, laboratory training, and clinical preparation, to say nothing of the thousands of licensed doctors of osteopathic medicine produced in the last decade by American medical schools. For the reasons just indicated we will henceforth refer to the medicine practiced by physicians trained in biomedicine as "cosmopolitan medicine," and other ethnomedicines will be referred to by the name of the group of which it forms part of the culture (for example, Bontoc medicine, Chinantec medicine, Zulu medicine).

CRITIQUES OF THE ETHNOMEDICAL APPROACH

Critiques of the rapidly growing field of ethnomedical studies (Fabrega 1974; Rubel 1983b) draw attention to its peculiarly mentalistic orientation. Horacio Fabrega (1974:40) wrote:

The implicit assumption adopted by the researcher is that he is dealing with a disorder that is either typically psychiatric or at least psychiatric-like. Excessive preoccupation with this dimension on the part of culturally oriented anthropologists has tended to obscure the influences that biological components have on [culturally defined] illnesses. Consequently, the potential of examining the reciprocal influences that psychocultural and biological factors have on instances of illness occurrence [as defined and categorized by subjects] has been missed.

Indeed, ethnomedical studies are often conducted in societies in which such "killer diseases" as infant diarrhea, pulmonary tuberculosis, "river blindness," and schistosomiasis are rampant with little if any attention to the local population's cultural response to these diseases. Instead, research fastens on concepts, prevention, and curing of folk diseases or diseases with psychiatric implications (see reviews by Lieban 1973; Landy 1983b; Wellin 1977).

As a consequence of this emphasis, the impact of ethnomedical studies on cosmopolitan medicine and, in particular, the culturally relativistic analyses of health institutions and practices in diverse societies[2] have been primarily in broadening and making more flexible the psychiatric categories of the International Classification of Disease and the Diagnostic and Statistical Manual (Devereux 1956; Simons and Hughes 1985; Hufford 1988; Kapur 1987; Prince and Tcheng-Laroche 1987). The growing number of cosmopolitan physicians engaged in studies of how illness in other ethnomedical systems is constructed and responded to by patients promises new efforts to examine the implications of comparative studies for the diagnosis and treatment of patients (Lewis 1975; Helman 1984; Like and Ellison 1981).

CURRENT APPROACHES: THE CASE OF HUMORAL MEDICINE

Humoral medicine is one of the most thoroughly studied topics in ethnomedicine and one that remains a subject of controversy. The concept of opposing humoral qualities affecting health is a prominent premise of Latin American and other ethnomedicines. According to this theory, health is a matter of balance between the opposites: hot-cold and wet-dry, for example (Browner 1985a; Escobar, Salazar, and Chung 1983; Graham 1976; Hart 1969; Kay 1977b; Kendall, Foote, and Martorell 1983; Nations and Rebhun 1988; Rubel 1960, 1966a; Schreiber and Homiak 1981; Scheper-Hughes 1988a).

One orientation to the widespread humoral concepts among Amerindians is to attribute their origins to the pre-Christian eras of Greek and Arabic history (Foster 1953, 1978a, 1978b). Proponents consider that this humoral theory of health and illness was introduced to indigenous America in the sixteenth century by the Spanish conquerors. Four humors—hot, cold, wet, and dry—constituted this important system; a person's state of health was to be attributed to a state of balance between such opposite qualities as hot-cold, wet-dry. Reference to these humoral qualities appears again and again in ethnographic accounts of Spanish- and Portuguese-speaking peoples' efforts to engage in preventive health and to cure themselves or others of disease.

Compelling data have been marshaled, however, to show that prior to the arrival in America of Europeans, the concept of opposite qualities played a prominent role in health care of indigenous American societies (Colson and de Armellado 1983; Lopez Austin 1975, 1980; Ortiz de Montellano 1987). More radical criticisms question whether such understandings of opposite qualities were systematically distributed among these populations, much less systematically applied as measures of preventive and curative health (Weller 1983).

Although none dispute that the concepts of hot and cold are remarkably widespread in Latin America or that they undergird much of the diagnostic and healing practices of these populations, of both Indian and non-Indian cultural background, our concern is the extent to which this critical system is systematically distributed and used within these groups. For instance, we know (Kay 1977a: 162) that in one Spanish-speaking barrio in Tucson, Arizona, "No woman under 30 could make such a distinction [between qualities of hot and cold] or seemed to be aware of this system of classification." In Guatemala, although women recognize hot and cold conceptual categories and their applications to nutritional and medicinal decisions are widespread (Weller 1983), they are not systematically distributed and perhaps never were. On the other hand, the free recall task Weller used by which to make salient the respondents' own domains of illness may not have provided an adequate key to tap the womens' concepts of humoral qualities. When the humoral categories of disease provided by a sample of urban Guatemalans are compared with those elicited from women who live in the countryside, "the disease terms that were categorized beyond the chance level by the rural women were not necessarily the same ones significantly categorized by the urban women, nor were they necessarily categorized in the same manner." Inasmuch as a reader might conclude that these women fail to order things or concepts such as humoral qualities into categories, it is important to realize that these same women did systematically agree in their assessments of the levels of severity and contagion associated with familiar disease names (Weller 1983:255; Cf. Young 1980; Logan 1977).

Among highland Chinantecs of Mexico, although the concept and utilization of humoral categories is widespread (Browner 1985a), another more encompassing mechanism crosscuts that of hot and cold. This underlying, crosscutting system is based on mechanical understandings of human physiological processes. In the Chinantec-speaking municipality of San Francisco, the physiological processes of reproduction are managed by the use of medicinal plants, some of which are of a hot quality and others cold. Rather than using these qualities according to some arcane logic, however, townswomen pragmatically select humorally hot or cold plants to stimulate bodily processes—for example, to cause the uterus to evacuate its contents (whether to facilitate labor, prevent a conception, or cause a miscarriage) or to retain them (to prevent miscarriage or to arrest excessive menstrual flow or spontaneous menstrual hemorrhaging).

This analysis is important because it interprets the use of hot and cold concepts as facilitators of another, underlying, system by means of which essential physiological mechanisms are regulated. Those results also provide reason to investigate similar efforts to manage physiological processes in other indigenous groups. However, in another Mexican group (Fabrega and Silver 1973:85), there is "no indication anywhere in Zinacanteco curing that *h'iloletik* [shamans] or their patients think or act about illnesses on the basis of concepts that involve the body as a system composed of functionally interrelated parts and processes— with the possible exception of body temperature." These investigations raise the question of why the results and conclusions of so many investigations of the same humoral categories of disease are in conflict.

Several students of the problem have asked the same question (Logan 1977; Weller 1983). The former suggests that the problems attaching to research in humoral qualities plague ethnomedicine in general:

Most ethnographic accounts of humoral medicine are descriptive, in that no specific hypotheses or set of relationships are central to the given research. It is of limited use simply to report that a given people classify certain items or conditions as hot and others as cold. For without explanation, that is, without relating the data to some fact of the group's culture, ecology, or biological adaptations, the data tell us little more than certain items and conditions are judged, by some informants, to be hot or cold. (Logan 1977:95)

It is also possible that the questions asked about humors are phrased ambiguously (Weller 1983), leading to different answers to apparently similar questions. Unfortunately, this cannot be evaluated inasmuch as readers are seldom provided information as to the questions asked. Neither are readers provided the criteria by which respondents are included in a sample, the sample size, or how the data were collected (Logan 1977). In view of the fact that organizing hypotheses are seldom utilized, and interviews or information as to the constitution or size of a sample are commonly unavailable, collection of a comparable body of data to permit cross-cultural comparisons of ethnomedical phenomena has been problematic. Furthermore, earlier studies mistakenly assumed homogeneous understandings of humoral categories, failing to account for intracultural variability or variation within individuals' accounts influenced by such life events as sickness, pregnancy, and lactation (Logan 1977:102, 104; Weller 1983:256). Until such methodological problems are resolved it is too soon to conclude that ethnomedical concepts are not systematically distributed within a social group (Weller 1983:255).

CURRENT USE OF ETHNOMEDICAL PARADIGMS

Much of the research on ethnomedical systems has focused on the issues of classificatory characteristics of ethnomedical phenomena, the meaning of illness, and how ethnomedical knowledge influences health seeking behavior.

Classificatory Dimensions of Ethnomedical Phenomena

The language of ethnomedical systems can be used to good advantage to gain access to how a group classifies ethnomedical phenomena. In one pioneering study of Subanun diagnosis of skin disease (Frake 1961), it is assumed that cognitive structures underlying illness behavior and decision making are implicit in utterances that can be systematically elicited from informants with standardized questions. That approach was subsequently improved by making the question asked even more specific (Metzger and Williams 1963). In a study of curers and curing in highland Chiapas, Mexico, D. Metzger and G. Williams formulated their questions in terms of the informants' own concepts and categories rather than their own. They discovered unforeseen subtle distinctions in Tzeltal illness categories, illuminating a classificatory system far more complex than previously suspected.

Other researchers, however, argue that not all of a people's knowledge about health and disease can be accurately represented by unidimensional semantic representations (D'Andrade et al. 1972). These researchers introduce multidimensional scaling instruments that show how members of different cultural groups cluster diseases on the basis of a number of attributes or features. Comparing English-speaking Americans' and Spanish-speaking Mexicans' disease classifications, it was found that for both subject groups, diseases were not organized conceptually on the basis of the features that formally defined them but on the basis of pragmatic dimensions such as type of victim, consequence or impact of the disease, and kind of remedy indicated. This conclusion marked a shift away from features that define disease to the way people perceive the impact of disease on their lives.

The Meaning of Illness

The influential concept of explanatory models of illness also recognizes the importance of context. Explanatory models are sets of beliefs or understandings that specify for an illness episode its cause, time and mode of onset of symptoms, pathophysiology, course of sickness, and treatment. Explanatory models are "formed and employed to cope with a specific health problem, and consequently they need to be analyzed in *that* concrete setting" (Kleinman 1980:106; emphasis added). Although others have invoked the concept of an explanatory model of illness as a cultural construct (Friedl 1982), Arthur Kleinman makes it clear that his explanatory models are attributes of individuals, drawing upon general cultural knowledge but remaining at least partially idiosyncratic and situational. Kleinman's work and that of many others influenced by his approach, however, fail to specify in any detail the extent to which individual explanatory models are shaped by culture and the extent to which they are idiosyncratic formulations.

A major innovative effort to analyze this important issue is found in a study of the Canadian Ojibway (Garro 1988). Combining in a single study the explanatory model and the cognitive approach to health understandings, Linda Garro found that an average of 78 percent of the personal explanations—explanatory models—reflect the shared Ojibway cultural model. Using this approach to understand Ojibway explanation of high blood pressure, we now know that individual Ojibway have explanatory models that draw from the group's shared cultural knowledge about high blood pressure.

Another limitation of the explanatory model approach is that models focusing on designation and classification do not inform us about the links between illness and social context. On the basis of fieldwork in the Iranian city of Maragheh, Byron Good examined the complaint of heart distress in its social and cultural context. Using information on the distribution of heart distress in a stratified sample of 750 persons from Maragheh and the surrounding area in conjunction with an explanatory model drawn from local traditions of Galenic-Islamic and sacred-Islamic medicine, he described the social and affective context of the experience in terms of a semantic illness network—the "words, situations, symptoms and feelings which are associated with an illness and give it meaning for the sufferer" (Good 1977:39). In his view, heart distress not only served as a vehicle for the expression of social stress but was also used instrumentally to bring about action to relieve it. Others (Lindenbaum 1979; Morsy 1978; Rubel 1960; Turner 1967) have also written of how symbols of ill health serve multiple social purposes.

In another study about the ways in which a group speaks and thinks about sickness, Gilles Bibeau (1981) observed that over the course of an illness episode, villagers change the labels assigned the signs and symptoms of the condition. In these observations among the Ngbandi of Zaire, Bibeau concluded that to understand medical language, one must examine it in context. Bibeau's observation that the Ngbandi name for a disease changed from one context to another (for example, when discussing the site at which the condition is located, the extent to which it resembles an animal, or if it is assumed to represent a social sanction for inappropriate behavior) led him to develop the idea of a network of names associated with a particular disease. Each name in the network refers to a different feature or characteristic of the disease, changing from one context to another. Bibeau discusses six principles that underlie the origins of the different labels used contextually, or what he refers to as "speech situations." Like Roy D'Andrade, Bibeau emphasizes the productive or generative capacity of language systems. Bibeau attempts to contextualize verbalized medical categories and forge links between them and the social settings in which they occur. Yet another effort (Early 1982:1491) to contextualize health knowledge is focused on "therapeutic narratives"—"commentary on illness progression, curative actions, and surrounding events"—that occur naturally among members of the lay therapy management group.

Whereas ethnomedicine's insistence on providing the cultural context in which an illness is analyzed has enriched our understanding of how cultures construct illness and has expanded the forms that illness can assume, that emphasis has inhibited cross-cultural comparison. A methodology recently proposed (Browner, Ortiz de Montellano, and Rubel 1988) might render certain types of cross-cultural comparison both ethnographically valid and systematic. Where cultural processes are anchored to physiological mechanisms, the same species-wide responses to those referents by different cultural groups can be more readily compared. For example, comparative ethnographic descriptions of illness in infants in which diarrhea is a salient physiological process illustrate what might be done with this approach. Many ethnomedical studies describe chronic infantile diarrhea, accompanied by a depressed fontanel, eyes seemingly sunken in the face, apathy, and sometimes vomiting. Cosmopolitan medicine refers to this congeries of symptoms as dehydration associated with diarrhea. Other cultural groups, such as the sixteenth-century Aztec, contemporary Hondurans, Peruvians, Brazilians, Mexican-Americans of Texas, Shona and Ndebele of East Africa, and East Indians, respond in diverse ways to the same signs and symptoms of biological dysfunction.

Some of these ethnomedical systems attribute the condition to the escape of the infant's vital force through the still-open fontanel (Lopez Austin 1967; Ortiz de Montellano 1987:392). In others it is attributed to pressure or trauma, which depresses the fontanel, in turn causing the upper palate to block the oral passageway (Rubel 1960). Elsewhere the condition is attributed to the child's mother's breastfeeding too soon after she has been exposed to a woman who has recently experienced a miscarriage (Lozoff, Kamath, and Feldman 1975). In another system, biomedicine, the same condition is explained by intrusion of an enteric pathogen, causing the infant an infection, of which loose stools is a consequence (Jelliffe 1966), and in parts of Brazil it is a consequence of the evil eye (Nations and Rebhun 1988). It is striking that some ethnomedical systems explain the condition as dehydration, of which a depressed fontanel is a manifestation, while others understand the characteristic runny stool, fluid loss, sunken eyes, and fitfulness to be caused by the depression of the fontanel.

Ethnomedicine and Health-Seeking Behavior

Ethnomedical research has made a significant contribution to the understanding of how knowledge about illness influences health-seeking behavior. But recent investigations have emphasized that verbalized illness categories, explanatory models, and other knowledge are not predictive of consequent behavior. Two studies, one in urban Nepal and the other in rural Mexico, provide strong evidence that illness beliefs are not good predictors of the health-seeking strategies of patients and their families. Nepalese, who have access to alternative forms of treatment, behave according to two basic patterns: illness specific, in which they seek out different kinds of therapy for different disorders, and multiple use, in which assistance is sought from a variety of medical resources during a single episode of illness. When asked, Nepalese informants expressed a preference for an illness-specific strategy; when observed, their behavior reflected a multiple-use strategy (Durkin-Longley 1984). The discrepancy may occur because therapeutic choices reflect the beliefs and preferences not only of the patient but of family and friends as well.

In rural Mexico, Young and Garro (1982) seized on an opportunity presented by two rural, Tarascan-speaking villages similar in medical beliefs but differing in degree of access to cosmopolitan medical facilities. In this quasi-experiment the researchers tested two competing explanations of why Indians fail to utilize cosmopolitan health services: because it is too costly in time and money to gain access to those services or because their health understandings are incompatible with those guiding clinic services. The village with easy access to cosmopolitan health services proved to use them at approximately twice the rate of the other. Other studies seeking to distinguish the influence of ethnomedical beliefs and ease of access on utilization of cosmopolitan medical clinics have failed, however, to reproduce Young and Garro's results (Stock 1980:385–86; Pearson 1982:229–36).

The many health services available to Detroiters (Hunt 1985) and the diverse sources of information from which they select information to comprehend their illness indicates that linkage between medical knowledge and social context becomes considerably more complicated the more medically pluralistic a society is. For example, in Belize there are a variety of medical resources available to residents (Staiano 1981). They include cosmopolitan medicine in the form of a hospital, out-patient clinic, and pharmacy; bush medicine consisting of traditional practitioners outside the cosmopolitan framework; Catholic or Pentecostal spiritualist healers; and household lay knowledge. Kathryn Staiano argues that in a pluralistic setting such as Belize, there are alternative systems of interpretation from which the patient and healer can select. Two case studies serve to illustrate the continuing process of negotiation that goes on as patients seek therapies and etiologies consistent with their understandings of illness. In both cases, the patients and their families accept some aspects of the cosmopolitan health care system as presented to them by a government physician, but they supplement this with information gathered in consultation with traditional healers.

The dynamic process by which patients accept, reject, and adapt information provided by health care providers is exemplified in research from urban Michigan (Hunt et al. 1989). In this study of middle-class women of Detroit, all diagnosed as hypoglycemic, the women incorporate the physician-provided diagnosis, adapt it to their preconceived concepts of disease, and utilize it to meet the needs and exigencies of their established life-styles.

Healers

From the earliest periods of anthropology there has been a marked interest in the recruitment, training, and personality of traditional healers. Indeed, interest in the varied ways in which cultures permit manifestations of psychopathology extended to speculation that the behavior of healers who cured their patients with dramatic ritual procedures was to be explained by emotional aberrance (Anisimov 1963:86, 102. 103, 120; Kroeber 1948:298–299). One authority (Sigerist 1951:172) has even defined shamanic procedures in Siberia as evidence of mental illness: "The Siberian shaman . . . undoubtedly is psychopathic. Mental illness plays a great part in his life and behavior." That view is no longer accepted.

Although many popular books and much of the medical literature makes reference to "*the* traditional healer," it is abundantly clear that there is no such universal entity.

Traditional healers are recruited in several ways. One common way is by divine selection in which an individual has a dream in which it is indicated that the dreamer is to undertake healing responsibilities (Joralemon 1985:5). Another form of divine selection is the normative obligation of a person who must accept such a responsibility in return for his or her recovery from an acute or life-threatening illness (Rubel 1966a; Turner 1967:282; Steedly 1988:855). An elected person who fails to become a healer is thought to be subject to divine sanctions, including serious illness and death. In contrast, in many societies, individuals who aspire to healing apprentice themselves to established practitioners.

The apprentice learns through didactics as well as observation of the master's conduct. In such situations, the student usually provides compensation for the training by assisting the senior healer and the latter's family; there are other instances in which a neophyte seeks out a noted healer, paying a fee to be trained (Rubel, field notes among Chinantec). Finally, there are some societies in which individuals who wish to embark on a curing career and possess the necessary self-confidence to engage in such risky behavior (Shweder 1965; Metzger and Williams 1963) initially test their abilities on household members and close family and subsequently expand their practice to cure nonrelatives.

There are several important differences between divine selection and formal training by means of apprenticeship. For one, people who are divinely selected or elect to learn informally are less subject to social control than those who undergo an apprenticeship or other formal training program. Inasmuch as traditional healing often includes considerable management of supernatural forces, the fear that healers who gain such control through efforts not publicly bestowed and largely unsupervised may use such potent forces for antisocial as well as helpful purposes (such as sorcery or witchcraft) is realistic (Brown 1988:102–20).

Some research has looked specifically at the relationship between healers' empirical knowledge and that of nonhealers (Garro 1986; Browner 1989a). Anthropological attention has also focused on the personal characteristics that differentiate healers from nonhealers. In one ethnomedical study (Fabrega and Silver 1973) shamans and nonshamans who reside in the Tzotzil-speaking town of Zinacantan were compared, using projective tests and data such as economic level, participation in the *cargo* system, levels of formal classroom education, and acculturation to Spanish-speaking Ladino culture. The shamans identified with the sociopolitically dominant Ladino culture less than did laypersons and were more likely to perceive human figures and themes of interpersonal conflict in inkblots. The knowledge about sickness utilized by shamans in Zinacantan proved not substantially distinct from the comprehensions of lay persons, but the shamans were more willing to utilize that knowledge (Garro 1986; Browner and Perdue 1988). In another provocative study of Zinacantan healers (Shweder 1965), it was concluded that there was little to differentiate laypersons and specialized healers in their store of healing knowledge and little differentiation in knowledge among healers but a considerable cognitive difference between healers and nonhealers. The healers were more likely than laypersons to impose their own sense of order on ambiguous stimuli, presented in the form of blurred photographs—less frequently saying "I don't know," giving greater variety of responses, and tending to respond with their own categories rather than choices presented by the interviewer.

Elsewhere, among Tarascan-speakers in Mexico, whereas the medical knowledge of women curers and noncurers was substantially the same, the curers demonstrated far more consistency and agreement among themselves (Garro 1986).

Although there is little in the reports to indicate how healers acquire their knowledge, a study from South Africa reports an unusual learning process (Ngubane 1977). There, "informal networks or associations of healers do exist, and these provide for the exchange of techniques and information, and monitoring of each other's behavior. . . . Meetings take place regularly between diviners to share ideas, experiences, and techniques. Each diviner has the opportunity to meet the ex-students, teacher, and neophyte of each other neighboring diviners, as well as more distant ones."

The extent to which knowledge is common among healers has received little attention, but in one interesting study, a Peruvian shaman was asked (Joralemon 1985) to comment on the symbolism employed in the altar of another local shaman: "His reaction was quick and definite: 'He's a spiritist. The *mesa* [altar] doesn't have power, it's pure stone, with no herbs whatsoever. There aren't any images! Mine is superior; his isn't the half of mine.' " When the other was shown photographs of his rival's altar, he called it "fetishistic" and implied that it was founded on superstitions: "With a disdain no less intense than Paz's, he asserted that Jose Paz does not really understand the illnesses he treats or the significance of the objects on his mesa" (Joralemon 1985:5; cf. Levi-Strauss 1963c:175-79).

By contrast, in Thailand, those who aspire to study with an established curer must often travel great distances to find a willing teacher. Aspirants who reside in a curer's region are not accepted as disciples because of the threat of future competition. Consequently Thailand is criss-crossed by master-disciple networks that often cross regional boundaries (Golomb 1986).

The studies of how healers are recruited to serve crucial societal functions, how they acquire their knowledge, and how they practice medicine are fascinating. Such studies represent some of the most traditional interests in anthropology. Yet our inability to make generalizations or predictions as to the kinds of sociocultural environments that will produce one or more category of healer is disappointing.

RESEARCH FOR THE FUTURE

Ethnomedical researchers have shown a troubling "reluctance to explore the interface between biology and culture [which] derives from their belief that previous efforts to do so using the biomedical paradigm were failures because they forced rich, complex ethnographic data into artificial categories" (Browner, Ortiz de Montellano, and Rubel 1988:682). However, by building on the anthropological tenet that human physiological processes are the same species-wide, studies of cultural responses to such physiological processes as maturation, aging, gestation, pregnancy and delivery, and disease offer the opportunity to maximize the equivalence of the processes to which cultural responses are being made (Browner, Ortiz de Montellano, and Rubel 1988:682). The effort is, first, to design standardized comparable units into which characteristics of an illness, gestation period, and maturational changes can be placed and then to compare the response to them across cultural groups. Efforts to accomplish these goals have been few but noteworthy (Jordan 1978; Fabrega 1977; Rubel, O'Nell, and Collado Ardon 1984; Clark and Anderson 1967). Future ethnomedical research might profitably focus on the following themes:

1. The incidence and distribution of particular illnesses within a population: Skewed distributions may be clues to underlying social or emotional mechanisms (Rubel 1964; Carey 1988). Is a stipulated illness widespread or confined to one or several segments of the population? Do women and men suffer it in equal measure? Does it affect persons without respect to their social and political status? Is it confined to a particular ethnic group or social class? For example, in ethnically pluralistic villages in Nicaragua, susceptibility to the illness *grisi siknes* distinguishes the Miskito-speaking residents from others (Dennis 1981). In Guatemala, discovery that two Cakchiquel villages with a common understanding of *susto* suffered significantly different attack rates contributed to in-

sightful analysis of the differential severity of socioeconomic stresses each was experiencing (Logan 1979).

Among Egyptian peasants, analysis of how the common illness known as '*uzr* was distributed showed that it serves as an index of asymmetrical power relations and gender status (Morsy 1978:143). Soheir Morsy commented that in view of the assumption that the appearance of '*uzr* is associated with subservient social status, "Validation of the assumption that the higher frequency of illness among women results from stress should involve not only a demonstration of a higher frequency of illness among females than males, but more fundamentally, it should show that a higher frequency of illness occurs among women who are identified as less powerful and as experiencing greater stress than their cohorts" (1978:144). She further comments (1978:146) that because power relations change in accordance with changes of a family's developmental cycle, the susceptibility of particular family members will vary accordingly (cf. Swagman 1989). O'Nell and Selby capitalized on their finding that *susto* was found primarily among women in two Zapotec towns, concluding that because norms permitted fewer social escapes for women than for men, becoming ill with *susto* was more socially legitimate for women than for men.

2. The effects of healing procedures: It is vitally important to discover the extent to which goals to which a healing procedure is directed have been attained, whether those goals are improved social relationships, improved social well-being, or improvement in an individual's biological or mental health status (Browner, Ortiz de Montellano, and Rubel 1988; Kleinman and Sung 1979; Kleinman and Gale, 1982; Helman 1984b:49). Where individual healing is a metaphor for the alleviation of social difficulties that threaten rupture of structural ties or of social solidarity (Lindenbaum 1979; Marwick 1964; Steedly 1988), do participants feel or acknowledge that social ties are less threatened following the procedure? In societies whose social structures are otherwise similar, do those that possess such metaphoric mechanisms experience less threat or disruption than those that lack them?

3. Healing implications of patient support groups: Although it is conventionally accepted (Frank 1963) that healing procedures that include patient support groups have better outcomes, the importance of this assumption demands empirical assessment. Does social support in a healing ceremony ensure better results and, if so, in what kinds of social organizations?

Similarly, it is reasonable to question the extent to which the gender of either patient or healer influences the performance and success of treatment procedures. Future research can provide a corrective to earlier tendencies to present healing procedures as virtually uniform no matter the gender, social status, or other important social characteristics of the participants.

4. The choice of nonprofessional care when cosmopolitan physicians are available (Harwood 1977c:201; Landy 1983a:235; Helman 1984a:49): Speculation that people prefer nonphysician healers because they share with them a paradigm of health and healing or because lay healers take more time in treatment of patients than biomedical physicians is unproductive. In several interesting studies

(Finkler 1985; Kleinman and Sung 1979) of the patient-healer relationship, it has been discovered that healers of whatever persuasion who are in great demand treat their patients impersonally and quickly. Furthermore, in one investigation, it is reported that these popular healers "generally fail to explain the etiology of the illness for which the patient is being treated, fail to share similar etiological beliefs with their patients, and frequently fail to uphold the patient's claim to the sick role" (Finkler 1985:6; see also 54, 84–89). Similarly, Kleinman writes of "Chinese-style doctors" on Taiwan that "unless a patient asks they rarely explain about cause, pathophysiology, or course of illness. They may not even name the illness" (Kleinman 1980:261; see also 262, 289).

5. The differences between healers locally identified by distinctive labels (Such as *curandero* and *empirica* [midwife], *espiritista* and *espiritualista*, "Chinese-style doctor," *tang-ki* and *ch'ien* interpreters) should be specified: whether they are recruited from the same segments of society, gain healing power in the same manner, and undergo similar training. Studies of this kind may eventually permit cross-cultural generalizations about categories of healers that can help guide further fieldwork on the subject (see, for example, Montgomery 1976:272–84; Topley 1976).

6. Symptoms of sicknesses: It is only through tabulation and description of the symptoms reported by all patients suffering a particular sickness that we can hope to discover a consistent assemblage of indicators and identify the relationships among them (Fabrega 1977; Marwick 1964:263–68; Prince and Tcheng-Laroche 1987). This kind of study can inform us whether two individuals who complain of *susto*, for example, share more symptoms than do a person who complains of *susto* and another who complains of *mal de ojo*. We need to know, as well, to what people are responding when complaining of illness; for example, Gilbert Lewis (1975:141) says that although the Gnau complained of being ill, they based their reports not on the signs and symptoms but on other characteristics of the sufferer: "since in their view causes were not discernible from the clinical signs, exact description of these [signs] was not relevant" (Lewis 1975:142).

7. The range of applicability of ethnomedical hypotheses: Such studies as Richard Lieban's test among Filipinos of B. Whiting's linking of attribution of sickness to form of social organization and Carl O'Nell and Henry Selby's (1968) test of Arthur Rubel's hypothesis of a relationship between failure to meet role expectations and heightened susceptibility to *susto* contribute to the comparative study of ethnomedical systems and eventually to a testable theory of illness and healing.

NOTES

We wish to acknowledge the constant encouragement and constructive comments of Carole Browner. Barbara Metzger proved an astute and helpful critic in the final organization of these materials. We are most grateful to them both.

1. In contrast, D. M. Landy's impression was that, prior to 1960, "despite the fact that every human society faces critically and daily the often life-and-death questions of

health and disease, coverage of institutional means of coping with these vital problems in most ethnographic reports had been generally unsystematic, often handled in a casual, fragmentary, and even confusing manner, and in some cases almost completely neglected. Of course, some classic ethnographies did include substantial accounts of the medical aspects of the cultures observed, but these were distinguished by their rarity'' (Landy 1977:4). Fabrega (1975:969) also concluded that ''ethnomedicine as an area of inquiry has been either bypassed and neglected or handled indirectly.''

2. By ''cosmopolitan medicine'' we mean biomedicine, the ethnomedicine in which physicians are trained, as distinguished from other ethnomedicines (Dunn 1976:355–37).

CHAPTER 7

ETHNOPSYCHIATRY

Charles C. Hughes

As an academic discipline, anthropology was in its beginnings and continues to remain ambitious in scope and perspective. Not only are biological origins and the evolution of human beings as a species included as objects of study; of interest also are the varied social forms and symbolically based cultural systems made both possible and necessary by such a biological matrix. Of preeminent theoretical interest are questions concerning the interrelationships among human biology, society, culture, and the individual life careers of the human organisms who are the very agents of the entire process, questions persuasively formulated and examined by La Barre, for example, in his important book, *The Human Animal* (1968).

Biology includes both "normal" and "abnormal" physiologic and developmental processes as these are structured and influenced by genetic and environmental stimuli (although, of course, such a dichotomy is overly simplistic in view of the demonstrable continua that comprise most natural processes). While disease states and conditions have been the object of study by anthropologists at the biological, social, or cultural levels of analysis, so too have disorders affecting the individual person become a field of study enlisting the intellectual curiosity of many anthropologists. Influenced, for example, by developments in psychology and particularly the medically oriented field of psychoanalysis (Kluckhohn 1944), the so-called culture and personality studies began in the 1920s, especially in the United States, and represented a forthright assertion of anthropology's appropriate, but certainly not proprietary, application to questions of how the evolving human personality is shaped in its diverse sociocultural contexts, ranging from the first babblings of infancy through the value-structured and socially channeled vicissitudes of adult life and old age.

Inevitably culture and personality investigations—dealing, as many of them were, with the person-based web of daily events and perceptions—came into intimate touch with behavioral tendencies and mental perspectives that raised the question of the normality of such tendencies and perspectives as these might be viewed in a Western psychiatric framework. Is the shaman, for example, when performing the seance and acting in a decidedly bizarre and non-"normal" manner, merely playing a role in a culturally familiar healing drama, or is he (or she) acting out the deep-based tensions of the neurotic personality? Or, in another domain of inquiry, what are the long-range structural effects of the manner in which the personality is shaped, cajoled, rewarded, or coerced in the early and formative years? Do all Alorese, for example, because of neglectful and inconsistent patterns of treatment in infancy, emerge as hostile, distrustful, and emotionally starved adults?

These and numerous other questions have become embedded in the broad institutional fabric of anthropology as a discipline. This chapter will sketch the most salient of the interests that have driven research in the field: What are the essential semantics of the term *ethnopsychiatry*? Does it differ from *ethnomedicine* (and, if so, on what basis)? How are "normal" behavior and thought—as contrasted to "abnormal" or "deviant" thought and behavior—culturally constituted and assessed from an insider's as well as outsider's point of view? What are the culture-bound syndromes (if there are such empirically discoverable entities)? Can we assess "craziness" in other societies and cultural settings by using the theoretical constructs of Western psychiatry? Are there "mental disorders" in other societies, especially small-scale, non-Western societies; and, if so, what cultural resources and social procedures (and roles) exist to ameliorate distress and disorder?

ETHNOPSYCHIATRY

The prefix *ethno-* (from the *ethno-* in *ethnology* and *ethnography*, the comparative analysis or descriptive study of ways of life of different societies) has proliferated to such an extent in the social and behavioral science literature of recent years that its semantic thrust may be at risk of becoming dulled through overuse and cursory familiarity. That would be most unfortunate, for the term signally serves as a reminder of the pervasiveness of the cultural structuring of all knowledge and experience. We have *ethnomedicine, ethnopharmacology, ethnologic, ethnosemantics*, and so many other uses that one expects an article soon on "ethnoethnology." Indeed, that would also be an apt usage, for, as with its other instances, the reader may properly infer that the given substantive subject matter is being considered as a subset of the total way of life of a people. In the case of ethnoethnology, the term would refer to the study of assumptions concerning and strategies for knowing about other people found in the particular group being studied—their out-group attitudes and behavior. How did the Zulus, for instance, learn about, perceive, evaluate, and define the Boers? or how did the Angles, the Celts of King Arthur's time?

Thus the word *ethnology* points the way to a conceptual approach in which one attempts to describe the world through the cultural lenses of the group being studied (their "assumptive world," as Frank calls it, 1973:24ff.), an avowedly phenomenological position. But beyond facile reiteration of the prefix in connection with a substantive subject matter, it does not necessarily follow that the investigator wishes to do so or is capable of success when looking at a problem vicariously through the constructs provided by the cultural system of another people. After all, when setting out into new cognitive territory, it is easier—and far more comforting perhaps—to render the unfamiliar into one's own familiar terms rather than approach the task with such tacit categories suspended. This is well known from studies of culture change: the exotic is adapted, modified, transformed in label, perhaps even appearance, to conform with what has existed up to this point; note the syncretism between the Catholic saints of the conquistadors and the preexisting indigenous gods and spirits of pre-Columbian Meso-American peoples.

What the investigator may do instead is study a problem in a group other than his or her own comparatively—as is often done in ethnology—anchoring such a study in the conceptual categories derived from his or her own cultural system, an approach that often has meant using those of a Western scientific approach. In this case, a categorical system of what is often presumed to be a higher order of generalizability is the grid imposed upon the particularistic concepts of a given group or groups being analyzed.

What is being discussed here is the by-now-familiar distinction between an "emic" and an "etic" approach to understanding human behavior. Over the past couple of decades there has been considerable discussion in the anthropological and cognate literature about the importance of the investigator's being aware of the implications the distinction has not only for the initiation of inquiry but also for a heuristic analysis and interpretation of results. Such an awareness is critical not only for the study of group behavior but also the psychodynamics of the individual person, as the fields of personality psychology and psychopathology illustrate.

While "emic" and "etic" came into more general usage in the last generation from their origin in linguistics, it may be noted that more than a century ago in anthropology, essentially the same need to distinguish between an "inner" and an "outer" perspective was underscored and a technique developed to do just that. The problem was that of understanding the degree of correspondence between genetically created biological relationships and culturally structured kinship designations in a society other than one's own, and the technique, that of the genealogical method for deriving indigenous kin terms (cf. *Notes and Queries* 1951:54ff.). Use of that technique led to the greatly varied sets of emic kin terms found in different societies being translated into a common matrix of structural categories that could allow for valid and theoretically fruitful comparative study of kinship systems.

In attempting to derive the social categories of the widely ramifying set of people to whom a person is biologically related, one does not, for example, ask of an informant: "What is the name of your uncle?" What does the term *uncle* mean? Does it refer, as in American society, to father's brother, father's sister's husband, mother's brother, or mother's sister's husband? A single term, *uncle*, here refers to four discriminably different biological relationships. Rather than proceeding from an ethnocentric base, one asks for the term designating other male children born to the informant's father's mother, the term for the man who married mother's sister, and so on; that is, one develops a set of more abstract categories based on biological relationships to use as the semantic niches into which to put the local, the emic, terms used by societies in elaborate patterns to define social relationships and shape behavior. To ask, "Who are your uncles?" without realizing, for example, that there might be only one term referring to only one position is to be an unwitting prisoner of one's own cultural constructs.

The point is not that one should always resolve all emic terms to etic terms, or vice versa. But to remain only at the emic level is to be locked into a theoretical stance that appears to offer no possibility of reaching across that presumed impermeable barrier between the world as I see it and the world as others see it. Generalization is stultified, if not impossible. Yet one need not be satisfied with a simple solipsism, as Robert MacLeod (1969:194) reminded us: "The task of the phenomenologist is to penetrate the world of the other person, to describe it and analyze it in such a way that its structure, properties, relations, and dimensions can then be correlated meaningfully with independently defined physical, biological and social variables. Phenomenology in this sense is always propaedeutic to a science, never the science in itself. Its scientific function is to generate questions, not to answer them."

What is needed is a research acumen capable of either or both approaches when the issue being addressed requires such flexibility. The method of choice will depend upon the specificity of the problem being investigated and the level of analysis to which the results are intended to refer. But it is clear that for optimal understanding in many of the problems studied by anthropology and the other behavioral sciences, the emic must inform the etic.

The reason the constructs *emic* and *etic* have been examined here in what to an anthropological readership may appear so prolix a manner is that the difference implied between ethnomedicine and ethnopsychiatry in the chapter titles in this book can be taken to illustrate the need for a constant self-monitoring vigilance in order to avoid the insidious entrapments of one's own emic world. To separate ethnopsychiatry from ethnomedicine when adopting a cross-cultural perspective on the conceptualization of diseases of any kind, on the labeling of disorders, and on the manifest as well as possible latent techniques of healing in societies other than one's own is to become hoist on one's own petard. The petard in this instance is the institutionalized distinction in Western societies between medicine ("real" medical processes and problems) and psychiatry, the subdiscipline of medicine dealing with disorders of the mind and behavioral abnormalities and deviations, all of which are usually given secondary consideration in any (Western medicine) patient history after thorough examination of "primary" causes of the presenting complaint have been ruled out.

While in the Western world psychiatry is formally included as one branch of science-based medicine, its status remains anomalous. In that branch of medicine, more than any other, potentially capable of bringing to problems of understanding and treating human illness and distress an integrated psychobiological conceptual framework, its practitioners are often so buffeted by peers wedded to a philosophy of biomedical reductionism that the easier course of searching for disease "entities" and tissue- or molecular-level etiologies is chosen over a broader, multilevel conceptual framework for understanding the totality of human problems of adaptation. Of course there are those who continue to speak out in an attempt to counter the trend toward biomedical reductionism (Engel 1977, with his call for a "biopsychosocial model," or White 1988), but when compared to the comprehensive character of indigenous or "folk psychiatry," Western psychiatry is narrowly circumscribed in conceptual scope and etiological considerations. And it may be suggested that, as Marshall McLuhan noted (1964), the medium is the message; the structure in which ideas are presented (for example, chapter titles such as "Ethnomedicine" and "Ethnopsychiatry") may be more influential in the semantic outcome than is the substance, the ideas contained therein.

Overwhelmingly non-Western, indigenous medical systems (those not based on Western science-derived concepts and techniques) are holistic in scope and basic premises. Not for them the seductive Cartesian division between body and mind. Rather, an affliction, a discomfiture of mind, an accident of nature is seen in a context of not only ailment-in-body but also of possible soul loss, spirit intrusion, taboo violation, malevolent acts of other persons or agents, or any number of other constructs that define the world of unseen power (Clements 1932), those emic constructs analogous to such designations as "anxiety." Such constructs include "empirical" causes (Ackerknecht 1944, 1946; Foster and Anderson 1978:51ff.).

Thus to speak of ethnomedicine and ethnopsychiatry separately when considering the great majority of the world's medical systems is, in effect, simply to take two different points of entry (of our own contriving) into what has been for the vast span of human history and what is now phenomenologically—emically—a unity: illness-disease-sickness, anxieties, forebodings, gnawing frustrations, grief, unfulfilled wishes that characterize human life. But to the extent that such conceptual points of entry become rigidly fixed and presumed to reflect natural as contrasted to social categorizations, they can quickly obfuscate rather than help, thus becoming further instances of the sin of emic projection.

An example comes to mind. A native healer in Sokoto, Nigeria, advertises that he can provide "medicine" (for specified prices, of course) for some 50 listed human problems, afflictions, desires, and quandaries, some of which are

scorpion medicine, market medicine, learn medicine, medicine for prevention of evil powers, medicine to drive witchcraft, medicine for gonorrhoea, medicine for ring worm, medicine for motor accident, medicine for record pen, medicine for promotion, medicine for progress, medicine for general love, medicine for examination, medicine for guinea worm, medicine for prevention of bad dreams, for measles, for information [sic] disease or "coughous" disease, chest pain and nerviousness [*sic*], commanding tongue, eye sight prevention, stomach trouble, medicine for office love, medicine for within, to prevent bad juju, medicine for fever, medicine for woman conciption [*sic*], medicine for life aboundant [*sic*], medicine to play ball, medicine to drive away poverty, medicine to catch thieves, medicine for tired penies [*sic*], medicine for cough, medicine for backache, medicine for headache disease. (Hughes, printed advertisement, Nigerian fieldwork)

The intent of this chapter is to comment on the evidence from "folk" societies (and occasionally other societies) about what—for convenience only—one can term topics of "psychiatric" (etically speaking) interest, for instance, "abnormal" behaviors, thoughts, and emotions; ethnotheories regarding diagnosis, labeling, and causation; and modes of treatment for such deviant instances or patterns.

"NORMAL" AND "ABNORMAL" BEHAVIOR

All human societies have notions, however varied, of what constitutes the normal behavior expected—indeed, demanded—of group members, as contrasted to abnormal behavior, that which is different from the mode and often socially disvalued. The most comprehensive rubric for such behavior is that of social deviance from norms in all institutionalized sectors of society—whether those are focused on performing expected tasks in the division of labor, behaving properly toward kinsmen, taking on marital obligations, obeying custom as well as law, showing proper reverence to the spirits conceived to constitute the very basis of empirical reality, exchanging goods and services, or any of the multitudinous obligations that are the costs standing in dialectic relationship to the benefits of belonging to a social group. The existence of a constellation of shared norms of behavior is quintessential to the survival of any society (Aberle et al. 1960), although there are reports in the ethnographic literature of groups that would appear to be dangerously close to approximating the Hobbesian state of anarchy, the "war of all against all" (perhaps the Ik and the Yanomamo).

Like the more general sick role as a "legitimated" form of deviance (Parsons 1951:436ff.), "behavioral disorders" or "mental disorders" or "psychopathology" represent a subset of the broad category of social deviance. But the clear specification of when a pattern of norm-violating behavior passes from being an instance of mere chicanery or criminality to that of pathology is one of the most vexing issues in the fields of psychiatry and social deviance (cf. "sociopaths" and the McNaughton rule of not guilty by reason of insanity). However, any attempt to devise a universalistic specification or listing of patterns of abnormal behavior (whether representing pathology or not) quickly becomes blunted when held against a cultural relativistic framework. A major shaper of American anthropology, Edward Sapir, commented that "cultural anthropology has the healthiest of all skepticisms about the validity of the concept of 'normal behavior.' . . . [It] is constantly rediscovering the normal" (Sapir 1949:514, 515).

In the same decade, another influential figure in American anthropology who also went beyond the narrow confines of discipline, A. Irving Hallowell, underscored the need for an outsider studying "deviant" or "abnormal" behavior to know the baseline against which such putative acts or patterns were being assessed. He stipulated that such an investigator should have an "intimate knowledge of the culture as a whole, he must also be aware of the normal range of individual behavior within the cultural pattern and likewise understand what the people themselves consider to be extreme deviations from this norm. In short, he must develop a standard of normality with reference to the culture itself, as a means of controlling an uncritical application of the criteria that he brings with him from our civilization" (1934:2).

Accepting that there can be a wide range of culturally structured definitions of what is normal, does this mean all members of that given social group adhere to such norms? Both the available literature and shared human experience say no. The subfield of deviant behavior is a major area of research in the discipline of sociology, a subfield that includes not only such topics as criminality but also illness and behavioral disorders that depart from the functional norm. Much literature has been developed pointing to varying patterns of nonadherence to norms, structural motivations for noncompliance, and the types of sanctions brought against offenders (cf. Blake and Davis 1964). Curiously, although individual behavioral deviations from prescribed norms are discussed in the anthropological literature, there appears to be no established rubric in cultural anthropology comparable to that in sociology (if one can judge, among other indicators, by the lack of indexing of "deviance" or "social deviance" in the last couple of decades of the *Annual Review of Anthropology*).

What happens when, for whatever reason, a given person does not act in accordance with the norms expected of him or her in such a specified social status—and there is always a specified social status, a role or variegated collection of roles or behavioral niches in terms of which behavior is judged to be either appropriate or inappropriate, with the connotation in the latter instance being that of behavioral or mental pathology? Typically, depending on the social salience of the institutionalized norm that was violated, a person may be forgiven for a momentary transgression of a culturally prescribed code of conduct; most societies recognize and tolerate a fairly wide range of deviations from the ideal. However, if, over time, a given person persists in not living up to the appropriate set of norms prescribed for any one of his or her several roles in society, a number of questions are raised: is that person simply and willfully violating the code of conduct expected of a proper member of the group, or are there more serious issues at stake, such as illness, bewitchment, or soul loss?

So far as evidence shows, no society is free from mental disorders (cf. Murphy 1982b), and it may be assumed that all human societies recognize and accept the possibility that under certain conditions some of their members may not be totally responsible for their behavior; they may be "out of mind," unable to conform to social expectations appropriate for the rest of society, and therefore in need of special designation and, possibly, special tolerance and treatment, or, contrarily, be subject to banishment or even execution.

THE "PSYCHIATRY" OF "ETHNOPSYCHIATRY"

Henry Wegrocki (1953) drew a distinction critical for understanding the difference between deliberate norm breaking and deviance, on the one hand, and abnormality of psychiatric interest on the other. He spoke of statistical abnormality (which depends on the parameters that define the object of interest—and there are always outliers in any frequency distribution) and functional abnormality, which is based on an assessment of how a given behavioral pattern figures in the total context of the personality, the purposes it serves. Does the behavior represent denial, repression, delusion, or any of a number of other psychodynamic defense mechanisms?

In a short and distinguished statement about the difference between deviance and psychiatric abnormality, John Honigmann (1956) succinctly presents the generic conceptual and referential differences between these two approaches to sorting out the implications of the term *deviance*:

The deviant does not stand out because of his high level of anxiety, sensori-motor dysfunctions, or reality distortion. He is conspicuous through the fact that he underplays or overplays socially standardized behavior or innovates behavior. The policeman who becomes an authoritarian colossus overplays his role; the Crow Indian who holds back from battle because of the fear that he may be killed underplays a role. The purveyor of a new religion represents an innovator. All are deviants, but we cannot without further information classify them as also psychopathic. To classify the policeman, warrior, and prophet as psychiatrically abnormal, each must be judged by the criteria which we adopted from psychiatry—anxiety, regression and the others.

Thus, the generic question becomes, What patterns of behavior in any given society are candidates for consideration as pathology? Along what must be considered as a continuum and not necessarily quantum steps, what is normal behavior as contrasted to abnormal? And in a cross-cultural framework, the operative question must be, Whose criteria are being used to define abnormal behavior: those of the group itself (the so-called emic categories) or those of an outside group (etic categories), such as the cultural constructs of Western psychiatry? For example, the behavioral episodes often termed possession (in Western etic psychiatric terms often diagnosed as dissociation) are widely found in human societies of all times and places. There is a vast literature dealing with such matters as ritualized healing cults, for example, and periods of out of awareness prescribed by various social and ceremonial occasions (Prince 1968; Crapanzano and Garrison 1977). Sometimes the behavior of persons in such situations is clearly of psychiatric relevance (demonstrates entrenched dissociative pathology), but often it is simply the playing out of a publicly viewed and socially prescribed role. It is "normal" behavior. How does one begin to understand such behavior? Perhaps by applying the etic concepts of Western psychiatry?

As a medical profession, psychiatry models itself in its approach to classification and diagnosis after the medical system of nosology, an "eclectically assembled, chronologic polyglot of different terms and ideas that reflect every layer of nosologic thinking and technologic data from antiquity to the present" (Feinstein 1977:193). Much of the implicit focus in such a diagnostic approach has been based on the search for disease "entities," an approach that appears to suggest the reification of pathological processes independent of context. Indeed, the dialectic continues today between two different conceptual bases for viewing disease: that of the ontological approach (diseases are "real") and a processual or physiological approach ("diseases" are simply useful constructs that point to dysfunctional processes in given contexts; cf. Temkin 1963; Engelhardt 1975). As some modern commentaries on the meta-logics of diagnosis suggest, an ontological approach leads to quandaries in consideration of some of the major health issues of a society—the debilities of aging, for example. Dysfunctional, certainly; but is aging "a" disease? And in the domain of psychiatric or (possible) behavioral disorder, is grief a "disease," as George Engel (1977) asks?

Explicitly modeling itself on the structure of the diagnostic system in medicine, how much more at risk of conceptual confusion may be psychiatry, when its objects of inquiry—behavioral and mental events—are not so amenable to sharp operational specification as are tissue-level pathologies and may be confounded further by local cultural definitions and justifications of abnormality?

A recent major effort to bring rationality, order, and standardized operational definitions into psychiatry in the United States produced the *Diagnostic and Statistical Manual Of Mental Disorders* (DSM-III) (American Psychiatric Association 1980, 1987), which, although controversy continues, is unquestionably an advance over earlier approaches to diagnosis. Even so, however, in that diagnostic volume there are numerous areas in which attribution of pathology as contrasted to simple abnormality or deviance may not be warranted, the type of development that Ivan Illich (1976) referred to as the "medicalization" of everyday life (and which earlier, in a classic article, Ackerknecht noted: "One of the characteristic mental traits of our culture is the labeling of phenomena with psychiatric diagnoses"; 1943:30). The psychologist Sol Garfield, for example, is uneasy about the inclusion in DSM-III—as diagnoses of "developmental disorders"—of such abnormalities as "specific reading disorder" and "specific arithmetic disorder" (1986:109), not to mention "pathological gambling" (p. 110), about which he pointedly comments, "Whether or not such a problem should be considered a form of psychiatric disorder or mental illness would seem to be debatable. Certainly, pathological gambling can have all sorts of negative and distressing consequences, but does it have to be labeled as psychiatric disorder? Many other problems in everyday life may have distressful effects, but they may be viewed as economic and social problems rather than psychiatric ones."

THE CULTURE-BOUND SYNDROMES

The so-called culture-bound syndromes are a prime target for discussion in any chapter on ethnopsychiatry and represent an instructive focus for many of the issues already raised. For a generation or so, the term has been found in the literature (primarily that of medical anthropology and culture and personality, far less in psychiatry). The phenomena addressed by the conceptual construct and labeled culture-bound syndromes take us directly into the middle of any analysis of deviance and the possible utility of etic Western psychiatric concepts in understanding such syndromes. Indeed, as noted in another place (Hughes 1985a:3), the culture-bound syndromes seem to observers in the Western world to represent almost archetypical cases of deviant deviance; in other words, they are "crazy" (to us) ways of being "crazy."

The term *culture-bound syndromes* is a catching designation, one creating an aura of exoticism, redolent of deep mysteries. It seems to fit well those wild episodes of random, senseless killing called "amok"—those periods of a person's being "out-of-mind" and, in one particular group, said to be suffering *pibloqtok* (sometimes called Arctic hysteria by outsiders); or those theatrical displays of giggling and mindless imitation of gestures or sounds whose indigenous (Malay) term is *latah*. But what does (or may) the term *culture-bound syndrome* mean conceptually, analytically?

On the surface, it connotes some degree of determinative influence, in usually unspecified ways, between the cultural context of a given behavior and its diagnostic status as a mental disorder or putative psychiatric condition. The phrase has occasioned numerous articles, symposia, and books or book chapters dealing with its meaning, its possible meaning, and its utility in determining the extent to which, and in what ways, the sociocultural context of the behavior of a given person, quite aside from any biologic predispositions or risk factors, is of major significance in the etiology, symptomatology, expression, course, and response to treatment when the issue is that of understanding a presumed case of cognitive-emotional-behavioral disorder (Simons and Hughes 1985; Littlewood and Lipsedge 1985). (It may also be noted that, aside from implications for research into the relationship between cultural factors and psychiatric disorders, there are substantial implications raised for treatment and management of a reputed instance of a culture-bound syndrome when a Western-trained physician or health worker is confronted with such a case, an event possible not simply in the non-Western world but also in industrialized societies having minority groups of different ethnic backgrounds, such as native Americans, blacks, and Hispanics, in the contemporary United States.)

Despite increased discussion of the culture-bound syndromes in the literature, it is clear that the semantic status of the term is by no means unequivocal, and, among other sources of confusion, it seems to reside in a twilight zone (Hughes 1985a:3) with respect to the etic considerations of Western psychiatry. Perhaps one of the factors confounding its systematic incorporation into Western (etic) psychiatric categories is the extent to which the behaviors usually included under this rubric may not comprise a homogeneous class. The phrase almost seems to be a verbal Rorschach card, bringing forth a variety of interpretations and attributions.

It may be suggested that there are several conflicting "metatheoretical" assertions threading through the literature on culture-bound syndromes, and recognition of the semantic alternatives implied by such assertions should be the point of departure in any discussion of the term: (1) the syndromes do not necessarily represent pathology but rather (for the observer) are simply different culturally patterned behavioral events; (2) standard psychiatric diagnostic categories are useful and appropriate in sorting such syndromes; (3) perhaps the standard psychiatric categories are inadequate because they are the expression of a given cultural structuring of experience and therefore perhaps not universally generalizable; (4) the repeated use of the phrase *culture-bound syndromes*—almost, it seems, to the point of reification—does not necessarily validate or legitimate the implied status of these assorted behavioral complexes as a separate class of psychiatric disorders, even if they can be shown to be "pathologic" behaviors; and (5) perhaps there is such divergence in levels of abstraction and analysis to which the term *culture-bound syndrome* applies that the term itself should be abandoned if comparative discussion of structure, etiology, and social implications of these behavior patterns is to succeed (Hughes 1985a:3).

Regardless of the extent to which any given psychiatric disorder may be influenced in its etiology, symptomatic expression, course, and therapeutic potential by the cultural environment in which it occurs—and hence to that extent be bound, as some assert all such disorders are (Murphy 1977; Alarcon 1983; Marsalla 1982; Hughes 1985a)—there is a much more problematic interpretation and use of the term *culture bound*. This is the implication that any psychiatric disorder so designated is unique to a particular society or to a narrow range of societies in which it is found. Such an interpretation often has been stimulated by reports of behavioral patterns found in other societies (especially traditional, non-Western societies) that were strikingly bizarre and exotic as compared to the familiar behavior of one's own society, so different that they seemed to be one of a kind. (Indeed, when one thinks about it, it is clear that every phenomenon is unique; it is only through use of conceptual constructs that we create similarities or sameness among diverse phenomena at varying levels of abstraction.)

When the evidence is closely examined, many disorders once thought to be unique to a given society (such as *latah*, presumably confined to Malaysian village societies) have been found in their symptomatic expression (though not their behavioral appearance and indigenous labeling) in other parts of the world as well (Simons 1985a). A glossary and synonymy that systematizes data on 185 such "culture-bound syndromes" (Hughes 1985b) clearly establishes the nonuniqueness of many of the major asymptomatic constellations.

The central conceptual issue when the question is put as to the uniqueness of a given syndrome is that of the level of abstraction being used in such an analysis. Is it the level of emic, culturally specific labels for a cluster of behaviors (which would make any given culture-bound syndrome unique in that respect); the level of similarity in observable behaviors (symptoms) characteristically demonstrated in such episodes in different cultural contexts; or perhaps a level of a sorting based on inferred neurologic or biological mechanisms, as Simons has done (Simons 1985b; Simons and Hughes 1985).

Interpreting the term *culture-bound syndromes* in a psychodynamically informed manner, some authors have suggested that such syndromes are not confined to small-scale, underdeveloped societies but may also be found in industrialized social contexts as well. Cecil Helman (1987) discusses the Type A coronary-prone behavioral pattern as a response to pervasive and particular value emphases in American society, and Cheryl Ritenbaugh (1982) considers anorexia nervosa in the same fashion, to cite but two examples (see also Littlewood and Lipsedge 1985:122ff.). If the basic premise is accepted that salient values in the sociocultural environment of a given person have some degree of determinative relationship to personality dynamics—the literature on "culture and personality" (in anthropology) and "character and social structure" (sociology) strongly supports this—then there is no a priori reason to exclude industrialized societies from review in this respect.

How does the topic of culture-bound syndromes fare in the psychiatric diagnostic systems of the Western world? Not well (Hughes 1985a; Hughes 1989; Simons and Hughes in press). Fitting the culture-bound syndromes into conventional Western (etic) psychiatric nosological categories is procrusteanly problematic; the standard diagnostic manuals are of no help in this regard. Consider, for example, that the term *culture* is missing from the index of DSM-III and that the associated terms *cultural relativism* and *culture bound* are similarly absent. Further, the two features of the innovative multiaxial diagnostic system of the DSM-III, which are highly relevant for observing and recording behaviors infused with the "cultural" dimension—Axes IV (Psychosocial Stressors) and V (Highest Level of Adaptive Functioning in Last Year)—are apparently not being systematically used by clinicians or researchers (Spitzer and Williams 1983:342–43; Rey et al. 1988), perhaps as much due to lack of appropriate formats for patient charting as to inherent reluctance to accept a new paradigm. Even in the most recent version of the diagnostic manual (DSM-III-R), only two brief paragraphs touch explicitly on this issue. There it is, quite rightly, stated that "caution should be exercised in the application of DSM-III-R diagnostic criteria to assure that their use is culturally valid. It is important that the clinician not employ DSM-III-R in a mechanical fashion, insensitive to differences in language, values, behavioral-norms, and idiomatic expressions of distress" (1987: xxvi). And in the clinically oriented volume *International Classification of Diseases*, which one would think an appropriate framework for such cross-cultural data, the situation is even worse. The only references are to highly segmental uses of the term *culture* or related concepts, for example, as in "cultural deprivation" (1:880ff.), as a subcategory of "social maladjustment." Neither of these terms, or others that are prima facie psychosocial in nature (such as *family disruption*), are included as etiologic elements in the course and diagnosis of the disease process.

THE HEALING MODALITIES

Viewed cross-culturally, human societies have developed a variety of health care practitioners: herbalists, bonesetters, midwives, diviners, acupuncturists, magicoreligious healers, and others. In some groups there are even folk healers who specialize in mental disorders—the "ethnopsychiatrists"—and employ emically derived diagnostic systems relating to behavioral disorders (Lederer 1959; Leighton, Alexander et al. 1963:111, 117; Prince 1964) that are comparable in intent to the "ethno-nosologic" system of the Subanum noted by Charles Frake (1961). Usually the functions performed by such persons are overlapping; for example, the magicoreligious healer also frequently prescribes ingestion of herbal medicine, and non-Western folk medicines are rich in their indigenously developed pharmacopeia (Etkin 1986a, 1988a; Steiner 1986; Vogel 1973). It may be noted that the great bulk of the world's people continue to use such folk healers either exclusively or in conjunction with what Western-type health care may be available (cf. almost any issue of the journal *Social Science and Medicine*).

The magicoreligious type of healer is usually taken as the focus, indeed, the very prototype, when discussion turns to psychiatry in nonindustrialized societies. Although the term *shaman* is not culturally authentic for widespread use (the term actually comes from the name for such a healer in one of the Paleo-Siberian groups), the word has come to be used interchangeably with *native healer, medicine man* (or *woman*), and the like, and narrow academic quibbling would not serve anyone's interests. The term will be used here in a general sense to refer to the healer whose power and calling come from close contact with the spiritual world and who in his or her healing activity includes elements of materia medica in the treatment process. In anthropological discussions of religion, the other principal religious functionary, the priest, is usually one whose sources of supernatural power derive from either oral or written sacred texts and instructions rather than from spiritual inspiration, although the distinction is not absolute. (Further discussions can be found in any anthropological text on comparative religion.)

Probably every known human group has had such a personage as the shaman—that key and powerful resource for ensuring the stability of the group and its organized response to threat. And "threat" does not mean merely sickness. It also refers to threat of famine through failure of crops, bad weather, or poor hunting; or the quandaries and puzzlement that come from trying to decide on a proper course of action in a problematic situation, either for the group as a whole or for families within that group—whether to make war or peace, where to find lost objects or missing persons, and the multifarious other situations needing a firm and authoritative guide for action. Thus the shaman's role is wide ranging; indeed, one might suggest, it is an early exemplar of a social medicine perspective. As the medical historian Henry Sigerist, noted, "It is an insult to the medicine man [his term] to call him the ancestor of the modern physician. He is that, to be sure, but he is much more, namely the ancestor of most of our professions" (1951:161).

Morris Opler published a classic article (Opler 1936) on shamanism among the Apache, the principal analytic conclusions of which have stood the test of comparison and elaboration in subsequent interpretations of the powerful and emically omniscient role that particular type of healer has had in human society (see Torrey 1973; Prince 1980; and relevant sections in a number of edited volumes in medical anthropology, such as Kiev 1964; Landy 1977; Romanucci-Ross et al. 1983; and, among others, the journals *Social Science and Medicine* and *Culture, Medicine, and Psychiatry*).

His central points (though not the particularistic details) are widely generalizable: such features as the involvement of the family and kinship group in both etiological conceptions and therapy; the use of empirical remedies; the setting off of the diagnostic and therapeutic encounter as a special situation that transfigures normal role relationships; and, above all, the use of a comprehensive conception of what shall be accepted as "disease"—indeed, a working with the concept of "*dysease*" in its original etymologic sense rather than the more restrictive denotation, if not connotation, of "disease" in Western systems. Some of the highlights of Opler's analysis may be taken as a model for shamanism and its sociopsychological context.

The shaman's power was believed to come from an all-encompassing force pervading the world—perhaps the most ancient and widespread sentiment characteristic of the human species. But being privy to such power is not simply for the asking; rather, a signal must be given, an invitation offered. With the Apache, this was a bird, an animal, a plant, or some other animate object that would give the script for a healing ceremony, such as a program to include the details of proper offerings or sacrifices, prayers, songs, and behavior.

Although any group member (male or female) was a potential shaman, a subtle selection process occurred, and in practice the successful shaman turned out to have a number of behavioral characteristics that augured well for an ability to translate the putative supernatural basis of his or her healing power into the world of everyday events. For example, as Opler (1936) notes, "he [or she] is ... not a credulous dupe of his own supernaturalistic claims and boastings, who undertakes to cure any ailment, no matter how hopeless.... The seasoned shaman was a shrewd and wary person who had witnessed enough suffering and death to recognize serious organic disturbances when he sees them, and was often reluctant to accept responsibility for curing these" (1372–73). In such a case he finds a convincing reason for referring to someone else or indicates that the patient should prepare himself or herself in particular ways before the attempted therapy could be undertaken (perhaps thereby giving natural healing processes a chance to take effect).

The reputation of a healer (shaman or otherwise) depends upon success, and the Apache shaman was adept at understanding self-limiting disease processes, using herbal medication, and harnessing the power of the patient's belief in his ability to bring about a cure (or at least amelioration). Such a combination of knowledge and skill frequently resulted in successful outcomes; if that did not occur, there was always an explanation (such as the patient's or someone else's having "bad thoughts"; cf. *noncompliance* in Western medicine's etic terms). Opler continues: "What I am suggesting is that the Apache shaman is far from an inspired automaton who enters upon his ritual without regard to the nature of the complaint, the circumstances and the probable outcome. He is a circumspect and careful worker more often, a good judge of his fellow men and of the ills to which humankind is heir'' (1173–74).

The shaman would actively take steps to encourage and foster the patient's belief in his powers to heal, such as directing the patient's family (and kin were always extensively involved) to build a particular ceremonial structure for the ritual. When the arrangements were made, the first event was that of the shaman's once again reinforcing the belief of the patient (and the patient's family) in his own curative powers. He would recount how he had obtained his skill and knowledge and how many people he had helped (perhaps like the framed diplomas indicating past training and awards that decorate the modern physician's office wall): "The insistence upon belief in the shaman and his 'power' is one of the most dominant and omnipresent themes of Apache ritual life. There is no more common phrase in the ceremonial songs than the one which can be translated, 'I believe it.' It is assumed that the 'power' will scarcely be inclined to extend itself or to expose its representative [the shaman] to danger on behalf of a patient who lacks the requisite degree of faith'' (p. 1376).

Then the diagnostic process would begin, with the shaman trying to get at the root of the trouble. First he would set the background, reciting many events of the patient's life leading up to the appearance of the symptoms (which he would have gathered by listening to gossip, by unobtrusive interviewing, and by other data-gathering devices readily at hand in small communities). A competent shaman would have learned everything he possibly could before the ceremony; he would also urge the patient to contribute what might be useful information (to "give his own history") and remember things that might account for the sickness (comparable, perhaps, to the modern family physician). Sometimes by this simple recitation, the symptom itself might even disappear, though the underlying disorder might well remain.

The event seized on for etiological significance would be presented in familiar emic Apache symbols—the patient had come into contact, for example, with an owl, bear, snake, or other animal embodying evil or serving as the instrument of a sorcerer's malevolence. The shaman points out this contact or whatever else in the patient's history might seem to be the source of the trouble, and usually the patient eagerly accepts such an explanation. Against the background of the patient's belief in the shaman's powers and his or her commitment to the shaman's competence and power, it can be inferred that a substantial part of the therapeutic process consists of suggestion and displacement of vague problems onto some concrete object or situation. (Indeed, the panhuman power of the word, especially as embodied in the diagnosis, is well represented in this process; how comforting it is, for example, to be told one has a cryptogenic disease instead of being told, "I just don't know what it is").

But the shaman must go further: he must give a reason that the patient is ill, and he does so by consulting his spiritual helpers. Performing sacred songs and beseeching his powers to come to the aid of the patient, the shaman is told the reasons for the patient's illness—for example the sorcerer had sent an "evil" animal such as a bear to frighten him or had "shot" arrows into the patient.

Then ensues the climax of this diagnostic-therapeutic process, a contest between the powers of the shaman and those of the sorcerer or spirits or objects causing the distress:

In the place of his patient... the shaman substitutes himself. The battle between the malevolent power and the patient is transformed into warfare between the shaman and the sorcerer. As soon as the shaman has announced that the cause is sorcery, he declares against it... He consults with his "power" on tactics. He relates how the sorcerer is trying to balk him and is desperately trying to hold his own. The theory is that a sorcerer, if bested, forfeits his power and his life. If the sorcerer cannot prevent the shaman from sucking the bone arrows and other evidences of his malice from the body of the victim, these objects "come back on himself." A sorcerer whose "power" is bested is shot by his own "arrows" and dies soon afterward.

The strengthening psychological effect upon the patient of gaining a powerful ally can well be imagined. (Opler 1936:1382–83)

The setting for such a ceremony is a multimedia event: theatrics, suspense, and drama, with the family in attendance and as involved as the sick person. Jerome Frank extensively discusses the varieties of group settings that ritually serve the therapeutic process:

Healing ceremonies are highly charged emotionally... [Methods] of primitive [sic] healing involve an interplay between patient, healer, group, and the world of the supernatural; this serves to raise the patient's expectancy of cure, help him to harmonize his inner conflicts, reintegrate him with his group and the spiritual world, supply a conceptual framework to aid this, and stir him emotionally. The total process combats his demoralization and strengthens his sense of self-worth. (1973:66)

In a survey of "cultural psychiatry," John Kennedy (1973:1170) presents an amalgam of commonly found elements in what he quite pointedly calls the "dramatic healing ritual": "Rather than being a private encounter of two individuals, the trance ritual is a semipublic event made up of at least three elements—patient, therapist, and audience, all of whom actively participate. Frequently there are auxiliary helpers such as assistants, musicians, and masters of ceremony; and in the audience are people who know the patient and curer in their daily life roles." At the end of such a ceremony the shaman would impose special taboos upon the patient (a therapeutic regimen? "doctor's orders"?) and even family members. They may not eat a particular food, for example, must not perform certain acts, must avoid certain locations, and so forth. What this does is offer something concrete for the patient's troubled mind to focus on instead of remaining gripped by vague worry and anxiety. This is especially true when accompanied by requirements for the preparation and ingestion of particular kinds of empirical medicines.

Opler ends his article by discussing the extent to which the modern psychiatrist and the shaman are similar. Obviously details of pharmacopoeia differ, but many of the psychodynamics involved are congruent. Opler indicates (with apparent disapproval) that the shamanic healing process is conducive to—perhaps intended for—the creation of a high degree of dependence of the patient upon the shaman, what Prince (1969:33) referred to as the patient's coming under the "cone of authority." Arguments will continue among professionals as to whether the gaining of insight or a sense of autonomy, among other outcomes, should be the primary goal of psychotherapy in all cases. But what stands out clearly in discussions not only of shamanic healing in other societies but also as the effective ingredient in so much of the healing encounter in industrialized societies also is that the sociopsychological and cultural context of the encounter may well be the most critical factor of all in a successful outcome for at least the nonorganic types of disorders.

This has been referred to as the placebo effect: those powerful psychobiological (one of our etic words again!) processes conducive to healing, or at least amelioration, fostered by an aura of compelling and emotion-triggering symbols, theatric reaffirmation of a system of belief, and, above all, a profound sense of confidence in the healer, all of which have been noted in all societies. Along with other commentators (e.g., Moerman 1983a), Howard Brody notes that "placebo research suggests that the placebo response forms a part of virtually all healing encounters, and is not limited to circumstances in which a 'dummy' pill is used. This suggests, in turn, that the placebo effect has been important in medicine throughout history, and that the modern physician has important elements in common with... 'pre-scientific' predecessors" (Brody 1988:149). In a memorable metaphor that well expresses the demonstrably powerful ameliorative and health protective effects of a supportive human relationship, Michael Balint (1964) spoke of "the doctor as drug."

One theme has been background to my discussion: the artificiality of any ontological distinction drawn between ethnomedicine and ethnopsychiatry and the embeddedness of both in a sociocultural context. Perhaps, therefore, drawing on earlier formulations, one may once again suggest that "religion, medicine, and morality are frequently found together in the behavioral act or event, and 'folk medicine' becomes 'social medicine' to an extent not found in industrialized societies" (Hughes 1968:88).

CHAPTER 8

ETHNOPHARMACOLOGY: BIOLOGICAL AND BEHAVIORAL PERSPECTIVES IN THE STUDY OF INDIGENOUS MEDICINES

Nina L. Etkin

As pharmacology is the study of the chemistry and action of substances used to affect health, ethnopharmacology is more specifically concerned with medications used by people whose understandings of health and disease are not based in the precepts of Western science and biomedicine.[1] Because such medications are predominantly botanicals, ethnopharmacology has been most closely allied with medical botany, but it is related as well to studies of plant taxonomy, phytochemistry, clinical applications, and the social and cultural parameters of plant use. What direction a particular ethnopharmacologic study pursues has been defined more by the concepts and theories that distinguish the investigator's academic discipline than by some broader biobehavioral perspective. Anthropologists, for example, have studied medicinal plants as cultural objects in order to relate medical cosmologies to perceptions of the biological universe. And botanists have been more likely to investigate phytochemical constituents devoid of cultural and other contextual data. Thus, until recently, much of ethnopharmacology was either biologically disinterested or ethnographically naive. Increasingly, however, research in ethnopharmacology is shaped by a biobehavioral perspective that transcends disciplinary boundaries. This is consonant with some of the fundamental concerns of a medical anthropology that contemplates not only the meaning of human-environment interactions but also the physiologic outcomes of those behaviors.

THE RELEVANCE OF ETHNOPHARMACOLOGY FOR MEDICAL ANTHROPOLOGY

Ever since medical anthropology began to flourish in the early 1970s, prominent scholars in the field have emphasized the interface between culture and biology. They have asserted that medical anthropology is "a mediating nexus between biological and cultural aspects of anthropology'' (Landy 1977:12), that research should center on the "dialectic of nature and culture" (Hahn and Kleinman 1983), and that because the human body is " simultaneously a physical and symbolic artifact" (Scheper-Hughes and Lock 1987), one must pursue health-related inquiry with the view that biologic and behavioral data are inextricably linked. Ethnopharmacology falls clearly within the field's diverse methodological repertoire. As a basis, detailed ethnographic research explores plants as cultural objects to determine their symbolic import, contexts of use, preparation and application as medicines, and the outcomes intended by different therapies. Laboratory investigations and literature review can then relate pharmacologic activity to physiologic processes and to the specific illnesses those plants are used to treat.

But it has been questioned whether it is even legitimate to apply biomedical standards in the study of indigenous plant medicines (Hahn and Kleinman 1983). This is because medical anthropologists have been predominantly interested in interpretive studies of illness and health and because some believe that the use of biomedical referents depreciates other understandings of illness and therapeutics. Yet a growing number of studies demonstrate that such research can be as anthropologically meaningful as other conceptual frameworks. The application of biomedical standards to integrate ethnographic with biological data need not deny the validity of alternative medical realities. Moreover, through such investigations, we learn not only more about what people think about plants and why but also what relevance this has for their physical health (Etkin 1979a, 1986a, 1986b, 1988a, 1988b). Anthropologists who advocate this approach view it as one among a number of practicable ways of studying ethnomedicines. And as Carole Browner and coworkers (1988) have persuasively argued, with the development of even more rigorous methodology, ethnopharmacology will continue to contribute substantially to concept and theory in medical anthropology and will make it possible to compare medical phenomena cross-culturally more systematically.

Beyond what are published as explicitly anthropological studies of ethnomedicines, the literature of ethnopharmacology is vast, representing many and diverse academic disciplines, including botany, pharmacology, nutrition and dietetics, agriculture, natural history, and ecology. These works fill some of the research needs of medical anthropologists, largely by providing resources on which to draw for one's own study. Much of the literature of ethnopharmacology is represented by compilations that document medicinal uses of primarily plants and some animal and mineral substances as well. These lists are variably structured and detailed and may include taxonomic identification and local name(s); symptoms that a particular medicine is used to treat; plant part, preparation, and mode of administration; constituents and pharmacologic activities; and clinical observations. If plants have been identified only by taxonomic binominals (as in many botanical studies) or only by local name (as anthropologists are wont to do), there is no way to find corresponding literature on the constituents or activities reported for those species, and it is not possible to compare the use of those plants cross-culturally.[2] The more detailed an account is regarding part used, preparation, and mode of administration, the more confidently one can predict the biological outcomes of plant use. This is because the concentration and character of active constituents vary from one part of a plant to another, different modes of compounding medicines can affect pharmacologic activity, and route of administration (by mouth or topical application, for example) can markedly influence whether and how a substance will influence the occurrence or course of a disease.

Among the more recent ethnopharmacologic research outside anthropology are studies that focus on one plant or several related species or genera, such as *Cymbopogon citratus* (Carbajal et al. 1989), *Calotropis procera* (Mascolo et al. 1988), the family Euphorbiaceae (MacRae et al. 1988); plants used in the treatment of malaria (Gbeassor et al. 1989), diabetes (Ajabnoor and Tilmisany 1988), and other illnesses; particular constituents, such as alkaloids (Arbain et al. 1989) or activities, such as antibiosis (Rios et al. 1988) and fertility suppression (Rajasekaran et al. 1988); and plants of a particular geographic region or ethnic group, such as New Zealand (Brooker et al. 1989), Madagascar (Beaujard 1988), and Egyptian Bedouins (Goodman and Hobbs 1988). These can be useful references for documentation of the existence of particular species, uses by different populations, and known constituents or activities. But these are really little more than ethnobotanical inventories that pay only scant attention to the social contexts and meaning of plant use. Medical anthropologists need to recognize that the objectives of ethnobotanical research are different from and generally narrower than the conceptual and theoretical concerns of their own discipline and must gauge their use of those inventories accordingly. These sensitivities to research needs are embodied in Moerman's (1986) comprehensive work on native American medicinal plants. This is a unique and especially powerful research tool. Indexing and on-line access to the vast data base unlocks a wealth of taxonomically reliable information on specific use, preparation, and ethnic group for more than 2,100 species.

To illustrate the relevance of ethnopharmacologic research for the field of medical anthropology, the remainder of this chapter will discuss the creation and elaboration of herbal pharmacopoeias, cultural constructions of efficacy, the contextualization of plant use, and suggestions for future work.

THE ELABORATION OF HERBAL PHARMACOPOEIAS

How do people interact with and learn from plants in their environment? How were their earliest experiences with botanicals interpreted and the outcomes manipulated to develop the elaborate herbal pharmacopoeias used by many contemporary populations? We know that plant selection is largely purposive and depends on more than simple availability. The most abundant species are not necessarily or ever overrepresented in a pharmacopoeia (Alcorn 1981; Etkin 1988b; Johns 1986; Logan 1988; Moerman 1979a, 1989).

Studies of nonhuman primate feeding ecology and prehistoric and contemporary human dietaries have taught us quite a lot about the evolution of hominid subsistence and the biological and behavioral correlates of food and food-getting technologies (Gilbert and Mielke 1985; Glander 1982; Harris and Ross 1987; Johnston 1987; Waterman 1984). Because much of that research has to do with the application and modification of selection criteria for plants, we begin to learn about the evolution of medicinal applications of plants as well. In natural habitats chimpanzees use unique, nondietary strategies to acquire the leaves of special antibiotic-containing plants (such as *Aspilia* spp.) (Rodriguez et al. 1985; Wrangham and Nishida 1983). While one is loathe to elaborate models of ape therapeutics, it is at least compelling to consider that nonhuman primates also manipulate their environment in ways that both exercise some measure of control and affect their own health. Similarly, palynological evidence for prehistoric human use of what are contemporary indigenous medicines has been interpreted to reflect medicinal use of those same plants in the past (Lewis and Elvin-Lewis 1977).

This last point is especially interesting since diet has been the predominant perspective in analyses of human-plant interactions in prehistory. Much effort has been devoted to comprehending when, how, and why humans domesticated certain plant species. This has been confounded by the assumption implicit in much of this work that plants are either and always foods or something else— medicines, items of manufacture, cosmetics, and the like. In fact, there is considerable overlap (Etkin 1986a). Coca (*Erythroxylum* spp.), for example, may have first been a famine food that was adapted from wild stands in the Andes and only later used medicinally (Plowman 1986), whereas soybeans (*Glycine max*) are relatively recent additions to Chinese diet, having first been cultivated for medicine (Katz 1987). Thus, domesticated crops and other anthropogenic vegetation represent in part the selection of medicinal plants.

CULTURAL CONSTRUCTIONS OF EFFICACY

The selection of plants for medicine bears directly on questions of efficacy. Does the medicine work? Intuitively this seems simple, but the parameters that define whether and how something is effective vary considerably between and even within different societies. Perceptions of efficacy are shaped by both biological and behavioral variables, the interactions among which are often complex, sometimes idiosyncratic, and generally not predictable from one society to another.

For example, one gauge of efficacy of medicines is related to organoleptic qualities such as taste, olfaction, appearance, and texture. Colors are among the more predominant signatures that mark efficacy. Red plants are commonly identified by Hausa and others as wound treatments and blood fortifiers (henna, *Lawsonia inermis*; red root, *Lachnanthes caroliniana*; bloodroot, *Sanguinaria canadensis*), and yellow plants are often indicated in treatments for jaundice (*Cocholospermum tinctorium*; goldthread, *Coptis trifolia*; goldenrod, *Solidago juncea*). Nigerian Hausa and Ecuadorian Waorani select strong-smelling plants to deal with spirits and witches, using unpleasant odors to deter these disease agents (onion and garlic, *Allium* spp.; cat's whiskers, *Gynandropsis pentaphylla; Siparuma* spp.) and fragrant plants to mollify them (ginger, *Zingiber officinale*; clove, *Eugenia caryophyllata*; spice bark, *Xanthoxylum senegalense*). The milky latexes of other plants (heliotrope, *Heliotropium undulatum; Euphorbia* spp.; swallow-wort, *Calotropis procera*) signal utility in stimulating lactation. Fertility-enhancing plants are marked by profuse flower or fruit and seed production (broom weed, *Scoparia dulcis*; fig, *Ficus capensis*; sesame, *Sesamum indicum*). Plants that readily shed their ripe fruit (mango, *Mangifera indica*; hog plum, *Spondias monbin*) or that contain oily or mucilaginous constituents (shea tree, *Butyrospermum parkii*; castor oil plant, *Ricinus communis*; beniseed, *Ceratotheca sesamoides*) are understood to facilitate childbirth. Liver disorders are treated with plants that have multilobed leaves (hepatica, *Hepatica nobilis*; camel's foot, *Bauhinia thonningii*). Aphrodisiacs are phallus shaped (deleb palm, *Borassus aethiopum*; mandrake, *Mandragora officinarum*), contain stimulants (kola nut, *Cola acuminata*; qat, *Catha edulis*), or have a sweet taste (wild amaranth, *Amaranthus spinosus*) (Davis and Yost 1983; Etkin et al. 1988; Kennedy 1987; Lewis and Elvin-Lewis 1977; Moerman 1986; Morgan 1981).[3]

Compellingly graphic as these associations may be, one must consider that more than sympathetic magic is involved. Plants are more than their mnemonic signals. For example, the quinones that impart red color to plants are antimicrobial and hemostatic (Delaveau 1981), suggesting additional or even different motivations for the use of those species in wound treatment. Similarly, the bitter Hausa plants that are selected to treat stomach disorders (calabash, *Lagenaria vulgaris*; buffalo thorn, *Zizyphus mucronata*) are emphatically disallowed during pregnancy because of their potential abortifacient actions. The bitter plants (cinnamon, *Cinnamomum zeylanicum*; parsley, *Petroselinum crispum*) that Colombian women select to treat amenorrhea and to precipitate abortion have oxytocic, counterimplantation, and abortifacient activities (Browner and Ortiz de Montellano 1986). To make sense of this, we need not invoke some fortuitous conjunction of sign (color or taste, for example) with pharmacologic activity. It suffices that indigenous populations are at least as keen observers of their biological universe as biomedical scientists pride themselves to be.

Other qualities of plants that affect the interpretation of their efficacy have to do with cognitive principles that are based in such binary oppositions as hot-cold, acid-sweet, bitter-sweet, yin-yang, male-female, and the like. In principle these humoral models conceptualize health and disease as balance and imbalance, respectively, of contrasting pairs of qualities. For example, Hausa ascribe some forms of obstructed labor to excess sugar, the treatment for which includes acidic plant medicines (lime, *Citrus aurantifolia*; lemon, *C. limon*; tamarind, *Tamarindus indica*). Rigid and absolute binary contrasts are partly the methodological artifact of interview protocols that present only pairs of terms, whereas the space between two poles may in some cases be better described as a continuum (Foster 1984a; Furbee and Benfer 1983; Tedlock 1987).

In addition to qualities of the medicine itself, a second gauge of efficacy is related to its physiologic effect. While the therapeutic strategies of all peoples are directed ultimately at illness resolution, symptom diminution may not be sufficient or may be expected only as the terminus of some series of therapeutic events. One can speak, then, of one or more proximate outcomes that are intended as the first stage(s) of healing and an ultimate outcome. What marks each stage of healing and the rules for moving through and interpreting stages of the healing sequence vary cross-culturally.

Evidence of disease egress is a required proximal outcome in medical systems that range geographically from Mexico and Honduras to Nigeria, Swaziland, and Bangladesh (Dominguez and Alcorn 1985; Kendall et al. 1984; Etkin and Ross 1982, 1983; Green 1985; Shahid et al. 1983). Physiologic reactions such as vomiting, sweating, diarrhea, and skin rash are signs that a disease or its agent leaves the body. It follows, then, that Hausa treatments for gastrointestinal disorders include, first, plants with emetic and diuretic action (kola nut, *Cola acuminata*; false kola, *Garcinia kola*; garden egg, *Solanum melongena*). These are not the "irrational and merely exacerbating" outcomes that biomedical observers describe. Indeed, they are based in empirical observations of plants and their pharmacologic actions and are, moreover, followed by use of other plants that have emollient and costive actions (tamarind, *Tamarindus indica*; jujube, *Zizyphus jujuba*; horseradish tree, *Moringa pterygosperma*) and that kill intestinal parasites (wild custard apple, *Anona senegalensis*; desert date, *Balanites aegyptica*; loincloth fig, *Ficus thonningii*) (Etkin and Ross 1982, 1983).

In other cases biomedical and ethnomedical ascriptions of efficacy are more conspicuously aligned, although perceptions of disease etiology and mode of drug action are different. Populations in New Guinea and Ecuador who use nettles (*Dendrocnide* spp., *Laportea* spp.) to lash painful body areas understand the mode of action to be the consolidation of disease substance at some internal locus to facilitate its expulsion or to chase the pain away (Johannes 1986; Davis and Yost 1983). Such treatments are consistent with biomedical understandings of efficacy through counterirritation—superficial irritation at the skin that relieves the inflammation of deep-lying structures. Wild peonies (*Paeonia lactiflora, P. moutan*) have long been used for what Chinese medicine refers to as "stagnant blood" and what biomedicine calls "standing blood in vessels" (intravascular hemostasis) and have the anticoagulant, pain-relieving, and anti-inflammatory activities (Kawashiri et al. 1986) that both medical systems regard as efficacious for this condition.

A note of caution should be interjected here. Phytochemical and clinical investigations of plants processed in ways different from preparation in the study population tell us something interesting about the plant and its pharmacologic potential but not necessarily about how it affects the health of populations in which it is used. Since most indigenous medicines are prepared as aqueous solutions that are either ingested or rubbed on the body, what are we to make of the following cases? Low rates of cardiovascular disease in Spanish populations have been attributed to their use of saffron (*Crocus sativus*) after discovery that intramuscular injections of extracts of this plant have a cholesterol-lowering effect (Basker and Negbi 1983). Similarly, the efficacy of an Italian plant medicine (black byrony, *Tamus communis*) that is topically applied for skin irritations was "confirmed" by laboratory studies that found anti-inflammatory activity for orally administered ethanol extracts (Caspasso et al. 1983). And methanol and acetone extractions are the preparatory modes used in "corroborating" the ulcer-protective actions of Chinese (*Atractylodes lancea*) and Japanese (*Saussurea lappa*) medicines for indigestion and stomachache (Nogami et al. 1986; Yamahara et al. 1985).

Ethnomedicines, unlike their pharmaceutical counterparts in biomedicine, are frequently composed of more than one constituent. Whereas biomedical interpretations of plant mixing invoke "merely magical" associations or the embellishment of some active constituent by "ballast" and "inert constituents," it has been shown repeatedly that compound medicines can be pharmacologically different from their individual plant constituents. In plant combinations, the activities of two plants may be additive; the action of one constituent may be potentiated by another so that the effect is greater than additive; one constituent may diminish the activity of another through antagonistic interaction; or the effect may be synergistic when one constituent substantially amplifies the activity of another. For example, an Ayurvedic medicine that combines several plants (black pepper, *Piper nigrum*, long pepper, *P. longum*, and ginger, *Zingiber officinalis*) potentiates the actions of additional plants in the medicine by markedly increasing the bioavailability of their active constituents (Atal et al. 1981). In other cases, the association of plants may diminish the toxicity of their individual constituents (such as tannins and saponins) (Freeland et al. 1985) while enabling the low-concentration activities of those same constituents or the beneficial actions of other substances in the mixture. On the other hand, whereas straightforward pharmacologic interpretation would predict anti-inflammatory activity for licorice (*Glycyrrhiza glabra*) and antibiosis for barberry (*Berberis vulgaris*), the combination of these two plants in a single medicine results in the precipitation of berberine by glycyrrhizin, thus neutralizing the actions of both substances (Noguchi 1978).

Because efficacy is culturally constructed, it must be understood first within the specific contexts in which therapeutic behaviors have evolved. But it is also appropriate to apply external criteria—for example to evaluate indigenous plant medicines by applying the standards of biomedicine. The significance of this has been obscured by medical anthropologists who have created or who perpetuate a false dichotomy between biomedicine and ethnomedicines. This occurs partly through contention that whereas biomedicine cures physiologic disorders ("diseases"), indigenous medicines treat the mere secondary reactions to disease (that is, treat the subjective "illness") (Kleinman and Sung 1979; Young 1983). This view ignores that plant medicines may be pharmacologically active and/or that non-western peoples are capable of empirically judging the biologic outcomes of their behaviors.

THE CONTEXTUALIZATION OF PLANT USE

Precisely because we can interpret plant medicines in both biological and behavioral frameworks, we come to appreciate the implications of their use under all circumstances, not just in medicinal contexts. Additional circumstances of plant use in Hausa society are illustrative. The most substantial impact that plants have on human physiology outside medicinal use is through dietary consumption, although these two categories are not always clearly differentiated, especially when one talks about healthy foods, nutritious medicines, tonics, and the like. Cosmetics, adornments, and items of hygiene include substances that come into prolonged contact with the body. One can also use plants to influence social relationships—for example, popularity or family harmony—by ingesting or applying them to oneself or covertly to someone else. Other plant materials are used to ensure prosperous market ventures, healthy livestock, or success in farming. The list is long because for Hausa it is possible to influence all aspects of life with *magani*—"medicine" in the broadest sense, which includes anything that one uses to change the course of or to prevent happenings in one's life. These categories of use and their biologic implications are relevant for other populations as well. But medicines that are directed at social relationships or that are otherwise not explicitly related to physiologic outcomes are likely to be overlooked by studies more narrowly concerned with disease. When assessing pharmacologic potential, distinctions among these categories are best blurred. The point is that pharmacologically active substances can affect one regardless of why they are consumed or applied.

Because foods are usually consumed in relatively large quantities compared to medicinal and other uses, the pharmacologic implications of their use are especially noteworthy. For Hausa, plants used in both medicine and diet act in concert to suppress malaria infection. Not only do extracts of fetid cassia (*Cassia tora*) and Egyptian mimosa (*Acacia arabica*) apparently generate oxidants, which are known to have antimalarial action, but also the seasonal fluctuations of Hausa diet result in maximum consumption of those plants during the period of highest malaria risk (Etkin 1979b, 1981; Etkin and Ross 1982, 1983). Similarly, in the case of gastrointestinal disorders, plants that are Hausa foods as well as medicines have costive, antimicrobial, and anti-inflammatory properties. Hausa use leaves of balsam apple (*Momordica balsamina*), horseradish tree (*Moringa pterygosperma*), and fig (*Ficus polita*) to treat stomachache because of their pungent, bitter, or astringent tastes; and they use the same signals to meet culinary objectives with these plants—that is, to season the otherwise bland grain-based foods that are the mainstay of Hausa dietaries (Etkin and Ross 1982). Among the Nekematigi of New Guinea, medical treatment encompasses the consumption of ceremonial meals that include plants with a variety of pharmacologic activities, such as antimicrobials (clove, *Eugenia carophyllata*) and stomachics (coleus, *Coleus* spp.; ginger, *Zingiber officinale*) (Johannes 1986). And the antiatherogenic effects of dietary and "tonic" plants—ginger (*Zingiber officinale*), garlic, and onion (*Allium sativum, A. cepa*)—likely contribute to a low rate of cardiovascular disease in some Chinese populations (Hammerschmidt 1986; Okuyama et al. 1986).

SUMMARY AND SUGGESTIONS FOR FUTURE WORK

Whereas interpretations of the social and cultural dimensions of medical systems have become increasingly sophisticated, there have been few efforts to understand the biological outcomes of those behaviors. Where such physiologic investigations were undertaken, cultural elements were so abbreviated and eclipsed by quantified data and technical language that anthropologists from the sociocultural camp projected onto these studies an ambience of biological determinism. Although there has been considerable recent progress in that direction, much more needs to be done to articulate the biological and behavioral aspects of health and to develop more evincive laboratory analyses and especially more rigorous field methodologies that enable cogent cross-cultural comparisons (Browner et al. 1988; Kyerematen and Ogunlana 1987; Verpoorte 1989). Ethnopharmacology is in a particularly good position to contribute to such endeavors. To the extent that medical anthropologists seek to comprehend the health of populations that they study, pharmacologic interpretations of the substances that they ingest or apply medicinally advance that knowledge. This has some more practical implications as well.

Some advocates of ethnopharmacologic research cite the important role that plants and natural products research have played in the development of biomedicine, the continued inclusion of a small number of natural compounds in biomedical therapeutics, and the contemporary manufacture of synthetic compounds modeled on natural products (Phillipson and Anderson 1989). The implication is that there is much more to be discovered and that ethnopharmacologic research can advance the interests of biomedicine. But in fact as the interval and costs increase between the time of discovery of a new plant or constituent and its eventual manufacture and marketing, pharmaceutical companies find it economically difficult to develop new drugs in this way. An increasingly compelling argument for seeking new pharmacologically active products is the growing rate of drug resistance among parasites, such as malaria and *Streptococcal* infections.

Others champion ethnopharmacologic investigations for their potential contributions to improving health throughout the world (Akerele 1987; Oyeneye 1985; Pelaez and Uribe 1986). Because plant medicines constitute most of the primary health care for rural populations worldwide and because biomedicines are difficult to acquire even in areas where they have become the preferred therapy, it is incumbent upon health-concerned agencies and individuals to assess thoroughly whatever medicines are in use. Plant medicines that are efficacious by indigenous and biomedical standards can be encouraged, especially where no comparably effective pharmaceuticals are available. Given the unambiguous effects of their consumption, it is not likely that acutely toxic plants are included in herbal pharmacopoeias for any human use other than poisoning. But chronic toxicity after protracted use is a possibility that might be worth exploring through ethnopharmacologic study.

Finally, and with some irony, the pharmacologic study of indigenous medicines will help us to understand as well the health impact of introducing pharmaceuticals (biomedical drugs), an indisputable and accelerating trend worldwide (van der Geest and Whyte 1988). As pharmaceuticals become readily available through informal (nonbiomedical, out-of-hospital) networks, local populations interpret and adapt those drugs in much the same way that they have been using plant medicines. Pharmaceuticals come to be used to treat diseases for which they are not intended. Albeit interesting, this transposition of indigenous criteria onto materials created within another cultural framework raises health concerns that include creative methods of drug administration and the coupling of diseases with inappropriate pharmaceuticals. For Hausa, the color, texture, and induction of disease egress through diarrhea are more compelling attributes of penicillin capsules than are arguments about its intrinsic merits as a broad-spectrum antibiotic. Further, since these pharmaceuticals are used concurrently with pharmacologically active plants, the potential for drug interactions is high, sometimes with grave outcome (Etkin et al. 1988). International and local health programs have a great deal to learn about what indigenous local populations expect from the medicines that they use. This will ensure that pharmaceuticals are used in ways intended by their manufacturer and in ways that neither duplicate effective indigenous medicines already in use nor biologically compromise the efficacy of either indigenous medicines or introduced pharmaceuticals.

NOTES

1. This is not to imply that biomedicine and other therapeutic systems are categorically different or that "ethnomedicine" should be understood as some single homogeneous system of knowledge any more than biomedicine is everywhere the same.

2. In the field, one must collect a pressed voucher specimen of each locally identified plant and have those vouchers taxonomically identified. For example, the Hausa plant *cediya* corresponds to the botanic genus and species names *Ficus thonningii*.

3. Aspects of Hausa nosology and therapeutics that appear in this chapter without specific citation have been drawn from my observations in northern Nigeria during two extensive periods of field research in 1975–1976 and 1987–1988.

CHAPTER 9

STUDYING BIOMEDICINE AS A CULTURAL SYSTEM

Lorna Amarasingham Rhodes

Western biomedicine and medical anthropology are intimately connected.[1] Many medical anthropologists work in biomedical settings or study problems that have been defined in biomedical terms. Medical anthropologists also study biomedicine itself, exploring the ways in which it is socially, culturally, and historically constructed and showing how its perspectives influence the lives of its patients. In addition, most medical anthropologists are members of societies in which biomedicine provides the dominant forms of explanation and treatment for illness and are thus participants in as well as observers of the culture of biomedicine.

In this chapter I explore some of the implications and paradoxes of this relationship. My focus is on the ways medical anthropologists and others in related fields (mainly history and sociology) approach biomedicine as an object of study. My emphasis is on biomedicine as it is understood by these writers; discussing the diversity, internal complexity, and changing conditions of current biomedical practice in the United States is beyond my scope here.

Recently a good deal of discussion and controversy has arisen within medical anthropology about its relationship to biomedicine. Often the issue is phrased as a difference between "clinically applied" and "critical" medical anthropology. Clinically applied medical anthropology has been described as "serving to clarify specific issues in health maintenance and response to sickness" (Chrisman and Maretzki 1982b:2). Its orientation is the application of anthropological perspectives to particular clinical situations and problems. Critical medical anthropology, on the other hand, defines itself in terms of a concern with the macrolevel of political and economic forces that shape medicine and determine the nature and extent of its interventions. Margaret Lock describes the critical approach as one that pays attention to "macro-structural questions, the role of power in social life, and the way in which biomedicine is culturally constructed" (Lock 1986a:110). Biomedical theory and practice is problematic not simply when it fails to address cultural and social issues involved in individual patient care but because of its embeddedness and (often) sustaining role in dominant political and economic systems.

The precise nature of the division between clinically applied and critical medical anthropology is by no means a matter of agreement among medical anthropologists, and there are numerous variations on these definitions. Morsy (1989a) points out that critical analysis is common in other disciplines and objects to using a label that sets it apart as special. On the other hand, M. Singer, Lani Davis, and Gina Gerdis (1988:373) make a case for separating "critical" analyses that "explicate culture in non-cultural terms" from "culturalist" approaches that avoid economic or political forms of explanation. In fact, many studies in medical anthropology are not easily assigned to particular camps. Nevertheless, the argument between clinically applied and critical medical anthropology reveals a central problematic issue: how is biomedicine understood and described from within medical anthropology?

I begin the exploration of this question by considering the anthropological concept of the cultural system, showing how several recent works illuminate biomedicine's cultural construction and the ways it functions as a system for producing as well as expressing cultural meanings. I then turn briefly to clinically applied approaches, showing how they deal with the cultural dichotomies contained in clinical practice. Finally, I explore some of the premises of the critical perspective as it touches on the issue of biomedical knowledge and practice. I end by discussing some of the research strategies implied by each of these orientations and suggest some directions for future work.

BIOMEDICINE AS A CULTURAL SYSTEM

In a series of classic articles, Clifford Geertz (1973c:108) suggests that cultural systems can best be understood in terms of their capacity to express the nature of the world and to shape that world to their dimensions. Thus, for example, religion "formulates, by means of symbols, an image of a genuine order of the world." This simultaneous shaping and expression produces a congruence between culture and experience that provides an "aura of factuality" within which cultural systems "make sense" and seem "uniquely real" to their participants. For our purposes, the crucial phrase here is "aura of factuality." The implication of Geertz's analysis is that cultural systems achieve a feeling of factuality, of realness, that is, in part or whole, a by-product of their symbolic forms.

In Western society biomedicine is generally believed to operate in a realm of "facts"; many people experience their most intimate contact with science through the biomedical description of the facts of bodily function and disease. This realm of bodily fact is often perceived to be quite separate from other cultural and social domains. "To a degree perhaps unique to segmented Western society, the participants of this ethnomedicine [biomedicine] emphatically distinguish their medicine from other aspects and institutions of their society. Illness is thought of as a 'natural' occurrence" (Hahn and Kleinman 1983:312). Given this assumption that nature and the body exist in a directly apprehendable realm of fact, the problem for a cultural analysis of biomedicine is the delineation of the "aura" in the "aura of factuality" that it promotes. The issue is not simply the description of biomedicine but the discovery of strategies that will make visible its nature as a cultural system. As Emily Martin points out (1987:52), it takes a "jolt" to see the "contingent nature" of biomedical description.

Several recent explorations of biomedicine undertake specific and deliberate strategies to provide this jolt by making visible the culture of biomedicine. One strategy is historical contextualization; biomedicine is shown as the historically embedded product of particular cultural and social assumptions, thereby highlighting the "arbitrariness of institutions" (Foucault 1988:11). Another strategy is to uncover, through analysis of metaphor and other forms of speech, ways in which social meaning is embedded in biomedical categories. Attending to the life worlds of clinicians is a third strategy; the daily practice of clinicians is revealing of biomedicine's theoretical and pragmatic foundations. All of these forms of analysis aim to recover from the domain of the "natural" and the "given" those aspects of biomedicine that are cultural and constructed.

Most historical discussions of biomedicine emphasize its origin in an elaboration of the Cartesian dichotomy between mind and body. Biomedical theory developed out of the possibility, following René Descartes, of a separation of the physical body from the mental and social. The body, as part of the natural world, becomes knowable as a bounded material entity; diseases similarly are physical entities occurring in specific locations within the body. Robert Hahn and Arthur Kleinman (1983:313) describe the consequence: physical reductionism is a central tenet of biomedicine. This medicine also radically separates body from nonbody; the body is thought to be knowable and treatable in isolation.

As Nancy Scheper-Hughes and Margaret Lock (1987:10) point out, even those who try to take an integrated perspective on illness "find themselves trapped by the Cartesian legacy. We lack a precise vocabulary with which to deal with mind-body-society interaction and so are left suspended in hyphens." This is not just a matter of vocabulary but of epistemology; biomedicine participates in deep-seated cultural assumptions about what it means to know the body.

The particularity of this way of knowing the body can be seen in biomedical texts and practices that provide a mechanistic and desocialized imagery of bodily processes. For example, in a section of *The Woman in the Body* (1987) entitled "Science as a Cultural System," Martin examines the images of women's bodies found in medical textbooks and suggests that several metaphors of the body permeate their seemingly "scientific" (that is, in this context, neutral or value-free) descriptions of physical processes. Thus the processes of menstruation and menopause are described in terms of production and control. The female reproductive system is geared to "production" and is organized as a hierarchical system of communication among hormones, cells, and the brain. This imagery corresponds to that of our economic system. In menopause, "what is being described is the breakdown of a system of authority . . . at every point in this system, functions 'fail' and 'falter.' Follicles 'fail to muster strength' to reach ovulation. As functions fail, so do the members of the system decline" (1987:42). The key to this metaphor, Martin says, is "functionlessness"; "these images frighten us in part because in our stage of advanced capitalism, they are close to a reality we find difficult to see clearly: broken down hierarchy and organizational members who no longer play their designated parts" (1987:44). In these images, the "natural" functioning of the body is described in a way that fits a wider social view of women as defined by their reproductive function.

A similarly circular relationship between social and medical imagery can be seen in Rayna Rapp's (1988a:149) description of the process of genetic counseling. She points out that "statistics and medical terminology are genres of communication, not simply neutral vocabularies.... Much of the scientific information that counselors want to convey is technical and invisible." The visual aids used by counselors, such as charts and graphs, have an effect in "shaping the perceptions of the client" and thus, for some clients, redefining what is known in terms congruent with the biomedical definition of the "natural." The "codes, genres and assumptions construct the conversations genetic counselors may have with their patients" (1988a:151), producing as natural a particular way of seeing the body and its reproductive life.

A revealing account of the historical embeddedness of biomedical knowledge is provided by Michel Foucault. For Foucault, medicine is one of a number of related disciplines that have shaped the body as a vulnerable site for the articulation of social relationships. In *The Birth of the Clinic* (1975) Foucault argues that modern medicine had its birth in the period around 1800 when medicine became clinically based and concerned with both the inside of the body and the control of the health of populations. Foucault's thought is complex, and my discussion here limited, but two examples can perhaps give some idea of the sense in which he perceives that medicine both shapes and expresses its historical context.

Foucault describes the period around 1800 as one in which medicine shifted not from a less to more accurate understanding of the body but from one kind of knowledge to another. Before 1800 Europe had a "medicine of species" that depended on classification; diseases were organized into families and species and related more to one another than to the body of the patient. Medicine after 1800 was dominated by what Foucault calls "the gaze," a new way of seeing that looked into the body and focused on what was individual and abnormal.

Suddenly doctors were able to see and to describe what for centuries had been beneath the level of the visible. It was not so much that doctors suddenly opened their eyes; rather the old codes of knowledge had determined what was seen (Sheridan 1980:39). A new way of seeing produced a new kind of knowledge: ... "clinical experience sees a new space opening up before it; the tangible space of the body... the medicine of organs, sites, causes, a clinic wholly ordered in accordance with pathological anatomy" (Foucault 1975:122). For Foucault the historical context, and particularly its shaping of what is possible, of what can be seen, determines what at any time is considered to be true. Practitioners of the early nineteenth century did not suddenly become better observers and therefore better able to discover the truth about the body; rather, there was a fundamental change in what constituted observation. This change brought about profound changes in medicine, and these in turn shape the body we perceive. In this argument, the issue of shaping goes deeper than "what is said." Foucault is interested in what can be said and in the mutual shaping of perception and possibility that gives rise to a particular medicine at a particular historical moment.

Foucault later extends this argument to show that in the nineteenth century, the body became an object of social control in a new sense. Minutely observed in clinics, prisons, and hospitals, bodies could be made into docile instruments of and for the exercise of power. One tactic of discipline is the dossier, the collection of documents that locates, describes, and accounts for each prisoner, patient, or child. As Foucault (1979:192) puts it, "The turning of real lives into writing functions as a procedure of objectification and subjection." Thus, for Foucault, neither "objective" description nor the case format in which such description is often framed constitutes value-neutral aspects of medicine. Rather than functioning to delineate a reality that exists independently of its description, they are techniques for the shaping of reality that create patients as individuals susceptible to a particular kind of judgment. Thus, people are profoundly shaped by disciplinary mechanisms that permeate our society, with medicine primary among them.

Issues of the relationship between mind and body, questions about what is knowable, and integration into the discipline of institutional life are enacted in the daily practice of clinicians. An example of a study that explores the lived world of a practitioner is Robert Hahn's "Portrait of an Internist" (1985a). Hahn portrays the symbolic world of a clinician; the internist uses and reflects on biomedicine's categories, and his practice is revealing of how these categories exist in the larger culture. Hahn's strategy is to explore the interface between the personal and social that is provided by the world of work, showing how "persons at once express themselves and reciprocally absorb those parts of the world touched by their expression" (1985a:53). Thus the physician enacts in work the production of both self and society.

The internist described in Hahn's portrait engages directly the questions of realism and nominalism inherent in biomedicine's Cartesian origins. Thus the internist "refers to his conception of the patient's problem, most often a physiological one, as 'a picture' . . . a 'thing' "; sometimes "pictures" "make sense" and sometimes he "makes sense of" them. As Hahn points out, "If purported facts fail to make sense, the anomaly must inhere in the facts; but, if Barry is unable to make sense of the facts, it may be . . . that the difficulty lies in Barry's sense-making activity. . . . These are respectively metaphors of realism and nominalism, of naturalism and constructionism" (1985a:80). Thus, this physician enacts, through work and in relation to the bodies of his patients, some of the fundamental issues embedded in the history of medicine itself.

The assumption behind Geertz's definition of a cultural system is that "culture can be explained primarily in terms of itself" (Singer, Davison, and Gerdes 1988:370; Good and Good 1981; Fabrega 1979). However, these examples suggest that the ulture of biomedicine does not lend itself to explanation in terms of itself. One problem is the same as that of Hahn's internist in the passage quoted: the relationship between constructed and natural fact. Hahn complains that "while participants in Biomedicine have often been blind to the ideal and cultural facets of their work . . . social science observers in the settings of Biomedicine have commonly ignored its materiality" (1984a:321). Biomedical practice depends on the assumption of an objectified nature subject to scientifically formulated "reality testing," and although, as Hahn points out (1984a), reality testing is fundamental to all healing traditions, we find our particular brand especially compelling. Thus, from the perspective of patients, practitioners, social scientists, and laypeople in our society and despite much evidence of limitations or confusion, nature as it is understood by biomedicine demands to be taken seriously (that is, not questioned) in studies of biomedicine. This paradox, usually not in evidence in studies of other medical systems—for example, most studies of Ayurveda do not generally consider its disease categories as descriptive of actual diseases but of socially constructed ones (see, for example, Obeyesekere 1978)—means that the categories of the culture under study are also the categories used to study it.

A second difficulty arises not so much in connection with factuality as with its aura. The closed circle of belief and expression suggested by the notion of cultural system appears flawed, even fragile, in several of these accounts. This may result in part from the way illness itself threatens the cultural order with chaos and loss of meaning and thus "calls into question particular socio-cultural resolutions" of the dilemmas of human existence (Comaroff 1982:51). Paradox and doubt may be intrinsic to the experience of the body; "physical form . . . generates, from its own internal contradictions, the potential basis for critical awareness" (Comaroff 1982:51).

In addition, however, biomedicine participates in a cultural separation of mind and body, nature and culture, in ways that may produce a sense of dissonance expressed in increasing criticism and doubt. Martin, for example, found that women she interviewed expressed diverse images of their bodily processes, contradicting and resisting biomedical formulations (1987). Similarly, Rapp's work suggests a complex interplay between social context and the expression of medical "information," with some counseling recipients unwilling to accept the language of risk in which advice was proffered and with that language itself constantly modified in interaction (1988a). Thus, as Jean Comaroff puts it, "there has been an awareness that 'factual' knowledge might imply social values, that medicine has bequeathed us powerful metaphors along with its 'natural' truths and that these might . . . reinforce the deep-seated paradoxes raised by illness" (1982:56). The examples given here suggest that critical perspectives tend to emerge out of the cultural analysis of biomedicine.

BRACKETING BIOMEDICINE

One solution to the problem posed by medicine's grounding in "fact" is to segregate biomedical and social science ways of knowing. Most of clinically applied anthropology, and much research in medical anthropology as a whole, is based on a bracketing of biomedical expertise as referring to areas of knowledge not within the purview of the anthropologist.

This bracketing is the basis for the well-known distinction between disease and illness proposed by Leon Eisenberg (1977) and Arthur Kleinman (1980) (see also Young 1982; Hahn and Kleinman 1984). This distinction is created by dividing up the field of "sickness" into a domain of disease, considered to be pathology as biomedically defined, and illness, which encompasses the cultural meaning and social relationships experienced by the patient. Allan Young sums it up thus: "Disease refers to abnormalities in the structure and/or function of organs, pathological states whether or not they are culturally recognized." This is the "arena of the biomedical model." Illness, on the other hand, "refers to a person's perceptions and experiences of certain socially disvalued states including, but not limited to, disease" (1982:264). Thus illness includes the experiences and beliefs of individuals; disease is what biomedicine discovers "in" the person regardless of his or her (personal or cultural) awareness.

The disease-illness distinction has provided the basis for much work in medical anthropology on the explanatory models and semantic illness networks of patients and, to some extent, of practitioners. These studies set aside the disease half of the distinction and concentrate on understanding the illness experiences and behavior of individuals and cultural groups. By setting aside I do not mean that disease itself is not considered problematic for those who experience it but that the definition of disease—its status as a real, natural phenomenon—is considered nonproblematic. This has allowed medical anthropologists to study culture (beliefs, issues of meaning, experience of illness) in medical settings without dealing with questions of the cultural construction of medicine itself. It also allows for the defining of research problems (for example, the study of groups of patients suffering from a particular disease or the study of the relationship between cultural and physical aspects of causation in a particular disorder) in ways that are relevant to the social context supporting the research. As Noel Chrisman and Thomas Maretzki say, "In our research, anthropologists have explicitly or implicitly drawn on clinical medicine as the standard for judging the 'real' world of sickness" (1982b:22).

One consequence is that medical anthropologists have been able to do research and teaching in medical settings, finding ways to incorporate anthropology into practice while respecting the orientation and commitments of clinicians. For the anthropologist who is, as Chrisman and Maretzki describe, bicultural in anthropology and medicine, the ideal is a translation of perspectives, enabling clinicians to make use of anthropological insights. Often these insights have to do with negotiation among perspectives (as in, for example, Kleinman's use of explanatory models, 1980); at other times they have to do with patient advocacy (as in, for example, obstetrics) or with the clarification of ways that the biomedical perspective influences the cultural interpretations of patients.

On the other hand, the disease-illness distinction is a variant of the mind-body and culture-nature dichotomies (Hahn 1984a). By using it to separate natural facts from cultural constructions, medical anthropology runs the risk of taking on characteristics of biomedicine itself. Instead of offering a perspective that comes from a position of stranger (Chrisman and Maretzki 1982b), the anthropologist may be a kissing cousin in disguise. For example, the emphasis on case studies reproduces in anthropology the individual-centered, "objective," and nonnarrative approach of the medical case study. Similarly, the use of scientific language to describe disease reproduces the position "from the outside looking over or into a space" (Pratt 1986) that is fundamental to the medical gaze. The anthropologist is also influenced by the premise of biomedicine that "it is *the* medicine, real medicine; only other ethnomedicines are specially denominated, 'osteopathic medicine,' 'Chinese medicine'" (Hahn and Kleinman 1983:312). In both biomedical settings and the study of other kinds of medicine, it is hard to avoid the assumption that what needs to be explained are the "alternatives," the "other" perspectives, the "misunderstandings" or "misuses" of biomedicine rather than biomedicine itself.

An interesting recent development is that as biomedicine expands its definitions of physical disorder, incorporating problems with recognizably large social components (as in, for example, alcoholism and posttraumatic stress disorder), the position of the anthropologist becomes problematic. These conditions, with their roots in problematic social environments, seem to be ripe for anthropological analysis and understanding. However, attempts to bring social and cultural considerations to bear on biological phenomena tend to participate, often unwittingly, in a process of naturalization that turns them into things comparable to diseases. The bringing of chronic or behavioral conditions into the domain of biomedical treatment (the very thing that brings them to the attention of the biomedically based medical anthropologist) tends to result in their naturalization and "reinterpretation as events requiring medical intervention." Thus, the more they are translated into the reified, concrete terminology of "disorders," the less room there is for the anthropologist's perspective on the cultural shaping of both the symptoms and their interpretation. As Young has shown for posttraumatic stress disorder, the production of "knowledge" about such disorders is itself a cultural process (1988).

CRITICAL PERSPECTIVES

Much work in anthropology has explored the positive aspects of cultural systems in providing and sustaining meaning in human social life. But there is another perspective from which the congruence between the shaping and expressive aspects of culture can be seen as perverse. Religion, for example, appears in this view as an "opiate" preventing people from recognizing the truth of their situation. Medicine, in its powerful mediation of human physical and emotional frailty, can similarly be understood in terms of its relationship to a larger social (political and economic) system in which it serves to conceal sources of injustice and suffering. From this point of view, medicine cannot be described apart from the relations of power that constitute its social context. As Howard Waitzkin puts it: "Major problems in medicine are also problems of society; the health system is so intimately tied to the broader society that attempts to study one without the other are misleading. Difficulties in health and medical care emerge from social contradictions and rarely can be separated from those contradictions" (1983:41).

There are two aspects to this relationship. One is that health problems themselves may be socially caused, creating what Waitzkin calls "the second sickness" (1983). The other, related, aspect is that medicine may function to conceal the social origins of sickness and to suppress the possibility of protest.

When biomedicine is seen in this light, clinical knowledge itself becomes problematic; its connections to the larger system mean that it "cannot be either evaluated or transformed in any simple, decontextualized manner" (Comaroff and Maguire 1981:121). Nor can it be seen merely as a "web of significance" (following Geertz) approachable through understanding; it must also (or perhaps, instead) be considered as a "web of mystification" (Singer et al. 1988).

Critical analyses of biomedicine are attempts at demystification. One strategy aims to uncover the incidence and causes of the "second sickness" by exploring ways in which medical care fails to reach, to recognize, or to correct socially created problems. Many analyses stress the relationship between capitalist production (and the profit motive inherent in it) and the failure to protect workers and others from its effects (Waitzkin 1983; Michaels 1988; Taussig 1978). Others focus on the maldistribution of medical care and the effects on the health of populations created by the dominance of complex technology (Young 1978; Navarro 1976).

A second strategy aims to uncover how biomedicine mystifies sickness through its participation in the nature-culture dichotomy. Medicine, because of its bias toward the uncovering of natural facts, represents the body in ways that are powerfully suggestive of a natural reality separate from the social. The effect, if not the intention, is to make the social invisible and to place sickness, as a natural process or entity, inside the individual.

Martin's point in her argument about menopause is that the "shriveling" of the ovaries is a metaphor that rests on and reinforces the social representation of the "shriveling" of production in the older woman. Because medicine has clothed the social representation in scientific language, it is difficult to discover its origins (1987). Similarly, Michael Taussig (1980a) describes the way a hospitalized patient is convinced of her own helplessness in the face of disease. She minimizes her own strength because she has been taught to rely on experts who function to invalidate her intuitive understanding of the social origin of her problem. Her disease is treated as a thing, part of a natural world separate from the social world that oppresses her. Thus Taussig considers medicine to express a hidden ideology, one that reifies the social and separates it into a natural domain where it cannot be understood for what it is.

By placing the body and bodily experience in the realm of nature, biomedicine conceals both the social causes of sickness and the social embeddedness of the experience of sickness. Thus, for example, the diagnostic category of premenstrual syndrome (PMS) creates a "disorder" that may serve to obscure the social relations that are the context of women's suffering (Martin 1987; Johnson 1987a). Similarly, the processes of childbirth and dying may be isolated from their social contexts and treated in largely technical terms that prevent those involved from taking care of themselves and each other (Illich 1976; Osherson and Amarasingham 1981; Comaroff 1982).

Recent cross-cultural and historical studies suggest that these tendencies toward reification and mystification are widely associated with biomedical practice. Lock's work on school refusal and on menopause in Japan shows that Japanese biomedicine similarly describes social problems as "syndromes" to be treated (Lock 1986a). In northeast Brazil, medical treatment, especially in the form of tranquilizers, serves to conceal the economic and social origin of starvation (Scheper-Hughes 1988b). An example from the history of psychiatry comes from Andrew Scull (1979), who shows that asylums in nineteenth-century England had the effect of isolating and controlling those in the population who could not survive under the conditions of early industrialization. Asylums maintained a distinction between the mad and the able-bodied, who could not be given relief for fear of undermining their value as surplus labor. Medical definitions of insanity contributed to and perpetuated the separation of "useless" from "useful" individuals. Scull sees the current move toward deinstitutionalization to be similarly motivated by economic policy; welfare and disability payments make it cheaper for the state to maintain disabled people outside asylums (Scull 1977).

Other areas of medicine have also been seen as fostering dependence in order to conceal and support class and gender interests. E. Richard Brown (1979), for example, shows that late nineteenth-century capitalism in the United States deliberately fostered biomedical definitions of problems that might otherwise have been seen as related to industrial development. The notion of the body as a mechanism that could be repaired corresponded in important ways to factory production (Scull 1979). Similarly, nineteenth-century medical theories about the fragility and emotionality of women served to bolster male dominance and the creation of the home as a domain separate from the workplace (Ehrenreich and English 1978).

These analyses regard biomedicine's aura of factuality as precisely its source of power. Medicine can describe events in a value-neutral language that makes them appear to be part of the natural world and thus neutralize what are, in reality, social problems. In the nineteenth century, villagers whose ability to support aging relatives had been undermined by social change were convinced that asylum care was provided by "experts" (doctors) and thus superior to their own; women who rebelled against restrictive conditions could be persuaded that bed rest was the only remedy for their restless female organs. Similarly, today,

Brazilian peasants believe tranquilizers to be "medicine" for starvation (Scheper-Hughes 1988b) and women angry over the unfair distribution of domestic work regard their anger as a "symptom" of PMS (Martin 1987).

For some writers this analysis of the embeddedness of biomedical categories in social life (and their tendency to perpetuate sickness-causing aspects of social life) is not enough. Additionally, it is important to recognize the ways in which biomedicine also gives rise to resistance. Martin attempts to make visible, through the analysis of women's speech, the way ordinary women resist the biomedical description of women's bodily life. For example, women may refuse to go to the hospital for childbirth, or they create original metaphors to describe bodily processes. Brigitte Jordan, in an analysis of the medical "training" given to Maya midwives (1989), shows that the midwives ignore much of what is presented to them and instead use medical supplies (masks, birth control pills) as props and symbols. They are resistant to changes in their way of delivering babies, preferring their own situated knowledge. Foucault suggests that this kind of "subjugated," situated knowledge, arising out of practice at a local level, forms the basis for a potential resistance to biomedical domination (1980b); however, he refuses to speculate about the ultimate shape that any change might take, insisting that while we can critique our system, we cannot be programmatic in our approach to change (1984).

Those who emphasize the misuse of medicine are more prescriptive. If the problem is the creation of sickness under capitalism and the maldistribution and misappropriation of biomedicine, then the solution does not lie so much with changes in biomedicine itself or with pockets of resistance among patients or practitioners as in larger-scale changes in the system. Hans Baer, Merrill Singer and John Johnsen issue this challenge: "attention to the influence of class-interests as well as to the workings of power in large-scale organizations is vital for a truly critical medical anthropology. . . . An approach that is sensitive to these issues will not cater to the furtherance of 'medical cultural hegemony' of the capitalist world system, but will help create a *new medical system*" (1986:97; emphasis in original).

Criticism of biomedicine—regardless of whether the stress is on discovering resistance or on creating a new system—often seems to involve a paradox. On the one hand, biomedicine as part of society (the "medical establishment") is seen as failing to serve the real best interests of that society. On the other hand, the techniques of biomedicine (its science) are seen as one means for discovering these real best interests. In some instances biomedical categories themselves are employed to critique the use of biomedicine. For instance, Nancy Scheper-Hughes uses biomedical definitions of starvation to challenge the misuse of biomedicine to conceal it. This sidesteps the question, raised by those who consistently question biomedical categories (for example, Foucault), as to whether the science of biomedicine itself does not contain intrinsic assumptions about society and about the nature of reality that are, at best, disempowering and, at worst, harmful to body and society (as in, for example, Illich's 1976 critique of medicine's iatrogenic effects).

As an example of the complexity of this problem, consider Jordan's account of the training of Mayan midwives (1989). Jordan suggests that these midwives are competent in their own right, rarely losing a mother or baby; she also suggests a few areas in which their management of labor and delivery is questionable by modern obstetrical standards. Is there a way to take what is "good" (useful? relevant?) from biomedicine and incorporate it into their practice? Who should decide what that usefulness or relevance is, especially as medical standards themselves change rapidly? Is it not possible that a few seemingly benign changes might undermine the midwives' entire practice? On the other hand, can Jordan, who knows, for example, that encouraging pushing too soon may damage the mother or baby, simply consider this aspect of the midwives' practice a part of their "culture," thereby refusing to acknowledge the possible benefits of medical training? In a situation like this it, becomes clear that we are torn between our own belief that the body can be considered part of the natural world, with at least part of its truth discoverable by biomedicine, and our (often also strong) belief that biomedical intervention can be either oppressive or outright wrong.

CONCLUSION

When I teach medical anthropology I often point out that illness entails an intensity and vulnerability that reveal the most basic attitudes of the society in which it occurs. This is what makes medical anthropology particularly interesting. The study of life and death situations often throws into relief issues and contradictions that are less visible when there is less at stake. In this chapter I have been concerned with what happens when we turn our gaze on our own medical system. Not surprisingly, we find that fundamental attitudes of our society and, in fact, our very epistemology, emerge as problematic. At the same time, the vulnerability of self, body, and society to illness engages us, to a greater or lesser extent depending on context and inclination, in the same problem faced by clinicians: the need to act, to provide useful understanding or in some other way to contribute to the alleviation of suffering.

How one thinks of biomedicine makes a difference in medical anthropology, influencing research, teaching, and one's orientation in one's own society. When biomedicine is contextualized and regarded as a cultural system, what Scheper-Hughes and Lock call the "as-ifness" of our "ethnoepistemology" is revealed (1987:30). A researcher oriented to this perspective is likely to be interested in how medicine's aura of factuality is achieved, focusing on historical, social, or linguistic contexts. She or he is likely to adopt a questioning stance toward the biomedical definitions of health problems. Thus Young (1988), for example, takes posttraumatic stress disorder as his object of study, not as the definition of what he should study. Similarly, Howard Stein (1982b) questions, not "cultural influences" on alcoholism but how "alcoholism" is a socially constructed category. Comparative work is particularly congenial to this perspective because movement through time or space reveals the arbitrary and culturally constructed nature of medical categories. On the other hand, it may be difficult to persuade those engaged in direct care of the usefulness of epistemological doubt; nor do problems framed in terms that "explain culture in terms of culture" always make sense to those accustomed to a biological bottom line for research.

The second approach takes the environment created by biomedicine—clinics and professional schools—as given and tries to contribute an anthropological understanding that will enhance the treatment of patients. Often this understanding is in the form of analyses of the meanings patients attribute to illness and of the process of care seeking; more rarely, understanding extends to the meanings clinicians attribute to their work. A medical anthropologist working within this framework is likely to do research on a "medical problem"—a disease or diseaselike entity or a clinically defined issue like doctor-patient relationships. The aim may be to discover certain facts about the problem or to show how cultural and social factors contribute to it. Conclusions are likely to point to useful changes or interventions. The point here is not that these steps do not result in criticism of biomedical practice—they often do—but that they rarely lead to an examination of biomedical knowledge itself as culturally constructed. What is made visible are likely to be problems within medicine, not medicine itself.

Finally, the third approach I have outlined attempts to shift the focus of attention to larger (macro) social problems such as class and gender inequality, corporate domination, and the health-destroying features of capitalism. The starting point is different; the clinic is no longer a bounded site for research but part of a larger system of domination or mystification. The improvement of the doctor-patient relationship is not the issue; rather, the question is how it reflects and augments relationships of power in the larger society. The medical anthropologist with this perspective is likely to focus on an area of social injustice and suffering and show how medicine contributes to mystifying the social forces involved. This perspective seems to require Gramsci's "pessimism of intellect, optimism of will" (Frankenberg 1988b:331) in the face of resistance to change at the macrosocial level. Or, as Taussig (1980a:7) puts it, "It is essential to pose the challenge [of developing a critique] but it is utopian to believe we can imagine our way out of our culture without acting on it in practical ways that alter its social infrastructure."

Since the contradictions in medical anthropology's relationship to biomedicine are reflective of contradictions in the society in which we work, they are unlikely to be resolved through any sort of agreed-upon theoretical framework for the discipline. In fact, it would probably be to the detriment of the liveliness and self-reflection evident in current medical anthropology were there easy solutions to the differences between clinical and critical approaches. Nor can we avoid the discomfort of "suspension in hyphens" when we consider the ways in which our epistemology mires us in the time-worn dilemmas of our culture. However, there are several fruitful directions for research that address some of the problems raised in this chapter.

The first is to press on with the study of biomedicine. The studies I have described here suggest the enormous richness of biomedical practice and history as areas for research in medical anthropology. Others, such as Charles Bosk's study of error on a surgical ward (1979), Donna Haraway's work on the immune system (1988), and much recent work on professionalization (cf. Light and Levine 1989), point to areas (the less "social" medical specialties, the imagery of biological science, recent developments in the medical profession's relationship to its work) that have barely been touched on by medical anthropology.

One promising direction is the close examination of practitioners. Their world of work, their formation of professional identity, and their situated knowledge provide a counterpoint to our already extensive study of patients (see, for example, Hahn 1985a). The practice of biomedicine often differs significantly from the standard descriptions of biomedicine as a system of knowledge, and these differences need to be explored (see, for example, Gordon 1988). In addition, such a close reading of practice is likely to discover seeds (if not a full-blown flowering) of criticism within biomedical practice itself and, perhaps, the basis for a critical analysis arising from below.

Second, we need to shift our perception of boundaries. We can seek out ways to define our object of study that avoid some of the more obvious contradictions in our own culture. This is what Scheper-Hughes and Lock suggest in their article, "The Mindful Body: A Prolegomenon to Future Work in Medical Anthropology" (1987). They propose that we make the body our object; by including its capacity to express and reflect emotional, social, and political life, we may be able to escape the "mind/body, nature/culture, individual/society epistemological muddle" (1987:28). Hahn makes a similar suggestion, proposing that we give our attention to "suffering" rather than "disease" or "illness." This, he says, creates a framework based on a "pan-human phenomenon" that can encompass various kinds of medical knowledge as "accounts for suffering" (1984a:22). These proposals aim to shift our vision, to create a larger framework within which problems of society and problems of individuals can be seen as mutually illuminating.

Third, we must experiment with mixed forms of analysis. Often we present our work in ways that reflect the epistemological muddles we are trying to escape. Medical anthropology might benefit from closer attention to recent work on reflexivity and experimental ethnography that explores the roots and implications of writing styles in anthropology (for example, Clifford and Marcus 1986; Marcus and Fischer 1986). Another possibility is to experiment with combining close phenomenological analysis of individual situations with a "reading out" of the social criticism embedded in such situations. In a recent paper on stroke patients, for example, Kaufman shows how their situations reflect medical and societal limitations (1988). This approach requires a shifting of attention back and forth from the close-up involvement required to understand the details of individual lives to the more distanced view necessary to see the social forces expressed and reflected in them. This leap may be hard to make because of the difficulty of showing precisely how the microlevel and macrolevel are connected; there is also the difficulty of knowing how far to go beyond the interpretations offered by those involved (see, for example, Csordas 1988b). Nevertheless the attempt is worth making if it allows us to be specific about the complexities of the body-person-society connection.

Medical anthropology speaks of, and speaks from within, the complex intersection of social institutions and the bodies and selves of individuals. Our concern with the connections among person, culture, and society places us squarely in the midst of fundamental anthropological debates about the nature of culture and the construction of social reality. At the same time, our involvement in illness and care leads to a concern with criticism and social action. These issues are likely to impinge, whether recognized or not, on theory and practice in the field of medical anthropology.

NOTES

1. All the terms we have for our medicine—*biomedicine, allopathic* medicine, *Western* medicine—are limited and inadequate. *Biomedicine* seems the best choice, though it implies, as Frankenberg points out, "an unjustifiable identity of biological (itself far from unitary) thinking and the medical gaze" (1988c:455). In this chapter I use *medicine* interchangeably with *biomedicine*.

2. The fact that "criticism" is an issue in medical anthropology—named, defined, argued over—may reflect the association between medical anthropology and biomedicine. There seems to be a sensitivity and defensiveness about "criticism" of a medicine with which we (as individuals and as a field) are, to varying degrees, intimate.

3. It is not my intention to provide a classification of medical anthropologists by type. In fact, there is variation within many individuals' work in terms of their alignment with one or another of these perspectives.

4. Many older studies of medicine do not make visible its aspect as a system of knowledge. For example, earlier studies of medical settings (e.g., Fox 1959; Caudill 1958b), while illuminating social relationships and issues of meaning within the clinic, do not examine the theoretical premises on which the clinical practice itself is based.

5. Interestingly Sontag (1978), who has given us a rich description of the metaphors associated with illness, exempts biomedicine itself (as theory) from her analysis. She replicates the cultural assumption that only patients and wrong-headed clinicians have "beliefs"; true science is metaphor free.

6. Kleinman's views of the relationship between disease and illness have changed (e.g., 1983) to reflect an increasing emphasis on the ways in which illness is converted to disease by biomedical practitioners.

CHAPTER 10

NURSING AND ANTHROPOLOGY

Molly Dougherty and Toni Tripp-Reimer

Parallel and complementary developments in nursing and anthropology suggest that the potential for collaboration continues to be excellent. As an academic discipline, anthropology is concerned largely with furthering knowledge and is primarily a theoretical field with an applied aspect. Although major theoretical growth is occurring, nursing is mainly an applied field. Perspectives on contributions of anthropology and nursing to one another and issues of professional identity are discussed here.

THE IDENTITY OF NURSING

Nursing is defined as "the diagnosis and treatment of human responses to actual or potential health problems" (American Nurses' Association 1980). There are important facets of this definition. Human responses to health problems are often multiple or continuous and are less discrete than medical diagnostic categories. Examples of human responses that focus nursing interventions include self-care limitations, pain, emotions related to disease and treatment, and changes related to life processes (birth, growth and development, and death). Physicians diagnose and treat pathology; nurses are concerned with actual and potential needs that emerge in response to illness or health states.

The central concern of biomedicine is not general well-being, or individual persons or simply their bodies but their bodies in disease (Kleinman 1982a). Medicine is primarily (and properly) concerned with disease—its etiology, pathophysiology, and treatment. The medical frame of reference is based on models of normal and abnormal human conditions and of methods for diagnosing and treating diseases and pathologies. While physicians are concerned with disease, clients are concerned with illness (Kleinman 1982a). This distinction defines a crucial domain for nursing. Nursing uses the model of illness and the model of disease and mediates the two. Nursing education emphasizes social and biological sciences; nurses integrate the two models in practice. Nursing deals with treating disease, assisting the client in coping with discomforts, and adapting life-styles to the illness or treatment. Anthropologists are recognizing slowly that nurses mediate the biomedical and client orientations.

Because nurses operate within two models, the nursing role is more difficult to define. The disease-illness distinction helps to show that some ambiguity in nursing results from the differential importance given to each model in diverse clinical situations. When a situation is life threatening, the biomedical model takes precedence; during a cardiac arrest, little consideration is given to sociocultural dimensions. Conversely, when clients experience life changes that accompany many diseases, the illness model assumes primacy. The consistent orientation of nurses is the provision of care that promotes well-being.

A NATURAL AFFILIATION

Nurse-anthropologists identify the natural alliance between nursing and anthropology in a number of ways. In 1968 the Council on Nursing and Anthropology (CONAA) was formed in relationship with the Society for Medical Anthropology. Later, other organizations formed, including the Transcultural Nursing Society (1974) and the American Nurses' Association's Council on Inter-Cultural Diversity (1980). M. Leininger's (1970) work, an important milestone in the development of the relationship between nursing and anthropology, delineates the disciplines of nursing and anthropology and areas of common interest and proposes common research interests.

The National League of Nursing mandates the inclusion of cultural content in nursing curricula. Cultural considerations in clinical practice and research are featured in nursing journals (Chinn 1982; Koshi 1977; Tripp-Reimer 1984c). The fusion of nursing and anthropology (Bauwens 1978; Brink 1976; Leininger 1978) and the inclusion of cultural content in nursing care (Clark 1978; Spector 1979) are addressed in several books for nursing audiences.

Similarities and differences in the approaches of nursing and anthropology are reflected in research problems and approaches. Nursing and anthropology focus on normalcy. Anthropology is concerned with shared beliefs, values, and behavior. Similarly nursing practice addresses normal growth and development, wellness promotion, and health education. During illness, the concern of nursing is in the client's behavioral response and in helping to modify patterns of daily living to promote a return to a normal life-style. When illness occurs, factors influenced by cultural patterns such as dependency, pain, fatigue, fear, personal physical care, diet modification, and stigma are the purview of nursing.

Nursing differs from anthropology in the customary level of analysis. Anthropological research focuses on cultural norms, a macrolevel of analysis; nursing concentrates on individuals and uses cultural norms as a background from which to understand client behaviors. In nursing practice cultural assessment includes an understanding of the values, beliefs, and behaviors of the client's reference group and the fit of the client to this normative pattern. The literature on ethnicity and health is deficient in its explication of intraethnic variation. Stereotypes arise occasionally when materials that describe cultural norms are used to direct practical action with individuals from cultural or ethnic groups (Harwood 1981; Tripp-Reimer 1984a).

Anthropology generally rejects positivist approaches and gives emphasis to the social determinants of knowledge (Young 1978). Much medical anthropological research is based on a systems approach, a view of health and disease in the context of cultural systems. Participant observation emphasizing qualitative data has been the most productive research method.

In nursing research and theory development, the received view holds less dominion than previously (Omery 1983; Silva and Rothbart 1984). Nurses, participant observers in home and hospital environments, learn the intimate details of health and illness through their physical proximity and temporal relationships with patients; this parallels the fieldwork setting used by anthropologists. Presence with clients in intensive care units for days or in nursing homes for months results in qualitative data; the nature of understanding is transformed by the intimacy of the interaction, a function of being there. Similar to anthropologists, community health nurses are part of the natural environment of clients and their families. Nursing and anthropology rely on observation, on "being with" and "understanding other" (Aamodt 1982).

Nursing and anthropology share a commitment to holism. Anthropology, the holistic study of human behavior, offers nursing and other fields information not available from any other discipline. More than other professions, nursing is committed to the total care of the patient, which parallels the anthropological study of humankind. The contrast between the holistic approach of anthropology and nursing is in the level of analysis; it is used to study culture and individuals, respectively.

ACADEMIC AND PROFESSIONAL DISCIPLINES

Noel Chrisman (1982) states that anthropology is solely a discipline, while nursing is a discipline and a service profession. However, anthropology is an academic discipline with a professional aspect. For academic disciplines like anthropology, the goal is to know, regardless of whether the research is basic or applied. In anthropology, theory is descriptive and explanatory in nature. Fields that apply research are more correctly termed applied disciplines, or applied branches of academic disciplines (Donaldson and Crowley 1978) rather than professional disciplines, which have prescriptive theories. For example, the nurse who deals with alleviating pain may choose from several alternatives, including talking to the patient to decrease anxiety, giving a back massage, or giving an ordered medication. Prescriptive theories characteristic of professional disciplines deal with application of knowledge in a practical sense.

In professional disciplines, there is a need to work from descriptive theory in addition to prescriptive ones. Prescriptive theories posit the ways practitioners should act in certain situations to achieve practical aims and involve implied values and goals. Theory from academic disciplines is used to guide practice, but practitioners must select among competing or contradictory theories. Professional disciplines such as law, engineering, and nursing are directed toward practical aims, and they generate prescriptive theories.

Failure to recognize the discipline's body of knowledge as separate from the activities of its practitioners has contributed to confusion about the role of research in nursing practice and the role of research in applied anthropology. The purview of academic nursing is the holistic study of health in humans, including cultural influences; a practical aim is optimizing human environments to promote health. The contribution of medical anthropology is in theory and research on comparative analysis of human responses.

Some anthropologists who teach nursing students believe they translate anthropological principles in systematic and applicable ways; most, however, neglect the distinction of nursing as both an academic and a professional discipline. The objectives of cross-cultural nursing courses are that students make assessments and interventions that are astute and culturally appropriate, such as caring behaviors that conform to the patient's ethnosemantic description of what care should be in that particular subculture (Thompson 1981). Through translated anthropological perspectives, nursing students are taught to understand, and implicitly to accept, the sociocultural conditions that produce variation in life and in health.

Professional nurses must make choices among prescriptive theories to understand and accept the circumstances of clients or to promote change in those circumstances. When a curriculum includes experiences that teach students skills to maintain the status quo and to foster adaptation to sickness, then it makes a political statement. As a discipline and a profession, nursing must choose perspectives that make nursing curricula and nursing practice reflect the social values of nursing (Thompson 1981). A similar point is made about medicine (Young 1982); medical practices are simultaneously ideological practices when they justify the social arrangement through which disease, healing, and curing are distributed in society and the social consequences of sickness (for example, the clients's liability for disease acquired in the workplace). The professional with recognized treatments and associated explanatory model is powerful and persuasive with the client who is simultaneously sick and vulnerable. The Western clinician becomes the agent of class interests, and medicine becomes a means of social control. These points can be illustrated more poignantly in nursing because nursing more intensively engages the poor, the ill, and the dying.

The value of anthropology to the discipline of nursing is undisputed; the translation of anthropology to the profession of nursing is less clear. Professionals function on the basis of prescriptive theories. Theory in anthropology is largely descriptive.

The role of the anthropologist as a clinician has evoked interest in recent years, but no clear direction has emerged. Issues to be resolved include the development of prescriptive theories with values and goals, content of programs of instruction, selection of students, supervision of practice, and professional certification and licensure. The clinical anthropologist may be an advocate; advocacy may result in the anthropologist's negotiating on behalf of the clients without a clear contractual relationship that specifies such a role. The clinical anthropologist may be a consultant, a situation that permits an emphasis on recommending, of allowing the client to select among alternatives (Maretzki 1980). The tendency of anthropologists to discredit Western medicine and to put forward a one-sided client advocacy may be an effort to put clinical anthropology forward as the "real medicine" (Stein 1980b).

The professional, or clinician, prescribes within a set of alternatives; he or she is limited by the institutional arrangements within which he or she functions and within known legal constraints. Much of the confusion that has marked clinical anthropology stems from the lack of recognition of the differences between an academic discipline and a professional discipline. Implicit in a clinical role is dependence on medical doctors and health care management, loss of autonomy, and tacit support of the biomedical enterprise. Future progress depends on clarification of the roles filled by clinicians and academicians in the milieu of client encounters.

Socialization into professional roles helps to explain shared values in the context client encounters. In E. Olesen and V. Whittaker's (1968) landmark study of socialization of student nurses, three questions guided the research: (1) How did the students become aware of themselves in their roles as nurses, students, women, and adults? (2) What strategies did the students work out for themselves personally and in company with their fellow students for managing the vicissitudes of the institution and how these strategies related to the process of becoming a nurse? (3) How did the students accommodate and integrate multiple facets of roles and selves? This analysis of the intermeshing of roles with the process of becoming reveals the complexity of socialization into a professional role, the importance of prior socialization, and the influence of societal values on the process.

Socialization of nurses has been studied extensively. In a recent ten-year period, over 102 research articles appeared (Conway 1983). Many studies emphasize differences between programs and measurable psychosocial changes within student groups during their formal education. These studies provide direction for curriculum content, pedagogic techniques, and intradiscipline planning. There is a lack of studies that evaluate socialization into the professional role after basic education is completed. P. Benner's (1984) investigations offer an exciting opportunity to understand expert clinical nursing and the optimal experiences to guide nurses into this role. The anthropological perspective on socialization goes beyond the educational process per se and is valuable for assessing the role of nursing in society. The study of socialization within careers in the health fields is a potentially fruitful area for collaboration.

CONTRIBUTIONS OF ANTHROPOLOGY TO NURSING

Anthropological theory guides research on client belief systems, care in multicultural context, and nursing as a subculture. The majority of the research on client belief systems is descriptive accounts of the beliefs and practices of specific groups (Byerly, Molgaard, and Snow 1979; Kay 1979a). These studies provide baseline data on beliefs and point out the important differences between the subjective perception of the client's health state and objective pathology that may be evident.

Investigations that focus on folk health beliefs of a specific group (Bauwens 1977; Kay 1977a), beliefs regarding specific conditions such as wind illness (Muecke 1979), evil eye (Tripp-Reimer 1983a), hypertension (Ailinger 1982; Binn 1980), and vitamin use (Johnston and Sarty 1978) contribute to our understanding of particular syndromes by integrating the emic and etic perspective, the importance of cultural diversity when investigating traditional beliefs, and the importance of generational depth in studies of ethnic populations. Study of the syncretic nature of beliefs (Byerly, Molgaard, and Snow 1979; Kay 1979; Ragucci 1981) leads to refinements of the definition of folk health beliefs.

Theory derived from anthropology helps to guide nursing research. Cognitive dissonance, exchange theory, cultural relativism, and ethnocentrism are examples of concepts commonly used in anthropology that serve as the base for descriptive nursing research on various aspects of several cultures. Qualitative methods from anthropology guide research for theory development in nursing.

A few studies (Glittenberg 1981; Osborne 1972) specifically examine the relationship of health care behaviors to other aspects of the social structure. With few exceptions, these studies have little direct applicability to nursing practice, but they broaden nursing research into sociocultural analysis and bring together the approaches of the two fields.

Generally research in cross-cultural nursing results in limited theoretical contributions because few investigators build progressively on research in one or two cultures. Cross-cultural nursing research tends to neglect the comparative theory building characteristic of ethnology. However, some contributions (Aamodt 1978; Leininger 1978) provide a basis on which to pursue the ethnography of transcultural nursing and to develop a body of knowledge on which theory can be built.

Studies of culture and nursing include the way in which nurses perceive clients from different ethnic groups and the culture of nursing. Contributions include the study of the transition from the novice to the expert role (Benner 1984), personality variables of the nurse (Bonaparte 1979), and nursing faculty (Ruiz 1981). Comparisons of nurses in the United States and abroad on sick role and patient behavior (Bhanumathi 1977) and nursing care (Kayser-Jones 1979, 1982; Klein et al. 1978) show that nurses from different cultures demonstrate differences in values, expectations, and caring behaviors. Studies of cross-cultural differences in nurses' assessment of physical pain and psychological stress (Davitz and Davitz 1978; Davitz, Davitz, and Higuchi 1977; Davitz, Sameshima and Davitz 1976) supported the hypothesis that nurses in different cultures vary in the degree of suffering they infer. These studies show cultural variables that directly influence nursing care. Nursing is studied as a subculture in a teaching hospital (Taylor 1970), a cancer unit (Germain 1979), a neonatal intensive care unit (Hutchinson 1984; Myers 1982), and walk-in clinics (Chafetz 1981). The results indicate that U.S. nurses share definable beliefs, values, and patterns of behavior.

A discipline is not global, but it is characterized by a unique perspective, a distinct way of viewing all phenomena, that ultimately defines and limits the nature of its inquiry (Donaldson and Crowley 1978). This distinct perspective determines what phenomena are of interest and in what context such phenomena are to be viewed. In nursing, the theoretical base is partially self-generated and partially drawn from other fields. As a professional discipline, nursing uses the results of research and selects theories from other sciences on the basis of their explanatory power in relation to the phenomena nurses diagnose and treat.

There is general agreement concerning the phenomena of interest to the discipline of nursing. Leading writers on nursing theory have identified four critical elements in the domain of nursing: human nature, environment, health, and nursing (Chinn 1983; Fawcett 1980; Flaskerud and Halloran 1980; Hardy 1983). The way these four major components are conceptualized and interrelated frames the different theories of nursing. However, the conceptual structure of a discipline is subject to change and evolution.

Elements in a discipline can be extended by incorporating additional knowledge or can be narrowed or refined as more precise conceptualizations become possible. Information from other disciplines is incorporated into nursing knowledge and is transformed by the unique view of nursing science. Anthropological theory has been adopted and integrated into all four elements of nursing's disciplinary matrix.

Human Nature

Nursing models describe human nature in terms of individual attributes, wholeness, and integrity. Sociocultural anthropology conceptualizes humans through a focus on ethnocentrism and cultural relativism (Edgerton 1965; Herskovits 1972), which posit differing ways of viewing human interactions and denote the perspective from which characteristics are interpreted. In nursing, this denotes whether data are interpreted from the perspective of the client or the nurse (Bonaparte 1979; LaFarque 1972; Ruiz 1981).

Environment

In nursing models the term *environment* refers to all the influences affecting the behavior and development of people. Here the major contribution of anthropology has been the concept of culture. Basic nursing texts address cultural affiliation—the background from which client values, beliefs, and practices can be anticipated. Nursing has extended the concept of culture in cultural assessment models (Aamodt 1978; Leininger 1977; Tripp-Reimer 1984a; Tripp-Reimer, Brink, and Saunders 1984).

Health
The concept of health in nursing has been enriched by the disease-illness distinction described in medical anthropology. Disease is defined in terms that are thought to be objective and quantifiable. Illness is a personal phenomenon concerning an individual's altered perception of self (Chrisman 1977; Fabrega 1974; Kleinman, Eisenberg, and Good 1978). Health is perceived differently by the client and by the health professional, and the physiologically based definition of disease is inadequate for the discipline of nursing. These perspectives are reconciled through the concepts of illness and disease into the broader construct of health, which identifies areas of practitioner and client congruence and incongruence and posits different intervention strategies in these situations (Tripp-Reimer 1984b).

Nursing
Conceptualization about nursing diagnosis and intervention is influenced by anthropological theory. The construct "culture broker" (Wolf 1956) is applied to several roles that link various sectors of society and to health care delivery. As a nursing intervention, culture brokerage involves the nurse as mediator between clients and health professionals (Brink 1984; Tripp-Reimer and Brink 1985). The unique perspective of nursing is enhanced by the essential constructs of anthropology.

CONTRIBUTIONS OF NURSING TO ANTHROPOLOGY

The education of nurses in anthropology is important for both disciplines. It allows nursing to profit from anthropological theory and research findings. Anthropology benefits from the understanding of health care delivery and applied physiology that nurses bring to anthropology.

Nursing Contributions for Anthropological Theory
Caring is a theoretical construct in cross-cultural nursing research that provides a basis for cross-cultural investigations. M. Leininger (1981) defined caring in a generic sense as "those assistive, supportive, or facilitative acts toward or for another individual or group with evident or anticipated needs to ameliorate or improve a human condition or lifeways." The conceptualization of care illustrates ways in which "taking care of" is a culturally relevant domain that organizes human experience. The concept of care is viewed as the central focus of nursing behaviors, processes, and intervention modalities. Generally the literature on caring is conceptual, but empirical studies on the Papago Indians (Aamodt 1972), Norwegian-Americans (Aamodt 1981), and Older Order Amish, Czech, and Greek (Tripp-Reimer and Schrock 1982) show cultural diversity in the definition and behaviors of caring. Exploration of the fit of health and healing in a cultural

system and the multicultural environment of caring is seen in research on alternative healing systems in an Anglo-American subculture (Molgaard and Byerly 1981).

The role of care is important in the study of culture and to the discipline of nursing. Conceptualization of care involves examining care in cultures that do not include the professional role of nurse. Three aspects of care found cross-culturally are receiver of care, giver of care, and self-care (Aamodt 1984). In the cycle of human development, each person passes through periods in which one aspect or another is dominant. It may be that research on care has been deemphasized in anthropology because males in Western culture are not attuned to its pervasive nature, and thus the importance of caring in social support has not been examined. Investigations of care in cultural context point to its role in promoting cohesion in society, the range of activities that are caring, and the reciprocal role that giving and receiving care has in culture.

Methodological Considerations

Anthropology traditionally is slow to validate theory; it is difficult to do so in ethnographic settings. Explication of research methods in anthropology is increasing because more research is conducted in interdisciplinary settings where fieldwork methods are examined by other disciplines. Nursing provides an arena in which theory and research methods are refined. The explication and implementation of qualitative methods are major strengths of cross-cultural nursing studies. The importance of the investigator's initial entry into the research setting and establishment of rapport with subjects (Aamodt 1981; Byerly 1969; Byerly, Molgaard, and Snow 1979) and the issues and the dilemmas involved in participant observation (Byerly 1969; Byerly, Molgaard, and Snow 1979) are acknowledged.

Combining ethnographic methods with the use of historical materials introduces a diachronic dimension to ethnography essential in settings where culture change is a factor. The diachronic perspective is demonstrated in research on Mexican-Americans in Arizona (Kay 1979) and on Italian-Americans (Ragucci 1981). Ethnographic accounts establish the contemporary culture; examination of language and history provides further documentation of the social history.

A major difficulty in conducting cross-cultural nursing research is lack of precision and delineation of differences in such areas as ethnic identity, cultural differences, and caring behavior. Vignettes, used to differentiate a minority group's normative behavior from the mainstream cultures' deviant behavior (Flaskerud 1979, 1980b) and a tool to compare the perceptions of problematic behavior for use by other researchers (Flaskerud 1980a, 1980b), are significant contributions toward precise work on ethnicity. These steps toward valid measures of ethnic differences are important to nursing and anthropology because both disciplines interact with disciplines, such as medicine, where quantification is overwhelmingly favored.

The literature in nursing and anthropology contains detailed descriptions of participant observation (Byerly 1969; Byerly, Molgaard, and Snow 1979) and ethnoscience (Bush, Ullom, and Osborne 1975; Byerly, Molgaard, and Snow 1979; Evaneshko and Bauwens 1976; Evaneshko and Kay 1982; Molgaard and Byerly 1981). Methodological contributions in cross-cultural nursing research are in ethnography, including ethnographic interviewing, participant observation, and the ethnoscience method.

Much descriptive research in nursing and in anthropology is influenced by the tradition (Weber 1947) in which meanings assigned by informants are described and analyzed. Describing the experiences of informants so that the reader understands how it feels to walk in the shoes of the informants is consistent with the empathic client-focused orientation of nursing. More problematic and less successful is research on clients groups in which the culture of the client is addressed. Difficulty arises because ethnic groups, subcultures, and other subgroups within the wider culture are difficult to describe as separate entities or to define operationally. Therefore, it is difficult to clarify the effect of "culture" on client behavior. The interrelationship between the social environment (culture) and observed behaviors requires intensive and extensive analysis. Culture as defined by Clifford Geertz (1973a)—to consist of a context within which social events, behaviors, institutions, or processes can be described and interpreted—leads to analysis that allows the interplay between culture and informants to unfold. Anthropologists bring this level of analysis to research. Research in nursing that addresses methods directly has helped to push anthropology toward greater specificity in methods (Agar 1986; Bernard 1988; Fielding and Fielding 1986).

Research Themes

Political and Economic Anthropology. Nursing is a discipline represented by women. Among the 112,000 nursing students in the United States, 5 percent are male (American Nurses' Association 1983). In the past 30 years there has been a concerted effort to move nursing education into institutions of higher learning, especially universities. The embrace of academia may be seen as a way to improve social status, employ science to separate nursing from medicine, and establish a knowledge base distinguishing it as a discipline. The higher status ascribed to male-dominated professions suggests that professional disciplines disproportionately represented by women would embody characteristics of interest to anthropologists. Nursing provides a setting in which economic and political theory may be tested. The practice of nursing in many cultures is on a continuum with indigenous care providers, including midwives. Of importance is the attention given to the cultural context of childbirth and the role of midwives cross-culturally (Cosminsky 1977; Dougherty 1982; Jordan 1980; Harrell 1981; Paul 1978). Care in indigenous populations, care providers as represented by women, the status of care providers cross-culturally, and the development of professional nursing in other cultures are areas for inquiry.

Biases in anthropological theory built in from the male orientation of the discipline have come under scrutiny. There is a call for research on culture from the perspective of women, even women's culture as separate from men (Reiter

1981). A number of questions have been raised about male bias in anthropology: How is the enthnographer perceived by the people, and what kind of information is given and what kind denied? How does the anthropologist's own culture act to structure perceptions and interactions in the field? How do anthropological theory, hypotheses, and values direct the search for significant data and the analysis of what is discovered (Bourguignon 1983)? Fruitful areas of study have been the personal strategies that nurses use to manage the intensity of workplace stresses (Hutchinson 1984) and ways society places conflicting demands on women with regard to home and employment (Reiter 1981).

Physiological Regularities. Sound cross-cultural research depends on identifying similar points of comparison in cultures under study. The variety in ethnographic research reflects the difficulty that anthropologists have in agreeing upon points of comparison. Physiological regularities across human populations provide a basis for comparison. Ironically, one of the strengths of the medical model is that it begins with human biology and proceeds to the insight that the human body is one of the most potent symbols in all health-illness systems (Stein 1980b).

There are physiological regularities in human experience surrounding birth, sexual maturity, sexuality, pregnancy, menopause, aging, death and altered states of consciousness. A more rigorous approach to physiology and the ways culture is used to modify physiological regularities provides a useful way for anthropologists to approach cross-cultural research. In recent years there has been some attention to this approach (Brown 1982; Flint 1975; Harrell 1981; Jordan 1980; Kaufert 1982).

The interrelationship between cultural and biological variables may be studied in relationship to the influences of cultural patterns on fertility (Urdaneta 1975), culture and disease transmission (Byerly and Molgaard 1982), blood pressure (Segall 1965), and postsurgical convalescence (Williams 1972). Research combining physiological and social variables has high potential; it combines the holistic approach of anthropology and nursing. Combined approaches to research is one outcome of increasing numbers of nurses with doctorates in anthropology or nursing.

Symbolic Anthropology. The meanings and forms of language attached to nursing are rich areas for research in symbolic anthropology. In Western culture those who care for the sick are identified with a lexicon that is profoundly female. The term *sister* is applied to the religious functionary, and in many European languages also identifies the nurse, suggesting a personal closeness in the nurse-patient relationship (Coser 1962). The expressions, "nursing the sick" and "nursing the baby" denote a metaphorical similarity between care of the patient and nurturance of the child. S. Schulman (1958) contrasted two roles of the nurse-healer and mother surrogate. Healing activities center on those specifically necessary to treat the patient's affliction. In contrast, mother surrogate activities center about the everyday tasks of living that the patient must have others do. Other fruitful lines of inquiry have been investigations of mythology in nursing (Ford and Stephenson 1954), pretending to be the physician's handmaiden (Stein

1967), the meaning nurses attach to their work (Clarke 1978), ritual and magic in practice (Roth 1957), and the social and historical base of ideologies in nursing (Williams and Williams 1959).

THE POTENTIAL FOR COLLABORATION

The striking similarities between nursing and anthropology in research topics, methods, conceptual approaches, and perspective point to a natural alliance. Nursing benefits from the social sciences and anthropology and has emerged with models for illness and health care distinct from medicine. Financial support affects the development of disciplines and the research conducted. Funding depends on the social environment and the ability of discipline leaders to assess societal priorities and influence legislative bodies and funding sources. Medical anthropologists are drawn to the prestige of medicine and to the availability of research funding in medicine. In comparison to medicine, nursing has limited resources and fewer well-prepared scientists.

Nationally major changes are before us. Growth of the for-profit health care sector and curtailment of third-party payment for hospitalization is resulting in changes that affect medical anthropology and nursing. For-profit hospital corporations, which are efficiently managed and provide services to the insured, employ professionals who historically have been self-employed (Starr 1982). Increasingly physicians are employees of conglomerate health corporations and are in greater supply. From the management perspective and in terms of decision making surrounding patient care, medicine is becoming more like nursing. The provision of health services to the uninsured and underinsured is reverting to local agencies, which are traditionally overextended and underfunded.

With recent federal regulations, including diagnostic-related groups, nursing is returning to home and out-of-hospital settings and is resuming a more independent role, though management is monolithic and centralized. The impact of these changes on the public and on the profession offers a focus for collaboration in nursing and anthropology. Changes in the age structure in the United States (proportionately fewer young adult college students and more older persons needing health services) affects anthropology and nursing. Anthropology is attracting mature adult learners and nonmajors. Demographic shifts are recognized as a significant contributing factor in the current nursing shortage. The rise of Ph.D. programs in nursing promotes the development of nursing as an independent academic discipline, yet there will be opportunities for nurses with Ph.D.s in anthropology for several years (Dougherty 1985). The preference for persons with Ph.D. degrees in nursing as faculty in schools of nursing will eventually affect the number of nurses who pursue Ph.D. degrees in anthropology. Nurses studying anthropology at the Ph.D. level represent an important opportunity for anthropologists to influence nurse academicians and for anthropological perspectives and methods to reach an audience whereby anthropological theory may be tested and applied.

Critical issues facing anthropology and nursing are affecting the development of both disciplines. A significant number of nurse-anthropologists are making important contributions to the anthropology literature. The readiness with which nursing incorporates theory and content from diverse academic disciplines reflects its vigor and an opportunity for anthropology to have a significant impact on this young academic discipline. More effective collaboration with anthropology would enhance the quality and volume of the literature and the ability of the two disciplines to adapt to and thrive in a changing societal environment. Anthropology has not seized the opportunity to collaborate with nursing; a closer relationship between these disciplines would benefit both.

NOTE

The concepts contained in this chapter were addressed in our article in the *Annual Review of Anthropology* (1985).

SECTION 3
HEALTH ISSUES IN HUMAN POPULATIONS

CHAPTER 11

DISEASE, ECOLOGY, AND HUMAN BEHAVIOR

Peter J. Brown and Marcia C. Inhorn

Disease is an inevitable part of life, and coping with disease is a universal aspect of the human experience. During the course of their lives, all humans harbor infections by disease organisms and suffer the consequences of those infections. The experience of disease, by individuals or whole populations, is as inescapable as death itself. Yet the particular diseases that afflict people, as well as the way in which symptoms are interpreted and acted upon, vary greatly among cultures. Understanding the nature of interactions between disease and culture can be a productive way of understanding humanity and is therefore an important topic in medical anthropology. From an anthropological perspective, diseases cannot be explained as purely things in themselves; they must be analyzed and understood within a human context—that is, in relation to ecology and culture.

The distribution of disease in a population is neither constant nor random. Both the type and severity of diseases that characteristically afflict members of a population vary significantly among societies as a result of differences in culture, ecological setting, and historical period. More important, within a single society, there may be striking variations in terms of the nature and severity of diseases that afflict individuals of different ages, sexes, social classes, and ethnic groups. Understanding these social epidemiological patterns presents a challenge to medical anthropologists because disease distributions often reflect culturally coded behaviors.

Culture plays a major role in determining the patterns of disease and death in a population, for two reasons. First, culture may shape important behaviors (with respect to diet, activity patterns, sexual practices, and so forth) that predispose individuals to certain diseases. Second, through culture, people actively change the nature of their environment, often in ways that affect their health. The archeological and historical record clearly demonstrates that the environmental changes caused by humans can have profound effects, positive and negative, on disease rates. Although humans have a dual system of inheritance through both genes and culture, it is culture that is the the primary mechanism for survival. Culture is a mechanism of adaptation to environmental threats, such as diseases, that act as agents of natural selection in the evolution of both human biology and culture.

Ecology is the study of the relationship of organisms in an environment. Human societies coinhabit their environment with many other organisms, including those producing disease. An ecological approach to human health and illness emphasizes the fact that the environment and its health risks are, to an extent, created by the culture. In many cultures, people think of themselves as masters of their environment because within the food chain they exploit so many plants and animals as sources of energy and nutrients. Yet at the same time humans are being exploited by microorganisms, including those that cause disease, as a source of food and shelter.

The study of disease and human behavior in an ecological setting is a fundamental task for medical anthropology. The approach contributes to basic and applied research in the field by providing a strategy for answering some of the major questions raised by general anthropology and epidemiology. For example, it can be applied to anthropological questions concerning the interaction of biology and culture in human evolution or to questions of why particular cultural behaviors may make sense and be retained in an ecological setting. This type of research strategy is truly biocultural and can help to bridge the gap between biological and cultural anthropology. In epidemiology, the contribution of an anthropological focus on human behavioral patterns can aid in unraveling fundamental questions of disease causality. The study of disease, ecology, and behavior also has important implications for public health programs. Through the study of behavioral patterns related to the social epidemiology of disease, it is possible to design health programs that are both effective and culturally acceptable. Moreover, the ecological approach can help to anticipate the health implications of technological change and political-economic policies.

This chapter discusses basic concepts and methods in the study of disease, ecology, and behavior. Although it covers both basic and applied research issues, it is not an exhaustive review of the literature. It summarizes many illustrative examples of this kind of research, focusing on particular diseases in particular cultural settings. These examples emphasize infectious diseases for several reasons: first, the etiology (causation) of these diseases is the best understood; second, the ecological approach described here is most applicable to this category of disease (although it is also applicable to the study of chronic diseases with complex etiologies, which are characteristic of industrialized societies); and, finally, infectious diseases still represent the major cause of morbidity and mortality in nonindustrial societies.

This chapter is divided into three general sections. First, we introduce some of the most important theoretical concepts. Second, from a diachronic perspective, we discuss the role of disease in biocultural evolution. And finally, using contemporary examples, we develop a typology of diseases and analyze examples of the interaction of cultural behaviors and disease prevalence rates, from both a micro- and macrosociological perspective. The study of disease, ecology, and behavior remains relatively undeveloped in medical anthropology; thus, there is much opportunity for important research to be done. The anthropological study of disease, we believe, can contribute to both the understanding of the human experience and to the solution of basic human problems.

THE THEORETICAL ORIENTATION OF DISEASE ECOLOGY

What Is Disease?

In the enormous literature of biomedicine, there is no universally accepted definition of disease. Like many theoretically important concepts, "disease" is essentially left undefined and is used in ambiguous ways. For example, it is often defined by what it is not. It is generally seen as a failure of normal physiological activities and a departure from a state of health. But such a definition is uninformative because within it is hidden the problematic concept of normal. Yet it is clear that normality must be considered as culturally constructed, and hence variable. For example, conditions that have been considered as normal in particular populations include persistent diarrhea (Desowitz 1981), malaria (Ackerknecht 1945), the bloody urine of schistosomiasis (Heyneman 1979), and the skin discolorations of pinta (Ackerknecht 1943). "Health," of course, is so notoriously difficult to define that the World Health Organization's (WHO) utopian phrase, "a state of complete physical, mental, and social well-being," has little use for those who wish to measure health.

Medical sociologists have often made the distinction between disease and illness. Disease refers to a set of objective, clinically identifiable symptoms, while illness refers to an individual's perception of those symptoms. This perception motivates the individual to seek medical care or to assume the sick role (Mechanic 1978). A persistent paradox in modern medical systems is the fact that many patients seeking medical care (those who have an illness) do not have any identifiable disease, while at the same time, many people with disease do not define themselves as ill and thus do not seek medical help (Zola 1972). Although the distinction between disease and illness is useful, it is based on a questionable assumption that the biomedical definition of disease is objective and culture free.

When defining disease, it is useful to compare the conceptions of the layperson, the biomedical specialist, and the disease ecologist. Most people, even in complex societies, conceive of diseases as invisible entities "out there," which attack victims and cause discomfort, loss of vitality, and even death. Although diseases can be named, they cannot usually be controlled by ordinary individuals. From this emic perspective, there is little difference between a disease caused by a "germ" and one caused by supernatural agents. In either case, the sick person may be a completely innocent victim of the disease (as in most pediatric cases) or may have partly encouraged it to attack by way of irresponsible behavior (such as breaking postpartum taboos or smoking cigarettes). For most people, the large number of unknown diseases "out there" makes the world a dangerous place. In this regard, disease can function as a symbolic metaphor for social and cultural issues (Sontag 1978).

For the practitioner of biomedicine, disease is the expression of pathology alone. Diseases can be identified by discrete sets of signs and symptoms or by diagnostic tests. Diseases can be categorized, within the taxonomy of biomedicine, primarily in terms of the biological characteristics of the etiological agents. Both the taxonomic and diagnostic systems of biomedicine, however, are based on certain cultural assumptions about causality and the nature of reality. For example, in the clinical setting, the disease often takes on an existence (from the viewpoint of the practitioner) quite apart from the patient; the disease is treated rather than the person. The idea that biomedicine is itself a cultural construction of reality is a basic insight of "critical medical anthropology" (Baer et al. 1986).

In contrast, from an ecological perspective, disease does not exist as a thing in and of itself. Disease is a process triggered by an interaction between a host and an environmental insult, most often a pathogenic organism or "germ." Disease is one possible outcome of the relationship between the host and the potential pathogen. Since the advent of bacteriology and germ theory, it has been recognized that infection is a necessary but not sufficient condition for disease to occur. Normal, healthy individuals typically harbor many different colonies of viruses and bacteria that are not pathogenic (disease producing) primarily because these agents are held in check by the human immune system. Indeed, individuals are constantly being challenged by microorganisms in their environment (Burnet and White 1978); disease occurs only when the host's immunological system is unable to keep pace with the reproduction of the pathogen, a process that can be accelerated through malnutrition or immunosuppression (Scrimshaw et al. 1968).

According to Jacques May in his classic volume, *The Ecology of Human Disease*, disease is "very simply that alteration of living tissues that jeopardizes their survival in their environment" (1958:1). This means that disease is the temporary expression of maladjustment of an individual trying to cope with the challenges of his or her environment. In this model the eventual outcome of this maladjustment is, on the level of the population, a mutual accommodation between host and pathogen.

What Is Ecology?

Ecology is the study of the relationship between a species and its total environment. Most often considered a subfield of biology, ecology deals with the interactions between organisms and their environment on the population, community, and ecosystem levels of organization (Ehrlich et al. 1973; Orlove 1980). Integral to most ecological studies is the idea that the complex set of interactions between organisms in an ecological niche (territory) makes up a system (Odum 1971). This "ecosystem" includes not only natural resources (water and minerals, for example) but also plants, animals, and humans. Two of the assumptions of this model are that the ecosystem is maintained through mutually dependent interactions between members of the system and that the common goal of the various species in the system is homeostasis. The primary benefit of homeostatic balance is the prevention of environmental degradation.

In this view, human activities such as agriculture create imbalances in natural ecosystems. Humans are capable not only of ecological change but, potentially, of ecological destruction. There is no doubt that humans have often been responsible for radical changes in their environment and that such ecological changes have had negative effects on health. But this observation does not require the assumption of a cooperative, mutually dependent "system" in nature, which would maintain itself if not for human disruption. Modern evolutionary theorists, in fact, question whether community ecosystems are a biological reality at all (Ayala 1983). With few exceptions, the apparent "system" may be nothing more than the sum total of individual behaviors aimed at the maximization of reproductive success.

What Is Disease Ecology?

Disease ecology focuses on the interactions between two organisms: the pathogen and the host. Unlike the more general ecological approach, however, the emphasis is not on the harmonic cooperation between humans and agents of disease (Armelagos et al. 1978). This is because diseases are most often viewed as serious threats to human health. Humans are, from the viewpoint of a disease organism, the environment in which the disease organism lives and reproduces and to which it must adapt. The disease ecologist tries, metaphorically, to understand the disease organism's "worldview" and its adaptive strategies for survival and reproduction. The ecological model is much more easily applied to diseases caused by infectious agents than the diseases of life-style that characterize modern affluent populations.

The notion of adaptation is a fundamental principle of disease ecology—adaptation from both the perspective of the disease agent and the host. As Richard Lieban states, "health and disease are measures of the effectiveness with which human groups, combining cultural and biological resources, adapt to their environments" (1973:1031).

Disease ecology is one of the foundations of medical anthropology and is, by definition, a biocultural enterprise, as are the closely related disciplines of medical geography and epidemiology. The study of disease ecology both allows and requires a bridging of the biological and cultural paradigms in anthropology. This approach in medical anthropology owes much to the pioneering work of A. Alland, whose book, *Adaptation in Cultural Evolution* (1970), used evolutionary theory to examine how cultural behaviors enhance hygiene, health and reproductive fitness. While an emphasis on disease ecology may be widespread in the current teaching of medical anthropology (McElroy and Townsend 1989), we agree with David Landy (1983) that the ecological approach has been more an unquestioned paradigmatic orientation than the basis of actual research.

DISEASE AND BIOCULTURAL EVOLUTION

Evolution refers to the process of change over time. Human evolution includes changes in biology, through modification of gene frequencies, and cultural forms. It is the latter, cultural change, that accounts for the tremendous success of our species. An important but often misunderstood point is that evolutionary change does not imply progress; evolution, whether biological or cultural, does not necessarily mean that things get better. Furthermore, evolutionary change occurs only in relation to a particular environment. The classic example of this fact is the evolution of the gene for the sickle-cell trait that was context dependent on an environment characterized by *Plasmodium falciparum* malaria.

Natural selection is the primary driving force for evolutionary change in biological and cultural systems. This means that, in general, traits that improve the chance of survival and reproduction in an environment will be maintained or increase in frequency. Conversely traits that result in premature death or decreased fertility will become very rare or disappear in the long run. These generalizations do not imply that biological or cultural traits are always able to solve environmental problems. It is important to remember that selection occurs only upon preexisting variations of genetic or cultural forms; in evolution, necessity is not the mother of invention. In both biological and cultural evolution, traits are selected that enhance reproductive fitness. However, there are important differences between these two processes because biological and cultural evolution differ in terms of units of variation, sources of variation, and measures of adaptive value (for an extended discussion of these differences, see Brown 1986).

The actual agents of natural selection are seldom specified in studies of biocultural evolution, but there appears to be tacit agreement that the most important factors are ones that cause differential mortality. Five major categories of agents of natural selection should be considered: diseases, food shortages, trauma and accidents, predation and competition with conspecifics (same, similar or related species); and thermoregulation. The geneticist J. B. S. Haldane (1949) was one of the first theoreticians to emphasize the importance of the first source, disease, in evolution. Disease is important in human biocultural evolution for the simple fact that it causes death—or, to put it in Darwinian terms, it results in differential rates of mortality and fertility.

Disease and Evolution: Three Mechanisms

There are three main mechanisms through which disease affects human biological and cultural evolution: large-scale mortality from epidemics, excess mortality from endemic diseases, and parasitism (Brown 1987).

The primary way in which disease affects the process of natural selection has been through the massive mortality caused by epidemics. Evolution can occur very rapidly in the context of the enormously strong selective pressure of an epidemic because it carries the possibility of extinction (Haldane 1949). A well-studied example of this phenomenon involves myxomatosis, a viral disease of rabbits that was introduced in 1950 to the wild rabbit population of Australia as a means of controlling overpopulation (Fenner and Ratcliffe 1965). In the first year after introduction, the die-off of the rabbit population was 99.8 percent; in the second year, it was 90 percent; and, by the seventh year, it was only 25 percent. Fifteen years following the introduction of the disease, the rabbit population was only one-fifth its original size, but the mortality due to myxomatosis was nearly zero. This change was the result of powerful selection of both the rabbit population and the virus. If rabbits had been eradicated in Australia, then the virus would have become extinct there too; thus, mutual adaptation was to the advantage of both species. The myxomatosis example illustrates an important process in which virulent epidemic diseases eventually become benign endemic diseases in a population through the process of mutual accommodation.

The massive mortality associated with epidemic diseases has also had an important effect on human cultural history. The most comprehensive treatment of this theme is in W. H. McNeill's landmark volume, *Plagues and Peoples* (1976), in which he demonstrates the active role that epidemics have played in the expansion of empires throughout history. Such expansion was facilitated, McNeill argues, by the "confluence of disease pools"; that is, infectious diseases were unwittingly spread from state-level societies with a complex repertoire of endemic childhood diseases to smaller and simpler societies, for which the introduction of these new diseases brought massive population losses and socioeconomic disorganization.

McNeill argues that disease played a crucial role in accelerating the conquest, subjugation, and acculturation of tribes and chiefdoms. This historical process depended on the biological transition of introduced epidemic diseases into local endemic diseases characteristic of childhood. In addition to diseases of obvious historical importance, like plague, smallpox, and syphilis, McNeill suggests that less dramatic agents such as measles, chicken pox, diphtheria, and unnamed respiratory and gastrointestinal disorders (which he generally calls "microparasites") followed this pattern. The well-known example of infectious epidemics and the depopulation of North American Indian groups (sometimes before actual face-to-face contact with Europeans) is a case in point: disease played an important role in the saga of how the West was won (see Krech 1978).

The second mechanism by which disease affects the processes of natural and cultural selection is through gradual population losses from endemic diseases. Endemic diseases can have important demographic effects that are often not recognized by the population itself. High infant mortality rates, for example, may be considered an uncontrollable fact of life and may be compensated for through high birthrates and associated cultural beliefs regarding child spacing and ideal family size. The negative demographic and socioeconomic effects of endemic childhood diseases can be significant. For example, endemic malaria in a tropical environment usually has a low case-fatality ratio (approximately 1 death per 100 cases), especially for adults (Bruce-Chwatt 1980). However, because malarial infections are so widespread, debilitating victims who eventually succumb to other diseases, the demographic impact of endemic malaria can be remarkably strong. This can be seen in "natural experiments" of malaria eradication in which health improvements have resulted in sudden and unprecedented increases in population growth rates. Such effects have been seen following malaria control programs in Sri Lanka (where malaria control appears to have accounted for 26 percent of the increase in population growth rates [Gray 1974]) and in Sardinia (Brown 1986). In a different type of study, conducted in communities with endemic malaria along the northern shore of Lake Victoria, Kenya, the single health intervention of insecticide spraying resulted in a 50 percent overall reduction in child and infant mortality rates in four years (Payne et al. 1976).

The third mechanism through which disease can affect the process of natural selection is parasitism, a concept generally neglected by medical anthropologists (Brown 1987). Parasitism refers to an evolutionary strategy in the struggle for life in which the underlying problems are eating and being eaten. The relationship of hosts and parasites is usually one of mutual adaptation through interactions that produce a state of equilibrium. It is disadvantageous for a parasite to kill its host, although most parasites cause some degree of real damage to their hosts, manifested through diseases that may affect the growth rate of the host population (Anderson and May 1978).

It has often been assumed, particularly in the literature of public health, that parasitic diseases sap the energy of individuals and therefore limit the possibility of cultural advancement. This vicious circle argument—that "people are sick because they are poor and they get poorer because they are sick" (Winslow 1951)—is an underlying tenet of international health policy. There is much research yet to be done by medical anthropologists to understand better the effects of parasitism on human behavior.

Disease and Cultural Evolution

Cultural systems have evolved from the original human life-style of food foraging to modern industrialized states. Anthropologists have long recognized a general pattern of cultural evolution from simple to complex societies and from low-energy- to high-energy-harnessing economies (Sahlins and Service 1960). This is simply a pattern of general historical change (evolution) from prehistory to the present that has been characterized by four processes: increased population size, expansion of technology, increased social inequality, and increased transformation of the environment.

Disease ecology and epidemiological patterns are correlated with stages in cultural evolution (Armelagos and Dewey 1970; McElroy and Townsend 1989). In general, food-foraging populations throughout history had relatively low rates of infectious diseases due to their small population size and mobility, although the total morbidity and mortality from disease varied with ecological setting (Dunn 1968). Diseases that require larger contiguous populations in order to be transmitted (such as measles, mumps, smallpox, and influenza) were probably nonexistent until the introduction of agriculture and preindustrial cities. Paleopathological studies of the health implications surrounding the introduction of agriculture have demonstrated that in virtually every society on record, the new economic form was associated with increases in malnutrition and infectious disease (Brothwell and Sandison 1967; Cohen and Armelagos 1984). The high prevalence of infectious diseases in the preindustrial cities of ancient civilizations resulted in consistent labor shortages and population decline (McNeill 1976; Knauft 1987). Today, despite advances of biomedical science since the eighteenth century, modern complex societies are characterized by a new epidemiological pattern—the Western diseases of obesity, hypertension, cardiovascular disease, and so forth (Trowell and Burkitt 1981; Brown and Konner 1987). In short, throughout history, new cultural patterns brought new disease problems.

Biological and Cultural Adaptations to Disease

The concept of adaptation refers to a fundamental process of evolution in which particular traits are selected in a given environment because they increase an organism's chances for survival and reproduction. Adaptation implies that the environment poses certain "problems," which organisms in the environment must "solve." Natural selection is the mechanism by which such solutions are found (Lewontin 1978, 1984). The concept does not imply that the resulting biological or cultural traits are the only or optimal solutions to environmental problems. Most important, it does not mean that adaptations exist for every environmental problem (or disease). Indeed, the fact that cultural behaviors play a direct role in disease transmission and can hinder disease control programs is an important theme in the third section of this chapter.

Although primarily used in evolutionary biology, the concept of adaptation has been central to discussions in both medical anthropology and cultural ecology (Alland 1966, 1970; Alland and McCay 1973; Brown 1986; Ellen 1982; Landy 1983a; Netting 1965; Rappaport 1976, 1979). Anthropologists have been concerned with describing examples of the successful outcome of adaptations on a genetic or cultural level. In terms of genetic adaptation to disease, the most comprehensive work focuses on polymorphisms of the hemoglobin system, such as sickle-cell trait and other hereditary disorders of the blood, which are most likely the result of natural selection by malaria.

Similarly, the human immune system can be viewed as the product of genetic adaptation to disease pressures. A primary biological characteristic of the immune system is its adaptability; in other words, it is a generalized mechanism capable of providing protection against potential (yet-to-evolve) pathogens (Baker 1984). The evolution of the immune system is the product of human adaptation to disease; at the same time, the immune system has required that disease organisms adapt to their host-victims. This pattern of mutual adaptation is an important feature of the relationship between humans and disease (Dubos 1965). From this perspective, agents of acute, lethal infectious diseases are less well adapted to their human environment than the agents of endemic or chronic infections. Thus, more lethal forms of a disease are probably younger and have had a shorter history of adaptation to the host.

Cultural adaptations to diseases include behaviors and beliefs that function to limit morbidity and mortality in two general ways. First, some behaviors and beliefs have preventive functions by reducing exposure to disease organisms for certain segments of society. Second, others involve appropriate therapy for diseases, generally termed ethnomedicine.

Particular patterns of social organization and behavior may have latent functions in preventing the spread of disease, even though their conscious purpose may be unrelated to health. Examples of such preventive adaptations include settlement patterns in elevated locations removed from malaria-endemic lowlands (Brown 1981); storage of night soil before its use as fertilizer (Alland 1970); and traditional laundry soaps with molluscicidal properties in schistosomiasis-endemic areas (Kloos and McCullough 1982). Another way of looking at this is to consider the ways in which the presence of disease in various ecological settings has limited economic or productive possibilities. For example, the presence of endemic malaria may make lowland areas unsuitable for human habitation, thereby restricting subsistence strategies that are too costly in terms of health.

In contrast, the cultural behaviors related to curative medicine are usually the result of conscious attempts to control sickness and death. Yet there is little evidence to suggest that either traditional curative medicine or modern scientific medicine has had any significant impact on general health or fecundity. T. McKeown (1976a, 1976b) has conclusively demonstrated that changes in life-style (such as better sanitation, nutrition, and birth control), and not the advancement of medicine, best account for improvements in health over the last two centuries.

Examples of Cultural Adaptations to Disease: Malaria

Anthropologists interested in cultural adaptations to disease have paid particular attention to the problem of malaria. This may be due to the fact that malaria has reportedly killed more people than any other single disease (Livingstone 1971) and that genetic adaptations to this disease have been well studied. The importance of human behavioral factors in malaria control has long been recognized by malariologists (see bibliography by Sotiroff-Junker 1978). The identification of culturally adaptive behaviors to malaria requires knowledge of the biological etiology of the disease, the social distribution of the disease, and local variation in the ecology of insect vectors of the disease.

The medical anthropological literature includes a number of examples of cultural adaptations to malaria. J. M. May (1960), for example, has suggested that the traditional house type of the hill tribes of Vietnam, where cooking and sleeping platforms are elevated on stilts, reduced exposure of the population to the mosquito vector *A. minimus*, which has a flight ceiling of about 10 feet.

P. J. Brown, in his analysis of traditional Sardinian culture (1981), argues that the nucleated settlement pattern, particularly the pastoral pattern of inverse transhumance (flock movement to high elevations in summer), reduces exposure to malaria. In the ecological context of a nondomestic vector (*A. labranchiae*), social groups that are expected to stay within the confines of the nucleated settlement have the lowest rates of the disease. In addition, traditional behaviors based on the folk etiology of miasma also have a preventive effect (Brown 1986).

C. P. MacCormack (1984, 1985) has studied cultural traditions and behavioral factors related to malaria control in Tanzania. This work has led to further explorations of preventive adaptations, which reduce exposure to the vector. In Sierra Leone, for example, individuals envelope themselves at night, the prime mosquito feeding period, in a thick cotton cloth, which is inpenetrable by the local malaria vector (*A. albimanus*). Similarly, in many other parts of Africa, people traditionally sleep under locally woven bed nets, which can be impregnated with mosquito repellent.

In a different vein, S. V. Katz and J. Schall (1979) have examined the practice of fava bean consumption and its relationship to malaria in the circum-Mediterranean region (where populations have high gene frequencies of glucose–6-phosphate dehydrogenase ([G6Pd]) deficiency). This dietary staple appears to have antimalarial qualities. However, for males with the G6Pd deficiency trait, fava bean consumption can trigger a potentially fatal hemolytic crisis. Through an analysis of the biochemistry of the gene-bean interaction, Katz and Schall argue that the combination of nonexpressed gene and fava bean consumption provides significant protection from malaria death in females.

A final example of cultural adaptations to malaria is the herbal medicines of the Hausa of Nigeria. N. L. Etkin and P. J. Ross (1982a, 1982b) have identified thirty-one "antimalarial plant medicines" used by either herbal specialists or the general population in response to the symptoms of malaria. Some of these medicinal plants have been shown to change the oxidation-reduction status of red blood cells, a physiological condition known to impede the development of the malaria parasite (Eaton et al. 1976). Empirical tests of the traditional medicines, using an animal model of malaria, also demonstrate that three of these substances were highly effective cures.

These are five examples of disease-limiting cultural behaviors illustrating the general principles suggested by the current theory of biocultural evolution. However, this discussion should not imply that cultural behaviors always or regularly enhance health. There are many examples, from both the historical and ethnographic record, in which cultural behaviors function to increase the prevalence of diseases. Such cases represent a challenge to both theoretical and applied medical anthropology.

DISEASE AND HUMAN BEHAVIORAL PATTERNS

As the field of epidemiology has made clear since its inception in the late 1800s, diseases are not distributed randomly in human populations. Some individuals—and some groups of individuals—are at increased risk from various diseases, for reasons that are often unclear. Epidemiologists describe patterns of disease occurrence through space and through time and attempt to elucidate disease etiology through the search for risk factors that appear to be significantly associated with disease outcome.

Disease risk factors are of two major types. Endogenous risk factors are those that are biologically intrinsic to the human host. For example, genetic diseases, such as sickle-cell anemia or hemophilia, have, by definition, an endogenous etiology. More commonly, however, genetic inheritance implies a predisposition to a disease that requires other variables or cofactors for expression to occur. Exogenous risk factors are those that are extrinsic to the body of the human host. Some of these may be biotic, such as microorganisms that cause infectious diseases, and others are nonbiotic substances present in the environment, such as toxic chemicals in the workplace. In most cases of disease, both endogenous and exogenous factors are involved—hence, the notion of multiple causation or multifactorial etiology (Dunn and Janes 1986).

Humans may unwittingly increase the likelihood of disease by exposing themselves or others to risk factors of both the exogenous and endogenous variety. In many cases, this enhanced exposure potential occurs through disruption of existing ecological relationships among the host, the agent(s) of disease, and the environment. In this way, human behavior itself may be said to be a risk factor for disease in that human activity may be a necessary component in the chain of events leading to a disease outcome.

Anthropologists, as professional observers and interpreters of human behavior, have an obvious and crucial role to play in the understanding of disease etiology: they can facilitate risk factor identification by describing distinctive patterns of human behavior related to the social distribution of disease. In this capacity, anthropologists may contribute directly to the generation of causal hypotheses, as they did in the case of kuru and cannibalism in New Guinea (Hunt 1978). In addition, anthropological descriptions of risk factor exposure based on long-term ethnographic observation may be more valid than those normally obtained through the standard epidemiological technique of questionnaire surveys.

Perhaps most important, anthropologists are especially equipped to understand disease-promoting human behaviors in sociocultural context. This includes the distribution of these behaviors through space and time, as well as the ideological and political-economic factors that serve to legitimate these behaviors. It is in this latter capacity—as interpreters of human behavior who elucidate how and why people act the way they do—that anthropologists may contribute directly to medical anthropological theory building and indirectly to disease prevention and control.

DISEASE ETIOLOGY: CATEGORIES AND CASE EXAMPLES

Human behavioral factors play a role in every major category of disease causation, although their role is sometimes subtle or indirect. Six major etiological categories are described in this section, and examples of these disease types are provided. Where applicable, examples of anthropological interest are presented to highlight the behavioral components in the etiological causal web and the ways in which anthropologists have contributed to their understanding.

Genetic

Genetic abnormalities that are heritable or occur as a result of mutation may be responsible for disease if they interfere with the normal functioning of the affected individual. So-called genetic diseases must be distinguished from congenital diseases, which, although appearing at birth, may be due to factors in the intrauterine environment acting upon the fetus (Sheldon 1984).[1]

Among the most thoroughly understood of the genetic diseases is a group of conditions called hemoglobinopathies, including the sickle-cell trait (Hb^S), G6PD deficiency, thalassemia, and hemoglobins Hb^C and Hb^F (Livingstone 1985). These hemoglobin defects have received the most attention from anthropologists, who have been interested in their potentially protective effects against *P. falciparum* malaria.

In the 1950s, researchers began to suspect that various heritable human biochemical polymorphisms conferred protection to affected individuals against specific infectious diseases. Through descriptive epidemiology, A. C. Allison (1954) was the first to hypothesize that the heterozygous condition known as sickle-cell trait appeared with greater frequency in areas of Africa in which potentially lethal *P. falciparum* malaria was present. This association led Allison to hypothesize that hemoglobin S, when present in the heterozygous condition, conferred protection from death by malaria; this association has only recently been systematically confirmed (Durham 1983).

In a now-classic anthropological work that followed, F. B. Livingstone (1958) related the widespread distribution of the sickle-cell trait in West Africa to the history of human behavior, technological transfer, and ecological disruption in that region. He suggested that falciparum malaria did not spread widely in West Africa until the introduction of iron tools and, subsequently, swidden agriculture. The diffusion of the new technology, leading to changes in production capacity and the alteration of the forest habitat, effectively increased the available breeding grounds for *Anopheles gambiae*, the major mosquito vector of *P. falciparum*, as well as the density of sedentary human populations. This, in turn, allowed falciparum malaria to become established as an endemic disease among agricultural groups in West Africa and as a significant selective agent for the sickle-cell allele. In short, human behavior (swidden agriculture), through its effect on the environment (destruction of forest habitats and creation of *A. gambiae* breeding sites), affected the distribution and incidence of not only one but two endemic diseases in West Africa (falciparum malaria and sickle-cell anemia), as well as the structure of the gene pool in this region. (See Livingstone 1976 for a historical reconstruction.)

In a refinement of Livingstone's work, S. L. Wiesenfeld (1967) demonstrated that the particular type of agricultural system utilized significantly affected the rates of both sickle-cell trait and falciparum malaria. Specifically, societies heavily reliant on root and tree crops (the Malaysian agricultural complex) created a more malarious environment, leading to a selective advantage for individuals with the heterozygous condition in those societies.

Nutritional

Disease may result from malnutrition—either from dietary deficiency or excessive (or otherwise harmful) consumption patterns. The most common worldwide cause of disease attributable to nutrition is malnutrition due to inadequate caloric intake (protein-energy malnutrition) (Sheldon 1984). However, protein-energy malnutrition must be understood not only as a biomedical "disease" but as a reflection of social inequality and consequent hunger (Cassidy 1982).

In addition, nutrition plays a major role in most of the diseases of civilization, including diabetes mellitus, coronary heart disease, hypertension, and even some forms of cancer. Yet because of the etiological complexity of these conditions, the magnitude of the contribution of nutritional risk factors has yet to be fully delineated. Furthermore, the nutritional component in, for example, coronary heart disease may vary from one population to the next and even between individuals.

Despite the current uncertainty surrounding nutritional factors in these First World diseases, it is clear that a number of specific vitamin- and mineral-deficiency diseases, largely eliminated in the industrialized world, continue to plague populations in poorer nations. These include the five major vitamin-deficiency diseases: beriberi (lack of thiamin); pellagra (lack of niacin); scurvy (lack of vitamin C); rickets (lack of vitamin D); and keratomalacia (lack of vitamin A). In addition, two of the mineral-deficiency diseases, anemia and goiter (from inadequate intake of iron and iodine, respectively), are found widely throughout the Third World.

In a study of nutritional deficiency and its effects on social organization in the Andean region of Ecuador, Greene (1973, 1977, 1980) has shown how the neurobiological consequences of nutritional-deficiency diseases are related to the development and continuation of a highly stratified social system. In this context, adequately nourished landowners exploit the malnourished rural populace (*indigenas* and *mestizos*) for cheap labor. Indigenous diets low in iodine and protein have led to high rates of goiter and protein-energy malnutrition, the latter exacerbated in this case by the early weaning of children to low-protein diets. The problem of endemic goiter is serious because of its association with cretinism and deaf-mutism. As Greene explains, the large number of mentally deficient individuals in this population has led to a redefinition of normalcy to markedly lower levels of cognitive functioning and an attempt by society to integrate behaviorally impaired individuals into the community (see also Buchbinder 1977).

In a somewhat different vein, anthropologists and clinicians have suggested that dietary habits in southern China may be responsible for the high rates of an otherwise rare cancer, nasopharyngeal carcinoma (NPC). H.C. Ho (1972) first proposed that consumption of salted marine fish may be responsible for the high rates of NPC in Guangdong province, where salted fish is commonly used to supplement rice among the lower social classes. Furthermore, in this region, infants are fed a mixture of salted fish with mushy rice during the weaning and postweaning period, which may account for the relatively young age at onset of this tumor (Anderson et al. 1978). According to D. P. Huang and colleagues (1978), the process of salting and drying fish leads to the production of volatile nitrosamines, which are known carcinogens in animals. In four major epidemiological studies of the association between Cantonese salted fish and NPC in humans, researchers have found increased risks of the disease ranging from 2.6- to 40-fold, depending on the timing and intensity of salted fish consumption (Henderson et al. 1976; Geser et al. 1978; Armstrong et al. 1983; Yu et al. 1986).

Environmental

Agents occurring naturally or as a result of human intervention in the external environment may cause disease. Physical agents, including unusual temperatures, electrical hazards, and irradiation, as well as trauma, may produce pathology (Sheldon 1984).

Of great interest to epidemiologists in the past 20 years has been the effect of exposure to various substances, especially toxic chemicals, in the workplace. For example, occupational epidemiologists have shown that exposure to the dust of asbestos, a substance once commonly used in construction, is a primary causal factor in the development of mesothelioma, an otherwise rare tumor (Selikoff et al. 1968). Moreover, exposure to asbestos appears to exacerbate the carcinogenic effects of cigarette smoking in the development of lung cancer (Hammond et al. 1979). In another major occupational study of Pennsylvania steelworkers, investigators have shown that men who work on the coke (liquified coal) ovens and are exposed to coke oven fumes over an extended period of time suffer significantly higher rates of mortality from respiratory cancers (Lloyd et al. 1970; Lloyd 1971). As with the previous example, coke oven workers who also smoke appear to be at increased risk.

Numerous other occupational groups have been shown to be at higher risk of various diseases because of workplace exposures, including miners, agricultural laborers exposed to various pesticides, and workers in cotton mills, dry cleaners, and the reinforced plastics industry, to name only a few. In addition, contaminants in the air and water, especially in urban, industrial areas, may place the general public at increased risk of disease, although the long-term health effects of environmental pollution remain speculative.

Psychogenic

It is now recognized that "psychogenic" factors may cause organic disease. "Psychosomatic illness" is the broad rubric under which somatic complaints of unknown etiology with a presumed psychological component are often placed. Unfortunately, etiological explanations for these conditions have tended to be reductionistic, involving either mental models or biological models but rarely synthetic models.

Anthropologists have perpetuated this dualism through an ongoing debate about the nature and etiology of voodoo death. Some anthropologists have argued that voodoo death occurs when the psychosocially traumatized victim gives up the will to live, thereby experiencing a form of "social" death (Thompson 1939; Warner 1958; Lewis 1977), while others have concluded that voodoo death occurs as the result of demonstrable biological mechanisms, such as dysfunction of the automatic nervous system (Cannon 1942), surgical shock from terror (Yap 1974, 1977), difficulty in swallowing (Lex 1974), or dehydration (Eastwell 1982). Although the cause of voodoo death probably involves some combination of biological, psychological, and culturally determined behavioral factors, such a synthetic model has yet to be fully developed.

Iatrogenic

With the expansion of medicine, iatrogenic factors, or the deleterious effects of medical interventions, have been recognized as a growing cause of disease (Illich 1975). Perhaps the most common type of clinical iatrogenesis involves the negative effects of medications (such as stroke following the administration of oral contraceptives, congenital limb defects following the administration of the tranquilizer thalidomide to pregnant women, blindness following the administration of antiparasitic medications, involuntary facial and other body movements following the administration of antipsychotic drugs). However, nondrug therapies and even diagnostic procedures may be iatrogenic. For example, the common therapeutic practice during the first half of this century of irradiating the head and neck region for the treatment of, among other things, adolescent acne was later found to be a cause of thyroid cancer in individuals who had undergone this procedure 10 to 35 years earlier (Jackson 1984).

Criticism of the iatrogenic nature of medical practice has been directed most vociferously at Western biomedicine (Illich 1975). Yet evidence from the ethnographic and clinical literature suggests that iatrogenesis is not an exclusively Western phenomenon. For example, on the Guinea Coast of West Africa, where infection with the subcutaneous tissue-dwelling guinea worm (*Dracunculus medinensis*) is endemic, traditional healers' practices, which include piercing the guinea worm ulcer with a red-hot metal rod, are partly responsible for the high rates of secondary infection and considerable morbidity accompanying this helminthic parasitic disease (Edungbola and Watts 1985). Similarly, in Egypt, where the chlamydial eye disease trachoma is endemic and leads to visual impairment and blindness in rural populations, traditional healers' practices may lead to further ocular injury (Lane and Millar 1987; Millar and Lane 1988). These "ethno-ophthalmological" practices include, among other things, scraping the inner surface of the eyelid with an unsterilized shaving blade or slicing open an infant's eyes with the blood-drenched tip of a goose or pigeon feather in order to ensure that the child's eyes are "big and beautiful." Robert Trotter (1987) has shown that the Mexican-American remedies for the folk illness *empacho* (caused by food sticking to the stomach lining), *azaron* and *greta* (red lead oxite paint and lead protoxite, respectively) contain about 90 percent lead tetroxide and are a cause of lead poisoning. Anthropologists have recently been involved in alerting the local and medical communities to the dangers of these two folk remedies.

Infectious

Biologic agents, ranging in complexity from microscopic, obligate intracellular viruses to large and structurally complex helminthic parasites, are the cause of

Table 11.1
Infectious Diseases: Classification and Definitions

Class	Types	Examples of Diseases Caused
Viruses	RNA viruses	Poliomyelitis
	DNA viruses	Smallpox
	Unclassified viruses	Hepatitis B
	Slow viruses	Kuru
Bacteria	Gram-negative cocci	Gonorrhea
	Gram-positive cocci	Streptococcal, staphylococcal infections
	Gram-negative bacilli	Cholera
	Gram-positive bacilli	Diphtheria
	Spirochetes	Syphilis
	Anaerobic bacteria	Tetanus
	Mycobacteria	Leprosy
	Miscellaneous forms	Donovanosis
Agents intermediate between viruses and bacteria	Chlamydial agents	Trachoma
	Mycoplasmal agents	Mycoplasmal pneumonia
	Rickettsial agents	Typhus
Fungi	No major subclassification	Candidiasis
Parasites	Helminths	Schistosomiasis
	Protozoa	Malaria
	Ectoparasites	Lice

Adapted from Mandell et al. (1985)

infectious diseases in humans. Disease occurs when the interaction between the human host and the infectious agent, or the host-parasite relationship, is no longer symbiotic, shifting in favor of the agent. The most successful agents are not those that overcome and kill the host quickly, thus preventing their own reproduction. Rather, all the infectious agents, including viruses, bacteria, fungi, parasites, and several classes of intermediate forms, are more successful as either symbionts or commensals—that is, as agents infecting the human host without causing disease (Sheldon 1984).

The variety and complexity of the infectious agents, in terms of their biological characteristics, their reproductive strategies, and their modes of transmission, are impressive (Burnet and White 1978). Table 11.1 provides a basic taxonomy of the five major classes of infectious agents, with an example of each subtype. Table 11.2 summarizes the major routes of transmission of the infectious agents, providing examples of diseases spread through each pathway.

Whether infection with a specific microorganism results in disease depends upon a number of intervening variables, the most important of which are the pathogenicity of the agent (its inherent ability to cause disease), the route of

Table 11.2
Infectious Diseases: Routes of Transmission

Exogenous routes	Definition	Examples
Contact		
Direct (person-to-person)	Source of infection and host come in physical contact, allowing for direct transfer of infectious agents	Sexually transmitted diseases (e.g., gonorrhea, syphilis)
Indirect	Agents transmitted from source to host via passive transfer, usually on inanimate object	Diphtheria
Droplet	Relatively large microorganisms (> 5 um) spread over very short distances (< 1 meter) on droplets produced by talking, coughing, or sneezing	Measles
Common vehicle	Single inanimate vehicle, usually food or water, acts as medium of transfer of infectious agent to multiple hosts	
Active vehicle	Medium in which agent multiples	Clostridium Perfringen in contaiminated gravy
Passive vehicle	Medium is agent of transmission only	Hepatitis A
Airborne	Small (< 5 um) infectious agent is transmitted through air from disseminating source (human, animal, or inanimate object) to host over distances > 1 meter in dust or droplet	Tuberculosis
nuclei Vector-borne	Vector is intermediate host, usually an insect, which "carries" infectious agent from one host to another	
External	Infectious agent is carried **on** body of vector to host, without undergoing any physiological changes during transmission	Trachoma (fly carries Chlamydia trachomatis)
Internal	Infectious agent is carried **within** body of vector, where it is either harbored without undergoing physiological changes or where it undergoes biological trans mission phase (reproduction accompanied by physiological changes	Plague (Yersinia pestis within flea); Malaria Plasmodium spp. in female mosquito

Adapted from Brachman (1985b) and Evans (1982a)

Table 11.3
Patterns of Acquired Immunity to Infectious Agents

Type of Immunity	Definition	Examples
Natural immunity	Follows the natural occurrence of an infectious disease and involves one or both of host's two basic defense mechanisms, antibody production (both humoral and local) and cell-mediated immunity	Rubella
Artificial immunity		
Active	Results from vaccination using killed vaccines, attenuated vaccines, Poliomyelitis toxoids, Tetanus	Typhoid fever
Passive	Acquired through artificial transfer of antibodies from one person (or animal) to another or by natural transfer of maternal antibodies to fetus via placenta	Hepatitis A (gammaglobulin)

Adapted from Evans (1982a) and Brachman (1985b)

transmission of the agent to the host, and the nature and strength of host defense mechanisms (Brachman 1985b). All of these factors are affected by the environment. Environmental factors, including such natural factors as temperature, moisture, altitude, and indigenous plants and animals, as well as such artificial factors as dams and irrigation schemes, human dwellings, and domesticated animals, may serve to promote the transmission of an infectious disease or, conversely, to limit or prevent its occurrence. Typically the infectious diseases are categorized into two major types, acute and chronic, according to the ways in which they affect susceptible populations through space and through time.

Acute infectious diseases, like measles and influenza, are generally characterized by sudden onset, marked symptomatology, and, most important, rapid resolution, either through death of affected individuals or the self-limiting nature of the illness. In many cases, natural immunity to subsequent infection is acquired following recovery (Table 11.3). When this occurs on a community-wide level, it is known as herd immunity.

In so-called virgin-soil populations (those without herd immunity), acute infectious diseases tend to occur in epidemics, which are said to exist when an unusual number of cases of the disease occurs in a given time period and geographic area as compared with the previous experience with the disease in the same area (Evans 1982a). The classic diagnostic features of an epidemic are listed in Table 11.4.

Table 11.4
Diagnostic Features of an Epidemic

Feature	Definition
1. Index Case	the primary case of an illness that may serve as a source of infection to others
2. Incubation Period	the definable interval between exposure and the appearance of the first detectable sign or symptom of the illness
3. Attack or Case Ratio	the incidence rate in the affected population during the outbreak
4. Epidemic Curve	the temporal pattern of the epidemic as illustrated by a histogram plotting number of cases against time interval

(Adapted from Evans 1986).

For diseases already present at some identifiable level in the community, it is necessary to know the total number of existing cases (prevalence), as well as the total number of new cases in the population still at risk (incidence), in order to determine whether an increase over normal levels of disease (an epidemic) has occurred. When such increases occur over a widespread area (such as a region, a continent, or globally), the term *pandemic* is used to designate the widespread geographic distribution of the epidemic.

Chronic infectious diseases, on the other hand, pose more difficult problems in definition because their course of occurrence and diffusion in susceptible populations must be viewed over years rather than days, weeks, or months (Evans 1982b). Chronic infectious diseases, such as schistosomiasis and tuberculosis, not only lack the short course of the acute infections, but they typically, although not invariably, lack the classic diagnostic features of an epidemic.[2] In general, chronic infectious diseases are endemic, a term denoting the constant or usual presence of an infection or a disease in a community (Evans 1982a).

From the standpoint of disease and human behavioral studies, the chronic infectious diseases are of greatest inherent interest. Although acute, epidemic infectious diseases are potentially devastating, they tend to burn themselves out quickly in populations, before behavioral and ideological responses on the part of the affected population are typically called into play. Chronic infectious diseases, on the other hand, are often associated with high morbidity, which may result in the incapacitation of members of affected populations. Because of their morbidity and their continual presence in the community, chronic infectious diseases may trigger adaptive responses, including culturally conditioned behavioral changes that may reduce, intentionally or unintentionally, disease transmission.

Such behavioral change is most likely to occur when affected populations are aware of the nature of the infectious agent, its route of transmission, and human behavioral factors involved in this transmission cycle (Alland 1970). Information of this sort, usually the domain of Western biomedicine, is not regularly or effectively communicated to those most in need of understanding. Moreover, health education programs designed to prevent infectious diseases through behavioral change have had a limited impact because of a variety of complex problems, ranging from lack of voluntary community participation in prevention efforts (Philips 1955; Barnes and Jenkins 1972) to health educators' lack of understanding of local channels of communication and authority (Hanks and Hanks 1955).

The parasitic infection echinococcosis (hydatid disease) provides an instructive example of the complex behavioral dimensions of a chronic infectious disease. Echinococcosis is a zoonosis, an infectious disease transmitted from animals to humans. The disease occurs in areas of the world where humans, dogs, and domesticated livestock (primarily sheep) live in close association with one another. Areas of high prevalence include the Middle East, the Mediterranean region (especially Cyprus and Sardinia), East Africa, New Zealand, Argentina, and among scattered indigenous tribal and Basque populations living in the United States and Canada (Matossian et al. 1977; Shantz 1983).

Both humans and livestock contract the life-threatening larval parasitic infection through accidental ingestion of *Echinococcus granulosus* eggs. These eggs are excreted in dog feces and may be present on an infected dog's fur or in contaminated food and water resources (Katz et al. 1982). Dogs, the usual final host of the tapeworm parasite, contract the infection primarily through consumption of the offal of infected livestock. Although they harbor the adult tapeworms in their intestinal tracts, dogs do not normally suffer apparent disease. Humans and livestock, on the other hand, serve as the host of the immature larval forms of the parasite. When a human or a sheep accidentally ingests an *E. granulosus* egg, the larval parasite is liberated in the small intestine, where it penetrates the intestinal wall, enters the portal (and rarely the lymphatic) circulation, and then passes to the lungs or some other organ (including the brain). In the organs, echinococcal larvae grow into hydatid cysts, or large fluid-filled lesions, enclosed in a relatively delicate membrane and virtually brimming with daughter generations of infectious larvae (hydatid sand). If ruptured, these cysts release their metastatic contents, resulting in the "seeding" of new sites in the body. Patients often die when this occurs, usually as a result of shock.

Unwittingly, humans create the conditions by which they contract the infection. The crucial behavioral variables involved in transmission are as follows: (1) using dogs to tend livestock; (2) permitting these dogs to defecate in livestock grazing areas, thereby allowing livestock to become infected; (3) slaughtering infected livestock and feeding the viscera to working dogs, thereby allowing dogs to become infected; and (4) treating infected working dogs as pets and companions, thereby promoting the risk of human infection through accidental ingestion of *E. granulosus* eggs present on dog fur.

This last point is crucial, for numerous epidemiological studies conducted in echinococcosis-endemic areas have shown that prevalence rates are highest among groups whose working dogs also function as pets. Nowhere is this more apparent than among the highly infected Turkana of Kenya and the neighboring tribes of southwestern Ethiopia. In richly detailed reports by medical geographers (French et al. 1982; French and Nelson 1982) and anthropologists (Fuller and Fuller 1981), cultural practices thought to promote echinococcosis in this region have been described. For example, dogs are the constant companions of men (who use them for sheepherding and protection), women (who use them as babysitters and nursemaids), and children (who use them as play companions). Of particular interest from the standpoint of echinococcosis transmission are the women's "nurse dogs," which are specially trained to care for children. These animals not only lick up the vomit and feces deposited by infants in the living quarters but also lick the face and anus of infants who soil themselves, thereby transmitting *E. granulosus* eggs from dog to human via the contaminated fur and muzzle. Moreover, these dogs sleep and sometimes defecate in the house, thereby disseminating infective material throughout the domestic environment.

Among the Turkana, potentially infective dog feces are highly valued as a traditional medicinal and cosmetic substance. Wounds are dressed with a baked mixture of dog feces and charcoal and a mixture of colored earth and dog feces, smeared over the face and body, is used to ward off evil spirits, as well as to protect women from the dermatologically damaging effects of their heavy layered necklaces, which are rarely removed (French, et al. 1982). Interestingly, the Turkana make no ethnomedical association between the symptoms of human echinococcosis, hydatid cysts in livestock, and dogs but rather believe the illness to be transmitted by supernatural curses resulting from social tensions (Fuller and Fuller 1981). This situation makes cultural adaptations to the disease less likely.

TWO PERSPECTIVES ON DISEASE AND HUMAN BEHAVIOR: THE SCHISTOSOMIASIS EXAMPLE

Human behavioral factors in disease causation have been viewed largely from a microsociological perspective. That is, the individual manifestations of culturally prescribed behavioral patterns are seen as risk factors for individual contraction of disease.

Certainly understanding human behavior is extremely important for a thorough description of disease etiology. However, the danger of viewing disease and human behavior on a microsociological level is that individuals may be incorrectly considered responsible, even culpable, for their own diseases. Even worse, entire societies may be blamed for maintaining unhealthful practices in their cultural repertoires.

To avoid such victim blaming and to understand disease causation, adoption of a macrosociological perspective is necessary. From this standpoint, disease is viewed on the level of the population, and disease rates are seen as the result of political and socioeconomic forces, operating through time and in some cases on a worldwide level. The macrosociological perspective emphasizes larger social forces and not the cumulative effects of individual behaviors as the ultimate causes of poor health.

Any medical anthropological study that hopes to shed light on the disease-behavior connection must ultimately adopt both perspectives. Unfortunately, the social scientific literature contains many examples of studies undertaken from one perspective or the other, but synthetic studies that attempt to evaluate behavioral patterns and to place these patterns in macrostructural context are rare. Furthermore, the current tendency within medical anthropology is to blame the overarching social-political-economic system for the health problems experienced at the local level without first describing in detail what those local health problems are and how behavioral risk factors may be involved.

The social scientific literature on the parasitic disease schistosomiasis is a particularly useful illustration of this problematic dualism. Furthermore, the rapid spread of schistosomiasis on the African continent today is largely due to the interaction of human behavioral and ecological factors, which must be viewed within a larger political-economic context.

Schistosomiasis (bilharzia) is a life-threatening blood fluke infection of humans. Like malaria and a number of other parasitic diseases, it is water based in that the three major species of schistosomes (*Schistosoma haematobium, S. mansoni*, and *S. japonicum*) share a developmental life cycle in which water plays a major role (Katz et al. 1982; Jordan 1985). Briefly, infected humans pass the eggs of the parasite, which are contained in their urine (*S. haematobium*) or feces (*S. mansoni* and *S. japonicum*), into the water, particularly in areas lacking modern sanitation. The eggs develop in the water, hatch, and release larval forms of the parasite. If the appropriate form of snail is present, these larvae penetrate the snail tissue, where they continue development. After several weeks, infective larvae (cercariae) are released from the snail into the water, where they live independently for up to 48 hours. These motile larvae seek out and penetrate human skin; once inside the human circulatory system, they mature into adult worms, mate, and pass to the veins of the bladder (*S. haematobium*) or mesenteric venules (*S. mansoni* and *S. japonicum*). Attached by their suckers to the walls of the veins, the adult worms, coupled for life, mate continuously during their five-to-ten-year life span and produce hundreds to thousands of eggs each day. These eggs cause morbidity in humans, adhering to the vessel walls and causing damage to the bladder or intestine. After they are eliminated in human waste, these eggs allow the parasitic life cycle to continue.

Because of the obvious human role in the perpetuation of the schistosomal life cycle, numerous studies of human water-contact behavior and schistosomiasis transmission have been undertaken within the past 30 years. These studies, advocated and supported by WHO (1979), can be characterized as microsociological in nature because of their primary focus on human behavioral factors in schistosomiasis transmission.

The first studies of this type were undertaken in the 1960s in locations ranging from Surinam (Van der Kuyp 1961) and Puerto Rico (Jobin and Ruiz-Tiben 1968) to Rhodesia (Husting 1970, 1983) and Egypt (Farooq 1966; Farooq et al. 1966; Farooq and Mallah 1966; Farooq and Samaan 1967). The most extensive investigations were carried out in Egypt, where M. Farooq and his colleagues performed elaborate observational studies of the daily social, occupational, and religious uses of water in a Nile Delta village. Their most striking finding was that Muslims had higher schistosomiasis prevalence rates than Christians due to the frequent practice of *wudu*, or ritual ablution before prayer, among the Muslims. Furthermore, the researchers concluded that swimming, a popular summertime activity for children, was responsible for the high rates of infection in the younger age groups.

Following a decade-long gap in research activity, a new generation of schistosomiasis investigators began to undertake water-contact studies in Africa (Kloos et al. 1977, 1980–1981, 1983; Dalton and Pole 1978; Polderman 1979; Edungbola 1980; Fenwick et al. 1982). As with the earlier studies, most of these more recent works examined the ways in which individuals became infected through water contact rather than the ways in which individuals infected water through urination and defecation in waterways. A notable exception was provided by an anthropologist, Ann Cheesmond, who with a colleague studied human excretory behavior in a schistosomiasis-endemic area of the Gezira, Sudan (Cheesmond and Fenwick 1981). From the standpoint of schistosomiasis transmission and control, Cheesmond's findings were heartening: 70 percent of the urination episodes and 93 percent of the defecation episodes observed occurred in sites far removed from any body of water, privacy being a more important consideration than proximity to water for the purposes of ablution. In fact, only 31 percent of those observed washed themselves after excretion, despite Islamic prescriptions to do so.

Despite the large number of water-contact studies undertaken and the recent major impetus for future water-contact studies from WHO, such studies are limited by their reliance on observation alone. As anthropologist Frederick Dunn aptly noted in an essay, "Behavioural Aspects of the Control of Parasitic Diseases":

Let us consider human water contact, as one important element in the epidemiology of schistosomiasis. Any study of water contact must take into account at least the following: consumption of water (drinking, cooking, etc.); excretion and postexcretory ablutions in the water; bathing for hygienic reasons and laundering; swimming and other play in the water; ritual bathing; health education efforts to minimize water contact through changes in behaviour; technical efforts to minimize water contact by providing alternatives, e.g., bridges, safe laundry sites, and latrines; fishing; agricultural practices involving water use and contact; washing and watering of domestic animals; and travel practices, especially stream-crossing and boating, that require contact with water.... In so far as the programme may require change in human behaviour it will not suffice to have only this detailed description. A further series of studies, *essentially anthropological and psycho-*

logical, will be needed in each situation to specify why people behave as they do, where and when.... Any effort to change human behavior must rest on such studies. (1979:503, emphasis added)

Unfortunately, few of the behavioral studies surrounding schistosomiasis have assessed the underlying cultural logic of water-contact patterns or, for that matter, whether groups affected by schistosomiasis associate this condition with water and water-related activities. In three studies in which community members were questioned about their knowledge of schistosomiasis and its transmission, investigators found high levels of awareness of the disease and its symptoms but varying levels of knowledge about transmission or ways in which individuals could protect themselves from infection (Kloos et al. 1980–1981; Tiglao 1982; Zumstein 1983). Furthermore, as H. Kloos and colleagues noted, villagers in rural Ethiopia perceived schistosomiasis, with its vague symptoms, to be a relatively minor health problem, considering their struggle with more readily apparent helminthic infections, such as *Ascaris* (giant roundworm).

Most of these schistosomiasis studies have attempted to quantify behavior and correlate disease-promoting behavior and disease prevalence. However, few are truly anthropological because they fail to place the behavioral patterns observed in sociocultural context. Moreover, few of the studies successfully bridge the micro-to-macro gap by contextualizing water-contact patterns in terms of political, economic, or ecological origins of unsafe water itself.

This last issue can be raised in terms of water-resource development projects and their effect on the spread of schistosomiasis. Research on this issue can be characterized as macrosociological because it focuses on the ecological disruption and health hazards engendered by politically and economically motivated development schemes. As Charles Hughes and John Hunter (1970) note in their review of disease and development in Africa, few of the economic development projects initiated on that continent over the past two centuries have been undertaken within a preconceived, ecological framework. This lack of ecological foresight has resulted in the escalation of "developo-genic" diseases, including schistosomiasis, onchocerciasis, trypanosomiasis, and malaria.

Of these diseases, schistosomiasis is the most rapidly spreading (Heyneman 1983a), a spread attributable almost entirely to the construction of high dams for hydroelectric power, artificial lakes for fish breeding, reservoirs for water storage, and irrigation systems for agriculture (Heyneman 1971, 1979, 1983a; Scudder 1973; Kloos and Thompson 1979). The expansion of old waterways and the creation of new ones has provided an ecological free zone for snails, the intermediate hosts. As the snail population has spread into new aquatic environments, so have schistosomal parasites and human infections.

The spread of schistosomiasis has been the most severe in Africa, and particularly in Egypt. This is largely due to the construction over the past century of the Aswan Dam–Lake Nasser complex (designed to provide hydroelectric power and perennial irrigation to the country). In a cross-sectional survey carried out in the 1950s in four selected sites in Egypt, schistosomiasis prevalence rates increased an average of 51 percent in three years (Lanoix 1958). Although the Egyptian government has made efforts over the past two decades to control the schistosomiasis problem among the rural population through mass treatment campaigns and mollusciciding (chemical extermination of the snail population), a recent report by Egyptian scholars has suggested that few, if any, real gains in schistosomiasis control have been made (Abdel-Salam et al. 1986).

Egypt is not alone in its predicament. The schistosomal upsurge witnessed there has been repeated over and over again in Africa following the construction of virtually every major dam and reservoir complex, irrigation system, and artificial lake (Desowitz 1981). In studies undertaken in the Awash Valley of Ethiopia, H. Kloos and his colleagues have described the expanding distribution of schistosome-transmitting snail populations and escalating rates of human infection following government-sponsored creation of large, irrigated farming estates (Kloos 1977, 1985; Kloos and Lemma 1977; Kloos et al. 1978; Kloos and Thompson 1979). In Sudan, the disease cycle was established within a few years of the start of the Gezira scheme, a large-scale, irrigated cotton project south of Khartoum (Kloos and Thompson 1979; Fenwick et al. 1981; Gruenbaum 1983). In this case, the change in irrigation methods from seasonal flooding to the use of pump irrigation created more extensive and stable snail habitats and intensified human water contact during periods of crop irrigation. In Nigeria, *S. haematobium* prevalence rates soared following construction of a low earth dam and perennial access to a large body of infective water (Pugh and Gilles 1978). This increase was likely to continue, researchers predicted, given government plans to build more dams in the area.

CONCLUSION: DIRECTIONS FOR FUTURE RESEARCH

The study of disease and human behavior from an ecological perspective has contributed, and should continue to contribute, to the solution of theoretical questions in general and medical anthropology and practical problems in public health. The research strategy described in this chapter has two complementary dimensions: (1) analysis of the social and ecological distribution of disease as it affects human culture and biology and (2) analysis of human behavior, and its sociocultural determinants, as it affects the changing distribution of disease. Both approaches require the crossing of the subdisciplinary boundaries that currently divide anthropology, for they examine the interaction of cultural and biological phenomena from both a diachronic and synchronic perspective. We believe that this "biocultural" orientation, stemming from an earlier, holistic tradition in anthropology, continues to be theoretically attractive and is directly applicable to the improvement of health, particularly in less-"developed" countries. Furthermore, because this biocultural approach to problems of disease and human behavior concerns all of the subdisciplines of anthropology (as well as epidemiology and medical geography), it has the potential to provide a synthesizing theoretical framework and, in so doing, to unify the now fragmented discipline itself.

This chapter on the study of disease and human behavior from an ecological perspective has emphasized five major themes:

1. Diseases occur within ecological settings and thus are context dependent.
2. Cultural practices can directly alter ecological relationships between hosts and agents of disease and can thereby influence, either positively or negatively, human health.
3. Biological and cultural traits with adaptive value against disease will generally be selected for and be maintained in a population, according to evolutionary theory, because they enhance reproductive fitness.
4. Human behavior plays a significant role in the etiology of every major category of disease and particularly the infectious diseases.
5. The understanding of the influence of human behavior on disease rates requires a synthesis of micro- and macrosociological perspectives.

Although a significant amount of exemplary research on the interaction of disease and human behavior in ecological context has already been conducted, the opportunities for future medical anthropological research in this field are great. Of the numerous diseases that now plague populations and individuals around the world, an inordinately small number of them have been studied by anthropologists, despite the fact that many of these diseases are significant causes of morbidity and mortality and are recognized as such by those afflicted, who may view the disease with great alarm. Moreover, many of the anthropological studies of disease that have been conducted to date have not been undertaken for their own sake; rather, they have been part and parcel of biomedical initiatives to elucidate the causes of diseases or to eliminate them in a "culturally appropriate" manner. Finally, both diseases themselves and the culturally determined behaviors influencing them are constantly changing; new diseases, such as acquired immune deficiency syndrome (AIDS), continue to appear. The introduction of new diseases and the appearance of new twists on old ones present major challenges to anthropologists interested in biological and cultural adaptations to disease threats. Nowhere is this more apparent today than with AIDS, which provides a graphic and tragic example of the complex interactions between a disease agent and human behavior within varying ecological contexts.

Given this scenario, three research priorities stand out as particularly important. First, bioculturally oriented medical anthropologists must attempt to refine the definition of disease so that it is no longer defined by what it is not (the absence of "health") or by juxtaposing it as the objective counterpart to the more subjective concept of "illness." If bioculturally oriented medical anthropologists are to study diseases without being labeled handmaidens of the biomedical establishment by so-called critical medical anthropologists, then disease models that acknowledge and incorporate the fundamental differences in culturally constructed notions of disease (including, necessarily, the Western biomedical construction) must be formulated.

Second, studies of cultural adaptations to disease threats must progress beyond the level of description to quantitatively rigorous analyses of the effects of particular behaviors on disease morbidity and mortality. Such work has recently been forthcoming in the study of AIDS with respect to the various practices involved in the spread of the human immunodeficiency virus (HIV) (Gorman 1986; Feldman and Johnson 1986).

Finally, future studies of the disease-culture interaction must begin to combine the micro-and macrosociological levels of analysis. There is a paucity of, and hence a pressing need for, synthetic models to describe disease problems. Most research today tends to focus either on individual behavioral risk factors for various diseases (often based on observational or questionnaire survey data alone) or on the overarching political-economic system that allows such diseases to be maintained (even in the absence of supportive ethnographic data). Unfortunately, such either-or research may lead to victim blaming—if not by the researchers themselves (who may never have intended to assign culpability for the disease problems under study), then by those who use the research to justify their own political and economic biases and objectives. Synthetic models, which examine in detail the interaction of disease and culture on a local level and frame this interaction in terms of the regional, national, and global forces impinging upon it, are needed if disease problems are to be fully understood.

NOTES

1. Research on genetic diseases perhaps overemphasizes endogenous risk factors, and differences in disease prevalence between racial groups are often misinterpreted as being purely genetic rather than reflecting socially generated behavioral differences (Krieger and Basset 1986). For example, sickle-cell anemia accounts for a very small fraction of mortality among American blacks and is a comparatively minor public health problem, whereas hypertension and stroke, both major causes of morbidity and mortality among blacks, are largely related to such exogenous factors as diet, smoking, exercise, and stress.

Furthermore, genetic diseases are based, in part, on cultural assumptions of normality and a failure of the biomedical community to recognize the range of physiological variation among humans. For example, the finding of S. Garn et al. (1975) that normal levels of iron in circulating blood are lower among American blacks necessitated a change in clinical definitions of anemia. This definitional broadening made an "epidemic" of anemia among American black women disappear.

2. Epidemic outbreaks of chronic infectious diseases may also occur following population movements, changes in vector or animal reservoir populations, environmental disruption, or any event that increases exposure of human populations to a given infectious agent.

CHAPTER 12

ANTHROPOLOGY AND STUDIES OF HUMAN REPRODUCTION

Carole H. Browner and Carolyn F. Sargent

Human reproduction is never entirely a biological affair; all societies shape their members' reproductive behavior. This cultural patterning of reproduction includes the beliefs and practices surrounding menstruation; proscriptions on the circumstances under which pregnancy may occur and who may legitimately reproduce; the prenatal and postpartum practices mothers-to-be and their significant others observe; the management of labor, the circumstances under which interventions occur and the form such interventions may take; and comparative study of the significance of the menopause.

Despite the fact that the way a society structures human reproductive behavior inevitably draws upon and reflects that society's core values and structural principles, such links have seldom been explicated in the anthropological literature. There is instead the sense that anthropological studies of human reproduction are isolated from the broader currents that shape social and medical anthropological research. In contrast, we hope to show that reproductive studies can provide a particularly powerful lens through which to view broader social processes. Not only does the domain bridge the biological and the cultural, as does much other medical anthropological research, but it inevitably articulates with a society's patterns of gender role organization and its associated ideological and sociopolitical dynamics. In the following account we describe how anthropological studies of human reproduction can inform larger medical and social anthropological concerns and how, in turn, insights from medical and social anthropology have influenced analyses of human reproductive behavior. Our focus is primarily on women's roles, experiences, and perspectives rather than on those of men. Traditionally women have been neglected in the medical and social anthropological literature; our goal is to diminish this bias. We will draw upon examples from our own work and that of colleagues who employ similar theoretical perspectives. This chapter, then, is not a comprehensive review of the anthropological literature, which instead can be found in Carol McClain's (1982) excellent account.

We first consider the concept of reproduction in its diverse meanings in order to contextualize the discussion that follows. This concept has been inconsistently used in the literature, and its varied meanings are often conflated (Edholm, Harris and Young 1977). Moreover, the nature of the relationships among different types of reproductive and productive processes has not been distinctly detailed. Nevertheless, the reproduction-production distinction continues to appeal to social scientists because, Jane Collier and Sylvia Yanagisako suggest, "it represents a symbolically meaningful and institutionally experienced opposition that our own culture draws between the production of people and the production of things" (1987:24).

REPRODUCTION AS BIOLOGICAL PROCESS

Biological reproduction is the production of human beings; it is a necessary condition for the perpetuation of society. The term refers to the physiology of human reproductive processes, including menstruation, coitus, conception, gestation, pregnancy, parturition, infertility, abortion, and menopause. Yet these species-wide physiological processes are not invariant but rather are experienced through cultural filters. Biological reproduction is inevitably a social activity, determined by changing material conditions and social relations (Petchesky 1984:8).

Research on biological reproduction has been dominated by medical- and health-related concerns, such as identifying the nature of normal and abnormal gestational processes (Annis 1978). There has also been extensive research on the psychological correlates of reproductive disorders such as infertility (Edelmann and Connolly 1986; Leader et al. 1984), spontaneous abortion (LaRoche et al. 1984; Llewellyn-Jones 1986), and prematurity (Fuchs and Stubblefield 1984; Elder and Hendrix 1981). Recent attention has been devoted to uncovering the psychological, social, or cultural factors that may contribute to aberrant reproductive behavior such as teenage pregnancy (Phipps-Yonas 1980; Jones et al. 1986; Ooms 1981) or repeat therapeutic abortion (Gibb 1984; Lewin 1985). An additional large body of literature beyond the scope of this chapter concerns demography and the dynamics of population processes (see Handwerker, this volume).

REPRODUCTION AS SOCIOCULTURAL PROCESS

Reproduction also refers to the activities and relationships involved in the perpetuation of social systems. Following Marx, the term is used to describe the progressive continuity of production itself, that is, the perpetual processes of production-circulation-consumption-production that account for the ability of social systems to endure over time (Harris and Young 1981:114). In a separate but related sense, the term also refers to the relationships and activities involved in feeding, socializing, and otherwise sustaining the members of a society who carry out its productive activities (Edholm, Harris, and Young 1977). More recently feminist scholars have broadened the concept of reproduction to include the entire set of social relationships associated with the maintenance of a society's political and ideological structures and the sustenance of its nonproducing members (Beneria and Roldan 1987; Gailey 1987; Stephen 1988).

Recent controversies concerning use of the reproduction concept underscore the need for continued exploration as to how its distinct dimensions are interrelated and determined culturally and socially. Such studies could profitably elucidate the relationship between a society's structural and symbolic principles and its paradigms of maternity, that is, the socially and culturally constructed forces that shape maternal roles, childbirth, and related reproductive activities and that link culturally constituted notions of femininity and maternal behavior.

EARLY ETHNOGRAPHIES AND SURVEYS

When the goals of many anthropologists were primarily ethnographic, research on reproduction also took on a strong ethnographic cast. Most of the data early researchers collected on reproduction are contained within comprehensive ethnographies, rather than in works devoted exclusively to the subject. Notable exceptions are M. F. Ashley Montagu's (1949) detailed analysis of Australian aboriginal concepts of conception and fetal development and Bronislaw Malinowski's (1932) account of Trobriand Islanders' understandings and practices regarding human reproduction.

Prior to 1970, several comparative surveys of the world ethnographic literature on reproduction appeared (Engelmann, 1883; Ford 1945; Lorimer 1958; Mead and Newton 1967; Nag 1966; Spencer 1949–1950). They ranged in quality from carefully detailed efforts by Clellan Ford and Moni Nag that demonstrate broad theoretical principles (such as how particular birth practices might be biologically or socially adaptive) to superficial accounts like Robert Spencer's that primarily provide a laundry list of reproductive customs around the world.

More recent surveys by Niles Newton and Michael Newton (1972) and Ann Oakley (1977), while also employing a cross-cultural comparative approach, further sought to demonstrate how insight into reproductive behavior in preindustrial societies might contribute to the solution of maternity care problems in the industrialized world. While providing much valuable information on the management of reproduction cross-culturally, none of this work linked the domain of reproduction to broadly determined sociocultural or political-economic processes.

PARADIGMS OF MATERNITY

The proliferation of international public health efforts devoted to maternal and child health following World War II and the second wave of feminism that began in the 1960s drew attention to the reproductive domain as a neglected area of investigation. The best research produced during this period documents how cross-cultural constructions of gender articulate with maternity. Sheila Kitzinger's work offers the first extended discourse on how the experience of motherhood is structured by broader sociocultural dynamics. She observes, for instance, that many ritual dances in preindustrial societies are not primarily expressions of the power of sexuality per se but rather of the power of fertility; successful performance of the female role in such societies is inexorably tied to a woman's reproductive behavior. She writes, "In such cultures young girls learn that pregnancy is fruition and that they will become more, not less, beautiful when pregnant" (Kitzinger 1978:36).

Ann Oakley's extensive writings (Oakley 1972, 1976, 1979a, 1979b, 1980) on the ways that motherhood is socially and culturally shaped have had an enormous impact on the field. Using twentieth-century Great Britain as an example, she describes the multitude of ways men idealize motherhood while simultaneously manifesting hostility toward women and female culture (Oakley 1980:284). Other important recent feminist scholarship on the topic has similarly been concerned with the relationship between women's status and motherhood in industrial and preindustrial societies. Some of these studies draw on the cross-cultural literature to argue that women's universal oppression is explicitly rooted in constraints that maternity and child rearing impose (Beneria 1979; Brown 1974; Ortner 1974; Rosaldo 1974, 1980; Rosaldo and Lamphere 1974). Others use cross-cultural data to offer alternate constructions to our own society's version of appropriate maternal role behavior (Jordan 1978; Kitzinger 1978).

The nature of the relationship between women's status and maternity is evident in the vast majority of the world's societies, where a woman's worth is measured by the number of children she bears; her status may be further enhanced if she prolifically produces male offspring. Throughout the Middle East, for example, a woman is

raised for marriage and procreation, [she] acquires her own social status only by fecundity. ... The young woman [is inevitably] ... taken to be responsible for the sterility of the couple, [and] will do everything to change her state: pilgrimages, magic practices ... and so forth. If she does not succeed, she will have only a diminished status. (Vieille 1976: 456–57)

Similarly, Denise Paulme observes, "An African woman sets greater store by her children than by her husband, for it is only by becoming a mother that she feels truly fulfilled" (Paulme 1960:14).

Accounts such as these blur the distinction between the prestige a mother accrues by virtue of successfully bearing and rearing live offspring and the feelings of satisfaction she may experience as a result of these accomplishments. A growing literature documents, however, that women may derive important self-esteem from performing the maternal role while responding to powerful societal- or community-based pronatalist pressures. In pre–World War II Japan, for instance, childbearing was considered woman's most important function, as reflected in the aphorism "a woman is a borrowed womb" (Bernstein and Kidd 1982:101–2). Similarly, writing of Jamaica, Edith Clarke reports that "the childless woman is an object of pity, contempt or derision" (Clarke 1957:95), and in Egypt, Soheir Morsy found that women who do not become mothers are considered useless (Morsy 1982:150).

The pressures to be prolific that are imposed upon women throughout the world take both positive and negative forms. Analysis of their intent can cast important light on the differential value societies place on children (Handwerker, this volume). In agrarian societies, for instance, pressures on women to reproduce are overt and relentless as a consequence of those societies' enormous need for labor (Caldwell 1981; Nag et al. 1978). These pressures are reflected in paradigms of maternity that glorify fertility, childbearing, and maternal role. But it is not only agrarian societies that manifest pronatalist pressures. In industrial societies, says Judith Blake, "people make their 'voluntary' reproductive choices in an institutional context that severely constrains them not to choose non-marriage, not to choose childlessness, not to choose only one child" (Blake 1974:30).

But not all societies value women primarily for their reproductive potential. Jane Collier and Michelle Rosaldo show that in many hunter-gatherer and hunter-horticultural societies, themes of motherhood and biological reproduction are far less central to cultural conceptions of the female role than are women as sexual beings. They write, "Contrary to our expectation that motherhood provides women everywhere with a natural source of emotional satisfaction and cultural value, we found that neither women nor men in very simple societies celebrate women as nurturers or women's unique capacity to give life" (Collier and Rosaldo 1981:275).

Analysis of the cultural construction of pregnancy can illuminate not only the myriad of ways women are pressured to become mothers but also the broader contexts within which women perform the maternal role. Working in a Colombian city, for instance, Carole Browner found pregnancy to be a time of increased anxiety and vulnerability, for many pregnant women are abandoned by their conjugal partners and they lack ready access to alternative sources of income. After interviewing over 100 pregnant women, Browner found that those who were socially isolated were much more likely than those who were not to perceive their partners' minor health disturbances as "caused" by the woman's pregnancy, that is, as an empathic response that symbolized to the women their partner's willingness to assume paternal responsibility. She concluded that women with very few of their own kin or friends in their active social networks were much more likely than the rest to perceive their partners' health problems as "pregnancy" symptoms, presumably because these women experienced greater economic and social dependency (Browner 1983).

Analyzing conjugal behavior during pregnancy can also cast light on tensions between the sexes seen in parts of the Caribbean. As in the Colombian case, most Caribbean women regard pregnancy as a time of heightened vulnerability. This is because men, who may father children with several mates, are not impelled to support them all regularly. In the absence of a sustained financial commitment from their male partners, women forge extended social networks, often maintaining exceptionally strong bonds with kin, particularly female relatives (Moses 1977:152; also Powell 1982; Roberts and Sinclair 1978). While providing important sources of reassurance and other emotional support, such networks also serve as a dependable source of financial assistance.

Paradigms of maternity may also influence cultural constructions of female virtue. Carolyn Sargent (1982), for instance, shows that in Bariba society, female virtue is displayed during parturition through stoicism and thereafter through self-sacrifice for one's children. Elsewhere women gain important prestige from maternal self-sacrifice as well (Lewin 1974). "Stories of mothers' deaths aptly illustrate this, as they usually focus on the lifelong suffering of the mother, the martyrdom of her last days, and the never-ending admiration such behavior gained for her in the eyes of those who knew her" (Browner and Lewin 1982:68).

Members of societies do not always share reproductive goals. Kin, neighbors, and members of other social collectivities may have reproductive goals that conflict with one another—and with the goals of women themselves. There have been surprisingly few studies of conflicts between the reproductive desires of a society's fertile women and other individuals, groups, or larger entities (Browner 1986). In her review of the subject, Rosalind Petchesky observes, "Utterly lacking is any sense that the methods and goals of reproduction, and control over them, may themselves be a contested area within [a] culture—particularly between women and men" (Petchesky 1984:10). Also absent is an awareness that differential access to a society's sources of power and prestige will determine how conflicts over reproduction are conducted—and even whether resolution ever occurs.

Recent research has shown that analyzing a society's attitudes toward and management of menstruation and menopause can also illuminate the social position of women. Accounts by Thomas Buckley (1982), Marla Powers (1980), Ruth Underhill, (1965), and Anne Wright (1982) of menstrual taboos in diverse native American societies reveal an important new perspective. Ethnocentrism led early Western researchers to interpret erroneously native American menstrual taboos as signs of female defilement and degradation. Yet, in reality, the female reproductive role was highly valued in those societies; a menstruating woman was considered to be at the height of her creative powers. Said one of Powers's male informants, "During their monthly time women *separate themselves* from men. Men must . . . [take a sweat bath] once a month while women are naturally purifying themselves to keep their medicine effective" (Powers 1980:57; emphasis in original). Buckley's reanalysis of Yurok data and Wright's of data from the Navaho show that menstrual blood is a generative substance, which, when not occupied for reproduction, was considered dangerous to other things with creative potential (Buckley 1982; Wright 1982). Secluding menstruating women, then, is not necessarily a mark of their defilement; it can also express women's power.

Similarly, literature on the menopause reveals the importance of reproduction in its broadest sense for structuring the social position of women. Accounts from a recent volume by Judith Brown and Virginia Kerns (1985), for instance, show that once menopausal, roles previously closed to women, such as midwife or healer, become open to them.

The postmenopausal women Elyse Barnett interviewed in rural Peru indicated that they were satisfied with their present lives because of the enhanced status their society granted adults over forty and because menopause signaled the end of women's responsibilities for child care (Barnett 1988:40-41). Bariba women in Africa also experience positive status changes with the onset of menopause. Bariba women of reproductive age are prohibited from contact with medicines and other activities associated with healing. But postmenopausal women can serve as healers and thereby attain status and power outside their own households (Sargent 1982:61). The status changes that accompany menopause in industrial societies are typically less positive. In such societies, menopause often represents not only a loss of fertility but a commensurate loss of life's meaning (Kaufert 1985:185).

The reasons for these differences in the postmenopausal statuses of women in traditional and industrial societies are not entirely clear. In part, the diminished status seen in postmenopausal women in industrial societies reflects the negative attitude toward biological aging that both sexes experience in those societies (Secunda 1984). But while for men the loss of status that accompanies biological aging may be compensated for by the prestige they may accrue by virtue of occupational achievements women are denied equivalent treatment. This large group of studies demonstrates that paradigms of maternity have an impact both narrowly upon women, in societal expectations of maternal role performance, and broadly because women's social position is explicitly tied to the significance of children in their society.

THE MANAGEMENT OF OBSTETRICAL EVENTS

Considerable research has been devoted to the cultural patterning of childbirth. Some scholars have addressed the epistemological status of childbirth and the degree to which the birth process is physiological event or cultural production (Jordan 1978; Oakley 1980; S. Romalis 1981b). Others have elucidated the beliefs and behaviors characteristic of pregnancy, labor, and the puerperium (Mead and Newton 1967; Newton and Newton 1972). These works demonstrate that human reproductive behavior is as highly patterned culturally as is any other societal domain. "The act of giving birth to a child is never simply a physiological act but rather a performance defined by and enacted within a cultural context" (S. Romalis 1981a:6). The increasing medicalization of childbirth in industrial societies has attracted the attention of such authors as William Arney (1982), Rita Arditti and associates (1984), Susan Irwin and Brigitte Jordan (1987), Judith Leavitt (1986, 1987), Oakley (1986), Emily Martin (1987), and K. Michaelson et al. (1988). These authors show that childbirth experiences even in advanced industrial societies are shaped by broad sociocultural, political, and economic processes.

As a cultural and social event, childbirth has consequences not only for the new mother but for others in her social milieu. This fact has received proportionately less research attention than has the significance of reproduction for the mother herself. In the discussion that follows, therefore, we consider how analyses of the cultural patterning of obstetrical events can deepen our understanding of such broader anthropological issues as how gender roles and relations are organized cross-culturally, the nature of domestic power relations, the forces that shape ritual behavior, and the components of ethnomedical systems. To do so we offer two extended case studies of childbirth.

A Case of Protracted Labor in Rural Benin

Adama, having recently remarried, was pregnant for the twelfth time.[1] Because all but one of her previous children had died soon after birth, she was worried about this pregnancy too. She and her new husband had no living children; she feared that loss of her current pregnancy would jeopardize their marriage. Labor began when she was only eight months pregnant. This frightened Adama, in part because eight-month babies are considered likely to be witches.

When her labor failed to progress, Adama sought advice from her older brother's wife and two of her husband's elderly female relatives. In an effort to accelerate labor, they gave her aromatic herbs to smell. This treatment proved ineffective, and a renowned local midwife was summoned. She administered additional aromatic herbs and massaged Adama's back and abdomen. A healthy baby was born soon thereafter, but the placenta did not closely follow. Aware of the danger of this condition, the midwife and other birth attendants quickly began a series of interventions. These included gagging Adama with a porridge stick, massaging her abdomen with a straw broom, pulling on the umbilical cord, and having her squat over burning herbs. When none of these treatments brought forth the placenta, the midwife filled a gourd with water and threw a needle into its skin while reciting incantations. She then instructed Adama to drink the water from the gourd and dropped the gourd onto the baby. The placenta was then promptly delivered (Sargent 1982:111–14).

Analysis. This case contains several themes of anthropological interest. Adama's desire to bear a healthy child for her husband stems in part from her recognition of the relationship between female adult status and successful childbearing. It also derives from the fact that a respected position as a wife in a polygynous household is dependent on that woman's ability to bear healthy children.

Adama's fears of a witch birth resulted from the fact that witches are primary agents of misfortune in Bariba cosmology. Because they are believed to present themselves at birth, any problematic birth, including an eight-month pregnancy, can be a potential witch baby. Since witches are thought to kill their patrilineal kin, any witch birth is of concern to a baby's patrilineage. Although in principle witch births are viewed as acts of God, in actuality, the women who produce them are likely to be blamed by their husband's kin. Because her union was recent and in the light of her unfortunate reproductive history, Adama felt particularly vulnerable to such accusation.

Among the Bariba, a midwife is not usually summoned unless complications occur. Should a birth attendant be needed (many Bariba women deliver alone), elderly female kin from either side of the family may be called. When they have exhausted their own knowledge, it is they who recommend whether, when, and who to call for additional help. However, these relatives lack authority to compel the parturient to comply with their advice. In Adama's case, a midwife from her husband's ethnic group and social network group was called. That choice illustrated the importance of ethnic loyalty in the selection of a health care specialist. It also illuminated the nature of more general Bariba principles of community alliance and organization.

The obstetrical procedures followed during Bariba childbirth are consistent with more general therapeutic principles. For instance, aromatic herbs are often burned to treat a variety of afflictions, especially those characterized by protrusions from the body, such as hemorrhoids or hernia. In the case of Adama's labor, aromatic herbs were burned to accelerate delivery of the baby and the placenta. Among the Bariba, incantations are recited not only during labor and delivery but at other times when spiritual assistance is needed, such as during illness or other uncertain times. Among the Bariba, as well as elsewhere in West Africa, words themselves carry power that may be instrumental in eliciting good fortune.

A Case of Birth and Death in Rural Malaysia

Asmah, a healthy woman in her early twenties, was pregnant with her first child. As is usually the case, a village midwife was called when labor began. When her labor failed to progress, Asmah's husband called a government-trained midwife. The government midwife examined Asmah, listened for the fetal heartbeat, and declared that if the birth were to occur that day, it would take place within the next hour. Asmah asked the village midwife to tie a wrapped sarong around her waist to encourage the baby to descend. Meanwhile, the village midwife recited prayers and massaged Asmah's abdomen. The government midwife then reexamined Asmah, said delivery was not in fact imminent, and promised to return later.

When the government midwife returned, she found Asmah's contractions still irregular and weak. Upon physical examination, she noticed meconium escaping from Asmah's vagina, a sign of fetal distress. She communicated her concern to Asmah and her husband and recommended that the woman be hospitalized. The couple refused. The government midwife then left, telling the family to call her again when the pains became stronger.

When the government midwife was called again several hours later, a ritual specialist in difficult labors was already there. He recited Koranic verses, but to no avail. A second ritual specialist, who recited native incantations and threw rice to repel noxious spiritual presences, was then called.

Eventually Asmah delivered an underdeveloped dead infant whose umbilical cord was looped three times around its neck. Relatives in attendance consoled one another saying, "It's nothing, it's all right." No visible signs of emotion were displayed by anyone at the sight of the dead child, nor did Asmah express pain, discomfort, or distress during her entire 22-hour labor (Laderman 1983:159–66).

Analysis. This case illustrates principles fundamental to Malay culture and social organization. Two of the most prominent concern the importance of female modesty and emotional restraint. "The Malay womanly ideal is circumspect, modest, and deferent, and those who deviate too far from the norm run the risk of divorce" (Laderman 1987:295). During parturition, Asmah's attendants respected her modesty by keeping the doors and windows shut and putting mats against the walls so that outsiders could not see in. It was only as the labor grew unusually protracted that the midwife suggested opening the windows and doors. This was because considerations of feminine modesty "outweigh the possible benefits that a magical correspondence between open windows and open wombs might confer" except in the case of especially threatening circumstances (Laderman 1983:165)

Display of strong emotions is strongly discouraged throughout rural Malaysia (Laderman 1983:166). During one labor that Carol Laderman observed, a young woman about to deliver her first child was slapped lightly on the face when she cried out. Those in attendance admonished her, asking rhetorically if she had no shame, to cry out in that manner. Laderman subsequently sought to determine whether the villagers with whom she worked believed that strong emotional expression could negatively affect physical health. "I never have any strong emotions," she was almost invariably told. Emotional restraint was plainly evident in both Asmah's behavior and that of all others present during delivery.

The treatment practices used during Asmah's parturition are consistent with the larger body of Malay ritual practice in which sympathetic magic as well as humoral reasoning is a therapeutic principle. Loosening the hair of the laboring woman and opening the cupboards, windows, and doors are two strategies most commonly employed. Recitation of incantations is another prominent therapeutic intervention. It is used during childbirth to enhance the safety of mother and child. These interventions are designed to evoke a more harmonious relationship between the laboring woman and the universe and to distract the woman from her pain (Laderman 1987a:296).

The preceding cases illustrate how analyses of the management of obstetrical events can increase our understanding of broader cultural and social principles. There are additional principles that can also be elucidated through interpretations of obstetrical events. For example, analyzing the roles and activities of obstetrical care providers can cast light on the nature of occupational specializations in a society (Browner 1989a; Cosminsky 1976; McClain 1989; Paul 1975; Sargent 1982:44–46). Similarly, examining the allocation of responsibility and authority during labor and delivery can provide insight into a society's broader patterns of stratification. The differential involvement of women and men during par-

DECISION MODELS AND COGNITION

There are two bodies of literature pertaining to the anthropology of reproduction that have enhanced the comparative study of belief and cognition. The first concerns "folk" concepts of ethnophysiology and their relationship to reproductive, therapeutic, and ritual practice. The second deals with the structure of decision making and the considerations that inform reproductive choices.

Some of the earliest ethnological research sought to articulate ethnophysiological understandings of human reproductive processes. While beliefs about conception are well represented in that literature, far less attention has been paid to menstruation, perceptions of pregnancy (cf. Jordan 1977; Browner 1980), gestation and fetal development, and menopause.

Most early ethnographers devoted only a sentence or two to the ethnophysiology of reproduction. Ashley Montagu's (1949) classic description of the embryological beliefs of primitive peoples and ancient societies through the eighteenth century is a rare exception; it provides remarkable detail about emic understandings of conception, fetal development, and embryology. Margaret Mead's work is another rare exception. Even Montagu and Mead, however, fail to provide the depth of detail seen in subsequent research on the subject.

Works by Margarita Kay (1977a), Arthur Rubel and associates (1975), Michelle Shedlin and Paula Hollerbach (1978), Clarissa Scott (1975), Loudell Snow (1974), Gisele Tucker (1986), and Carol McClain (1975), among others, demonstrate that many cultures possess well-developed understandings about conception, gestation, and parturition. To date, little of this work has considered the relationship between ethnophysiological understandings and those of biomedicine (Browner et al. 1988). Instead, however, some anthropologists have shown that analyzing folk concepts of reproduction can have important practical applications for understanding reproduction behavior. McClain, for example, found that many of the Mexican women with whom she worked refused to accept injections during pregnancy because they understood that injections cause the cervix to close. Because those women believe that the fetus breathes through its mother's cervix, they decline injections rather than jeopardize the well-being of their fetus (McClain 1975). A comparative study of indigenous fertility regulating practices in seven societies (Newman 1985) details relationships between ethnophysiological concepts and fertility regulating behavior. Interestingly, many of the herbal remedies women use for the management of pregnancy and the treatment of female reproductive health problems appear in several societies, with similar ethnophysiological rationales often provided for the selection of those particular substances.

Research on the ethnophysiology of reproduction holds the potential for illuminating more general ethnomedical principles, but to date little work has elucidated the connections. Instead, researchers have shown how folk concepts of reproduction are informed by the broader ethnomedical systems of which they are part (Kay 1982; Newman 1985). One exception is Browner's (1985a) article on the criteria used in an indigenous Mexican village for selecting herbal remedies for reproduction and reproduction health. She shows that within the domain of reproduction, the hot-cold theory is subsumed by a broader set of therapeutic practices intended to help the body expel or retain certain substances.[2] She suggests that these more comprehensive folk principles of expulsion and retention may also be fundamental to health care concepts and practices beyond the reproductive domain.

Laderman's account of Malay ethnophysiology of pregnancy, childbirth, and the postpartum period is valuable for the insight it provides not only into general Malay therapeutic understandings but also into core concepts of Malaysian culture.

The birth of a baby is much more than just a physiological event. . . . It is also the most important rite of passage, requiring spiritual prophylaxis and ritual expertise. . . . Cultural signposts furnish [Malay women] and their husbands with information about the advantages and risks of following subsidiary paths, or even leaving the highroad altogether. . . . Some of these signposts are phrased in humoral terms and others are not; theirs is a metalanguage, the language of Malay *adat*, custom in its widest and deepest sense, embodying all the shared norms, values, beliefs and traditions of the society. (1987b:359)

The second body of literature that has informed cognitive research focuses on reproductive decision making and the considerations that shape fertility-related behavior. There has been extensive research by anthropologists and researchers from other disciplines designed to investigate the social, psychological, and cultural dimensions of population growth and the reasons poor women throughout the world often seem reluctant to use modern contraceptives.

Much of this work consists of cross-cultural surveys designed to determine women's (and occasionally men's) knowledge, attitudes, and practices with regard to modern birth control techniques (see Berelson 1966). A few in-depth studies have looked at the relationship between birth control methods or the organization of contraceptive clinics, and women's decisions about whether to use contraceptives (Coleman 1983; Marshall 1977; Polgar 1971; Polgar and Marshall 1976; Scrimshaw 1980). Additional research has focused on the considerations women take into account in deciding whether to terminate a pregnancy (Browner 1976, 1979; Friedlander et al. 1984; Lee 1969; Luker 1975). Other aspects of reproductive decision making have been less fully studied by anthropologists, although demographers have developed a considerable literature on the subject (see Handwerker, this volume).

Given the extensive ethnographic literature on medical choice (see Sargent 1982, 1989), the scant anthropological contribution to the study of reproductive decision making is surprising. One interesting study that does address this issue is Bonnie Nardi's analysis of reproductive decision making in Western Samoa. Nardi articulates how the value of child labor, old age security, husband's approval, and the intrinsic desirability of children influence women's fertility decision-making behavior (Nardi 1983).

Other recent cross-cultural research has been devoted to analyzing factors that influence women's decisions about the use of obstetrical services. McClain (1985) investigated how a group of California women decided whether to attempt trial of labor instead of elective repeat cesarean section. She found that the women did not assess their potential delivery outcomes in strict probabilistic terms. Instead, they based their decisions on their previous childbirth experiences and their expectations concerning the two types of delivery. Goforth's (1988) research on women's choice of birth attendants in a Yucatec Maya community demonstrated that access to economic resources was the best predictor of pregnant women's decisions to use traditional or biomedical obstetrical practitioners. Sargent's (1989) study of obstetrical decision making in rural and urban Benin describes how Bariba women's diverse objectives and goals, most of which are nonmedical in nature, lead them to make particular obstetrical choices.

One strength these studies share is the fact that their implications extend beyond the reproductive domain. Each author has explicitly delineated her study's larger significance, either for decision theory or social organization more generally. We are encouraged by this trend and hope that it stimulates additional research linking reproductive behavior to broader social processes.

DIRECTIONS FOR FUTURE RESEARCH

There are several directions that anthropological research on the patterning of reproduction could profitably take. Still urgently needed is a fuller understanding of how ethnicity and social class mold women's wishes, expectations, and behavior within the reproductive domain. This will move us toward more accurately articulating the multiple paradigms of maternity held by different groups within heterogeneous societies. Until now, where paradigms of maternity have been detailed, researchers have described unitary models rather than ones that reflect the diversity of women's and men's experiences, attitudes, and values. It will be through rich ethnographic data of the sort we have discussed in this chapter that we will come to understand how ethnographic research can compellingly elucidate diverse paradigms of maternity and their relationships to broader societal principles and structural processes.

To their detriment, the early ethnographic studies generally ignored reproductive issues or failed to provide detailed accounts of women's roles, activities, and attitudes within the reproductive domain. In contrast, most recent analyses of reproduction totally neglect men. Exceptions such as C. Romalis's (1981) description of a father's role in labor and delivery, V. Eban's (1982) work on the activities of male reproductive specialists, and two recent studies of men's adaptation to the paternal role (Briesemeister and Haines 1988; Whiteford and Sharinus 1988) illustrate an encouraging trend.

Human reproductive behavior is socially constructed and formed by political and economic processes. Many anthropologists and others who study human reproductive behavior are concerned about the development and dissemination of new technologies for prenatal testing, fertility enhancement, and selective reproduction. In many parts of America, ultrasonography is now a routine part of prenatal care; other forms of prenatal screening are also quickly becoming the norm. But since most genetic disorders have neither treatment nor cure, selective abortion is the only means to reduce their impact. This has made the technology controversial, particularly for Catholics and others who advocate fetuses' "rights to life" (Lawler 1988; Peel 1985). Feminist scholars and advocates for the handicapped are also concerned about technologies that can be selectively used to abort fetuses by sex or for other reasons (Arditti et al. 1984; Callahan 1986; Corea et al. 1987; Overall 1987; Spallone and Steinberg 1987; Stanworth 1987). Meanwhile, progress in developing new techniques to treat infertility holds the potential for dramatically redefining American paradigms of maternity (Blank 1984; Overall 1987).

But despite these technologies' actual or potential impact, there are still very few firsthand data on what users think and feel about them and the associated issues their widespread use will inevitably entail. Rayna Rapp's (1987, 1988b, n.d.) work on amniocentesis is an important exception in its analysis of the meaning of the procedure to women who choose it and in its consideration of how race and social class help to shape that experience. Barbara Rothman (1986, 1988) deals with related issues in her penetrating comparative study of women who accepted and those who refused the amniocentesis procedure. But as both the historical and cross-cultural literature unequivocally show, neither the use of technology to influence reproductive outcomes nor concern about the meanings of such interventions is new (Devereux 1976; Himes 1970; Lorimer 1958; McLaren 1984). What is new are the implications for totally reshaping human society that these types of technology hold.

Throughout contemporary society, these wide-ranging technological developments and pressing debates will have profound implications for the future of motherhood and the status, role, and experience of all women. The insight anthropologists could contribute by virtue of their cross-cultural knowledge and relativistic perspective can be crucial in charting these debates' future course. Exciting new research by Lynn Morgan (1989) on cross-cultural perceptions of when human life begins and Anna Tsing (n.d.) on the cultural meanings of infanticide are examples of directions such work could profitably take. We began this chapter by showing that analyzing patterns of human reproductive behavior revealed latent dimensions of broader cultural and sociopolitical dynamics. Similarly, studying the characteristics and shape of reproductive activities as we move toward future society will cast important light on social organization, gender politics, and symbol and ritual.

NOTES

We thank Ellen Lewin and Carol Laderman for their helpful comments on an earlier draft of this chapter.

1. All proper names are pseudonyms.
2. This theory, common in many parts of the world, holds that the essence of good health is somatic equilibrium, which is achieved by balancing intakes of heat and coldness that enter the body. Hot and cold refer to substances' metaphorical qualities; they are not necessarily equivalent to physical temperature.

CHAPTER 13

DRUG STUDIES

Linda A. Bennett and Paul W. Cook, Jr.

A penchant for challenging common assumptions about substance use and abuse runs through anthropological work on alcohol and other drugs (Agar et al. 1981; Douglas 1987; Dreher 1984c; Heath 1987b; Leland 1976; MacAndrew and Edgerton 1969). In this chapter, we delineate this theme by highlighting a select number of areas where the uniqueness of anthropological contributions to understanding drug use and abuse is clearly seen. We have not reviewed the entire field of anthropological research in the area; given the enormous body of literature, especially in alcohol studies, such a review would constitute a project beyond the scope of this book. Furthermore, several excellent reviews have been published on specific topics within this research domain. Instead, we have selectively chosen a limited number of issues in anthropological drug research that are pertinent to medical anthropology generally.

Because anthropologists have a tendency to take a different tack in approaching studies of substance use and abuse, their work is often controversial to policymakers and treatment providers. Controversy—and sometimes skepticism—frequently surround the approach and methods applied (Bennett 1988; Heath 1985; Room 1984, Stall 1985), interpretation of data (Fisher 1987; Schaefer 1981), and recommendations for policy (Dreher 1984c, Levy and Kunitz 1981). In certain instances, their orientation is congruent with that of colleagues in other disciplines. In recent years, in fact, some anthropologists have created or joined interdisciplinary research groups and are working as team researchers (Marshall 1982, 1983: 11; True 1984:95; Bennett et al. 1987; Brown et al. 1988; Hall et al. 1983; Lex et al. 1984; Marshall 1982).

Anthropological interest in studies of drug use and abuse has been apparent for several decades (Heath 1976; Marshall 1987). Until the 1970s, however, most of this research was a by-product of broader ethnographic studies of small societies in Latin America, Africa, Oceania, and the North American Indian and

Eskimo tribes. In this tradition, data collected on the use of mind altering substances formed one component of an overall study, such as noting the use of plants for medicinal purposes or describing curing ceremonies where sacred plants were employed. A basic theme in anthropological drug studies developed that stresses the importance of viewing drug use practices and beliefs as part of broader sociocultural patterns.

Cross-cultural research on substances has been conducted through the use of data housed in the Human Relations Area Files (Barry 1982; Horton 1943; Narroll 1983; Schaefer 1976), by in-depth analysis of available ethnographic data (MacAndrew and Edgerton 1969), through special conferences in which drug use data were presented for a variety of societies, communities, or ethnic groups (Bennett and Ames 1985; Everett et al. 1976; Marshall 1982), or through projects in which the anthropologists conducted a controlled comparison or contrasted different drug use traditions cross-culturally (Bunzel 1940, 1976; Levy and Kunitz 1974).

In addition, by the 1960s several articles had been published in which alcohol data from wider ethnographic research were specifically highlighted (Doughty 1971; Holmberg 1971; and Simmons 1968). Significantly, these anthropologists did not explicitly identify themselves as alcohol researchers, though they had collected and reported data that deepened our understanding of the role of alcohol use within the wider sociocultural contexts of these Peruvian communities.

Thus, it is fair to conclude that as of the early 1970s, anthropology had not yet developed an explicit drug research tradition, especially with respect to abuse of drugs (Heath 1976, 1987b). With increased funding available for such studies and with the expansion of applied anthropology, the situation has changed dramatically over the past two decades. Today in the United States alone, at least sixty anthropologists would identify themselves as students of alcohol and another twenty as students of other drugs (based upon information from the membership of the Alcohol and Drug Study Group and from publications). The field of drug studies has developed into several subspecializations among anthropologists concerned with family, AIDS, treatment, and special populations (such as North American Indians, Hispanic groups, black Americans, the working class, and women). During the past decade, several doctoral dissertations have been written on alcohol and culture (Ames 1982; Gilbert 1980; P. Marshall 1982).

Up to the present, anthropological discussions of substance use and abuse are almost always treated separately with respect to alcohol and other drugs. This tendency reflects wider patterns in national and international policy and research, as well as treatment of substance abuse. For example, the National Institute on Alcohol Abuse and Alcoholism was established in 1970 separate from the National Institute on Drug Abuse, and the World Health Organization continues to separate alcohol from the "illicit" drugs in most of its working conferences and publications. In anthropology, it is also rare for more than one drug to be encompassed in anthropological studies and publications although there are exceptions (Agar et al. 1981; Douglas 1987; Lex et al. 1984, 1986, 1988, Marshall 1987; Strug et al. 1985).

Anthropologists in the substance use-abuse field have focused primarily on studies of alcohol, reflecting, in part, the relative order of usage of particular drugs throughout the world: first, ethanol; second, nicotine; third, caffeine; fourth, betel; and fifth, marijuana (Marshall 1987:38). Over the past fifteen years, however, a substantial tradition has developed in cannabis research, mainly conducted in the Caribbean and Latin America (Carter 1980; Rubin 1975a, Rubin and Comitas 1975). Similarly, there has been an increasing interest in tobacco studies, and trends in publications and recently organized symposia at anthropology meetings seem to indicate that this line of research is gathering momentum. Some research has focused on the role tobacco plays in social relationships (Black 1984). Another theme has been the interaction of transnational tobacco companies seeking new markets in Third World countries (Stebbins 1987). Several researchers with roots in early studies of religious experience and hallucinogens (Wallace 1959) have specialized in the cultural context of the ingestion of hallucinogens such as peyote and mescaline in the past two decades (Dobkin de Rios 1975, 1977, 1984; Furst 1972, 1976; Hill 1988; La Barre 1970, 1980).

Due in part to American society's definition of heroin, opium, marijuana, and cocaine use as clearly deviant behavior—in contrast to alcohol consumption—and in part to demand for legal and/or clinical intervention, studies on such drugs by anthropologists have attracted considerable attention. The street culture around the use of heroin and the use of methadone in the treatment of heroin addiction has, for example, drawn a kind of interest that is perhaps more curious than serious. The typical anthropologist's emic focus on the drug user's cognitive and social worlds is often at odds with the clinician's and policymaker's perception of the problem. The clinical and policy domains of our society take a more etic stance with respect to use of these "illicit" drugs and thus express impatience, at the very least, with arguments that suggest the use of these substances is not necessarily deviant from the user's perspective (Agar et al. 1981; Dreher 1984c). Regardless of the position taken regarding the deviance of such drug use, it is becoming apparent that prevention and treatment programs must do more than remove the drug in order to be lastingly effective. Drug use fits into a cluster of behaviors and beliefs, and treatment agendas must deal with that reality in proposing alternative ways of life to a recovering addict. Thus, a lucid understanding of the cognitive and social worlds of drug users is highly pertinent to preventive and intervention efforts.

In addition to twenty years of research on heroin addicts (e.g., Agar 1973, 1977, Carlson 1977, Preble and Casey 1969, and Smits 1980), anthropologists have more recently undertaken studies on cocaine, as cocaine has gained popularity as the drug of choice for many Americans. One such study examines the ways in which cocaine users interpret their environment, and the resultant influences of the user subculture on drug use patterns (Morningstar and Chitwood 1984). Another combines interest in issues of multiple drug use by investigating cocaine use among methadone clients (Strug et al. 1985). Thus far, only a small body of research on cocaine exists in anthropology. This body of research will likely increase, given the drug use patterns of clients seeking treatment for substance abuse (combined cocaine and alcohol addiction is currently a widespread pattern among clients under the age of 40 in most treatment programs throughout the country). Because of the relatively widespread indigenous use of kava and betel in Oceania, anthropologists working there have in the course of ethnographic research reported on the use of these substances (e.g., Iamo 1987, Lindstrom 1987b, Marshall 1987).

As noted at the beginning, anthropologists tend to approach a research problem in drug use and abuse by first questioning whether the basic issues being posed by policy makers and funding agencies are really the most important questions. For example, in the widespread concern about children of alcoholics over the past decade, the assumption was made that growing up in an alcoholic family automatically places a child at greater risk for many problems—including alcoholism. Some anthropologists, and other behavioral scientists, have asked why the culture of particular alcoholic families poses greater risk for children than other alcoholic families (Bennett et al. 1987).

Similarly, while American society has dramatically moved in an antitobacco direction, some anthropologists have recently called attention to the functional role of tobacco use (Robbins and Kline 1988). Consequently, anthropologists at times have been seen as rabble-rousers and troublemakers who rock the boat of cherished assumptions about the pathology or deviancy of drug use (Heath 1987b. For example, anthropologists have been taken to task for overstressing the functional role of alcohol in culture and ignoring its dysfunctional use (Room 1984). Over two decades ago, David Mandelbaum clearly articulated the anthropological slant on functional and dysfunctional use of alcohol: "Drunkenness cannot be understood apart from drinking in general, and drinking cannot be understood apart from the characteristic features of social relations of which it is part and which are reflected and expressed in the act of drinking" (1965). More recently, Mac Marshall has similarly stressed the essential value in examining deviant drug use within the context of normal patterns: "All the ethnographic accounts ... show the necessity of understanding the variety of normal drinking styles in any social setting before attempting to deal with abnormal (or addictive) drinking" (1979a: 10).

In the published research of the past decade, it is clear that while anthropologists have remained true to the principle of examining drug-related problems within the context of normal use, there has been a definite shift in some quarters to focus also on drug abuse as a primary interest in research.

As colleagues in other disciplines have taken a greater interest in the role of culture in drug use and abuse, they have understood and applied the concept of culture in ways that are sometimes discrepant with the concept in anthropology (Bennett 1988, 1989; Heath 1986). Specifically, in the minds of many scholars outside anthropology, "culture" has become synonymous with presumed membership in a particular ethnic group, nationality, racial group, religious affiliation, class, and so forth as related to particular drug use and abuse patterns. This perspective stands in contrast to the more traditional anthropological view of culture as a dynamic process through which individuals and societies learn the sum total of their society's behaviors and associated belief systems, including those encompassing drug use practices and beliefs.

CURRENT TRENDS IN ANTHROPOLOGICAL STUDIES OF SUBSTANCES

In addition to the notable increase in the number of anthropologists working in the drug field and identifying themselves as specialists in the area, certain trends in research approach characterize much of the work being conducted in studies of substance use and abuse that indicate a shift from the field of twenty years ago. First, anthropological research on drug use and abuse has garnered the attention of many experts in other disciplines. Anthropologists are in growing demand to serve on peer review committees for federal grants, to join editorial boards of journals, to participate in conferences, and to contribute to published collections on substance abuse. Second, anthropologists are conducting research more and more with colleagues in adjacent disciplines such as sociology and psychiatry, often leading to larger and more complex projects. Third, anthropologists are combining qualitative and quantitative methods within their studies, partly as an outgrowth of the increasingly interdisciplinary nature of the work and in part due to changes within anthropology itself. Fourth, greater attention is being given to problems of drug use and the application of solutions to abuse rather than to only the "normal" use of substances within particular cultural settings. Fifth, as drug use patterns have changed, some anthropologists are moving away from studies of a single drug only, such as alcohol, into substance use and abuse generally. This trend is very recent; it remains to be seen how far it develops. Sixth, emphasis in anthropology on the importance of culture in understanding drug use patterns and beliefs persists. This aspect remains the core feature of much anthropological research in the area, sometimes entailing cross-cultural comparisons and sometimes in-depth examination of drug use and/or abuse within a particular cultural context. The seventh trend is a growing interest in developing and applying a biocultural approach—drawing upon the sociocultural and biological knowledge bases within anthropology in better understanding the complex etiology of drug abuse problems. Thus far, however, this goal is more vision than reality (Bennett 1988).

In reviewing the plethora of studies on substance use and abuse, we have decided to focus on two drug categories: hallucinogens, including cannabis and such sacred plants as peyote, mescaline, and mushrooms; and alcohol. Anthropological research on these drugs has a long history (Bunzel 1940; Wallace 1959). Over the past two decades, an interest in applied issues having to do with the abuse of these substances has been added to the traditional consideration of the sociocultural integration of drug use in the behavior and belief systems of Western and non-Western societies.

We follow our discussion of anthropological work on hallucinogens and alcohol with suggestions as to the direction future anthropological work on drugs and drug abuse may take. We identify three possible directions: conducting treatment studies around the question of efficacy of culturally appropriate programs, developing a biocultural synthesis of alcoholism etiology, and playing a mediator role between research and application in practical concerns of the drug field.

HALLUCINOGENS

The Role of Sacred Plants in Traditional Societies

Fieldwork focusing on the magicoreligious use of hallucinogenic plants is perhaps the (nonalcohol) drug field's best representative of traditional academic anthropology, as distinct from the growing applied area of the discipline. In the case of the sacred plant hallucinogens—such as peyote, mescaline, and mushrooms—traditional ethnographic research is not typically undertaken to improve treatment or to inform policy. Its aim is to broaden the understanding of the human experience by illuminating the perspectives and experience of others. The vantage point of cultural relativism has especially influenced this line of anthropological research. While this influence has helped provide fresh insight into the cross-cultural use of hallucinogens, it has also reinforced the controversial posture of much anthropological research on drug use.

Cross-cultural assessments of the role of hallucinogen use illustrate how controversy may take form. While most people in Western society typically believe that the use of hallucinogenic drugs is dysfunctional, ethnographies of tribal cultures have often shown that these substances have been used for generations without disruptive effects to the society. In Western and some non-Western societies, drug users have divergent experiences apparently related to wider cultural differences. Comments from Marlene Dobkin de Rios illustrate this point: "Lacking specific cultural traditions of drug use which program their experience, Westerners often report idiosyncratic patterns. . . . There seems to be good evidence that in a society where plant hallucinogens are used, each individual builds up a certain expectation of drug use which, in fact, permits the evocation of particular types of visions" (1984:9, 197).

Other ethnographers have written similar accounts of the user experience in traditional societies, noting the power of culture to shape the drug encounter, to "determine the nature and intensity of the ecstatic experience and how that experience is interpreted and assimilated" (Furst 1976:10). Both Dobkin de Rios (1984) and Peter Furst (1976) find such elements as ritual preparation for and ritual control of the drug experience common to societies with magicoreligious traditions of hallucinogen use. In these societies, the substances are used to evoke visions or stir insight; as sacred plants, they rate a level of regard not accorded recreational drugs in complex societies.

In comparing mainstream American and North American Indian societies, Weston La Barre (1980:65) observes that in some tribal groups, American Indian adolescents receive drugs and guidance in their use from adults through socially established and respectable channels. This procedure differs considerably in intent from that of many other American adolescents who are resisting the influences of the dominant culture. In the former case, the adult order is reinforced; in the latter, it is assailed.

La Barre (1980:82–83) draws on a body of anthropological knowledge about hallucinogens to connect "altered states of consciousness," including dreams, hallucination, and similar states with the origins of religion. He finds such altered states to be genuine human universals and asserts that the experience of shamans while in such states, often induced by hallucinogens, shapes the revelations on which religions are based.

Cannabis Use: Functional or Dysfunctional?

Cannabis is a widespread drug of ancient vintage, usually classified as a hallucinogen based on its effects on mood and perception (Brill 1981). Anthropologists have studied its use and its role in social structure in a number of cultures. Jamaica, for example, has a high rate of regular users of cannabis, making it an excellent place to study the issues that unfold around the use and abuse of this drug, known to Jamaicans as *ganja*.

In Jamaica, *ganja* use is integrally linked to all aspects of working-class social structure: cultivation, cash crops, marketing, economics, consumer-cultivator-dealer networks; interclass relationships and processes of avoidance or cooperation; parent-child, peer and mate relationships; folk medicine; folk religious doctrines; . . . gossip sanctions; personality and culture; interclass stereotypes; legal and church sanctions; perceived requisites of behavioral changes for social mobility; and adaptive strategies. (Rubin and Comitas 1975:161).

Ganja figures strongly in the economic realm. On the lowest rung of the Jamaican socioeconomic ladder, poor families with few marketable skills make their living however they can, often engaging in several diverse economic activities. One of these activities may be the cultivation of cannabis. Vera Rubin and Lambros Comitas point out that vendors of cannabis typically lead a stable family life and are otherwise law abiding and conservative.

Working-class Jamaicans often believe that use of *ganja* makes work go more pleasantly and allows them to work harder; however, the middle and upper classes, who employ the lower classes and supervise their work, believe the drug is detrimental to work performance. Melanie Dreher (1983) has investigated the interplay of these differing views in the setting of a Jamaican sugar estate. Three farms were contrasted, all having different proportions of cannabis smokers to nonsmokers. Dreher examined productivity figures by categories of smokers and nonsmokers and found no significant differences in the work performance of smokers and nonsmokers. The results support neither the views of the workers nor of the managers (1983:4).

Dreher's study illustrates the increasing use of quantitative data in anthropological work on drug use, but it also points to the levels of subtlety and sophistication that can be added to research by the inclusion of qualitative material. This dimension of research is one of anthropology's strongest assets; it allows for deeper and more accurate understanding of complex questions and helps restrain impulses to hasty generalization (Agar 1980). Evidence for the value of such methods in interpreting data has led to the inclusion of an ethnographic or qualitative component in many of the interdisciplinary studies of drug use and abuse currently underway and to the explicit request for proposals forthcoming from the National Institute on Alcohol Abuse and Alcoholism and the National Institute on Drug Abuse (Stall 1989).

Dreher has also studied the use of cannabis among Jamaican women (1984a, 1987). She examined the different patterns of *ganja* use among women in two similar Jamaican villages, where women in one village seemed more inclined to smoke cannabis than in the other. At the time of this study, smoking was contrary to norms for Jamaican women, although they routinely made cannabis teas for medicinal purposes. In the village with the higher rate of smokers, women were found to have more economic opportunity and thus more independence. Women in the village with fewer smokers found it adaptive to conform to the norms, so that they would not alienate men who were potential husbands and sources of support.

By taking a cross-cultural look at what is considered to be a growing problem in the United States, Dreher has undertaken applied research to shed light on an important policy question. A common conceptual framework for the behavior of drug users whose conduct is outside society's usual limits is the social-psychological notion of deviance. Dreher argues that the behavior of the women she studied is better understood anthropologically in terms of intracultural variation. Again, we see a contextual focus, a perspective that, instead of looking solely at individual action, allows for the connecting of individual action to sociocultural structure. Currently more tolerance for *ganja* smoking has developed among lower-class Jamaican women. Use of the substance fits into a constellation of personal characteristics to which the term "roots daughter" has been given. Connected to the ideas generated by the Rastafarian religion about what is "natural" and African, a "roots daughter" is dignified, independent, and intelligent (Dreher 1987). Findings of this later research indicate changing attitudes and thereby remind us of culture's dynamic nature.

Anthropological research often probes the role of ritual in human action, as in the case of the Colombian work of William Partridge (1977). He found that smoking of cannabis was associated with work life through the action of ritual. An important part of worker comradeship is sharing cannabis when one can afford it; those who have it share it with whomever may not have it at that time. Workers who use but do not provide cannabis for sharing at work breaks are considered undependable and isolate themselves from the social networks from which work gangs are developed in the agricultural economy. In this fashion, meaning is shifted from one social context to another. In a domain similar to ritual, Rubin (1975b) has looked at the first experience of smokers as a rite of passage, an experience that strongly influences whether boys become regular smokers. If their first experience is a good one, they will probably become regular smokers; if not, they tend not to become users.

The practice of learning about the cultural intricacies of studied groups makes the anthropological enterprise often more time-consuming than other research approaches. In the Costa Rican work of J. Bryan Page, for example, a command of "proper" Spanish was not adequate to the task of following conversations in the argot of the drug culture on the street (1977). The arcane vernacular was found to be useful to the speakers; one use was the concealment of illegal economic activity, economic activity again motivated by need. Research in Costa Rica involved life histories, participant observation, and ethnographic interviews and subdivided smokers into different categories whose members found their smoking experiences to be shaped considerably by conditioned expectations and socioeconomic factors. Users who enjoyed economic stability and good social support found the smoking of cannabis to enhance activity; those users with less secure lives did not have universally pleasing experiences (Carter 1980; Page et al. 1988; True et al. 1980).

In her keynote address to the Alcohol and Drug Study Group, Dreher documented several theoretical and methodological contributions from anthropology, especially as distinct from the research forthcoming from sociology and social psychology. Not surprisingly, the use of cannabis in modern society is viewed by anthropologists as a "sociocultural phenomenon rather than an individual characteristic" (1984c:7). The holistic and comparative approach, the use of society or community as the unit of analysis, the reliance upon ethnohistorical and ethnographic studies, and the combination of qualitative and quantitative methods make anthropological research on cannabis unique.

The cannabis question is obviously a loaded issue in American society at the present, and therefore it is not surprising that there is resistance to accepting the results of these "controversial" anthropological findings. However, the same skepticism regarding these conclusions about the potential functional role of *ganja* use in certain cultural contexts is remarkably familiar to some of the resistance alcohol researchers in anthropology have encountered when they call into question certain widespread assumptions about the the etiology and diagnosis of alcoholism. The question of where to draw the line between acceptable usage— if usage of a particular drug is thought ever to be acceptable—and dysfunctional-pathological usage is extremely complicated. This message is probably one of the most important ones that anthropology offers, especially on controversial drugs such as cannabis.

ALCOHOL

From their early writings on alcohol, anthropologists have stressed the value of examining drinking patterns and the meaning of those behaviors firmly within their cultural context. This proclivity holds for both "normal" drinking as well as drunkenness and alcohol-related problems.

Sociocultural Context

In 1940 Ruth Bunzel pioneered the way for anthropological research on alcohol through the publication of the results of a controlled comparison of the role of drinking in two different Central American societies where she had conducted in-depth ethnographic fieldwork. She had not set out to study drinking *or* alcoholism specifically. Applying psychoanalytic concepts, Bunzel connected drinking behavior to its wider sociocultural context. By identifying positive functions within these drinking patterns as well as explicating drunken behavior, Bunzel found that drinking seemed to help lubricate social relations in the village of Chamula in Mexico. In comparison, in the Guatemalan village of Chichicastenango, alcohol provided a release from anxieties related to a stressful environment (Bunzel 1976:22).

In the late 1950s Dwight B. Heath took up the gauntlet of this genre of research in his study of culture change following the Bolivian revolution of 1952 (Heath 1958). One area of investigation was change in drinking behavior as an indication of shifting interethnic social relations between the peasants and the mestizos: "drinking is a useful index, being both highly visible and an integral part of the etiquette of relations between men" (1971: 180). With this work and an earlier study among the Navaho Indians, Heath began the first sustained effort in anthropology to advance alcohol studies.

The number of ethnographies concerned with drinking practices and beliefs has proliferated since the 1950s. In Peru alone, three publications during the late 1960s and early 1970s focus on alcohol. In one example, Ozzie Simmons offers a description of the sociocultural integration of alcohol use within Lunahuana, a Spanish-speaking coastal village in Peru: "the meshing of drinking with a configuration of culture and social structure [gives] alcohol positive symbolic and functional roles" within the society (1968:168). Similarly, Paul Doughty found that "the use of alcoholic drinks was highly patterned and integral to normal social interaction" within the mestizo community of Huaylas in highland Peru (1971: 187). Allan Holmberg summarizes that for the agricultural peasant village of Viru on the north coast of Peru, "traditional patterns of drinking are such an integral part of the value structure of Viru that they are not likely to change in the near future" (1971:198).

A more recent example of basic ethnographic research out of which alcohol data developed but was not the central theme or intent of the research is Ndolamb Ngokwey's fieldwork among the Lele of Kasai in the Republic of Zaire (1987) in which he analyzes the drinking of palm wine: when it is drunk and within what contexts, types of wine drunk, drinking manners, and its connection with health and illness. By concluding that "Lele rules and practices concerning palm wine reproduce cultural values, notions, and categories" (1987:119), Ngokwey clearly articulates the sociocultural integration theme. He also raises another issue, which runs through much of the literature on alcohol (as well as other drugs): gender differences in consumption.

Gerald Mars, an anthropologist focusing on occupational issues, is another recent researcher whose studies uncovered distinctive patterns in drinking styles. Among longshoremen in Newfoundland, Canada, two distinct groups emerged: the "regular men" and the "outside men." The regular men were regularly hired and rehired to work on the docks at the port of St. John's, where one of the requirements to be a "regular man" was to learn the proper drinking behavior for members of the group. These patterns were so fundamental to the continuities between nonwork and work roles that in Mars's research the men rarely mentioned the importance of drinking roles without explicit questions because "I didn't think you counted drinking! *Everyone* always drinks with their buddies!" (1987:93).

The consumption of alcohol is always subject to rules and regulations, and breaching those rules arouses strong emotional response (Heath 1976:43). Currently we see such intense emotionality expressed through the Mothers against Drunk Driving (MADD) campaign. Over the past decade MADD has garnered phenomenal support in American society, to the point of strongly influencing such formal legal controls as blood alcohol levels permissible for drivers, and the penalties for exceeding those levels.

Acculturation and Culture Change Studies

By the 1960s, anthropologists had developed an increased interest in applying their ethnographic and often emic approach in order better to understand the problematic use of alcohol. This was particularly the case with respect to American Indians. As part of the interdisciplinary team at the Tri-Ethnic Research Project at the University of Colorado, Theodore Graves contrasted Spanish-American, Anglo-American, and Ute Indian groups living in the same area as a means for addressing the question: "under what conditions is acculturation accompanied by symptoms of social and psychological disorganization, and under what conditions it is not?" (1967:306). Stark differences in drinking practices and problems with alcohol as well as other types of social problems existed among these three cultural groups.

Graves and his colleagues combined ethnographic observations with structured and unstructured interviews conducted with a randomly selected sample from the three groups. He found that the relatively unacculturated Spanish-Americans and Indians evidence patterns of alcohol use and abuse distinct from each other. While the Spanish-Americans retained strong controls socially and psychologically, the Indians were weak on this dimension. Furthermore, while the unacculturated Indian groups displayed excessive drinking patterns and problems associated with heavy drinking, the Spanish as a group did not (1967:317).

With this study, a long tradition in acculturation studies of American Indians and other ethnic groups in the United States was well underway (Bennett and Ames 1985). Paradoxically, acculturation is sometimes hypothesized to be a protective factor against dysfunctional drinking practices and at other times a risk factor. As Graves pointed out in 1967,

Acculturation is obviously not the unqualified evil that some observers regard it. When traditional cultural strategies for personal satisfaction have become inapplicable, a reorientation toward a set of new and potentially attainable goals appears to be a promising path to mental health. Furthermore, where traditional social and personal control systems are weak, . . . acculturation may also serve to promote the development of new controls,

Drug Studies

and thereby make the group better able to prevent disruptive individual behavior. (1967:319)

Change in drinking patterns under conditions of culture change and/or acculturation has been an ongoing theme of some alcohol research in the past two decades. The Institute of Applied Social and Economic Research (ISAER) Alcohol Project in Papua New Guinea is an example of an ambitious two-year research project directed by anthropologist Mac Marshall and undertaken to address a growing problem with alcohol there (1982, 1988). A notable feature of the resulting conference and monograph is the fact that most presentations were made by scholars—including many anthropologists—who had conducted in-depth ethnographic research at a particular field site on Papua New Guinea. While none of these researchers had intentionally undertaken a study of alcohol and culture, each discovered that alcohol consumption was important enough to collect data on the topic (Marshall 1982:xxiii). In 1982 Marshall edited a monograph on changes in drinking patterns in highland and coastal villages and urban areas of Papua New Guinea and problems associated with drinking. The significance of this project is seen in the fact that it constitutes "the first time anywhere that such a large body of ethnographic information has been assembled specifically in the service of public policy decisions on alcohol" (Marshall 1982: xxiii).

The Application of Anthropology to Alcohol-Related Problems

This line of research and applied anthropological activities signal a shift in the field of alcohol studies already noted: that of application of research on the role of alcohol in cultural context to emerging public health concerns regarding the abuse of alcohol. With this shift, anthropologists have entered the field of prevention (Ames and Janes 1987; Klee and Ames 1987; Page 1987; Stall 1988) and of formal and informal alcohol control policies (Anderson 1988; Brady 1988a; Hill 1988; Waddell 1988). At the same time, anthropologists have continued to ask hard questions about the effectiveness of formal alcohol control policies in changing consumption patterns (Heath 1988), and we are currently in the midst of a lively cross-disciplinary and within-anthropology debate on the subject.

Drunken Comportment

These two issues—the extent to which alcohol consumption poses serious social problems and the extent to which available alcohol control policies help to stem the tide of those perceived problems—have historical reference in anthropology in the "drunken comportment" concept. In their 1969 book, psychologist Craig MacAndrew and anthropologist Robert Edgerton examine the phenomenon of drunkenness cross-culturally using ethnographic and ethnohistorical data to evaluate several assumptions held about behavior under the influence of alcohol. First, drawing upon ethnographic data reported from five societies, they evaluate evidence for the "disinhibiting" effects of alcohol. They found that "even during periods of extreme intoxication, the inhibitions that are normally in effect *remain* in effect. Drunken persons in these societies . . . may stagger, speak thickly, and become stuporous, without any corresponding display of changes-for-the-worse . . . In a word, if alcohol were a 'superego solvent' for one group of people due to its toxic action, then the same disinhibiting effect *ought* to be evident in *all* people. In point of fact, however, *it is not*" (1969:36). In short, MacAndrew and Edgerton call into question the common assumption held by many people in American society that alcohol serves as a disinhibitor, a point of view often perpetuated by medical science (Marshall 1985:68). Thus, even in the midst of increasing cross-disciplinary cooperation, anthropologists continue to find themselves in a position to question seemingly entrenched viewpoints about alcohol and alcohol-related behaviors. Unfortunately, noncritical thinking about alcohol and alcoholism also characterizes some of the research on alcohol. As Heath has succinctly put it, "polemic masquerades as science in much of what is written on alcoholism" (Bennett 1988:110).

Seemingly everyone is an expert on alcoholism in that virtually everyone has some direct experience with alcoholism or alcohol-related problems and, based upon that experience, holds strong opinions about its etiology and the connection between alcohol-related behaviors such as drunkenness and other undesirable behavior patterns. Consequently, drunkenness is used as "an excuse for antisocial behavior ranging from rowdiness to wife-beating to homicide" (Marshall 1985:70). Thus, while MacAndrew and Edgerton's book is cited in a recent survey as the most useful book by anthropologists on alcohol studies (Bennett 1988), the basic message of that book has not become become widely accepted.

The Disease Concept of Alcoholism

Perhaps nowhere else do we find such a powerful and pervasive example of a commonsense mentality in the understanding of alcohol as in the disease concept of alcoholism, as propounded by alcoholism treatment professionals and some members of the medical establishment. This is an area in which the essential need to examine cultural context in understanding the complex etiology of alcohol-related problems seems to fall on deaf ears. Dogmatism about alcoholism is often expressed in either-or opinions. In their discussion of "the mindful body," Nancy Scheper-Hughes and Margaret Lock (1987:9) note how the tendency to treat the body separately from the mind harks back to René Descartes' writings in the sixteenth century.

In understanding alcohol abuse—how it develops, how it is diagnosed, and how to prevent it or intervene in it—alcohologists tend to rely upon simplistic oppositions such as the nature-nurture or genetic-environment contrasts. Similarly the disease concept is often contrasted with the moral model concept in which alcoholism is seen to stem from weaknesses of individuals, which keep them from controlling their drinking. Historically, American society experienced a long period in which the moral model reigned supreme—during the 150 years of strong temperance and prohibition movements (beginning in the late 1700s with the rum trade, and continuing through the repeal of prohibition in 1933) (Ames 1985b).

With the founding of the Yale Center for Alcohol Studies after World War II under the leadership of E. M. Jellinek, the disease or biomedical model was developed as a counter to the moral model. The disease model, according to Jellinek, explains alcoholism as a progressive disease with clear symptoms and certain recognizable, inevitable phases (1960). The insistence on fidelity to the disease concept in the treatment of alcoholism, however, is a more convenient, established theory than scientific understanding based upon scholarly work. In reality, American society has superimposed the disease model upon the moral weaknesses model in popular understanding of the etiology and nature of alcoholism (Ames 1985b). Thus, alcoholics can be held responsible for their addiction based on personality features while at the same time be excused based on a presumed physiological predisposition. Either facet of this combined belief system can be referred to whenever the situation warrants.

In addition to the confusion around the moral-medical distinction, many well-meaning professionals (researchers and clinicians alike) and the general public operate with a vague idea of what is really meant by the disease concept and assume that whatever it is is clearly supported by scientific evidence. Contrary to some popular beliefs, the same symptoms are not always present in all alcoholics or in those seeking treatment for alcoholism. The course of alcoholism varies widely. Also, from a disease point of view, we might expect that biomedical criteria would be used to diagnose alcoholism. In fact, however, mainly behavioral criteria are applied. Drinking patterns and behavior under the influence of alcohol figure more prominently in diagnostic criteria established to distinguish moderate, heavy, and alcoholic drinking than do strict biomedical indicators such as organ damage and withdrawal signs (Levy 1984:182).

We recently surveyed a group of anthropologists as to their points of view about the disease concept of alcoholism. This is far from a neutral topic—some respondents commented on its sensitivity—but responses were frank. David Strug noted that he had never "felt comfortable . . . with the disease concept of alcoholism based on a biomedical model. . . . The cultural component will always remain a contextual constant that must be considered" (Bennett 1988:115). In connecting the idea of alcoholism with disease, Merrill Singer concludes that it reflects "broader patterns of medicalization, privatization of suffering and politically-endorsed individualized problem-solving patterns" (Bennett 1988:116). While virtually all respondents expressed skepticism about the disease concept, Dwight Heath was the most clearly dubious among these reports: "If alcoholism is a disease, it is a most unusual one inasmuch as an individual can often bring an end to it by modifying his/her behavior even in the absence of any other intervention. Most of the reasons commonly given for calling it a disease are fallacious" (1988:117).

Interestingly, these opinions are generally consistent with the World Health Organization's (1980) position that alcohol problems do not necessarily follow a coherent pattern throughout the general population and do not necessarily have to do with a physiological dependence on alcohol. Anthropologists insist, as do some other alcohologists (Room 1983), that alcoholism is a complex phenomenon, perhaps having predisposing factors (genetic and physiological) in combination with a series of precipitating factors (including psychological, social, and cultural) contributing to etiology. The need for a biocultural synthesis of studies of individual and cultural variation is compelling (Bennett 1988).

The "Firewater Myth"

The "firewater myth" is a major arena where the genetic versus environment debate with respect to population-level differences has been waged for decades and continues to attract the attention of anthropologists and others concerned with these issues. Here conventional wisdom states categorically that North American Indians cannot handle alcohol because of their physical constitution, an idea going back to the nineteenth century. Joy Leland has traced the history of the argument and examined the available published data as of the mid-1970s (Leland 1976).

One explanation for widespread disagreement as to the extent of alcohol addiction among American Indians is the lack of a set of agreed-upon symptoms of alcohol abuse. Leland points out that we are far from having such a list of symptoms for the "dominant society," let alone distinctive cultural groups such as American Indians. In her review, Leland tabulates the presence or absence of 44 symptoms of alcohol addiction proposed by E. M. Jellinek (1952) that are documented in the available literature on North American Indian groups. Using the symptoms checklist, it was not possible to confirm the firewater hypothesis. On the other hand, the reverse of that hypothesis cannot be decisively supported or discredited (Leland 1976:104, 123). Much more scrutiny is necessary before any firm conclusions can be drawn about the extent of alcohol addiction among American Indian groups, let alone the potential biocultural basis for such addiction.

The term *firewater myth* uses the word *myth* in the sense meaning "misconception," or a notion based on something other than fact. Myths of this kind can mold attitudes, and thus actions, as can myths of a more traditional stripe, such as creation myths: "Myths are powerful influences in human affairs: they condition situations, their preconceptions create consequences" (Leland 1976:123).

POSSIBLE DIRECTIONS FOR THE FUTURE

In addition to maintaining its well-established course of explicating the cultural context of drug use and abuse, anthropology might target three areas for special attention: evaluation of the efficacy of culturally appropriate treatment programs; biocultural studies of alcoholism; and mediation between research and application.

Culturally Appropriate Treatment

Anthropologists have argued that knowledge about cultural variation in drug use and abuse patterns—as well as the wider cultural context—is important for planning effective prevention, intervention, and treatment strategies (Ames 1982; Gilbert and Cervantes 1987; Hall 1986; Heggenhougen 1984; Trotter and Chavira 1978; Weibel-Orlando 1984, 1987, 1988; Westermeyer 1982). In fact, Joan Weibel-Orlando asserts that "we accept, as a disciplinary mission, the role of revealer/advocate. We advocate the right of a people to heal themselves in any manner they see fit. . . . [To do so is a] noble cause consistent with long-established anthropological ethics and belief in the cultural relativity of all institutions including those that attempt to heal and bring people back into 'balance' " (1988: 11, 13).

What is the evidence for the efficacy of treatment programs designed with the cultural background of the clients in mind? H. K. Heggenhougen (1984:3-5) points out that traditional systems of healing have been applied to addiction for some time. In Hong Kong, for example, acupuncture has been used to treat withdrawal. He also notes that conventional treatment programs do not have outstanding success in treating addiction and that they are not available to all who need them. Although the efficacy of alternative treatment for addiction is still uncertain, he argues that treatment provided through traditional or indigenous medical system is a needed resource.

Joseph Westermeyer (1982) has made a similar point. He studied Laotian opium addicts in voluntary treatment at a Buddhist monastery in Thailand. Alternatively, treatment at a medical center was available, where patients were slowly withdrawn from opium through methadone therapy. Clients of the monastery's program underwent "cold turkey" withdrawal, yet many addicts continued to seek it out because of its "traditional and reassuring location" (1982:217). Some difficulties arose at the monastery due to language barriers between the Thai monks and some of the Laotian tribal people: clients at the medical facility complained of the same problems. Both groups, however (monastery and medical center), had good overall feelings about their treatment experiences (1982:222-23). Both have similar long-term outcomes in client abstention. The monastery had a substantial cost advantage over the medical facility but lost favor because of the mortality among older addicts in the withdrawal (1982:249-50). A combination of the best features of both might be optimal.

Many anthropologists have posited the increased efficacy of treatment programs that take into account the cultural milieu of patients. This hypothesis, however, has not been solidly tested. Weibel-Orlando—after acknowledging her own strong support of this position, especially with respect to treatment programs for North American Indian groups—then calls into question the research base for the argument: "Most of our enthusiasm for indigenous curing strategies as viable contemporary alcohol and drug interventions is based on anecdotal materials. . . . More systematic and observational investigations of the efficacy of such interventions are needed" (1988:16).

Biocultural Synthesis of Alcoholism Etiology

Discussion of the firewater myth debate leads directly to the question of why anthropologists have not led the way in studies combining biological and cultural factors in presumed population-level differences in the incidence and prevalence of alcoholism. On an individual and family level, a biocultural synthesis might help unravel some of the thorny questions around the interplay between predisposing (genetic) and precipitating (personal, social, and cultural) factors in alcoholism etiology. With its integrative approach, anthropology would seem to be in a particularly good position to design and conduct such studies.

James Schaefer, in his recent update on the firewater myth, proposes two types of studies that would address these issues (1981). He points out the need for both general population and large family pedigree studies. If both were to be conducted in a well-conceptualized manner, together they could provide fresh insights into the "biophysiological or sociopsychological predispostions to alcoholism" (1981:106).

With respect to existing data about differences between North American Indian groups and other ethnic groups, Schaefer strongly contends that "we are a long way from having conclusive evidence of differences in ethanol metabolism by racial group" (1981:106). In addition to the methodological problems with existing studies, he highlights the basic point—too often overlooked in these discussions—that hypothesized physiological differences between groups in ethanol metabolism cannot be automatically presumed to place the group at increased or decreased risk for alcoholism; certain questions must first be addressed. For example, what are the consequences of relatively greater physical discomfort after drinking, and what are the likely consequences of more rapid metabolism of ethanol upon actual drinking patterns for a group? Do these differences provide increased or decreased protection from possible addiction? "A paradox thus emerges. Biophysiologically based hypersensitivity reactions may be 'protective'; however, in some cases social, psychological and cultural factors may transcend the 'protection.' Indeed, a wide spectrum of behavioral evidence points to increased amounts of cultural stress, powerlessness and anxiety as conditions which exacerbate alcohol use" (1981:109). The family pedigree study approach would be a fruitful direction in attempting a biocultural investigation of alcoholism etiology. To date such studies have focused on biophysiological measures, drug use histories, and social-demographic variables. If the cultural orientation of anthropology is to be a core component of such studies, anthropologists must participate in projects from their beginnings in the design phase of research. Otherwise, the dynamic or processual bent of anthropology tends to get relegated to a less prominent status in the project.

Anthropologist as Mediator

The need for a biocultural approach to studies of the etiology of alcoholism leads to another future direction that anthropology might take. As we have noted elsewhere in this chapter, much anthropological evidence has not been incorporated into professional and lay understanding of drug use and abuse. There is a major gap between the research end of the spectrum and the application of conclusions from studies. At least three things are responsible for the breakdown.

One, the issues are complex, and it is truly difficult to sustain the attention of a reader or listener long enough so that he or she can make an informed decision. The more that anthropologists—and other scientists—clearly present the evidence for and against a position and the more that it can be interpreted in real-life terms, the better the chances are to make changes in public opinion. Second, conclusions from anthropology often seem to go against the grain of common sense, making the business of influencing people's thinking an uphill struggle. An open acknowledgment of those differences is perhaps more constructive than assuming audiences will be swayed by a solid argument.

Third, anthropologists may not be placing enough importance on presenting their arguments to the right audiences. It is essential that anthropologists not limit their written and oral presentations to other researchers. Courses and workshops in the area of drug studies can, for example, draw students who are hungering to explore the relationship between culture and biology in the development of drug-related problems. They also provide a good forum for expanding the dialogue between researchers and clinicians. Publication in popular contexts and delivering public talks are also critical to advancing the general understanding of drug use and abuse. Anthropology can and should be an active force in expanding informed discourse on drugs, leaving its distinctive imprint on the process of inquiry.

CHAPTER 14

CULTURE, STRESS, AND DISEASE

William W. Dressler

The literature on stress and disease has grown at a geometric rate over the past decade (Vingerhoets and Marcelissen 1988). Research on stress and disease focuses on those social and psychological factors that are related to health outcomes, independently from behavioral factors that mechanically increase individual exposure to physical or chemical insults (such as smoking or poor diet). It is well established that a portion of the risk associated with the development of diseases such as depression, hypertension, and coronary heart disease is due to the social and cultural circumstances in which a person lives, as well as the beliefs and attitudes held by that person. The research issue now is not to demonstrate merely that this is so but rather to work out in a refined and systematic way the process involved. This includes identifying the variables of greatest relevance to the prediction of disease, determining the interactions among those variables, and examining how relationships are modified by the social and cultural contexts in which they occur.

Quite a bit of work has been done with respect to identifying relevant variables and pursuing the interactions among those variables, but very little has been done with respect to examining in a systematic way how those relationships vary across different social and cultural contexts (Dressler 1989a). For many researchers, the effects of "cultural factors" are thought to be those demonstrated by the classic work of John Cassel and his colleagues (Cassel, Patrick, and Jenkins 1960; Henry and Cassel 1969), who showed how rates of essential hypertension and related health problems (Cassel and Tyroler 1961) increased with culture change or "modernization." In this research, "culture change" is synonymous with "stress"; extending the model involves breaking down the imperfect indicator of "stress" into smaller and more discrete pieces, which in turn can be related to disease. Precisely the same, and essentially reductionist, strategy can be seen in the sociological literature on stress and disease, where the starting point has been the relationship of social class and disease, and the aim has been to break down the concept into discrete psychological-behavioral elements that are more directly related to disease (Kessler and Cleary 1980; Pearlin 1982).

These research strategies have resulted in what Allan Young (1980) refers to as an "asocial" stress model. Little or no consideration is given to how psychosocial risks and resistance resources are embedded in contexts of different social relationships or in how specific historical circumstances have generated specific configurations of stress, adaptation, and disease. A small amount of work has been devoted to the "content" of the stress model across cultures (Fairbank and Hough 1981; Dressler 1984b). By this I mean the cultural contribution to differences in the perception of what is stressful or what is helpful in coping with stressful circumstances. But relatively little work has been done on how the social and contextual nature of stress and disease can alter the relationships of various factors in the model. If there is to be serious cross-cultural study of stress, the central problems to be solved must involve how the content of stressors and adaptive factors varies by cultural context and how the relationships among stress, disease, and adaptation are modified by the social and cultural contexts in which these occur.

The contribution of such a research program to an understanding of disease in human populations should not be underestimated. The study of stress and disease is generally thought to be an excellent example of George Engel's (1977) "biopsychosocial" model, which has been proposed as an alternative to the reductionist "biomedical" model. However, much of the research on stress and disease fits quite comfortably into the confines of the biomedical model because psychosocial factors are treated as if they were independent of social and historical contexts. What is currently thought important is, for example, whether there has been a recent life crisis for an individual, not the significance of that particular crisis in the larger cultural context of the community or the meaning of the crisis in the context of the recent social or economic trends in the community. A more explicit focus on these issues would lead to a serious consideration of the broad range of influences on disease. My aim in this chapter is to review selectively the literature on stress and disease from this vantage point, both to clarify what is or is not known about psychosocial and behavioral risk factors and to understand better needed future directions in research.

THE CONCEPT OF STRESS

Discussions of the concept of stress sometimes engender in participants in such discussions the very phenomena of interest; in other words, some people find the concept of stress frustrating, upsetting, and worrisome. Mostly this stems from the inconsistent and uncritical use of the idea in many areas of research. Some persons use the term to refer to outside pressures brought to bear on an individual. Sometimes the "stress" is very specific, such as particular occupational arrangements, and at other times it is very vague, as in the "stress of modern society." Other persons use the term to refer to a response of the individual to some environmental stimulus. This was the sense in which the concept was originally defined by Hans Selye (1975)—to refer to a generalized physiologic pattern in laboratory animals in response to a wide variety of environmental stimuli.

In reviewing the concept of stress, John Mason (1975) pointed out two things. First, over the years the concept has gained a decidedly psychological connotation and lost much of its physiological utility. Second, research has progressed to a sufficient degree to classify or categorize different stimuli and responses more precisely rather than lumping them together all under the rubric of "stress". This latter observation has been amplified by a number of writers. Sidney Cobb (1976) and Cassel (1976) led the way in pointing out that what gets lumped under "stress" actually involves two linked sets of factors related to health in different ways. On the one hand, there are events and circumstances that occur and increase the probability that an individual will become ill. There are risk factors or "stressors." On the other hand, there are social relationships and beliefs and values that, when present or possessed by an individual, lower the risk of falling ill. These are "resistance resources." The point is that the concept of stress per se becomes less useful in describing actual variables of interest or relationships and becomes instead a broad term descriptive of an entire process. It was this trend in research and theoretical development that led Mason (1975) to suggest that the term *stress* be thought of analogously to the concept of pathogen in infectious disease. When one speaks of pathogens in infectious disease, everyone is generally aware of what is being referred to, but it is very clear that there are many specifics left unstated. Similarly, when one speaks of stress, or perhaps more accurately, the stress process, it should be clear that these descriptions just orient one's thinking toward a type of process leading to disease, and these terms do not refer to any concrete entity. "Stress" is not an "it" (see also Lazarus and Folkman 1986).

What, then, is the stress process? Robert Scott and Alan Howard (1970) provided an excellent description of a formal model of the stress process. Every organism, every individual human being, lives in an environmental context that has both a physical and a social environment. Human life is a continuing transaction between the individual and these environments. The individual seeks to maintain a preferred state of existence, balancing energy intake and discharge, and involving a preferred activity level, both physiologically and psychobehaviorally. This preferred state can be referred to as homeostasis, although it must be recognized that the precise homeostatic state, which people think of as normal daily activities, can change.

Difficulties can arise from a variety of sources in this process. The environment, whether physical or social, can change. If this change involves something salient to the maintenance of the individual's preferred adjustment, such as the loss of his or her job, the individual must intensify activity in that area in order to return to a preferred state. In order to deal with this threatened loss of adjustment, a person must be able to recognize it, accurately identify a solution, and above all have resources in the environment that can be brought to bear on the problem (such as live in a community where other jobs are available). Where a person can successfully meet an environmental challenge, then adjustment has occurred, and "normal" life is maintained. Where a person cannot—where environmental challenges are too great or resources are too meager—adjustment cannot occur, and some sort of breakdown of the system—the individual—occurs. Often, but not necessarily, this breakdown is what we refer to as disease. If any single event or circumstance could accurately be termed stress, it should be the simultaneous confluence of environmental demands and inadequate resources for adaptation.

Two things should be made explicit about this theoretical orientation. First, it is highly abstract. Clearly, demands and resources can be found in many levels of human life, including human biology, psychology, social relationships, and culture. It becomes the task of the researcher to analyze specific situations and to determine the specific factors involved in the process. Second, there is a great emphasis in this abstract model on the environment. Commonsense thinking about "stress" carries with it a strong "mentalistic bias" (Dressler et al. 1987). By that I mean a bias toward thinking of stress as a metaphor for psychological upset, worry, anxiety, and frustration. Also implicit in this bias is the notion that what is stressful depends on what individuals perceive or feel to be stressful (that is, "one man's meat is another man's poison"). Carried to an extreme, this bias can lead us to ignore the social environment. The mentalistic bias in conceptualizing stress amounts to saying that appropriate variables cannot be identified except insofar as factors are consciously perceived by the individual. The emphasis on the environment in the theoretical perspective applied here is essential because social, cultural, and historical processes generate the stressors that place individuals at risk of disease. Individual beliefs, values, and perceptions may (and do) modify the impact of those stressors, but the stressors, arising from environmental constraints, exist and exert influences, often quite apart from what individuals think about them.

The task of research is one of providing substance for this abstract theoretical sketch. Already various schools (to use the term loosely) of thought have developed in stress research, including theories emphasizing "person-environment fit" (French, Rodgers, and Cobb 1974), "person-environment transactions" (Lazarus and Folkman 1986), "transition" models (Jacobson 1986; Parkes 1988), "social readjustment" models (Dohrenwend and Dohrenwend 1981), and models derived from "social role theory" (Pearlin 1982). These various models are not mutually exclusive, and all are compatible with Scott and Howard's (1970) systems theory formulation; indeed, as Benjamin Colby (1987) has recently shown so well, models of stress are one part of a larger theory of human adaptation. Rather than be detained by the details of any of these middle-range theories, my concern will be with empirical results, and especially with results that bear on the fundamental questions of the social and cultural definition of stressors and resistance resources and on the contextual modification of relationships among stressors, adaptation, and disease. This is also in keeping with

Caudill's (1958a) observation that these stress factors operate at different phenomenal levels and will spill over (in his terms) and have different effects at different levels.

ACUTE STRESSORS AND DISEASE

Two broad categories of stressors have been investigated: acute stressors and chronic stressors. Acute stressors include natural disasters, such as tornadoes (Wallace 1956), and life events that are part of the normal life cycle (Holmes and Rahe 1967). Probably three-quarters of all research on stress and mental health since the publication of the famous Holmes-Rahe article has focused on these factors. These life events include major points of crisis or transition in the life cycle, such as death of a spouse or child, divorce, and loss of a job, as well as fairly minor events, such as Christmas and getting a parking ticket. The number of events studied for etiologic significance varies in different studies, ranging from as low as 15 to over 100. The key to the inventory, whatever the size, is that these events place new adaptive demands upon the individual experiencing them. The person whose spouse dies is faced with readjustments in many spheres of life. The individual who loses his or her job must change normal daily activities and begin to search for new employment, which may mean a complete alteration of regular life. Even something seemingly positive and small-scale like a holiday means change in habit and social interaction (such as reunions with family members) that can have profound social-psychological implications. As the amount of social readjustment required increases, either through the accumulation of many small events or through the occurrence of one or two major events, the risk of mental illness increases. This risk is increased because the likelihood that an individual's adaptive capacities will be overwhelmed is correspondingly increased.

The predictive efficacy of life events has been demonstrated in many studies (Dohrenwend and Dohrenwend 1973, 1981; Barrett 1979). This relationship has been replicated in both retrospective and prospective studies, so there can be little doubt about the role of life events in the etiology of mental illness. What has been disappointing about life events research, however, has been the relatively small magnitude of the effects and the small amount of research on the definition of significant "events." Studies have confirmed that the correlation of life events and symptoms is only about 0.20 (Rabkin and Streuning 1976; Taussig 1982). A great deal of research effort has been expended to define the psychosocial parameters of life events that may improve this strength of association. Parameters such as the perceived predictability, controllability, desirability, and subjective impact of life events have been investigated (McFarlane et al. 1980; Thoits 1981). None of these dimensions has been shown to improve markedly the predictive efficacy of simple counts of life events.

There is some intriguing evidence that using a brief inventory of events that are culturally regarded as undesirable accounts for most of the association of life events and depression. In research with American samples, using a brief inventory (about 20 events) of life events that includes truly major events in the adult life cycle, such as deaths of relatives, divorce or other marital separations, or unemployment, accounts for essentially all of the effect of life events on depression (Taussig 1982).

Research investigating the variation in the definition of stressful events in different societies has not been extensive. William Dressler (1984a) found that life events were grouped and ranked differently in a West Indian society than they were in published accounts from American samples and that those most strongly related to hypertension were also most salient within West Indian culture. Similarly, Dressler (1986a) argued that unemployment could not be treated simply as another in an inventory of life events in an African-American community in the rural South of the United States because of the cultural salience of work; unemployment was found to have an effect on depression in that community independent of other life events. Scheder (1988) found life events to occur more frequently among diabetic Mexican-American migrant farmworkers than among nondiabetics. The simple count of the number of life events was related to disease status more strongly than individual perceptions of the stressfulness of events, and the kinds of events reported were all related to the problems of the migrant way of life.

An extensive cross-national study of stressful life events and schizophrenia has been carried out within the World Health Organization's larger studies of psychiatric disorder (Day et al. 1987). Samples of patients were drawn from India, Colombia, Denmark, Nigeria, Japan, Czechoslovakia, and the United States and were diagnosed as schizophrenic using standardized criteria. A standardized methodology for identifying and evaluating the impact of stressful life events, modeled on the work of George Brown (Brown 1974; Brown and Harris 1978), was employed: "The conceptual approach embodied in the WHO life event schedule... was 'objective' (or 'sociological') in orientation; that is to say, it assumed that the influence of life events on episodes of illness could be defined and measured without taking into account the patient's idiosyncratic (i.e. 'subjective') perception of the significance of things occurring in his/her life world. Instead, 'life events' were defined to be changes that would have been considered stress provoking by an average member of the patient's group" (Day et al. 1987). It was found that life events could be reliably assessed across these diverse contexts using this methodology, especially with respect to events likely to have a large impact on patients. Consistent with the hypothesis that life events play a triggering role in the onset of florid schizophrenic symptoms, in each of the societies studied, life events clustered in a two-to-three-week period before the onset of symptoms.

There is some evidence that the risk produced by the occurrence of life events is a function of the social class context in which they occur. In a community study in an American city, Ronald Kessler and Paul Cleary (1980) found that the effect of life events on depression was concentrated among lower-class respondents; there was no effect in the middle-class group. Similarly, in research in an African-American community, the effect of unemployment (Dressler 1986a) and noneconomic life events (Dressler 1987) on depression was concentrated among low-income persons. These studies point to the importance of social context and social meanings as determinants of the etiologic significance of life events, determinants more important than idiosyncratic perceptions of life events.

CHRONIC STRESSORS AND DISEASE

Richard Rahe and Ransom Arthur (1978) explicitly note that life events are only one category of stressors, acute stressors; chronic social stressors are risk factors that do not have the discrete and identifiable onset as do life events but rather persist in the structure of everyday social roles and circumstances. The social disorganization hypothesis (Leighton et al. 1963) and the life stress hypothesis (Langner and Michael 1963) are classic examples of chronic and ongoing stressful circumstances.

More recent and more explicit attempts to study chronic social stressors have been made by Leonard Pearlin and his associates (Pearlin and Schooler 1978; Ilfeld 1977; Pearlin 1982). They examined the ways in which the basic social roles of spouse, parent, worker, provider, and neighbor are perceived as difficult by individuals. Where conflict, worry, and upset are seen as enduring in these roles, the risk of depression is greater. Richard Lazarus and his colleagues (Kanner et al. 1980) have also investigated common and seemingly mundane persistent concerns, which they call "hassles," and have found them to be related to depression. Dressler (1985a, 1987) examined chronic social role stressors in an African-American community in the rural southern United States. He found some interesting differences in the content of the chronic social role stressors in that in each social role, problems associated with racism and discrimination were part of the definition of chronic difficulties. These chronic stressors were found to be related to more depressive symptoms. Furthermore, in Leonard Pearlin's largely Euroamerican sample, marital stressors were most strongly related to depression (Ilfeld 1977); in the black community, economic stressors were the strongest correlate (Dressler 1985a), in keeping with the general cultural salience of economic adjustment.

Theodore Graves and Nancy Graves (1985) examined the impact of a kind of hybrid stressor measure in their study of Polynesian migrants to New Zealand. This measure included some life events (such as the death of a close family member), as well as chronic role difficulties, such as work and family problems. The correlation of stressors with more reported psychosomatic symptoms was about the same ($r = .37$) for migrants from Samoa and the Cook Islands and for European New Zealanders.

A chronic stressor that has been investigated cross-culturally is "life-style stress" (Dressler 1982; Dressler, Mata et al. 1987; Dressler, Dos Santos et al. 1987), or, as it has been referred to more recently, "life-style incongruity" (Dressler 1988, 1989b). Drawing on earlier work (Chance 1965; Graves 1967), Dressler defines this factor as the degree to which style of life exceeds occupational class; these two variables are defined, respectively, as the consumption of material goods and services and the individual's relationship to the market economy (Weber 1946). Operationally, life-style is measured by the ownership of material culture and the adoption of "cosmopolitan" behaviors, and occupational class is measured with standard occupational rankings. Life-style incongruity is related to higher blood pressure in St. Lucia, Brazil, Mexico, and Alabama and is related to higher depressive symptoms in Alabama. One of the most intriguing aspects of this factor is that it is related to disease independently from individual perceptions of stressful events, feelings of relative economic deprivation, or perceptions of chronic economic stressors.

Similar inconsistencies have been investigated elsewhere. Norman Chance (1965) found a similar discrepancy to be related to emotional symptoms among Alaskan Eskimo, and Graves (1987) found that this discrepancy predicted problem drinking among native Americans and Mexican-Americans. Stephen McGarvey and Diana Schendel (1986) found that blood pressures among Samoans were higher among those persons with inconsistencies in education and occupation. M. Beiser and coworkers (1976) found that blood pressure among women in Senegal was higher if they were oriented toward urban, Western culture but did not have the language skills (in French) to participate in that culture. Craig Janes and Ivan Pawson (1986) found, in a study of the Samoan community in northern California, that individuals with few economic resources who were attempting to achieve higher prestige in the community through extensive social participation had higher blood pressures.

When the effects of acute and chronic stressors have been compared, it has generally been found that they have independent effects on depression (Aneshensel and Stone 1982; Dressler 1986a). Similarly, different kinds of chronic stressors have independent effects as well (Dressler, Santos et al. 1987; Dressler 1988). These latter studies are especially intriguing since life-style incongruity has been measured "objectively," in the sense that there is no verbal report from the respondent of the stressfulness in any sense of life-style, and chronic social role stressors have been measured "subjectively," in the sense that this measurement relies explicitly on verbal reports by the respondent of problems or difficulties. These appear to be two distinct phenomena with parallel effects on depression and blood pressure. Furthermore, the effects of life-style incongruity are invariant across communities.

RESISTANCE RESOURCES

Since the mid-1970s, with the publication of two very influential review papers (Cassel 1976; Cobb 1976), a focus of research has become those factors that directly reduce and/or moderate the risk of disease. The topic of most interest has been social support (Cohen and Syme 1985; Henderson 1984; Cohen and Wills 1985; Orth-Gomer and Unden 1987), with considerable interest given also to personal coping resources (Folkman 1984; Gore 1985). These two factors fall under the general rubric of "resistance resources" (Antonovsky 1979), and interest in these factors derives from theoretical perspectives and from common sense. With respect to the latter, it is clear that everyone who experiences some kind of stressful event or circumstance does not necessarily fall ill, just as some people exposed to an infectious disease agent fail to become sick. On a more theoretical level, since the publication of Emile Durkheim's (1951; original 1897) classic study of suicide, it has been clear that the sense of social solidarity, of mutual support and aid within a social group, is a fundamental dimension of social interaction that contributes to better functioning and individual health. Since Durkheim, modern life, with its social centrifugal forces, has been seen as a threat to this sense, or as contributing to anomie, a feeling of the loss of this integrative system and attendant sentiments. In a sense, this classic model sees the stress process as unidimensional, with positive and healthy individual functioning occurring under conditions of high social solidarity and negative and unhealthy functioning occurring under the loss of that social solidarity. Contemporary models of the stress process simply make this a two-dimensional, as opposed to one-dimensional, process. The first dimension is the risk or stressor dimension; the second and counterbalancing dimension is the resistance resource dimension, including both social supports and personal coping resources.

A further emphasis in contemporary models is the "buffering" hypothesis. This hypothesis states that, in terms of the prediction of mental illness, the availability of social support or personal coping resources has no particular effect for those who are not experiencing some kind of stressful event or circumstance. For persons exposed to stressors, however, the effect of those stressors is dependent on the level of available resistance resources; persons with high resources will be unaffected by stressors, and persons with low resources will experience a considerable impact of stressors. Put differently, persons with meager resources for coping with demands are most vulnerable.

SOCIAL SUPPORT

What are these resources? Social support may be defined as the perceived availability of help or assistance from other persons during times of felt need. A few additional definitions are in order for putting this in the proper context. Social structure is a set of norms and values that define the range of behaviors and kinds of interactions permissible within a culture for specified classes of individuals. Social organization is the observable and statistically quantifiable manifestation of these norms. Social networks are the concrete relationships among a defined set of individuals. A social support system is a subset of an individual's ego-centered social network, upon whom that individual relies for social support as defined above.

As in any other fresh area of inquiry, social support has been assessed in a bewildering variety of ways; only recently have programmatic reviews begun to appear recommending the best approaches to the concept (House and Kahn 1985; Bruhn and Phillips 1984; Berkman 1985; Orth-Gomer and Unden 1987), although these programs are not necessarily in agreement. Sheldon Cohen and Thomas

Wills (1985) distinguish studies that examine structural measures of social support (those describing the existence and/or quantity of relationships) from functional measures of social support (those describing the kinds of supportive transactions occurring); in my terminology these two alternatives are network measures versus support measures.

Earlier studies relied heavily on network or structural measures of support, finding that individuals who are married or who live with other persons are at a lower risk of depression if a life event occurs (Eaton 1978; Kessler and Essex 1982; Monroe et al. 1983). More recently attention has shifted to the perception of support available within a network, and this research consistently demonstrates a buffering effect of the perceived availability of support on stressors (Wilcox 1981; LaRocco, House, and French 1980; Caldwell and Bloom 1982). Some (Jacobson 1987) have argued that the actual support received in a social transaction must be taken into account to understand the stress-buffering effect of support, reasoning that if support perceived to be available was not forthcoming, this would negate any beneficial effect. Surprisingly, available research (Wethington and Kessler 1986) indicates this is not the case; the perception that support is available reduces the impact of stressors regardless of actual support received.

A number of interesting cross-cultural studies of social support demonstrate the influence of cultural context in terms of the definition of social support, and in terms of the modification of the support-disease relationship. Soheir Morsy (1978) found that individuals in an Egyptian village who reported the poorest overall health status were those who had the least status, and hence could anticipate the least amount of support, within a household. These were young women who had married and resided in the extended family households of their husbands but who had yet to have children of their own and gain status associated with childbearing.

Dressler, Mata, and others (1986) used similar reasoning in their study of social support and blood pressure in a Mexican town. They assessed social support by asking respondents to whom they might turn for assistance in response to a set of six problems. Each respondent was asked about each of the following relationships as potential supporters: relatives, friends, neighbors, or *compadres/comadres*. Four measures of perceived support were found by counting the number of problems for which a person would seek aid from each kind of social network member. It was found that, for males, perceived support from each kind of supporter was related to lower blood pressure, and the strongest correlation was observed for *compadre* support. For all females, there were no significant effects. When women were divided into younger and older age groups, a pattern emerged. Older women had lower blood pressure if they perceived support available from their relatives; younger women had higher blood pressures if they perceived support available from friends. This was interpreted as evidence of the threat to family integrity posed by the formation of friendships by young women outside the domestic group, when normative expectations were that they should be submersed within the family. For older women, this was evidence of their gain in family power and prestige with age.

As the role and status of women change with economic development and urbanization, this pattern of correlations also changes. In a study in urban Brazil, using precisely the same measurement of social support, Dressler (1986b) found that for men, support from relatives was related to lower blood pressure, while for women, support from nonkin (especially neighbors) was related to lower blood pressure. As the roles and status of women change, their power in forming enduring relationships outside the context of kinship also changes.

These contextual modifications of the social support–disease relationship have also been observed in research in Polynesia and among Polynesian migrants to urban centers. In traditional villages in Polynesia, greater involvement in the salient social groups (primarily large kindreds) of the community is associated both with lower secretion of "stress" hormones (Hanna, James, and Mantz 1986) and with fewer reported psychosomatic symptoms (Graves and Graves 1979). Graves and Graves (1980) argue that the adaptation to urban settings places different demands on individuals, which in turn alters the nature of support systems. These hypotheses were supported in a study of migrants to New Zealand; Samoans reported more symptoms in association with reports of more relatives in the community (Graves and Graves 1985). Similarly, in a study of Samoan migrants to California, Craig Janes and Ivan Pawson (1986) found that involvement in "core social networks" of siblings was related to lower blood pressure, while involvement in larger kin and other social groups was related to higher blood pressure.

Research in African Caribbean (Dressler 1979) and African-American (Dressler 1985a) communities also demonstrates the cultural specificity in the definition and effects of social support systems. In each setting, it was hypothesized that only support systems organized in terms of extended kinship relationships would be related to better health status because of the specific meanings attached to those relationships in these cultural contexts. This hypothesis was supported in each setting.

Research on social support and health indicates that the definition of social support systems, and the relationship of support and disease, is more variable across social and cultural contexts than are the definitions or effects of stressors.

PERSONAL COPING RESOURCES

A second major category of resistance resources is the beliefs, attitudes, and behavioral strategies individuals use in coping with stressful events and circumstances. The study of coping is most often associated with Lazarus and his cognitive appraisal model of the coping process (Lazarus and Folkman 1986). In this model, coping, consists of attempts through cognitive restructuring and behavioral changes to alter the impact of a stressful circumstance. The recent work of this group has shown that an active and intentional approach to problem solving and a redefinition of stressful events as less threatening are both related to less negative emotional reactions (Folkman and Lazarus 1988; see also Pearlin and Schooler 1978).

A number of studies have examined the cultural context of these coping styles.

These styles are often distinguished as an "active" or "problem-focused" style, characterized by direct problem solving, versus a "passive" or "defensive" or "emotion-focused" style, characterized by attempts to control negative emotional reactions. Some cross-cultural research is consistent with the hypothesis that an active coping style is related to better health status (Dressler 1980; Wheaton 1983; Colby et al. 1985). In certain contexts, however, it has been found that emotion-focused coping can lead to better mental health status. This was suggested in a study of a black community in the rural South (Dressler 1985b) in which it was found that men, but not women, who used emotion-focused coping had fewer depressive symptoms. A similar finding came from a study of university students dealing with the threat of final examinations in India (Caplan et al. 1984). Sherman James and his associates (James et al. 1983, 1987) have observed that an active coping style, when coupled with few economic resources in a black community, was related to higher blood pressure. These studies suggest that there are particular social-environmental circumstances in which the anticipated effects of a particular coping style can change, depending on available resources and thus the meaning of coping.

Several studies of more specialized institutional resources deserve mention here. Robert Ness (1980) found that faith healing activities in a fundamentalist church in Newfoundland could have beneficial mental health effects. Similarly, Vivian Garrison (1977a) and Kaja Finkler (1981), in studies of spiritualist healing centers in Hispanic cultures in the United States and Costa Rica, provide evidence that these provide emotionally supportive environments for individuals coping with chronic stressors. Diane Brown and Lawrence Gary (1987) found religiosity to moderate the impact of stressful life events on the depressive symptoms of black Americans in a southern city. And Henry Murphy (1982), reviewing cross-cultural evidence on hypertension, speculates that societies in which blood pressure levels are low may have compensatory mechanisms, including ritual activities, that help to discharge autonomic nervous system arousal that might otherwise result in peripheral vascular resistance. All of these studies help to emphasize that a diversity of personal and institutional resources may prove to be important in accounting for disease resistance cross-culturally.

INTEGRATIVE STUDIES

Finally, a few more comprehensive studies need to be mentioned within the specific rubric of stress research. No review of social and cultural components of the stress process would be complete without noting the seminal contributions of George Brown and his associates (Brown and Harris 1978). Brown set out to understand how life events, chronic stressors, social supports, and other vulnerability factors interact to precipitate major depression. This work cannot be easily summarized, but in it he has demonstrated that stressors and supports interact to predict depression (the so-called buffering model) and that these factors are embedded in the context of individual lives. Brown's concept of embeddedness, and especially his approach to the perception of stress and support, varies considerably from received wisdom. He argues (Brown 1974) that individual perceptions of stress or support are necessarily distorted and of little utility for understanding the etiologic significance of those factors. What is important is the socially patterned meaning of those factors, a meaning embedded in a symbolic network that the individual subject is in little position to apprehend. Therefore, Brown exploits the shared culture of subject and observer to define what is a "stressor" or "support" and goes on to demonstrate the considerable empirical value of doing so. Brown also challenges current notions of endogenous versus reactive depressions, suggesting instead that the contextual vulnerability factors distinguishing the two have been overlooked. These contextual factors can be delineated with a replicable method developed by these investigators, and anyone interested in this area should explore Brown's work.

John Bruhn and S. Wolf (1979) describe the exploration of the epidemiologic puzzle of a remarkably low cardiovascular disease mortality rate among Italian-Americans in a Pennsylvania community, a group that by conventional (mainly dietary) measures of risk should have had a much higher mortality rate. These investigators attribute the findings to the highly integrated social organization of the community and show that as that organization has changed over time, heart disease has increased.

Dressler (1982) studied the interaction between chronic stressors generated in the process of economic development and the counterbalancing forces of social and cultural resistance resources, in the risk of high blood pressure in St. Lucia, a Caribbean society. The incongruity between life-style and economic class was the major risk for high blood pressure and was shown to have been generated by the nature of social change occurring over a thirty-year period. But individuals who had access to traditional forms of social support and had active styles were effectively protected from stressors. This study serves as an example of the buffering model of stressors and resistance and shows how all elements of the process are embedded in specific social and historical processes.

Arthur Kleinman (1986) provides a detailed analysis of neurasthenia and depression in the context of profound social change in the People's Republic of China. He finds that an understanding of the development of depression requires an understanding of how social change, and especially the Cultural Revolution, generated specific kinds of stressful experiences and altered the nature of traditional social support systems for many individuals. Notable in this work is the combination of social scientific theory and detailed psychiatric case analysis to generate a comprehensive model of depression in a specific cultural context.

SPECIAL TOPICS AND PUZZLES

There are a number of directions in the cultural study of stress and disease that cannot be fitted neatly into the categories of the stress model I have outlined above or that form a separate literature. Cross-cultural research has also generated specific puzzles that call into question some of the received wisdom of social and behavioral epidemiology. One special topic is the study of the adaptation of migrants to their host culture. A number of studies have demonstrated that following migration, individuals are in poorer health than in their premigrant status or compared to nonmigrants (Salmond et al. 1985; Hackenberg et al. 1983; Baker 1986).

In one sense migration could be treated as a stressful life event or acute stressor, but a variety of studies have shown that the stressful effects of migration can persist for years if an effective adaptive strategy within the host culture is not established (Graves and Graves 1980, 1985). Much of this research has looked at immigrants to the United States. Dressler and Bernal (1982) and Joseph Westermeyer and coworkers (1984) found that increasing length of residence in the host culture was related to more symptoms of emotional maladjustment if individuals did not have either personal or social resources to assist in coping with the novel environment (see also Kuo 1976).

Premigration experiences also influence adjustment. In a study of Southeast Asian immigrants, Lynn August and Barbara Gianola (1987) found that these migrants exhibited posttraumatic stress disorder, much as Vietnam War veterans do. William Vega and colleagues (1987), emphasizing a quite different premigration experience, found that Mexican migrant women were better adjusted in the United States if they had stronger premigration support and were able to maintain some contact with their premigration support network.

Thanh Tran (1987), Lucia McSpadden (1987), and Anthony Walsh and Patricia Walsh (1987) explored the importance of social relationships in facilitating immigrant adjustment. In a study of Vietnamese refugees, Tran (1987) found that participation in ethnic organizations and the availability of close confidants of similar ethnicity were related to better mental health. Other resources, such as English-language ability and education, were found to be important primarily through the indirect effect of increasing income. Walsh and Walsh (1987), in a study of blood pressure among a diverse group of immigrants, found generalized perceptions of the availability of social support to be related to lower blood pressure, independently of a variety of other variables. McSpadden (1987) found that Ethiopian refugees who were assisted in their settlement in the United States through a voluntary association (such as a church congregation) exhibited better mental health status than those who were assisted by individual caseworkers.

Studies of "acculturation" are complementary to studies of migrants, often being carried out on groups of migrants to a new cultural setting. What distinguishes acculturation from migration studies is the emphasis on a precise set of measurements of "acculturation" in the former studies as opposed to the group-level comparisons in the latter studies. Also, acculturative processes may be occurring in situations of political and economic change, such as when marginal and minority populations are gradually drawn into increased participation in larger national social structures.

Richman and associates (1987) and J. W. Berry and associates (1987) review studies of acculturation, drawing on the classic statement of Robert Redfield, Ralph Linton, and Melville Herskovits (1936) to define the process. Berry and others (1987) also review a series of studies conducted by a group of cross-cultural psychologists, led by J. W. Berry, of acculturation as a predictor of symptoms of emotional stress. What ties all of these studies together is mainly the operational definition of acculturation: the adoption of a new language, new material life-styles, exposure to new information through the media, and, sometimes, the adoption of new forms of employment. The "new" forms of these behaviors are those of the dominant culture, and the adopters are members of a subordinate group, whether migrants, members of an ethnic minority, or members of a peripheral and dominated community.

In the studies reviewed by Berry and associates (1987), higher education predicts lower symptom levels, as does an attitude that traditional cultural identity can be maintained in the context of the dominant culture. Furthermore, when the variables listed above were combined into a single index, it was related to lower symptoms. As the authors note, this finding runs counter to traditional wisdom, since more behavioral acculturation is thought to be related to more symptoms; however, they note that a combined index is dominated by measured years of formal education, which, as we have already seen, is related to access to the larger culture, and hence fewer symptoms.

Studies of acculturation and cardiovascular disease provide a different picture. Studies of coronary heart disease among Japanese-Americans in California (Marmot and Syme 1976) and Hawaii (Reed et al. 1982) show that the more acculturated (more Western education, more English-language use, more participation in Western institutions) have higher rates of cardiovascular disease. Similarly, in a study of elderly Navaho, Stephen Kunitz and Jerrold Levy (1986) found a greater prevalence of hypertension among the more acculturated, especially for women.

Recently M. Audrey Burnam and associates (1987) examined acculturation in relation to diagnostic categories of psychiatric disorder among Mexican-Americans in Los Angeles. Using an acculturation scale, they found that the more acculturated had higher rates of a variety of disorders, until migrant status was controlled for. All of the predictive strength of acculturation was accounted for by the fact that U.S.-born Mexican-Americans had a higher prevalence of mental disorders than immigrant Mexican-Americans.

If studies of migration and acculturation represent special topics in the cultural study of stress and disease, the study of social class and disease presents a special puzzle. It is widely accepted that nearly all forms of disease, but especially various forms of cardiovascular disease and mental illness, are inversely related to social class, whether that is assessed on the basis of occupation, income, education, or some combination of these variables (Macintyre 1986). Most would agree with Horacio Fabrega's (1974:56) observation that "social class" is an abstract category that masks more precise psychosocial factors more closely related to disease. This leads to the attempt to reduce the social class–disease effect to more precise, and usually individual-level, variables.

But the historical and cross-cultural evidence presents a different picture. I have referred to studies (Kessler and Cleary 1980; Dressler 1986a) showing that more precise measurements of stressful events and circumstances do not supersede the effects of social class, but rather their effects are contingent upon social class. G. Rose and M. G. Marmot (1981) and H. Morgenstern (1980) found in Great Britain and the United States that the inverse effect of social class on cardiovascular disease mortality has emerged only within the past thirty years; prior to 1950 or so, higher mortality rates were found in the highest social classes. The current inverse pattern in Britain is found only among Britons and Irish immigrants; mortality is higher among higher-class Caribbean immigrants (Marmot and Theorell 1988).

Reviewing cross-cultural studies of blood pressure, Dressler (1984b) observed that in some societies, there was an inverse relationship between social class and blood pressure, and in other societies there was a direct relationship. Most recently Janis Hutchinson (1986) and Dressler and coworkers (1988), in intracultural studies in the Caribbean, found an interaction effect between gender and social class in relation to lower blood pressure. For females, increasing social class was related to lower blood pressure, and for males, increasing social class was related to higher blood pressure. Taken together, these studies are confusing, but there does appear to be a systematic pattern to them. At some point in the process of social change, the patterning of disease and disease risk by social class changes, going from a direct to an inverse relationship. The parameters of this process remain to be determined.

Another risk factor worth mentioning here but on which there has been little sociocultural research is the Type A behavioral pattern. This is a pattern of behavior characterized by a chronic struggle to achieve, a heightened sense of time urgency, and chronic hostility; it is also the most well-researched behavioral predictor of coronary heart disease, and it is clear that the meaning and impact of the behavioral pattern vary across different cultural contexts (Dressler 1989a). Allan Young (1980) and Cecil Helman (1987) have offered excellent theoretical analyses of the Western cultural principles underlying the development of the behavioral pattern, and future empirical work should follow these leads in cross-cultural research.

DISCUSSION

My major aim in this section is to explore more fully some of the implications of the results of the research reviewed here and to point out some places of potential convergence in separate traditions of research, with the goal of outlining a future direction for empirical work. A striking pattern in these findings is the relatively small amount of cross-cultural variability in the definitions and effects of stressors. Whether stressful life events, chronic social role stressors, or structural imbalances like life-style incongruity are examined, there is a fair agreement between research conducted in disparate settings that these are important risk factors for disease. Of course, the precise definition of particular stressors does vary, as, for example, when problems associated with racism are emphasized as chronically stressful circumstances in an African-American community. But it is striking that once these definitional matters are taken into account, there is a consistent and replicable effect of stressors on disease. This even extends to the finding that the effects of stressful life events vary by social class in different cultural settings (Kessler and Cleary 1980; Dressler 1986a, 1987).

A common denominator to all this research, whether it has been carried out among women in London (Brown and Harris 1978), Polynesian migrants to New Zealand (Graves and Graves 1985), or African-Americans (Dressler 1986a), is that Western, industrial, "modern" society provides the macrolevel historical context in which these studies are conducted. Fundamental to the definition of this context is the differentiation of systems of social stratification and the changing values emphasis described so well by Peter Worsley (1981). What I am suggesting is that this particular pattern of development, as described by world systems theory, carries within it specific structural relationships that generate stressful events and circumstances that vary only a little depending on the setting in which they occur.

The effects of stressful events are one example of this. Consistently across studies it is the occurrence of these life events, regardless of respondents' idiosyncratic reports of the "stressfulness" of those events, that increases disease risk. In studies in developed countries, the important events are the truly major, disruptive transitions involving the loss of valued statuses. As the WHO international study found, these truly major events can be reliably identified and predict disease onset in both developed and developing countries. It seems likely that these events come to be socially and culturally defined as transitions to valued statuses in the process of economic change and development and that the occurrence of an event signifying the loss of a valued status results in increased risk of disease.

This can perhaps be seen more clearly in the example of life-style incongruity. Mass consumption of material culture is a pattern that has diffused widely throughout the Western world in the linked process of development and dependency. It is also well known that productive capacities that can absorb labor are outstripped by consumption values in the process of development, thus virtually ensuring the structural imbalance described by life-style incongruity. The only changes from setting to setting are the precise items consumed and the degree of socioeconomic differentiation (contrast Dressler, Mata et al. 1987 and Dressler, Santos et al. 1987). More important than these local variations is the general pattern that the imbalance between the valued status defined by material consumption and the valued status defined by occupational class reliably predicts disease risk across these settings.

These same arguments extend as well to chronic social stressors. These stressors are defined as perceived problems in major social role areas such as spouse, worker, and economic provider. As occupational and domestic roles organized within an industrial mode of production supplant the more culturally variable social roles of traditional cultures, it is the perceived difficulties associated with these "modern" roles that generalize across settings as predictors of disease. Two points are important here. First, there is evidence that conventional notions of stress are important to disease risk. These perceived difficulties are precisely what people usually mean by the term, and there is consistent evidence that they are important. Second, it is striking that these perceptions themselves generalize across cultural settings and are consistently associated with disease (Graves and Graves 1985). This implies that these individual perceptions are a function of the socially patterned meanings of major social roles in an industrial mode of production. All of this evidence, for events, role stressors, and structural imbalances, suggests that the sociocultural risk of disease is more importantly a function of the socially defined, rather than idiosyncratically defined, impact of events and circumstances. While these observations may seem heretical to a conventional understanding of stress and disease, not to mention to the particular variant of cultural determinism in current vogue in anthropology, it nevertheless is consistent with the available empirical evidence, as well as a historical materialist theoretical orientation. What would be useful now is a well-designed program of cross-cultural studies to examine these ideas with greater specificity, including societies not within the Western sphere of development.

Where the definition of variables, and the relationships of those variables to disease outcomes, appears to vary most dramatically across cultural contexts is in the study of resistance resources. This is especially true in the study of social support systems. Assuming for the moment that the perception of social support is the most important feature of support systems, and this can be only a tentative assumption, those relationships defined as supportive vary considerably within and between cultures. The available evidence suggests that an important factor in this regard is the kin-nonkin distinction (Dressler, Mata et al. 1986), although even within categories of kin, a kind of distance function can assume prominence (Janes and Pawson 1986).

Even more remarkable is the cross-cultural variability in the effects of social support (Graves and Graves 1985; Dressler 1989c). As we have seen, in some settings, social support is related to a lower disease risk and buffers the effects of stressors; in other settings social "support" is related to a higher disease risk. It would be convenient simply to redefine some forms of social "support" as social "stress," but this replaces empirical analysis with semantic juggling that will not extend our understanding. If in particular circumstances an individual states that he or she believes support to be available and that belief in turn is related to a greater likelihood of disease, we must accept that belief and search for the contextual circumstances that determine why it is risk enhancing rather than risk reducing. It is this contextual effect of support that led me to propose that there is a particular valence to certain relationships (Dressler 1989c). By that I mean a particular meaning or significance in a supportive transaction that transcends the support provided (such as information or material assistance) and activates instead a set of psychophysiologic pathways that reduce the risk of disease. Some relationships will be supportive in the sense of providing actual support but will not have this valence. These support relationships will be neutral, or even perhaps deleterious, with respect to disease, while the perceived support that carries that valence will provide the protective function expected of social support. Of course, this concept of valence is now purely descriptive, to provide some way of discussing that of which we know little. Its only utility is to urge researchers to explore dimensions of support that have yet to be explored.

Some (e.g., Jacobson 1986, 1987) have argued that what is important in the study of social support is the specific timing of support in relation to different stages of the onset and unfolding of a stressful transition and that this process is best investigated phenomenologically. This hypothesis provides a useful starting point for the investigation of social support and specific kinds of risk factors, such as migration, where there is a definite onset and unfolding of the stressor. It fails to provide a useful model for investigating either the direct effects of social support or the other kinds of moderating effects that support might have with respect to chronic or structural stressors, nor can a phenomenological study of support stand alone without careful epidemiologic studies that relate support factors to measured disease outcomes.

Everything said thus far about the study of social support applies equally, or perhaps more heavily, to the study of personal coping resources. At least with respect to social support, there is a preliminary taxonomy of what variables are relevant to the investigation. With respect to personal coping resources, a wide range of factors could be important, as Lazarus (1966) argued in his seminal work on the topic. The most interesting lead in this respect is Colby's (1987) work on the adaptive potential of a particular structure of beliefs and values regarding personal efficacy, creativity, and altruism. Not only does Colby ground his perspective in a theory with enough generality to be of considerable utility for the cross-cultural study of disease, he has taken important initial steps in defining adaptive potential in operational terms and has tested it in several preliminary studies. Cross-cultural researchers in stress and disease should follow this lead.

Overall, research using an explicit model of stress has progressed well beyond a simplistic reductionist model in which all of the impact of the social and cultural setting on disease risk can be condensed to what individuals can consciously report as their perceptions (a model that, as Young 1980 shows, primarily recapitulates Western notions of personhood). Rather, social and individual meanings combine in complex interactions between stressors on the one hand and resistance resources on the other. Elsewhere I have argued that social constraints and individual beliefs and values ultimately are resolved and bridge the gap between society and human biology through the definition of individual identities (Dressler 1985c). More theoretical work in refining the stress model needs to be done to understand this process better.

Research on migration, acculturation, and other factors such as the Type A behavioral pattern needs to be incorporated into more comprehensive models of stress and disease. These have so far represented a separate literature with respect to stress and disease. A better approach would be to develop more complex models where, for example, migration could be contrasted with the occurrence of other stressful events or chronic stressors in the prediction of disease outcomes. Similarly, is "acculturation" per se a stressful experience, or does acculturation influence access to valued rewards within a society, thus making this process one component of larger social class processes (Graves 1967; Dressler 1988)? The epidemiologic puzzle of the cross-cultural variability of the social class–disease relationship can also be worked out only if more complex models are developed, requiring a cumulative empiricism all too rare in anthropological research.

One topic that has not been addressed at all in this review has been the nature of the outcome variable studied. I have freely assumed a definition of disease following Arthur Kleinman, L. Eisenberg, and B.J. Good (1978), further assuming that outcome variables such as depression and high blood pressure could be equally unambiguously defined. This is clearly not the case, as shown in a variety of ways (Good and Kleinman 1985). A paper by Good, Good, and Moradi (1985) makes the problem explicit in the study of depressive disorders. In a carefully combined interpretive and quantitative analysis of depression among Iranian migrants, they show that symptoms associated with a Western definition of depressive disorder can be distinguished from symptoms that serve an expressive-interpretive role in Iranian culture. Only the former show a patterned association with migration experience. This raises the possibility that stress factors predict "disease" but perhaps not "illness." Other studies (Dressler 1985c; Kleinman 1986) suggest that both disease and illness are related to stressors and resistance resources but that there are additional factors distinguishing the epidemiology of the two outcomes. There are fertile fields for future findings here.

Finally, future research should follow the lead established by Kleinman (1986) and others in which the relationship of stress and disease is investigated within a context of solid ethnography. It is by grounding the study of stress and disease in a larger understanding of historical change, unequal relations of power and status, and a refined definition of social organization that the intersection of human behavior and human biology in the process of evolutionary change can be better explained.

SECTION 4
METHODS IN MEDICAL ANTHROPOLOGY

CHAPTER 15

FIELD METHODS IN MEDICAL ANTHROPOLOGY

Pertti J. Pelto and Gretel H. Pelto

Medical anthropology is primarily an applied subdiscipline, as should be apparent from many of the materials covered in this book. The roots of the subdiscipline reach back to an intellectual, academic interest in describing and understanding the ways in which different non-Western peoples have explained illness and given treatment to the sick, but the preponderance of research in the 1970s and 1980s centered on pragmatic issues of improving the health and health care situations of people, both "Western" and "non-Western."

Health problems throughout the world constitute a sector of applied research that is by nature interdisciplinary; most health issues use data from biological sciences, clinical medical practices, and social-behavioral sciences. Research in health problems often requires other types of expertise as well; for example, the role of entomology is often central to understanding various vector-born diseases such as malaria, typhus, and dengue fevers, and the growing interest in research on health care systems requires information from economics and political science. Although there are many instances of research in which individual anthropologists, medical doctors, or biologists did it on their own, such solo performances are increasingly suspect, given the complex data involved in health issues.

The interdisciplinary nature of the illness and health care sector is partly responsible for the fact that methodological issues are strongly affected by national and international agencies and organizations that sponsor research. In the United States, a large share of health-related research is funded from the National Institute for Mental Health, National Institute for Drug and Alcohol, National Cancer Institute, National Institute on Aging, and other federal agencies. On the international health scene, the World Health Organization (WHO), the U.N. International Children's Emergency Fund (UNICEF), the U.S. Agency for International Development (USAID), and a variety of other organizations sponsor health-related research.

Proposals for research in any of these national and international agencies are judged by interdisciplinary review panels, often (but not always) dominated by biomedical scientists. These factors have had considerable influence in shaping the directions of research methodology in medical anthropology. Also, increasing numbers of medical anthropologists are based in medical schools, schools of public health, and other health agencies in which collegial relations are strongly interdisciplinary.

On the other hand, a considerable portion of research in medical anthropology continues to be funded by the anthropology division in the National Science Foundation, the Wenner-Gren Foundation, and other sources in which the review panels are primarily anthropologists. These anthropology-oriented sources are especially likely to be tapped for funding by medical anthropologists whose primary bases of operations are in anthropology departments. In such cases the research designs and other methodological features are somewhat less affected by the interdisciplinary, especially the biomedical, realm of discourse. It is probably fair to say that such "anthropology-oriented" medical anthropology is also less often applied in nature; however, one can find many exceptions to these patterns.

The growth of medical anthropology over the past two decades has been especially evident in the applied, interdisciplinary realm. In applied research, the solutions to specific practical questions about health and illness are the central concern, and development of theory plays a secondary role. Theoretical concerns are not totally ignored, but the areas of theoretical interest are often in theories of the middle range, where theoretical issues are strongly intermingled with methodological strategies. Medical anthropologists may pay lip-service to aspects of grand theory, but the research is usually at a considerable remove from direct linkage to broader theoretical abstractions.

In any case it is possible to examine a great many issues in methodology of medical anthropology without direct commitment to a particular theoretical position. In fact, much of anthropological method is essentially theory-less, in the sense that the basic methods of data gathering are the same regardless of the theoretical system adopted by the investigator (Bernard et al. 1986; Plattner et al. 1989). In field research it appears that practically all anthropologists use a mixture of interviewing (both structured and unstructured) and direct observation (again, both structured and unstructured). Specific questions asked, and specific targets for observation differ, depending on theoretical interests, but the processes of data gathering are broadly similar regardless of theoretical orientation. It is in the language of theoretical discourse that anthropologists differ markedly, even when discussing basically similar data. This is not to say that two different theoretical discourses necessarily disagree with one another; quite often the different theoretical vocabularies are in some sort of complementary, noncontrastive relationship.

Our examination of field methodologies in medical anthropology will be presented in a generally nontheoretical, or theory-neutral, manner. However, certain methodological tools and techniques will be presented with reference to particular research examples, which may include some of the theoretical language of the authors of the research.

BASIC RESEARCH QUESTIONS IN MEDICAL ANTHROPOLOGY

Research methodology becomes specific when we address specific questions. In the research in health care as carried out by medical anthropologists and others, the basic questions very often consist of variations on the following (applied) themes:

1. What are the causes (or important factors) in the variations in frequencies-appearances of a particular illness or pathology (for example, who gets malaria, diarrhea, asthma, hypertension, and so forth)?
2. What are the variations in treatment forms with relation to particular illnesses or pathologies?
3. What (and why) are the variations in peoples' choices of forms of treatment with relation to particular illnesses or pathologies?
4. How can the organization of prevention and treatment forms be made more effective in relation to the health of specific populations?

Although they are not the only forms of basic questions in medical anthropology, a very large share of research is intended to focus on specific issues related to these fundamental concerns. In a great many instances of research, then, the dependent variable of interest centers on a particular illness or condition—quite often the actual frequency of the illness. A great deal of medical and health care research, after all, is directed to lessening the frequency (incidence or prevalence) of specific illnesses. Just as frequently, however, the dependent variables center on peoples' choices of forms of treatment. Who uses "indigenous" treatments versus "cosmopolitan" resources to "do something" about a particular health problem?

The independent variables are much more varied, and they are by nature more directly reflective of basic theoretical approaches. The following hypotheses concerning "causes" or "factors" affecting treatment choices are all in the same grammatical form and can be examined with basically similar methodology, but they reflect different theoretical assumptions and language:

1. People [in community x] avoid cosmopolitan health care because of their traditional health beliefs.
2. People [in community x] choose indigenous versus cosmopolitan health care depending on their assessment of the severity of the illness and their ability to meet the costs of the specific health care.
3. People [in community x] will go to cosmopolitan health providers and will follow the medical advice to the extent that the information fits with their explanatory models of a specific illness.

4. People [in community x] see health care as a political expression, and they choose or reject cosmopolitan health care on political and ideological grounds.

5. People [in community x] are likely to be more accepting of the newly introduced primary health care (cosmopolitan) if they have the opportunity to participate actively in the planning of the health service system.

Although these are only a small fragment from all possible research statements, generalizations, or hypotheses, they are useful in illustrating ways in which different researchers, with different theoretical approaches, often have the same implicit or explicit dependent variable (a behavioral outcome) in mind, and they will use basically similar methodological approaches to gather the relevant data. In the five hypothetical cases, each researcher would presumably collect data on peoples' choices of health care alternatives through direct observation or interviewing and would also collect information about the network of independent variables specified in their particular theoretical model. Some researchers may adopt a strategy of direct observation plus unstructured interviews; others might rely mainly on quite structured interviews; still others will opt for various mixtures of quantified and qualitative data-gathering.

CONCEPTS AND DEFINITIONS

Before exploring the inventory of basic research methods in medical anthropology, it will be useful to present some definitions of terms central to methodological discussions. These terms play a central role in the structure of research proposals, so they constitute a key element in the vocabulary of grantsmanship, as well as in the analysis of different approaches to theory building and problem solving in medical anthropology.

Data are the recorded results of empirical observations in fieldwork, both quantitative and qualitative. All field notes are data; the recorded responses to structured interviews, and their transformations in, for example, computerized data sets, are data. Photographs, documents, and other physical materials also constitute data. Note that we use the term *data* to refer to both the physical materials (including tape recordings) and to the variables or "themes" or other attributes extracted from the primary materials. Sometimes we use the term *raw data* to refer to the actual physical materials, including unprocessed field notes.

A *dependent variable* is an outcome or condition or phenomenon that is to be explained or accounted for, or predicted, by reference to presumed "causal factors," "prior conditions", "determinants," "disposing features," or other conceptualizable antecedents.

An *independent variable* is any presumed "causal factor," "prior condition," "determinant," "disposing feature," or other conceptualizable antecedent thought to account for, predict, explain, or contribute to the existence, specific pattern or form of, or characteristics of an outcome or condition or phenomenon.

In experimental and quasi-experimental research designs, it is always the independent variable that is manipulated. If a research project has an experimental and a control group, the nature of those two groups constitutes, or embodies, the major independent variable. (Although many researchers have come to associate the notion of variables with statistical analysis, all empirical research can be usefully conceptualized in terms of variables, however implicit they may be in the actual research reports. Thus, data concerning particular variables may be "highly quantitative" or they may be quite qualitative in presentation.)

A *hypothesis* is a more or less explicit statement of a hunch or expectation or prediction of relationships or patterns that one seeks to test or examine in the course of a specific research project. Hypotheses are best seen as aspects of specific research projects.

The *methodology* is the logic-in-use in any research project whereby "raw" empirical observations are assembled and transformed into successively more abstract descriptive and analytic statements. Methodology may be thought of as a series of transformational rules and processes (including definitions of key concepts) that guide data gathering and relate the resulting data systematically to the hypotheses and other conceptual models in terms of which research results are expressed. Statistical procedures are one type of transformational system for arranging complex arrays of numerical data into patterns that can be expressed as theoretical models.

A *model* is any representation of the interrelationships among a series of variables or constructs in a research domain. A model is thus an analogic, simplified, physical representation of the phenomena in a particular instance of research. Commonly encountered models include maps, diagrams, scale models of physical things, as well as verbal descriptions that aptly portray essential elements of a complex domain. A famous model is the physical representation of the double helix used by the biologists James Watson and Francis Crick in arriving at the description of the DNA molecule (Watson 1968). In anthropology, particularly in earlier decades, the most commonly encountered models were representations of kinship terminologies. For our purposes, the term *model* is the meeting ground between the theoretical and methodological realms of discourse. A model embodies the elements derived from a particular theoretical perspective. Thus, the terms or features of a model are simplified portions of a general theory. The model also includes the elements or details about which specific data are to be gathered in a research project. Each element or concept in a model requires some sort of "operationalized" representation in the research activity.

An *operational definition* (of a variable) is the presentation of any dependent or independent variable in a specific research project as it is embodied through data-gathering procedures, whether explicit or implicit—for example, "Socioeconomic status [in this research] was dichotomized into two groups, landowners and the landless." As in the case of variables, some researchers feel that the idea of operational definitions refers only to quantitative research. However, the logic of the concepts in research is the same whether quantified or not. Any concepts reported by a researcher arise from data. The reader of any research can always ask, "What data serve as evidence for this particular construct?" Much of the writing in anthropology, including medical anthropology, presents information without specifying details of research methodology. Often we are left to guess at the operational definitions. But they are still part of the research structure, even if they remain unreported.

THE ANTHROPOLOGICAL APPROACH

Compared to most other disciplines, the hallmark of anthropology, medical anthropology included, is the so-called holistic approach. This takes many forms, but in most research there is the assumption that for any particular outcome or phenomenon to be explained, a great many interrelated factors are at work. In practice this means that medical anthropologists are likely to collect a great deal of data about economic features, social relationships, cultural belief systems, political processes, and other aspects of a community, even if the research intention is focused on a specific health question. This holistic perspective often leads anthropologists to be highly critical of other disciplines when they appear to adopt single-factor explanations or seemingly simple explanations for illness conditions, health care responses, and other issues.

The holistic perspective has important effects on research design. Whenever numerical analysis is involved, medical anthropologists are likely to be concerned with a large number of variables, requiring fairly complex statistical procedures. Also, attention to large numbers of factors, or variables, requires a considerable investment of time for each case, patient, illness episode, or other unit of analysis. The time limitations (and limitations of personnel) in turn constrain the anthropologist to limit sample sizes severely. The typical project in medical anthropology is likely to have much smaller samples than, for example, corresponding research projects by epidemiologists and sociologists.

Another hallmark of medical anthropology is the central role played by the culture concept in most research. To varying degrees most other researchers recognize the idea of cultural differences and cultural effects in relation to health care, but for anthropologists, the concept has much greater importance in shaping the directions of research.

Earlier, before the subdiscipline of medical anthropology came into being, many anthropologists who studied matters of health and illness among non-Western peoples regarded the detailed description of traditional healers and cultural beliefs about illness as the primary ethnographic objective, usually paying little attention to instances in which people used cosmopolitan medicines and practitioners. That is, the primary emphasis of earlier work was on the abstracted belief system, "the culture," rather than on actual behavior. In such studies, then, "the culture" was seen as the sole topic of data gathering.

More recently the concept of culture has assumed a somewhat more modest place in the theoretical and methodological works of many medical anthropologists. "Culture" and cultural differences have come to be seen as one major cluster of variables among complex networks of factors that account for, or explain, peoples' actual behaviors. This shift in the use of the culture concept constitutes a major achievement in anthropological methodology and "metatheory," as the idea of "culture" distinct from "behavior" has made it methodologically possible to speak of (and carry out research on) the variable effects of culture on peoples' behaviors.

Not all anthropologists share this definition of culture, but there is a widespread tendency to consider culture as idea systems, systems of symbolic meaning, or other variations in language that focus on peoples' mental processes. For example, a widely cited book by Arthur Kleinman states, "We can view medicine as a cultural system, a system of symbolic meanings anchored in particular arrangements of social institutions and patterns of interpersonal interactions" (Kleinman 1980:24). Similarly, Horacio Fabrega, in his book *Disease and Social Behavior*, commented that "illness, for example, offers an additional opportunity to study how behavior is structured and organized by underlying cultural rules" (Fabrega 1974:3). He then noted that "culture by definition represents a 'manmade,' socially relevant, experientially derived set of rules for living."

Regardless of researchers' specific definitions of culture, one of the central contributions of anthropology to applied studies of health issues is the delineation of the complex ways in which peoples' cultural belief systems interact with other factors in affecting rates of disease, definitions of illness, differential responses to illness, and other outcomes of interest. Although other disciplines pay some lip-service to the idea of culture in relation to health and illness, medical anthropologists are thought to be the methodological experts in study of cultural factors. To a considerable extent, the continued increases in acceptance of medical anthropologists in the interdisciplinary community of health research are due to increased recognition of the "cultural factor" as crucial to understanding all aspects of illness and health care.

The concept of culture has led to a generally accepted distinction between disease and illness. Illness refers to the culturally defined feelings and perceptions of physical and/or mental ailment and disability in the minds of people in specific communities. Disease is the formally taught definition of physical and mental pathology from the point of view of the medical profession. Both terms are, of course, "culture." The terms refer methodologically to the contrasts between two distinct cultures that meet when patients interact with physicians, whether in modern urban settings or in Third World health systems.

A large share of the research in medical anthropology of the 1980s focuses on situations of cultural pluralism in which populations with various indigenous health cultures are in more or less extensive contact with the trappings of cosmopolitan health culture. Accordingly, their cultural systems (or "rules for living") include beliefs and rules about the introduced cosmopolitan medications and practitioners, intermingled with the cultural ideas concerning the indigenous healers and treatments. Studies of health care and health issues in urban communities in North America are set in a context of cultural pluralism—as most "mainline" and middle-class people are aware of various alternative health care choices.

EXPLANATORY MODELS: CULTURAL VIEWS OF ILLNESS

Kleinman's formulation of the explanatory model (EM) of illness has taken a central place in research on particular illnesses, as medical anthropologists and others have sought to present a coherent picture of the cultural features that affect peoples' health behaviors. The EM for a particular illness should ordinarily consist of signs and symptoms by which the illness is recognized, presumed causes of the illness, recommended therapies, the pathophysiology of the illness, and prognosis (Kleinman 1980:105–7).

As Kleinman points out, individuals are likely to have quite vague and indefinite models of explanation for their illnesses, depending on past experiences of the patient and her or his circle of kin and friends. Some individuals in a community may have quite coherent explanations and expectations concerning a specific illness, and the "experts," the healers in the community, would probably on average have more coherent definitions with regard to the illnesses and the relevant therapies.

In any case, recent research among medical anthropologists has frequently made use of the EM construct as a focus around which a variety of questions can be raised concerning treatment behaviors and other features.

Intracultural Diversity as a Methodological Aid

In the past two decades researchers have increasingly recognized the methodological importance of intracultural and intracommunity diversity in peoples' beliefs and practices. This tendency in research arose in part in relation to the growth of cultural pluralism, especially in matters of health and illness. Medical anthropologists have come to realize that, even in seemingly isolated communities, individuals and families differ in their degree of adherence to traditional, indigenous health practices, as well as in their attitudes about medical and health ideas and materials newly introduced into their regions.

As a direct consequence, researchers have recognized the need for representative samples of individuals and households from whom cultural data are collected. The older ethnographic methodology based on a few selected key informants is not entirely abandoned, however. In-depth interviewing of key informants, along with participant observation, are still essential aspects of anthropological research, particularly in exploratory phases of study. The qualitative, descriptive materials from this ethnographic work are essential for making sense of the more quantified materials gathered from samples of observations or structured interviews.

Clinical and Community Populations

A clinical population can be defined as any group of patients, clients, or cases selected from the persons found at a particular health center, hospital, or individual healer's location. Clinical populations are selected for research whenever a portion of the research issues focus directly on the activities of the clinic or when it appears that a substantial part of the cases of a particular illness are to be found at the clinical setting.

Much of contemporary medical anthropology is concerned directly with the cultural systems, technical workings, and other aspects of health care in hospitals and other health care settings. For example, in his wide-ranging studies of sickness and healing in Taiwan, Kleinman has observed the practices of various kinds of healers and has interviewed their patients. To study the effects of shamanistic healing, he observed therapeutic sessions conducted by a *Tang-ki* (shaman) at a shrine called the Saintly Emperor's Palace. In addition to direct observation of the proceedings, "We attempted follow-up evaluations of nineteen consecutive clients treated for complaints of sickness over a three-night period in this shrine ... All patients were visited at their homes two months after their initial visit to the shrine" (Kleinman 1980: 313, 319).

A more systematic and larger sampling from a clinic population was utilized by Sharon Kaufman in her study of rehabilitation of stroke victims. "Data are drawn from a three-year investigation (1983–1986) of patterns of rehabilitation among 102 stroke patients over the age of 45. The study was carried out in an urban community hospital" (Kaufman 1988: 341). In both examples, the focus of research was on aspects of therapies in the specified clinical setting, as well as on the patients' responses and reactions to treatment. Also, in both instances, research included follow-up interviews with the patients in their home environments.

Direct observation of practitioner-patient interactions has become an important methodological focus as researchers seek to define more precisely the interactions that occur in therapeutic encounters. Such interaction studies have also been directed to the work of other practitioners besides doctors and healers. Rayna Rapp recently conducted an extensive study of genetic counselors, during which she "observed five genetic counselors working for New York City's Department of Health during their counseling sessions ... sitting in on more than 200 intake interviews" (Rapp 1988:145).

Where specific aspects of the client-provider interaction are studied, the sample unit is often the specific encounter rather than the population of individuals. Accordingly, in some cases, the sampling frame is specified as "all client-provider interactions occurring during _____ period," and a system of randomizing can be applied to the time periods themselves.

A study by W. Trevathan of childbirth events in a bicultural community, El Paso, Texas, illustrates the kind of research in which the data can be gathered only in a clinic setting. In the case of childbirth, the significant questions often center on the expectations of mothers in relation to a particular clinic regimen. Accordingly, Trevathan selected a particular birth center with a large flow of clients. She enrolled in the one-year midwifery training program of the birth center, after which a study of mother-infant interaction was initiated. "Every woman who registered for prenatal care at the Birth Center and whose delivery was expected between October 1978 and May 1979 was informed of the bonding study ... Volunteers were also recruited during childbirth education classes ...

In the eight-month period, 152 women agree to be in the study, approximately 50 percent of all those who delivered during that time period'' (Trevathan 1988:220). In this example, focus on cases in a particular clinical setting, where the researcher was a participant, permitted her to maintain close control of the research environment. On the other hand, the generalizations—for example, concerning differences between Spanish-speaking and Anglo mother-infant pairs—cannot be extrapolated to the general population.

In the cases mentioned, the clinic populations were appropriately selected because of the nature of the research topic; however, clinic populations should never be considered as representative of the general (community-based) population. In almost every case, a particular hospital or other health setting receives only a selected, nonrandom portion of the population that exhibits a given illness or condition. Other cases may remain home, untreated; still others are found at the various alternative treatment facilities. Even an exhaustive tally of all cases in all facilities does not produce a representative picture of a given health problem, except perhaps with illnesses so severe, and so clearly identified, that nearly all of them can be found.

Clinic-based samples, if used as the sole data collection strategy, also have another potential weakness. Patients at health facilities appear as individuals, separated from the family networks in which they normally reside. Full, holistic understanding of peoples' expectations and reactions concerning illness and health care requires consideration of the household setting as it affects peoples' cultural responses.

Generalizations about the frequencies of health care problems and peoples' choices of treatment usually require sampling from the relevant community population. Epidemiologists often refer to that community-based population as the denominator, which is essential to study if one is interested in understanding problems of health and illness in precise estimation of rates of particular illnesses or health care practices.

Clinical Samples with Matched Controls

Generalizations from clinic-based samples can often be greatly strengthened by selecting a control group from the same population that the clinic patients represent. Kaja Finkler introduced this method in her extensive study of spiritualist healers and their patients in the state of Hidalgo, Mexico: "Interviews were conducted on Tuesdays and Fridays, the two principal curing days in Spiritualist temples. While the interviewers were administering the questionnaires at the entrance of the temple, I sat in the curing room recording the number of patients that arrived... I also timed and recorded the verbal exchanges'' (Finkler 1985:200). Follow-up interviews were also conducted with the patients in their homes.

The data from the clinic (temple) sample were systematically compared with a control group (N = 372), which "was geographically matched with subjects interviewed in the temple corresponding to the villages... [from which the patients originated]'' (Finkler 1985:201). Use of the control group permitted

Finkler to state that the regular clientele of the temples did not differ significantly from the general population in perceived illness (Finkler 1985:130).

Strategies for Community-based Samples

Most research in medical anthropology has been structured primarily in terms of communities or various communities within communities. One or more communities in a particular region are chosen as primary sites for research, usually (not always) because of the prevalence of a particular health issue or problem in the selected region. Once the community or communities have been selected, sampling and other aspects of research design depend a great deal on two main factors: the nature of the specific health problem addressed and the geographic characteristics of the communities.

Community-based research is particularly congenial to medical anthropologists because the holistic methodological perspective practically requires a research context in which the field researcher enters into fairly long-term contacts with the people and is able to combine a great deal of firsthand participant observation with equally extensive interviews and conversations with people. Regardless of the specific topical focus, fieldworkers usually immerse themselves in the daily living of the people they study.

Often the researcher focuses on a single, well-chosen community of intermediate size. Where local villages and hamlets contain small numbers of households, it becomes necessary to include several such communities. Research concerned with a particular illness of a specific population segment—such as asthma among small children—requires that the population be large enough to contain an adequate sampling of households with small children experiencing the illness.

Sizes of study samples vary greatly, depending on overall community size, prevalence of specific illnesses studied, the types of data gathered, and the resources (including time) available. Mark and Mimi Nichter described a survey carried out in south India in which a small number of questions concerning food intakes during pregnancy, preferred size of baby, and relations of food intake to baby size constituted the very simple interview protocol. The simplicity of the interview schedule made it feasible to manage a sample size of 282 participants (Nichter and Nichter 1983). In research on cultural constraints on fertility transition and other aspects of women's roles in a Tunisian town, L. Stamm carried out an extensive survey in 107 households during 15 months of fieldwork (Stamm and Tsui 1986). Approximately 100 households appears to be a common ballpark figure in medical anthropology research.

On the other hand, it is not uncommon that intensive studies are carried out with smaller samples. Logan examined the role of pharmacists and over-the-counter medications in a Mexican city through detailed interviews with 48 informants. In addition, she carried out key informant interviews with "several local pharmacists" and also observed transactions in the pharmacies (Logan 1983). Sargent and associates interviewed Kampuchean refugee women in Dallas, with a total sample of 42 respondents (Sargent, et al. 1983; Sargent and

Marcucci 1988). M. L. Welch carried out in-depth, repeated interviews with a sample of 30 serious trauma victims, all of whom were initially treated at a New England hospital. Repeated interviews with the patients continued over a period of nine to fourteen months, as some individuals required very long periods of convalescence (Welch 1989). In the Logan and Sargent studies, the data were presented as primarily descriptive materials, with statistics limited to presentation of frequencies of particular response categories. In the study of trauma victims M. L. Welch was primarily interested in collecting a wealth of textual material for qualitative analysis, though she presents a few characteristics in terms of numerical frequencies.

In all three studies the data are useful primarily for the planning of applied programs, but the data also suggest specific hypotheses of theoretical interest that could be the focus of further research. Studies involving small samples occur frequently in situations where the total population is small (such as the Kampuchean population in Dallas), where large amounts of information are to be gathered from each individual case (such as the trauma victims), and in situations in which appropriate respondents or cases may be quite difficult to locate in the general population (such as in case of a particular rare illness). Prospective case monitoring is another type of research that usually results in small samples, particularly when the types of cases are relatively infrequent.

When researchers have sufficient coinvestigators and/or research assistants, samples can be quite large. Carole Browner and associates carried out research on reproduction and health in a township of 1,800 inhabitants in highland Oaxaca, Mexico: "In addition to participant observation and intensive interviewing of selected key informants, single interviews were conducted with a 54 percent sample of the *municipio*'s adult women and their husbands. One-hundred eighty women and 126 men were interviewed, with the sample constructed to represent the age, residential, and linguistic backgrounds of . . . [the] adult population" (Browner and Perdue 1988:85–86).

Many anthropological studies utilize multiple community samples. In some cases several communities or hamlets must be included simply for representativeness in a complex population. J. Gittelsohn, in a study of intrahousehold food distribution patterns, defined his research population in rural Nepal in terms of a network of six villages in order to include all relevant caste groups (Gittelsohn 1989).

Quite often the selection of multiple communities is used to operationalize a significant, usually independent, variable. M. E. Bentley chose three villages in north India as the population for study of household management of childhood diarrhea in order to have an experimental and control group. One village was the site of an oral rehydration therapy (ORT) intervention program, and two villages nearby were selected as controls in order to test the efficacy of the program (Bentley 1988).

In a study of "ethnicity, ecology and mortality in northwestern Thailand," Peter Kunstadter gathered data from a number of different communities, both highland and lowland: "Community type is the basic unit of comparison. Disaggregation of the population according to type of community shows that fertility and mortality patterns are systematically associated with ethnicity and ecology (location and basic economy). . . . Populations in the study area allow control of ecological and ethnic variability by comparing, for example, the same ethnic group in different ecological settings (Northern Thai in Town, Suburb, and Lowland Rural communities, and different ethnic groups in the same ecological setting (e.g., Highland Skaw Karen, Po Karen and Lua' with similar swidden economies)'' (Kunstadter 1986:125). In a similar vein, Robert Hackenberg and associates selected four communities in the Philippines—two sedentary and two migrant groups—for testing specific hypotheses about the effects of migration and modernization on hypertension levels (Hackenberg et al. 1983)

B. Gebrian has used a multicommunity design in a study of nutrition, rates of immunization, and other characteristics in a thirty-four-community zone in southwestern Haiti. She compared communities in terms of "distance from health center," "level of community participation," "size of population," and other independent variables (Gebrian 1989).

SAMPLING IN URBAN COMMUNITIES

Medical anthropology in urban sites, particularly in North American settings, often focuses on one or more ethnic groups within the general population. The selection of such ethnic (or other) subcommunities poses special problems, particularly in identifying the total population of ethnic households from which sampling will occur. A typical strategy is to identify one or more urban neighborhoods thought to be concentrations of the particular ethnic group. In Hartford, Connecticut, S. Schensul and associates selected two neighborhoods, one a public housing project and the other an area of privately owned dwellings. After arbitrarily delimiting the two neighborhoods, a system of random sampling was adopted by which 143 households were selected for interviews (Schensul and Borrero 1982).

Craig Janes described the difficulties in selecting a sample of Samoan migrants in northern California for study of hypertension: "The sample selection process involved the following steps: a list of the church membership of two large church congregations was obtained, numbering about 130 households. From this pool, 60 households were chosen at random. This resulted in 89 interviews with men and women in these households . . . In addition, with the aid of a Samoan research assistant, who was also a well-known and respected member of the community, I selected a sample of 25 individuals from other religious denominations" (Janes 1986:205).

The contrast in style between intensive, small-sample research and the collection of survey data in an urban setting is particularly striking in the work of Susan Scrimshaw in the Ecuadorian city of Guayaquil. In the ethnographic phase of research, "Sixty-five families in one small area of the squatter settlement were studied for six months . . . using . . . participant observation, conversation, informal interviewing, and observation" (Scrimshaw 1985:125). An interview schedule was then designed for gathering quantitative data on migration, fertility, and induced abortions and was administered to approximately 2,000 households in a squatter settlement and the central city slum area, using probability cluster sampling. Scrimshaw demonstrated that her ethnographic sample of fewer than 100 households was in many ways quite similar to the large-scale sample in terms of frequencies of fertility attitudes and behaviors.

The Household as the Basic Unit of Analysis

In all but a tiny fraction of situations, the people of interest to medical anthropologists experience their health and illness, and make decisions about health care, in the nexus of the household. The specific operational definition of household may vary for different kinds of populations, but the general term refers to a group of people living together in a single domicile, sharing food and other resources, whether or not consanguineally related. Often researchers seek to delineate households as the people "who eat from the same pot," even in cases in which more than one such cooking or eating group may be found within a compound or other complex domicile.

Common practice in many community-based studies is some sort of census or enumeration of all the households in order to define the universe from which samples may be selected. Even in cases where research is mainly qualitative participant observation and unstructured interviewing, it is common to establish a baseline census. Where large numbers of households are involved, the basic census is usually limited to a small list of key items of information:

1. name, age and sex of each person (and their relationship to household heads)
2. ethnic identification of household heads
3. occupations of adult members (including cash crops)
4. education of adult members
5. religious affiliation of adult members
6. physical indicators of house quality (usually number of rooms, floor material, roof and walls, number of windows)

The physical indicators of house quality are useful as an approximate measure of socioeconomic status.

In addition to these items, each household (and usually each individual), must be designated with a unique identification number to relate all subsequently collected information, and the selection of research samples, to the correct units. Commonly the identification number is composed of community, household, individual, as follows: 01 (community) /001 (household) /01 (individual) = 0100101 (the first person in the first household in the first community.)

In many countries the health ministry or one of the government health research institutes may have a standard census form that they want all researchers to use. Such "nationwide" formats have the advantage that they permit some comparisons between the specific research population and other populations in the country. On the other hand, the standard forms often include portions that are obsolete or inappropriate for given regions. If possible, researchers will use the "official protocol," with additions and modifications to fit with local conditions.

If resources are available for gathering more information in each household, the additional items will reflect the specific research concerns, as well as special ecological and other local features important to specific health-illness issues. Some usual basic items are:

1. sources of water supplies
2. sources and types of heating fuel
3. types of toilet facilities
4. immunization status of children and women
5. physiological status of women (pregnant, etc.)
6. usual source(s) of health services
7. labor migration of family members
8. recency of arrival to area and community
9. community of origin of adult members
10. foods produced by household
11. animals owned or maintained by household members
12. ownership of selected consumer items, such as radio, television, and vehicles

Many other items can be added to the list of basic questions concerning the universe of households. However, very few researchers can afford to collect even this much information from all households in their study communities. Quite often a researcher (or research team) will direct the extra questions to a subsample—perhaps every tenth household of the overall census. In this way at least approximate frequencies will be obtained for a variety of features that can then be studied in greater depth as research progresses.

The census, or enumeration, of all households in a study population has other functions besides the collection of specific data. Regardless of whether the process occurs at the outset of research or later, the census is an important opportunity to introduce the research group, and purposes of the research, to all households in the area. In addition to information about the researchers, each household can be given information about any health interventions connected with the study. The census enumerators can distribute health education leaflets and information about clinic times and places and can recruit volunteers for local health committees. Census contacts can often help in identifying potential key informants, such as local healers.

Qualitative Interviewing in Selected Households

Unstructured conversations and interviews should always be carried out in the research population before the census is initiated. The forms of even the most routine questions should be shaped by knowledge of the local language and ecological conditions. After the census has been carried out, it becomes possible to select types of families from the census lists. Small numbers of representative families—such as families with children under 5, households with pregnant women, nuclear versus extended households, or other categories—can then be visited for in-depth ethnographic interviewing.

Ethnographic interviewing and unstructured observations in homes is the crucial stage in many projects, during which the complexities of health care decision making, types of home treatments, attitudes and relationships to health facilities, economic and political issues, and many other details of local life are studied extensively in preparation for carefully designed structured observations and interviews. The informal contacts with selected households can also include some pretesting of portions of data-gathering formats intended for the later, more structured portions of the study.

Structured Data Gathering in Samples of Households

Unlike many other types of field researchers, medical anthropologists generally are loathe to begin highly structured data gathering until they have significant ethnographic experience in the local communities. Detailed ethnographic field research is essential for a number of reasons:

1. Many of the most significant variables can be effectively identified and operationalized only on the basis of specific information about local conditions.
2. Nuances of local language use must be known if specific questions are to elicit useful data. Misuse of local language can easily lead to embarrassing errors that reduce peoples' willingness to take questions seriously.
3. Several weeks of ethnographic fieldwork usually lead to familiarity and improved rapport with local people, increasing the likelihood of cooperation with structured questions.

Many field research projects include several different structured data-gathering operations, sometimes using somewhat different samples for the various observations. For example, Bentley, in her research on diarrhea management in north India, interviewed a random sample of 199 households to collect data on beliefs and knowledge about the causes and prevention of diarrhea and other aspects of explanatory models. In a later phase of research, mothers of children with diarrhea episodes were interviewed as well as observed in 50 households to get actual behavioral data (Bentley 1988:75–76). In his research on intrahousehold food distribution in Nepal, Gittelsohn selected six villages within a *panchayat*, from which he identified a random sample of 115 households. A number of different interviews and observations were carried out, including a socio-economic interview, 24-hour dietary recalls, anthropometric measurements of children and adults, repeated direct observation of meals (total of 354 meals recorded), collection of morbidity data, in addition to key informant interviews and informal chats with many of the people in the sample. The resulting data set contained 21 separate subfiles, totaling 70,000 lines (Gittelsohn 1989).

COLLECTION OF STRUCTURED DATA: CASE ILLUSTRATIONS

Case I: Explanatory Models of Illness and Decision Making

One of the more thorough and impressive studies of peoples' modes of choosing among health care alternatives is that of James Young, in the town of Pichataro in western Mexico (Young 1981) The study is important because it illustrates structured interviewing with small numbers of key informants, after which the methodology shifted to collection of actual illness episodes.

In the first phase of research, Young and Linda Garro carried out a census of the 509 households in the community and began key informant interviews concerning common illnesses and their characteristics. General ethnographic interviewing was necessary to identify specific types of health care resources utilized by the people, as well as to develop the basic list of locally recognized illnesses concerning which cultural models of explanation and choice making could be derived.

With a provisional set of 42 physical and behavioral symptoms of illness (each written on a separate card), the researchers asked five literate informants to sort these into piles in terms of severity. The same informants were also asked to sort the illnesses (diagnostic labels) into piles in terms of severity.

The researchers also carried out paired-comparison interviews in which questions were posed in the basic form: "[In case of illness] . . . when—for what reason—would you (consult) (use) [type of practitioner] instead of (consulting) (using) [another type of practitioner]?" The possible alternatives in the blanks were: "1. self-treatment; 2. a folk curer; 3. a pharmacy (with consultation only with the clerk or pharmacist; 4. a local *practicante*; 5. the Patzcuaro Health Center; and 6. a private-practice physician" (pp. 132–33). Each of the six alternatives was paired with every other, resulting in 30 choice questions. "The interview was completed with fifteen persons, eight men and seven women, of varying age, occupation, and economic status" (Young 1981:133).

In order to get in-depth information concerning the culturally defined characteristics of each of the illnesses, a set of 43 different illness attributes (questions) were asked of each of the 34 illness terms identified in early stages of the research. This very time-consuming interview required a number of sessions with each of the ten informants, (six women and four men) (Young 1981:81).

The most time-consuming portion was the collection of a corpus of actual illnesses for testing the decision model derived from analysis of the data on illness definitions and characteristics. From the original census data, a representative sample was drawn: "Over a six-month period, sixty-two households were visited on an approximate biweekly basis and records were made of each illness occurring among its members" Young 1981:77) A total of 323 cases were collected.

This study includes a thorough mixing of qualitative and quantified procedures, progressing from pattern identification (of illnesses), to the testing of models concerning the ways in which the patterns influenced actual behaviors (in the 323 episodes).

Case 2: Modernization and Arterial Blood Pressure

"Hypertension," or more accurately, differential blood pressure, is particularly interesting as a focus of research because the disease is relatively symptom free, so in most indigenous communities there has been no "traditional" concept. Nonetheless, a great many cultural groups, including many native American communities, now have cultural models of hypertension, learned (and modified) from the doctors, nurses, and others in cosmopolitan medical services. Studies of factors affecting differences in blood pressure levels (and outright hypertension) involve (require) use of an overt biomedical measurement (a sphygmomanometer), plus the observation of cultural, psychological, social, and other factors thought to be factors affecting arterial blood pressure levels. The following case is important because it exemplifies an increasingly frequent type of study in which medical anthropologists collaborate with epidemiologists and other biomedical researchers in projects sponsored by international agencies.

William Dressler and associates chose an urban area in the city of Ribeirão Prêto, Brazil, with a population of 400,000, for the research. "A variant of cluster sampling was used to draw a sample of 139 individuals. Four broad clusters based on residential and economic sector... were chosen, and then random samples of 20 households were chosen from each cluster" (Dressler et al. 1987:400). The clusters that the researchers selected represented agricultural day laborers, continuously employed plantation workers, factory workers, and a fourth cluster of bank employees (Dressler et al. 1987:400–401).

For the dependent variable, the research group used the mean values derived from five separate measurements of blood pressure using a DINAMAP Vital Signs Monitor Model 845XT. The automated equipment for measuring blood pressure is much more reliable than ordinary sphygmomanometers because it "virtually eliminates inter-observer variability" (p. 401). This is an example of use of state-of-the-art equipment and methods to manage the biomedical variables in an interdisciplinary project. Other variables were "index of style of life," composed of ownership of items of material culture, and "economic resources," representing occupations of all adult members of the households. From these two measures, an index of "life-style stress" was computed based on the discrepancies between the two indexes. Dietary data were collected using a series of four 24-hour recalls. Other variables included individual perception of "relative deprivation," "life changes," and the usual age, sex, education, and race, as well as height and weight.

The life-style index in this study is particularly interesting because it includes ownership of consumer goods—color television, vehicle, food blender, camera, telephone—and also items such as yearly trips to São Paulo, vacation trips, magazines read per month, newspapers read per week, and number of books read per year (Dressler et al. 1987:402).

The statistical analysis (multiple regressions) replicated Dressler's previous study of hypertension in St. Lucia, again demonstrating the importance of lifestyle stresses as predictors of differences in blood pressures. In his earlier research Dressler had carried out extensive qualitative ethnographic research in addition to the quantified data gathering. The Brazilian study, on the other hand, included very little qualitative data gathering.

Case 3: Diarrhea Research of the 1980s

This case departs from the focus on individual projects in order to examine features of a concerted program of research on diarrhea that now occupies a central role in the child survival programs of the 1980s, particularly involving ORT. Infant and childhood diarrheas have been a leading cause of mortality in most parts of the developing world. Beginning in the 1980s it became apparent that a major reduction in infant and small child mortality could take place if ORT were regularly used to offset the dehydrating effects of diarrheas, although ORT is not itself a cure for the illness.

Practically every developing country now has a program for promotion and dissemination of ORT. In most cases the emphasis is on teaching people to use ORT packets disseminated throughout the primary health care systems; however, some programs have sought to train people to mix home-made oral rehydration solutions, following simple recipes. Despite the apparent success in some of these campaigns, most national programs have encountered difficulties in convincing the majority of people to use ORT. And in many instances even those who accept the therapeutic regimen do not use it appropriately.

Problems with peoples' acceptance and proper use of ORT in most developing countries have led to widespread realization of the need for research, including anthropological data gathering, to identify the points of difficulty and to develop ways for improving programs. The study by Bentley in north India is one of a large number of studies by anthropologists during the 1980s. Several of these studies were published in a special edition of *Social Science and Medicine* (Coreil and Mull 1988).

Biomedical thinking and directions of research with regard to childhood diarrhea have progressed from a simple focus on ORT, to the realization of complex issues around breastfeeding and other dietary behaviors, patterns of use (and misuse) of pharmaceutical remedies, and many other culturally mediated beliefs and behaviors. With this realization of complexity has come a greatly increased interest in the possibility that specifically anthropological methods may hold the keys to better management of the diarrhea issue.

A major first step to disentangling the diarrhea problem was the shift of focus from the biomedical construct, "diarrheal disease," to the variety of cultural constructions—the emically defined patterns related to diarrhea as illness. One of the more influential studies earlier in the decade was Marilyn Nations's study in an economically impoverished area of northeast Brazil. She noted the points of incongruity between the prevailing allopathic approaches to diarrhea and the perspectives of the mothers and local healers among the people. She called for new approaches to diarrhea control:

In short, the foremost concern of this alternative approach to diarrheal disease control is to support rather than suppress popular village healing. Doctors must adapt medical terminology to popular usage . . . They must learn the popular folk explanations for childhood illnesses and explore their relation to biomedical etiologies. Health professionals must also give villagers dietary advice in a way that does not violate harmless food beliefs and that assures the traditional healers power in village medicine. Still, peasant families must also have easy access to effective modern means to save children dying from severe dehydration. (Nations 1982:155).

Key informant interviewing to elicit varied emic terminology for diarrhea, types of diarrhea, and the exploration of the explanatory models (EM) for diarrhea in given cultures have become core elements of most community-based diarrhea research, even by nonanthropologists (Weiss 1988). In north India Bentley found that mothers identified five types of diarrhea: "bloody," "watery," "bits-and-pieces," "green," and "yellow" (Bentley 1988: 76–77). Susan Scrimshaw and E. Hurtado (1988) found that explanatory models of diarrhea in Guatemala included those caused by the mother (due to, for example, emotion or physiological condition), food-related diarrhea (hot, cold, "bad," excess), as well as those due to tooth eruption, "fallen fontanel," evil eye, worms, and "cold enters the stomach." This complex array of different causes is associated with different choices of therapies. In Baluchistan, Elizabeth Herman and associates found that rural mothers identified 13 different folk types of diarrhea, mostly identified in relation to perceived cause (Herman n.d. personal communication).

Recently P. Hudelson found that mothers and caretakers in Managua, Nicaragua, have fairly complex knowledge of parasites and other causes of diarrhea, along with extensive information on pharmaceuticals, which they much prefer to ORT (Hudelson 1989). Mark Nichter demonstrated that terms for diarrhea in Sri Lanka (Sinhalese) differ for adults and children and that the concept (and terminology) of dehydration is not recognized in the rural population he studied: "The 3 most prominent impressions of the function of ORS were that it was (1) a medicine for diarrhea, (2) a purification agent for the body—like chlorine for a well and (3) a medicine providing strength when a child was weak" (Nichter 1988:47).

In recent ethnographic research in rural Mexico, H. Martinez asked mothers to sort into groups the various foods that had previously been identified as "foods given to children during diarrhea." The pile-sort task results were then submitted to multidimensional (MD) scaling. H. Martinez asked his community health workers to examine the MD scaling results and to interpret the dimensions. The general result included the finding that women were differentiating between foods that were appropriate during acute phases of diarrhea and those that are usually fed during the recovery phase (Martinez 1988:39–40).

Most of these ethnographic researchers have used some sort of sampling procedure, but the exploration of folk taxonomies, explanatory models, and other aspects of emic views of diarrhea does not generally depend on statistical analysis other than, at most, frequencies of recognition of taxonomic categories. While some variations are always found in the numbers and types of categories identified by different informants, the range of variation is not usually extensive.

Quantitative survey techniques, on the other hand, are generally used to assess the strength and prevalence of beliefs about causes of diarrhea, and especially for assessing frequencies of crucial elements such as cessation of breastfeeding, curtailment of solid foods, and other potentially harmful behaviors arising from cultural belief systems. Survey techniques have also been used to find out the percentage of people who have heard of ORT, as well as the rates of recent use of this therapy. J. Coreil and E. Genece report a survey concerning adoption of ORT among Haitian mothers, carried out in the coastal town of Montrouis and the surrounding villages. As is usual in this kind of study, ethnographic investigation was carried out for several weeks before the survey was initiated: "A random sample of 300 mothers or caretakers of children 0–5 years were interviewed. . . . Census records allowed us to identify all the 1714 families in the health program with preschool children" (Coreil and Genece 1988:88–89). The researchers made use of two survey teams, "each consisting of 3 interviewers and a supervisor. The project director (author) trained and closely monitored the teams. . . . The 65-item questionnaire was pretested on 15 mothers from an adjacent community" (Coreil and Genece 1988:89). The statistical analysis consisted of a multiple regression to examine the relative strengths of several hypothesized predictors of ORT knowledge and use.

The third major sector of anthropological research on diarrhea has been directed to prospective study of behaviors in the case of actual diarrheal episodes. This methodology requires three main elements: (1) a representative sample of households containing small children of the requisite age, (2) a method for monitoring households so that episodes of diarrhea are quickly identified as they occur, and (3) a well-designed protocol for direct observations and interviewing concerning the identified cases. In the north India study, Bentley was able to follow 50 episodes of diarrhea: "Where possible, household visits were made either daily or every other day until the diarrhea had stopped for 2 days. Post-recovery visits were also done to compare feeding practices during and after the diarrhea" (Bentley 1988:76).

Monitoring and follow-up of diarrheal episodes is time-consuming; each visit should include direct observation if possible, as well as interviews of caretakers concerning modes of treatment, visits to health care facilities, feeding behaviors, present condition of the child, and many other details. As studies of diarrhea have shifted toward possible prevention strategies, interest is focusing on direct observation of hygiene and sanitation in households, including hand washing, modes of cleaning up after childrens' diarrhea, maintenance of drinking water, and other behaviors. All of the recent studies of actual behaviors have demonstrated wide discrepancies between peoples' answers to surveys as opposed to actual behavior observed directly by the researchers. At the same time, direct observation of complex health-related behaviors is a relatively under developed aspect of anthropological research. More experimentation is needed to refine the methodology.

The Applied Diarrheal Disease Research Program (ADDR) at Harvard, the Diarrhoeal Diseases Control Program of WHO, and other international programs devoted to health care in Third World countries are sponsoring new research projects on childhood diarrhea with participation from clinical medicine, epidemiology, medical anthropology, health education, and other disciplines. Most of these international research programs provide funds primarily for Third World research groups, based in the countries in which the research is carried out. On the other hand, a number of North American anthropologists have been involved as consultants and proposal developers, particularly in workshops in which methodological training is imparted in the context of refining specific research projects developed by the Third World research groups.

Collaboration of medical anthropologists with epidemiologists, biomedical researchers, and others has been particularly fruitful in the sector of diarrhea control. This is partly because of the widespread realization that qualitative ethnographic work and other anthropological research tools play a vital role in furthering practical understanding of key issues, particularly about the ways in which complex health beliefs, or explanatory models, affect health care decision making.

Discussion of the Cases

The three cases illustrate a few of the many trends in contemporary medical anthropology, particularly in fieldwork in primary health care in developing countries. To an increasing extent, medical anthropological research is directed to intensive study of specific sicknesses—either in emic, culturally delimited terms of illness or through study of a biomedically derived disease for which the relevant cultural explanations, behaviors, and other features are explored. Research directed to specific pathological states has the large advantage of delimiting and controlling the universe of relevant health behaviors to be studied. Also it permits the anthropologist to become at least moderately knowledgeable about the relevant biomedical aspects without having to spend months in studying medical textbooks.

Most field research in medical anthropology—in these cases and other studies like them—includes varying mixtures of the following ingredients:

1. Initial selection of field site where the sickness condition of interest is of some concern and prevalent enough to be studied (more than one may be of interest). Quite often the field site is selected because of an ongoing health care program.

2. General descriptive field research in the area, much like other anthropologists in the first phases of getting acquainted with the local environment and its people.

3. Census or enumeration of the local population in order to gather general descriptive information and to acquire the framework for later representative sampling.

Field Methods in Medical Anthropology 291

4. Key informant interviewing and participant observation focused on the particular pathology, to explore explanatory models, taxonomies, and a variety of other areas of cultural knowledge concerning the topical focus.
5. Use of pile sorts, triad sorts, sentence frames, or other structured methods with small numbers of informants in order to refine various aspects of the explanatory models and other aspects of the cultural belief systems.
6. Structured direct observations of management of illness, hygienic-sanitation behavior and conditions, provider-patient interactions, and/or other behaviors central to the research.
7. Structured interviews with representative samples of respondents to elicit data on main independent and dependent variables in order to test specific hypotheses and to verify major patterns and processes tentatively identified in earlier, qualitative phases of the research.
8. Extraction of data from patient records in hospital, clinic, or other health care facility where available. In the usual case, extraction of such data requires permission not only from the administrative personnel who control the records but also from the individual patients or their families. Such records may also include data from special bioclinical observations, including blood pressures, blood samples, urinalysis, X-rays, clinical assessments by doctors, and other procedures.
9. Analysis of both qualitative and quantitative data, using microcomputers or mainframe computers, and often both.
10. Presentation of results of research and policy recommendations to persons in the research community and/or other groups involved in health program operations.

In addition to these specific items, medical anthropologists generally collect large amounts of descriptive, contextual information about the community, environmental features, political and economic structures, and other relevant material. Most research projects do not, of course, include all of the qualitative and quantified procedures mentioned. Depending on the time frames of research, the specific questions studied, and personnel and funding available, individual projects can range from small-scale studies using one or two of these basic tools, all the way to comprehensive, multiyear programs of data gathering that expand beyond this core list.

RAPID ETHNOGRAPHIC ASSESSMENT PROCEDURES

Applied ethnographic research is frequently seen as a desirable first step before health care programs are put into operation. Also, increasing numbers of epidemiologists and other quantitative researchers are realizing the importance of ethnographic research for fine-tuning their approaches to planning structured interviewing and other research operations. There are three main reasons for initial ethnographic research:

1. To provide locally relevant cultural information for use in improving health care programs.

2. To provide a baseline of data from which to measure change and effectiveness in such programs.
3. To identify locally relevant cultural taxonomies and explanatory models in order to frame meaningful questions in structured interviewing and observations.

Often initial ethnographic research must be completed in a few weeks so as not to delay the introduction of the health care program itself. However, anthropologists have traditionally resisted what some people have referred to as "quick and dirty" applied research. Based on the general holistic principle common to most sociocultural anthropology, some ethnographers have argued that many months are required to become familiar with all the relevant cultural features and to become known in a given community setting. Also, learning the local language(s), often thought essential to good ethnographic work, requires a great deal of time.

Despite some trepidations concerning rapid ethnographic research, the 1980s saw a substantial increase in sophistication in systematizing this type of data gathering. In several instances, the guidelines for specific data gathering have been set forth in field manuals, particularly in instances in which similar data were to be gathered in several sites by different research groups. One of the early examples of such a field manual was prepared by T. Marchione for the Infant Feeding Practices Study, undertaken by a consortium of researchers from the Population Council, Cornell University, and Columbia University School of Public Health (Marchione 1981). The plan of research called for approximately ten weeks of ethnographic reconaissance, with a suggested sample of 30 to 50 informants. The informants were to be selected from the same communities in which a later, structured interview survey was to be carried out.

A similar manual, which was used in a six-week period of rapid assessment of infant feeding practices in northern Cameroon (1982), was designed by G. Pelto for a project sponsored by the Educational Development Council (Pelto 1984).

A more comprehensive manual for rapid anthropological assessment was designed by Scrimshaw and Hurtado for use in an ambitious program of research sponsored by the United Nations University, initiated in 1983–1984. Social science researchers in 15 countries carried out projects that ranged from two to three months to six or eight months, using the draft set of guidelines. The researchers and their methodological consultants convened in Bellagio, Italy, in 1985 to review the resulting data and to modify aspects of the methodology. The revised set of research guidelines, the *Rapid Assessment Procedures* manual, was then published for general use in health and nutrition programs. The manual contains an appendix with data collection guides, including morbidity history of adult household members, inventory of household remedies, use of health resources, interview with health staff, provider-patient interaction, and others (Scrimshaw and Hurtado 1987: Appendix 1).

Scrimshaw and Hurtado commented in their manual that "a great deal of practical, diagnostic, and applied work can be accomplished in a shorter time and by using a simpler approach" (Scrimshaw and Hurtado 1987:1). The authors of the manual point out that a great many health care programs have been initiated without any sort of "culture-specific map" to guide health personnel in adjusting to local belief structures, ecological conditions, economic restraints, and other factors affecting peoples' health-seeking behaviors.

Rapid assessment procedures of varying styles have been developed, with varying degrees of specificity of purpose. For example, Schensul and associates reported a "commando raid technique" in which a number of observers were "deployed" to selected community sites with instructions to collect a carefully delimited package of information (Schensul and Borrero 1982). Bentley and associates developed a field guide for "rapid ethnographic assessment" in an intervention program aimed at dietary management during childrens' diarrheal episodes (Bentley et al. 1988): "Because the data were urgently required for subsequent phases of research, the time allotted for data collection and analysis for each site was six weeks" (Bentley et al. 1988:110).

Among these several different examples of rapid research techniques, there are some common methodological themes:

1. It is commonly assumed that some descriptive materials on the local cultural system(s) are available so that the researcher does not need to spend time finding out about the economic system, kinship and social organization, and other general features.
2. Familiarity with the local language on the part of the researchers or use of local research workers as interviewers is generally assumed.
3. The extensive version of the holistic assumption is rejected in favor of a more limited style of multifactor research. In research on diarrhea as carried out by Bentley and coworkers, it was assumed that data gathering can focus specifically on the illness itself, plus a clearly specified list of contextual factors. Very little general ethnography is needed.
4. The specific ethnographic data to be collected are thought to require small numbers of informants. Samples of informants are seldom more than 25 or 30—often substantially fewer.
5. When research is limited to small numbers of informants, contacted during a fairly short time period, considerable care is usually exerted to ensure representativeness of the sample in terms of local subgroups, age and sex distribution, socioeconomic status, and other dimensions of variation.
5. Focus group interviews or group discussion sessions are commonly used in the exploratory phases of the research.
6. Inferential statistical analysis is seldom appropriate in the rapid ethnography methodology, but descriptions often include frequencies of responses in various categories.
7. The methodologies sometimes include limited use of survey methods near the end of the data-gathering process.

The rapid methodologies have developed primarily in response to the requirements of applied primary health care programs. In many cases the rapid ethnographic assessment is needed to produce basic data for designing health care intervention programs. However, the *Rapid Assessment Procedures* manual of Scrimshaw and her associates was developed in relation to evaluation of ongoing nutrition and health care programs (Scrimshaw and Hurtado 1988).

Use of Microcomputers

A second major methodological development of the 1980s is the ongoing rapid evolution of computer utilization in research. To an increasing extent, medical anthropologists (and many other types of researchers) are carrying microcomputers into fieldwork for qualitative and quantitative data management. The most common use of microcomputers is in writing field notes. The legendary tediousness of writing field notes, and analysis of them, is somewhat lessened through use of versatile word processing software. However, failures with microcomputers in fieldwork in the 1980s were numerous (Gittelsohn 1989); fieldworkers are urged to print out hard copy notes frequently and to make backup copies onto floppy diskettes. The newest portable microcomputers appear to be more reliable than earlier models and are increasingly important for data management even in relatively remote field locations.

In a comprehensive longitudinal nutrition research program in rural Mexico, microcomputers were introduced to community research assistants for entering quantitative data from a wide variety of interviews and other protocols (Allen Chavez, and Pelto 1987). With proper team organization, data entry at the research site makes it possible to check computerized data against the original raw data and to send researchers back to households to retrieve missing data. For community-based data capture, it is advisable that database programs be tailor-made so that the blanks for entering numbers or words mimic the interview forms. In B. Gebrian's primary health care project in Haiti, the field-based computer allows the program coordinator to send printouts of household data summaries back to individual communities so that health committees receive feedback concerning local health status (such as the percentage of malnourished children) for planning purposes. Pie charts that graphically illustrate percentages of vaccinations and other data have proved effective in communicating with local health committees (Gebrian n.d.).

In rare instances anthropologists take their portable computers directly to informants or respondents for direct data entry. Literate respondents, even if they have no previous experience with computers, can be taught fairly easily to answer question frames in the computer. H. R. Bernard is currently (1989) using this technique for gathering data about networks in Mexico City (Bernard, personal communication). While some researchers might object that the computer makes the interview artificial, the interactive computer program is often quite interesting for respondents and might be seen as no more artificial than the usual structured interview.

Database management software of various types is the standard for entering numerical data in the field. On the other hand, quantified data can also be entered with an ordinary word processor program, provided the program can produce files with no hidden codes. Some statistical programs such as SYSTAT include a data editor to facilitate the tedious process of transferring raw data into computer files.

A major advantage of the microcomputer in fieldwork is the ability to carry out data analysis, both qualitative and quantitative. For extensive text data (field notes), most word processing programs include at least minimal search or find routines. Full-scale indexing of field notes, for more complex searches of keywords, can be done with programs such as ANYWORD and ZYINDEX. Researchers who want to code field notes, using the Outline of Cultural Materials or another system, can use ETHNOGRAPH, which mimics the familiar manual coding process (Bee and Crabtree, forthcoming).

High-powered statistical analysis for microcomputers is available in SAS and SPSS versions. Somewhat less expensive and much easier to use, SYSTAT offers a wide range of statistical procedures (including factor analysis, multidimensional scaling, loglinear modeling, and the familiar nonparametric analyses) (Crabtree and Pelto 1988). Many anthropologists find that simple statistical programs such as EPISTAT and MYSTAT are sufficient for field-based data analysis (MYSTAT manual 1988).

Until recently anthropologists had no simple microcomputer programs available for construction and analysis of triad sorts and pile sorts or for developing and testing Guttman and Likert scales. However, a new program developed by S. Borgatti, ANTHROPAC, is now available for these fieldwork operations. The program is menu driven and quite easy to use (Borgatti 1989).

Communications from field sites to home base often depend on slow-moving mails, but large amounts of data and voluminous reports can be conveniently shipped on floppy diskettes. Where telephone services are reliable, a great deal of communication, including transmission of data files, can be accomplished through the electronic mails, directly from computer to computer. R. T. Trotter and his fellow researchers used electronic communications between field sites and the principal investigator's office for rapid data sharing recently in a multisite project in the Southwest (Trotter n.d.). Electronic mail requires that each end of the system have a modem for connecting computer to telephone, plus appropriate software to facilitate sending and receiving. In addition some researchers use the BITNET communications system for messages and data file transmissions, both domestic and international.

Microcomputers have come into a such a wide variety of uses, specialized and not so specialized, that a full review of electronic tools and processes would require a large book. M. S. Boone and associates are compiling a wide-ranging set of papers on contemporary computer users and uses, both micro and mainframe (Boone and Woods forthcoming). Many medical anthropologists still continue to rely on mainframe computers for complex data analysis and other operations, but fieldwork operations are increasingly microcomputerized.

SUMMARY AND CONCLUSIONS

The 1980s saw impressive advances in research methods in medical anthropology. These developments are due in part to influences outside anthropology, through expanded interdisciplinary collaboration in research. Widespread acceptance of medical anthropology as an essential ingredient in research on illness and health care has brought about increased sharing of methodological techniques among biological, clinical, epidemiological, and social sciences. The mutual interactions of anthropology and epidemiology have been particularly important, as documented in the book *Anthropology and Epidemiology* (Janes, Stall, and Gifford 1986). Cooperation between epidemiologists and anthropologists has led to methodological shifts on both sides. Medical anthropologists have come to pay more attention to matters of sampling and representativeness, along with new techniques of statistical analysis. The ADDR, Pan American Health Organization, WHO, as well as the National Institutes of Health and other organizations have insisted that ethnographic fieldwork should be described in concrete, easily understood terms, and these influences have led anthropologists to be more specific about techniques, leading in turn to increased standardization of procedures.

In the area of structured direct observations, anthropologists, epidemiologists, nutritionists, and psychologists seem to have learned from each other. Earlier anthropological observations tended to be unstructured and ad hoc, without much concern for representativeness. Some of the other disciplines, on the other hand, had developed methods that were highly structured but poorly suited to specific field conditions. Medical anthropologists have played an important role in helping to develop culturally appropriate modes of observation that can be structured sufficiently to permit statistical analysis.

The advent of microcomputers, basically phenomena of the 1980s, has had a direct technological impact on medical anthropology. The availability of easy-to-use statistical software has encouraged researchers to develop more numerical data gathering. Some of the impetus for improvements in computerized data gathering and analysis has come directly from anthropologists with long experience at mainframe operations. Researchers in other disciplines also contributed techniques and tools that anthropologists have found useful.

The primary motivation for improved methodologies, both qualitative and quantitative, has continued to be the natural effect of requirements in applied programs. Whenever data gathering is intended to have direct programmatic consequences, within organizations whose personnel are largely nonanthropologists, there is a considerable pressure to improve the credibility of data gathering and data analysis. Even the conventions of report writing and oral presentations of research results foster consciousness of methodology.

Our impressions, based on many recent experiences and informal communications among medical anthropologists, are that the transmission of effective research methodology is not strongly developed in our graduate training programs. Most medical anthropologists have improved their methodological skills by trial and error in the course of work in interdisciplinary projects. As a result, colleagues who are not involved in interdisciplinary team research can find themselves with fewer resources for keeping abreast of methodological developments.

Methodological skills are scarce resources and have direct economic value—in employment, promotion, and the like—in addition to their contribution to excellence of research output. To an increasing extent, researchers who are marginalized in relation to main communications centers may be falling behind in methodological terms, leading to relatively weaker, less useful research. The problem of effective dissemination of research methodologies is especially important for anthropologists in Third World countries. The tendency for Euro-American hegemony in research methods and technology is offset to some extent by the conscious efforts of the ADDR, United Nations University, WHO, and other international research-sponsoring organizations. These agencies are promoting expanded research capabilities, including use of microcomputer hardware and skills, through workshops and research grant programs in the developing countries (cf. Trostle et al. in 1989 AAA annual meeting).

The 1980s ushered in an era of rapid change in research methodology among medical anthropologists. The central importance of ethnographic interviewing and participant observation has been enhanced despite the expansion of new methodological techniques. We venture to predict that the 1990s will bring an even more extensive refinement and elaboration of field research methods in the arena of health, illness, and healing.

CHAPTER 16

EPIDEMIOLOGY AND MEDICAL ANTHROPOLOGY

William R. True

Epidemiology has established a place for itself in the health sciences by providing both perspectives and methods for documenting and measuring the occurrence of health phenomena. Early victories over an array of infectious diseases such as cholera, smallpox, polio, tuberculosis, and syphilis emboldened epidemiology to move into the study of more complex, multifactorial, chronic disease processes, where the range of inquiry is more encompassing and progress has been more elusive.

Nevertheless, whether discovering single sources of infirmity or unraveling the multifactorial webs of causation for a multitude of other disorders, epidemiology has not only relied on quantitative methods but also has embraced a qualitative perspective. Because it utilizes comparative methodologies for studying the spectrum of health and disease and includes a holistic perspective encompassing environmental attributes, biological parameters, human physical endowments, and social resources, epidemiology compares in breadth and range, if not in focus and application, with medical anthropology.

The perspectives of epidemiology offer a bridge between medical anthropology's traditional focus on the social and environmental aspects of disease etiology and the focus on classification, definition, and etiology of specific disorders more typically the domain of interest of biomedical colleagues. The purpose of this chapter is to focus on the contribution epidemiology can make to medical anthropology in the definition and specification of research questions encompassing disorders as they are distributed among people.

Although the lesson of this chapter is what epidemiology has to teach anthropology, it does not provide a precis of specific epidemiological methods, which are well covered in a number of excellent textbooks reviewing the fundamental assumptions and methods of the field (Mausner and Kramer 1985; Friedman 1987; Lillienfeld 1976; Rothman 1986, for an especially up-to-date account of current thinking; and Slome et al. 1986 for an excellent workbook of basic quantitative methods).

Further, it does not cover the subfield of social epidemiology, which takes as its specialized focus the role of social factors in disease etiology. This topic is similarly well represented in the literature (Marmot and Morris 1984; Berkman 1981; Kaplan 1985), with several excellent review articles discussing a number of areas of interest to anthropologists, such as the effects of networks and social support (McKinlay 1981; Berkman and Syme 1979), social stress (Brown and Harris 1978), and economic risks such as unemployment (Kasl 1979; Stern 1981) on disease processes. The natural interests and methods of anthropology are quite consistent with work that has defined a number of important social and cultural variables that have had considerable impact in the study of disease etiology.

What has not been well developed in the literature is the potential for cross-fertilization in perspectives between the fields of epidemiology and anthropology. The relationship between epidemiology and anthropology has been the subject of recent treatments (Janes et al. 1986; Rubenstein and Perloff 1986; Rubinstein 1984). While these anthropological commentaries emphasize the different methods of epidemiology and the nature of epidemiological data, anthropologists have not recognized that the roots of epidemiology place the field squarely in the anthropological tradition of understanding how the well-being of human beings is directly affected by their physical, social, and cultural environments. By not availing ourselves of epidemiological training or perspectives and by engaging in the all-too-familiar occupational hazard of talking to ourselves about the problems of other disciplines, we lose a valuable opportunity to move our discipline in exciting new directions.

A HISTORICAL VIEW OF EPIDEMIOLOGY AND MEDICAL ANTHROPOLOGY

Historically epidemiology is rooted in the fundamental observation that disease occurs in patterned ways rather than randomly. Epidemiology portrays the occurrence of disease and ascertains susceptibility to risk, viewed in the context of cultural and social processes, environmental attributes, and historical sequence. From the earliest formulations of epidemiology, it was clear that understanding these patterns demanded comparative investigations of social and cultural contexts of both the afflicted and the nonafflicted. Early writings are now seen as establishing this precedent for the field, though the authors were not formally identified as epidemiologists.

For example, Louis Villerme documented in 1840 (reprinted in Buck et al. 1988) the patterns of morbidity and mortality among textile workers in Amiens, France, and in so doing described the living conditions of the afflicted. While the effects of noxious working conditions, the human costs of child labor, and the growing burden of industrial pollution were becoming serious concerns, Villerme noted direct connections between such variables and particular categories of illness or causes of death. His work provides precedent for both social epidemiologists and medical anthropologists.

A classic early example of the development of social epidemiological perspectives is found with tuberculosis (Susser 1988:33–34). Rudolph Virchow, who seeded so many of our notions of social medicine, described tuberculosis as a social disease. Later, however, after Robert Koch isolated the tubercle bacillus and established a new paradigm with the germ theory, thinking of the day came to focus on relationships between specific agents and diseases. We now understand that single-factorial reasoning was not adequate to explain tuberculosis. Today, science again is required to include such nonmicrobial factors as family characteristics, health status, housing and genetic susceptibility to the etiological equation because single factorial models are not sufficient to account for occurrence of an increasing number of disorders.

Historically, epidemiologists were among the first to note the pernicious health consequences of industrialization, occupational exploitation, and urbanization. These perspectives emerged from the search to explain why certain diseases tended to occur at higher rates in these new social settings. In conceptual terms, these early investigations were defining disorders and relative risks.

For example, Carolyn Merchant (1980) has traced the history of coal workers' pneumoconiosis in terms of detailing the parallel history of establishing the dangerous aspects of the workers' environment and the tragically difficult task of translating that knowledge into political and regulatory action. These kinds of issues are familiar to anthropologists. Where epidemiologists go further than anthropologists is in defining, measuring, and analyzing the pathologies that are implicated and arraying these data in terms of assessment of comparative health status.

Given research goals of describing and discovering the etiology of disorders, epidemiologists characteristically use methods and analyze data differently from anthropologists. These differences have precipitated some tension between epidemiologists and anthropologists because of conflicting values about types of data and has led to accusations by anthropologists that epidemiology is guilty of "scientism" (Rubenstein 1984) and of "rigor mortis" (Nations 1986).

Traditionally anthropologists have been critical about kinds of data employed by epidemiologists, asserting, for example, that "[epidemiological data] run a serious risk of being inaccurate by excluding a vital human element: the way people really approach illness and cope with death" (Nations 1986:97). Marilyn Nations's specific example is a moving description of an infant's death in her area of research in northeast Brazil. While it is true that epidemiologists portray such vital events as birth, death, and morbidity in statistical form, which indeed does not permit the rich ethnographic texture Nations captured in her work, to assert the relative merit of one kind of datum over the other is to ignore that data serve specific purposes and that purposes can vary. It is ironic that Nations criticizes the epidemiologist's conception of infant mortality as missing much of the meaning of the event when, in fact, epidemiologists have long recognized infant mortality as the most sensitive indicator of the health of a population (Windom 1987).

Anthropological and epidemiological data have the potential of complementing each other when the contrasting ideas and methods are framed in terms of an appropriate research question. In its adherence to a specific research question, epidemiology seems to anthropologists to be limiting itself to the most superficial of data, while to epidemiologists, depth of data without adherence to principles of generalizability and without specification in terms of a particular question seems excessive and of limited utility.

Yet in spite of these difficulties, there is much common ground for collaboration, where both medical anthropology and epidemiology may profit from increased shared perspectives. Indeed, many medical anthropologists are now receiving postdoctoral training in epidemiology (Thomas Johnson 1984). As I hope to demonstrate, the two fields share a holistic view of the processes of disease and health, and this provides the basis for further collaboration. To illustrate, I begin with a sketch of how I work as an anthropologist-epidemiologist.

MEDICAL ANTHROPOLOGIST AS EPIDEMIOLOGIST

As an epidemiologist, I work in a different setting from those that are typical of most academic medical anthropologists. I have an appointment with three institutional affiliations. The first is the Veterans Administration Medical Center, where I am a funded investigator. The second is at my university medical center, where I am a faculty member in the Center for Health Services Education and Research, a program that gives masters' degrees in public health and hospital administration and has a Ph.D. program in health services research. The third is an appointment in the Psychiatry Department of the School of Medicine, where I participate in research and train residents. I detail my work setting to emphasize that while anthropologists are finding themselves in a wide array of jobs, those with an epidemiological bent also find that their working relationships are with a variety of health professionals, often in an array of clinical and research settings.

Epidemiological research typically is conducted by multidisciplinary teams, which often include the divergent viewpoints of physicians, social scientists, biostatisticians, research methodologists, and administrators. Medical anthropologists today work in such interdisciplinary research teams to a much greater degree than anticipated in traditional anthropological training, which too often presumes that anthropologists will work alone in the field. The professional and personal skills necessary for anthropologists to accommodate to a team approach to research are usually learned by trial and error (unfortunately, often by error) while on the job. Group process training is available, however, and should be employed far more than it has been in graduate anthropology training.

Expertise on epidemiologic research teams is arrayed along formal lines: deciding on research design and analytical strategies, defining the outcome or dependent variable (usually a disorder of some type), and speculating about the etiological dimensions or risk conditions represented in the independent variables. Teams work through a committee format and meet regularly to make decisions about all matters pertaining to the project. In lively and searching team meetings, I often have been struck by how holistic, in an anthropological sense, these deliberations are. Participants speculate and explore many hypotheses as they attempt to resolve the puzzles presented in choosing and estimating the independent variables or in specifying and verifying the dependent variable outcome conditions or disorders.

Each participant represents his or her own primary interests and concerns, knowing that, in the end, the team must choose from among the emphases of the individual participants. This is necessary because if each member of the team could include all the questions he or she personally prefers on a questionnaire or do all the analyses of interest, accomplishing the basic shared goals would be impossible. What is shared in epidemiological investigations is that all components must have clear, measurable dimensions and have to be integrated into a coherent statement or statements comprising hypotheses. The participants, whatever their disciplines, must argue for the importance of their views and contributions while sharing the common focus of the primary research question.

In my experience, where epidemiology sharply differs from anthropology is in the emphasis on the full implications of the statement of the research question. Research questions point directly to research designs. This is because certain designs answer particular questions. Questions about the nature and extent of a condition in a population suggest certain cross-sectional approaches. Questions about potential etiological factors suggest case control design approaches and subsequently the development of powerful prospective designs. Further, each of these designs has different requirements: in methods, procedures, financial demands, personnel requirements, and institutional support. Formal training in epidemiology focuses on analyzing alternative designs and strategies and weighing the attendant strengths and limitations of each.

Anthropologists tend to see such activities as characteristic of other fields, but training in epidemiological perspectives affords anthropologists the opportunity better to structure their own inquiries. Some anthropologists may want to make major contributions to epidemiological research. Both approaches are appropriate because epidemiology provides a model for asserting the role of anthropology in research on health and illness and for assessing the role of social and cultural factors in health and disease.

THE RESEARCH QUESTION

Although all scientists are concerned with the issue, "What is the research question?" it has seemed to me that epidemiologists ask the question as a first reflex in a way that I have not experienced in other research settings. For epidemiologists, the specification of the research question suggests the specific research design that is appropriate, constrains the range of data that are directly applicable and relevant for answering the question, provides the basis, through analysis of the proposed instruments and predicted statistical parameters of the anticipated answers, for determining sample size, and suggests budget requirements.

Although anthropologists propose research projects, specify research questions, and delineate research designs, epidemiologists and anthropologists seem to have different notions of this process. A particular point of contention is the issue of data gathering. In epidemiological research meetings, the purpose and utility of each piece of datum is usually clear, given the chosen design. Additional potentially interesting avenues for data gathering often are ruled out early in research planning. Anthropologists, on the other hand, tend to be less willing to eliminate a priori certain avenues of data gathering simply because they do not seem initially to contribute directly to answering the research question. For an anthropologist, the test of whether data-gathering techniques should be considered to assist in answering the research question is tempered by the thought that it is always prudent to gather more data and subsequently to modify the research question. Anthropologists do not want to preclude unanticipated results that may emerge.

As a way of conveying my sense of this difference in perspective, I have written a short dialogue that captures the flavor of innumerable conversations I have had with colleagues around these topics.

Epidemiologist: You folks write the most interesting stuff. Who would have imagined that you could have learned so much about those practices no one has ever heard of. I would never have thought even to ask the questions. Take a look at my questionnaire. The Office of Management and Budget would never have approved the questions you asked.

Anthropologist: That's a difference between us. I didn't have a questionnaire.

Epidemiologist: How did you know what to ask everybody? How were you sure you got the same information from everyone you talked to?

Anthropologist: I was looking at healing rituals. I found some practitioners and got to talk to their clients. I let them lead much of the interview.

Epidemiologist: So your study was a survey of a kind of healers. We call that a cross-sectional study.

Anthropologist: No, it wasn't a survey. I have no idea how many healers like these there are. I just talked to some of them—enough to see what they had in their minds. I wanted to know what their patients were looking for.

Epidemiologist: You don't know how many there are? But aren't the ones you talked to at least typical?

Anthropologist: In the sense that there are a lot more like them.

Epidemiologist: No, no. I mean typical in the sense that at least the ones you talked to are like the others you didn't talk to.

Anthropologist: I have no way of knowing that. There aren't any lists to start with and choose informants from. I can try to cover the area geographically, but we don't sample the way you do.

Epidemiologist: It's not just sampling. I know that I'm looking at a particular disorder. I can get a dozen physicians to agree with me on how to define it. Then I want to know a lot about risk. You seem to me to ask everything. What is your outcome variable? What exactly is it that you are trying to predict?

Anthropologist: You see, we ask different questions. I'm looking at a range of behaviors and beliefs on the part of both the healer and the patient. I don't even call him a patient. And I probably couldn't get two physicians to agree with any of my categories.

Epidemiologist: When I read your work, I'm never sure exactly who you're talking about. So I'm to generalize to whom?

Anthropologist: Don't you see I'm trying to portray the range of beliefs and behaviors that are out there? That they are believed and acted upon is what matters. I can't put a statistic on that.

Epidemiologist: So what's your research question? What is the research design that you picked to answer it?

Anthropologist: I have a problem that I was trying to answer, but when you ask that question, you have something really specific in mind, right?

Epidemiologist: Yes, there are only a few basic designs. The most well-known epidemiological designs are case control and cohort studies. They are very different from each other. We also do descriptive studies and experimental studies.

Anthropologist: I don't think they are relevant to what I'm looking at. But I'm curious. You see, anthropologists are always curious about unusual worldviews. So what are the differences among the different designs, and what are they good for?

Epidemiologist: Ah, this is at the heart of my business. I love talking about designs and research questions. How much time do you have?

We leave the medical anthropologist as he is about to embark on a crash course in epidemiology. The notion that, for epidemiological questions, there is a defined array of research design options is foreign to anthropology. I refer here to those types that may be further defined under categories of cross-sectional, retrospective, or prospective designs. We could return in a couple of hours and find a colleague either glazed and shellshocked with such an onslaught of epidemiological principles and methods or perhaps intrigued, pondering the possibility that, behind the different methods and perspectives, there might be grounds for possible collaboration.

One theme of the conversation is that anthropologists and epidemiologists warm up to different aspects of research endeavors and that there are ample opportunities for profound misunderstandings. When an anthropologist examines epidemiological data and finds rates, prevalence odds ratios, etiologic fractions, and complex standardization procedures, he or she may be intimidated by the apparent quantitative rigor but at the same time may take solace in the fact that the data are sparse compared to the rich ethnographic information available after a year of intensive fieldwork.

Epidemiologists see in anthropological data important information about the range and depth of phenomena but ask about generalizability and want to know the specific research question that the data purport to answer. Epidemiologists think in terms of the total population, the study population, and the sample to be studied. The concept of normality and abnormality serves to differentiate the members of these populations into those that are affected and those that are not. Descriptive and analytical procedures may then be conducted in order to place the disorder into a complete, population-based context. Therefore epidemiology constitutes, with the clinical profile, biological characteristics, and pathology markers, an essential aspect of the description of a disorder.

The question of etiology raises another key issue for anthropologists. I have been asked by an anthropologist who had just heard a presentation about epidemiological views of response to trauma that was rich in quantitative graphics and terminology: "But are these kinds of data better than a richly detailed case series such as a fieldworker in a clinic might gather?" The answer can be found in the theme of this chapter: it depends on the research question. The anthropologist in the clinic, documenting with thick description a problem seen in patients, is performing a role similar to that of clinicians' presenting case reports of their treatment experiences. These kinds of data establish the importance of a question by documenting that certain clinical patterns exist but cannot answer a question. No progress toward establishing etiology or causal factors can be made, however, until the case material is arrayed in terms of a research question, an appropriate research design is selected, and followed by an orderly execution of the design.

BASIC EPIDEMIOLOGICAL PERSPECTIVES

Normality-Abnormality

There are major underlying differences between anthropological and epidemiological perspectives. Perhaps first among these are conceptions of normality and abnormality. Typically, in epidemiological thinking, those being studied are sorted into two groups: those with and those without the condition under question. Something has to be amiss. The epidemiological questions have as a touchstone a "something" that needs to be defined and understood. Therefore, in epidemiological thinking, "normal" is thought of as "unaffected" or "noncase," and "abnormal" is thought of as "affected" or "case."

I would like to relate one of my own moments of enlightenment during my training as an epidemiologist as my "Aha" experience, even though my naiveté at the time now makes me uncomfortable. I was fresh from anthropological training, steeped in ethnomedicine and sick roles and indoctrinated into the blindnesses of Western medicine when I was taking a required year-long seminar in a major disease process, in my case the epidemiology of coronary heart disease. The second class session appropriately dealt with anatomy and physiology, and the speaker, an anatomy professor, came to class carrying a dissecting tray, covered in a green cloth. After a dense but interesting lecture on the anatomy and physiology of the heart and its arteries, he turned to the tray. Upon uncovering it, I saw that it contained a human heart. He dissected it, and we studied its arterial structures.

My own heart was beating rapidly; I was facing many issues well known to medical students who have to confront the human body in all sorts of permutations. But finally, the lesson of the class struck me: those coronary arteries were really blocked (I believe the professor said approximately 80 percent). That very blockage was the dependent variable, the case definition, the abnormality that was in question. The rest of the course was to look at the medical, social, psychological, dietary, and familial factors that shed light on the development of those blockages, either by increasing the likelihood that those blockages would occur, and thereby become risk factors, or would diminish that likelihood and become protective factors. Thereby, as we have learned, oat bran, negative family history, and exercise are "good," and excessive job stress, obesity, and cigarettes are "bad."

My thinking on outcomes changed that moment as I realized that my future research interests would be with colleagues with whom we would dissect different areas of interest to measure and analyze, trying always to retain a sense of the whole, whether that whole is the individual, the study sample, or the population from which both the individual and the sample were drawn.

In epidemiological designs, the abnormality is called the outcome—the unhealthy condition. The outcome condition does not necessarily have to be a diagnosis, such as type of depression or diabetes. It does not have to be a structure as dramatic or obvious as those atherosclerotic plaques we observed. It may be a diagnostic sign (such as a blood chemistry value like cholesterol or high-density lipoprotein levels), a syndrome, or a symptom cluster (such as might be found in the example of coronary artery disease risk factors). The role of hypothesized etiologic factors in the disease process may be unclear or even of uncertain importance, and the purpose of the research may be to illuminate whether there is an etiological role for the outcome.

This epidemiological conceptualization of affected and unaffected was born out of the discipline's roots in infectious disease analysis and indeed is now incorporated into some of the most useful and powerful of the epidemiologist's analytical tools such as case control studies and the concept of relative risk. The binary logic of normality and abnormality is also a traditional product of a clinician's approach to a patient as therapeutic decisions are made.

We know that disease processes are not all-or-none phenomena and that case definition is highly complex. This has come about because the increasingly sophisticated detection of precursor states, subclinical manifestations of disease, presence of risk factors, and even positive family histories may justify defining a case or an abnormality even in the absence of frank clinical pathology. To epidemiologists, the notion of abnormality or case therefore does not necessarily imply a practitioner-defined case, which would justify specific treatment. It is a concept that alludes to a replicable (reliable) definition of a state of health that can therefore be the focus of a defined research question, to be operationalized and tested. A current example is the case of an HIV-positive individual, with no clinical symptoms, and an unknown probability of progressing to immunodeficiency syndrome (AIDS).

It is important to detail several common ways to define abnormality and the attendant difficulties with each. The issue is complex because the definition of abnormality suggests different kinds of reality. Following an effective and succinct review of conventional approaches (Rose and Barker 1978), I will characterize these as statistical, clinical, prognostic, and operational. The point of presenting these different perceptions of the problems of defining normality and abnormality is to show that each may be appropriate for different purposes. The researcher must make these definitions in terms of the research question motivating the inquiry.

Using statistical criteria, standardized laboratory practice often defines normal as within two standard deviations of the mean value, thereby fixing abnormal scores as comprising approximately 5 percent of each stratum. Such an approach does not establish the content for such a definition but specifies the tails of the distribution as defining a case. Another application of the statistical approach is to define an arbitrary score as a case, as, for example, all individuals in the top quartile of a symptom scale. This reasoning describes the definition of standard normal that is used in a range of diagnostic procedures.

The definition of cases, as contrasted with statistical findings, often provides research teams with much to talk about. The biostatisticians on a team may find that there is a statistically significant difference between groups of cases and controls. Following the example of the last paragraph, this difference may be a difference of 5 millimeters of mercury on systolic blood pressure. The biostatisticians say, "This is significant," meaning that there is less than a 5 percent (or 1 percent) chance of the findings occurring by chance. "But," the clinicians on the team reply, "that isn't a clinically important difference," meaning that the magnitude observed would not be enough to begin a treatment course or change one already in place. "However,'" the dietitians who have defined a pressure-lowering dietary intervention may interject, "that may translate into a much lower incidence of strokes in the study group." What is "significant," "clinical," or "important" is what research team members spend much time defining and interpreting.

The conception of prognostic cases and noncases is based on probabilistic assumptions about the likelihood of developing a disorder based on an aspect of current health status. Consequently this approach is quite sensitive to ongoing research that constantly redefines these thresholds. For example, clinicians used to consider a normal systolic blood pressure as one's age plus 100. Thus, a 50-year-old man with a systolic blood pressure of 150 would have been considered both asymptomatic and normal. Following the well-known Veterans Administration clinical trial on borderline hypertension (Veterans Administration 1970), the risks of even slightly elevated blood pressures became known, and now the conception of normal blood pressure is one that is clinically normal and does not increase with age.

The final perspective is the operational one. The referent is to the clinician as one who makes decisions about when to treat and how to treat. Thus, regardless of the research criteria for defining a particular disorder, the thresholds for treatment may be different. For example, in a research project, borderline hypertension may be defined as 140 millimeters of mercury, but the threshold for treatment, the clinicians' operational definition, may be 150.

These ideas are summarized by physicians writing about clinical epidemiology (Fletcher et al. 1982) to define abnormality in three ways: as unusual, as associated with disease, and as treatable. These authors discuss the utility and limitations of the clinicians' available quantitative data for arriving at case definitions. Using data for defining criteria raises issues of validity (accuracy) and reliability (repeatability) and sources of variation in observation. The message from these sophisticated treatments of the conceptions of normality and abnormality is that the distinction can be made but must be done with thought and care and in terms of the research question at hand. Clearly decisions using any of the approaches would not likely agree with the others.

There are factors implicated in the etiology of outcomes or abnormal conditions. I have called these risk factors; in the language of research designs, they are labeled independent variables and to epidemiologists are captured in the term exposure. Thus, smoking cigarettes is the risk factor or exposure associated with the development of lung cancer. A measured level of smoking, operationalized, for example, as lifetime "pack-years," therefore can be entered into analysis as an independent exposure variable.

These notions about normality and abnormality contrast sharply with the anthropological doctrine of cultural relativity, which was the lodestar for my own training in anthropology. This is surely the minimal message from anthropology that most faculty would agree must emerge from the freshman course. Therefore most anthropologists are uncomfortable with the discussion about abnormality. Yet there is nothing comparable in anthropology to the occluded artery that I discovered in my epidemiology seminar. We as anthropologists are trained to see what is before us as a natural sample that is explicable in its own terms. Once we would have said the system was functional. We as anthropologists are not to judge, not to categorize into such notions, so foreign to the emic point of view, as normal or abnormal, and especially for our own purposes as inquiring scientists.

Causation

In focusing on risk and exposure, epidemiologists are using terminology and concepts that focus on etiology, or cause. Thus in addressing the scientific and philosophical issue of what is causation, epidemiologists also are in territory that is typically not comfortable ground for anthropologists. Epidemiologists are asking about the contribution to developing a health outcome of certain risks or exposures.

The issue of how epidemiologists view cause is well summarized in a major textbook of epidemiology (Mausner and Kramer 1985:185–91) and in a recent edited treatise (Rothman 1988). J. S. Mausner and S. Kramer discuss the criteria with reference to the evidence for the relationship between cigarette smoking and lung cancer, a presentation I will summarize here.

The first criterion for ascertaining causation is evaluating the strength of the association between the hypothesized causal factor and the disease. Technically this is calculated as the ratio of the disease rates for two groups: those with and those without the causal factor. This ratio is called the relative risk, and high ratios indicate strong strength of association. With reference to smoking and cancer, Mausner and Kramer cite two studies that report relative risks for cancer in heavy smokers of 20 to 1 and one study that reports 40 to 1 relative risks.

The second criterion, dose-response relationship, is related to the first and refers specifically to whether the increasing gradient of exposure is related to an increase in disease outcome. For example, the increase in risk for lung cancer increases from a 4.4-fold greater risk of mortality at fewer than 10 cigarettes per day to 43.7-fold increased risk at 40 cigarettes or more per day (Mausner and Kramer 1985:188).

Consistency of the association refers to the fact that if a causal relationship is present, it will be replicated in different settings, with different populations, and with different study methods. With tobacco, replications have been conducted with consistent findings in different countries, with study populations of contrasting demographic characteristics, and with both retrospective and prospective designs.

A claim of causation requires evidence of temporal association between exposure and outcome. While obvious, this observation cannot generally be made in cross-sectional studies, when an interview is administered to a sample at a single point in time. Individual reconstruction of history may not be accurate, and claims from cross-sectional studies about temporality are not convincing. Evidence for tobacco is indicated by studies that have demonstrated the onset of disease after long exposure and decreased mortality following longer periods of time of abstinence for those who have stopped smoking.

The next criterion, specificity of the association, is a difficult point. Ideally this criterion would hold that there is always a relationship between an exposure and the outcome. Rarely in industrial chemical exposure, such as chloracne following exposure to dioxin, can this association can be asserted. Usually, however, an exposure or exposures can lead to more than one outcome, and further, disease causality is now discussed as part of the web of causation. The postulate that a single cause is both necessary and sufficient to precipitate a disease outcome may be applicable only to a very few disease processes. In the case of smoking and lung cancer, this criterion has been the basis for much of the dispute between the Tobacco Institute and the epidemiological community. The tobacco interests point out that the claims for disease causation are negated by the fact that a multitude of diseases are attributed to tobacco. The epidemiologists respond that a case for each can be made following the thinking about causation summarized here. Another argument of the Tobacco Institute is that most smokers do not develop lung cancer and that some cases of disease occur in nonsmokers. Both statements are true. Epidemiologists respond that disease

Figure 16.1
The Basic Epidemiological Perspective

		Disease/outcome		
		+ (cases)	− (non-cases)	
Condition/exposure	+ (exposed)	A	B	A + B
	− (not exposed)	C	D	C + D
		A + C	B + D	

processes are embedded in a multifactorial web of causation where the single factor of tobacco exposure is neither necessary nor sufficient to explain all cases of lung cancer. Still, they argue, the evidence is overwhelming for a causal relationship.

The final criterion specifies that the postulated association be coherent with existing information (biological plausibility). This point does not require that the biological link be proved or specified, only that it be plausible. Thus, chronic smoking can be understood as a continual irritant to the lung, the organ receiving the smoke, and the link to pulmonary pathology is plausible.

Epidemiologists' Tool Kit: Research Designs

The logic of the preceding discussion is embodied in Figure 16.1. The distinctions between case and noncase and between exposure and nonexposure are defined according to criteria explicated by the investigator. The reason that this figure characterizes a basic epidemiological perspective is that it embodies the thinking about normality and abnormality as it is applied in the definition of cases and the thinking about causation as it is represented in questions and definitions of etiological agents. Thus, the basic epidemiological question is what kinds of noxious things (conditions or exposures) are associated with causing sick outcomes (diseases or precursor states).

Before I define what the cell designations mean, I want to point out another reason that this figure is a basic key to epidemiological thinking: it also embodies an epidemiologist's notion of temporality, as this gets expressed in research designs.

Epidemiological research can be approached from either the left side of the figure or from the top. Beginning at the top of the figure implies a completely different kind of research approach. Here we are conditioning on disease, which will be defined as either present or absent. Therefore a sample of affected persons

Table 16.1
Cell Definitions

Cell	Prospective	Retrospective
A	Exposed/develops disease	Diseased (case) with exposure
B	Exposed and does not develop disease	Not diseased (control)
C	Non-exposed and develops disease	Diseased (case) without exposure
D	Not exposed and does not develop disease	Not diseased (control) without exposure

will be matched with a group of unaffected controls, and a retrospective examination will be conducted among these matched case controls to determine what exposures might account for the presence of the disease state.

From the left side of the figure, we are conditioning on exposure—either present or absent. This means that we have done the preliminary investigation to determine who among our study subjects can be counted on during the study to be either exposed or not exposed. An example will be persons defined as smokers or nonsmokers or factory workers who either are or are not in a place where they will be exposed to vinyl chloride. The key is to follow an identified cohort in a prospective manner in order to determine who develops the outcome or health state of interest. This is the fundamental idea of a cohort or prospective study. The study conceptually begins at a point in time and continues into the future.

The definitions of who is in each cell therefore varies according to the kind of temporal approach the researcher is employing. I have summarized these definitions in Table 16.1. Note that cells A and D conform to the logic that the epidemiological approach is in fact testing. Thus in a perfect world, which ran according to immutable epidemiological logic, the diseased would all be exposed (cell A) and the healthy would be not exposed (cell D). Here all smokers would become ill, for example, and those with good, healthy habits are forever protected from infirmity. Alas, such a perfect chi-square distribution is rarely seen. Rather, as epidemiologists note, the key data are located in the off-diagonals, that is, cells B and C, which provide the data to establish the appropriate measurement of risk that can be attributed to the factor or exposure. The intricacies of such calculations are best studied in the epidemiological texts cited at the beginning of the chapter. I will now discuss some further details about these basic epidemiological research designs. First I will address retrospective, or case control studies.

Case Control Designs

Case control designs address the issue of trying to ascertain the etiology of rare conditions where normal sampling procedures would be too inefficient to conduct a study. Also, the latency of disease onset often makes a prospective study an interminable and excessively expensive venture (Greenberg and Ibrahim 1985; Schlesselman 1982). In this design, a group of people who has the outcome or condition of interest (cases) is defined and might be recruited from a clinic or hospital population on the basis of a screening technique applied to a given at-risk group or an entire community or from listening on a register of one kind or another. These cases must be matched with controls: similar individuals but who are assuredly free of the pathological condition being investigated.

The process of defining matching criteria and of performing the pairing of cases with controls presents questions familiar to anthropologists. Who would be appropriate controls? Often these decisions are based on categorical criteria: age within a bracket, sex, some rough economic status indicator, or other similar marker. Sometimes controls are defined as those in the same patient lists as the cases, or neighbors. Fallacies through incorrect matching are the Achilles heel of case control studies, and the errors made should seem obvious to those with anthropological training.

The crux of the design is a systematic elicitation of past history, exposures, experiences, or treatments from both cases and controls. The sensitivity and care required for these elicitations will be familiar to anthropologists, whose techniques might add much to common methods used, which are questionnaires or highly structured interviews. These different histories are then systematically compared to detect differences in any of a multitude of exposures that might distinguish cases from controls. In the references cited, the multiple subtleties and complications of the design are discussed.

The most critical problem with case control studies is selective recall. The design requires that comparable histories be elicited from cases and controls. Imagine the complication in a case control study of birth defects, however. When the mother of an affected child (a case) is interviewed and asked to search her memory for some drink, drug, or experience that might account for a birth defect in her child, she will likely be especially vigilant in trying to remember. This woman's control, who might be down the hall of the hospital enjoying her new, healthy baby, would not feel the same urgency to remember every glass of wine, use of prescriptions or over-the-counter medication, or every unusual event or circumstance.

Cohort Designs

The second broad category of epidemiological study begins with healthy people who are differentially exposed to a suspected etiological factor. Whether exposures are noxious in one way or another is the specific question for study. Cohort studies are a logical follow-up to case control studies. A case control study may discover that the cases showing a disorder share a common factor, as R. Doll and A. Hill (1950) found with smoking and lung cancer. Although the link may be biologically plausible, as discussed in the context of causation, the case control method shows only the correlation of the outcome and the supposed exposure. The sequence of exposure to outcome can be shown only in a cohort study, which follows exposed and nonexposed cohorts over time, in a type of natural experiment to see if the exposed group, in fact, develops higher levels of disorder. Doll and Hill (1964) followed up their case control study with a cohort study, confirming their original observation.

Epidemiologists see these designs in terms of the differences in the logistical requirements they demand. The case control study can be fast and inexpensive, requiring relatively few subjects and the gathering of limited data and utilizing relatively straightforward analytical techniques. In contrast, a cohort study is a long-term project, usually of high cost, and characterized by problems in minimizing attrition (dropouts) from the study, usually accomplished only by great expenditure of effort to keep in touch with study subjects.

What do these observations about the two basic kinds of epidemiological research designs say to medical anthropologists? The basic message from discussing research question and research design is that hypotheses about antecedents and sequelae can be addressed. For example, anthropologists who track a community or group over many years are conforming to one of the attributes of a cohort study. Whether the full attributes of a cohort may be of use to an anthropologist would depend on the nature of the question and whether definition issues around exposure and outcome would contribute to answering that question.

What is abnormal in either of the two basic research designs is a defined condition and a defined exposure. Epidemiological research designs focus on studying abnormal conditions and exposures in systematic and replicable ways. A priori conceptions of abnormality do not flow easily from the tongues of medical anthropologists, who usually conduct a study with the goal of discovering the natural categories of abnormality as the subjects themselves portray them. Medical anthropologists have continuously pointed out that illness as it is experienced by those afflicted may not conform to the categories of those doing the treating. In an epidemiological design, there must be agreement about what is wrong.

In whatever design employed, epidemiologists are concerned that the definition of abnormality is repeatable or replicable when in the hands of different investigators, even in different research settings. It is crucial that the definitions be consistently applied by both participants and researchers. Analyses of such reliability may seem tedious, but these efforts should seem familiar to anthropologists who constantly ask if their categories have utility in other, usually cross-cultural, settings.

The next question asked by epidemiologists is, Are the categories accurate or valid? Do they reflect field or clinical reality? The issue of validity is a crucial one for all scientists, but for epidemiologists the definitions are the basis for specifying the outcome or dependent variable and therefore are the keys to understanding the different research designs. The concept of validity has become even more complex as the nosological coding schemes, such as the *Diagnostic and Statistical Manual* (American Psychiatric Association 1980, 1987), have become increasingly concrete in terms of the kinds and numbers of specific criteria determined to be necessary for the diagnosing of certain mental and emotional disorders. In addition to research designs, there is an additional tool essential to the epidemiologist: the rate.

Epidemiologists' Tool Kit: The Rate

The fundamental measurement for relating and describing occurrence of disease is the ratio of affected cases to the total population at risk, or the rate. The concept of the rate is a deceptively simple one. A rate consists of three parts. With no more complexity than that encountered in high school algebra, the basic rate consists of a numerator, a denominator, and a standard constant (such as per 1,000) to yield comparability. Therefore, the form of a rate is:

$$\frac{\text{Numerator (event or condition of interest)}}{\text{Denominator (population at risk)}} \times \text{Standard factor.}$$

The numerator represents the case and refers back to the discussion of abnormality. Thus, there are a number of bases for defining a case, including statistical, clinical, prognostic, and operational. These criteria are embedded in the concept of the "natural history of disease," which posits that disease processes move through stages (see Mausner and Kramer 1985:6–9).

First among these is the stage of susceptibility, where disease is not present, but fertile soil for the development of disorder is present. These factors may include malnutrition, high cholesterol levels, or maladaptive living circumstances. Next is the stage of presymptomatic disease, where atherosclerotic plaques may mark the onset of coronary artery disease but without any symptoms of the disorder. The onset of clinical disease may mark various functional levels of health, from no limitations to complete bed rest. Finally, for some there is the stage of disability that marks a change to life under altered conditions. The point is that caseness may be defined at any point in the natural history of disease, depending on the nature of the research question. This definition will reflect issues of definition in the concept of abnormality as discussed.

Corresponding to issues in defining the numerator are those that pertain to the denominator. The denominator is so important to epidemiologists and controversies about it occur so often that there is a term shared among practitioners: the denominator problem. The issue is one of definition. If the numerator consists of cases, then the denominator must consist of all those at risk of being cases. Thus the denominator consists of the population at risk. Mistakenly defining the population at risk can modify rates and change the description being presented.

I will present an example from literature about adolescent pregnancy. There is a controversy about the effectiveness of the increased availability of contraceptives for lowering teen pregnancy rates. A fundamental issue is what the trend has been over time in the adolescent pregnancy rates. Figure 16.2 (Childrens' Defense Fund 1988) presents data showing two trends in rates: an increasing rate (that calculated for all women 15–19) and a decreasing rate (that calculated for all sexually active women).

Those uncomfortable with providing contraceptives to adolescents have been

Figure 16.2
Estimated Adolescent Pregnancy Rates

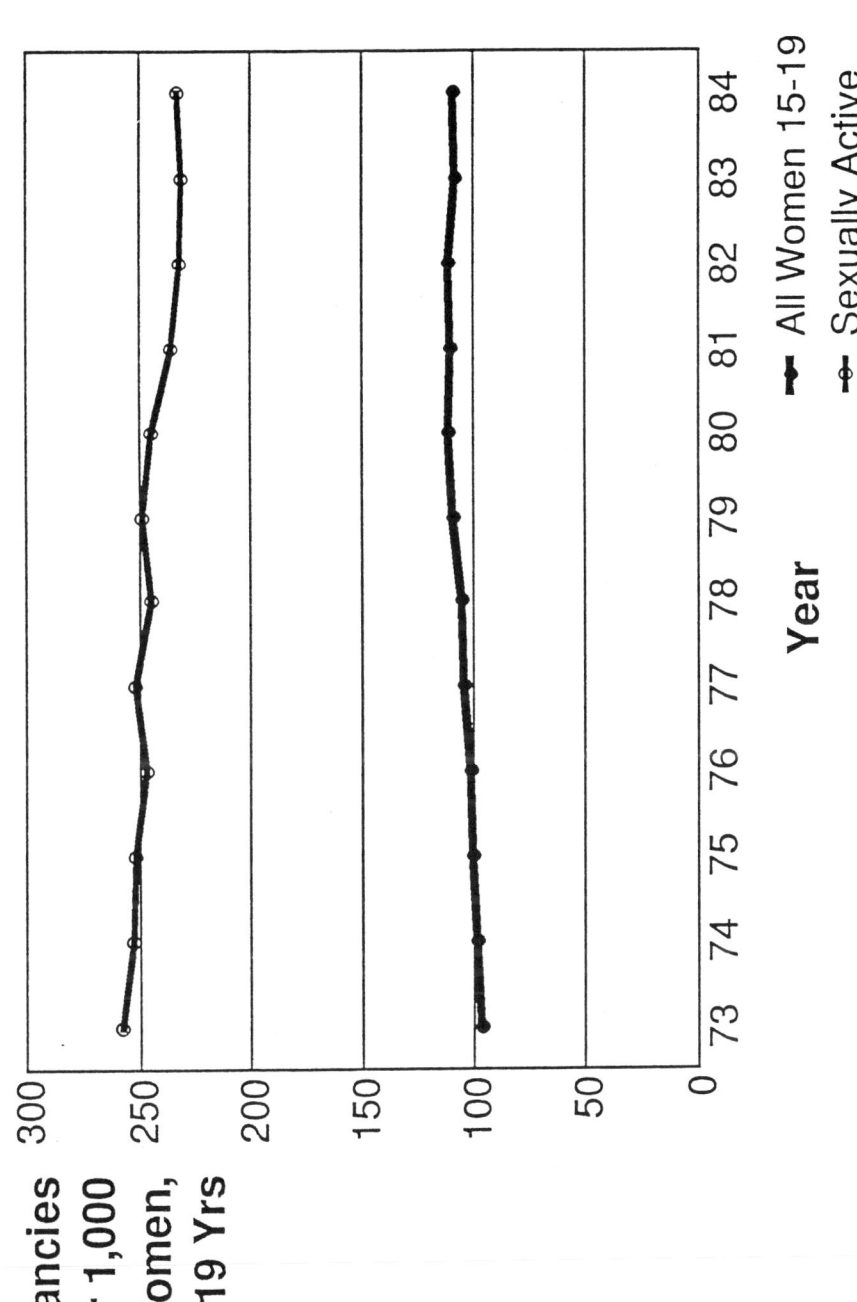

able to cite the increasing pregnancy rates as evidence that contraceptive programs are not working. But there is a denominator problem because the rate for all adolescent women obscures the fact that the proportion of sexually active adolescents has increased substantially over the same period of time. That is, out of 1,000 adolescent women in 1971 and 1,000 in 1981, there are more exposed to the risk of pregnancy in 1981. When recalculated with sexually active adolescent women as the denominator, the trend reverses. The denominator problem stems from the fact that not all women 15–19 were at risk of being in the numerator (being pregnant.) When the denominator is changed to those actually at risk of pregnancy, those who are sexually active, the rate is dropping, and a policy issue would then turn to defining how the declining rate could be reduced further (Flick n.d.). Thus, a technical epidemiological principle can have considerable policy impact.

There are a number of important rates, which are routinely defined in epidemiology texts (Hennekens and Buring 1987:54–98). Most epidemiologists would agree that the most sensitive and most important rate for indicating the overall health of population is the infant mortality rate, which I will use to illustrate the terminology. The infant mortality rate is calculated as follows:

$$\frac{\text{Number of deaths in a year of children less than 1 year of age}}{\text{Number of live births in that year}} \times 1{,}000 = \text{Yields infant deaths per 1,000 births per year.}$$

Obviously such a rate is more accurate for a society that has complete reporting of vital events than a developing country without complete data. Still, in spite of the problems of complete and accurate reporting, there is little ambiguity about a mortal event, or age. I am claiming that there is little difficulty in defining the outcome, or establishing the age, even if these data do not end up properly recorded for retrieval.

Similarly, the problem for the denominator is tallying the number of births, not identifying whether a birth has occurred. Even in the United States, with the increasing utilization of home deliveries and other nonstandard delivery of obstetrical services, the recording of births is not automatically handled in the way that once licensed hospitals consistently reported births. Thus, there may be delayed reporting or even missed vital events.

These examples are intended to illustrate the kind of reasoning epidemiologists use when examining data. I have emphasized rates in the seminar I teach about epidemiology. The students come to see that the apparent obvious simplicity of the rate conceals much subtlety and sophistication in presenting data and describing reality.

CONCLUSIONS: HOLISM AND EPIDEMIOLOGY

I began this chapter talking about the fact that I felt there were shared grounds for collaboration between epidemiologists and anthropologists. Whether these thoughts convince readers that this is fact or fantasy I cannot say. I conclude with some personal observations I have had in the course of a nontraditional anthropological career.

Epidemiology is a field of science that bridges what are usually biologically and clinically oriented outcomes and a range of etiological factors associated with the development of those outcomes. As etiological factors may encompass many candidate variables, social scientists are often involved in the research endeavor. Epidemiology embodies a set of methods and approaches for answering questions concerning the distribution of disease. The field systematically approaches causation while drawing widely from a range of disciplines through the integrative mechanism of focused research questions. Therefore, the field operationalizes the concept of holism in an instructive and powerful way.

My anthropological training emphasized anthropology as a holistic science, and therefore we studied the traditional four fields. Yet we have seen the field become more atomized, not less, as the recent reorganization of the American Anthropological Association is demonstrating. Epidemiology has seemed to me to be a way to carry out some of the holistic message of anthropology. In thinking about outcomes and physical illness and health states, epidemiology clearly has shared ground with physical anthropology, including considerations of genetics, biological processes, and measurement. Epidemiology shares interests with social and cultural anthropology when considering risk factors, exposures that encompass environmental dimensions, and parameters about work and family: the whole constellation of variables that define human settings.

Epidemiologists seem little concerned with matters that would draw from linguistics and archaeology. However, diagnostic schemes, such as the *Diagnostic and Statistical Manual* (American Psychiatric Association 1980, 1987), embody nuances of nosology and discrimination among similar disorders, which invites linguistic analysis. Inquiries in epidemiology would be enriched by a historical, archaeological view, particularly in the area of environmental issues. I see areas where there is now much cross-fertilization and areas where there are potential mutual contributions.

Epidemiology, which was defined as a discipline only quite recently, provides explanations for health phenomena that have presented a range of presumed etiology from moral turpitude (tuberculosis) to contagion associated with poverty (pellagra). Now, in a time when human ills are increasingly chronic and when the etiologies are understood to be of extreme multifactorial complexity, any cross-fertilization of these two fields may contribute new perspectives and approaches.

Anthropologists need to judge work by the questions asked, not by the methods used. I have heard the criticism, "But that is not anthropology," when the research question at hand in fact posed a coordinated inquiry about social and biological factors involved in an outcome of considerable impact. I suspect what was meant by the statement was, "But the methods employed are not those traditionally used by anthropologists." By shifting emphasis to the questions, not the methods, we will be able to define unique anthropological contributions to a wide range of human concerns where we will interact with colleagues who will teach us new perspectives and involve ourselves with other disciplines that will enrich our science and widen the scope of our endeavors.

CHAPTER 17

DEMOGRAPHY

W. Penn Handwerker

Demography is the study of the causes and consequences of population growth and decline. Its central concepts refer to numbers—population size, age structure, sex ratios, density, growth rate, and the rates of births, deaths, and movements that generate these characteristics. Consequently demography relies heavily on numerical analyses, and it requires distinctive methodological tools to capture its central concepts.[1] Nonetheless, demographic analysis invokes most of the concepts used in any social and cultural analysis, and it bears on some of the most intriguing problems in the social sciences. Thus, demography intersects the study of technological changes in the Paleolithic, the origins of agriculture, the rise of the state, the origins and dissolution of feudalism, the growth of a world industrial economy, and, consequently, the causes and consequences of "development" when that term is conceived broadly.

The latter issues raise policy concerns of immense importance. These center on the question of whether the world is, or is soon to be, overpopulated and on its policy corollary of how national and international resources should be allocated. Should they be expended on family planning facilities that may reduce fertility, on medical care that will reduce morbidity and mortality, on job creation that will reduce unemployment and may increase real incomes, or on educational systems to create a more informed population? If we send food to starving families in Africa, do we contribute to human welfare, or do we exacerbate a world population crisis?

Medical anthropologists must interpret the significance of demographic conditions in nearly all of the work they carry out, even if they do not directly confront issues of global significance. The incidence, distribution, and severity of disease in human communities, as Chapter 11 by Peter Brown and Marcia Millar made clear, reflects population size, structure, density, and mobility, and the patterns of migration that link different communities. Different rates of birth, death, and migration will generate differences in the number of children, of the young to middle-aged men and women who carry out most of the productive tasks, and of older men and women in the household production units in farming communities. The age and sex composition of these units thus influences their susceptibility to illness and disability and the demands placed on the primary work force, particularly women. Age and sex composition thus influences productive capabilities and consequently will affect the quality and level of diets. Reproductive patterns and rates may reflect complex relationships with mortality and migration; shortened intervals between births may reflect reductions in infant mortality in one community but may reduce nutritional quality and levels and so raise infant mortality in another. The role and social position of the elderly will reflect how many of them exist relative to their children and so will reflect levels of mortality and migration. Any change in the level or character of migration, mortality, or fertility and subsequent changes in the size, structure, and density of populations necessarily change the content and efficacy of social support networks. Virtually any demographic change thus alters both the physical and mental health of a community. Some diseases will become less common, and others will increase in incidence and severity. The stress levels to which people are subject will increase, as may substance abuse. Both the content and efficacy of prevention and therapeutic procedures utilized by the community can be expected to change as people adjust to the new diseases in the environment. One can even expect that the dynamism, efficiency, and effectiveness of medical organizations will reflect their rates of growth and age structure.

Thus, for medical anthropology, the demography of human populations is best understood as human population ecology. The health of a human population is both cause and consequence of its vital rates and growth or decline in its numbers. This chapter introduces the fundamental concepts of demography and outlines ways in which variations in demographic conditions both shape and reflect the broader environmental, cultural, and social framework within which health issues arise and take on meaning.

CONVENTIONAL OVERSIMPLIFICATIONS

The causes and consequences of human population growth have been the subject of speculation for at least 2,000 years, and probably for much longer.[2] Eugene Hammel and Nancy Howell (1987) point out that, today, analyses of population issues tend to express either the Malthusian view that technological innovations that occur independently of population increase allow populations to grow and that too much growth creates misery, or the Boserupian view (see Boserup 1965, 1981; Simon 1977, 1986) that population growth forces a more intensive use of resources and thus generates the technological innovations that improve human welfare. These views are not irreconcilable (Lee 1984), although they are usually associated with irreconcilable policies. Where some people look at misery and see a population problem, others see a production and distribution problem that further population growth can help alleviate. Where some people believe that effective family planning programs are essential to fertility reduction, others believe that socioeconomic development will bring about fertility reduction and that family planning programs have little or no impact on fertility. Where some people believe that cultural changes associated with modernization bring about fertility reductions, others believe that economic development is the primary force that reduces fertility.

The real issues are more subtle than these common policy positions, of course. For example, population growth may be associated with reductions in the supply of specific resources, which make feasible the exploitation of others, as when coal substituted for wood in the centuries prior to the industrial revolution (Boserup 1981). Such growth may affect environmental conditions adversely, as when political constraints on movement or technological change lead to a denuded landscape (Haiti and much of the African Sahel are good examples; on the latter, see Monod 1975; Galaty et al. 1981; Talbot 1986). On the other hand, population growth creates conditions that can increase the efficiency of distribution (Handwerker 1979, 1980). The growth of a potential market of specialists makes agricultural intensification profitable (Netting 1985). Light population densities in Africa unduely increase the costs of development (Amin 1972).

Subtleties such as these elude both Malthusian and Boserupian hypotheses because they share a common weakness: a concept of population pressure and an associated concept of a boundary on population size set by resources, which have never been shown to exist outside our imaginations and which, in fact, merely disguise our ignorance about the relationship between population and resources. Life itself implies population pressure because each living thing requires and thus puts pressure on resources. This does not tell us anything useful about the relationship between population and resources, only that it exists all the time, everywhere.

In fact, we have no clear evidence that any real population has ever brought misery upon itself merely because it was too large. Migration, reductions in fertility (or increased infanticide), and intensification of food production always seem to keep population sizes from reaching the Malthusian resource boundary if, in fact, it exists. Where it exists, misery can be best explained by the conjunction of several conditions, including unexpected fluctuations in climate or other environmental parameters (Galloway 1986), poor distribution systems (Morgan 1979; Garnsey 1988), the expropriation of surplus by controlling elites (Ross 1986), and constraints imposed by elites or infrastructual inadequacies on a population's ability to fission or reduce its fertility (Laughlin and Brady 1978; Mellor and Gavian 1987). Since no population has ever been shown to exert pressure on resources, just how population growth forces more intensive use of resources remains a mystery. More people, we might agree with Julian Simon, imply more ideas. But what process transforms new ideas, which may originate in contexts far removed from problems of subsistence, into effective actions that push back the resource bound and increase carrying capacity?

DON'T UNDERESTIMATE THE HUMAN CAPACITY FOR SCREW-UPS

One answer to this question, an appeal to human foresight and rationality, appears to be more utopian than realistic. It is not at all clear that human rationality can effectively sort through problems of even moderate complexity (Hogarth and Reder 1987). This does not bode well for economic theories of fertility (see Crosbie 1986). It is clear that we regularly blind ourselves to effective courses of action even when we have at our disposal enough information to identify them, as Barbara Tuchman pointed out in her book, *The March of Folly* (1984). Even if we are prescient, the complexities of power relationships make it virtually impossible to direct the course of human events in ways that we might like (Skocpol 1979).

A DARWINIAN THEORY CAPTURES ELUSIVE SUBTLETIES

A Darwinian theory of population helps clarify these issues because it recasts the entire argument. Darwin extended a Malthusian argument to all living things when he pointed out that all organisms face the problem of having the capacity to produce far more offspring than could possibly survive. But he added two observations: organisms vary and many of these variations are inherited by their offspring, and variations differ in their effects on survival and reproduction in particular environments. It followed that variations that contribute to survival and reproduction will accumulate in populations by selection.

Darwin thus created a revolutionary image of life. The contrast between a Malthusian view and a Darwinian view perhaps is clearest if we imagine a petri dish to which we add one bacterium. From a Malthusian perspective, the bacterium becomes bacteria, all of which will ultimately die because all the resources will ultimately be consumed. From a Darwinian perspective, the bacterium becomes bacteria, which, by mutation and selection, become a myriad of new species that may consume, along with uncounted other possibilities, the petri dish itself.

Darwin argued that nature simply exists. It is a physical system. As such, it is a system regulated by clear principles that operate independently of and without regard to the intentions, purposes, or rationality of the organisms subject to those principles. The driving force of evolution is an interaction between innovations and selective criteria dictated by the properties of living things.

Our knowledge of the genetics of living things reveals that, although existing species may be discrete in one sense or another, all species share a common ancestor. This means that all current species are merely the endpoints of a continuous growth trajectory for the population of lifeforms as a whole. The history of life on earth has revealed an infinite supply of resources over some 3 billion years, not because environmental conditions elicit specific innovations or because living things are prescient but because selection creates relatively advantageous means for using resources. The genetic innovations that may differentiate the offspring of common parents, which selection may concentrate into different species, change the definition of what constitutes a resource or the means used to acquire resources and creates new niches in the environment of our earth.

NEW IDEAS HELP

So can new ideas and new ways of acting. The innovations that become part of evolutionary processes need not be genetic. Humans think "intelligently" (Sternberg 1985). We do not change our behavior merely because we sense material stimuli with particular physical qualities. On the contrary, we construct conceptual models of reality by a process we call inference because the genes that control the processes by which concepts form do not control the conceptual outcome of those processes. We thus possess a built-in mechanism—the very process by which people experience the physical properties of material stimuli—that continuously generates new and unexpected ways to look at and act in the world (Handwerker 1989b).

BUT FIRST WE NEED TO EAT

Living things are distinguished by being open energy systems controlled by nucleic acids. All living things by definition require regular inputs of energy and nutrients. *Resource* is a cover term that encompasses all energy and nutrients and all means (*access channels*) by which they can be acquired. Perhaps the vast majority of conceptual and behavioral innovations are not very useful, and many constitute errors of varying magnitude. Nonetheless, it follows that selection must favor any innovation that improves or optimizes resource access, that selection will concentrate innovations that do so, and that selection will build relatively advantageous means of acquiring resources and will eliminate innovations that interfere with the process of resource acquisition.

The resource access hypothesis thus stipulates that selection operates by reference to the costs attached to various resources and to the means (the channels) by which people may gain access to those resources (see Handwerker 1989a,c). Resources are the energy and nutrients necessary for life, the foods that provide energy and nutrients, and the things, behavior, concepts, and other forms of life that facilitate resource access. Money, land, labor, education, berries, hoes, nets, cattle, husbands, or friends all may constitute a resource, depending on the time and place one analyzes. Any means by which a resource can be accessed can be thought of as a channel to that resource. Resource access channels may be sets of activities, a person or people, an organization, or some combination of activities, people, and organizations. For example, access channels to the resource of a job may include the activities that constitute "education," a school organization, or individual teachers, employers, friends, or relatives.

Gatekeepers are individuals or organizations that function as resource access channels. Illness, disability, and death reduce resource access or threaten to do so. Thus, people and organizations who can alleviate medical problems or control access to the people, organizations, or knowledge that can do so function as gatekeepers. They acquire significant social power as a result (Handwerker 1989a), and medical care systems constitute systems of power that have the potential to shape human relationships far beyond the confines of the medical system itself.

Changes in selective pressures are changes in the access costs of one resource relative to another or to others. The presence and intensity of selective pressures thus may be measured as resource access cost differences. Selection, which is only one mechanism of cultural evolution and social change, does not operate in the absence of such cost differentials. Selection generates cultural and social continuity when cost differentials do not change. Selection generates cultural evolution and social change when cost differentials change. The intensity of selection, and the rate of cultural evolution and social change, is a function of the size of those cost differentials. We may be able to explain more precisely the specific currents in human cultural evolution and social change once we identify the changes in resource access costs that they reflect. Consequently, the resource access hypothesis may make it possible to identify more precisely both the conditions that affect the health of specific communities and the social and cultural implications of specific medical innovations.

Changes in resource access costs come about when people create new ways to think about and act in the world, when environmental conditions change, and when fertility, mortality, or migration rises or falls and changes population density or composition and produces either population growth or population decline. Culture evolves and social changes occur with any demographic change because the behavioral strategies that optimize or improve resource access change accordingly. Thus, population pressure is not a special property of large, dense, or rapidly growing populations; it is merely the changes in selective pressures generated by demographic change.

The direction of cultural evolution, the specific nature of social change, and, hence, the specific health implications of either, is dictated by which resource access cost differences change and the new power relationships that they create. For example, population collapse following the Black Death effectively destroyed the English manorial system (Bolton 1980); in Eastern Europe, it destroyed smallholders' ability to maintain their freedom (Brenner 1976). Similarly, in some situations, large families enhance the material well-being of both individual parents and their affiliated descent groups or villages (Weil 1986; Cleveland 1986; Schumann 1986; Odell 1986). In other situations, small families have the same effect (Whiteford 1986; Handwerker 1989a). Women in the former situation may use family planning services, but they do not use birth control to reduce the number of children they have (Handwerker 1986b:404). Women in the latter situation do use birth control to reduce their family size even when family planning services are not available (Schneider and Schneider 1984).

Populations vary enormously. They might be a family or household, a band of foragers, an ethnic unit, the people who live within the confines of a village or a region, the citizens of a state, the employees of a ministry of health or a hospital, or all the people who live on our planet. Populations are distinguished primarily by characteristics such as their size and density, their age and sex structure, and their rate of growth (or decline). The physical and mental health conditions of populations vary with each of these characteristics.

THE BASIC COMPONENTS OF POPULATIONS

Do We Respect Our Elders or Dislike Them?

A population that consists of a relatively large number of older people will exhibit very different life-styles and medical problems than will a population that consists of a relatively large number of young people. Thus, the high death rates and youthfulness that have characterized all human populations until the last century imply a very different view of social relationships and different standards for viewing death and the aged (Fourastié 1972). Infants may not be considered real people in societies in which 25 to 30 percent (or more) of all who are born die before they reach their first birthday. Death and suffering take on immense social significance where 50 percent of the people who were born during the same year die before they are 15 years old and 80 percent may die by their early fifties. Elders may achieve respect merely because they have survived. Young populations in contemporary less developed countries (LDCs) imply a high demand for government investment in education and other services for children and adolescents who contribute little to government revenues. Older populations in the more developed countries (MDCs) imply a demand for services for the aged, including distinctive health care facilities, and an increasing burden on younger, employed taxpayers. The young may come to see their parents and other older people with less respect merely because there are so many of them. Older populations grow slowly, and newcomers to the population—the young—may have fewer chances for upward economic and social mobility than their seniors. Conflicts arise in which seniors who continue to work may block opportunities for their juniors or in which employment policy requires that active seniors retire before they wish to.

The age structure of populations that create these differences is commonly measured in two ways: as the count of people in one-year age categories and, in an abridged form, as the count of people in five-year age categories. In either case, age categories encompass people of exact age x to the exact age $x+n$ that begins the succeeding age category. Thus, in an abridged table of ages, the category 0–1 encompasses all living people from the moment of birth to exact age 1; the succeeding category 1–4 encompasses all living people from exact age 1 through exact age 4 (up to exact age 5); the succeeding category 5–9 encompasses all living people from exact age 5 through exact age 9 (up to exact age 10). When age structure is measured by five-year age categories, it is conventional to distinguish age 0–1 and 1–4 and to measure all subsequent ages by five-year age categories (5–9, 10–14, . . . , 60–64, . . . , 85 and older) to recognize that the probability of dying varies significantly over the first five years of life.

Can Each Woman (or Man) Marry? Or, Is There a Shortage of Mates?

The health issues that are important in a community reflect its sex composition as well as its age structure. The sex composition of populations is commonly measured by the sex ratio, which conventionally is expressed as the ratio of males to females, multiplied by a convenient numerical constant, normally 100. Sex ratios at different ages reflect sex-specific migration and mortality rates. On average, about 48.8 percent of all births in large populations are females, which gives rise to a sex ratio at birth of approximately 105; 105 males are born for every 100 females. Estimates of the sex ratio at conception range from about 110 to 170 (McMillen 1979).

Age and Sex Together Describe the Basic Structure of Populations

The age and sex structure of populations is commonly summarized in population pyramids (Figure 17.1). Population pyramids consist of two histograms placed back to back, one of which expresses the relative frequency of males of different ages and the other of which expresses the relative frequency of females of different ages. Together they express the sex and age composition of a population, and they reflect the birth, death, and migration processes that have affected it. The width of the pyramid base reflects the level of fertility; it will be wide if the birthrate is high and relatively narrow if the birthrate is low. Mortality and migration at successive ages determine the pyramid slope.

Figure 17.1 illustrates three distinctive forms of population structure. The first, from Liberia in West Africa, illustrates the very young populations common in LDCs that experience high birthrates. The second, from the United Kingdom, illustrates the structure of aging populations, which experience very low birth and death rates. The third, from the United States, illustrates the structure of a population that experienced a pronounced decline in fertility following the baby boom of the late 1940s through 1960. Note that a change in fertility creates a wave of people that will work its way through the population. Especially high levels of emigration or mortality, or a birth deficit, such as occurred in both England and the United States during the Great Depression (see the proportions of men and women aged 40–49) creates a pyramid constriction, which also works its way through the population.

Variation in age and sex structures creates variation in resource access costs and thus creates very different social and cultural patterns, in addition to differences in medical problems and health issues. For example, the sex ratio influences the probability that a woman or man will be able to marry, the incidence of extramarital sexual activity, the birthrate, marriage duration, the composition and character of work and friendship groups, the intensity of competition among and between men and women, and, through these and other avenues of influence, the tenor and character of social relationships (Guttentag and Secord 1983; Chagnon 1968, 1977; Marino 1970). The exodus of men aged 15–40 to towns, mines, and plantations has radically altered the sex ratio and

Figure 17.1
Population Pyramids for Liberia (1974), the United States (1981), and the United Kingdom (England and Wales, 1980).

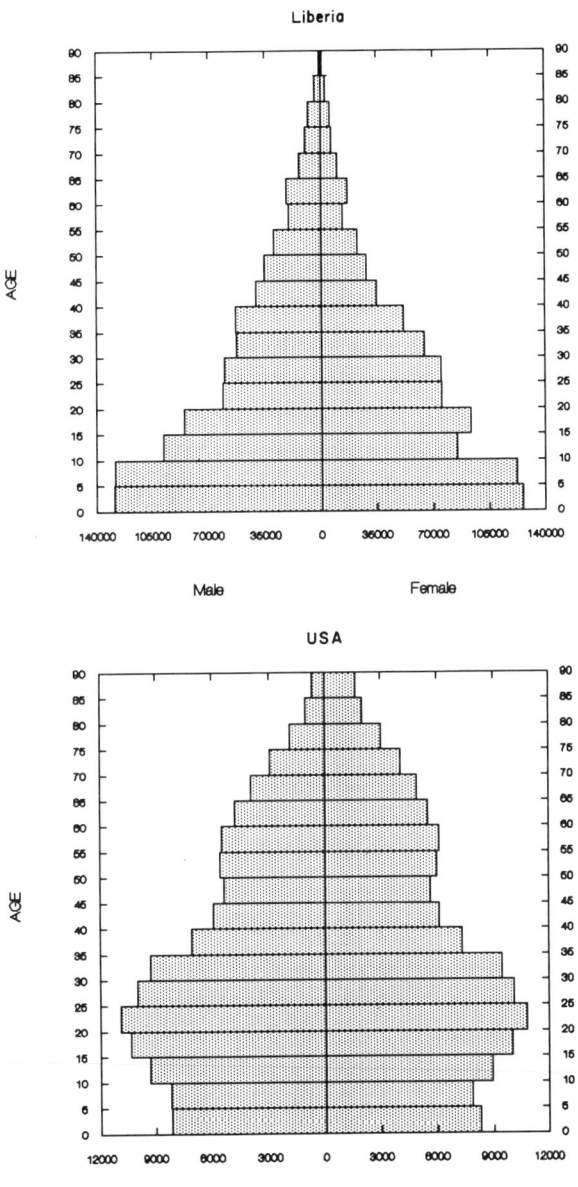

Figure 17.1 (continued)

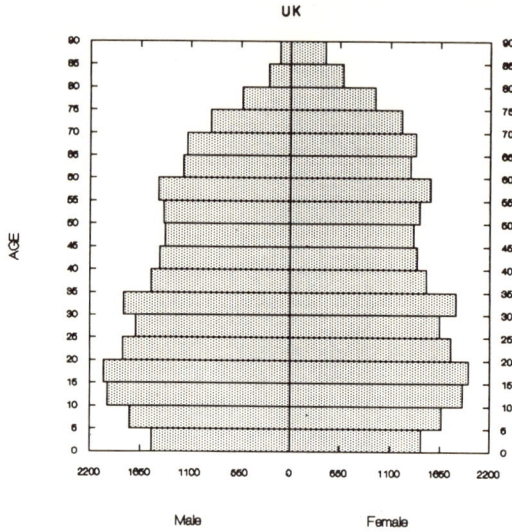

Source: U.N. Demographic Yearbook, 1985.

the age composition of African rural areas (Figure 17.2) in ways that have markedly increased the work load on women and the elderly, changed the division of labor, reduced the variety of crops grown, changed crop scheduling, acreages planted, and productive technologies, restructured power relationships both within villages and with households, contributed to the disappearance of certain kinds of work groups and fostered the creation of new ones (Handwerker 1974; Wilson 1977; Hart 1982), and have led to significant changes in reproductive behavior (Cleveland 1986; Weil 1986).

POPULATION PROCESSES GENERATE DEMOGRAPHIC CHARACTERISTICS

The physical and mental health of communities reflects the size, structure, and growth rate of their populations, but these demographic characteristics arise from population processes—fertility, mortality, immigration, and emigration. A convenient way to study the effects of population processes is to assume that a population experiences no migration. Populations that experience no migration are characterized by an age and sex structure and rate of population growth that is stable from generation to generation, if birth and death rates do not change. Stable population theory reveals that each combination of birth and death rates generates a distinctive age and sex structure and rate of growth. Characteristically, high fertility rates generate young populations irrespective of the expectation of life at birth; low fertility rates generate old populations.

Births, deaths, and movements thus constitute the fundamental population

Demography

Figure 17.2
Population Pyramid for the Village of Saboke, Republic of Liberia, 1967

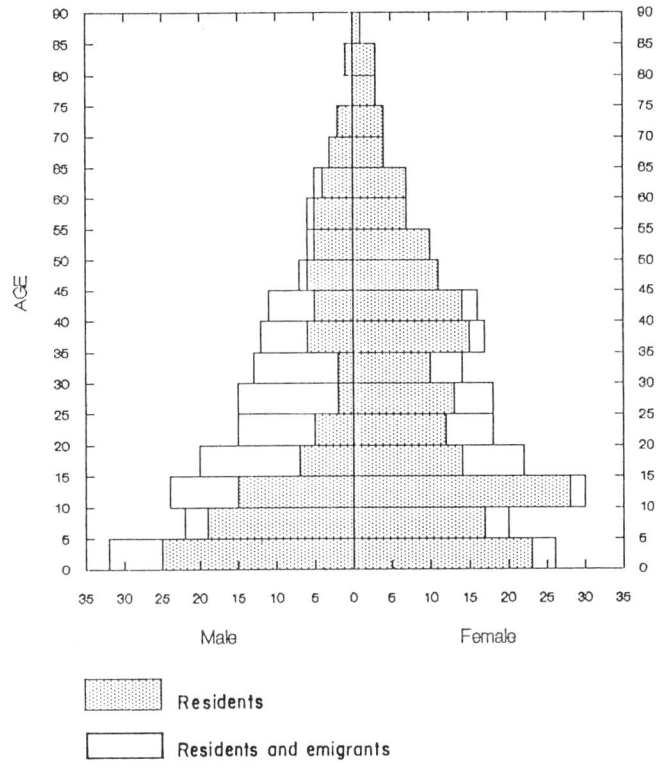

Source: McEvoy (1971: Table 3–14).

events. Population events are commonly measured not by absolute counts but as exposure rates in which the number of times a particular population event occurs is expressed relative to the number of people exposed to the possibility of that event. For example, perhaps the most commonly cited demographic rates express the number of children who are born and the number of people who die relative to the total number of people in a population. Both statistics are usually computed for a particular year as the number of births (or the number of deaths) divided by the size of the population in midyear, multiplied by a convenient numerical base (usually 1,000). These statistics are the crude birthrate (CBR) and the crude death rate (CDR). They tell us the number of births and deaths that occur for every 1,000 people in a population, and thus they make it possible to compare the fertility and mortality experiences of different-sized populations. They are crude rates because the probability of birth and death varies significantly with the age and sex composition of populations. More refined measures of fertility and mortality take cognizance of these variables.

Figure 17.3
Fertility Rates by Age

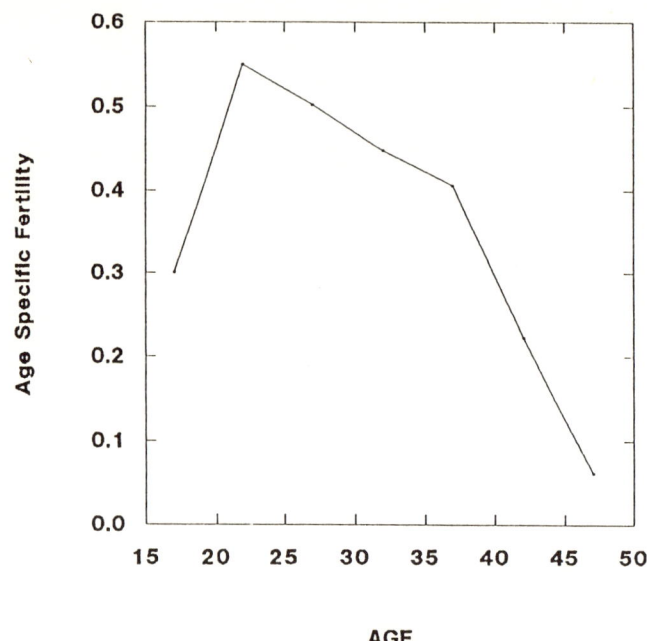

WHEN AND HOW FAST ARE BABIES PRODUCED?

The general fertility rate (GFR) partially controls for the age and sex composition of populations because it is calculated by dividing the number of children who are born by the number of women who are most likely to bear a child. These are women aged 15–49, for the human reproductive span begins with the onset of menarche around age 15 and extends through menopause at average age 48–50.

Fertility in human populations exhibits characteristic variation by age, however (Figure 17.3). Women experience very low levels of fertility at the very beginning of the reproductive period and a gradual increase in fertility as they approach age 20. Women experience the highest probability of birth from approximately age 20 through age 29. Thereafter the probability of birth falls increasingly rapidly. The age pattern of childbearing that characterizes human populations is determined by factors that are poorly understood at this point. Genetic factors dictate the length of the human reproductive span and the length of gestation, but we have only begun to speculate about how they evolved (Lovejoy 1981). Biological variables, which are influenced by nutrition and disease in ways that are only now being uncovered, lead to characteristic periods of reduced reproductive capacity before the onset of regular ovarian function, age-specific intrauterine mortality rates, age-specific proportions of women who are sterile, and declining ovarian function by age. Age-specific fertility rates (ASFR) and total fertility rates (TFR) control for the age and sex composition of populations and thus constitute the most useful measures of individual and population fertility.

Age-specific fertility refers to the number of children born alive to a woman during a specific age range and historical period. Age-specific fertility may be computed for individual women as the average number of children they bear alive relative to a specific age range and period of time:

$$\text{ASFR} = \sum_{x}^{x+n} (\text{births} \div \text{woman-years}).$$

For example, a woman who gives birth to two children over a five-year period exhibits an age-specific fertility rate of $2 \div 5$, or 0.4 children per woman-year over that period. A woman who gives birth to three children over that period exhibits an age-specific fertility rate of 0.6 children per woman-year over the same period. A woman who gives birth to only one child over the five-year period exhibits an age-specific fertility rate of 0.2 children per woman-year over that period.

Total fertility refers to the total number of children born alive to a woman by the end of her reproductive years. A woman's total fertility is the sum of her age-specific fertility:

$$\text{TFR} = \sum_{15}^{49} (\text{births} \div \text{woman-years}).$$

Thus, the first woman's total fertility for the five-year period is 0.4 child per year $\times$ 5 years, or 2 children. The second woman's total fertility is 0.6×5, or 3 children. The third woman's total fertility is $0.2. \times 5$, or 1 child.

Age-specific fertility rates may be computed for a population or a segment of a population as an average of the age-specific fertility for all women of a specific age or age range (from 15 through 49) in the population or population segment. Sum the individual age-specific fertility rates and divide by the total number of women who belonged to a specific age category for the pertinent historical period. Thus, the three hypothetical women mentioned above exhibit an average age-specific fertility of $(0.2 + 0.4 + 0.6)/3$, or 0.4 children per woman-year. The total fertility rate of a population or segment of a population is the average number of children born alive to women of reproductive age. The population total fertility rate is computed as the sum of the population age-specific fertility rates. The total fertility (over the five-year period) of the three hypothetical women mentioned above is $0.4. \times 5$, or 2 children. Alternatively, the population total fertility rate is computed as an average of the individual age-specific fertility rates—$[(0.2 + 0.4 + 0.6)5] \div 3$, or 2 children.

ASFRs are commonly computed for five-year intervals (15–19, 20–24, 25–29, 30–34, 35–39, 40–44, 45–49). The computation procedures may be short-cut by dividing the number of live births that occurred to women of a particular age range by the total number of women in the population who belonged to that age group during the five-year interval. When ASFRs are computed for five-year intervals, a population's TFR continues to be the sum of the pertinent ASFRs and is found by multiplying the sum of ASFRs for ages 15–19 through 44–49 by 5.

WHAT ABOUT THE SMALL SAMPLES THAT ANTHROPOLOGISTS NORMALLY USE?

Age-specific fertility rates and total fertility rates often cannot be calculated from secondary sources, including census data. Indeed, they can be computed from anthropological field surveys and censuses only when detailed birth history data are collected. Even when such data have been collected, the small samples anthropologists and historical demographers frequently work with may prohibit the computation of ASFRs and TFRs that accurately estimate fertility parameters. One study of the sampling variability of fertility statistics (Handwerker 1988) suggests that population TFR values may be accurately estimated from birth histories collected from as few as 50 women and that population ASFR values may be accurately estimated so long as the number of woman-years in any cohort or period age-group is 35 or larger. But these findings need to be confirmed by further, more detailed studies.

WHAT TO DO WHEN YOU CAN'T CALCULATE AGE-SPECIFIC FERTILITY RATES

In the absence of appropriate data, indexes of fertility may be calculated. These include the GFR, child-woman ratios (the number of children below age 5 relative to the number of women of child-bearing age, multiplied by 1000), and Ansley Coale's comparative indexes of general fertility, I_f; of marital (legitimate) fertility, I_g; of illegitimate fertility, I_n; and of the proportion of women married. I_m; Coale's indexes express observed fertility and marriage rates relative to the standard age-specific marital fertility rates experienced by the Hutterites between 1921 and 1930, which, at a total marital fertility rate of 12.44, are the highest such rates ever recorded (Wunsch and Termote 1978:270 present the standard ASFRs for the Hutterites).

CONSTRAINTS ON THE RATE OF BABY PRODUCTION

Kenneth Campbell and James Wood (1987) point out that almost none of the variation in total fertility from one population to another appears to be explained by variation in the age at menopause, the level of intrauterine mortality, or the length of gestation. Likewise, variation in the age at menarche appears to explain little of the variation in fertility. Variation in the incidence of sterility, which may be significantly affected by the incidence of gonorrhea and other sexually transmitted diseases, may dramatically reduce the fertility of particular populations during specific historical periods (Pirie 1972; Belsey 1976). Variation in total fertility from population to population is believed to be explained primarily, however, by only five *intermediate fertility variables* (cf. Bongaarts 1982, 1983): (1) the duration and intensity of breastfeeding (and periods of postpartum abstinence linked with breastfeeding), (2) the proportion of women who are married (sexually active), which may function primarily as a proxy for the frequency of coitus (Trussell 1979), (3) fecundability[3] (as determined, for example, by the length of the ovarian cycle, the proportion of cycles that are ovulatory, and the duration of the fecund period), (4) the effectiveness and use rate of contraception, and (5) the incidence of induced abortion. The effects of contraception and induced abortion may negate the importance of other proximate fertility determinants.

Intermediate fertility variables reflect the costs of resource access and fluctuate with cost changes brought about by climate fluctuations, real wage rates, landownership, and other variables (Wrigley and Schofield 1981; Wilmsen 1986; Borgerhoff Mulder 1987). Constraints imposed by the means people use to access resources affect the operation of intermediate fertility variables and may lead to distinctive levels of fertility even among people who do not intentionally contracept or abort (such as possible differences in fertility among foragers, between foragers and settled agriculturalists, and between farming populations in Africa and those in Europe; see Handwerker 1983).

Births are political events (insofar as variations in resource access costs reflect social and cultural rather than environmental conditions), and the incidence of births both reflects and changes power relationships. Thus a birth may be part of a strategy to acquire or extend power, or it may be used to create new ties of dependence, as in contemporary West Africa (Bledsoe 1988) and Central America (Odell 1986). Births may provide a means to break ties of dependence, as on Barbados during the 1950s where support from children made it possible for women of middle age and older to escape subservience from autocratic mates (Handwerker 1989a). The most dramatic changes in fertility may reflect fundamental changes in women's power relationships with their spouses, parents, and children (Greenhalgh 1985b). High fertility appears to exist where women are dependent on their offspring for their material well-being; fertility transition occurs when this dependence is broken (Handwerker 1989a).

THE THREE-DIMENSIONAL EFFECT: COHORT AND PERIOD ANALYSIS

As the discussion of age-specific fertility makes clear, population events such as birth, illness, and death occur in three simultaneous dimensions: (1) to a group of people (a cohort), (2) at a particular age, and (3) during a particular historical period. The three dimensions of population events give rise to two distinctive styles of demographic analysis: cohort analysis and period analysis. Cohort analyses focus on the life-trajectory experiences of particular groups of people (such as all the people born during a specific period or all those who marry or move). Period analyses focus on the experiences of an entire population during

Figure 17.4
Lexis Diagram

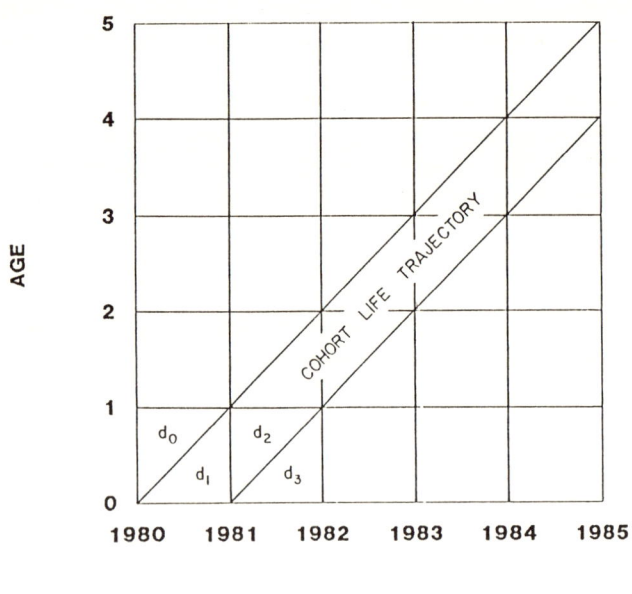

a particular historical period (for example, during 1988 or from 1985 to 1990). Demographic statistics are computed differently in the two styles of analysis. The differences between the two styles of demographic analysis and the distinctive characteristics of population events are most clearly analyzed in Lexis diagrams (Figure 17.4).

Lexis diagrams such as the abbreviated one in Figure 17.4 make explicit the three dimensions of population events. The vertical axis identifies the age of people exposed to a population event. The horizontal axis identifies the historical period during which time a population event may occur. The diagonal identifies the life trajectory of a particular cohort exposed to a population event over that historical period.

The Lexis diagram in Figure 17.4 defines a cohort as all people born during the course of a particular year (1980). Populations and cohorts are subject to attrition by death once they come into being, but the number of deaths that occur to the whole population are not the same as the number of deaths that occur to a specific cohort of that population. Deaths that occur to members of the population and to members of the specific cohort examined in Figure 17.4 are represented by a subscripted d. If we were to compute an infant mortality rate for the population, we would compute the rate for a particular historical period—say, for 1980. We would add together all the deaths that occurred to infant members of the population during this period ($d_o + d_1$), divide that sum by the number of people born during that year, and multiply the result by 1,000.

Infant mortality rates are normally computed in this fashion, as period rates. So are crude birth rates and crude death rates. Period rates are not the same as the comparable rates computed solely for a cohort. If we computed the infant mortality rate experienced by the cohort born during 1980, we would add together all of the infant deaths that occurred only to members of the cohort $(d_1 + d_2)$, divide that number by all of the people born into the cohort, and multiply the result by 1,000. This statistic is a cohort measure of infant mortality and constitutes the probability of dying before age 1 experienced by the cohort (q_o).

All demographic statistics may be computed either as cohort measures or as period measures, and fertility statistics commonly are. For example, ASFRs and TRFs may be computed for cohorts to study how the birth histories of a group or groups of women (for example, those who were age 15 in 1980, 1981, 1982, and so forth) may have been affected by war, migration, epidemic, famine, economic depression, or new economic opportunities. Alternatively, the birth experiences of all women of reproductive age may be aggregated into a fictitious cohort to study the reproductive events of a specific historical period. Period rates are commonly computed for individual years, and thus "woman-years" in the equations already presented would be equivalent to the midyear population of women who belonged to pertinent age classes. Midyear populations are commonly estimated as one-half of the sum of population size at the beginning of the year, P_1, and the population size at the end of the year, P_2 $(.5[P_1 + P_2])$, and thus assume that mortality probabilities do not change significantly over the course of the year. With small samples, however, period rates may be computed for five or ten year time periods (Cleveland 1986). Moreover, we can summarize the fertility experience of a population by aggregating the birth histories of all women, although we might miss significant historical fluctuations if we did not also compute period rates by years or by five or ten year time periods. When period rates are computed for periods greater than one year, each year a woman belonged to a particular age group over that time period would have to be entered into the denominator of the equations.

Cohort mortality rates are rarely calculable because appropriate data often do not exist. Instead, period age-specific mortality rates, which are calculated by dividing the sum of the deaths that occur to people of a given age range at a particular point in time by the total number of people of that age range ($M_x = d_x/P_x$), are transformed into probabilities of dying (q_x). These probabilities of death can then be used to create a fictitious cohort and an especially valuable tool for analyzing the mortality experience of a population—a life table (Table 17.1).

HOW DO WE KNOW YOUR LIFE EXPECTANCY?

Life tables measure the health risks faced by specific populations or subpopulations (for example, all men, women during their reproductive careers, or children from birth to exact age 5). Life tables such as the abridged one for the United States in Table 17.1 have seven commonly reported functions, although

Table 17.1
Life Table for the United States, 1980

Age	q_x	l_x	d_x	L_x	T_x	e_x
0	0.0127	100.000	1.270	98,794	7,368,044	73.7
1	.0025	98.730	247	394,426	7,269,250	73.6
5	.0015	98,483	148	492,045	6,874,824	69.8
10	.0015	98,335	148	491,305	6,382,779	64.9
15	.0049	98,187	481	489,732	5,891,474	60.0
20	.0066	97,706	645	486,918	5,401,742	55.3
25	.0066	97,061	641	483,702	4,914,824	50.6
30	.0070	96,420	675	480,412	4,431,122	46.0
35	.0091	95,745	871	476,548	3,950,710	41.3
40	.0139	94,874	1,319	471,072	3,474,162	36.6
45	.0222	93,555	2,077	462,582	3,003,090	32.1
50	.0351	91,478	3,211	449,362	2,540,508	27.8
55	.0530	88,267	4,678	429,662	2,091,146	23.7
60	.0794	83,589	6,637	401,375	1,661,484	19.9
65	.1165	76,952	8,965	362,348	1,260,109	16.4
70	.1694	67,987	11,517	311,142	897,761	13.2
75	.2427	56,470	13,705	248,087	586,619	10.4
80	.3554	42,765	15,199	175,828	338,532	7.9
85+	1.0000	27,566	27,566	162,704	162,704	5.9

Source: q_x from *Vital Statistics of the United States*, 1980.

not all of them are always presented. The most important is q, the probability of dying between age x and exact age $x+n$. The function q generates the remaining six functions once the life table radix, l_0 is specified. The function q is an attrition rate, unlike age-specific mortality rates M_x, which are exposure rates.

This Is How You Can Convert People Who Die into Death Probabilities

Mortality rates (Mx) can be transformed into attrition rates (q_x) because they have the following equality: $q_x = 2nM_x \div (2 + nM_x)$ where n = the exposure interval (five years for most age intervals in abridged tables). Period infant mortality rates (M_o) and child mortality rates (M_1) are converted to probabilities of dying before age 1 (q_o) and between age 1 and exact age 5 (q_1) by formulas that are slightly modified in recognition that the probabilities of death vary significantly through these one- and four-year exposure intervals. Acceptable estimates for these early exposure intervals may be computed as follows: $q_o = 2M_o \div (2 + 1.82M_o)$ and $q_1 = 4M_1 \div (2 + 4.88M_1)$. Mortality rates for the age interval 5–9 (M_s) are converted into the probability of dying over that interval q_s by the equality: $q_s = 10M_s \div (2 + 5M_s)$. The same equality holds for all succeeding five-year age intervals. The probability of dying during the terminal age interval (age 65 and over, or age 85 and over) is 1.000.

This Is How You Can Count People Who Do Not Die

The function l_x gives the number of cohort survivors at exact age x. The radix, l_o specifies the size of the originating cohort as a convenient numerical base (100, 1,000, 100,000). The complement of the function q_x $(1-q_x)$ is the probability of survival, p_x. q_o tells the proportion of the radix who will not survive the first year of life; its complement, $p_o = 1 - q_o$ tells the proportion of the radix who will survive the year (l_1). q_1 tells the proportion of the survivors at exact age 1 (l_1 who will not survive to exact age 5; its complement, $p_1 = 1 - q_1$, tell the proportion of the survivors at exact age 1 who will survive to exact age 5 (l_5). q_5 tells the proportion of the survivors to exact age 5 (l_5) who will not survive to exact age 10; its complement $p_5 = 1 - q_5$, tells the proportion of the survivors at exact age 5 who will survive to exact age 10 (l_{10}).

This Is How You Can Count the People Who Do Die

The function d_x tells you the number of deaths that occur between exact age x and exact age $x+n$, and is simply the product $q_x l_x$ the probability of dying between age x and age $x+n$ multiplied by the number of survivors at exact age x. Note that l_x is simply the number of survivors at the beginning of the previous age interval minus those who died: $(l_{x-n} - d_x)$.

This Is How You Can Count the Total Number of Years of Life Experience

The function L_x estimates the number of person-years lived by cohort members and so exposed to the risk of death (or illness, disability, marriage, divorce, migration, or birth) between age x and exact age $x+n$, based on estimates of mortality over the time period n. L_x for the four-year age category 1–4 and for all five-year age categories may be calculated to an acceptable level of accuracy as the mid-period population size: $n/2$ $(l_x + l_{x+n})$, where n = the number of years in the interval (4 or 5), on the assumption that the probability of death remains constant throughout these periods.

The probability of dying falls significantly over the first year of life, although this decline is moderated when infant mortality levels are very low. When infant mortality is very low (about 15 or lower), as in contemporary MDCs, L_o may be calculated as $.05 l_o + .95 l_1$. These weights (.05, .95) need to be adjusted when infant mortality is higher (Shryock and Seigel 1973). When infant mortality is about 25, as it is in many upper-middle-income countries, L_o may be calculated as $.15 l_o + .85 l_1$. When infant mortality is about 100, L_o may be calculated as $.25 l_1 + .75 l_1$. When infant mortality is about 150, as in many contemporary African countries, L_o may be calculated as $.33 l_o + .67 l_1$.

The probability of dying is 100 percent for the terminal life table age interval. The number of person-years lived during this last period, L_w, is estimated as the number of cohort survivors to the beginning of this period (l_{65+}, or l_{85+}) divided by the period mortality rate of people at or above the age that begins the terminal age interval (M_{65+}, or M_{85+}). Note that the number of people who survive to the beginning of this age interval equals the number of people who die by the end of that interval.

This Is How You Can Summarize the Life Experience of an Entire Cohort

The function T_x is the count of the number of person-years lived by all members of the fictitious cohort through age x and is the sequential sum of L_x from the terminal age interval (L_{65+} or L_{85+}) through the initiating age interval (L_o). Note that the value of T for the terminal age interval (e.g., T_{65+}) equals the value of L for that age interval.

Now It Is Easy to Compute Your Life Expectancy

The function e_x is the average number of years cohort members live beyond age x. The total number of years of life experienced by cohort members who survived to age x is equal to T_x; the number of cohort members who survive to age x is equal to l_x. Thus, e_x is T_x divided by l_x.

e_o estimates life expectancy at birth. e_1 estimates the additional number of years that cohort members who survive to age 1 can expect to live. e_{15} estimates the additional number of years that cohort members who survive to age 15 can expect to live. e_x added to the age of cohort members at the beginning of a specific age interval constitutes their expected age at death.

Your Life Expectancy Does Not Tell You When You Will Die

Figure 17.5 plots the expected age at death for !Kung foragers, whose life expectancy at birth is about 35 years (Howell 1979), and for U.S. citizens, whose life expectancy at birth (in 1980) is about 74 years. Note that life expectancy converges very rapidly after the first few years of life. A life expectancy at birth of 35 years does not mean that everyone dies by the time they are 35 years old. A significant number of people in such populations live long, healthy, and productive lives and far outlive many people in our society. Life expectancy numbers are averages. These numbers constitute our best guess about how long you will live once you have attained a particular age. These numbers also reveal that your life expectancy at birth is heavily influenced by deaths among infants who have not yet reached their first birthday. Public health measures aimed at infants and children have a profound impact on a population's longevity. The sophisticated medical technologies aimed at prolonging life among older people have relatively minor impacts on population longevity.

Life tables cannot always be constructed because of deficient primary data. In these cases, the mortality experience of a population may be estimated from model life tables such as those of Coale and Demeny (1983). Nancy Howell's report on !Kung demography (1979) illustrates their use.

Demography

Figure 17.5
Expected Age at Death by Age

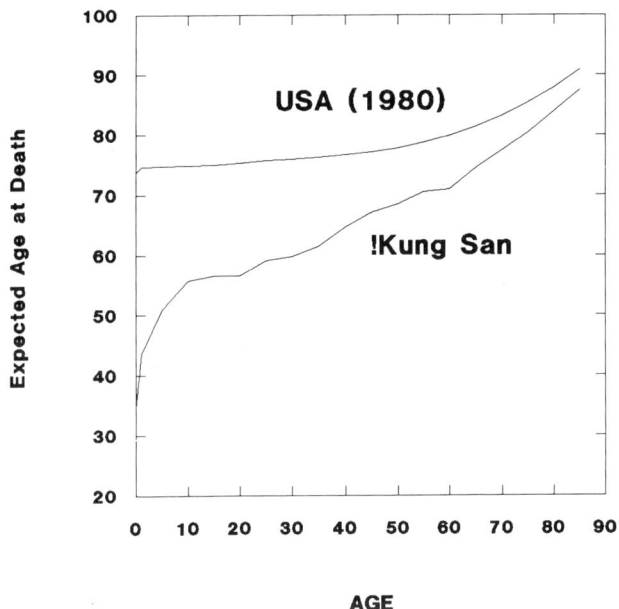

Sources: Table 17.1; Howell (1979).

LIFE TABLES AND PERIOD TOTAL FERTILITY RATES APPLY TO FICTITIOUS COHORTS

It is important to emphasize that all life tables apply to fictitious cohorts. They tell what would happen to a birth cohort subject to a specific set of age-specific mortality (or morbidity) probabilities. Mortality probabilities experienced by real populations vary over time, of course. Also it is important to emphasize that period age-specific and total fertility rates also apply to a fictitious cohort. These rates tell what would happen to a cohort of women subject to a specific set of fertility probabilities. On average, women of this cohort would experience a certain number of births at different ages and at the end of their reproductive years would have borne a specific number of children.

THESE FICTIONS HAVE MANY IMPORTANT USES THAT MEDICAL ANTHROPOLOGISTS HAVE NOT YET TAPPED

These rates are useful nonetheless. Life table death probabilities effectively summarize the life trajectories experienced by a population at a particular point in time that controls for its age and sex composition. Life tables may be constructed to control for other individual and population characteristics as well and thus may be used to evaluate the life trajectories of subpopulations, the personnel turnover in health organizations, the loss of production time due to illness or disability or the efficacy of a specific therapy or preventative measure, among many other applications that do not require extensive and detailed national census data (see Namboodiri and Suchindran 1987 for an introduction to many of the advanced applications of life table methods).

Spatial, cross-sectional, and historical variations in resource access opportunities and costs generate variations in mortality. Fluctuations in resource flows and power dependencies, for example, may generate infanticide, overt or disguised (contrast Scrimshaw 1978, 1983, and Scheper-Hughes 1984a with Weil 1986), selective or not (Eng and Smith 1976, Scheper-Hughes, ed. 1987). Cross-population or time-series comparisons of age-or sex-specific mortality probabilities reveal differences in the effects of mortality determinants from one population or time period to another. Such comparisons can be used to study the time- and age-or sex-specific manifestation of public health measures; such comparisons are essential for obtaining a detailed understanding of the ecology of disease, as Brown and Millar point out, including the modern mortality transition.

Keeping Track of Migrants Is Very Important and Exceedingly Difficult

Life tables, together with a count of births, also can be used to estimate migration into or out of a region. Migration, like the production of new generations, provides resources that governments may use, but it also provides in one location a population that must be fed, clothed, and housed and for which medical care will be required, while it takes it away from another. Migration changes population size, density, and composition in both sending and receiving areas in ways that may generate new migration flows (Little 1973; Massey and España 1987), as well as social, political, and economic change in both regions (Richardson 1985; Kearney 1986; Gulliver 1958: Dorjahn 1975). Different sectors of a population may grow (or decline) at different rates. Differential growth of this kind shifts the basis of political power and may change profoundly the political complexion of a society, whether it occurs by natural increase (as among the Arab population in contemporary Israel) or migration (as in the contemporary United States and Western Europe; Borjas and Tienda 1987; Therborn 1987). Migration exerts an increasing influence on local demographic conditions and thus on local health conditions and the demand for medical facilities and services, especially as mortality and fertility decline.

Spatial differentials in resource access costs generate migration flows (Stenning 1957; Berg 1965; Skinner 1960; Southall 1961; Mitchell 1961; Gulliver 1957; Handlin 1951; Dunn 1972; Richardson 1985). But migration is notoriously difficult to measure even in field surveys that collect first-hand reports of migration histories because such reports necessarily exclude reports from migrants who died. The simplest way to estimate migration over a specific period of time is to subtract the natural increase in a population (births − deaths) from the total population change (population size at the beginning of the period − population size at the end of the period). This estimate of net migration has its own shortcomings, one of which is that the measure of natural increase includes births and deaths to in-migrants, excludes deaths and births to out-migrants, and thus is not independent of the total population change. Life table mortality probabilities by age and sex tell us the attrition that we could expect from a population with a given age and sex structure, if that population were subject to those death probabilities over a specified period of time. A census count at a later time would reveal a distinctive population age and sex structure. The differences between the expected population structure generated by life table mortality probabilities and the observed population structure provide an estimate of immigration and emigration by people of different ages and sexes. This method to estimate migration also has shortcomings, of course. Perhaps the most important of these is that the method does not adjust for changing death probabilities, which usually are not known.

These Are Some Ways to Measure Demand for Reproductive and Child Health Services

Similarly ASFRs and TFRs permit us to evaluate childbearing trajectories of women at different stages of life, and they provide a direct measure of a population's childbearing trajectory, which controls for its age and sex composition. Childbearing trajectories thus measure the demand for health care services devoted to reproduction and children. Changes in these trajectories can be used to estimate future demand for these medical services. If we express the age-specific fertility rate of women at ages 25–29, 30–34, 35–39, 40–44, and 45–49 as a proportion of the age-specific fertility rate at age 20–24 and plot the results, we reveal the age pattern of childbearing that characterizes a population. Such a plot of relative birth trajectory by age clearly discriminates target fertility populations in which people deliberately stop childbearing or reduce the rate of childbearing after they have reached a particular (a "target") number of births, from "natural" fertility populations in which this practice is absent (see Knodel 1983; Figure 17.6). Ansley Coale and James Trussell (1974, 1975) have worked out an index of fertility control (m) that expresses observed age-specific fertility rates relative to a standard "natural fertility" age pattern of fertility. Birth trajectories also may be plotted by parity progression ratios, which express the proportion of all women who experience a first birth, the proportion of all women who experience a first birth who subsequently experience a second, and so forth (see Howell 1979). Birth trajectories of these kinds are useful indicators of the proportion of women of different ages who are engaged in childbearing. These trajectories thus constitute measures that can be used to estimate women's medical and dietary needs over time and the need for particular health care facilities or services.

POPULATION GROWTH AND DECLINE

Life table probabilities, age-specific fertility rates, and total fertility rates also can be used to estimate the long-run growth potential of populations. The growth

Figure 17.6
Contrasts in the Age Pattern of Childbearing

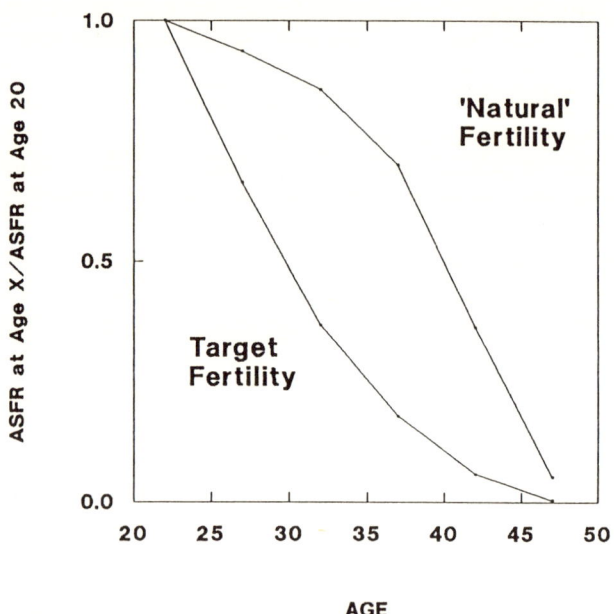

Source: Adapted from Handwerker (1983).

or decline of a population may be expressed as a proportion or percentage of population at an earlier time period and, thus, as the ratio of the size of the population at a given point in time (t) to the size of the population at a previous point in time ($t-n$): $\Delta P = P_t / P_{t-n}$. For example, in 1980 the world's population was about 4.4 billion people. In 1950, the world's population was about 2.5 billion. Our population in 1980 was (4.4/2.5), or about 176 percent larger in 1980 than it was in 1950. This population growth also is conveniently expressed as a percentage change: $100 \, (P_t - P_{t-n})/P_{t-n}$. Between 1950 and 1980, the world's population grew by 100 (4.4−2.5)/2.5, or by about 76 percent.

The Intrinsic Rate of Population Growth

Human populations grow continuously, unlike the populations of organisms that have distinct breeding seasons. The rate of population growth is appropriately expressed as an instantaneous compounding rate. This rate, the intrinsic rate of population growth r, may be computed as the nth root of the proportional change in population between time $t-n$ and time t, minus 1: $r = (\sqrt[n]{\delta P}) - 1$. Thus, the world's population grew at an average rate of $(\sqrt[30]{1.76}) - 1 = .0190225$, or about 1.9 percent annually from 1950 through 1980.

A population that increases at rate r will grow by a factor of e^r at the end of one year and by a factor of e^{rn} at the end of n years, where e is the base of natural logarithms (2.71828 . . .). Thus, if a population of 2.5 billion people at a given point in time grows by a rate of 1.9 percent annually for 30 years, at the end of that period,

$$P_t = P_{t-30}e^{rn} = 2.5\ (2.71828^{(.019)(30)}) = 4.4 \text{ billion people.}$$

Population Doubling Time and Half-Life

If a population doubles, $e^{rn} = 2$. If we take logarithms, $Ln2 = rn$. The number of years (n) that it will take for a population to double in size when it grows at a rate r will be: $n = Ln2/r$, or $n = .693/r$. Thus, a population doubles itself in about 693 years if it grows at an annual rate of about 0.1 percent, as the human population appears to have grown during the origins of agriculture 10,000 years ago. The world's population doubles in about 36 years when it grows at its 1950–1980 rate of 1.9 percent annually. A country will double its population size in only about 21 years when it grows, as many African countries currently do, at 3.3 percent annually. Kenya's population will double in just over 17 years if it continues to grow at its estimated rate of around 4 percent annually. Conversely, if a population is declining at rate r, its half-life is $e^{rn} = .5$. The number of years (n) it will take for population to decline to one-half of its original size will be: $n = -.693/r$

Natural Increase Is the Difference between Births and Deaths

The change in population size over a given period of time is the number of births that occurred over that period minus the deaths over the same period, plus immigration and minus emigration. In a closed population (one that experiences no migration), the change in population size is births minus deaths. The difference between birth and death rates (CBR − CDR) is the rate of natural increase of a population.

Women Determine a Population's Growth Potential

Not all births count the same for the long-run growth potential of a population, however. A population's growth potential is a function of the number of women in the population, and population growth may be expressed as the ratio of the size of a cohort of mothers to the size of the cohort of their daughters. A cohort of mothers smaller than the succeeding cohort of daughters creates a growing population. A cohort of mothers larger than the succeeding cohort of daughters creates a declining population. A cohort of mothers the same size as the succeeding cohort of daughters creates a population that neither grows nor declines without migration.

The growth potential of a population thus may be expressed as the ability of a cohort of mothers to replace themselves in the succeeding cohort of their daughters. The average number of daughters born to women in a population is known as the gross reproduction rate (GRR). Because human sex ratios at birth average 105, GRR may be estimated as .488TFR. However, the gross reproduction rate does not control for female mortality. Populations may produce large numbers of girls but may still decline if female mortality is high. The net reproduction rate (R_o) controls for female mortality and may be calculated directly as the sum, from the beginning to the end of the reproductive period, of the female births that occur to women who survive to reproduce through a given age interval: $l_x b_x$. Alternatively, R_0 may be estimated as the product GRR • l_m, which estimates the number of daughters produced by women who survive to the mean age of reproduction. The mean age of reproduction is (approximately) the average generation length, t^4. The average generation length is about 28 years where women tend to bear children throughout the reproductive span (although English historical data suggest that the average generation length will be longer when the mean age at marriage is high; cf. Wrigley and Schofield 1981). The average generation length is about 25 years where women sharply restrict their childbearing to the early years of their reproductive span, as in contemporary Europe and North America.

The population growth factor $e^{rt} = R_0$ when $t =$ the mean generation length. If we take logarithms, $Ln R_0 = rt$. Thus we can estimate a population's intrinsic rate of growth if we know the net reproduction rate, R_0. If $R_0 = 1$, the population neither grows nor declines without migration. If $R_0 = 2$, the population doubles each generation unless migration offsets or adds to the natural increase.

Special Properties of Stationary Populations

Stationary populations (closed populations that neither grow nor decline over time) are ones in which the number of women who reach the mean age of reproduction does not change from one generation to another ($R_0 = 1$). Important functional relationships hold for such populations. The crude birth rate equals the crude death rate, and the birthrate is the reciprocal of the expectation of life at birth ($1/e_o$). The proportion of women who survive to the mean age of reproduction (l_m) can be estimated from life expectancy at birth,[5] and the number of daughters produced by these women, the gross reproduction rate (GRR), is the reciprocal of the proportion of women who survive to the mean age of reproduction (l_m). Since 100 females tend to be born for every 105 males, the total fertility rate (TFR) of the stationary population is approximately 2.05GRR. These interdependencies allow us to estimate the total fertility rate at which a population will neither grow nor decline over the long run. Figure 17.7 plots these estimates and reveals that populations cannot replace themselves without high levels of fertility (TFR = 5 or higher) where life expectancy at birth is low (e_0 = 20–25), as it appears to have been through much of human history. Conversely, total fertility rates must fall below TFR = 3 as life expectancy increases to age 50 and beyond, or the rate of population growth will rise dramatically.

Research on the Implications of Below-Replacement Fertility Is a Major Prospective Growth Field

Once life expectancy at birth rises to age 75 or older, as it does in the MDCs, zero population growth is achieved by total fertility rates of about 2.1. As of the mid-1980s, in fact, total fertility in the industrial market economies of North

Figure 17.7
Total Fertility Rates by Life Expectancy at Birth for Stationary Populations

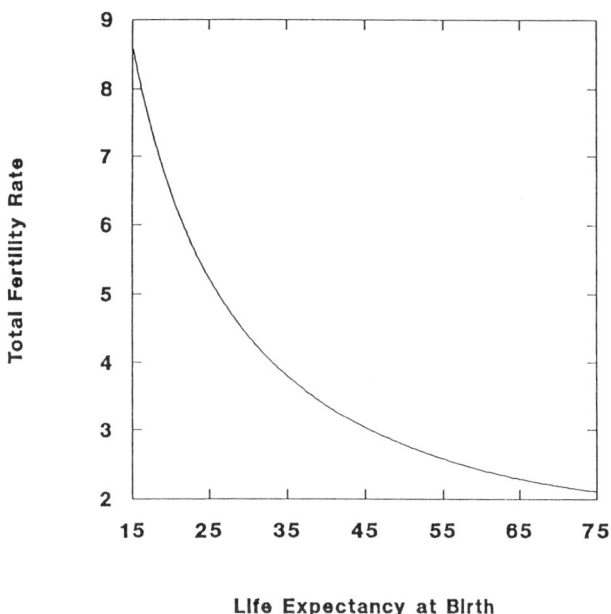

America, Europe, and Asia tended to be below 1.8, well below population replacement levels (see the current World Development Reports published by the World Bank). These populations currently replace themselves or grow only by immigration. The implications of below-replacement fertility are profound and are only beginning to be explored (Davis, Bernstam, and Ricardo-Campbell 1986). Medical anthropologists who address these issues will be engaged in work that will have theoretical and policy implications that extend far beyond the confines of our discipline.

IMPLICATIONS FOR THEORY, POLICY, AND RESEARCH

There are around 5.2 billion people in the world today (1989), and we may add another 1.3 billion people, for a total human population of 6.5 billion, by the year 2000, if the human population growth rate has remained constant since 1950. If the rate of human population growth falls significantly, as it probably has, world population may not grow too much beyond 8 billion people; but if it does not, we may have as many as 12 billion people in the world in only 50 years.

We are now in a poor position to evaluate the implications of such growth or even to know whether there will be such growth because conventional theory does not adequately capture the subtleties of demographic change and its implications. Our ability to design policy that can effectively contribute to human welfare is crippled accordingly. A Darwinian perspective on human population ecology may be able to capture the subtleties of demographic change and increase our ability to design policy that more effectively addresses issues of human welfare.

The validity of Darwin's conception of life is supported by more than 3 billion years of empirical evidence. Yet it does not follow that unlimited population growth is desirable, that we will, in fact, create the means to support an indefinitely large future population, or that current policy now points in the right direction. Selection guarantees neither survival nor success. Selection only guarantees that change will exhibit discernible patterns when we view the historical record in retrospect. Short-run mistakes must pervade all activities carried out under the guidance of cultural constructs (Handwerker 1989b). Moreover, selection tends to be shortsighted; innovations that improve or optimize resource access over the long term are unlikely to be incorporated into human sociocultural systems unless they also yield improvements in resource access to individuals in the short-term.

Darwin's conception of life does mean that population growth rates, sizes, and densities are not in themselves the issues. Population processes generate demographic conditions, and population processes respond in clear ways to resource access cost differences and the power relationships that they create (Handwerker 1989c). Development policy thus needs to recognize explicitly its potential to free people from constraints imposed by existing power differentials and the role it may play in maintaining those differentials. So does research. We need to develop effective measures of resource access costs and power relationships and apply these to population and health issues. Our global future is being shaped profoundly by reductions in mortality, reductions in fertility that lead to below-replacement fertility, and migration at levels that are unprecedented in human history. The questions for future research thus appear to be these:

1. What changes in resource access costs and power relationships do these processes reflect?
2. What changes in resource access costs and power relationships do these processes generate?
3. What social and cultural processes do these changes in power relationships set in motion, with what effect on health conditions, medical systems, and the content and distribution of medical services and facilities and, more generally, with what effect on our planet's ecosystem?

Our species may well become extinct because we confront unexpected events and circumstances that our previous evolutionary history has not well equipped us to handle, as have most of the species that have lived on our earth (Raup 1986). In the event that we manufacture our own extinction, however, it will not be because there are too many of us. It will be due to the political dynamics that dictate how we produce and distribute resources.

NOTES

The quality of this chapter has been improved immeasurably by helpful criticism provided by Tom Johnson, Carolyn Sargent, and Martha Ward.

1. This chapter cannot substitute for the specialized training required to conduct effective demographic research. The texts by Barclay (1958), Pressat (1972), and Wunsch and Termote (1978) provide sound introductions to the basics of demographic analysis. Keyfitz (1977) provides a useful introduction to the mathematics of population. Readers should note that demographic techniques apply to the study of any population, including populations of nonliving things like light bulbs or textbooks.

2. Keyfitz (1972) provides an excellent review of the development of demographic theory up through the 1960s. Lee (1982) reviews changes in demography over the last 30 years. Hammel (1983) is also useful. Greenhalgh (1989) reviews the relations between anthropology and demography and identifies new directions for research. Harris and Ross (1987a) provide a useful review of the problem of population regulation.

3. Readers interested specifically in infant mortality should also consult Mosley and Chen's (1984) discussion, which treats five categories of variables that have been shown to affect, directly and, occasionally, synergistically, infant mortalities. Good sources on the biology and proximate determinants of fertility include: Leridon (1977), Gray (1983), Blake and Davis (1956), Bongaarts (1980, 1982, 1983), Bongaarts and Potter (1983), Leridon and Menken (1979), Sheps and Menken (1973), Mosley (1978), Moghissi and Evans (1977), and Zatuchni, Sciarra, and Speidel (1979).

3. The importance of fecundability is only beginning to be realized. Fecundability usually is defined as the probability of conception within a specific time frame. The concept confounds a number of different variables, and its measurement still needs much work (Campbell and Wood 1987; Wood and Weinstein 1988). Almost certainly we will create a new way to think about proximate determinants of fertility as we come to understand this phenomenon more fully. We will also be able to understand better populations that experience unusually low fertility, such as those in Zaire (Ellison, Peacock, and Lager 1986) and the Kalahari (Wilmsen 1986). We may also come to understand better why fertility appears to vary consistently positively with income once we control for confounding variables.

4. The mean age of reproduction, m, is not identical to t. The relationship is: $t = m - \sigma 2 \, \text{LogGRR}/2m$; where $\sigma 2$ may be estimated as 50.

5. The proportion of women who survive to the mean age of reproduction is estimated from life expectancy at birth by the following empirical relationship (from Coale 1974):

$$l_m = .001272727 + .015710909 e_o + .000015091 e_o^2 - .000000691 e_o^3$$

SECTION 5
POLICY AND ADVOCACY

CHAPTER 18

PROFESSIONALIZATION OF INDIGENOUS HEALERS

Murray Last

In an anthropological context, "profession" takes on a set of meanings wider than those used in sociology. Even within sociology, after nearly a century, the range of definitions remains large and the debate continues. Our concern here, however, is not with professions per se but with medicine—the way it is organized, the way its systems of knowledge are structured—and comparison is sought not with other occupations but with medicine as it is practiced in different cultures. Nonetheless, it needs to be noted that, among professions, medicine is an extreme case, more regulated and more exposed to public scrutiny, with stricter social closure (through stiff requirements for qualifications that take long to acquire in higher education) and with particular privileges in courts of law. While the church, perhaps the oldest of professional institutions, has lost its monopoly and while lawyers have multiplied and diversified, medicine has become increasingly specialized, with numerous health-related services seeking similar forms of organization and regulation in order to become "professional." It has also retained an unusually high social status (Becker 1970; Larson 1977; Freidson 1986; Johnson 1972; Dingwall and Lewis 1983; Jacob 1988).

The detailed history of the professionalization of medicine and related occupations in Britain and the United States (the paradigmatic examples of professionalism) is the subject of a large literature (for example, Mapother 1968; Carr-Saunders 1933; Shryock 1967; Parry and Parry 1976; Burrow 1977; Gelfand 1980; Starr 1982; Ramsey 1988; Spree 1988. On the current range, and absurdities, of licensing practice generally in Britain, see Mason 1988). The way professions have been elaborated there, as nowhere else in the world, has led sociologists to treat "profession" as a culture-bound folk concept (Becker 1970:92). Yet that Anglo-American folk concept has gone into circulation worldwide, as indeed has so-called Western (or cosmopolitan) medicine. As a consequence, in a wider anthropology of medical professions, we need to retain the broader senses of the English term *profession* (as a full-time occupation locally recognized for its specialized skills), if we are to compare contemporary processes and structures in the practice of medicine beyond America and Europe.

The criteria employed here for inclusion as a profession are that it be an extended self-conscious grouping of healers with defined criteria for membership (whether through licensing, certification, or registration), and an expertise over which it seeks primary control, and an expertise that claims to be more than a craft and has in addition an esoteric, theoretical basis. These criteria, used here in lieu of a formal definition of a profession, reflect the attributes of the conventional professions of Europe and America, since de facto the agenda under which all these therapeutic organizations have to operate has already been set by the existing agreements between government and the conventional professions after nearly a century of political debate and lawmaking. This is as true of India or Nigeria as it is of Europe or America; the detailed history of these debates, though, is particularly well documented only for Europe and America, with some valuable literature on India and China (Leslie 1972, 1975, 1976; Jeffrey 1988; Hillier and Jewell 1983; Unschuld 1975).

The spread of professionalism in medicine has been especially notable in Anglophone countries—both in nations that had once been part of the British Empire and in states more recently affected by American influence. In such countries, professional associations modeled on British or American associations have been set up, initially as branches and subsequently as autonomous but mutually recognized institutions (Johnson 1973; Grey-Turner and Sutherland 1982). Furthermore, since 1948 the World Health Organization (WHO) has played an increasingly significant part in attempts to foster a worldwide medical profession, though because of its size and internal diversity, it has not always spoken with a single voice. For example, its attitude toward "traditional medicine" and its policy of encouraging member-states to organize their traditional practitioners was finally adopted in 1978 despite internal debate and controversy; today, that policy is once again in doubt and subject to review. Yet overall the consequences are clear: the potential professionalization of indigenous practitioners is firmly on the agenda (Bannerman et al. 1983; WHO 1976, 1978).

The issues are not academic. With the much-proclaimed target of health for all by the year 2000, the shortage of medical manpower in the present period of economic crisis in the Third World is so acute that medical practitioners of all kinds are potentially acceptable recruits to national health services. Add to this the extra demand on resources posed by the AIDS epidemic, and issues such as the training and licensing of auxiliary practitioners come to the fore as matters of urgency. In such a context, there is a particular relevance in an anthropology of professionalism in medicine that extends beyond the limited experience of Europe and North America.

Three arguments are presented here. First, professions of medicine function primarily within a national medical culture, with certain professions claiming for themselves a universal validity. These claims are significant in the struggles over professional recognition and dominance within the national culture. But despite the claims, all systems of medicine are in varying measure culture specific.

Second, these national medical cultures are partly the product of a nation's ruling political philosophy and partly the product of the ways people express their health needs and find solutions to them. Worldwide there are broadly three types of political philosophies that affect medical practice and seek to determine the role of healers in society and how (if at all) they will be organized. Yet popular support, from patients and their kin, is also a crucial factor in formulating the diverse medical subculture labeled indigenous or "traditional medicine" (the term conventionally used to replace the earlier "native medicine" and "folk medicine"; it includes practices that may in fact not be traditional). The two perspectives—the one from above, the other from below—are often at odds.

Third, professionalization is one solution to the dilemma of practitioners of traditional medicine in the face of unequal competition from other systems of medicine. It requires being organized in a form, recognized and respected within the national culture, that can best represent the interests of practitioners and their clientele, both now and in the future. The problem is by no means limited to Third World countries, though it is there that the issues are being most clearly articulated and the possibilities for developing "traditional medicine" most practicable (Velimirovic 1984; Chambers 1986; cf. Vaskilampi and MacCormack 1982).

MEDICAL CULTURES: NATIONAL AND INTERNATIONAL

I use the concept of a national medical culture here to denote the national arena in which competition between medical systems takes place, with professionalism as one factor in that competition. The nation-state is an appropriate unit of analysis, for although the term *cosmopolitan medicine* (as modern hospital-based medicine is often called, e.g., in Leslie 1976) suggests it has become today's universal medical system much as humoral medicine was before it, in practice even such an apparently rigorous scientific system is subject to national cultural variations.

Attempts to foster a worldwide medical profession are nonetheless significant for the support a wider profession can give to the local status of national medical groupings. Not only do agencies like WHO and UNICEF act as forces for unification, but international congresses and working parties are set up to seek agreement on such issues as the proper definition (and treatment) of schizophrenia or updated nomenclatures for diseases and anatomical structures (WHO 1973, 1974; Warwick 1977). Indeed for AIDS, WHO has resorted to publishing "consensus statements" in an attempt to avoid controversies among national experts (Panos 1988:105). These attempts, however, only betray how nationally oriented the medical professions are. For example, other countries' medical qualifications are rarely recognized as adequate in themselves; thus the United States requires a further comprehensive examination for foreigners, and Indian medical degrees after May 1975 are refused direct recognition in Britain (Stevens et al. 1978;

Jeffery 1988:207). A limited step toward a common international profession is being taken by the European Common Market, but doubts are being expressed about whether this will actually work and what changes to national regulations will be involved. Whether the result is more or less regulation (for example, of practitioners of alternative medicine) remains to be seen.

Hospital medicine is not the only system of medicine that has sought to organize itself worldwide. The most successful is homeopathy, though it lacks the sort of funding that gives WHO its authority (Salmon 1984:75). Patients' self-help groups, most notably Alcoholics Anonymous, have also succeeded in crossing national and cultural boundaries to provide common techniques of treatment (Janzen 1982b:158; Kurtz 1979:226–27). The international status of these groupings and others like them gives them an added weight within the politics of national health services.

Indigenous practitioners of traditional medicine, by contrast, have few if any such links and tend to emphasize instead not the universality of their therapies but their cultural or regional specificity. Pan-African associations of healers have been only of limited scope and short duration, while international congresses (to which less culture-specific herbalists are often invited) have tended to be dominated by professionals from pharmacology and pharmacognosy intent on incorporating into their own universal systems any traditional expertise that is available (Sofowora 1979, 1982). Indeed even WHO's patronage has served mainly to encourage national ministries of health to try to incorporate healers into the hospital-based profession, offering them retraining and a minor role in state health services (Sargent 1986; Twumasi and Warren 1986). In short, any tendency to "universalize" or even internationalize traditional medicine seems to call into question practitioners' autonomy. Within a national medical culture, this issue is not so apparent.

One reason that there does not yet exist any worldwide profession of medicine, with uniform credentials that permit holders to practice clinically anywhere they wish, is that clinical practice varies in detail from state to state, with the variation due as much to historical and cultural differences as to any scientific rationale (O'Brien 1984; Payer 1988). Indeed, in all clinical practice, traditional or scientific, there is a significant element that is culture specific.

Some national differences in medical practice are notorious. Disputes over the definition of schizophrenia, let alone its proper treatment, have already been mentioned (Leff 1981). The different ways in which countries collect medical statistics are reflected in the various national nomenclatures of disease; the terminology of medicine, and with it the etiological and anatomical categories, reveal how basic assumptions in medical thought vary (Royal College of Physicians 1948). So too in research; the recent academic dispute between French and American research teams over the AIDS virus proved to be more a national political (and economic) issue than a serious question of medical science, despite the common discourse (Connor and Kingman 1988).

Finally, practice also is subject to national custom. Well known is the French preference for pessaries over pills (a preference that extends to francophone

Africa) or the particular German interest in hydrotherapy (Payer 1988). Soviet bloc medicine prefers terminations to contraceptive devices; and, uniquely, sanatoriums for treating asthma and emphysema there have long been sited in disused deep-mine workings, with great success. In Third World countries where nationals have been trained in a range of institutions abroad and foreigners are regularly employed, the diversity is readily apparent, and, though doctors seldom know it, the different national styles are the subject of critical evaluation by patients locally.

Again "cosmopolitan" medicine is not the only medical system with a worldwide distribution that is subject to national variation. In homeopathy some of the national variations reflect which edition of Hahnemann's *Organon* was originally used when homeopathy was first introduced, while, for example, in its Indian or Brazilian forms, homeopathy has been identified by nationalists as an indigenous modern medicine and has been absorbed and modified accordingly (Santos 1981). Similarly the practice of acupuncture and Ayurvedic medicine in Europe and America varies considerably from that practiced in China or India; both have been adapted to local conditions, whether climatic or scientific, and the subtle theoretical basis of each system is usually ignored by patients and practitioners alike (Kao and Kao 1979).

For these reasons, a comparative analysis of national medical cultures is a necessary starting point. No one should take for granted that what is normative according to the textbook (which textbook?) is in fact the practice in any one locality; it may be so. There can thus be no adequate discussion of the comparative efficacy of the different systems. In theory, no doubt, all systems may "work"; in practice, all have successes and failures, with some systems scoring much higher in particular areas of medicine. Yet all too frequently, when comparisons are made between the different systems of medicine practiced in any one state, a normative model is used for one system while observed practice is used for the other. We lack enough detailed ethnographies of the various systems at work.

Within a national medical culture, then, are included all the various medical systems and practices available to patients. These often quite distinct systems of medicine are competing for custom, for privileged access to government finance, for bureaucratic recognition of their certificates as competent to certify sickness or health; they are competing too for the "truth" of their particular understanding of the nature of life and how best to sustain it. By using the nation as the analytical unit, emphasis is being put on the political aspect of professionalism in medicine, for it is through the political process that the most significant variations in professionalism have come into being—and through it too will come (if ever) the professional recognition of indigenous practitioners.

PROFESSIONS OF MEDICINE AND THE MARKET

In this wider anthropology of medical professions I will include three distinct groupings:

1. The conventional medical professions privileged by almost every state and by WHO as the scientifically efficacious system for a nation's health services. Included in this category are professionals such as nurses and midwives, as well as those in occupations formally labeled in Britain as "professions supplementary to medicine," alias physiotherapy, occupational therapy, radiotherapy, ophthalmic opticians, and others (Larkin 1983; MacNab 1970).

2. Professions of alternative medicine, such as homeopathy, Ayurveda, acupuncture, or osteopathy, which may be recognized by government and public alike as a formal system of therapy, with a set curriculum taught in special colleges or as a special subject.

3. Professions of traditional medicine, where there is an attempt to create a new professional grouping—amalgamating ordinary, individual healers of varying kinds and specialties into a single body as the basis for obtaining government recognition and for improving public acceptance of its members.

It is important to recognize that a great deal of healing takes place outside the purview of governmental or professional regulations. The largest segment, self-medication (including home remedies), accounts for the great majority of ailments, injuries, and malaise. Where a range of drugs is readily available over the counter (for example, as antibiotics are in France), the scale of self-medication is vast. In addition, in countries like Nigeria where such drugs are not restricted to registered pharmacists but form part of a trader's ordinary merchandise, injection sets are also available; and with razor blades for scalpels, rudimentary surgery is undertaken at home. Given that people's commonsense knowledge normally includes herbal medicines and tonics available in the habitat; given too that people have always coped with wounds from fights and hunting, lancing boils and reducing fractures, contemporary self-medication is simply an expansion of ordinary practice. (The other important area of healing outside medical or bureaucratic regulation, church healing, will be discussed below.)

The professions in medicine, then, are dealing with a relatively restricted field. Indeed, until recently (and still today in the Soviet Union; Ryan 1978:44–45) the majority of licensed doctors have not always found it easy to make a living from medicine full time. The development of new drugs and equipment has given doctors a considerable technical (if not always therapeutic) edge in most fields of medicine. But it is only with the provision by the state of free medicine, and the establishment of government hospitals and dispensaries, that the demand for medicine (and the expectations of good health) expanded the market for medicine. Thus in India, people's present widespread use of "Western" medicine is attributed to its ready availability at low cost in rural areas, whereas before Ayurveda and homeopathy had a greater share of a smaller "market" (Jeffery 1988:57–58).

The limited market in which the various medical professions operate is not, however, a free one. Regulatory systems of one sort or another are found governing the provision of health care in every modern state.

THE MATRIX FOR PROFESSIONALISM: REGULATIONS AND THE STATE

The range of subcultures permitted within a national medical culture varies greatly, from the Soviet Union's monolithic system of state-controlled health to, say, Nigeria's, India's or Britain's where pluralism is at its most extreme. In practice there are three broad types of regulatory systems that help to determine politically the nature of a state's medical culture, and with it the organizational possibilities for indigenous practitioners (Stepan 1985; Ramsey 1984).

Exclusive Systems: Medical Monopolies

Soviet Model. Developed out of the autocratic tradition of Eastern European government, and greatly expanded under a Soviet administration, medicine is a monopoly of the state (Konrad and Szelenyi 1979; Ryan 1978; Field 1976b). The Ministry of Health, both at the center and in the republics, employs medical practitioners as civil servants and attaches them to public clinics or to specific ministries and industries, where they form part of a management team concerned with productivity. All other forms of healer have been formally banned since 1923. The only "professional" association is the Medical Workers Union, in which paramedicals outnumber doctors; any other professional groupings dating from before the revolution had disappeared by the 1930s, under strong pressure from other medical workers. In an otherwise apparently uniform medical system, it is the patient's political merit, rather than just wealth or clinical need, that determines the way different medical facilities (such as a bed in the special hospitals run by the "Fourth Department") are allocated (Matthews 1978:47).

The bureaucratically rational, total monopoly model has been adopted, with variations, in Third World countries influenced by the Soviet Union and by Marxist modes of planning. The status of doctors is usually higher (they form part of the intelligentsia "class") and their numbers lower, and the ban on traditional healers is usually ineffective. Nonetheless, opposition to healers remains linked ideologically to the role they played in supporting the "feudal" social systems of the past, while the endorsement healers receive elsewhere is put down to the bourgeoisie's predictable preference for the cheapest possible health care for the masses (Barker and Turshen 1986). Furthermore traditional medicine is seen as reinforcing the class divide, by helping to prevent people having a proper scientific understanding of their condition and pandering instead to superstition.

French Model. This model starts from the premise of centralized state control with all unlicensed healers illegal; the state employs doctors in official positions as civil servants, to practice medicine, to teach, and to conduct research. In addition, registered doctors can practice privately; pharmacists routinely advise customers and sell a wide range of drugs. The result is a mixed state and professional system in which some doctors attain high social and political status by playing both sides of the system (Bourdieu 1988; Jamous and Peloille 1970). Licenses are granted only to those qualified in state-run schools of medicine, and prosecutions are brought against the unlicensed if they are practicing regularly (Stepan 1985:288).

The Third World countries that follow the French model have tended to emphasize that aspect of the model that favors a state monopoly. Colonial regimes were by nature autocratic, and the Napoleonic legal code that sanctioned centralized control has been carried over into the new independent states. In Cameroun, in particular, control reaches down to district levels, and any attempt to set up an alternative healing practice, even under church auspices, is likely to be closed rapidly by the police. Elsewhere in francophone Africa, no such tight control exists. Indeed in Côte d'Ivoire, government makes use of the healing cult run by Albert Atcho (Piault 1975:45–72). Nonetheless, professional associations of traditional healers get little or no encouragement (as, for example, in Benin; Sargent 1986), and the legality of their practice remains in question until the relevant laws are changed.

The basic French model is not confined to former French colonies. Variations of the model are found in Spanish- and Portuguese-speaking areas, particularly in Latin America, though in practice restrictions on indigenous practitioners have proved unenforceable. Further modification has come through American influence, whether in the form of missionary medicine or through local doctors receiving their training in the United States or through the establishment of private American-funded medical institutions,

American Model. While the French model assumes government could be bureaucratically rational (and not just seeking to monopolise power), the American model seeks to modify, through strict and detailed regulation at the state (not national) level, a free medical market (Freidson 1986; Starr 1982; Navarro 1986). Both models in the process, however, greatly enhanced the privileges of the dominant medical subculture, hospital medicine, at the expense of alternative systems and practices. Osteopathy, for example, allied itself with hospital medicine so as to gain recognition, and a version of it has been integrated into the educational system. Other systems have fared somewhat better under a religious umbrella (because of federal provisions for freedom of religion) so long as they do not use drugs. But refusal on religious grounds to seek adequate treatment is a matter of contention; people have fewer rights over their bodies than over their minds or souls.

The rationale for the state's policing role in medicine is the maintenance of public health. In practice, however, curanderos and similar practitioners serving specific minorities have been left to function as normal, though it seems regulation of them too will eventually become an issue despite the political climate against regulation and monopolies. Debate is likely to focus on the legal problems surrounding malpractice suits, just as it did in the nineteenth century before states introduced their various regulations (Burns 1977; Shrylock 1967; Department of Health, Education and Welfare 1973; Forbes 1948; Rosenthal 1987).

An important difference between the American and other state-centered models is the lack of standardization due to privately run institutions in all aspects of medicine. In theory the hallmark of the bureaucratically run system is that its standards should be uniform throughout the nation. Despite an important public health sector, it is privately funded medicine—schools, research institutes, hospitals, health insurance systems—that dominates the American system and marks it out as distinctive. In other countries the state runs more or less directly the institutions that award the credentials of individual doctors; in the United States the state accredits independent institutions, which in turn form regional groupings in order to raise their status collectively. The result is a competitive market within the medical profession rather than a market between the medical and other therapeutic professions. It is to this latter market that we now turn.

Tolerant Systems: Medical Markets

British Model. In the British model, instead of outlawing all other forms of healing, regulations merely define who can legally be described by a specific professional label, "doctor" (Ramsey 1984; Parry and Parry 1976). The formal rationale of the legislation is to prevent fraudulent description so that the customer-patient can make an informed choice; a patient who wants the services of a nondoctor is free to do so, and healers of any persuasion (except in the fields of surgery and dentistry) are free to offer their services. The state-financed National Health Service, for which the majority of doctors work on contract, does not pay for alternative or traditional treatments, though doctors may practice such treatments themselves or formally supervise others doing so. A further, crucial degree of regulation is achieved through controls over the sale of drugs, making access to most significant medicines possible only through a doctor's prescription. Yet another regulatory mechanism is a restriction on the right to incise the skin to any depth. Similarly certain diseases have to be referred, as a matter of public health if nothing else, to doctors. Thus self-medication or treatment by unqualified healers is in fact more restricted than it might at first seem.

Professional autonomy in this model is maintained through a series of institutions that distance the government (which provides effectively all the funds for both medical practice and for medical education) from detailed policymaking, structuring, and disciplining of the profession. The compromise works only insofar as there is a consensus between government and profession; when resources are scarce and the consensus breaks down, professional autonomy proves hollow. On an individual basis, autonomy does, however, allow the doctor, once qualified, to practice as he or she thinks fit; licensing does not in itself prohibit unorthodox practice. Professional knowledge in this system, then, is not exclusive of quite alien medical beliefs or even practices beyond the point of entry into the system. An unorthodox doctor (who may have to work in private practice if no one is willing to appoint him or her to a post) is thus free to compete for patients on an open medical market, though he or she is still bound by professional restrictions on advertising services.

It follows from this that other systems of medicine are free to form professional associations, set up special colleges, and issue qualifications (but not to describe themselves as doctors) without reference to any other profession. Thus osteopathy in Britain (but not in the United States) remains independent of orthopedic medicine, and in principle it retains its distinct theoretical basis, though there is no evidence that its clientele is particularly interested in those theories or in their development (Inglis 1964:94–122). Indeed people's therapeutic pragmatism—their willingness to divorce therapeutic practice from therapeutic theory—is essential in understanding how the medical market works, for efficacy is not seen to depend on "truth"; a mode of treatment can be right for the wrong reason.

Anomalies reveal a similar pragmatism in the model itself. For example, homeopathy has won for itself the privileged position of being officially included, if only marginally, within the state's health service, despite numerous professional commissions of inquiries rejecting its scientific status. Political patronage is an important factor since in this instance the Royal National Homoeopathic Hospital has long received royal support (Inglis 1964:85; Nichols 1988). But the anomaly extends even to veterinary medicine, which is otherwise much more strictly regulated in Britain (as elsewhere in formerly British-run territories) than human medicine in that homeopathic vets have a growing, and legal, share of the market for treating both domestic and farm animals.

In the numerous Third World and other countries that follow the British model (the majority of them former colonies), the conventional medical profession has proved politically to be relatively weak (Johnson 1973; Macleod and Lewis 1988; Last and Chavunduka 1986:9–12; Schram 1971). Private practice cannot be a substitute for government employment for the majority of doctors until there is a large enough middle class to provide the demand. Demand is further weakened by people's ability to buy without prescription the drugs that in Britain are on the restricted list; in this doctors have lost a crucial monopoly. Furthermore it is in these countries that there has come the strongest pressure from traditional practitioners for government recognition. Nonetheless, the social status of doctors is very high—constitutionally, since colonial times, the medical officer has been the second-ranking official in the community should a crisis arise—and the informal influence of the profession remains in spite of its lack of monopoly. The success of alternative medical systems in establishing themselves in developing countries has been patchy. Apart from India where homeopathy has thrived, the main areas have been where Anglophone immigrants have settled—for example, in southern and eastern Africa, where they have been subject to special legislation, distinct from that covering either indigenous practitioners or doctors.

German Model. The importance here of the German model lies in the unique way German indigenous practitioners of any kind are licensed (Unschuld 1980; Stepan 1985). They merely have to pass an examination to show that they know the state law regulating medical practice; the actual content of the expertise they claim to exercise is not otherwise restricted or examined. Not surprisingly no overall profession of *Heilpraktiker* (as lay practitioners are called) exists, and given their diversity it is unlikely that one would be practicable. Schools, however, exist to teach would-be lay practitioners the relevant information to pass the examination.

The model has left no legacy in the Third World. (Indeed, when Germany established colonies in Africa, the colonial authorities never apparently applied this model. Local practitioners were considered instead to be resistance leaders and were closely controlled, to the extent of prices being fixed [Feierman 1986:208].) Nonetheless, it is surely one possible model—should a model be needed—if licensing of indigenous practitioners is to be introduced elsewhere.

Integrated Systems: Asian Pluralism

Indian and Chinese Models. Under British imperial legislation, Indian practitioners of Ayurvedic, Siddha, and Unani medicine were at liberty not only to practice but to develop associations and schools of medicine. For nearly a century these alternative medical institutions have developed to rival those set up for "cosmopolitan" (or "Western") medicine by the imperial regime (Jeffery 1988). All the formal trappings of professionalism—theoretical texts for teaching in university courses, research institutes, an autonomous governing council with statutory powers, hospitals, state funding, a specialized drug industry—have long been in place. Nonetheless, since independence the government of India has built up the "cosmopolitan," hospital-based services, not only supporting a strong medical profession with qualifications that met international standards but also developing a network of rural dispensaries and related services to such an extent that use of "Western" medicine is reported to be as widespread as Ayurveda. Not merely is it now as widely available, but it is offered at lower cost. In this situation, Ayurvedic colleges are said to be having difficulties recruiting applicants of comparable caliber. Homeopathy, with an origin that links it theoretically with Islamic medicine, has been adopted and adapted, particularly in Bengal, as an Indian system of medicine and similarly given rise to formal professional structures.

Other, less systematic therapeutic systems survive without professionalization on the margins of the national medical culture and meeting specific needs the various formal systems cannot adequately provide for. Many are religious in essence, using temples or festivals as focal points for healing and relying on charity rather than government or local state funds (Kakar 1982).

Legal models like India's are widespread in south and east Asia, with professional recognition given to more than one system of medicine (cf. Lock 1980 on Japan). In recent years the more restrictive legislation carried over from the colonial period has been replaced, in part as a response to nationalist feeling, in part to make the law match social reality. The degree to which all formally recognized medical professions are run as bureaucracies by the state depends on the local political matrix. India, with its open, democratic system, reflects that political tradition in its attitudes to medical politics and so leaves practitioners largely to regulate themselves. China, by contrast, being Marxist in ideology, has always recognized Chinese traditional medicine in all its variety but integrated it into the state-run services (Hillier and Jewell 1983). "Barefoot doctors" were one solution to the problem of integration; trained partly in traditional and mainly in "Western" medicine, they served as medical auxiliaries. Another solution was to maintain state-financed hospitals in which acupuncture, moxibustion, and herbal therapy were available as required. During the Cultural Revolution, the independence of practitioners of traditional systems was sharply curtailed and their associations closed down—only temporarily as it has happened. More recently priorities have once again changed; for example, now that the one-child policy is in force, parents in the countryside are reportedly seeking out the best-qualified urban obstetricians and pediatricians; traditional midwives and barefoot doctors—once the models for Third World medicine—are being spurned.

These two systems—Indian and Chinese—have provided models for incorporating indigenous practitioners elsewhere, but there are questions as to their appropriateness, particularly in Africa, where, historically, centralized states have tended not to create elaborate medical bureaucracies, with ancient written texts and systematic theorization. Furthermore, in both India and China there was considerable unity to the medical traditions, which had largely ceased to be as culture or region specific, as are many such traditions in Africa.

Third World Model. A final model which de facto (if not de jure) is integrative is to be found in Third World countries whose economic resources and colonial history have left them with the legacy of small, secondary professions not powerful enough to effect a monopoly. Although their legal traditions and the current political matrix may differ, these differences may count for less than the characteristics they have in common.

The characteristics of the Third World model are (1) a relatively weak and underfinanced system of hospital medicine, largely urban centered, staffed by doctors (nationals and foreigners) trained to different standards and routines in a number of different countries; (2) a legal system that privileges that hospital system yet is unable, in practical terms, to outlaw any alternative; (3) a very large number of local practitioners of traditional medicine, bonesetters, midwives, barber-surgeons, and so forth who have always tried to meet the health needs of the community; (4) a wide spectrum of modern alternative therapies, alongside a market in medical drugs imported, sometimes unmarked and instructionless, from all over the world; and (5) a population that is dispersed and often difficult of access yet has high rates of morbidity and mortality (Sanders 1985; Twumasi 1975; Good 1987).

It should be noted, too, that case law on medical, or indeed any other form of, negligence is virtually nonexistent in most Third World countries, and consumer rights remain to be defined either by new legislation after independence or by judicial decision (*Newswatch*, September 26, 1988:37). At present, in a country like Nigeria, death due to a healer's bold attempt at surgery can lead to his or her arrest by the police for manslaughter, but otherwise malpractice results at most in loss of reputation and earnings. Conventional doctors have been equally safe, though attitudes are apparently beginning to change (*African Guardian*, November 7, 1988). In Cameroun, witches have recently begun to be recognized as expert witnesses and required to testify in court against fellow witches (Geschiere 1988:60; Chukkol 1981; *Dar es Salaam Sunday News*, October 30, 1988:8). In time, then, as healers and other purveyors of medicines or medical services gain formal recognition, litigation is likely to be added to social pressure as a curb on fraudulent or negligent practice.

In this context, the practitioners of traditional medicine have been encouraged by their national ministries of health and by WHO either to organize themselves into professional associations or be organized into a role ancillary to hospital-based medicine. Their dilemma is the central theme of the remainder of this chapter.

THE SOCIAL MATRIX: PROFESSIONALIZATION FROM BELOW

The legal matrix is not the sole determinant; medicine is more than merely a matter of political culture. Strictly local realities are a factor in determining what is available to the sick. Seen from the perspective of the sick and their kin, the national medical culture takes on a much less orderly, systematic appearance, with matters like price, availability, efficacy, local experience, and sympathy all counting toward how a particular therapy for a particular case comes to be chosen. The issues are complex and likely to change as people alter their priorities and their perceptions of risk.

Seen from below, then, the legitimacy of a healing system is quite distinct from the kind of political legality so far discussed. This grass-roots legitimacy may arise, as Weber suggests, either from the community's own traditions or from the healer's personal charisma. Whatever the source, at this level it is clinical practice, not political philosophy, that is determinant. At the core of clinical practice is the therapeutic triangle of relationships of patient, healer, and a local public that includes both kin and others in the community. The structure of these relationships and the medical concepts that inform them vary widely within any country today, indeed even within communities. But taken together, the distinct patterns of relationships and concepts rendered visible in this therapeutic triangle constitute the various separate medical subcultures that, for convenience we can label as Ayurveda, for example, or homeopathy. Constituting more diffuse a subculture are those individual practitioners whose therapies we generally categorize together under the heading "traditional medicine."

Professionalization of this traditionally diffuse subculture seeks to give it not only a certain political unity but also at the community level a coherent image, akin to a successful trademark with its associated goodwill, that would guarantee a uniformly high quality of service. Contemporary sociological analyses are obsessed with the power of professions as interest groups within society at large, whereas earlier analysts were intrigued by the way ethical rather than commercial norms were (in theory at least) established and enforced, by the way too that unethical or incompetent practitioners were controlled. Unfashionable though these concerns may be (or simply taken for granted), nonetheless for patients at the clinical level, these concerns are central. The legality of a practice is less important than the practitioner's moral standing or trustworthiness. Where a community and its practitioners have worked together for years, this local legitimation is rarely problematic. Elsewhere, and particularly in towns, where practitioners or patients may be newcomers, initial legitimation of this kind might potentially come from professional membership.

In short, a professionalization from below has always existed in some form or other in long-established communities. The question is how to expand it to meet modern circumstances. Is politically orientated professionalization from above compatible with socially sanctioned professionalization from below? A major difference between the two perspectives on professionalization lies in the ways professional knowledge is perceived (whether bureaucratically from above or clinically from below) and what the relationship is between the two. It is to professional knowledge, then, that we now briefly turn.

PROFESSIONAL KNOWLEDGE

Conventionally, professions are characterized by their use of higher education for their specialist qualifications—by their control over the curriculum and staffing of the specialized institutions responsible for both teaching and developing their area of expertise on behalf of the nation (Freidson 1986). In the process an orthodoxy comes into being, consisting of a standardized body of knowledge that has been developed, disseminated, and accepted. It does not necessarily include the latest in therapeutic fashion or even the latest research ideas; indeed orthodoxy can be not only obsolete but wrong in terms of current sophisticated thinking (which is orthodoxy in the making). In short, while knowledge, both abstract and factual, constitutes a crucial element in professionalism, the professional medical knowledge that underwrites daily clinical practice is a bundle of "facts" and working hypotheses of uncertain truth value, if usually of proved efficacy. Furthermore, most of the knowledge is factual, not theoretical; scientific debates about the nature of life, matter, and time are not intrinsic to this professional knowledge.

From one angle, then, professional knowledge may look formidably systematic and complete, the bureaucratic requirements of licensing elaborate and foolproof. From below, as practitioners perform their daily work, the coherence is not so obvious or the logic so compelling. The differences at this low level between medical systems are not so marked. Indeed for many patients, the theoretical basis for a particular therapy is not only irrelevant but better left unknown; their confidence in the therapy is more important than an acceptance of its logic. Thus the dilemma facing practitioners of traditional medicine is whether they really need to match the systematization achieved by other professions in medicine— for example, by Ayurveda—so long as their own practice remains rooted in people's common sense knowledge of illness, its causes and its cures. For example, an attempt by Zimbabwe's ZINATHA at running a school for trainee healers was halted not only for financial reasons (which are surmountable) but also over the issue of an appropriate structure and content of the curriculum.

Nor was it clear that the traditional methods of training recruits through apprenticeships and of licensing through an initiatory experience were not more effective and publicly more acceptable than a school diploma (Chavunduka 1984, 1986).

Furthermore traditional medical knowledge is rarely uniform. Broadly speaking, traditional practitioners are considered specialists in one of the two main aspects of healing: divining or diagnosing the ultimate causes of an illness and identifying the nature of the illness and treating it, usually with an herbal or other empirical medicine. As a diviner, a healer practices usually in a specific locality where his or her social knowledge of the community is crucial; in contrast, a herbalist can ply the trade anywhere. Many practitioners (especially diviners) are skilled in both aspects of healing, but the theoretical premises are distinct. While herbal expertise can be acquired by anyone so inclined and is often an extension of people's ordinary knowledge of their habitat, diviners' skills are much more personal, even charismatic in origin and scarcely amenable to being taught or examined in schools. As a consequence, attempts to formalize the qualifications of practitioners through school education are likely to lose the support of many diviners, yet it is they who often have the widest public recognition.

Nonetheless, the elaboration of traditional knowledge into a formal system is proceeding among some groups—most notably, among Yoruba religious experts and practitioners in Nigeria. Here Yoruba traditional religion has already been elevated into an academically led philosophy (Abimbola 1976; Pearce 1986; Oyebola 1981). The literature on the subject is sufficient for university degree courses; initially oral, the central texts are now published along with a large exegetical literature and studies of healers in practice. Given the strong emphasis on schooling and certification generally in other aspects of Yoruba life, given too the plethora of privately owned schools and personally run churches, the problem will lie not so much in creating a suitable curriculum as in agreeing upon a common one. Finally, the Yoruba tradition has been maintained, and recently revived for political purposes, in both Brazil and many Caribbean states, thus giving the Yoruba system a potential international status. At present, it is seen primarily as a religious, not a medical system. Yet it is among Yoruba healers that the strongest pressure for formal government recognition comes; and such recognition has already been won in Lagos state (Oyebola 1986). In a national context, however, nurturing so culture specific a system of therapy provokes both opposition on the grounds that it is tribalistic and derision on religious grounds, and thus effectively strangles attempts to form a nationwide profession.

In short, the formal elaboration of traditional medical knowledge has so far proved difficult and divisive, and without obvious benefits. More success has been had in creating practitioners' organizations that can bridge the differences in styles of expertise. But not all countries recognize people's rights to form associations (or indeed churches), and those that do often require them to be registered under one category or another. There is not space here to go into the relevant national variables, but it can be a significant feature of the political climate in which popular but marginalized groups have to operate.

PROFESSIONAL ORGANIZATIONS IN THE THIRD WORLD

In recent years the number of practitioners' organizations has grown rapidly, with at least one attaining professional powers. Most, however, operate as networks or as pressure groups. The difficulty has been to expand beyond this and find leaders widely acceptable and able to unite the majority of healers; in older organizations the problem has been in ensuring continuity once the local founder has died. Furthermore, as one such leader complained, the "bureaucratic habit" necessary to run committees proved uncongenial to most healers. It is arguable that the organizations will develop stage by stage—from regional to national society, from society to licensing authority, from licensing to full professional institutions—and given time and continuing government support that may be possible. More detailed analysis, country by country, is necessary. The present range of organizational types is as follows, starting with those with the least professional powers:

1. Cultural societies for like-minded practitioners whose aim is the advancement of their particular therapy. Membership is voluntary and does not depend on any qualification; it carries no weight publicly except to demonstrate commitment to a common cause. Yet the society's officers may be influential in advising government and thereby profitably enhance their reputations. Such societies are common; often they are regionally organized and create a network through which practitioners can exchange remedies and experiences, place suitable apprentices, and even refer cases for specialist attention. Some of the earliest associations of traditional practitioners were of this kind but were not formally constituted. An example of such an informal, early association is described by Harriet Sibisi (1981); Gilles Bibeau (1980, 1982) has discussed a modern network of associations in Zaire.
2. Promotional groupings, membership of which is seen as a seal of approval, seeking to guarantee certain standards of competence. Membership is voluntary, but members submit themselves to some form of testing or at least undertake to comply with the grouping's code of conduct. Such codes of conduct may be displayed along with membership certificates. But the grouping has no statutory control over a particular therapy or its practitioners. Many of Nigeria's different associations of traditional medicine are of this kind, with some formally registered as commercial companies (Last and Chavunduka 1986: 22,93).
3. Unions to which persons employed in medical practice (for example, by the state) have to belong in order to practice legally, though the union does not itself do any testing of its members. The union defends its members' interests in relation to their employers, and acts as a vehicle for government to mobilize or instruct practitioners. Unions of this kind exist particularly in states with government-run health services employing practitioners such as traditional birth attendants and others in primary care as part-time auxiliaries (usually after some introductory retraining). The system ef-

fectively acts as a register of state-recognized healers and can take the form of an association run centrally by the ministry of health, as in Zambia (Twumasi 1986).
4. Professional associations, in which committees of the practitioners' organization have exclusive rights to license a practitioner. The organization undertakes to test the practitioner's ability to practice adequately and safely and to review (and, if necessary, revoke) any practitioner's license for malpractice or other misconduct. The business of the profession may be divided between a general council (a statutory body for traditional medicine established by government) and an association run by officers elected by practitioners and answerable to them. The profession's certificates are recognized by employers and insurers for certain benefits on a par with those issued by doctors.

Zimbabwe has established professional institutions of this last kind after much debate and delay. Though they do not have powers to prevent nonmembers from practicing, many in the rural areas believe that they have. At present testing procedures are carried out (orally) within each community by a committee of the leading local healers, and their recommendations are accepted centrally. Recognition by employers of certificates for sick leave and other matters has been won only recently through strike action (Chavunduka 1984, 1986).

Formal identification as a branch of medicine is not, of course, the only route practitioners can take to avoid the legal sanctions associated with medical practice. An alternative route is for healers to capitalize on their religious strengths and form a church instead of a medical profession. Where the political climate has been opposed to traditional medicine yet tolerant of church diversity, large numbers of Zionist or prophetic churches have sprung up to divine the causes of illness and to offer healing through prayer, exorcism, laying on of hands, or using incense or holy waters and oils. Historically, Christian churches have always been centers of medical care, pioneering some of the earliest hospital and ambulance services. Theologians' emphasis on Christ's role as a healer has ensured that the tradition of healing has continued into the present among both Catholics and Protestants, as shown most recently by the former archbishop of Lusaka Emmanuel Milingo or by the Filipino evangelists who perform "psychic surgery" (Milingo 1984; Hagey 1980).

Other healers, basing their practice not on church rituals but on the concepts of traditional religions, have the option of turning their practice formally into a cult, focusing on a shrine or a regular ritual like spirit possession. The successes of candomble in Brazil, vodoun in Haiti, or Lemba in Zaire are well known (Janzen 1982b). But they are dependent nonetheless on the vitality of traditional belief in the face of increasingly widespread, secular education, and the explicit hostility of churches, Muslim organizations, and Marxist parties. Where church and cult groupings have to be registered in order to be allowed to operate, such hostility has potentially severe consequences, such as an outright ban or the destruction by the police of the shrine (as can happen, for example, in Cameroun). Though the demand for their services may be strong—for example, at times when accusations of witchcraft grow particularly common and there is an epidemic of anxiety—yet the political clout of their clientele, especially if it is composed mainly of women, has in the past proved inadequate to protect them from closure. In this situation, better protection can come from redefining a religious cult as primarily therapeutic and joining a healers' association, run perhaps with links to the university and its hospitals. Thus the *zar* cult has continued to thrive in the Sudan despite an otherwise pervasive Islamic fundamentalism.

The final alternative is for practitioners not to organize themselves but to practice as individuals, train apprentices individually as before, and serve, as required, on government-run local health committees by virtue of their own public reputation. Thus the personal, almost idiosyncratic nature of their healing skill is recognized. Healers only in their spare time, many escape notice as they treat local patients privately. In this manner they survived through the colonial period unorganized. The danger now is that their skills will disappear with them—but not just their skills: the intellectual insight into how their society functions, its inner meanings and rituals, and, from that insight, how society's casualties can be repaired. Given the weakness in many Third World countries of university departments teaching "Western" psychiatry—a weakness that is both conceptual and practical—and given the scant psychiatric facilities made available by governments (Cohen 1988; de Jong 1987), surely no country can afford to lose the insight and creative abilities of its indigenous practitioners, in this field at least. It is not that professional organization is thought to be the solution (though it is politically achievable now as never before) but that it offers a framework within which new developments in traditional medical thought can be tried out and passed on. In the process, new forms of professionalism will no doubt emerge, reflecting the priorities of indigenous practitioners and the public that patronizes them.

CHAPTER 19

INTERNATIONAL HEALTH AND DEVELOPMENT

Robert A. Rubinstein and Sandra D. Lane

International health development work is among the most personally challenging, intellectually engaging, and potentially frustrating areas of medical anthropological practice. On a personal level, it can demand compassion and understanding in the midst of seemingly incredible amounts of disease, poverty, and suffering. Yet because an adequate understanding of the dynamics that lead to these conditions requires the integration of information from many spheres—biological, ecological, social, and cultural, for instance—using a variety of qualitative and quantitative methods, it engages the holistic commitment of anthropology as do few other anthropological activities. Notwithstanding this, it can be a frustrating area of work because the interaction of the broader political and economic contexts in which international health and development work is situated and the culture of the community of international health workers often lead to perverse outcomes.

These challenges, problems, and paradoxes are partly reflected in the following three examples:

1. In developing countries, 14 million children under the age of 5 died during 1987. More than 70 percent of these deaths were due to four main causes, all of which "are now susceptible to effective low-cost actions by well-informed and well-supported parents" (Grant 1988:3). These four are diarrheal diseases, malaria, measles, and acute respiratory infection. In fact, children die of multiple causes, and malnutrition contributes to many of these.

2. U.S. foreign aid to Egypt since 1974 has totaled $13 billion. The principal bureaucratic means for distributing these funds is the U.S. Agency for International Development (USAID). In part because of AID policies and practices, this massive investment has not yet yielded equally impressive results. One problem is that AID assistance requires that projects use costly U.S. materials and equipment: "One Egyptian government source has estimated that AID financed purchases are from 30 to 40 percent more

expensive than substitutes readily available even in U.S. markets. Goods must also be shipped on U.S. vessels, at a cost that is sometimes three times the going international rate" (Rodenbeck 1988:17; see also Sullivan 1984). And the annual cost of maintaining the Cairo USAID office is approximately $150 million.

3. After investing huge amounts of money in the basic laboratory work needed to develop effective low-cost oral rehydration therapy (ORT) for stemming the devastating effects of diarrheal diseases, these techniques are frequently unused or misused. In part this failure derives from the frustrating circumstance that research supporting health planning is constrained by bureaucratic commitments so that it necessarily fails to discover culturally appropriate ways of integrating low-cost technologies, like ORT, into peoples' daily lives. As Foster (1987a:715) observes, "The assumption that asking people about their health beliefs and behavior, and observing their health behavior, is not science unless the data are used to test hypotheses, often severely constricts research designs and research results" (see also Pacey 1982; Rubinstein 1984).

International health is the term most frequently used when health policy planners speak about health in the developing world. Although the United States, the Soviet Union, and other industrialized nations are normally included in the concept *international*, in the case of health development work they are most commonly the planners, and less developed nations such as Egypt, Liberia, and Bangladesh are the recipients. Thus, in practice, international health refers to the flow of advice, health professionals, and health technology from the wealthier nations to the poorer.

International health development began with the eighteenth- and nineteenth-century missionaries, who set up clinics and offered medicine to the people they were trying to convert. Following the missionaries, colonial governments established health services in their colonies. Leng (1982:411) argues that the development of medical care by the British colonialists in Malaya occurred mainly because the indigenous labor force was decimated by infectious diseases, and communicable diseases were threatening the lives of the colonizers. El-Mehairy (1984: 11) also stresses that "Western governments undertook international health work to protect their people from exotic diseases . . . [and in] . . . the hope of political and economic benefit from foreign aid."

In 1914 Charles Eliot set out these assumptions in a remarkably unself-conscious way in his report to the Carnegie Endowment for International Peace:

The fundamental object of Western colonization, or other form of occupation in the East, is, as it always has been, the extension of European trade and the increase of European wealth; but the opinion is beginning to prevail extensively in Europe and among Europeans who live in the East, that these objects can best be accomplished by increasing the intelligence, skill, and well-being of the Eastern populations controlled, by raising their standards of living, relieving them from superstitious terrors, social bondages and industrial handicaps, and by creating among them new wants and ambitions . . . The principle means to these worthy ends are . . . preventive medicine and an effective public health organization directed to the relief of current suffering, the prevention of sweeping pestilences, and the increase of industrial efficiency. (Eliot 1914:4)

Thus, although international health work has always drawn on the talents and energies of compassionate and caring health professionals, the social organization of international health work developed in the context of, and continues to be shaped by, the political and economic self-interests of powerful groups. In a real sense, international health development was not based on altruism but served the political and medical needs of the donor countries.

An unequal distribution of power is implicit in the relationship between the donors of medical assistance and its recipients. Arturo Escobar (1985), following Michel Foucault's analysis of the discourse of power, examines the jargon of international health. He argues that health development work was preceded by the "creation of abnormalities" such as the term *underdeveloped*, which held the West to be the "developed" goal to which other countries must aspire, and in doing so devalued more than half of the world (Escobar 1985:387). The standard on which development is based is largely arbitrary, culture bound, and one-dimensional. The basis of this evaluation, industrialization and wealth, assumes that the "underdeveloped" countries would benefit from becoming more like the developed countries and that they therefore must attempt to change in that direction. A rarely stated, but increasingly clear, point is that a scale based on development devalues, or discounts, some aspects of culture that promote quality of life, including "non-Western" traditions of art, religion, intellectual accomplishment, and social support (Rahnema 1986).[1]

Once these kinds of assumptions coalesced to form the "problem of underdevelopment," its professionalization soon followed. As Escobar (1985) notes, major universities formed departments focused on development studies. With this development, an institutionalized approach to the analysis and treatment of development projects grew up (Sen 1979; Silverberg 1986) that restricts the range of information considered legitimate. A particularly extreme view of this process is expressed by Allan Hoben, who argues that development studies are "a positivistic and ethnocentric interpretation of a particular historical process, the emergence of capitalism, and the industrial revolution in Western Europe" (Hoben 1982:352; see also Hill 1986). This situation has resulted in calls for expanding the kinds of information considered appropriate for use in health planning (Rubinstein 1984; Foster 1987a, 1987b; Justice 1987), and it has spawned more passionate responses as well.[2]

Since nearly all of the terms used in international health work reflect the unequal relationship between the haves and the have nots, it is problematic to chose non-value-laden terms. In an effort to modify the term *underdeveloped*, scholars have used *developing* and *less developed countries* (LDCs) in the World Health Organization (WHO) jargon. Marxists and others with a political-economic perspective often refer to the Third World to distinguish the First World (the United States and its allies) and the Second World (the Soviet Union and its allies) from the remaining polities in the world. The term *Third World* implies an understanding of the sociopolitical divisions between rich and poor nations, but it nonetheless lumps together quite diverse countries that often have little in common except poverty (Worsley 1984).

Since there are no nonpejorative terms to describe the major recipient countries of international health aid, in this chapter we use *less developed countries* and *Third World* interchangeably. The following section describes the assumptions and institutional arrangements, especially international health agencies, through which the big business of international health is organized.

ASSUMPTIONS AND ORGANIZATION OF INTERNATIONAL HEALTH WORK

The assumptions of international health work have, according to George Foster (1987a, 1987b), historically included the assumptions: (1) that wealthier countries have the capital, the talent, and the "know-how" to solve the health problems of the poorer countries; (2) that the wealthier countries should therefore plan and direct such efforts; and (3) that Western health care institutions and approaches will work in solving health problems in LDCs. These general assumptions are elements of a professional worldview that persists despite repeated demonstrations that it is inadequate. There is no reason to assume that development projects designed and implemented by Western experts will be either appropriate or useful in the Third World. Judithanne Justice (1983, 1984, 1987) demonstrates that in Nepal the primary health care model developed by the WHO, the United Nations Children's Fund (UNICEF), and USAID was applied without considering local cultural or political factors and failed as a result.

A further, perhaps more basic, assumption in international health development has been that the provision of health care will improve the health of the recipients. Although there have been successes in international health work—the most frequently cited being the eradication of smallpox during the 1970s—many projects have failed to improve health, and some have also worsened the health of the people they were trying to help.

Furthermore, in Europe the major improvements in infectious diseases (especially tuberculosis) occurred before the development of sophisticated health care technologies like antibiotics, vaccines, and modern medicine (Dubos 1959; Ratcliffe 1985).

T. McKeown (1976b) describes how the social movements of the nineteenth century in England led to the provision of clean water and improvements in nutrition and housing, which were responsible for the reduction in infectious disease. The resulting decrease in mortality rates, especially among infants and children, happened before the advent of antibiotics. Thus, health care alone may not be the best method of improving the health of people internationally, particularly when their health problems stem directly from poverty.

International health bureaucracies encompass four distinct types of organizations (Foster 1987a, 1987b).

1. International (multilateral) organizations, such as WHO, UNICEF, the Food and Agriculture Organization (FAO), the United Nations Fund for Population Assistance (UNFPA), the United Nations Educational, Scientific and Cultural Organization (UNESCO), the World Bank, and many others. It is at

conferences funded and organized by these agencies that major policy directions are charted. One of the most famous such meetings was the 1978 Alma Ata Conference, which officially inaugurated primary health care (WHO 1978). Following ratification of each new policy direction, the multilateral organizations, often in cooperation with bilateral and private organizations, fund projects in individual countries.

2. Governmental (bilateral) organizations, in which one country directly extends aid to a second country, usually through the ministry of health in the recipient country. The United States channels this assistance through USAID. Although this aid is officially for health projects, it also serves the needs of U.S. foreign policy and is used as an incentive to encourage others to act in accord with U.S. self-interests. Furthermore, USAID assistance often reflects U.S. concerns more than those of the recipient countries. For example, during the Reagan administration, USAID withdrew its support from UNFPA because of right-wing pressure against funding abortion services. The conservative trend toward privatization has influenced USAID funding as well. Although the bulk of USAID's support still goes to ministries of health, an increasing portion supports the health projects of private organizations and for-profit health services (Montague and Lamstein 1988).

3. Private and voluntary organizations (PVOs) or nongovernmental organizations (NGOs), which may be secular (for example, Save the Children Foundation and CARE) or religious (for example, Catholic Relief Services and the American Friends Service Committee). They may also be international, where the headquarters are located in the United States or Europe with local offices in recipient countries, or they may be indigenous. In India, for example, indigenous voluntary organizations are particularly strong. In many other countries, however, government control of indigenous organizations precludes their development of effective programs. In general, NGOs provide direct assistance to particular groups such as refugees, children, disaster victims, and the like. Since they often serve fairly small groups, NGOs may quite successfully improve the health of their target populations. When the same programs are attempted with a larger population with no increase in funding (for example, when a ministry of health attempts to replicate a successful pilot project on a country-wide scale), the projects often fail. This effect, called *upscaling* in the development literature, is one of the main reasons that pilot projects are so difficult to translate into large-scale strategies (Sohoni 1988:25–28).

4. Philanthropic foundations, which were among the first bureaucracies to become involved in international health. These include the Rockefeller Foundation, the Ford Foundation, Hewlett, Mellon, the Packard Foundation, and many others. Although U.S. based philanthropic foundations are private and not associated with the government, they have, especially in the past, been accused of serving the needs of American business and foreign policy. Indeed an entire body of literature examines the Rockefeller Foundation's heavy-handed approach to international development (Brown 1976, 1980; Donaldson 1976; Franco-Agudelo 1983). More recently, however, many philanthropic agencies have revised

their funding strategies. The Ford Foundation, for example, works primarily through indigenous institutions. It supports research, education, and action programs conceived of and conducted by local scholars to meet the needs of their own countries.

HEALTH PROBLEMS IN THE THIRD WORLD

Before discussing specific international health projects or the role of anthropologists in them, it is important to review the major health problems in the Third World that these projects are designed to address. Obviously the countries that make up the Third World are heterogeneous, as are the populations within those countries, so any overview that lumps them together does not do justice to their diversity. However, sociopolitical and ecological similarities exist among Third World countries that affect the health of their people.

Third World populations are usually characterized by pyramidal age structures, with the bulk of the people under age 15. High infant death is reflected in the infant mortality rates (Table 19.1)—for 1986, for example, 185 per 1,000 in Afghanistan and 171 per 1,000 in Mali, with 6 per 1,000 for Sweden and Finland and 10 per 1,000 for the United States (Grant 1988:64–65; International Bank for Reconstruction and Development 1988; Golladay and Liese 1980; Rohde 1983). High infant and childhood death is largely from such infectious diseases as neonatal tetanus, diarrhea, respiratory illnesses, and the diseases for which there are vaccinations: polio, diphtheria, pertussis (whooping cough), tetanus, measles, rubella, tuberculosis, cholera, yellow fever, and typhoid. Although immunizations are officially available in most countries, many children are unvaccinated. The reasons for this span the cultural and political spectrum. Nevertheless, these diseases are not limited to children and cause morbidity and mortality in adults as well. Two conditions that are more commonly thought of as adult diseases afflict infants who are born to infected mothers: hepatitis B and AIDS. Hepatitis B infection may induce chronic hepatitis and, years later, liver cancer (Horn 1986a). Babies infected with the human immunodeficiency virus rarely survive to their fifth year. Hepatitis B infection is already widespread in the Third World, and AIDS is a growing problem in many areas.

The major parasitic diseases (malaria, schistosomiasis, onchocerciasis, trypanasomiasis, leischmaniasis, filariasis, and the intestinal parasites) plague both children and adults with chronic infections that cause debility, loss of productivity, and shortened life spans (Katz, Despommier, and Gwadz 1982). Although much international health work has attempted to control these parasitic diseases, especially malaria, schistosomiasis, and trypanasomiasis, the failure of vector control measures and a number of other problems has contributed to the failure of these programs (Golladay and Liese 1980:18).

Accidents, particularly motor vehicle accidents, are common in cities where the traffic congestion rivals that in the industrialized world (Fenner 1980). Burns are frequent occurrences in makeshift housing, where open fires or small kerosene stoves are used for cooking and heating. Inadequate or completely lacking emer-

Table 19.1
Child and Infant Mortality Rates and Adult Literacy Rates

Country	1986 under 5 Mortality	1986 IMR	% Adults Literate--1985 male/female
Afganistan	325	185	39/8
Mali	297	171	23/11
Sierra Leone	297	171	38/21
Malawi	270	153	52/31
Ethiopia	255	151	.
Guinea	255	150	40/17
Somalia	255	151	18/6
Burkina Faso	241	141	21/6
Niger	233	137	19/9
Chad	228	134	40/11
Guinea-Bissau	228	134	46/17
Central African Republic	228	134	53/292
Senegal	227	134	37/19
Mauritania	225	129	.
Liberia	211	124	47/23
Rwanda	210	124	61/33
Kampuchea	206	132	85/65
Yemen	204	123	27/3
Yemen, Dem	204	123	59/25
Bhutan	202	130	.
Nepal	202	130	39/12
Burundi	196	116	43/26
Bangladesh	193	121	43/22
Benin	189	112	37/16
Sudan	182	108	33/14
Tanzania, U. Rep. of	179	107	93/88
Bolivia	179	113	84/65
Nigeria	178	107	54/31
Hati	176	119	40/35
Gabon	174	105	70/53
Uganda	174	105	70/45
Pakistan	170	111	40/19
Zaire	166	100	79/45
Lao People's Dem Rep	166	113	92/76
Oman	166	104	47/12
Cameroon	158	96	68/55
Togo	157	95	53/28
India	154	101	57/29
Cote d'Ivoire	153	102	53/31
Ghana	150	91	64/43
Zambia	132	82	84/67

Table 19.1 (continued)

Country	1986 under 5 Mortality	1986 IMR	% Adults Literate--1985 male/female
Egypt	131	88	59/30
Peru	128	91	91/78
Libyan Arab Jamahiriya	125	85	81/50
Morocco	125	85	45/22
Indonesia	122	76	83/65
Congo	119	75	71/55
Kenya	118	74	70/49
Zimbabwe	118	74	81/67
Honduras	112	71	61/58
Algeria	112	76	63/37
Tunisia	106	74	68/41
Guatemala	105	61	63/47
Saudi Arabia	105	74	35/12
South Africa	101	75	.
Nicaragua	100	64	.
Turkey	99	79	86/62
Iraq	98	71	90/87
Botswana	96	69	73/69
Viet Nam	95	68	88/80
Madagascar	94	61	74/62
Ecuador	90	64	85/80
Papua New Guinea	90	64	55/35
Brazil	89	65	79/76
Burma	89	64	.
El Salvador	88	61	75/69
Dominican Republic	86	67	78/77
Philippines	75	46	86/85
Mexico	71	48	92/88
Colombia	70	47	89/87
Syrian Arab Republic	68	50	76/43
Paraguay	63	42	91/85
Mongolia	62	46	93/86
Jordan	62	46	87/63
Lebanon	53	41	86/69
Thailand	53	41	94/88
Albania	50	41	.
China	47	34	82/56
Sri Lanka	46	34	91/83
Venezuela	44	36	88/85
United Arab Emirates	41	33	58/38
Guyana	39	31	97/95
Argentina	39	33	96/95
Malaysia	37	27	81/66
Panama	34	23	89/88

Table 19.1 (continued)

Country	1986 under 5 Mortality	1986 IMR	% Adults Literate--1985 male/female
Korea, Dem. Rep of	33	25	.
Korea, Republic of	33	25	96/88
Uruguay	31	27	93/94
Mauritius	30	24	89/77
Romania	30	24	.
Yugoslavia	30	27	97/86
USSR	28	23	.
Chile	25	20	97/96
Trinidad and Tobago	25	21	97/95
Jamaica	24	19	90/93
Kuwait	24	20	76/63
Costa Rica	23	18	94/93
Portugal	21	18	89/80
Bulgaria	20	15	.
Hungary	20	18	.
Poland	20	18	.
Cuba	19	15	96/96
Greece	17	12	97/88
Czechoslovakia	17	14	.
Israel	16	14	97/93
New Zealand	13	11	.
USA	13	10	.
Austria	13	10	.
Belgium	13	9	.
German Democratic Rep.	13	9	.
Italy	13	11	98/96
Singapore	12	9	93/79
Germany, Federal Rep.	12	9	.
Ireland	12	9	.
Spain	11	9	97/92
United Kingdom	11	9	.
Australia	11	10	.
Hong Kong	11	9	95/81
France	10	8	.
Canada	10	8	.
Denmark	9	7	.
Japan	9	6	.
Netherlands	9	8	.
Switzerland	9	7	.
Norway	8	7	.
Finland	7	6	.
Sweden	7	6	.

Abstracted from Grant 1988:64-65.

gency and fire vehicles, equipment, and personnel mean that people die who might otherwise be saved. Occupational exposures to such toxins as lead, pesticides, and other chemicals cause unknown amounts of disease, especially where safety equipment is inadequate or not even considered. For example, textile workers in Egypt frequently suffer from pneumoconiosis after years of inhaling fiber dust without any respiratory protective equipment (Lane 1985).

Illiteracy is often high, and in some countries a majority of women are illiterate (Grant 1988:76–77). Female literacy has a profound indirect effect on health. Illiterate mothers are unable to read directions on medicine containers and consequently may give the wrong medicine or wrong dose of medicine to a child (Lane 1987). Furthermore, increasing female literacy is associated with a decrease in the birthrate and decreased infant mortality rates (Herz and Measham 1987:35–37). In a remarkable study that examined data from 33 countries, a linear relationship was found between maternal education and child survival (Cochrane, O'Hara, and Leslie 1980). For every one-year increment in mothers' education, there was a 7 to 9 percent decline in child mortality.

Unemployment and underemployment are large problems in the developing world, where the labor force may be unable to absorb those who receive an education (Kepel 1985:85). Frequently the brightest and the best young graduates emigrate to seek their fortunes in other countries, often in the West (Saleh 1979). This brain drain disproportionately affects the ranks of physicians and nurses, the loss of whom directly affects a country's health care. According to Halfdan Mahler (1981:10) more than 75 percent of the world's migrant physicians now practice in five of the wealthiest Western countries: Australia, Canada, the Federal Republic of Germany, the United Kingdom, and the United States.

Sociopolitical conditions both cause some health problems and make a number of existing problems worse, including inadequate food, clean water, stress associated with migration, war, multinational business interests, and large-scale development projects.

Poor Access to Food

It is widely acknowledged that nutritional status is the most important determinant of health (Scrimshaw 1974). Nevertheless, due to lack of food, millions of children and adults in the developing world are malnourished. Dietary inadequacy often results from unequal distribution of food within a country and between countries, which occurs even when adequate food stores exist (Feder 1981). Susan George (1977) describes how price controls meant to increase profits result in planned scarcity, where millions starve while farmers in the United States are paid not to produce. Noting the unequal distribution of food internationally, the *Food and Nutrition Bulletin* commented: "No doubt everyone realizes how preposterous it is that the two most protein-needy continents, Africa and South America, are the main suppliers of animal protein food moving in the world trade—and they supply those who already have plenty" (cited in *Xerophthalmia Club Bulletin* 1983). In Egypt, for example, the rural delta has the highest density of animals per unit of land in the world (Horn 1986b);

however, the peasants rarely eat meat, mainly on religious holy days and when someone dies (Lane 1987). Nevertheless, a significant amount of acreage is devoted to fodder to fatten the livestock, which are then sold for cash (Adams 1986; Lane 1987).

In rural farming areas, the shift from subsistence agriculture to growing cash crops has worsened the diets of the farmers and their families (George 1977:15–19). The change in crops, often from food to nonfood items such as cotton or coffee, began under colonialism. For example, in 1832 during the British colonial period, Egypt began growing cotton, which is still its major cash crop (Owen 1969). The Sudan began cotton production in 1910 also under British colonial rule. With the completion of the Sennar Dam in 1925, more than 2 million acres in the Gezira scheme were irrigated for the production of cotton and other crops (Gezira Board 1987). Since cash crops are grown to be exported and since they are usually cultivated on the best land, farmers must then grow their families' food on smaller and poorer plots of land and purchase the remainder. Further, farmers must purchase seeds, fertilizer, pesticides, and the like to grow the next year's cash crop. The families' diet, which may have been relatively abundant and varied during subsistence farming, suffers, and the most vulnerable members of the family, the children and childbearing women, suffer the most.

The "green revolution" was a development strategy based on the assumption that producing more food per unit of land would be the answer to the world's food shortages (George 1977). In an attempt to increase crop yield, new hybrid plants were developed that produced twice their former yields. However, the green revolution replaced the varied traditional agriculture with monocrops of cereals (Taussig 1978; Schertz 1972). This switch decreased the peasants' dietary diversity and replaced much of the leguminous proteins that were the peasants' main protein source. Furthermore, the genetic diversity of the crops was decreased since the hybrids were developed in a few laboratories, such as the International Rice Research Institute in the Philippines (George 1977:88). The new hybrids needed enormous amounts of fertilizer and pesticides, which the developing countries were often forced to purchase from the West. The expense of these purchases forced many small farmers off their land, which was then bought by agribusinesses that used the green revolution technology to produce cash crops (World Agricultural Research Project 1980). In Colombia, for example, "the expansion of intensive large-scale farming has driven the bulk of the peasantry off the land in recent years, 50 percent of the children six years and under are said to be suffering from malnutrition" (Taussig 1978:101).

In many parts of the world, land tenure remains nearly feudal, with a small percentage of landlords owning the fields upon which tenant farmers grow crops. P. J. Brown (1987) examined such a situation in Sardinia and found that the energy taken from the peasants in the form of payment to the landlords was a much greater burden on them than the chronic malaria from which they suffered. He had originally gone to Sardinia to study the effect of malaria on impeding development and concluded that the land tenure system that so favored the few owners presented a much larger obstacle. A similar situation exists in many parts of India. Sandra Lane (1989) interviewed landless farmworkers in Gujarat state and found that they were paid only half of the official minimum wage (6 rupees per day rather than 12 rupees). When large expenses, such as providing a dowry for a daughter, forced them to borrow from the landlord, they and their entire families entered into a form of indentured servitude.

In Third World cities, rural-to-urban migrants have swelled the squatter settlements. Many of these residents were farmers who lost their land due to poverty and must now purchase all of their food. With high unemployment and lack of literacy and job skills to survive in a city, they and their children may starve due to lack of money. Charles Hughes and John Hunter (1970) describe this phenomenon as "urban malnutrition."

Even fuel for cooking of food is often scarce and expensive. In areas where women depend on wood for cooking, deforestation has complicated their lives enormously. In a village in Gujarat state, India, the women claimed to spend between two to four hours per day gathering sufficient firewood to cook the daily meal.

Lack of Clean Water

In many countries piped water and sanitation are luxuries of the urban middle and upper classes. In the rural areas and in the urban slums, residents may have to travel some distance to a crowded public tap or may have to drink from a stream polluted with human and animal waste. In 1987, for example, only 54 percent of people in India, 25 percent of people in Paraguay, and 9 percent of people in Mozambique had access to safe water (International Bank for Reconstruction and Development 1988:112, 184, 166).

David Sanders (1985) describes three types of disease associated with inadequate water supplies: water-borne diseases, which occur when drinking water is contaminated with fecal organisms, such as cholera, typhoid, amoebiasis, hepatitis A, polio, and diarrhea; water-washed diseases, which increase when washwater is inadequate, such as skin and eye infections; and water-based diseases, in which the infectious agent is present in the water and penetrates the skin during washing, such as schistosomiasis. The most ubiquitous water-borne disease, diarrhea, is the leading cause of death in children under 5 in developing countries and results in between 5 million and 18 million childhood deaths per year (Rohde and Northrup 1976:341). In addition to fatal dehydration, diarrhea contributes to malnutrition and weakened immunity in children who survive (Chen and Scrimshaw 1983). So detrimental is diarrhea to the child's nutritional status that it can cause malnutrition even when there is sufficient food available to the child (Chen and Scrimshaw 1983).

Increase in Disease due to Refugee Flight, Forced Relocation, and Rural-to-Urban Migration

Migration, especially refugee flight from war and natural disasters, has been increasing every year. Since 1945, 60 million to 70 million people have fled from their homes because of political repression and war (Beyer 1981:26); more than 14 million of these refugees fled in 1974 alone (1974 World Refugee Report, cited by Jacobson 1977:516). Forced relocation of entire communities is a consequence of the construction of such dams as the Kariba Dam (Zimbabwe), the Aswan High Dam (Egypt and the Sudan), and the Keban Dam (Turkey) (Scudder 1975).

In most Third World countries, a large proportion of the population is rural, with farming as its main occupation. However, rural-to-urban migration is increasing; the World Bank estimates that by the year 2000, the worldwide urban population will be 45 percent of the total (Golladay and Liese 1980:21). Due to this migration, the large cities in the Third World have swelled in recent years and are surrounded by squatter settlements of poor people who live without basic sanitation in crowded, makeshift housing (Peattie 1968). In many Third World cities, estimates of the proportion of the population that lives in squatter settlements range from 20 percent to 50 percent (Abrams 1970).

Thayer Scudder and Elizabeth Colson (1982) attribute the health effects of migration to three types of stress: physiological, psychological, and sociocultural. Such physiological stresses as crowding, inadequate food, water, and sewage disposal can both lower the migrants' resistance to disease and expose them to such infectious diseases as tuberculosis, parasitism, diarrhea, and respiratory illnesses (Hull 1979:32; McNeill 1980). Such psychological stresses as grief, anxiety, and emotional trauma contribute to both physical and mental illness (Murphy 1961). Such sociocultural stresses as language barriers and resettlement in an area where the habits, attitudes, and beliefs are unfamiliar and where xenophobia makes the host population negatively prejudiced toward the migrants may lead to such economic, family, and social problems as alcoholism (Scudder and Colson 1982; Ablon 1965).

Political Repression, Violence, and War

Directly and indirectly, political economic struggles affect health. War and violence, as parts of contemporary political realities, are now much different from the conventional wars of other eras of human history. Now combat between opposing armies is infrequent. In its place, "war is focused on the Third World, and pits guerrilla insurgences against state governments and states against indigenous nations" (Nietschmann 1987:1). The direct killing and maiming of combatants is the unfortunate goal of war. A less obvious effect is the loss of this human power for the society—the loss of teachers, engineers, and manual workers to carry on the daily tasks of the society. After the war the society must support and care for the disabled veterans and suffers the effects of angry men in its midst who have been trained to kill (Siegel, Baron, and Epstein 1985). It is not hyperbole to say, for example, that the young Israeli soldiers who are learning that it is acceptable to break the hands and skulls of West Bank Palestinians have become dehumanized—as one soldier stated, "The more I break other people's bones, the more I am broken myself" (Greenberg 1988:1)—nor is it difficult to imagine the future problems this brutality will create for Israeli society (Physicians for Human Rights 1988).

War profoundly affects civilian health as well. The civilians need not be members of the enemy; war may provide an excuse for genocide of a national minority population. The examples of such genocide are numerous, from the German Holocaust of European Jews to the Guatemalan extermination of the indigenous Indian peasants (Carmack 1988).[3]

Direct health effects on civilian enemies are also numerous but are often ignored since the people killed are typically women, children, and elders. The Mylai massacre of an entire village by U.S. soldiers is one example (Nagel 1972). During the war of 1948, 250 Palestinians were killed in the village of Dier Yassin to "liberate" the territory for the newly created state of Israel (Said 1979:44). And more recently, the use of poison gas by Iraq during its war with Iran is reported to have wiped out the entire population of a Kurdish village (Browne 1988; Physicians for Human Rights 1989).

A less obvious effect of war on civilian health is on disruption of food distribution and disruption of health care. In Sudan, the largest country in Africa, the effects of the brutal civil war between the Muslim North and non-Muslim South have resulted in significant losses in progress from past development efforts and in diminished prospects for development in the future (Ahmed et al. 1988). For example, for the South the war has meant the near cessation of the drilling of boreholes for freshwater after 1985 (Dodge and Ibrahim 1988:48–49), an exceptionally high infant mortality rate of 180 per thousand, prevalent malnutrition among children 12 and younger (Duku 1988:44) and the decimation of the infrastructure for primary and secondary health care in the region (Duku 1988:37–41).

In Zimbabwe from 1978 to 1980 the military carried out Operation Turkey, destroying crops, livestock, and food supplies in order to starve the guerrillas (Sanders 1982). The unfortunate consequence of this strategy was widespread malnutrition of rural children and increased infant and childhood mortality.

In Nicaragua the contra forces have explicitly targeted health workers and health institutions (Siegel, Baron, and Epstein 1985; Siegel, Baron, and Eitel 1985; Kreier and Baron 1987). From 1981 to 1985, 38 health workers were killed and 28 kidnapped while they were performing medical services; 61 health units have been destroyed and 37 others forced to close due to contra activity. Due to the decreased availability of health services immunization, sanitation, nutrition, and other health programs have been curtailed, and health, especially of the rural peasants, has suffered.

In the Guatemalan village of San Pedro, for instance, the effect of the burden of military operations on the economy is conspicuous. Between 1977 and 1987 the cost of one pound of rice increased fivefold, from .15 quetzal to .75 quetzal. Although there was a rise in wages during the decade, it was nowhere as great as the rise in prices. This means that one pound of rice rose from representing .25 percent to .71 percent of a laborer's average monthly wage. Similar increases occurred in the cost of other staple commodities (Table 19.2). The nutritional consequences of this situation are remarkable: "One impact of all this is that protein consumption dropped by at least 15 percent, caloric intake by 16 percent, and the per capita intake of eggs, meat and fat was reduced in 90 percent of the

Table 19.2
Price in San Pedro, Guatemala, as Percentage of Monthly Wages, 1977 and 1987

		1977				1987	
		Teacher	Laborer	Maid		Teacher	Laborer	Maid
Wage (1)	Price	240.00 %	60.00 %	12.00 %	Price	372.00 %	105.00 %	40.00 %
Black beans/lb	.08	.03	.13	.67	.70	.19	.67	1.75
Corn/lb	.05	.02	.08	.42	.22	.06	.21	.55
Rice/lb	.15	.06	.25	1.25	.75	.20	.71	1.88
Soap/ea	.04	.02	.07	.33	.22	.06	.21	.55
Meat/lb	.75	.31	1.25	6.25	3.75	1.01	3.57	9.38
Chicken feed/100lbs	8.40	3.50	14.00	70.00	33.80	9.09	32.19	84.50
Milk/liter	.08	.03	.13	.67	.50	.13	.48	1.25
Salt	.03	.01	.05	.25	.20	.05	.19	.50
Chicken/lb	.29	.12	.48	2.42	1.80	.48	1.71	4.50
Sugar/lb	.08	.03	.13	.67	.30	.08	.29	.75
Bread/six	.05	.02	.08	.42	.24	.06	.23	.60
Carrots/doz.	.40	.17	.67	3.33	1.00	.27	.95	2.50
Shrimp/lb	1.20	.50	2.00	10.00	8.00	2.15	7.62	20.00
Tomato paste/each	.15	.06	.25	1.25	.75	.20	.71	1.88
Hot sauce/each	.10	.04	.17	.83	.50	.13	.48	1.25
Gasoline/gallon	.95	.40	1.58	7.92	2.95	.79	2.81	7.38
Electricity/kwh	.07	.03	.12	.58	.21	.06	.20	.53
Antacids/each	.05	.02	.08	.42	.15	.04	.14	.38
Private school/month	4.00	1.67	6.67	33.33	15.00	4.03	14.29	37.50
Bus to Quezaltenango	.50	.21	.83	4.17	1.50	.40	1.43	3.75

Source: Adapted from Ehlers (1987:27).
aQuetzals, laborer's wage based on daily wage estimate.

population'' (Ehlers 1987:27). That devoting a disproportionate share of a nation's economy to maintaining a military effort has a negative effect on human services and on social supports in that nation has been well documented (Melman 1965, 1988; Pinxten 1986). Further, the devotion of resources to the procurement of military resources has worldwide effects, especially in the case of the development of nuclear arsenals.

The threat of nuclear war and the scientific study of long-term effects of dropping the atomic bomb on Hiroshima and Nagasaki have focused attention on the medical aspects of nuclear war (Ishikawa and Swain 1981). This has inspired a number of speculative reports on the potential health effects of nuclear war. Owen Greene and associates (1982) describe the effects of several different kinds of nuclear attacks on London, England. In their analysis, they calculate that "a single one-megaton bomb can destroy by blast and fire an area 10 miles across" (Greene et al. 1982:25), and they note that it would disrupt electrical and other utilities over a much wider area. As for casualties, they say that even in an attack "in which no bomb falls on Inner London, over one million die in seconds from blast injuries and more than 4 million from radiation over a period of up to two months after the attack. At least half a million people are injured by blast" (p. 55). More generally, in addition to deaths immediately attributable to blast, Elizabeth Schueler and George Armelagos (1989:108; Armelagos and Schueler 1986) point out that the "short term health effects on the population will be further exacerbated by the destruction of an estimated 80 percent of the medical resources." Further, aside from radiation-induced illness, there will be an increase in morbidity due to vitamin, mineral, and food deficiencies. On the social and cultural levels, the possibility of nuclear war suggests the likely disruption of social life on a dramatic scale (Rubinstein 1988).

Multinational Business Interests

Businesses often place profits above other considerations, including the health of unsuspecting consumers. The infant formula scandal is perhaps the most well-known example of this phenomenon. Following World War II infant formula companies such as Nestles and Unigate began increasingly intensive promotion of artificial milk as the healthiest choice for infant diets (George 1977:152–53; Jelliffe and Jelliffe 1977). This marketing involved not only print, radio, and television advertisements but also saleswomen dressed as nurses who demonstrated the products to new mothers in hospitals, frequently giving away the first tin for free (George 1977:153). For poor families, however, the formula was so expensive that one-quarter to one-third of the family's income might be required to purchase adequate amounts, forcing mothers to dilute the strength of the mixture (George 1977:153; Elling 1981). Furthermore, lack of refrigeration and contamination of the water used to mix the formula is the surest route to diarrhea. Finally, without the nipple stimulation of frequent suckling, the mother's breast milk dries up. Thus, the child is deprived of the immunoprotective factors intrinsic to human milk—factors that would protect it from infection—and if the parents lack money to purchase sufficient formula, the infant starves. The irony is how completely unnecessary artificial formula is for babies; breast milk is healthier than formula, and it is free and sterile.

A second example of multinational business interests directly impairing health is the dumping of drugs in the Third World. M. Silverman, P. Lee, and M. Lydecker (1982) have conducted extensive investigations of the marketing of drugs in the developing world. Specifically they called attention to the inconsistencies in drug indications and descriptions of side effects in the promotional literature. Powerful antibiotics such as chloramphenocol are used extensively in Latin America and the Middle East for childhood diarrhea, according to package directions. The package directions do not mention the potentially fatal side effect—aplastic anemia—which is the reason that chloramphenocol is reserved for only life-threatening infections in the United States. Since in many parts of the developing world it is possible to purchase drugs directly from the pharmacy without a doctor's prescription or advice, there is great danger that such inappropriate drugs are given to children and adults every day.

The companies that make these drugs are well aware of their side effects. For example Ciba-Geigy produces an antidiarrhea medication marketed as Enterovioform. The active ingredient, clioquinol, was found to cause a nerve disease, subacute myelo-optic neuropathy, characterized by numbness in the extremities and in some cases blindness and paralysis. In the 1970s the Ciba-Geigy company was forced to pay the Japanese victims of the drug $111 million in legal compensation. In 1985, Ciba-Geigy was still marketing Enterovioform in Egypt without sufficient warning on the package insert (Lane 1985).

Large-Scale Development Projects

Development projects are meant to improve the standard of living in developing countries, so it is at first surprising that they are responsible for much disease themselves. However, as D. Heyneman (1983b), Thayer Scudder (1973), and Charles Hughes and John Hunter (1970) point out, projects are often developed in the donor countries without considering the ecological cost of the endeavor. Indeed there has developed a culture of the development community that is heavily invested in providing technological solutions to the "problems of developing countries" (Pacey 1983:5–15). One result is that even when local planners are involved in projects, local information is not incorporated into project designs, as Justice's (1986) analysis of health development planning in Nepal shows.

We have already described the effects of forced relocation on migrants who must resettle to accommodate big dam projects. Heyneman (1983b) also describes how the construction of each major dam in Africa was accompanied by an upsurge of parasitic diseases. For example, more than half of the 85,000 new residents in fishing villages around the newly created Lake Volta have become infected with *Schistosoma haematobium*. This chronic parasite spends part of its life cycle in snails that live in slow-moving water. Whenever the water flow is impeded, such as with a dam, the snails flourish and provide the perfect ecosphere for the *Schistosoma* parasite. In humans chronic schistosomiasis or bilharziasis causes cirrhosis, enlarged spleen, and portal hypertension; infected adults frequently bleed to death when the overdistended veins in their esophagi burst (Plorde 1980:907–11). In 1937, just 12 years after the completion of the Sennar dam on the Blue Nile in the Sudan, these health problems were already apparent, and perceptively, if paternalistically, noted by Emil Ludwig (1937:37):

For disease, in an uncanny way, followed the dam, the cotton and the gold to which it gave birth. Bilharziasis, a severe parasitic affliction, which had broken out before the completion of the dam in Dongola Province, and been carried to Sennar by western pilgrims, then ague, malaria, and smallpox—all spread, to the horror of the people, who saw their suspicions of machines confirmed by Allah's wrath. In 1930, many thousands of sick passed through the Sudanese hospitals. Science and medical practice advanced vigorously from Khartoum against the pests; the locusts, which lay their eggs in light sand, were attacked by an army of chemists, policemen, and Arabs, who by means of poison and rapidly dug trenches, endeavored to keep the insects away from the crops. But when an aeroplane circled overhead, bringing fresh medicines from England, the natives looked up angrily and said that all the evil came from aeroplanes.

Here lies the terrible warning that will again thunder towards us in Egypt. It is true that the world crisis, rain, and sickness have upset a reckoning that at first seemed good and brought big profits. But what good is a new raw material to a country which, to export it, has to go without the bread which was its natural portion for thousands of years, and for the increase of which the dams and canals, the tractors and engineers' brains, would have been admirably employed.

Widespread clearing of the rain forests is another example of the destruction wrought by development. F. B. Livingstone (1958) first connected the cutting down of the rain forest with the increase in malaria because it gave the malaria vector—the mosquito—more open pools of stagnant water in which to breed. Commenting on how frequently the increase in malaria and other diseases are associated with changes in the ecosystem, J. R. Audy (1958) coined the term "man-made maladies." R. H. Adams (1986) described the World Bank–supported Polonoreste project in northeastern Brazil that cleared the rain forest for agriculture. Unfortunately, the exposed soil is not rich enough to support agriculture, causing the project to fail. However, the aboriginal populations who resided in these rain forests have witnessed the destruction of their homelands and have suffered from exposure to many diseases brought in by the project laborers.

TRENDS AND ANTHROPOLOGICAL PROSPECTS IN INTERNATIONAL HEALTH

Many of the health problems of the developing world result from inequality. It follows that the greatest improvement in health would be accomplished by education, the provision of adequate food, clean water, sanitation, housing, employment, and freedom from bombs, guns, and torture. The major improvements in health in Europe did not result from medicines or other technological advances or from the elaboration of health care per se but from improved water supplies, sanitation, nutrition, and housing. Nonetheless, the major themes of health development work involve the exporting by the West to the developing world its concepts of medicine and health care.

There have been historic trends in international health work, and anthropologists have played roles in two opposing camps: those who worked on the projects and those who became the critics. This section describes the major historical trends in international health projects.

Control of Tropical Diseases

In the early years of the twentieth century the Rockefeller Foundation and other agencies began national and international economic development projects. A major program rationale for these projects, which placed health development at their center, was that "tropical diseases" (especially hookworm, malaria, and yellow fever) were obstacles to development (Brown 1976). According to E. Brown (1976:898), the Rockefeller hookworm eradication campaign began when Charles Stiles, a zoologist, convinced the foundation that the parasite was the cause of "some of the proverbial laziness of the poorer classes," following which the *New York Sun* proclaimed that they had found the "germ of laziness." Significantly, health was defined as the capacity to work, and the program's successes were measured in increased productivity of workers. From Molina-Guzman's (1979) description of the projects, it appears that they employed many altruistic health professionals unknowingly to serve economic and political ends with which they may not have agreed.

Medical Education and Population Programs

Following World War II two trends emerged in international health work: development of medical schools, hospitals, and clinics based on Western systems (Molina-Guzman 1979) and population programs. F. M. Mburu (1981) shows that the introduction of curative, hospital-centered care was particularly ill suited to African countries. Such health care is urban based, while the bulk of the population is rural; it is expensive, while the majority are poor; it is highly specialized and focused on esoteric diseases, while most of these people suffer from communicable diseases, deficiencies in sanitation, and malnutrition.

Toward the end of the 1950s, international awareness focused on two factors: the world's population was rapidly increasing, and developments in fertility control had reached the point where it was becoming possible to control population growth (Greep, Koblinsky, and Jaffe 1976:372–79). A United Nations 1962 resolution, "Population Growth and Economic Development," recognized that the poorest people in the least developed nations had the highest fertility. It was assumed that poverty could be overcome if only the poor could control their fertility.

By 1965, President Lyndon Johnson's State of the Union message called for funding to "seek new ways to use our knowledge to help deal with the explosion in world population and the growing scarcity in world resources" (Johnson

1965:16). Following the president's call to action, the United States became a major donor in international population programs.

The correlation of high fertility with poverty may not indicate direct causation, however. In fact, John Ratcliffe (1978, 1985) suggested that rather than people being poor because they have many children, people may have many children because they are poor. He cites the example of Kerala state, India, where land reform, increased education, and availability of health services were followed by decreases in infant and child mortality and only then by declining fertility.

Nevertheless, such improvements in education and health services are exceedingly difficult if the population is increasing at a rapid pace. Such is the case with Egypt, where the population was 51 million in 1988 and is projected to reach 126 million before declines in fertility reach zero population growth (International Bank for Development and Reconstruction 1988: 76). Egypt's schools are overcrowded, the health care system can barely cope with the demand, and housing in Cairo is in such demand that there is a waiting list of people seeking to live in mausoleums in the cemetery known as the City of the Dead (Schiffer 1988).

Unfortunately, many of the population programs of the 1960s and 1970s concentrated on population control at the expense of human dignity and rights. Policies aimed at trying to control numbers of poor people convinced many in the Third World that such policies were a form of genocide. They found confirmation of these convictions too often in the use of medical technology in the service of project objectives. For example, in Puerto Rico many women were sterilized, often without their consent or knowledge (Henderson 1975). Furthermore, drugs and devices, such as Depo-Provera and the Dalkon shield, have been used in the Third World even after their safety was seriously questioned in the United States (Elling 1981). We are not suggesting that family planning programs are not needed. Clearly women need safe, reliable methods to control their fertility, and countries need to limit their populations so that they may better serve their existing citizens. However, to succeed, such programs must respect the humanity and choice of the consumer of family planning technologies.

Primary Health Care

Primary health care emerged in the 1970s with a growing realization that the supposed benefits of all the money spent on sophisticated curative medicine were not reaching the poor, mostly rural, populations who had the most disease (Golladay and Liese 1980). Its ambitious goal, proclaimed by the Alma Ata declaration of 1978 was, "Health for all by the year 2000" (Mahler 1981). The basic components of primary health care are community involvement, appropriate health technology, and reorientation of health services away from urban, hospital-based care toward country-wide health programs. It includes an emphasis on preventive medicine and employs community health workers to serve the needs of their communities. This model of primary health care has now been adopted worldwide but implemented with varying degrees of success. In highly motivated socialist societies, such as China (Mosley 1983) and Nicaragua (Donahue 1986b), great improvements in health indicators have been reported.

Elsewhere primary health care has been less impressive. Justice (1984) describes how the introduction of nurse-midwives failed because young women were stationed at health posts away from their home areas, without taking into account the social constraints that make it socially unacceptable for young Nepali women to travel or live alone.

David Werner (1983) argues that while Cuba has made great strides in health care, the system there remains highly centralized and dependent upon physicians. He also points out (1977) that in Mexico, primary health care was less successful where community health workers were appointed by the government rather than chosen by the village, and he argues that many programs fail because they only give lip-service to community involvement while remaining paternalistic and authoritarian.

In Bolivia, Libbett Crandon (1983) saw a USAID-sponsored primary health program disbanded by the government. It failed for the frequently cited reason that the imported model of health care was imposed on the local system without taking into account cultural or political realities (see, for example, Paul 1955). Moreover, many primary health care programs may never have had much chance to succeed. In areas where physicians dominate the governments and ministries of health, their suspicion of nontraditional alternatives may have truncated the system before it began (Mosley 1983). In addition, the community involvement and thus the level of organization demanded by primary health care may have alarmed governments that feared losing control to a newly militant peasantry (Davis 1988:6–20).

Child Survival

By the early 1980s it had become clear that unless existing strategies were revised, health for all, especially for the world's children, would not be achieved by the year 2000 (International Conference on Population 1984). Political economists like Vicente Navarro (1984) claimed that major health improvements are not possible without changes in economic, social, and political structures. Nevertheless, many international health specialists felt that the introduction of specific, inexpensive technologies could have a major impact on child mortality.

With this in mind UNICEF outlined its child survival strategy in a 1982–1983 report entitled *State of the World's Children* (Mandl 1983). This program included growth monitoring, oral rehydration therapy, breastfeeding, improved weaning foods, immunization, food supplements, and family planning. As before, this initiative focused mainly on exporting medical technologies to the developing countries. Massive investments were made in developing oral rehydration therapy, a simple solution (McQuestion 1983:ix) of 1 liter of water mixed with sodium chloride (3.5 grams), sodium bicarbonate (2.5 grams), potassium chloride (1.5 grams), and glucose (20 grams). So large was the investment that between 1980 and 1982 alone, at least 150 articles about ORT appeared in the scientific literature. Most of these focused on the technical aspects of

ORT, like the proper composition of the rehydration solution, clinical trials, or the measurement of the impact on nutritional status of treatment with ORT under controlled circumstances (McQuestion 1983).

As an easy-to-use, inexpensive, and life-saving technology that could prevent death from dehydration and could replace costly hospital-based intravenous rehydration, the value of ORT was unquestionable in principle. But because its development had emphasized "scientific" questions to the exclusion of sociocultural information, attempts at implementing its widespread use were often unsuccessful and frustrating. For instance, WHO recommendations for the implementation of ORT, based on technical researches, were often out of touch with the realities of peoples' lives. Richard Cash (1983:211) asserts that "the overall recommendation by WHO is that ORT be made with ordinary drinking water, and that prepared oral therapy should not be kept more than 24 hours. There is no apparent reason to alter this recommendation." Yet in many cases ORT is inaccurately mixed, infrequently used, and not often recommended by physicians.

Rather than focusing on the community, child survival emphasizes the mother and her children. It has influenced a great deal of research on the determinants of child health (see Mosley and Chen 1984). Anthropologists are increasingly being included in research teams investigating the question, "How can we change mothers' behavior?" This program is too new for extensive evaluations of it to have reached the anthropological literature. There have been some successes, notably the Egyptian National Control of Diarrheal Diseases Project (Rodenbeck 1988).

A preliminary examination of the problems with the program is that in some countries it has produced a series of vertical programs, each with its own staff, budget, and agenda. For example, in the Sudan there are separate programs for the Expanded Program of Immunization (EPI), the Control of Diarrheal Diseases (CDD), Growth Monitoring, and the like. Each program has its own bureaucracy, vehicles, and personnel. When the CDD people go to a village, they do not take vaccines along, and when the growth monitors weigh and measure children, they do not give out oral rehydration solution packets. Clearly this is inefficient at best.

Furthermore, John Briscoe (1987:103) argues that the "Child Survival Revolution gives low priority to improvements in water supply and sanitation because it has concluded that these interventions are not cost-effective." Such shortsighted planning results from programs that count success only in numbers of children vaccinated or numbers of oral rehydration solution packets distributed. Health improvements resulting from clean water, adequate housing, or fair wages are much more difficult to measure and are thus discounted in international development priorities.

Safe Motherhood

The beginning of the latest emerging trend in international health, safe motherhood, was initiated by a World Bank–supported conference in February 1987 in Nairobi. Between 1987 and 1988, in fact, twelve conferences on safe motherhood in Africa, Asia, Latin America, and the Middle East have been funded by international health agencies. Among the sponsors for these conferences have been the WHO, UNDP, UNICEF, the World Bank, and the Ford Foundation.

The slogan for this program—"putting the M back in MCH" (putting the mother back into maternal/child health)—indicates a recognition that women have been largely ignored in favor of children. Maternal deaths in developing countries range from 100 to 700 per 100,000 live births (Hertz and Measham 1987). In parts of the Sudan, maternal deaths reach 2,276 per 100,000 live births (Sudan Ministry of Health personal communication). Moreover, the health of women before and during pregnancy profoundly affects the health of their infants. Safe motherhood strategies include stronger community-based care (primarily nonphysician care), stronger referral facilities, and better transport systems for high-risk pregnancies (Hertz and Measham 1987).

The implementation of safe motherhood programs is just beginning. UNICEF is sponsoring training of traditional birth attendants in the hope of improving the community-based care of pregnant women, and research is beginning in many areas into how to improve women's reproductive health.

Anthropological Prospects

Just as the general area of development studies has evolved in a way that is consistent with the concerns of development professionals, so the development of international health programs takes place in an arena in which the concerns of the First World provide the major imperatives for action. Shifts in the focus of international health work have not taken place primarily because the problems were solved but rather because of political and economic considerations. Indeed, there is evidence that program shifts occur even at times when such changes frustrate the chances of success of the earlier programs (Justice 1986).

Trends in international health development can be traced in large part to the constraints within which programs are developed. These include organizational cultures that reward innovation rather than constancy, planning tied to short-term (fiscal year) cycles rather than to time periods that reflect realistic program spans, and a basic ethnocentrism involved in exporting technology and development based on "rational," "scientific" principles. Medical anthropologists working in international health must recognize these constraints, identify their effect on people's health, and work to ensure that bureaucratic and ethnocentric program rationales do not blind health professionals to the critical and dynamic role that culture and political processes play in enabling people to achieve satisfactory levels of health and well-being.

NOTES

The views expressed in this chapter are those of the authors, and no official endorsement by the Ford Foundation is intended or should be inferred. We thank Judith Justice, Daniel

Perlman, Robert Pickering, and Sol Tax for critical discussions of earlier drafts of this chapter and Rupa Goswami for bibliographical assistance.

1. Reflecting on his twenty years of experience working with USAID, Harrison (1985) states straightforwardly these premises. Introducing his retrospective analysis, *Underdevelopment Is a State of Mind*, he says: "I hope the book will demonstrate how one culture may make progress easier for its people than another. According to my values, which are, I believe, generally shared by most people in both the developed and underdeveloped worlds, progress-prone cultures are better places for human beings to live than traditional, static cultures. And the most progressive cultures that humankind has thus far evolved follow the democratic model of the West" (Harrison 1985:xvii).

2. Majid Rahnema, a former United Nations civil servant, summed up this aspect of development work when he wrote:

Ever since that restless little macho man, called *homo economicus*, was born to our planet, some 300 years ago, the economized societies of his creation have, in turn, given birth to a host of new varieties of humanoids, most of them frightfully dangerous: bureaucrats, strategists, entrepreneurs, developers and planners of all kinds; modern shamans and marabouts with professional degrees in every discipline, from animal psychiatry and bereavement counseling to genetic engineering; technowizards producing nuclear toys and statesmen and generals specialized in playing with them; heads of state who believe that nuclear war is the ultimate answer to peace-keeping, and those who would not speak the language of their peoples, yet master the language of anyone who provides them with arms and weapons in order to keep their people quiet and docile. All these figures and figureheads have pledged allegiance to a three-headed monster, the heads representing the new world empires of economics, politics, and technology. They are all pledged to save the 'Underdeveloped' world, through aid and assistance. (Rahnema 1988:117)

3. We do not consider here the effects of the participation of health professionals in political repression and violence through state-sanctioned torture and abuse of citizens. Nonetheless, the organization and consequences of such activities affect international health and are important for medical anthropologists practicing in such circumstances (see Claude, Stover, and Lopez 1987; Bloche 1987; Stover 1987; Rayner 1987).

REFERENCES

Aamodt, A. M.
   1972   The Child View of Health and Healing. In Communicating Nursing Research. The Many Sources of Nursing Knowledge. M. Batey, ed. Boulder, Colorado: Western Interstate Commission on Higher Education, 5:38–54.
   1978   The Care Component in a Health and Healing System. The Anthropology of Health. St. Louis: Mosby, 37–45.
   1981   Neighboring: Discovering Support Systems among Norwegian-American Women. In Anthropologists at Home in America: Methods and Issues in the Study of One's Own Culture. D. Messerschmidt ed. Cambridge: Cambridge University Press, 133–49.
   1982   Examining Ethnography for Nurse Researchers. Western Journal of Nursing Research 4:209–21.
   1984   Themes and Issues in Conceptualizing Care. In Care: The Essence of Nursing and Health. Thorofare, N.J.: Slack, 75–79.
Abaza, Mona, and Georg Stauth
   1988   Occidental Reason, Orientalism, Islamic Fundamentalism: A Critique. International Sociology 3(4):343–64.
Abdel Malek, Anwar
   1963   Orientalism in Crisis. Diogenes 44:107–8.
Abdel-Salam, E., P. A. S. Peters, A. E. Abdel Meguid, A. A. E. Abdel Meguid, and A. A. F. Mahmoud
   1986   Discrepancies in Outcome of a Control Program for Schistosomiasis Haematobia in Fayoum Governorate, Egypt. American Journal of Tropical Medicine and Hygiene 35:786–90.
Abel, Theodora M., Rhoda Metraux, and Samuel Roll
   1987   Psychotherapy and Culture. Rev. ed. Albuquerque, N.M.: University of New Mexico Press.
Aberle, David
   1952   Arctic Hysteria and Latah in Mongolia. Transactions of the New York Academy of Science 14:294–97.
Aberle, D. F., A. K. Cohen, A. K. Davis, M. J. Levy, and F. X. Sutton
   1960   The Functional Prerequisites of a Society. Ethics 60:100–111.
Abimbola, W.
   1976   Ifa: An Exposition of Ifa Literary Corpus. Nigeria: Ibadan University Press.
Ablon, Joan
   1965   American Indian Relocation: Problems of Dependency and Management in the City. Phylon 26:362–71.
   1976   Family Behavior and Alcoholism. In Cross-Cultural Approaches to the Study of Alcohol. Michael Everett et al., eds. The Hague: Mouton.
   1980   Thoughts on a "Clinical Anthropology." Medical Anthropology Newsletter 12(1):22–23.
   1984   Family Research and Alcoholism. In Recent Developments in Alcoholism, vol. 2. Marc Galanter, ed. New York: Plenum.
   1985   Irish-American Catholics in a West Coast Metropolitan Area. In The American Experience with Alcohol. Linda Bennett and Genevieve Ames, eds. New York: Plenum.
Abrams, Charles.
   1970   Man's Struggle for Shelter in an Urbanizing World. Cambridge: MIT Press.

Ackerknecht, Erwin H.
  1943 Psychopathology, Primitive Medicine and Primitive Culture, Bulletin of the History of Medicine 14:30–67.
  1944 Primitive Surgery, American Anthropologist 49:25–45.
  1945 Malaria in the Upper Mississippi Valley, 1760–1900. Bulletin of the History of Medicine, Supplement 4.
  1946 Natural Diseases and Rational Treatment in Primitive Medicine. Bulletin of the History on Medicine 19(5):467–97.
  1958 Primitive Medicine's Social Function. In Miscelanea, Paul Rivet, ed. Mexico City: Universidad Nacional Autonoma de Mexico, 3–7.
  1971 Medicine and Ethnology: Selected Essays. Baltimore: Johns Hopkins University Press.
Adams, F., trans.
  1939 Hippocrates: The Genuine Works of Hippocrates. 2 vols. Baltimore: Williams & Wilkins.
Adams, R. H.
  1986 Development and Social Change in Rural Egypt. Syracuse, N.Y.: Syracuse University Press.
Adams, Richard N., and Arthur J. Rubel
  1967 Sickness and Social Relations. In Handbook of Middle American Indians. Robert Wauchope, ed. Austin: University of Texas Press, 333–56.
Adams, Vincanne
  1988 Modes of Production and Medicine: An Examination of the Theory in Light of Sherpa Medical Traditionalism. Social Science and Medicine 27(5):505–13.
Agar, Michael H.
  1973 Ripping and Running: A Formal Ethnography of Urban Heroin Addicts. New York: Seminar Press.
  1977 Into That Whole Ritual Thing: Ritualistic Drug Use among Urban American Heroin Addicts. In Drugs, Rituals, and Altered States of Consciousness. Brian M. du Toit, ed. Rotterdam: A. A. Balkema.
  1980 The Professional Stranger: An Informal Introduction to Ethnography. New York: Academic Press.
  1981 The Commonality Quest: The Search for Parallels between Drug Use and Other Behaviors. Newsletter of the Alcohol and Drug Study Group, American Anthropological Association, no. 3.
  1986 Speaking of Ethnography. Sage University Series on Qualitative Research Methods vol. 2. Beverly Hills, Calif.: Sage.
Agar, Michael H., Charles Underwood, and Kathryn Woolard
  1981 The Commonalities Quest: Toward a Theory of "Problem Behavior." Journal of Psychoactive Drugs 13(4): 333–43.
Ahmed, Abdul Rahman Abu Zayd, et al.
  1988 War Wounds: Development Costs of Conflict in Southern Sudan. London: Panos Institute.
Ailinger, R. L.
  1980 Nursing—A Social Policy Statement. Kansas City: American Nurses' Association.
  1982 Hypertension Knowledge in a Hispanic Community. Nursing Research 31:207–10.
  1983 Facts about Nursing. Kansas City: American Nurses' Association.
Ajabnoor, M. A. and A. K. Tilmisany
  1988 Effect of Trigonella foenum graceum on Blood Glucose Levels in Normal and Alloxan-Diabetic Mice. Journal of Ethnopharmacology 23:45–49.
Akerele, O.
  1987 The Best of Both Worlds: Bringing Traditional Medicine up to Date. Social Science and Medicine 24:177–81.
Alarcon, Renato D.
  1983 A Latin American Perspective on DSM-III. American Journal of Psychiatry 140(1):102–5
Alcorn, Janis B.
  1981 Some Factors Influencing Botanical Resource Perception among the Huastec. Journal of Ethnobiology 1:221–30.
Alexander, Franz, Samuel Eisenstein, and Martin Grotjahn, eds.
  1966 Psychoanalytic Pioneers. New York: Basic Books.
Alexander, Jaqui
  1988 The Ideological Construction of Risk: An Analysis of Corporate Health Promotion Programs in the 1980's. Social Science and Medicine 26(5): 559–67.
Alexander, Linda
  1979 Clinical Anthropology: Morals and Methods. Medical Anthropology 3(1):61–109.
Alland, A.
  1966 Medical Anthropology and the Study of Biological and Cultural Adaptation. American Anthropologist 68:40.
  1970 Adaptation in Cultural Evolution: An Approach to Medical Anthropology. New York: Columbia University Press.
Alland, A., and B. McCay
  1973 The Concept of Adaptation in Biological and Cultural Evolution. In: J. Honigmann, ed., Handbook of Social and Cultural Anthropology (Chicago: Rand McNally), 143–178.
Allen, L., A. Chavez, and G. H. Pelto
  1987 The Collaborative Research and Support Program on Food Intake and Human Function: Mexico Project. Final Report. University of Connecticut and Instituto Nacional de Nutricion (Mexico).

References

Allison, A. C.
  1954 Protection Afforded by Sickle-Cell Trait against Subtertian Malarial Infection. British Medical Journal 1:290–94.
Altorki, Soraya, and Camilia Fawz El-Solh
  1988 Arab Women in the Field: Studying Your Own Society. Syracuse, N.Y.: Syracuse University Press.
Alubo, S. Ogoh
  1987 Drugging the Nigerian People: The Public Hazards of Private Profits. The Impact of Development and Modern Technologies in Third World Health. Studies in Third World Societies 34:89–114.
American Nurses' Association
  1980 Nursing- A Social Policy Statement. Kansas City: American Nurses' Association.
  1983 Facts about Nursing. Kansas City: American Nurses' Association.
American Psychiatric Association
  1980 Diagnostic and Statistical Manual of Mental Disorders. 3d ed. (DSM III). Washington D.C.:APA.
  1987 Diagnostic and Statistical Manual of Mental Disorders. 3d ed. rev. (DSM III-R). Washington D.C.:APA.
Ames, Genevieve M.
  1982 Maternal Alcoholism and Family Life: A Cultural Model for Research and Intervention. Ph.D. dissertation, University of California Medical Center.
  1985a American Beliefs about Alcoholism: Historical Perspectives on the Moral—Medical Controversy. In The American Experience with Alcohol. Linda Bennett and Genevieve Ames, eds. New York: Plenum.
  1985b Middle-class Protestants: Alcohol and the Family. In The American Experience with Alcohol. Linda Bennett and Genevieve Ames, eds. New York: Plenum.
Ames, Genevieve M., and Craig R. Janes
  1987 Heavy and Problem Drinking in an American Blue-collar Population: Implications for Prevention. Social Science and Medicine 25(8):949–60.
Amin, Galal
  1981 Some Economic and Cultural Aspects of Economic Liberalization in Egypt. Social Problems 28(4):430–41.
Amin, Samir
  1972 Under-Populated Africa. Manpower and Unemployment Research in Africa 5:5–17.
Anderson, E. N.
  1988 A Native-based Strategy for Alcohol Abuse Control. Paper presented at IUAES Congress, Zagreb, Yugoslavia.
Anderson, E. N., M. L. Anderson, and H. C. Ho
  1978 Environmental Backgrounds of Young Chinese Nasopharyngeal Carcinoma Patients. In G. de-The and Y. Ito, eds., NPC: Etiology and Control. Lyon: IARC, 231–39.
Anderson, R. M., and R. M. May
  1978 Regulation and Stability in Host-Parasite Population Interactions, I. Regulatory Processes. Journal of Animal Ecology 47:219–47.
Aneshensel, Carol S., and Jeffrey D. Stone
  1982 Stress and Depression: A Test of the Buffering Model of Social Support. Archives of General Psychiatry 39:1392–96
Anisimov, A. F.
  1963 The Shaman's Tent of the Evenks and the Origin of the Shamanistic Rite. In Studies in Siberian Shamanism. H. N. Michael, ed. Toronto: University of Toronto Press, 84–123.
Annis, Linda Ferrill
  1978 The Child before Birth. Ithaca: Cornell University Press.
Antonovsky, Aaron
  1979 Health, Stress, and Coping. San Francisco: Jossey-Bass.
Apprey, Maurice
  1986 Discussion: A Prefatory Note on Motives and Projective Identification. International Journal of Psychoanalytic Psychotherapy 11:111–16.
Arbain, D., et al.
  1989 Survey of Some West Sumatran Plants for Alkaloids. Economic Botany 43:73–78.
Arditti, Rita, Renate Duelli Klein, and Shelley Minden, eds.
  1984 Test-Tube Women: What Future for Motherhood? London: Pandora Press.
Armelagos, G. J., and J. R. Dewey
  1970 Evolutionary Response to Human Infectious Diseases. BioScience 157:638–644.
Armelagos, G. J., A. Goodman, and K. H. Jacobs
  1978 The Ecological Perspective in Disease. In Health and the Human Condition. M. Logan and E. Hunt, eds. North Scituate, Mass.: Duxbury, 71–84.
Armelagos, George, and Elizabeth Schueler
  1986 Biological Consequences of Nuclear Winter. In Nuclear Winter: The Anthropology of Human Survival. M. Pamela Bumsted, ed. Los Alamos, N.M.: Los Alamos National Laboratory, 23–29.
Armstrong, R. W., M. J. Armstrong, M. C. Yu, and B. C. Henderson
  1983 Salted Fish and Inhalants as Risk Factors for Nasopharyngeal Carcinoma in Malaysian Chinese. Cancer Research 43:2967–70.

Arney, William Ray
   1982   Power and the Profession of Obstetrics. Chicago: University of Chicago Press.
Arney, William Ray, and Bernard J. Bergen
   1984   Medicine and the Management of Living: Taming the Last Great Beast. Chicago: University of Chicago Press
Asad, Talal
   1973   Anthropology and the Colonial Encounter. London: Ithaca Press.
   1979   Anthropology and the Analysis of Ideology. Man, n.s. 14(4):607–27.
   1987   Are There Histories of Peoples without Europe? A Review Article. Comparative Studies in Society and History 29(3):597–607.
Atal, C. K., U. Zutshi, and P. G. Rao
   1981   Scientific Evidence on the Role of Ayurvedic Herbals on Bioavailability of Drugs. Journal of Ethnopharmacology 4:229–32.
Aubo, Ogoh
   1987   Power and Privileges in Medical Care: An Analysis of Medical Services in Post Colonial Nigeria. Social Science and Medicine 24(5):453–62.
Audy, J. R.
   1958   Medical Ecology in Relation to Geography. British Journal of Clinical Practice 12:102–10.
August, Lynn R., and Barbara A. Gianola
   1987   Symptoms of War Trauma Induced Psychiatric Disorders: Southeast Asian Refugees and Vietnam Veterans. International Migration Review 21:820–31
Ayala, F. J.
   1983   Microevolution and Macroevolution. In D. Bendall, ed., Evolution from Molecules to Men. Cambridge: Cambridge University Press, 387–402.
Badcock, C. R.
   1980   The Psychoanalysis of Culture. Oxford: Basil Blackwell.
   1986   The Problem of Altruism: Freudian-Darwinian Solutions. New York: Basil Blackwell.
Baer, Hans A.
   1982   On the Political Economy of Health. Medical Anthropology Newsletter 14(1):1–2, 13–17.
   1984   A Comparative View of a Heterodox Health System: Chiropractics in America and Britain. Medical Anthropology 8:151–68.
   1986a   The Replication of the Medical Division of Labor in Medical Anthropology. Medical Anthropology Quarterly 17(3):63–65.
   1986b   Sociological Contributions to the Political Economy of Health: Lessons for Medical Anthropologists. Medical Anthropology Quarterly 17(5):129–31.
   1988   How Critical Can Clinical Anthropology Be? Paper presented at the Annual Meeting of the Society for Applied Anthropology, Tampa, Florida.
   1989   The American Dominative Medical System as a Reflection of Social Relations in the Larger Society. Social Science and Medicine 28(11):1103–12.
Baer, Hans A., Merrill Singer, and John H. Johnsen
   1986   Introduction. Toward a Critical Medical Anthropology. Social Science and Medicine 23(2):95–98.
Bahr, Donald M., Juan Gregorio, David I. Lopez, and Albert Alvarez
   1974   Piman Shamanism and Staying Sickness. Tucson: University of Arizona Press.
Baker, P. T.
   1984   The Adaptive Limits of Human Populations. Man (n.s.) 19:1–14.
   1986   Rationale and Research Design in the Changing Samoans: Behavior and Health in Transition. Paul T. Baker, Joel M. Hanna, and Thelma S. Baker, eds. New York: Oxford University Press.
Balint, Michael
   1964   The Doctor, the Patient and His Illness. London: Pitman Medical Publications.
Banaji, J.
   1970   Crisis in British Anthropology. New Left Review 64:71–85.
Banerji, Debabar
   1984   The Political Economy of Western Medicine in Third World countries. In Issues in the Political Economy of Health Care. J. McKinlay, ed. New York: Tavistock, 257–282.
   1986   Comments on New Patterns in Health Sector Aid to India. International Journal of Health Services 16(2):309–11.
Bannerman, R. H., J. Burton, and C. Wen-Chief, eds.
   1983   Traditional Medicine and Health Coverage. Geneva: World Health Organization.
Bannoune, Mahfoud
   1984   What Does It Mean to be a Third World Anthropologist? Dialectical Anthropology 9(1–4):357–64.
Barclay, George W.
   1958   Techniques of Population Analysis. New York: Wiley.
Barker, C., and M. Turshen
   1986   Primary Health Care or Selective Health Strategies. Review of African Political Economy 36 (September):78–85.
Barnes, J. A.
   1973   Genitrix:Genitor:Nature:Culture? In The Character of Kinship. Jack Goody, ed. Cambridge: Cambridge University Press.

References

Barnes, S. T., and C. D. Jenkins
 1972 Changing Personal and Social Behaviour: Experiences of Health Workers in a Tribal Society. Social Science and Medicine 6:1–15.
Barnett, Clifford R.
 1980 Commentary (On Clinical Anthropology). Medical Anthropology Newsletter 12(1):23–25.
 1985 Anthropological Research in Clinical Settings: Role Requirements and Adaptations. Medical Anthropology Quarterly 16(3):59–61.
Barnett, Clifford, M. L. Poland, H. H. Weidman, H. F. Stein, I. Press, A. Kleinman, and O. von Mering
 1985 Symposium: Anthropologists in Clinical Settings—A Matter of Style. Medical Anthropology Quarterly 16(3):59–73.
Barnett, Elyse Ann
 1988 La Edad Critica: The Positive Experience of Menopause in a Small Peruvian Town. In Women and Health. Patricia Whelehan, ed. Granby, Mass.: Bergin and Garvey, 40–55.
Barrabee, Paul, and Otto von Mering
 1953 Ethnic Variations in Mental Stress in Families with Psychotic Children. Social Problems 1(2):48–53.
Barrett, James E., ed.
 1979 Stress and Mental Disorder. New York: Raven Press.
Barry III, Herbert
 1982 Cultural Variations in Alcohol Use. In Culture and Psychopathology. I. Al-Issa, ed. Baltimore: University Park Press.
Basker, D., and M. Negbi
 1983 Uses of Saffron. Economic Botany 37(2):228–36.
Basaglia, Franco
 1964 Silence in the Dialogue with the Psychotic. Journal of Existentialism 6(21):99–102.
Bassett, Ken
 1988 The Fetal Patient. Paper prepared for the Society of Medical Anthropology Invited Session on Reproductive Technology, Medical Practice, Public Expectations and New Representations of the Human Body. Annual Meeting of the American Anthropological Association, Phoenix, November 16–20.
Basso, Keith H.
 1969 Western Apache Witchcraft. Tucson: University of Arizona Press.
Bastien, Joseph
 1985 Qollahuaya-Andean Body Concepts: A Topographical- Hydraulic Model of Physiology. American Anthropologist 87:595–611.
Bateson, Gregory
 1972 Steps to an Ecology of Mind. St. Albans, England: Palladin Books.
Bauwens, E. E.
 1977 Medical Beliefs and Practices among Lower-Income Anglos. In Edward Spicer, ed. Ethnic Medicine in the Southwest. Tucson: University of Arizona Press.
 1978 The Anthropology of Health. St. Louis: Mosby.
Beals, Ralph L.
 1980 Intracultural Variation: Reflections Stimulated by George Foster. Human Organization 39:289–91.
Beaujard, Philippe
 1988 Plantes et Medecine Traditionnelle dans le Sud-Est de Madagascar. Journal of Ethnopharmacology 23:165–265.
Becker, H. S., ed.
 1970 Sociological Work. Chicago: Aldine.
Bee, R. L., and B. F. Crabtree
 1989 Using Ethnography in Fieldnote Management. In Computer Applications for Anthropologists. M. S. Boone and J. J. Woods eds. Belmont, Calif.: Wadsworth.
Beiser, M., H. Collomb, J. Ravel, and C. J. Nafziger
 1976 Systemic Blood Pressure Studies among the Serer of Senegal. Journal of Chronic Diseases 29:371–80
Belmonte, Thomas
 1979 The Broken Fountain. New York: Columbia University Press.
Belsey, Mark A.
 1976 The Epidemiology of Infertility: A Review with Particular Reference to Sub-Saharan Africa. Bulletin of the World Health Organization 54:319–41.
Benedict, Ruth
 1934 Patterns of Culture. Boston: Houghton Mifflin.
Beneria, Lourdes
 1979 Reproduction, Production and the Sexual Division of Labour. Cambridge Journal of Economics 3:203–23.
Beneria, Lourdes, and Martha Roldan
 1987 The Crossroads of Class and Gender. Chicago: University of Chicago Press.
Benner, P.
 1984 From Novice to Expert: Excellence and Power in Clinical Nursing Practice. Readings, Mass.:Addison-Wesley.

Bennett, John W.
　1985　The Micro-Macro Nexus: Typology, Process, and System. In Billie R. DeWalt and Pertti Pelto, eds. Boulder, Colorado, 23–54.
Bennett, Linda A.
　1984　Contributions from Anthropology to the Study of Alcoholism. In Recent Developments in Alcoholism, vol. 2. Marc Galanter, ed. New York: Plenum.
　1988　Alcohol in Context: Anthropological Perspectives. Drugs and Society 2 (3/4):89–131.
　1989　Family, Alcohol and Culture. In Recent Developments in Alcoholism, Volume 7. Marc Galanter, ed. New York: Plenum.
Bennett, Linda A., ed.
　1984　Ethnography, Alcohol, and South-Central European Societies. East European Quarterly 18 (4): entire issue.
Bennett, Linda A., and Genevieve M. Ames, eds.
　1985　The American Experience with Alcohol: Contrasting Cultural Perspectives. New York: Plenum.
Bennett, Linda A., Steven J. Wolin, David Reiss, and Martha A. Teitelbaum
　1987　Couples at Risk for Alcoholism Transmission: Protective Influences. Family Process 26:111–29.
Benoist, Jean
　1978　The Structural Revolution. London: Weidenfeld Nicolson.
Bentley, M. E.
　1988　The Household Management of Childhood Diarrhea in Rural North India. In J. Coreil and J. D. Mull, eds. Anthropological Studies of Diarrheal Illness. Special Issue of Social Science and Medicine 27 (1):75–86.
Bentley, M. E., et al
　1988　Rapid Ethnographic Assessment: Applications in a Diarrhea Management Program. In J. Coreil and J. D. Mull, eds. Anthropological Studies of Diarrheal Illness. Special Issue of Social Science and Medicine 27 (1):107–16.
Berelson, Bernard
　1966　KAP Studies on Fertility. In Family Planning and Population Programs, Bernard Berelson, et al., eds. Chicago: University of Chicago Press, 655–68.
Berg, Elliott J.
　1965　The Economics of the Migrant Labor System. In Urbanization and Migration in West Africa, Hilda Kuper, ed. Berkeley: University of California Press, 160–81.
Berkman, Lisa F.
　1981　Physical Health and the Social Environment: A Social Epidemiological Perspective. In The Relevance of Social Science for Medicine. Leon Eisenberg and Arthur Kleinman, eds. Dordrecht, Holland: D. Reidel, 51–75.
　1985　Measures of Social Networks and Social Support: Evidence and Measurement in Measuring Psychosocial Variables in Epidemiologic Studies of Cardiovascular Disease. NIH Publication 85-2270. Adrian M. Ostfeld and Elaine D. Eaker eds. Bethesda: National Institutes of Health.
Berkman, L.,F. and S. L. Syme
　1979　Social Networks, Host Resistance and Mortality: A Nine-Year Follow-up Study of Alameda County Residents. American Journal of Epidemiology 109 (2):186–204.
Berliner, Howard
　1977　Emerging Ideologies in Medicine. Review of Radical Political Economics 9(1):116–24.
Bernard, H. R.
　1988　Research Methods in Cultural Anthropology. Beverly Hills: Sage.
Bernard, H. R., et al.
　1986　The Construction of Primary Data in Cultural Anthropology. Current Anthropology 27(4):382–96.
Bernstein, Gale L., and Yasue Aoki Kidd
　1982　Childbearing in Japan. In Anthropology of Human Birth. Margarita Artschwager Kay, ed. Philadelphia: F. A. Davis Co., 101–18.
Berry, J. W., Uichol Kim, Thomas Minde, and Doris Mok
　1987　Comparative Studies of Acculturative Stress. International Migration Review 21:491–511
Beyer, Gunther
　1981　The Political Refugee: 35 Years Later. International Migration Review 15:26–34.
Bhanumathi, P. P.
　1977　Nurses' Conceptions of "Sick-Role" and "Good Patient" Behavior: A Cross-Cultural Comparison. International Nursing Review 24:20–24.
Bibeau, Gilles
　1980　Traditional Medicine in Zaire. Ottawa: IRDC.
　1981　The Circular Semantic Network in Ngbandi Disease Nosology. Social Science and Medicine 15B:295–307.
　1982　New Legal Values for an Old Art of Healing. Social Science and Medicine 16 (21):1843–49.
Binn, M.
　1980　Using the Explanatory Model to Understand Ethnomedical Perceptions of Hypertension and the Resultant Behaviors. In Transcultural Nursing Care: Teaching, Practice and Research. M. Leininger ed. Salt Lake City: University of Utah, College of Nursing, 60–76.

Binswanger, Ludwig
   1958   Insanity as Life-History Phenomenon. In Existence: A New Dimension in Psychiatry and Psychology. Rollo May, Ernest Angle, and Henri Ellenberger, eds. New York: Simon & Schuster.

Bion, W. R.
   1959   Experiences in Groups. London: Tavistock.

Black, Peter Weston
   1984   The Anthropology of Tobacco Use: Tobian Data and Theoretical Issues. Journal of Anthropological Research 40 (4):475–503.

Blacking, John
   1977   Towards an Anthropology of the Body. In The Anthropology of the Body. John Blacking, ed. New York: Academic Press, 1–17.

Blacking, John, ed.
   1977   Outline of a Theory of Practice. Cambridge Studies in Social Anthropology, vol. 16. Cambridge: Cambridge University Press.

Blake, Judith
   1974   Coercive Pronatalism and American Population Policy. In Pronatalism: The Myth of Mom and Apple Pie. Ellen Peck and Judith Senderowitz, eds. New York: Thomas Y. Crowell Co, 29–68.

Blake, Judith, and Kingsley Davis
   1964   Norms, Values, and Sanctions. In Handbook of Modern Sociology. Robert E. L. Faris, ed. Chicago: Rand McNally, 465–484.

Blank, Robert H.
   1984   Redefining Human Life: Reproductive Technologies and Social Policy. Boulder, Colorado: Westview Press.

Bledsoe, Caroline
   1988   The Politics of Children: People and Wealth Among the Mene of Sierre Leone. Manuscript.

Bloche, Gregg
   1987   Uruguay's Military Physicians: Cogs in a System of State Terror. Washington, D.C.: American Association for the Advancement of Science.

Bock, Philip K.
   1988   Rethinking Psychological Anthropology: Continuity and Change in the Study of Human Action. New York: W. H. Freeman and Co. (orig. 1980).

Boddy, Janice
   1988   Spirits and Selves in Northern Sudan: The Cultural Therapeutics of Possession and Trance. American Ethnologist 15:4–27.

Bolton, J. L.
   1980   The Medieval English Economy 1150–1500. London: J. M. Dent & Sons.

Bonaparte, B.
   1979   Ego Defensiveness, Open-closed Mindedness, and Nurses' Attitudes toward Culturally Different Patients. Nursing Research 28:166–72.

Bonfil-Batalla, G.
   1970   Conservative Thought in Applied Anthropology. In Applied Anthropology. J. A. Clifton, ed. Boston: Houghton Mifflin.

Bongaarts, John
   1980   Does Malnutrition Affect Fertility? Science 208:564–69.
   1982   The Fertility Inhibiting Effects of the Intermediate Fertility Variables. Studies in Family Planning 13:179–89.
   1983   The Proximate Determinants of Natural Marital Fertility. In Determinants of Fertility in Developing Countries. R. A. Bulatao and R. D. Lee, eds. San Francisco: Academic Press 1:103–38.

Bongaarts, John, and R. G. Potter
   1983   Fertility, Biology and Behavior. New York: Academic Press.

Boone, M. S. and J. J. Woods, eds.
   1989   Computer Applications for Anthropologists. Belmont, Calif.: Wadsworth.

Borgatti, S.
   1988   ANTHROPAC (microcomputer software).

Borgerhoff Mulder, Monique
   1987   Resources and Reproductive Success in Women with an Example from the Kipsigis of Kenya. Journal of Zoology (London) 213:489–505.

Borjas, George J., and Marta Tienda
   1987   The Economic Consequences of Immigration. Science 235:645–51.

Borrini, Grazia
   1987   Health and Development: A Marriage of Heaven and Hell? In The Impact of Development and Modern Technologies in Third World Health. Barbara Jackson and Antonio Ugalde, eds. Studies in Third World Societies 34. Williamsburg, Va: College of William and Mary, Department of Anthropology.

Boserup, Ester
   1965   The Conditions of Agricultural Growth. Chicago: Aldine.
   1981   Population and Technological Change. Chicago: University of Chicago Press.

Bosk, Charles L.
   1979   Forgive and Remember: Managing Medical Failure. Chicago: University of Chicago Press.
Bourdieu, P.
   1977   Outline of a Theory of Practice. Cambridge Studies in Social Anthropology, Vol. 16. Cambridge: Cambridge University Press.
   1988   Homo Academicus. Cambridge: Polity Press. French ed., 1984.
Bourguignon, Erika
   1976   The Effectiveness of Religious Healing Movements: A Review of the Literature. Transcultural Psychiatric Research Review 13:5–21.
   1983   Sex Bias, Ethnocentrism, and Myth Building in Anthropology: The Case of Universal Male Dominance. Central Issues of Anthropology 5(1):59–79.
Boyer, L. Bryce
   1979   Childhood and Folklore: A Psychoanalytic Study of Apache Personality. New York: Library of Psychological Anthropology.
Boyer, L. Bryce, George De Vos, Orin Borders, and Alice Tani-Borders
   1978   The "Burnt Child Reaction" Among the Yukon Eskimos. The Journal of Psychological Anthropology 1(1):7–56.
Brachman, P. S.
   1985a   Principles and Methods. In: G. L. Mandell, R. G. Douglas, and J. E. Bennett, eds., Principles and Practice of Infectious Diseases, Second Edition (New York: John Wiley), pp. 96–103.
   1985b   Transmission and Principles of Control. In: G. L. Mandell, R. G. Douglas, and J. E. Bennett, eds., Principles and Practice of Infectious Diseases, Second Edition (New York: John Wiley), pp. 103–106.
Brady, Maggie
   1988   Indigenous and Government Attempts to Control Alcohol Use among Australian Aborigines. Paper presented at the International Union of Anthropological and Ethnological Sciences Congress, Zagreb, Yugoslavia.
Bratton, Michael
   1982   Types of Development and Underdevelopment: Towards Comparison. Unpublished manuscript.
Brenner, Charles
   1974   An Elementary Textbook of Psychoanalysis. Rev. and exp. ed. New York: International Universities Press.
Brenner, Robert
   1976   Agrarian Class Structure and Economic Development in Pre-industrial Europe. Past and Present 70:30–75.
Briesemeister, Linda H. and Beth A. Haines
   1988   The Interactions of Fathers and Newborns. In Childbirth in America. Karen Michaelson, ed. South Hadley, Mass: Bergin and Garvey, 228–239.
Briggs, Jean
   1970   Never in Anger: Portrait of an Eskimo Family. Cambridge: Harvard University Press.
Brill, L
   1981   The Clinical Treatment of Substance Abusers. New York: Free Press.
Brink, P. J.
   1984   Key Issues in Nursing and Anthropology. Advances in Medicine Social Science 2:107–46.
Brink, P. J., ed.
   1976   Transcultural Nursing: A Book of Readings. Englewood Cliffs, N. J. Prentice-Hall.
Briscoe, John.
   1987   A Role for Water Supply and Sanitation in the Child Survival Revolution. PAHO Bulletin 21(2):93–105.
Brody, Howard
   1980   Placebos and the Philosophy of Medicine. Chicago: University of Chicago Press.
   1988   The Symbolic Power of the Modern Personal Physician: The Placebo Response under Challenge. Journal of Drug Issues 18(2):149–61
Brooker, Stanley G., Richard C. Cambie, and Robert C. Cooper
   1989   Economic Native Plants of New Zealand. Economic Botany 43:79–106.
Brothwell, D., and A. T. Sandison
   1967   Diseases in Antiquity: A Survey of Diseases, Injuries, and Surgery in Ancient Populations. Springfield, Ill.: Charles C. Thomas.
Brown, Diane R., and Lawrence E. Gary
   1987   Stressful Life Events, Social Support Networks, and the Physical and Mental Health of Urban Black Adults. Journal of Human Stress 13:165–74
Brown, E. L.
   1982   Cross-cultural Perspectives on Middle-aged Women. Current Anthropology 23(2):143–56.
Brown, E. Richard
   1976   Public Health in Imperialism: Early Rockefeller Programs at Home and Abroad. American Journal of Public Health 66:897.
   1979   Rockefeller Medicine Men: Medicine and Capitalism in America. Berkeley: University of California Press.

References

    1980   Rockefeller Medicine in China: Professionalism and Imperialism. In Philanthropy and Cultural Imperialism. Robert F. Armour, ed. Boston: G. K. Hall and Co, 123–146.
Brown, George W.
    1974   Meaning, Measurement, and Stress of Life Events. In Stressful Life Events: Their Nature and Effects. B. S. Dohrenwend and B. P. Dohrenwend, eds. New York: Wiley
Brown, G. W., and T. Harris.
    1978   Social Origins of Depression: A Study of Psychiatric Disorder in Women. London: Tavistock Publications.
Brown, Jr., Howard P., John H. Peterson, Jr., and Orville Cunningham
    1988   An Individualized Behavior Approach to Spiritual Development for the Recovering Alcoholic/Addict. Alcoholism Treatment Quarterly 5 (1/2): 177–91.
Brown, Judith K.
    1970   Note on the Division of Labor by Sex. American Anthropologist 72(5):1073–78.
Brown, Judith K., and Virginia Kerns, eds.
    1985   In Her Prime: A New View of Middle-Aged Women. South Hadley, Mass.: Bergin and Garvey.
Brown, Michael F.
    1988   Shamanism and its Discontents. Medical Anthropology Quarterly 2:102–20.
Brown, P. J.
    1981   Cultural Adaptations to Endemic Malaria in Sardinia. Medical Anthropology 5:313-339.
    1986   Cultural and Genetic Adaptations to Malaria: Problems of Comparison. Human Ecology 14:311–32.
    1987   Microparasites and Macroparasites. Cultural Anthropology 2:155–71.
Brown, Paul, and D. Carleton Gajdusek
    1978   Acute and Chronic Pulmonary Airway Disease in Pacific Island Micronesians. American Journal of Epidemiology 108:266–73.
Brown, P. J., and M. Konner
    1987   An Anthropological Perspective on Obesity. Annals of the New York Academy of Science 499:29–46.
Browne, M. W.
    1988   Poor Man's Atomic Bomb Is Once Again Used in Battle. New York Times, April 17.
Browner, Carole H.
    1976   Poor Women's Fertility Decisions: Illegal Abortion in Cali, Colombia. Ph.D. dissertation, University of California.
    1979   Abortion Decision Making: Some Findings from Colombia. Studies in Family Planning 10(3):96–106.
    1980   The Management of Early Pregnancy: Folk Concepts of Fertility Control. Social Science and Medicine 14B(1):25–32.
    1983   Male Pregnancy Symptoms in Urban Colombia. American Ethnologist 10(3):494–511.
    1985a Criteria for Selecting Herbal Remedies. Ethnology 24(1): 13–32.
    1985b Plants Used for Reproductive Health in Oaxaca, Mexico. Economic Botany 39:482–504.
    1986   The Politics of Reproduction in a Mexican Village. Signs 11(4):710–24.
    1989a The Management of Reproduction in an Egalitarian Community. In Women Healers. Carol McClain, ed. New Brunswick, N.J.: Rutgers University Press.
    1989b Women, Household, and Health in Latin America. Social Science and Medicine 28:461–73.
Browner, Carole, and Ellen Lewin
    1982   Female Altruism Reconsidered: The Virgin Mary as Economic Woman. American Ethnologist 9(1):61–75.
Browner, C. H., and Bernard R. Ortiz de Montellano
    1986   Herbal Emmenagogues Used by Women in Colombia and Mexico. In Plants in Indigenous Medicine and Diet. N. L. Etkin, ed. Bedford Hills, N.Y.: Redgrave, 32–47.
Browner, Carole, Bernard R. Ortiz de Montellano, and Arthur J. Rubel
    1988   A Methodology for Cross-Cultural Ethnomedical Research. Current Anthropology 29(5):11–32.
Browner, C. H., and S. T. Perdue
    1988   Womens' Secrets: Bases for Reproductive and Social Autonomy in a Mexican Community. American Ethnologist 15(1):84–97.
Bruce-Chwatt, L. J.
    1980   Essential Malariology. London: William Heinemann Medical Books.
Bruhn, John G., and S. Wolf
    1979   The Roseto Story: An Anatomy of Health. Norman: University of Oklahoma Press.
Bruhn, John G., and Billy U. Philips
    1984   Measuring Social Support: A Synthesis of Current Approaches. Journal of Behavioral Medicine 7:151–69
Buchbinder, G.
    1977   Endemic Cretinism among the Maring: The By-product of Culture Contact. In T. K. Fitzgerald, ed., Nutrition and Anthropology in Action Assem: Van Gorcum, 106–16.
Buck, C., Alvaro Llopis, Enrique Najera, and Milton Terris
    1988   The Challenge of Epidemiology: Issues and Selected Readings. Washington, D.C.: Pan American Health Organization, Scientific Publication No. 505.
Buckley, Thomas
    1982   Menstruation and the Power of Yurok Women: Methods in Cultural Reconstruction. American Ethnologist 9(1): 47–61.

Bulato, R. A. and R. D. Lee, eds.
  1983   Determinants of Fertility in Developing Countries. 2 vols. San Francisco: Academic Press.
Bunzel, Ruth
  1940   The Role of Alcoholism in Two Central American Cultures. Psychiatry 3: 361–87.
  1976   Chamula and Chichicastenango: A Reexamination. In Cross-Cultural Approaches to the Study of Alcohol. Michael Everett et al., eds. The Hague: Mouton.
Burnam, M. Audrey, Richard L. Hough, Marvin Karno, Javier I. Escobar, and Cynthia A. Telles
  1987   Acculturation and Lifetime Prevalence of Psychiatric Disorders among Mexican Americans in Los Angeles. Journal of Health and Social Behavior 28:89–102
Burnet, M., and D. O. White
  1978   Natural History of Infectious Disease, 4th ed. Cambridge: Cambridge University Press.
Burns, Chester, ed.
  1977   Legacies in Law and Medicine. New York: Science History Publications.
Burr, Angela
  1984   The Ideologies of Despair: A Symbolic Interpretation of Punks and Skinheads' Usage of Barbituates. Social Science and Medicine 19 (9):929–38.
Burrow, James
  1977   Organised Medicine in the Progressive Era: The Move Toward Monopoly. Baltimore: Johns Hopkins University Press.
Bush, M. T., J. A. Ullom, and O. H. Osborne
  1975   The Meaning of Mental Health: A Report of Two Ethnoscientific Studies. Nursing Research 24:130–38.
Byerly, E. L.
  1969   The Nurse-Researcher as Participant-Observer in a Nursing Setting. Nursing Research 18:230–36.
Byerly, E. L., and C. A. Molgaard
  1982   Social Institutions and Disease Transmission. In Clinically Applied Anthropology: Anthropologists in Health Science Settings. N. Chrisman and T. Maretzki, eds. Dordrecht: D. Reidel, 395–409.
Byerly, E. L., C. A. Molgaard, and C. T. Snow
  1979   Dissonance in the Desert: What to Do with the Golden seal? In Transcultural Nursing Care: Culture Change, Ethics and Nursing Care Implications. Proceeding of the Fourth National Transcultural Nursing Conference. M. Leininger, ed. Salt Lake City: University of Utah, College of Nursing, 114–33.
Caldwell, John C.
  1981   The Mechanisms of Demographic Change in Historical Perspective. Population Studies 35(1):5–27.
  1982   Theory of Fertility Decline. San Francisco: Academic Press.
Caldwell, Robert A., and Bernard L. Bloom
  1982   Social Support: Its Structure and Impact on Marital Disruption. American Journal of Community Psychology 10:647–67
Calestro, Kenneth
  1972   Psychotherapy, Faith Healing, and Suggestion. International Journal of Psychiatry 10:83–113.
Callahan, Daniel
  1986   How Technology Is Shaping the Abortion Debate. Hastings Center Report 16:33–42.
Cameron, A.
  1960   Folk-lore as a Medical Problem among Arab Refugees. Practitioner 185:347–353.
Campbell, Gregory
  1988   Historic Health Patterns on the Northern Cheyenne Reservation. Paper presented at the Annual Meeting of the American Anthropological Association, Phoenix, Arizona, November 16–20.
Campbell, Kenneth L., and James W. Wood
  1987   Fertility in Traditional Societies. In Natural Human Fertility: Social and Biological Mechanisms. P. Diggory and S. Teper, eds. London: Macmillan.
Cannon, J. R., A. Capasso, F. N. Mascolo, G. Autore, F. de Simone, and F. Senatore
  1983   Anti-inflammatory and Analgesic Activity in Alcoholic Extract of Tamus communis L. Journal of Ethnopharmacology 8(3):321–25.
Cannon, W. B.
  1942   "Voodoo" Death. American Anthropologist 44:169–81.
Capers, Cynthia Flynn
  1985   Cultural Diversity and Nursing Practice. Topics in Clinical Nursing 7:3.
Caplan, Robert D., R. K. Naidu, and Rama C. Tripathi
  1984   Coping and Defense: Contellations vs. Components. Journal of Health and Social Behavior 25:303–20
Carbajal, D., A. Casaco, L. Arruzazabala, R. Gonzalez, and Z. Tolon
  1989   Pharmacological Study of Cymbopogon citratus Leaves. Journal of Ethnopharmacology 25:103–7.
Carey, James W.
  1988   Folk Illness: Incidence Patterns and Household Health in the Southern Peruvian Andes. Paper presented at Annual Meetings, American Anthropological Association, Phoenix.
Carlson, Katherine A.
  1977   Identifying the Stranger: An Analysis of Behavioral Rules for Sales of Heroin. In Drugs, Rituals and Altered States of Consciousness. Brian du Toit, ed. Rotterdam: A. A. Balkema.

References

Carmack, Robert M., ed.
  1988 Harvest of Violence: The Maya Indians and the Guatemalan Crisis. Norman: University of Oklahoma Press.
Carr-Saunders, E. M. and P. A. Wilson
  1933 The Professions. Oxford: Clarendon Press.
Carter, William E., ed.
  1980 Cannabis in Costa Rica. Philadelphia: Institute for the Study of Human Issues.
Cash, Richard A.
  1983 Oral Rehydration in the Treatment of Diarrhea: Issues in the Implementation of Diarrhea Treatment Programs. In Diarrhea and Malnutrition: Interactions, Mechanisms, and Interventions. Lincoln Chen and Nevin Scrimshaw, eds. New York: Plenum Press, 203–10.
Cassel, John C.
  1955 A Comprehensive Health Program among South African Zulus. In Health, Culture, and Community. B. D. Paul, ed. New York: Russell Sage Foundation, 15–41.
  1976 The Contribution of the Social Environment to Host Resistance. American Journal of Epidemiology 104:107–23
Cassel, John C., Ralph Patrick, and David Jenkins
  1960 Epidemiological Analysis of the Health Implications of Culture Change. Annals of the New York Academy of Sciences 84:938–49
Cassel, John C., and H. A. Tyroler
  1961 Epidemiological Studies of Cultural Change. Archives of Environmental Health 3(1):25–33.
Cassidy, C. M.
  1982 Protein-Energy Malnutrition as a Culture-Bound Syndrome. Culture, Medicine and Psychiatry 6:325–45.
Caudill, William
  1953 Applied Anthropology in Medicine. In Anthropology Today. A. L. Kroeber, ed. Chicago: University of Chicago Press.
  1958a Effects of Social and Cultural Systems in Reactions to Stress. New York: Social Science Research Council.
  1958b The Psychiatric Hospital as a Small Society. Cambridge: Harvard University Press.
  1962 Anthropology and Psychoanalysis: Some Theoretical Issues. In Anthropology and Human Behavior. T. Gladwin and W. C. Sturtevant, eds. Washington, D.C.: Anthropological Society of Washington, 174–214.
Chafetz, L.
  1981 Aggressive Behaviors in Walk-in Settings: Nursing responses. In Developing, Teaching and Practicing Transcultural Nursing: Proceedings of the Sixth Transcultural Nursing Conference. P. Morley, ed. Salt Lake City: University of Utah, College of Nursing and the Transcultural Nursing Society, 96–114.
Chagnon, Napoleon A.
  1968 Yanomamo Social Organization and Warfare. In War: The Anthropology of Armed Conflict and Aggression. Morton Fried, Marvin Harris, and Robert Murphy, eds. New York: Natural History Press, 109–59.
  1977 The Fierce People. 2d ed. New York: Holt, Rinehart & Winston.
Chambers, Erve J., and Philip D. Young
  1979 Mesoamerican Community Studies: The Past Decade. Annual Reviews of Anthropology 8:45–69.
Chambers, Robert
  1986 Normal Professionalism, New Paradigms, and Development. Discussion Paper 227. Brighton: Institute of Development Studies.
Chance, Norman A.
  1965 Acculturation, Self-identification, and Personality Adjustment. American Anthropologist 67:372–93
Chasin, Barbara, and Richard W. Franke
  1979 The West African Sahel: Social Roots of Ecological Disaster. ARC Newsletter 3(2): 3.
Chavez, Leo R.
  1986 Mexican Immigration and Health Care: A Political Economy Perspective. Human Organization 45(4): 344–52.
Chavunduka, G. L.
  1984 The Zimbabwe National Traditional Healers Association (ZINATHA). Harare: .
  1986 The Organisation of Traditional Medicine in Zimbabwe. In M. Last and G. L. Chavunduka, eds. The Professionalisation of African Medicine. Manchester: Manchester University Press for the International African Institute, 29–50.
Cheesmond, A. K., and A. Fenwick
  1981 Human Excretion Behaviour in a Schistosomiasis Endemic Area of the Geizira, Sudan. Journal of Tropical Medicine and Hygiene 84:101–7.
Chen, Lincoln and Nevin Scrimshaw, eds.
  1983 Diarrhea and Malnutrition: Interactions, Mechanisms, and Interventions. New York: Plenum Press.
Children's Defense Fund
  1988 Teen Age Pregnancy: The Advocates Guide to the Numbers. A Publication of the Adolescent Pregnancy Prevention Clearing House. January/March. Washington, D.C.

Chinn, P. L.
  1983 Nursing Theory Development: Where We Have Been and Where We Are Going. In The Nursing Profession: A Time to Speak. N. L. Chaska, ed. New York: McGraw-Hill, 394–405.
Chinn, P. L., ed.
  1982 From the Editor. Nursing and Culture. Advance Nursing Science 4(3):xii-xiii.
Choukri, Ghari
  1985 Conceptual Problems on the Arab Road towards a Sociology of Knowledge. Al-Mustaqbal Al-Arabi 77(7):126–36 (in Arabic).
Chrisman, Noel J.
  1977 The Health Seeking Process: An Approach to the Natural History of Illness. Culture, Medicine, and Psychiatry 1(4):351–77.
  1982 Anthropology in Nursing: An Exploration of Adaptation. In Clinically Applied Anthropology: Anthropologists in Health Science Settings. N. Chrisman and T. Maretzki, eds. Dordrecht: D. Reidel, 117–40.
  1986 Transcultural Care. In Mosby's Comprehensive Review of Critical Care. Donna Zschoche, ed. St. Louis: Mosby, chap. 2.
In press a Cultural Systems. In Cancer Nursing. X. Baird, R. McCorkle, and X. Grant, eds. Philadelphia: W.B. Saunders, chap. 4.
In press b Culture Sensitive Nursing Care. In Medical Surgical Nursing: Pathophysiologic Concepts. 2d ed. M. Patrick, S. Woods, R. Craven, J. Rokosky, and P. Bruno, eds. Philadelphia: Lippincott.
Chrisman, Noel J., and Arthur Kleinman
  1983 Popular Health Care, Social Networks, and Cultural Meanings: The Orientation of Medical Anthropology. In Handbook of Health, Health Care, and the Health Professions. David Mechanic, ed. New York: Free Press, 569–91.
Chrisman, Noel J., and Thomas W. Maretzki
  1982b Anthropology in Health Science Settings. In Noel J. Chrisman, and Thomas W Maretzki, eds. Clinically Applied Anthropology: Anthropologists in Health Science Settings. Dordrecht: D. Reidel, 1–35
Chrisman, Noel J., and Thomas W Maretzki, eds.
  1982a Clinically Applied Anthropology: Anthropologists in Health Science Settings. Dordrecht: D. Reidel.
Chukkol, Kharisu, Sufiyanu
  1981 Supernatural Belief and the Criminal Law in Nigeria: A Critical Appraisal. Zaria: Ahmadu Bello University Press.
Clark, A. L., ed.
  1978 Culture, Child-bearing, Health Professionals. Philadelphia: Davis.
Clark, Margaret, and Barbara G. Anderson
  1967 Culture and Aging. Springfield, Ill: Charles Thomas.
Clarke, Edith
  1957 My Mother Who Fathered Me. London: George Allen and Unwin.
Clarke, M.
  1978 Getting through the Work. In Readings in the Sociology of Nursing. R. Dingwall, and J. McIntosh, eds. London: Churchill Livingstone, 67–86.
Claude, Richard, Eric Stover, and June Lopez
  1987 Health Professionals and Human Rights in the Philippines. Washington, D.C.: American Association for the Advancement of Science.
Clawson, Patrick
  1978 Egypt's Industrialization: A Critique of Dependency Theory. MERIP Reports 72:17–23.
Clements, Forrest E.
  1932 Primitive Concepts of Disease. University of California Publications in American Archaeology and Ethnology 32(2): 185–252
Cleveland, David
  1986 The Political Economy of Fertility Regulation: The Kusasi of Savanna West Africa (Ghana). In Culture and Reproduction, W. Penn Handwerker, ed. Boulder: Westview, 263–93.
Clifford, James, and George E. Marcus, eds.
  1986 Writing Culture: The Poetics and Politics of Ethnography. Berkeley: University of California Press.
Coale, Ansley J.
  1969 The Decline of Fertility in Europe from the French Revolution to World War II. In Fertility and Family Planning. S.J. Behrman, Leslie Corsa and Ronald Fredman, eds. Ann Arbor: University of Michigan Press.
  1974 The History of the Human Population. Scientific American 231:41–51.
Coale, Ansley J., and Paul Demeny
  1983 Regional Model Life Tables and Stable Populations. 2d ed. New York: Academic Press.
Coale, Ansley J., and T. James Trussell
  1974 Model Fertility Schedules. Population Index 40:185–258.
  1975 Erratum. Population Index 41:572–73.
Cobb, Sidney
  1976 Social Support as a Moderator of Life Stress. Psychosomatic Medicine 38:300–14

Cochrane, S. H., D. J. O'Hara, and J. Leslie
   1980   The Effects of Education on Health. World Bank Staff Working Paper 405. Washington, D.C.: World Bank.
Cohen, David
   1988   Forgotten Millions. London: Paladin Grafton Books.
Cohen, M. N., and G. J. Armelagos, eds.
   1984   Paleopathology at the Origins of Agriculture. New York: Academic Press.
Cohen, Sheldon, and S. Leonard Syme, eds.
   1985   Social Support and Health. Orlando, Fla: Academic Press.
Cohen, Sheldon, and Thomas Ashby Wills
   1985   Stress, Social Support, and the Buffering Hypothesis. Psychological Bulletin 98:310–57
Colby, Benjamin N.
   1987   Well-being: A Theoretical Program. American Anthropologist 89:879–95.
Colby, Benjamin N., et al.
   1985   Adaptive Potential, Stress, and Illness in the Elderly. Medical Anthropology 9:283–95.
Coleman, Samuel
   1983   Family Planning in Japanese Society: Traditional Birth Control in a Modern Urban Culture. Princeton, NJ: Princeton University Press.
Collier, Jane F., and Michelle Z. Rosaldo
   1981   Politics and Gender in Simple Societies. In Sexual Meanings: The Cultural Construction of Gender and Sexuality. Sherry B. Ortner and Harriet Whitehead, eds. Cambridge: Cambridge University Press, 275–329.
Collier, Jane Fishburne, and Sylvia Junko Yanagisako, eds.
   1987   Gender and Kinship: Essays toward a Unified Analysis. Stanford: Stanford University Press.
Colson, Audrey B., and Cesario de Armellado
   1983   An American Derivation for Latin American Creole Illnesses and Their Treatment. Social Science and Medicine 17:1229–48.
Comaroff, Jean
   1982   Medicine: Symbol and Ideology. In The Problem of Medical Knowledge: Examining the Social Construction of Medicine. Peter Wright and Andrew Treacher, eds. Edinburgh: Edinburgh University Press, 49–68.
   1985   Body of Power, Spirit of Resistance: The Culture and History of a South African People. Chicago: University of Chicago Press.
   1988   The Diseased Heart of Africa: Medicine, Colonialism and the Black Body. In Analysis in Medical Anthropology. S. Lindenbaum and M. Lock, eds. Dordrecht: Kluwer Academic Publishers.
Comaroff, Jean and Peter Maguire
   1981   Ambiguity and the Search for Meaning: Childhood Leukaemia in the Modern Clinical Context. Social Science and Medicine 15B:115–23.
Connor, S., and S. Kingman
   1973   Medical Malpractice: Secretary's Commission on Medical Malpractice. Washington, D.C.: Department of Health, Education, and Welfare.
   1988   The Search for the Virus. London: Penguin Group.
Conway, M. E.
   1983   Socialization and Roles in Nursing. In Annual Review of Nursing Research. H. H. Werley, and J. J. Fitzpatrick, eds. New York: Springer, 1:183–208.
Cooper, John M.
   1933   The Cree Witiko Psychosis. Primitive Man 6:20–24.
   1934   Mental Disease Situations in Certain Cultures: A New Field for Research. Journal of Abnormal and Social Psychology 29:10–17.
Corea, Gina, Renate Duelli Klein, Jalna Hanmer, Helen B. Holmes, Betty Hoskins, Madhu Kishwar, Janice Raymond, Robyn Rowland, and Roberta Steinbacher
   1987   Man-Made Women: How New Reproductive Technologies Affect Women. Bloomington: Indiana University Press.
Corbett, Kitty King
   1986   Adding Insult to Injury: Cultural Dimensions of Frustration in the Management of Chronic Back Pain. Ph.D. dissertation, University of California, Berkeley.
Coreil, J., and E. Genece
   1988   Adoption of Oral Rehydration Therapy among Haitian Mothers. In J. Coreil and J. D. Mull, eds. Anthropological Studies of Diarrheal Illness. Special Issue of Social Science and Medicine 27 (1) 87–96.
Coreil, J., and J. D. Mull, eds.
   1988   Anthropological Studies of Diarrheal Illness. Special Issue of Social Science and Medicine 27(1):87–96.
Coser, R.
   1962   Life in the Ward. East Lansing: Michigan State University Press.
Cosminsky, Sheila
   1976   Cross-Cultural Perspectives on Midwifery. In F. X. Grollig, and Harold Haley, eds. Medical Anthropology. The Hague: Mouton Publishers, 229–49.
   1977   Childbirth and Midwifery on a Guatemalan Finca. Medical Anthropology 1(3):69–104.

Crabtree, Benjamin F., and P. J. Pelto
  1988 Anthropologists Learn Systat Computer Program for Applied and Research Purposes. Practicing Anthropology, 18–21.
Crandon, Libbet
  1983 Grass Roots, Herbs, Promoters and Preventions: A Reevaluation of Contemporary International Health Care Planning. The Bolivian Case. Social Science and Medicine 17:1281–89.
Crapanzano, Victor
  1973 The Hamadsha: A Study in Moroccan Ethnopsychiatry. Berkeley: University of California Press.
Crapanzano, Vincent, and Vivian Garrison, eds.
  1977 Case Studies in Spirit Possession. New York: John Wiley and Sons.
Crawford, Robert
  1980 Healthism and the Medicalization of Everyday Life. International Journal of Health Services 10:365–88.
  1984 A Cultural Account of Health: Self Control, Release, and the Social Body. In Issues in the Political Economy of Health Care. J. McKinlay, ed. London: Tavistock.
Crick, Malcolm R.
  1982 Anthropology of Knowledge. Annual Review of Anthropology 11:287–313.
Crosbie, Paul V.
  1986 Rationality and Models of Reproductive Decision-Making. In Culture and Reproduction. W. Penn Handwerker, ed. Boulder, Colo.: Westview, 30–58.
Csordas, Thomas J.
  1983 The Rhetoric of Transformation in Ritual Healing. Culture, Medicine, and Psychiatry 7:333–75.
  1987 Health and the Holy in African and Afro-American Spirit Possession. Social Science and Medicine 24(1):1–11.
  1988a Elements of Charismatic Persuasion and Healing. Medical Anthropology Quarterly 2:445–69.
  1988b The Conceptual Status of Hegemony an Critique in Medical Anthropology. Medical Anthropology Quarterly 2:416–21.
Cunningham, Clark
  1973 Order in the Atoni House. In Right and Left: on Dual Symbolic Classification. Rodney Needham, ed. Chicago: University of Chicago Press, 204–38.
Currier, Richard
  1969 The Hot-Cold Syndrome and Symbolic Balance in Mexican and Spanish-American Folk Medicine. In The Cross-Cultural Approach to Health Behavior. L. R. Lynch, ed. Madison, NJ: Fairleigh Dickinson University Press, 255–73.
D'Andrade, Roy G.
  1976 A Propositional Analysis of U.S. American Beliefs about Illness. In Meaning in Anthropology. K. H. Basso, and H. A. Selby, eds. Albuquerque: University of New Mexico Press, 155–80.
D'Andrade, Roy G., Naomi R. Quinn, S. B. Nerlove, and A. K. Romney
  1972 Categories of Disease in American-English and Mexican-Spanish. In Multidimensional Scaling: Theory and Applications in the Behavioral Sciences. A. K. Romney, R. N. Shephard, and S. B. Nerlove, eds. New York: Seminar Press, 9–54.
Dalton, P. R., and D. Pole
  1978 Water-Contact Patterns in Relation to Schistosoma haematobium Infection. Bulletin of the World Health Organization 56:417–26.
Daly, Mary
  1978 Gyn/Ecology. Boston: Beacon Press.
Darity, W.A.
  1965 Some Sociocultural Factors in the Administration of Technical Assistance and Training in Health. Human Organization 24(1):78–82.
Davidson, William D.
  1986 Psychiatry and Foreign Affairs: A Vision and a Commitment. Psychoanalytic Inquiry 6(2):223–42.
Davis, E. W., and J. A. Yost
  1983 The Ethnomedicine of the Waorani of Amazonian Ecuador. Journal of Ethnopharmacology 9:273–97.
Davis, Kingsley
  1959 The Myth of Functional Analysis as a Special Method in Sociology and Anthropology. American Sociological Review 24:752–71.
Davis, Kingsley, Mikhail S. Bernstam, and Rita Ricardo-Campbell, eds.
  1986 Below-Replacement Fertility in Industrial Societies. A Supplement to Volume 12, Population and Development Review.
Davis, Kingsley, and Judith Blake
  1956 Social Structure and Fertility. Economic Development and Cultural Change 4:211–35.
Davis, Shelton H.
  1988 Introduction: Sowing the Seeds of Violence. In Harvest of Violence: The Maya Indians and the Guatemalan Crisis. Robert Carmack, ed. Norman: University of Oklahoma Press, 3–36.
Davitz L. J. and J. R. Davitz
  1978 Black and White Nurses' Inferences of Suffering. Nursing Times 74:708–10.
Davitz, L. J., J. R. Davitz and Y. Higuchi
  1977 Cross-Cultural Inferences of Physical Pain and Psychological Distress—2. Nursing Times 73:536–58.

References

Davitz, L. J., Y. Sameshima, and J. R. Davitz
1976 Suffering as Viewed in Six Different Cultures. American Journal of Nursing 76:1296–97.
Day, R., et al.
1987 Stressful Life Events Preceding the Acute Onset of Schizophrenia: A Cross-Cultural Study from the World Health Organization. Culture, Medicine, and Psychiatry 11:123–205.
Delaveau, P.
1981 Evaluation of Traditional Pharmacopoeias. In Natural Products as Medicinal Agents. J. L. Beal and E. Reinhard, eds. Stuttgart: Hippokrates Verlag, 395–404.
deMause, Lloyd
1974 The History of Childhood. New York: Psychohistory Press.
1977 Jimmy Carter and American Fantasy. In Jimmy Carter and American Fantasy: Psychohistorical Explorations. Lloyd deMause and Henry Ebel, eds. New York: Two Continents/Psychohistory Press, 9–31.
1982 Foundations of Psychohistory. New York: Creative Roots.
1984 Reagan's America. New York: Creative Books.
1987 Schreber and the History of Childhood. Journal of Psychohistory 15(1):423–30.
1988 What Incest Barrier? Journal of Psychohistory 15(3):273–77.
Dennis, Philip A.
1981 Grisi Siknis among the Miskito. Medical Anthropology 5:445–504.
Dentan, Robert Knox
1988 Reply to Paul. American Anthropologist 90(2):420–21.
Department of Health, Education and Welfare
1973 Medical Malpractice: Secretary's Commission on Medical Malpractice. Department of Health, Education and Welfare. Washington, D.C.
Dervin, Daniel
1987 Abandonment: A Dominant Pattern in the Development of Creative Writers, Philosophers and Scientists since the Seventeenth Century. Journal of Psychohistory 15(2):153–87.
1988 Freud's Baby and Ours: Notes toward a Psychohistory of Psychoanalysis. Journal of Psychohistory 16(1)79–87.
Desowitz, R. S.
1981 New Guinea Tapeworms and Jewish Grandmothers: Tales of Parasites and People. New York: W. W. Norton.
Devereux, George
1955 Charismatic Leadership and Crisis. Psychoanalysis and the Social Sciences 4:145–57.
1956 Normal and Abnormal: The Key Problem of Psychiatric Anthropology. In Some Uses of Anthropology: Theoretical and Applied. J. B. Casagrande and T. Gladwin, eds. Washington, D.C.: Anthropological Society of Washington, 3–48.
1967 From Anxiety to Method in the Behavioral Sciences. The Hague: Mouton.
1976 A Study of Abortion in Primitive Societies. New York: International Universities Press.
1978 Ethnopsychoanalysis: Psychoanalysis and Anthropology as Complementary Frames of Reference. Berkeley and Los Angeles: University of California Press.
1980a Basic Problems of Ethno-Psychiatry. B. M. Gulati and G. Devereux, trans. Chicago: University of Chicago Press.
1980b Female Juvenile Sex Delinquency in a Puritanical Society. In Basic Problems of Ethno-Psychiatry. B. M. Gulati and G. Devereux, trans. Chicago: University of Chicago Press, 155–84.
1980c Normal and Abnormal. In Basic Problems of Ethnopsychiatry. B. M. Gulati and G. Devereux, trans. Chicago: University of Chicago Press, 3–71.
1980d A Sociological Theory of Schizophrenia. In Basic Problems of Ethno-Psychiatry. B. M. Gulati and G. Devereux, trans. Chicago: University of Chicago Press, 185–213.
Devich, Renatt
1985 Symbol and Psychosomatic Symptom in Bodily Space-Time: The Case of the Yaka of Zaire. International Journal of Psychology 20:589–616.
De Vos, George A.
1973 Socialization for Achievement. Berkeley: University of California Press.
De Vos, George, and L. Bryce Boyer
1988 Symbolic Analysis Crossculturally: The Rorschach Test. Berkeley and Los Angeles: University of California Press.
DeVos, George, Anthony Marsella, and Francis Hsu
1985 Approaches to Culture and the Self. In Culture and Self. Anthony Marsella, George DeVos, and Francis Hsu, eds. London: Tavistock.
deVries, Martin, R. L. Berg, and M. Lipkin, eds.
1982 The Use and Abuse of Medicine. New York: Praeger.
Dewalt, Billie R., and Pertti J. Pelto, eds.
1985 Micro and Macro Levels of Analysis in Anthropology. Colorado: Westview Press.
DeWalt, Kathleen, and John Van Willigen
1984 Research Priorities for Medical Anthropologists in the 1980's. Social Science and Medicine 18(10): 845–46.

Dewey, Kathryn
　1989　Nutrition and the Commoditization of Food Systems in Latin America and the Caribbean. Social Science and Medicine 28(5): 415–24.
Diener, P., K. Moore, and R. Mutaw
　1980　Meat Markets and Mechanical Materialism: The Great Protein Fiasco in Anthropology. Dialectical Anthropology 5:171–92.
Dillon-Malone, Clive
　1988　Matumwa Nchimi Healers and Wizardry Beliefs in Zambia. Social Science and Medicine 26:1159–72.
Dingwall, R., and P. Lewis, eds.
　1983　The Sociology of the Professions. London: Macmillan.
Dobkin de Rios, Marlene
　1975　Man, Culture, and Hallucinogens: An Overview. In Cannabis and Culture. Vera Rubin, ed. The Hague: Mouton.
　1977　Plant Hallucinogens, Out-of-Body Experiences and New World Monumental Earthworks. In Drugs, Rituals, and Altered States of Consciousness. Brian M. du Toit, ed. Rotterdam: A. A. Balkema.
　1984　Hallucinogens: Cross-Cultural Perspectives. Albuquerque: University of New Mexico Press.
Dobzhansky, Theodosius
　1970　Heredity. Encyclopedia Britannica 11:419–27
Dodge, Cole P., and Siddiq Abdel Rahman Ibrahim.
　1988　The Civilians Suffer Most. In War Wounds: Sudanese People Report on Their War. London: Panos Institute, 45–52.
Dohrenwend, Barbara S., and Bruce P. Dohrenwend, eds.
　1974　Stressful Life Events: Their Nature and Effects. New York: Wiley.
　1981　Stressful Life Events and Their Contexts. New York: Prodist.
Doll, R., and A. Bradford Hill
　1950　Smoking and Carcinoma of the Lung: Preliminary Report. In The Challenge of Epidemiology: Issues and Selected Readings. Carol Buck, Alvaro Llopis, Enrique Najera, and Milton Terris, eds. Scientific Publication 505. Washington, D.C.: Pan American Health Organization, 475–91.
　1964　Mortality in Relation to Smoking: Ten Years' Observations of British Doctors. In The Challenge of Epidemiology: Issues and Selected Readings. Carol Buck, Alvaro Llopis, Enrique Najera, and Milton Terris, eds. Scientific Publication 505. Washington, D.C.: Pan American Health Organization, 631–67.
Dominguez, Xorge, and Janis B. Alcorn
　1985　Screening of Medicinal Plants Used by Huastec Mayans of Northeastern Mexico. Journal of Ethnopharmacology 13(2):139–56.
Donahue, John M.
　1983　The Politics of Health Care in Nicaragua before and after the Revolution of 1979. Human Organization 42(3): 264–72.
　1984　Studying the Transition to Socialism in the Nicaraguan Health System. Medical Anthropology Quarterly 15(3):70–71.
　1986a　The Nicaraguan Revolution in Health. South Hadley, Mass.: Bergin and Garvey.
　1986b　Planning for Primary Health Care in Nicaragua: A Study in Revolutionary Process. Social Science and Medicine 23:149–57.
Donaldson, Peter J.
　1976　Foreign Intervention in Medical Education: A Case Study of the Rockefeller Foundation's Involvement in a Thai Medical School. International Journal of Health Services 6:251–70.
Donaldson S., and D. Crowley
　1978　The Discipline of Nursing. Nursing Outlook 26:113–20.
Dorjahn, Vernon R.
　1975　Migration in Central Sierra Leone. Africa 45:29–49.
Dougherty, Molly C.
　1982　Southern Mid-Wifery and Organized Health Care. Medical Anthropology 6(2):113–26.
　1985　Anthropologists in Nursing-Education Programs. In Training Manual in Medical Anthropology. C. E. Hill, ed. Washington D.C.: American Anthropological Association, 58–70.
Dougherty, Molly C., and Toni Tripp-Reimer
　1985　The Interface of Nursing and Anthropology. Annual Review of Anthropology 14:219–41.
Doughty, Paul L.
　1971　The Social Use of Alcoholic Beverages in a Peruvian Community. Human Organization 30(2):187–97.
Douglas, Mary
　1966　Purity and Danger. New York: Praeger.
　1970　Natural Symbols. New York: Vintage.
Douglas, Mary, ed.
　1987　Constructive Drinking: Perspectives on Drink from Anthropology. Cambridge: Cambridge University Press.
Douglas, Mary, and Aaron Wildavsky
　1982　Risk and Culture: An Essay on the Selection of Technological and Environmental Dangers. Berkeley: University of California Press.

References

Douglas, William
  1969 Death in Murelaga: Funerary Ritual in a Spanish Basque Village. Seattle: University of Washington Press.
Dow, James
  1986 Universal Aspects of Symbolic Healing: A Theoretical Synthesis. American Anthropologist 88:56–69.
Doyal, Lesley, and Imogen Pennel
  1979 The Political Economy of Health. Boston: South End Press.
Dreher, Melanie C.
  1983 Marihuana and Work: Cannabis Smoking on a Jamaican Sugar Estate. Human Organization 42(1):1–8.
  1984a Marijuana Use among Women—An Anthropological view. Advances in Alcohol and Substance Abuse 3(3):51–64.
  1984b Schoolchildren and Ganja: Youthful Marijuana Consumption in Rural Jamaica. Anthropology and Education Quarterly 15:131–50.
  1984c Anthropology and Cannabis Research. Newsletter of the Alcohol and Drug Study Group, American Anthropological Association, 12.
  1987 The Evolution of a Roots Daughter. Journal of Psychoactive Drugs 19(2):165–70.
Dressler, William W.
  1979 Disorganization, Adaptation, and Arterial Blood Pressure. Medical Anthropology 3:225–48.
  1980 Coping Dispositions, Social Supports, and Health Status. Ethos 8:146–71.
  1982 Hypertension and Culture Change: Acculturation and Disease in the West Indies. South Salem, N.Y.: Redgrave Publishing Company.
  1984a Hypertension and Perceived Stress: A St. Lucian Example. Ethos 12:265–83.
  1984b Social and Cultural Influences in Cardiovascular Disease: A Review. Transcultural Psychiatric Research Review 21:5–42.
  1985a Extended Family Relationships, Social Support, and Mental Health in a Southern Black Community. Journal of Health and Social Behavior 26:39–48.
  1985b The Social and Cultural Context of Coping. Social Science and Medicine 21:499–506.
  1985c Psychosomatic Symptoms, Stress, and Modernization: A Model. Culture, Medicine, and Psychiatry 9:257–86.
  1986a Unemployment and Depressive Symptoms in a Southern Black Community. Journal of Nervous and Mental Diseases 174:639–45.
  1986b Blood Pressure, Sex Roles, and Social Support. Abstracts of the 85th Annual Meeting of the American Anthropological Association, December 3–7, Philadelphia.
  1987 Building Models and Testing Theories in Specific Contexts. Abstracts of the 86th Annual Meeting of the American Anthropological Association, November 18–22, Chicago.
  1988 Social Consistency and Psychological Distress. Journal of Health and Social Behavior 29:79–91.
  1989a Type A Behavior and the Social Production of Cardiovascular Disease. Journal of Nervous and Mental Disease 177:181–90.
  1989b Lifestyle, Stress, and Blood Pressure in a Southern Black Community. Paper presented at the 46th Annual Meeting of the American Psychosomatic Society, March 9–11, San Francisco,
  1989c Cross-cultural Differences and Social Influences in Social Support and Cardiovascular Disease. In Social Support and Cardiovascular Disease. Sally A. Shumaker and Susan M. Czajkowski, eds. New York: Plenum Publishing.
Dressler, William W., and Henrietta Bernal
  1982 Acculturation and Stress in a Low-Income Puerto Rican Community. Journal of Human Stress 8:32–38.
Dressler, William W., Jose Ernesto Dos Santos, Philip N. Gallagher, Jr., and Fernando Viteri
  1987 Aterial Blood Pressure and Modernization in Brazil. American Anthropologist 89:389–409.
Dressler, William W., Gerald A. C. Grell, Philip N. Gallagher, Jr., and Fernando E. Viteri
  1988 Blood Pressure and Social Class in a Jamaican Community. American Journal of Public Health 78:714–16.
Dressler, William W., Alfonso Mata, Adolfo Chavez, and Fernando E. Viteri
  1987 Arterial Blood Pressure and Individual Modernization in a Mexican Community. Social Science and Medicine 24:679–87.
Dressler, William W., Alfonso Mata, Adolfo Chavez, Fernando E. Viteri, and Philip N. Gallagher
  1986 Social Support and Arterial Blood Pressure in a Central Mexican Community. Psychosomatic Medicine 48:338–350.
Dubos, Rene
  1959 Mirage of Health. New York: Harper & Row.
  1965 Man Adapting. New Haven: Yale University Press.
Duku, Oliver M.
  1988 Cut Off from Health Care. In War Wounds: Sudanese People Report on Their War. London: Panos Institute, 35–44.
Dundes, Alan
  1984 Life Is Like a Chicken Coop Ladder: A Portrait of German Culture through Folklore. New York: Columbia University Press.
  1985 The American Game of "Smear the Queer" and the Homosexual Component of Male Competitive Sport and Warfare. Journal of Psychoanalytic Anthropology 8(3):115–29.

Dunn, F.
   1968   Epidemiological Factors: Health and Disease in Hunter Gatherers. In Man the Hunter. R. B. Lee and I. DeVore, eds. Chicago: Aldine, 221–28.
   1976   Traditional Asian Medicine and Cosmopolitan Medicine as Adaptive Systems. In Asian Medical Systems: A Comparative Study. C. Leslie, ed. Berkeley and Los Angeles: University of California Press, 133–59.
   1979   Behavioural Aspects of the Control of Parasitic Diseases. Bulletin of the World Health Organization 57:499–512.
Dunn, F. L., and C. R. Janes
   1986   Introduction: Medical Anthropology and Epidemiology. In Anthropology and Epidemiology. Craig Janes, et al., eds. Dordrecht: Reidel Publishing Co., 3–34.
Dunn, Richard S.
   1972   Sugar and Slaves. Chapel Hill: University of North Carolina Press.
Durham, W. H.
   1976   The Adaptive Significance of Cultural Behavior. Human Ecology 4:89–121.
   1982   Interactions of Genetic and Cultural Evolution: Models and Examples. Human Ecology 10:289–323.
   1983   Testing the Malaria Hypothesis in West Africa. In Distribution and Evolution of Hemoglobin and Globin Loci. S. J. Bowman, ed. Dordrecht: Elsevier Science, 45–72.
Durkheim, E.
   1951   Suicide. J. Spaulding and G. Simpson, trans. New York: Free Press (orig. 1897).
   1961   The Elementary Forms of the Religious Life. Joseph Ward Swain, trans. New York: Collier (orig. 1915).
Durkin-Longley, Maureen
   1984   Multiple Therapeutic Use in Urban Nepal. Social Science and Medicine 19:867–72.
Early, Evelyn A.
   1982   The Logic of Well Being: Therapeutic Narratives in Cairo, Egypt. Social Science and Medicine 16:1491–97.
Easley, Linda
   1983   Ethnography of a Neighborhood Organization: Analysis of the Neighborhood Movement. Ph.D. Dissertation, Michigan State University.
Eastwell, H. D.
   1982   Voodoo Death and the Mechanism for Dispatch of the Dying in East Arnhem, Australia. American Anthropologist 84:5–18.
Eaton, J. W., J. R. Eckman, E. Berger, and H. S. Jacob
   1976   Suppression of Malaria Infection by Oxidant-Sensitive Host Erythrocytes. Nature 264:758–60.
Eaton, William W.
   1978   Life Events, Social Supports, and Psychiatric Symptoms. A Reanalysis of the New Haven Data. Journal of Health and Social Behavior 19:230–34.
Eban, V.
   1982   Interpretations of Infertility: The Aowin People of Southwest Ghana. In Ethnography of Fertility and Birth. Carol P. MacCormack, ed. New York: Academic Press, 41–59.
Edelmann, Robert J., and Kevin J. Connolly
   1986   Psychological Aspects of Infertility. British Journal of Medical Psychology 59(3):209–19.
Edgerton, Robert B.
   1965   Cultural vs. Ecological Factors in the Expression of Values, Attitudes and Personality Factors. American Anthropologist 67:442–47.
   1967   The Cloak of Competence. Berkeley: University of California Press.
   1971   A Traditional African Psychiatrist. Southwestern Journal of Anthropology 27:259–78.
Edholm, Felicity, Olivia Harris, and Kate Young
   1977   Conceptualizing Women. Critique of Anthropology 3:101–30.
Edungbola, L. D.
   1980   Water Utilization and Its Health Implications in Ilorin, Kwara State, Nigeria. Acta Tropica 37:73–81.
Edungbola, L. D., and S. J. Watts
   1985   Epidemiological Assessment of the Distribution and Endemicity of Guinea Worm Infection in Asa, Kwara State, Nigeria. Tropical and Geographical Medicine 37:22–28.
Ehlers, Tracy B.
   1987   A Guatemalan Town Ten Years Later. Cultural Survival Quarterly 11(3):25–29.
Ehrenreich, Barbara, and Dierdre English
   1978   For Her Own Good: 150 Years of the Experts' Advice to Women. New York: Anchor.
Ehrlich, P. R., A. H. Ehrlich, and J. P. Holdren
   1973   Human Ecology. San Francisco: W. H. Freeman.
Eisenberg, Leon
   1977   Disease and Illness: Distinctions between Professional and Popular Ideas of Sickness. Culture, Medicine and Psychiatry 1:9–23.
   1988   Science in Medicine: Too Much or Too Little and Too Limited in Scope? American Journal of Medicine 84:483–91.
El-Mehairy, Theresa
   1984   Medical Doctors: A Study of Role Concept and Job Satisfaction, the Egyptian Case. Leiden: E. J. Brill.

El-Sayed, Mustafa Kamel
   1986   Reflections on Dependency: Its Status and Theories. Kadaya Fikriya 2:18-29.
Elder, M. G., and Charles H. Hendrix, eds.
   1981   Preterm Labor. Obstetrics and Gynecology, vol. 1. London: Butterworth International Medical Reviews.
Elgood, C.
   1962   Tibb-ul-Nabi. Medicine of the Prophet. Osiris 14:33-192.
Eliot, Charles W.
   1914   Some Roads toward Peace: A Report to the Trustees of the Endowment on Observations Made in China and Japan in 1912. Washington, D.C.: Carnegie Endowment for International Peace.
Ellen, R.
   1982   Environment, Subsistence and System. Cambridge: Cambridge University Press.
Elling, Ray H.
   1981   The Capitalist World-System and International Health. International Journal of Health Services 11:21-51.
Ellison, Peter T., Nadine R. Peacock, and Catherine Lager
   1986   Salivary Progesterone and Luteal Function in Two Low-Fertility Populations of Northeast Zaire. Human Biology 58:473-83.
Endleman, Robert
   1981   Psyche and Society: Explorations in Psychoanalytic Sociology. New York: Columbia University Press.
Eng, Robert Y., and Thomas C. Smith
   1976   Peasant Families and Population Control in Eighteenth Century Japan. Journal of Interdisciplinary History 11:417-45.
Engel, George L.
   1977   The Need for a New Medical Model: A Challenge for Biomedicine. Science 196:129-36.
Engelhardt, H. Tristram
   1975   The Concepts of Health and Disease. In Evaluation and Explanation in the Biomedical Sciences. H. Tristram Engelhardt, Jr. and Stuart F. Spicker, eds. Dordrecht: D. Reidel, 125-41.
Engelmann, George J.
   1883   Labor among Primitive Peoples. St. Louis: Chambers & Co.
Erikson, Erik H.
   1950   Childhood and Society. New York: Norton.
   1974   Dimensions of a New Identity. New York: Norton.
Escobar, Arturo
   1985   Discourse and Power in Development: Michel Foucault and the Relevance of His Work to the Third World. Alternatives 10:377-400.
Escobar, G. J., E. Salazar, and M. Chung
   1983   Beliefs Regarding the Etiology and Treatment of Infantile Diarrhea in Lima, Peru. Social Science and Medicine 17:1257-69.
Estroff, Sue E.
   1981   Making It Crazy: An Ethnography of Psychiatric Clients in an American Community. Berkeley: University of California Press.
   1988   Whose Hegemony? A Critical Commentary on Critical Medical Anthropology. Medical Anthropology Quarterly (n.s.) 2(4):421-26.
Etkin, Nina L.
   1979a   Introduction. In Biomedical Evaluation of Indigenous Medical Practices. N. L. Etkin, special ed. Medical Anthropology 3(4):393-400.
   1979b   Indigenous Medicine among the Hausa of Northern Nigeria: Laboratory Evaluation for Potential Therapeutic Efficacy of Antimalarial Plant Medicinals. In Biomedical Evaluation of Indigenous Medical Practices. N. L. Etkin, special ed. Medical Anthropology 3(4):401-29.
   1981   A Hausa Herbal Pharmacopoeia: Biomedical Evaluation of Commonly Used Plant Medicines. Journal of Ethnopharmacology 4(1):75-98.
   1986a   Plants in Indigenous Medicine and Diet: Biobehavioral Approaches. Nina Etkin, ed. Bedford Hills, N.Y.: Redgrave Publishing Co.
   1986b   Multidisciplinary Perspectives in the Interpretation of Plants Used in Indigenous Medicine and Diet. In Plants in Indigenous Medicine and Diet: Biobehavioral Approaches. N. L. Etkin, ed. Bedford Hills, N.Y.:Redgrave, 2-29.
   1988a   Ethnopharmacology: Biobehavioral Approaches in the Anthropological Study of Indigenous Medicines, Annual Review of Anthropology 17:23-42.
   1988b   Cultural Constructions of Efficacy. In The Context of Medicines in Developing Countries: Studies in Pharmaceutical Anthropology. S. van der Geest and S. R. Whyte, eds. Dordrecht: Kluwer, 299-326.
Etkin, N. L., and Ross, P. J.
   1982   Food as Medicine and Medicine as Food: An Adaptive Framework for the Interpretation of Plant Utilization among the Hausa of Northern Nigeria. Social Science and Medicine 16:1559-73.
   1983   Malaria, Medicine, and Meals: Plant Use among the Hausa and Its Impact on Disease. In The Anthropology of Medicine: From Culture to Method. L. Romanucci-Ross, D. E. Moerman, and L. R. Trancredi, eds. New York: Praeger, 231-59.

Etkin, Nina L., Paul J. Ross, and Ibrahim Muazzamu
  1988 The Indigenization of Pharmaceuticals: Therapeutic Innovations in Rural Hausaland. Presented at the 87th Annual Meeting of the American Anthropological Association, Phoenix, November 16–20.
Evaneshko, V., and E. E. Bauwens
  1976 Cognitive Analysis and Decision-Making in Medical Emergencies. In Health Care Dimensions: Transcultural Health Care Issues and Conditions. M. Leininger, ed. Philadelphia: Davis, 83–102.
Evaneshko, V., and M. A. Kay
  1982 The Ethnoscience Research Technique. Western Journal of Nursing Research 4:49–64.
Evans, A. S.
  1982a Epidemiological Concepts and Methods. In Bacterial Infections of Humans: Epidemiology and Control. A. S. Evans and H. A. Feldman, eds. New York: Plenum Press, 1–48.
  1982b Epidemiological Concepts and Methods. In Viral Infections of Humans: Epidemiology and Control. A. S. Evans, ed. New York: Plenum Press, 3–42.
  1986 Epidemic Investigation. In Methods in Observational Epidemiology. J. L. Kelsey, W. D. Thompson, and A. S. Evans, eds. New York: Oxford University Press, 212–53.
Evans-Pritchard, E.E.
  1937 Witchcraft, Oracles and Magic among the Azande. Oxford: Clarendon.
  1940 The Nuer. Oxford: Oxford University Press.
Everett, Michael W., Jack O. Waddell, and Dwight B. Heath, eds.
  1976 Cross-Cultural Approaches to the Study of Alcohol: An Interdisciplinary Perspective. The Hague: Mouton.
Fabrega, Horacio, Jr.
  1970a Dynamics of Medical Practice in a Folk Community. Milbank Memorial Fund Quarterly 48:391–412.
  1970b On the Specificity of Folk Illnesses. Southwestern Journal of Anthropology 26:305–14.
  1972 Medical Anthropology. In Biennial Review of Anthropology, 1971. Bernard J. Siegel, ed. Stanford: Stanford University Press.
  1974 Disease and Social Behavior: An Interdisciplinary Perspective. Cambridge: MIT Press.
  1975 The Need for an Ethnomedical Science. Science 189:969–75.
  1976 The Function of Medical Care Systems: A Logical Analysis. Perspectives in Biology and Medicine 20:108–19.
  1977 Group Difference in the Structure of Illness. Culture, Medicine and Psychiatry 1:379–94.
  1979 The Ethnography of Illness. Social Science and Medicine 13A:565–75.
Fabrega, Horacio, Jr., and Daniel B. Silver
  1973 Illness and Shamanistic Curing in Zinacantan. Stanford: Stanford University Press.
Fahim, Hussein
  1982 Indigenous Anthropology in Non-Western Countries. Durham, N.C.: Carolina Academic Press.
  1987 Anthropology and Contemporary Arab Thought. Paper presented at the Symposium, The Arab Intelligensia, Cairo, Egypt, March 26–31.
Fairbairn, W. Ronald D.
  1954 An Object-Relations Theory of the Personality. New York: Basic Books.
Fairbank, D. T., and R. L. Hough
  1981 Cross-cultural Differences in Perceptions of Life Events. In Stressful Life Events and Their Contexts. B. S. Dohrenwend and B. P. Dohrenwend, eds. New York: Prodist.
Farooq, M.
  1966 Importance of Determining Transmission Sites in Planning Bilharziasis Control. American Journal of Epidemiology 83:603–12.
Farooq, M., and M. B. Mallah
  1966 The Behavioural Pattern of Social and Religious Water-Contact Activities in the Egypt-49 Bilharziasis Project Area. Bulletin of the World Health Organization 35:377–87.
Farooq, M., J. Nielsen, S. A. Samaan, M. B. Mallah, and A. A. Allam
  1966 The Epidemiology of Schistosoma haematobium and S. mansoni Infections in the Egypt-49 Project Area. 2. Prevalence of Bilharziasis in Relation to Personal Attributes and Habits. Bulletin of the World Health Organization 35:293–318.
Farooq, M., and S. A. Samaan
  1967 The Relative Potential of Different Age-Groups in the Transmission of Schistosomiasis in the Egypt–49 Project Area. Annals of Tropical Medicine and Parasitology 61:315–20.
Fawcett, J.
  1980 A Framework for Analysis and Evaluation of Conceptual Models of Nursing. Nursing Education 5:10–14.
Feder, Ernest
  1981 The Deterioration of the Food Situation in the Third World and the Capitalist System. International Journal of Health Services 11:247–62.
Fee, Elizabeth, ed.
  1983 Women and Health: The Politics of Sex in Medicine. Farmingdale, New York: Baywood Publishing Company.
Feierman, S.
  1986 Popular Control over the Institutions of Health: A Historical Study. In The Professionalisation of African Medicine. M. Last and G. L. Chavunduka, eds. Manchester: Manchester University Press for the International African Institute, 205–20.

References

Feinstein, Alvan R.
  1977 A Critical Overview of Diagnosis in Psychiatry. In Psychiatric Diagnosis. Vivian M. Rakoff, Harvey C. Stancer, and Henry B. Kedward, eds. New York: Brunner/Mazel, 189–206.
Feldman, D. A., and T. M. Johnson, eds.
  1986 The Social Dimensions of AIDS: Method and Theory. New York: Praeger.
Fenner, F.
  1980 Sociocultural Change and Environmental Diseases. In N.F. Stanley and R.A. Joske, eds. Changing Disease Patterns and Human Behavior. London: Academic Press, 7–26.
Fenner, F., and F. N. Ratcliffe
  1965 Myxomatosis. Cambridge: Cambridge University Press.
Fenwick, A., A. K. Cheesmond, and M. A. Amin
  1981 The Role of Field Irrigation Canals in the Transmission of Schistosoma mansoni in the Gezira Scheme, Sudan. Bulletin of the World Health Organization 59:777–86.
Fenwick, A., A. K. Cheesmond, M. Kardaman, M. A. Amin, and B. K. Manjing
  1982 Schistosomiasis among Labouring Communities in the Gezira Irrigated Area, Sudan. Journal of Tropical Medicine and Hygiene 85:3–11.
Ferguson, Anne
  1981 Commercial Pharmaceutical Medicine and Medicalization: A Case Study from El Salvador. Culture, Medicine and Psychiatry 5(2):105–34.
  1986 Class Differences in Women's Roles as Health Care Managers: A Case Study from El Salvador. Paper Presented at the National Women's Studies Association Meetings, Champagne-Urbana, June 11–15.
Ferreira, Antonio J.
  1963 Family Myth and Homeostasis. Archives of General Psychiatry 9:55–61.
Field, M. G.
  1976a Comparative Sociological Perspectives on Health Care Systems. In Arthur Kleinman et al., eds., Medicine in Chinese Cultures. Washington, D.C.: U.S. Government Printing Office.
  1976b The Modern Medical System: The Soviet Variant. In C. Leslie, ed., Asian Medical Systems. Berkeley: University of California Press, 82–102.
Fielding, N. G., and J. L. Fielding
  1986 Linking Data. Beverly Hills: Sage.
Fields, A. Belden
  1988 In Defense of Political Economy and Systemic Analysis: A Critique of Prevailing Theoretical Approaches to the New Social Movements. In Marxism and the Interpretation of Culture. Cary Nelson and Lauren Grossberg, eds. Urbana and Chicago: University of Illinois Press, 141–58.
Finkler, Kaja
  1981 Non-medical Treatments and Their Outcomes. Culture, Medicine, and Psychiatry 5:65–103.
  1985 Spiritualist Healers in Mexico: Successes and Failures in Alternative Therapeutics. South Hadley, Mass.: Bergin & Garvey Publishers.
  1986 The Social Consequences of Wellness: A View of Healing Outcomes from Micro and Macro Perspectives. International Journal of Health Services 16(4):627–42.
Firth, Raymond
  1975 The Sceptical Anthropologists? Social Anthropology and Marxist Views of Society. In Marxist Analysis and Social Anthropology. Maurice Block, ed. New York: John Wiley, 29–60.
  1981 Engagement and Detachment: Reflections on Applying Social Anthropology to Public Affairs. Human Organization 40:193–201.
Fisher, A. D.
  1987 Alcoholism and Race: The Misapplication of Both Concepts to North American Indians. Canadian Review of Sociology and Anthropology 24(1):81–98.
Fisher, S., and S. Cleveland
  1958 Body Image and Personality. Princeton, N.J.: D. Van Nostrand.
Flaskerud, J. H.
  1979 Use of Vignettes to Elicit Responses toward Broad Concepts. Nursing Research 28:210–12.
  1980a Perceptions of Problematic Behavior by Appalachians, Mental Health Professions, and Lay Non-Appalachians. Nursing Research 29:140–49.
  1980b Tool for Comparing the Perceptions of Problematic Behavior by Psychiatric Professionals and Minority Groups. Nursing Research 29:4–9.
Flaskerud, J. H., and E. Halloran
  1980 Areas of Agreement in Nursing Theory Development. Advances in Nursing Science 3(1):1–7.
Fletcher, Robert H., Suzanne W. Fletcher, and Edward H. Wagner
  1982 Clinical Epidemiology—The Essentials. Baltimore: Williams & Wilkins.
Flick, L. H.
  n.d. Analysis of Adolescent Pregnancy Rates. Personal communication.
Flint, M.
  1975 The Menopause: Reward or Punishment? Psychosomatics 16:161–63.
Folkman, Susan
  1984 Personal Control and Stress and Coping Processes: A Theoretical Analysis. Journal of Personality and Social Psychology 46:839–52

Folkman, Susan, and Richard S. Lazarus
   1988   The Relationship between Coping and Emotion: Implications for Theory and Research. Social Science and Medicine 26:309–17

Fong, Carolyn Mae
   1985   Ethnicity and Nursing Practice. Topics in Clinical Nursing 7(3):1–11.

Forbes, R.
   1948   Sixty Years of Medical Defence. London: Medical Defence Union.

Ford, Clellan Stearns
   1945   A Comparative Study of Human Reproduction. Yale University Publications in Anthropology. New Haven: Human Relations Area File Press.

Ford, T. R., and D. D. Stephenson
   1954   Institutional Nurses: Roles, Relationships and Attitudes in Three Alabama Hospitals. Tuscaloosa: University of Alabama Press.

Fortes, Meyer
   1959   Oedipus and Job in West African Religion. Cambridge: Cambridge University Press.

Foster, George M.
   1953   Relationships between Spanish and Spanish-American Folk Medicine. Journal of American Folklore 66:201–17.
   1958   Problems of Intercultural Health Programs. New York: Social Science Research Council.
   1965   Peasant Society and the Image of the Limited Good. American Anthropologist 67:293–315.
   1974   Medical Anthropology: Some Contrasts with Medical Sociology. Medical Anthropology Newsletter 6(1):1–6.
   1978a   Hippocrates' Latin American Legacy: "Hot" and "Cold" in Contemporary Folk Medicine. In Colloquia in Anthropology. R. K. Wetherington, ed. Dallas: Southern Methodist University, 3–19.
   1978b   Humoral Pathology in Spain and Spanish America. In Homenaje a Julio Caro Baroja. A. Carreira, J. A. Cid, M. Gutierrez Esteve, and R. Rubio, eds. Madrid: Centro de Investigaciones Sociologicas, 357–70.
   1984a   The Concept of "Neutral" in Humoral Medical Systems. Medical Anthropology 8:181–94.
   1984b   Anthropological Research Perspectives on Health Problems in Developing Countries. Social Science and Medicine 18(10):847–54.
   1987a   World Health Organization Behavioral Science Research: Problems and Prospects. Social Science and Medicine 24:709–15.
   1987b   Bureaucratic Aspects of International Health Agencies. Social Science and Medicine 25:1039–48.

Foster, George M., and Barbara Gallatin Anderson
   1978   Medical Anthropology. New York: Wiley.

Foucault, Michel
   1973   Madness and Civilization: A History of Insanity in the Age of Reason. New York: Vintage.
   1975   The Birth of the Clinic: An Archeology of Medical Perception. New York: Vintage.
   1979   Discipline and Punish: The Birth of the Prison. New York: Vintage.
   1980a   The History of Sexuality, vol. 1: An Introduction. New York: Vintage.
   1980b   Power/Knowledge: Selected Interviews and Other Writings. New York: Pantheon.
   1984   Politics and Ethics: An Interview. In The Foucault Reader. P. Rabinow, ed. New York: Pantheon, 373–90.
   1988   Truth, Power, Self: An Interview with Michel Foucault. In L. Martin, H. Gutman, and P. Hutton, eds. Technologies of the Self. Amherst: University of Massachusetts Press, 9–16.

Fourastié, Jean
   1972   From the Traditional to the "Tertiary Life Cycle." In Readings in Population. William Petersen, ed. New York: Macmillan.

Fox, Renee
   1959   Experiment Perilous. New York: Free Press.

Frake, Charles O.
   1961   The Diagnosis of Disease among the Subanum of Mindanao. American Anthropologist 63:113–32.

Franco, Jean
   1988   Beyond Ethnocentrism: Gender, Power, and the Third World Intelligentsia. In Marxism and the Interpretation of Culture. Cary Nelson and Lawrence Grossberg, eds. Urbana: University of Illinois Press, 508–15.

Franco-Agudelo, Saul
   1983   The Rockefeller Foundation's Antimalarial Program in Latin America: Donating or Dominating? International Journal of Health Services 13:51–67.

Frank, Andre G.
   1975   Anthropology-Ideology, Applied Anthropology-Politics. Race and Class 17(1):57–68.
   1977   Dependence Is Dead, Long Live Dependence and the Class Struggle: An Answer to Critics. World Development 5(4):355–370.

Frank, Jerome
   1973   Persuasion and Healing. Rev. ed. Baltimore: Johns Hopkins University Press.
   1978   Psychotherapy and the Human Predicament. New York: Schocken.

Frankenberg, Ronald
   1974   Functionalism and After? Theory and Developments in Social Science Applied to the Health Field. International Journal of Health Services 4(3):411–27.

1978 Economic Anthropology or Political Economy? The Barotose Social Formation: A Case Study. In The New Economic Anthropology. J. Clammer, ed. New York: St. Martin's Press, 32–57.
1980 Medical Anthropology and Development: A Theoretical Perspective. Social Science and Medicine 14b(4):197–207.
1988a "Your Time or Mine?" An Anthropological View of the Tragic Temporal Contradictions of Biomedical Practice. International Journal of Health Services 18(1):11–34.
1988b Gramsci, Culture and Medical Anthropology: Kundry and Parsifal? Or Rat's Tail to Sea Serpent? Medical Anthropology Quarterly 2:324–37.
1988c Rejoinder. Medical Anthropology Quarterly (n.s.) 2(4):454–59.
Frazer, James George
1911 The Golden Bough. Vols. 1–2, Pt. 1. 3d ed. London: Macmillan.
Freeland, W. J., P. H. Calcott, and Lisa R. Anderson
1985 Tannins and Saponin: Interaction in Herbivore Diets. Biochemical Systematics and Ecology 13(2):189–93.
Freidson, Elliot
1970 Profession of Medicine: A Study of the Sociology of Applied Knowledge. New York: Harper & Row.
1972 Client Control and Medical Practice. In Patients, Physicians, and Healers. E. Gartly Jaco, ed. New York: Free Press, 214–21.
1986 Professional Powers: A Study of the Institutionalisation of Formal Knowledge. Chicago: University of Chicago Press.
Freidson, Elliot, and J. Lorber, eds.
1972 Medical Men and Their Work: A Sociological Reader. Chicago: Aldine.
French, C. M., and G. S. Nelson
1982 Hydatid Disease in the Turkana District of Kenya. II. A Study in Medical Geography. Annals of Tropical Medicine and Parasitology 76:439–57.
French, C. M., G. S. Nelson, and M. Wood
1982 Hydatid Disease in the Turkana District of Kenya. I. The Background to the Problem with Hypotheses to Account for the Remarkably High Prevalence of the Disease in Man. Annals of Tropical Medicine and Parasitology 76:425–37.
French, John R. P., Jr., W. Rodgers, and Sidney Cobb
1974 Adjustment as Person-Environment Fit in Coping and Adaptation. George V. Coelho, David A. Hamburg, and John E. Adams, eds. New York: Basic Books.
Freud, Anna
1936 The Ego and the Mechanisms of Defense. New York: International Universities Press.
Freud, Sigmund
1920 Beyond the Pleasure Principle. The Standard Edition of the Complete Psychological Works of Sigmund Freud (SE). London: Hogarth Press, 1955, 18:3–64.
1923 The Ego and the Id. SE. London: Hogarth Press, 1961, 19:3–36.
1927 The Future of an Illusion. SE. London: Hogarth Press, 1961, 21:5–56.
Freund, Paul, and Mac Marshall
1977 Research Bibliography of Alcohol and Kava Studies in Oceania: Update and Additional Items. Micronesia 13: 313–17.
Friedl, John
1982 Explanatory Models of Black Lung: Understanding the Health-Related Behavior of Appalachian Coal Miners. Culture, Medicine and Psychiatry 6:3–10.
Friedlander, Myrna L., Theodore J. Ksul, and Carolyn A. Stimel
1984 Abortion: Predicting the Complexity of the Decision- Making Process. Women and Health 9(1):43–54.
Friedman, G. D.
1987 Primer of Epidemiology. New York: McGraw-Hill.
Friedman, Paul
1983 The Relevance of Anthropology for Clinical Work: The Observations of a Physician-Social Scientist. In Clinical Anthropology. Demitri Shimkin and Peggy Golde, eds. Lanham, Md.: University Press of America, 239–45.
Fuchs, Fritz, and Phillip G. Stubblefield, eds.
1984 Preterm Birth: Causes, Prevention, and Management. New York: Macmillan.
Fuller, G. K., and D. C. Fuller
1981 Hydatid Disease in Ethiopia: Epidemiological Findings and Ethnographic Observations of Disease Transmission in Southwestern Ethiopia. Medical Anthropology 5:293–311.
Furbee, L., and R. A. Benfer
1983 Cognitive and Geographic Maps: Study of Individual Variation among Tojolabal Mayans. American Anthropologist 85:305–34.
Furst, Peter T.
1976 Hallucinogens and Culture. San Francisco: Chandler and Sharp.
Furst, Peter T., ed.
1972 Flesh of the Gods: The Ritual Use of Hallucinogens. New York: Praeger.
Gailey, Christine Ward
1987 Kinship to Kingship. Austin: University of Texas Press.

Gaines, Atwood D.
  1982 Knowledge and Practice: Anthropological Ideas and Psychiatric Practice. In Noel J. Chrisman and Thomas W. Maretzki, eds., Clinically Applied Anthropology: Anthropologists in Health Science Settings. Dordrecht: D. Reidel, 243–75.
Galaty, J. G., Dan Aronson, P. C. Salzman, and Amy Chouinard, eds.
  1981 The Future of Pastoral Peoples. Ottawa: International Development Research Center.
Galazka, S., and J. K. Eckert
  1986 Clinically Applied Anthropology: Concepts for the Family Physician. Journal of Family Practice 22(2):159–65.
Gallagher, Catherine
  1986 The Body versus the Social Body in the Works of Thomas Malthus and Henry Mayhew. Representations 14:83–106.
Galloway, Patrick R.
  1986 Long-Term Fluctuations in Climate and Population. Population and Development Review 12:1–24.
GAP (Group for the Advancement of Psychiatry)
  1987 Us and Them: The Psychology of Ethnonationalism. GAP Report 123 by the Committee on International Relations with H. F. Stein. New York: Brunner/Mazel.
Garfield, Sol. L.
  1986 Problems in Diagnostic Classification. In Contemporary Directions in Psychopathology toward the DSM-IV. Theodore Millon and Gerald L. Klerman, eds. New York: Guilford Press, 99–114.
Garn, S. M., N. J. Smith, and D. C. Clark
  1975 The Magnitude and the Implications of Apparent Race Differences in Hemoglobin Values. American Journal of Clinical Nutrition 28:563–68.
Garnsey, Peter
  1988 Famine and Food Supply in the Graeco-Roman World. Cambridge: Cambridge University Press.
Garrison, Vivian
  1977a Doctor, Espiritista, or Psychiatrist: Health Seeking Behavior in a Puerto Rican Neighborhood of New York City. Medical Anthropology 1:65–91.
  1977b The "Puerto Rican Syndrome" in Psychiatry and Espiritismo. In Case Studies in Spirit Possession. V. Crapanzano, and V. Garrison, eds. New York: Wiley, 383–449.
Garro, Linda C.
  1986 Intracultural Variation in Folk Medical Knowledge: A Comparison between Curers and Noncurers. American Anthropologist 88:351–70.
  1988 Explaining High Blood Pressure: Variation in Knowledge about Illness. American Ethnologist 15:98–119.
Gbeassor, M., Y. Kossou, K. Amegbo, C. de Souza, K. Koumaglo, and A. Denke
  1989 Antimalarial Effects of Eight African Medicinal Plants. Journal of Ethnopharmacology 25:115–18.
Gebrian, B.
  1989 Haitian Health Foundation Primary Health Care Program. Annual Report Unpublished.
  n.d. Personal Communication.
Geertz, Clifford
  1973a The Interpretation of Cultures: Selected Essays. New York: Basic Books.
  1973b Ideology as a Cultural System. In C. Geertz, ed. The Interpretation of Cultures. New York: Basic Books, 193–234.
  1973c Religion as a Cultural System. In C. Geertz ed. The Interpretation of Cultures. New York: Basic Books, 87–126.
  1980 Negara: The Theatre-State in Nineteenth Century Bali. Princeton: Princeton University Press.
  1984 From the Native's Point of View: On the Nature of Anthropological Understanding. In Culture Theory. Richard Shweder and Robert LeVine, eds. Cambridge: Cambridge University Press, 123–36.
Gehrie, Mark J.
  1976 Childhood and Community: On the Experience of Young Japanese Americans in Chicago. Ethos 4(3):353–83.
Geison, Gerald L., ed.
  1984 Professions and the French State, 1700–1900. Philadelphia: University of Pennsylvania Press.
Gelfand, T.
  1980 Professionalising Modern Medicine: Paris Surgeons and Medical Science and Institutions in the Eighteenth Century. Westport, Conn.: Greenwood Press.
Gelso, Charles, and Jean Canter
  1985 The Relationship in Counseling and Psychotherapy: Components, Consequences, and Theoretical Antecedents. Counseling Psychologist 13:155–243.
George, Susan
  1979 How the Other Half Dies: The Real Reasons for World Hunger. Montclair, N.J.: Allanheld, Osmun.
  1981 Feeding the Few: Corporate Control of Food. Washington, D.C.: Institute for Policy Studies.
Germain, C.
  1979 The Cancer Unit: An Ethnography. Wakefield, Mass.: Nursing Resources.
Geschiere, P.
  1988 Sorcery and the State. Critique of Anthropology 6(1):35–63.

References

Geser, A., et al.
   1978 Environmental Factors in the Etiology of Nasopharyngeal Carcinoma: Report on a Case-Control Study in Hong Kong. In G. de-The and Y. Ito, eds., NPC: Etiology and Control. Lyon: IARC, 213–29.

Gezira Board
   1987 The Gezira Scheme: Past, Present and Future. Wad Medani, Sudan: Gezira Scheme Board.

Gibb, G. D.
   1984 A Comparative Study of Recidivists and Contraceptors along the Dimensions of Control and Impulsivity. International Journal of Psychiatry 19(6):581–91.

Gilbert, M. Jean
   1980 Los Parientes: Social Structural Factors and Kinship Relations among Second Generation Mexican Americans. Ph.D. dissertation, University of California, Santa Barbara.

Gilbert, M. Jean, and Richard C. Cervantes
   1987 Mexican Americans and Alcohol. Monograph 11. Los Angeles: Spanish Speaking Mental Health Research Center.

Gilbert, Robert I., and James H. Mielke, eds.
   1985 The Analysis of Prehistoric Diets. Orlando: Academic Press.

Gish, Oscar, and Martin Godfrey
   1979 A Reappraisal of the "Brain Drain" with Special Reference to the Medical Profession. Social Science and Medicine 18C:1–44.

Gittelsohn, J.
   1989 Intrahousehold Food Distribution in Rural Nepal. Ph.D. dissertation, University of Connecticut.

Glander, K. E.
   1982 The Impact of Plant Secondary Compounds on Primate Feeding Behavior. Yearbook of Physical Anthropology 25:1–18.

Glick, Leonard B.
   1967 Medicine as an Ethnographic Category: The Gimi of the New Guinea Highlands. Ethnology 6:31–56.

Glittenberg, J. E.
   1981 Variations in Stress and Coping in Three Migrant Settlements—Guatemala City. Image 13:43–46.

Gluckman, Max
   1965 Foreword to Sorcery in Its Social Setting, by Max Marwick. Manchester: Manchester University Press.

Gluckman, Max, ed.
   1964 Closed Systems and Open Minds: The Limits of Naivety in Social Anthropology. Chicago: Aldine.

Goforth, Lynnel
   1988 Household Structure and Birth Attendant Choice in a Yucatec Maya Community. Ph.D. dissertation, University of California, Los Angeles.

Golde, Peggy
   1983a Foreword: Clinical Anthropology as a Committed Profession. In Clinical Anthropology. Demitri Shimkin and Peggy Golde, eds. Lanham, Md.: University Press of America, 27–37.
   1983b Anthropological Contributions to Psychotherapy: an Overview. In Clinical Anthropology. Demetri Shimkin and Peggy Golde, eds. Pp. 75–86. Lanham, Md: University Press of America.

Golde, Peggy, and Demitri B. Shimkin
   1980 Clinical Anthropology—An Emerging Health Profession? Medical Anthropology Newsletter 12(1):15–16.

Goldsmith, Douglas S., Dana E. Hunt, Douglas S. Lipton, and David L. Strug
   1984 Methadone Folklore: Beliefs About Side Effects and Their Impact on Treatment. Human Organization 43 (4):330–40.

Golladay, Frederick, and Bernhard Liese
   1980 Health Problems and Policies in Developing Countries. Washington, D.C.: The World Bank.

Golomb, Lewis
   1986 Rivalry and Diversity Among Thai Curer-Magicians. Social Science and Medicine 22:691–97.

Gonen, Jay, Y.
   1975 A Psychohistory of Zionism. New York: Mason Charter.

Good, Byron J.
   1977 The Heart of What's the Matter: The Semantics of Illness in Iran. Culture, Medicine and Psychiatry 1:25–58.

Good, Byron J. and Mary-Jo Delvecchio Good
   1981 The Meaning of Symptoms: A Cultural Hermeneutic Model for Clinical Practice. In L. Eisenberg and A. Kleinman, eds. The Relevance of Social Science for medicine. Dordrecht: D. Reidel, 165–97.

Good, Byron J., Mary Jo Del Vecchio Good, and Robert Moradi
   1985 The Interpretation of Iranian Depressive Illness and Dysphoric Affect. In Arthur Kleinman and Byron Good, eds., Culture and Depression. Berkeley, Calif.: University of California Press.

Good, Byron J., and Arthur Kleinman
   1985 Epilogue: Culture and Depression. In Culture and Depression: Arthur Kleinman and Byron Good eds. Berkeley, Calif.: University of California Press.

Good, C.M.
   1987 Ethnomedical Systems in Africa: Patterns of Traditional Medicine in Urban and Rural Kenya. New York: Guilford Press.

Good, Mary-Jo Delvecchio, and Byron J. Good
  1988 Ritual, the State, and the Transformation of Emotional Discourse in Iranian Society. Culture, Medicine and Psychiatry 12:43–63.
Goodenough, Ward
  1963 Cooperation in Change. New York: Russell Sage Foundation.
Goodman, Steven M., and Joseph J. Hobbs
  1988 The Ethnobotany of the Egyptian Eastern Desert: A Comparison of Common Plant Usage between Two Culturally Distinct Bedouin Groups. Journal of Ethnopharmacology 23:73–89.
Goody, Jack
  1977 The Domestication of the Savage Mind. Cambridge: Cambridge University Press.
Goonatilake, S.
  1984 Aborted Discovery: Science and Creativity in the Third World. London: Zed Press.
Gordon, Andrew J., ed.
  1978 Ethnicity and Alcohol Use. Medical Anthropology 2 (4): entire issue.
Gordon, Deborah
  1988 Tenacious Assumptions in Western Medicine. In Biomedicine Examined. Margaret Lock and Deborah Gordon, eds. Dordrecht: D. Reidel.
Gore, Susan
  1985 Social Support and Styles of Coping with Stress. In Social Support and Health. S. Cohen and S. L. Syme, eds. Orlando, Florida: Academic Press.
Gorman, M.E.
  1986 The AIDS Epidemic in San Francisco: Epidemiological and Anthropological Perspectives. In Anthropology and Epidemiology. C.R. Janes, R. Stall, and S.M. Gifford, eds., Dordrecht: Reidel, 157–72.
Gough, Kathleen
  1968 World Revolution and the Science of Man. In The Dissenting Academy. Theodore Rosak, ed. London: Chatto and Windus, Ltd.
Gough, Kathleen, and H. Sharma, eds.
  1975 Imperialism and Revolution in South Asia. New York: Monthly Review Press.
Gould, Harold
  1965 Modern Medicine and Folk Cognition in Rural India. Human Organization 24:201–8.
Graham, Joe S.
  1976 The Role of Curanderos in the Mexican-American Folk System in West Texas. In American Folk Medicine. W. D. Hand, ed. Berkeley and Los Angeles: University of California Press, 175–89.
Gran, Peter
  1979 Medical Pluralism in Arab and Egyptian History: An Overview of Class Structures and Philosophies of the Main Phase. Social Science and Medicine 13(B):339–48.
Grant, James P.
  1988 The State of the World's Children 1988. Oxford: Oxford University Press.
Graves, Theodore D.
  1967 Acculturation, Access, and Alcohol in a Tri-Ethnic Community. American Anthropologist 69: 306–21.
Graves, Theodore D., and Nancy B. Graves
  1979 Stress and Health: Modernization in a Traditional Polynesian Society. Medical Anthropology 3:23–59
  1980 Kinship Ties and the Preferred Adaptive Strategies of Urban Migrants. In The Versatility of Kinship. Linda S. Cordell and Stephen J. Beckerman, eds. New York: Academic Press
  1985 Stress and Health Among Polynesian Migrants to New Zealand. Journal of Behavioral Medicine 8:1–19
Graves, Theodore D., Nancy B. Graves, Vineta N. Semu, and Iulai Ah Sam
  1982 Patterns of Public Drinking in a Multiethnic Society: A Systematic Observational Study. Journal of Studies on Alcohol 43: 990–1009.
Gray, R.H.
  1974 The Decline of Mortality in Ceylon and the Demographic Effects of Malaria Control. Population Studies 28:205–29.
Gray, Ronald
  1983 The Impact of Health and Nutrition on Natural Fertility. In Determinants of Fertility in Developing Countries. R.A. Bulatao and R.D. Lee, eds. vol. 1, 139–63. New York: Academic Press.
Green, Edward C.
  1985 Traditional Healers, Mothers and Childhood Diarrheal Disease in Swaziland: the Interface of Anthropology and Health Education. Social Science and Medicine 20(3):277–85.
Greenberg, Joel
  1988 U.S. Doctors Find 'Epidemic of Army Violence' in Areas. Jerusalem Post 12 February: 1,4.
Greenberg, R. S., and M. A. Ibrahim
  1985 Epidemiological Techniques and Planned Investigation: The Case-Control Study. In Oxford Textbook of Public Health. vol. 3. Investigative Methods in Public Health. Walter W. Holland, Roger Detels, and George Knox, eds. Oxford: Oxford University Press.
Greene, L.S.
  1973 Physical Growth and Development, Neurological Maturation, and Behavioral Functioning in Two Ecuadorian Andean Communities in Which Goiter is Endemic. I. Outline of the Problem of Endemic Goiter and Cretinism. Physical Growth and Neurological Maturation in the Adult Population of La Esperanza. American Journal of Physical Anthropology 38:119–34.

1977 Hyperendemic Goiter, Cretinism, and Social Organization in Highland Ecuador. In Malnutrition, Behavior, and Social Organization. L.S. Green, ed. New York: Academic Press, 55–94.
1980 Social and Biological Predictors of Physical Growth and Neurological Development in an Area Where Iodine and Protein- Energy Malnutrition are Endemic. In Social and Biological Predictors of Nutritional Status, Physical Growth and Neurological Development. L.S. Greene and F.E. Johnston, eds. New York: Academic Press, 223–56.

Greene, Owen, Barry Rubin, Neil Turok, Philip Webber, and Graeme Wilkinson
1982 London after the Bomb: What a Nuclear Attack Really Means. Oxford: Oxford University Press.

Greenhalgh, Susan
1985a Is Inequality Demographically Induced? American Anthropologist 87:571–94.
1985b Sexual Stratification: The Other Side of "Growth with Equity" in East Asia. Population and Development Review 11:265–314.
1989 New Directions in Fertility Research: Anthropological Perspectives. Paper prepared for the General Conference of the IUSSP, September 20–27, New Delhi.

Greep, R. O., M. A. Koblinsky, and F. S. Jaffe.
1976 Reproduction and Human Welfare: A Challenge to Research. Cambridge: MIT Press.

Grey-Turner, E., and F. M. Sutherland
1982 History of the British Medical Association, vol.2, 1932–1981. London: British Medical Association.

Griaule, Marcel
1965 Conversations with Ogotemmeli. Oxford: Oxford University Press.

Grossinger, Richard
1980 Planet Medicine: From Stone Age Shamanism to Post- Industrial Healing. Garden City, N.Y.: Doubleday.

Gruenbaum, Ellen
1981 Medical Anthropology, Health Policy and the State: A Case Study of Sudan. Review 1: 47–65.
1983 Struggling with the Mosquito: Malaria Policy and Agricultural Development in Sudan. Medical Anthropology 7(2):51–62.

Gulliver, Philip H.
1957 Nyakyusa Labour Migration. Journal of the Rhodes-Livingstone Institute 21:32–63.
1958 Land Tenure and Social Change among the Nyakyusa. Kampala: East African Institute of Social Research.

Gussow, Zachary W.
1960 'Piblotoq' (Hysteria) among the Polar Eskimo: An Ethno-Psychiatric Study. In Psychoanalysis and the Social Sciences. W. Muensterberger and S. Axelrod, eds, New York, N.Y.: International Universities Press.

Guttentag, Marcia, and Paul F. Secord
1983 Too Many Women? Beverly Hills: Sage.

Guttmacher, Sally and L. Garcia
1975 Social Science and Health in Cuba. Ideology, Planning and Health. In Topias and Utopias. S. Ingman and A. Thomas, eds. The Hague: Mouton.

Hackenberg, Robert A., Beverly H. Hackenberg, Henry F. Mogalit, Esperanza I. Cabral, and Santiago V. Guzman
1983 Migration, Modernization, and Hypertension. Medical Anthropology 7:45–71.

Hagey, R.S.
1980 Healing Entrepreneurship in the Phillipines. PhD dissertation, Case Western Reserve University.

Hahn, Robert A.
1983 Biomedical Practice and Anthropological Theory: Frameworks and Directions. Annual Review of Anthropology 12:305–33.
1984 Rethinking "Illness" and "Disease." Contributions to Asian Studies 18:1–23.
1985a Portrait of an Internist. In Robert A. Hahn and Atwood D. Gaines, eds, Physicians of Western Medicine: Anthropological Approaches to Theory and Practice. Dordrecht: D. Reidel, 51–115.
1985b Culture-Bound Syndromes Unbound. Social Science and Medicine 21:165–171.

Hahn, Robert A., and Atwood D. Gaines, eds.
1985 Physicians of Western Medicine: Anthropological Approaches to Theory and Practice. Holland: D. Reidel.

Hahn, Robert, and Arthur Kleinman
1983 Belief as Pathogen, Belief as Medicine. Medical Anthropology Quarterly 14(4):3, 16–19.
1984 Biomedical Practice and Anthropological Theory. Annual Review of Anthropology 12: 305–33.

Haldane, J. B. S.
1949 Disease and Evolution. La Ricerca Scientifica 19:68–76.

Hale, Sondra
1981 History, Development, and Liberation: Northern Sudanese Women. Paper presented at the African Studies Association Annual Meeting, Los Angeles, November.

Halifax, Joan, and H. Weidman
1973 Religion as a Mediating Institution in Acculturation. In Richard Cox, ed., Religious Systems and Psychotherapy. Springfield, Ill.: Charles C. Thomas.

Hall, R. L., V. M. Hesselbrock, and J. R. Stabenau
1983 Familial Distribution of Alcohol Use: I Assortative Mating in the Parents of Alcoholics. Behavior Genetics 13: 361–72.

Hall, Roberta A.
1986 Alcohol Treatment in American Indian Populations: An Indigenous Treatment Modality Compared with Traditional Approaches. In Alcohol and Culture. Thomas F. Babor, ed. New York: New York Academy of Sciences.

Hallowell, A. I.
  1934   Culture and Mental Disorder. Journal of Abnormal and Social Psychology 29:1–9.
Halmos, P.
  1973   Professonalisation and Social Change. Keele, U.K.: Sociological Review.
Hammady, Iman
  1979   Islamic Medical Centers in Egypt: A Case Study. Unpublished abstract of research in progress.
Hammel, E.A.
  1983   The China Lectures. Program in Population Research Working Paper 10, University of California, Berkeley.
Hammel, E. A., and Nancy Howell
  1987   Research in Population and Culture: An Evolutionary Framework. Current Anthropology 28:141–60
Hammerschmidt, Dale E.
  1986   Chinese Diet and Traditional Materia Medica: Effects on Platelet Function and Atherogenesis. In Plants in Indigenous Medicine and Diet. N. L. Etkin, ed. Beford Hills: Redgrave, 171–85.
Hammond, E.C., I. J. Selikoff, and H. Seidman
  1979   Asbestos Exposure, Cigarette Smoking and Death Rates. Annals of the New York Academy of Sciences 330:473–90.
Handlin, Oscar
  1951   The Uprooted. Boston: Little, Brown.
Handwerker, W. Penn
  1974   Changing Household Organization in the Origins of Market Places in Liberia. Economic Development and Cultural Change 22:229–48.
  1979   Daily Markets and Urban Economic Development. Human Organization 40:27–39.
  1980   Market Places, Travelling Traders, and Shops: Commercial Structural Variation in the Liberian Interior prior to 1940. African Economic History 9:3–26.
  1983   The First Demographic Transition. American Anthropologist 85:5–27.
  1986   The Modern Demographic Transition. American Anthropologist 88:400–17.
  1988   Sampling Variability in Microdemographic Estimation of Fertility Parameters. Human Biology 60:305–18.
  1989a   Women's Power and Social Revolution. Newbury Park, Calif.: Sage.
  1989b   The Origins and Evolution of Culture. American Anthropologist 91(2): 313–27.
  1989c   Population, Power, and Evolution. manuscript.
Hanks, L. M., Jr., and J. R. Hanks
  1955   Diphtheria Immunization in a Thai Community. In: B. D. Paul, ed., Health, Culture, and Community. New York: Russell Sage Foundation, 155–85.
Hanna, Joel M., Gary D. James, and Joann M. Martz
  1986   Hormonal Measures of Stress. In The Changing Samoans: Behavior and Health in Transition. Paul T. Baker, Joel M.Hanna, and Thelma S. Baker eds. New York: Oxford University Press.
Haraway, Donna
  1988   The Biopolitics of Postmodern Bodies: Determinations of Self in Immune System Discourse. Manuscript prepared for the Wenner-Gren Foundation in Anthropology.
Hardy, M.
  1983   Metaparadigms and Theory Development. In The Nursing Profession: A Time to Speak. N. L. Chaska, ed. New York: McGraw-Hill, 421–37.
Haring, Douglas, ed.
  1956   Personal Character and Cultural Milieu. Syracuse: Syracuse University Press.
Harrell, B. B.
  1981   Lactation and Menstruation in Cultural Perspective. American Anthropology 83:796–823.
Harris, Grace
  1978   Casting Out Anger: Religion among the Taita of Kenya. Cambridge: Cambridge University Press.
Harris, Marvin, and Eric B. Ross, eds.
  1987a   Death, Sex, and Fertility. New York: Columbia University Press.
  1987b   Food and Evolution: Toward a Theory of Human Food Habits. Philadelphia: Temple University Press.
Harris, Marvin
  1974   Cows, Pigs, Wars and Witches. New York: Vintage.
  1979   Cultural Materialism: The Struggle for a Science of Culture. New York: Random House.
Harris, Olivia, and Kate Young
  1981   Engendered Structures: Some Problems in the Analysis of Reproduction. In The Anthropology of Pre-Capitalist Societies, Joel Kahn and Josep Llobera, eds., London: Macmillan, 109–47.
Harrison, Lawrence.
  1985.   Underdevelopment Is a State of Mind. Lanham, Md.: University Press of America.
Hart, Donn V.
  1969   Bisayan Filipino and Malayan Humoral Pathologies: Folk Medicine and History in Southeast Asia. Southeast Asia Data Paper. Cornell University.
Hart, Keith
  1982   The Political Economy of West African Agriculture. Cambridge: Cambridge University Press.

Hartmann, Heinz, Ernest Kris, and Rudolph M. Loewenstein
　1969　Some Psychoanalytic Comments on "Culture and Personality." In Man and His Culture. Warner Muensterberger, ed. New York: Taplinger (orig. 1951), 239–70.
Hartog, Joseph, and Elizabeth Ann Hartog
　1983　Cultural Aspects of Health and Illness Behavior in Hospitals. Western Journal of Medicine 139(6):910–17.
Harwood, Alan
　1971　The Hot-Cold Theory of Disease: Implications for Treatment of Puerto Rican Patients. Journal of the American Medical Association 216:1153–58.
　1977a　Puerto Rican Spiritism Part I—Description and Analysis of an Alternative Psychotherapeutic Approach. Culture, Medicine and Psychiatry 1:69–95.
　1977b　Puerto Rican Spiritism Part 2—An Institution with Preventive and Therapeutic Functions in Community Psychiatry. Culture, Medicine and Psychiatry 1:135–53.
　1977c　RX: Spiritist As Needed. A Study of a Puerto Rican Community Mental Health Resource. New York: Wiley.
Harwood, Alan, ed.
　1981　Ethnicity and Medical Care. Cambridge: Harvard University Press.
Hasan, Khwaja A.
　1975　What Is Medical Anthropology? Medical Anthropology Newsletter 6(3):7–10.
Head, Henry
　1920　Studies in Neurology. 2 vols. London: Hodder Stoughton.
Heath, Dwight B.
　1958　Drinking Patterns of the Bolivian Camba: Quarterly Journal of Studies on Alcohol 19:491–508.
　1971　Peasants, Revolution, and Drinking: Interethnic Drinking Patterns in Two Bolivian Communities. Human Organization 30 (2):179–86.
　1975　A Critical Review of Ethnographic Studies of Alcohol Use. In Research Advances in Alcohol and Drug Problems, vol 2. R. Gibbins et al., eds. New York: Wiley.
　1976　Anthropological Perspectives on Alcohol: An Historical Review. In Cross-Cultural Approaches to the Study of Alcohol: An Interdisciplinary Approach. M. Everett et al., eds. The Hague: Mouton.
　1983　Alcohol Use among North American Indians: A Cross-cultural Survey of Patterns and Problems. In Research Advances in Alcohol and Drug Problems, vol. 7. Reginald Smart et al. eds. New York: Plenum.
　1984　Cross-cultural Studies of Alcoholism. In Recent Developments in Alcoholism, vol. 2. Marc Galanter, ed. New York: Plenum.
　1985　American Experiences with Alcohol: Commonalities and Contrasts. In The American Experience with Alcohol. L. Bennett and G. Ames, eds. New York: Plenum.
　1986　Concluding Remarks. In Thomas F. Babor, ed. Alcohol and Culture: Comparative Perspectives from Europe and America. New York: New York Academy of Science, Volume 472, 234–236.
　1987a　A Decade of Development in the Anthropological Study of Alcohol Use, 1970–1980. In Constructive Drinking. Mary Douglas, ed. Cambridge: Cambridge University Press.
　1987b　Anthropology and Alcohol Studies: Current Issues. Annual Review of Anthropology 16:99–120.
　1988　Alcohol Control Policies and Drinking Patterns: An International Game of Politics against Science. Journal of Substance Abuse 1: 121–25.
Heath, Dwight B., ed.
　1985　Alcohol Studies and Anthropology: Methodological and Practical Issues. Abstracts published in the Drinking and Drug Practices Surveyor 20:48–53.
Heath, Dwight B., and A. M. Cooper
　1981　Alcohol Use and World Cultures: A Comprehensive Bibliography of Anthropological Sources. Toronto: Addiction Research Foundation. Bibliographic Series 15.
Heath, Dwight B., Jack O. Waddell, and Martin D. Topper, eds.
　1981　Cultural Factors in Alcohol Research and Treatment of Drinking Problems. Journal of Studies on Alcohol Supplement 9.
Heggenhougen, H. K.
　1984　Traditional Medicine and the Treatment of Drug Addicts: Three Examples from Southeast Asia. Medical Anthropology Quarterly 16 (1):3–7.
Helman, Cecil G.
　1984a　Interpreting the Evidence on Social Support. Social Psychiatry 19:49–52.
　1984b　Culture, Health and Illness. Bristol: John Wright & Sons.
　1985　Psyche, Soma and Society: The Social Construction of Psychosomatic Disorders. Culture, Medicine and Psychiatry 9:1–26.
　1987　Heart Disease and the Cultural Construction of Time: The Type A Behaviour Pattern as a Western Culture-Bound Syndrome. Social Science and Medicine 25 (9): 969–79
Henderson, B. E., E. Louie, J. S. Jing, et al.
　1976　Risk Factors Associated with Nasopharyngeal Carcinoma. New England Journal of Medicine 295:1101–06.
Henderson, P.
　1975　Population Policy, Social Structure and the Health System in Puerto Rico: The Case of Female Sterilization. Ph.D. Dissertation, University of Connecticut.

Hennekens, Charles H., and J. E. Buring
  1987 Epidemiology in Medicine. Boston: Little, Brown.
Henry, J. P., and J. C. Cassel
  1969 Psychosocial Factors in Essential Hypertension. American Journal of Epidemiology 90:171–200.
Henry, Jules
  1963 Culture against Man. New York: Random House.
Henry, Jules, and Melford E. Spiro
  1953 Psychological Techniques: Projective Tests in Field Work. In Anthropology Today. A. L. Kroeber, ed. Chicago: University of Chicago Press, 417–29.
Herman, Elizabeth
  n.d. Personal Communication.
Herrick, James
  1983 The Symbolic Roots of Three Potent Iroquois Medicinal Plants. In The Anthropology of Medicine. Lola Romanucci-Ross, Daniel Moerman, and L. Tancredit, eds. New York: Bergin & Garvey 134–55.
Herskovits, M.
  1972 Cultural Relativism: Perspectives in Cultural Pluralism. New York: Random House.
Hertz, Barbara and Anthony Measham
  1987 The Safe Motherhood Initiative: Proposals for Action. Washington, D.C.: World Bank.
Heyneman, D.
  1971 Mis-Aid to the Third World: Disease Repercussions Caused by Ecological Ignorance. Canadian Journal of Public Health 62:303–13.
  1979 Dams and Disease. Human Nature 2(2):50–57.
  1983a Development and Disease: A Dual Dilemma. Journal of Parasitology 70:3–17.
  1983b Development and Disease: A Dual Dilemma. Presidential address, American Society of Parasitologists, 58th annual meeting, December 7, San Antonio.
Hill, Carole E.
  1988 Review of Culture, Politics and Medicine in Costa Rica by Setha Low. American Ethnologist 15(1):173.
Hill, Carole E., ed.
  1985 Training Manual in Medical Anthropology. Washington, D.C.: American Anthropological Association.
Hill, Polly
  1986 Development Economics on Trial: The Anthropological Case for the Prosecution. Cambridge: Cambridge University Press.
Hill, Thomas W.
  1978 Drunken Comportment of Urban Indians: "Time-out" Behavior? Journal of Anthropological Research 34 (3): 442–67.
  1984 Ethnohistory and Alcohol Studies. In Recent Developments in Alcoholism, vol. 2. Marc Galanter, ed. New York: Plenum.
Hillier, S. M. and J. A. Jewell
  1983 Health Care and Traditional Medicine in China, 1800–1982. London: Routledge & Kegan Paul.
Himes, Norman
  1970 Medical History of Contraception. New York: Schocken Books.
Hippler, Arthur E.
  1974 The North Alaska Eskimos: A Culture and Personality Perspective. American Ethnologist 1(3):449–69.
  1977 Discussion and Debate: On Stein and Kleinman, and the Crucial Issues in Medical Anthropology. Medical Anthropology Newsletter 9(1):18–19.
Ho, H. C.
  1972 Current Knowledge of the Epidemiology of Nasopharyneal Carcinoma: A Review. In: Oncogenesis and Herpesviruses. Lyon: IARC, 357–66.
Hoben, Allan
  1982 Anthropologists and Development. Annual Review of Anthropology 11:349–75.
Hogarth, Robin M., and Melvin W. Reder, eds.
  1987 Rational Choice. Chicago: University of Chicago Press.
Holland, William R.
  1963a Medicina Maya en los Altos de Chiapas. Mexico City: Instituto Nacional Indigenista.
  1963b Mexican-American Medical Beliefs: Science or Magic? Arizona Medicine 89–102.
Holmberg, Allan R.
  1971 The Rhythms of Drinking in a Peruvian Coastal Mestizo Community. Human Organization 30 (2): 198–202.
Holmes T. H., and R. H. Rahe
  1967 The Social Readjustment Rating Scale. Journal of Psychosomatic Research 11:213–18
Honigmann, John J.
  1947 Witch-Fear in Post-Contact Kaska Society. American Anthropologist 49:222–43.
  1956 Toward a Distinction between Psychiatric and Social Abnormality. In Personal Character and Cultural Milieu, Douglas G. Haring, ed., Syracuse: Syracuse University Press, 429–445.
Hook, R. H.
  1979 Phantasy and Symbol: A Psychoanalytic Point of View. In Fantasy and Symbol: Studies in Anthropological Interpretation. R. H. Hook, ed. New York: Academic Press, 267–91.

References

Hopkins, Lawrence and Immanual Wallerstein
   1967   The Comparative Study of National Societies. Social Science Information 6.
Hopper, Kim
   1975   Of Language and the Sorcerer's Appendix: A Critical Appraisal of Horacio Fabrega's Disease and Social Behavior. Medical Anthropology Newsletter 19(3):9–14.
   1982   Discussant Comments following the Organized Session, The Lure and Haven of Illness, 81st annual meeting of the American Anthropological Association, Washington, D.C.
   1988   More Than Passing Stranger: Homelessness and Mental Illness in New York City. American Ethnologist 15(1):155–67.
Horn, G. H.
   1986a   Hepatitis B, a Serious Health Concern in Egypt. Cairo Today 8(1): 53–55.
   1986b   Feeding Egypt. Cairo Today 7(2):24–27.
Horn, James J.
   1985   Brazil: The Health Care Model of the Military Modernizers and Technocrats. International Journal of Health Services 15(1):47–68.
Horowitz, M. J.
   1966   Body Image. Archives of General Psychiatry 14:456–61.
Horton, Donald J.
   1943   The Functions of Alcohol in Primitive Societies: A Cross-Cultural Study. Quarterly Journal of Studies on Alcohol 4:199–320.
House, James S., and Robert L. Kahn
   1985   Measures and Concepts of Social Support. In Social Support and Health. Sheldon Cohen and S. Leonard Syme, eds. Orlando, Fla.: Academic Press.
Howell, Nancy
   1979   The Demography of the Dobe !Kung. New York: Academic Press.
   1986   Demographic Anthropology. Annual Review of Anthropology 15:219–46.
Huang, D. P., J. H. C. Ho, and T. A. Gough
   1978   Analysis for Volatile Nitrosamines in Salt-Preserved Foodstuffs Traditionally Consumed by Southern Chinese. In G. de-The and Y. Ito, eds., NPC: Etiology and Control. Lyon: IARC, 309–14.
Hudelson, P.
   1989   Management of Diarrhea in Managua, Nicaragua. Ph.D. dissertation, University of Connecticut.
Hufford, David J.
   1988   Review: Ronald C. Simons and Charles C. Hughes, The Culture-Bound Syndromes: Folk Illnesses of Psychiatric and Anthropological Interest. Culture, Medicine, and Psychiatry 12:503–12.
Hugh-Jones, C.
   1979   From the Milk of the River: Spatial and Temporal Process in Northwest Amazonia. Cambridge: Cambridge University Press.
Hughes, Charles C.
   1968   Ethnomedicine. In International Encyclopedia of the Social Sciences, David Sills, ed. New York: Crowell Collier and Macmillan, 10:87–92.
   1985a   Culture-Bound or Construct-Bound? In The Culture-Bound Syndromes: Folk Illnesses of Psychiatric and Anthropological Interest. Ronald C. Simons and Charles C. Hughes,eds. Dordrecht: D. Reidel, 3–24.
   1985b   Glossary of "Culture-Bound" or Folk Psychiatric Syndromes. In The Culture-Bound Syndromes: Folk Illnesses of Psychiatric and Anthropological Interest. Ronald C. Simons and Charles C. Hughes, eds. Dordrecht: D. Reidel, 469–505.
   1989   On Fabrega and "Cultural Relativism—Commentary" Journal of Nervous and Mental Disease 177 (7): 426–30
Hughes, Charles, and John Hunter
   1970   Disease and "Development" in Africa. Social Science and Medicine 3:443–93.
   1971   Disease and "Development" in Africa. In The Social Organization of Health. H. Dreitzel, ed. New York: Macmillan, 150–214.
Hughes, Charles C., and Donald A. Kennedy
   1983   Beyond the Germ Theory: Reflections on Relations between Medicine and the Behavioral Sciences. In Advances in Medical Social Science. Julio L. Ruffini, ed. New York: Gordon and Breach Science Publishers, 321–99.
Hull, Diana
   1979   Migration, Adaptation, and Illness: A Review. Social Science and Medicine 13A: 25–36.
Hunt, E. E.,Jr.
   1978   Ecological Frameworks and Hypothesis Testing in Medical Anthropology. In M. H. Logan and E. E. Hunt, eds, Health and the Human Condition. North Scituate, Mass.: Duxbury Press, 84–100.
Hunt, Linda M.
   1985   Relativism in the Diagnosis of Hypoglycemia. Social Science and Medicine 20:1289–94.
Hunt, Linda M., Brigitte Jordan, Susan Irwin, and Carole H. Browner
   1989   Compliance and the Patient's Perspective. Culture, Medicine and Psychiatry 13(38):315–339.
Husting, E. L.
   1970   Sociological Patterns and their Influence on the Transmission of Bilharziasis. Central African Journal of Medicine (July Supp.):5–10.

1983 Human Water Contact Activities Related to the Transmission of Bilharziasis (Schistosomiasis). Journal of Tropical Medicine and Hygiene 86:23–35.
Hutchinson, Janis
1986 Association between Stress and Blood Pressure Variation in a Caribbean Population. American Journal of Physical Anthropology 71:69–79.
Hutchinson, S. A.
1984 Creating Meaning Out of Horror. Nursing Outlook 32(2):86–90.
Hymes, Dell
1969 Re-Inventing Anthropology. New York: Random House.
1972 The Use of Anthropology: Critical, Political, Personal. In Re-Inventing Anthropology. New York: Random House, 3–83.
Ilfeld, Frederic W.
1977 Current Social Stressors and Symptoms of Depression. American Journal of Psychiatry 134:161–66
Illich, I.
1975 Medical Nemesis: The Expropriation of Health. London: Calder and Boyars.
1976 Medical Nemesis: The Expropriation of Health. New York: Bantam.
Imhof, Arthur
1985 From the Old Mortality Pattern to the New: Implications of a Radical Change from the Sixteenth to the Twentieth Century. Bulletin of the History of Medicine 59:1–29.
Inglis, B.
1964 Fringe Medicine. London: Faber.
International Bank for Reconstruction and Development
1988 Social Indicators of Development. Baltimore: Johns Hopkins University Press.
International Conference on Population
1984 New Hope in Dark Times: UNICEF's Assessment of Past Experience with a Child Survival Package: Its Effectiveness and Its Social and Economic Feasibility. United Nations Children's Fund, Expert Group on Mortality and Health Policy. Rome, May 30–June 3, 1983.
Irwin, Susan, and Brigitte Jordan
1987 Knowledge, Practice, and Power: Court-Ordered Cesarean Sections. Medical Anthropology Quarterly (n.s.) 1(3):319–34.
Isaacs, Hope
1983 On Teaching Medical Anthropology to Clinicians: Is It Clinical Anthropology? In Clinical Anthropology. Demitri Shimkin and Peggy Golde, eds. Lanham, Md.: University Press of America, 259–67.
Ishikawa, Eisei and David L. Swain, trans.
1981 The Committee on the Compilation of Materials on Damage Caused by the Atomic Bombs in Hiroshima and Nagasaki. New York: Basic Books.
Jachimowicz, Edith
1975 Islamic Cosmology. In Ancient Cosmologies. Carmen Blacker and Michael Lowe, eds. London: George Allen and Unwin.
Jackson, I. M. D.
1984 That Thyroid Nodule: Is It Cancer? Modern Medicine 52:88–94.
Jackson, J. A., ed.
1970 Professions and Professionalization. Cambridge: Cambridge University Press.
Jacob, J.
1988 Doctors and Rules: A Sociology of Professional Values. London: Routledge.
Jacobson, David
1986 Types and Timing of Support. Journal of Health and Social Behavior 27:250–64.
1987 The Cultural Context of Social Support and Support Networks. Medical Anthropology Quarterly 1:42–67.
Jacobson, Gaynor
1977 The Refugee Movement: An Overview. International Migration Review 11:514–23.
James, Sherman A., Sue A. Hartnett, and William D. Kalsbeek
1983 John Henryism and Blood Pressure Differences among Black Men. Journal of Behavioral Medicine 6:259–78.
James, Sherman A., David S. Strogatz, Steven B. Wing, and Diane L. Ramsey
1987 Socioeconomic Status, John Henryism, and Hypertension in Blacks and Whites. American Journal of Epidemiology 126:664–73.
Jamous, H., and B. Peloille
1970 Changes in the French University-Hospital System. In J. A. Jackson, ed., Professions and Professionalisation. Cambridge: Cambridge University Press, 111–53.
Janes, Craig R.
1986 Migration and Hypertension: An Ethnography of Disease Risk in an Urban Samoan Community. In Janes, et al., eds., Anthropology and Epidemiology. Dordecht: D. Reidel, 175–212.
Janes, Craig R., and Ivan G. Pawson
1986 Migration and Biocultural Adaptation: Samoans in California. Social Science and Medicine 22:821–34.
Janes, Craig R., Ron Stall, and Sandra M. Gifford
1986 Anthropology and Epidemiology. Dordecht: D. Reidel.

Janzen, John M.
  1978a The Comparative Study of Medical Systems as Changing Social Systems. Social Science and Medicine 12:121–29.
  1978b The Quest for Therapy in Lower Zaire. Berkeley: University of California Press.
  1981 The Need for a Taxonomy of Health in the Study of African Therapeutics. Social Science and Medicine 15B:185–94.
  1982a Drums Anonymous. In M. de Vries, R. L. Berg, and M. Lipkin, eds., Use and Abuse of Medicine. New York: Praeger, 154–66.
  1982b Lemba, 1650–1930: A Drum of Affliction in Africa and the New World. New York: Garland.
  1987 Therapy Management: Concept, Reality, Process. Medical Anthropology Quarterly 1:68–84.
Jeffery, R.
  1988 The Politics of Health in India. Berkeley: University of California Press.
Jelliffe, Derrick B.
  1966 Diarrhoea in Childhood. In Medical Care in Developing Countries. Maurice King, ed. Nairobi: Oxford University Press, 15:2–15:6.
Jelliffe, D. B., and E. F. P. Jelliffe
  1975 Human Milk, Nutrition, and the World Resource Crisis. Science 188:557–61.
  1977 The Infant Food Industry and International Health. International Journal of Health Services 7:249–54.
Jellinek, E. M.
  1952 Phases of Alcohol Addiction. Quarterly Journal of Studies on Alcohol 13:673–84.
  1960 The Disease Concept of Alcoholism. Highland Park, N.J.: Hillhouse.
Jobin, W. R., and E. Ruiz-Tiben
  1968 Bilharzia and Patterns of Human Contact with Water in Puerto Rico. Boletin Asoc. Medica de Puerto Rico 60:279–84.
Jocobsen, Rick
  1986 Using Organization to Pursue Political Economic Analysis: The Case for Primary Health Care for the Poor. Medical Anthropology Quarterly 17(5):131–32.
Johannes, Adell
  1986 Medicinal Plants of the New Guinea Highlands: An Ethnopharmacologic and Phytochemical Update. In Plants in Indigenous Medicine and Diet. N. L. Etkin, ed. Bedford Hills, N.Y.: Redgrave, 266–88.
Johns, Timothy A.
  1986 Chemical Selection in Andean Domesticated Tubers as a Model for the Acquisition of Empirical Plant Knowledge. In Plants in Indigenous Medicine and Diet: Biobehavioral Approaches. N. L. Etkin, ed. Bedford Hills, N.Y.: Redgrave.
Johnson, Adeline, and Stanislaus Szurek
  1952 The Genesis of Antisocial Acting Out in Children and Adults. Psychoanalytic Quarterly 21:323–43.
Johnson, Frank
  1985 The Western Conception of Self. In Culture and Self. A. Marsella, George DeVos, and F. Hsu, eds. London: Tavistock.
Johnson, Lyndon.
  1965 Transcript of the President's Message to Congress on the State of the Union. New York Times January 5.
Johnson, Terrence
  1972 Professions and Power. London: Macmillan.
  1973 Imperialism and the Professions. In P. Halmos, ed., Professionalisation and Social Change. Keele: Sociological Review, 281–309.
Johnson, Thomas M.
  1981 The Anthropologist as a Role Model for Medical Students. Practicing Anthropology 4:8–10.
  1987 Premenstrual Syndrome as a Western Culture-Specific Disorder. Culture, Medicine, and Psychiatry 11(3):337–56.
  1987a Practicing Medical Anthropology: Clinical Strategies for Work in the Hospital. In Applied Anthropology in America. 2d ed. Elizabeth Eddy and William Partridge, eds. New York: Columbia University Press, 316–39.
  1987b Consultation Psychiatry as Applied Medical Anthropology. In Encounters with Biomedicine: Case Studies in Medical Anthropology. Hans A. Baer, ed. New York: Gordon and Breach Science Publishers, 269–93.
Johnson, Thomas, ed.
  1984 Perspectives on Post Doctoral Public Health Training for Medical Anthropologists. Medical Anthropological Quarterly 15(4):90–101.
Johnston, Francis E., ed.
  1987 Nutritional Anthropology. New York: Alan R. Liss.
Johnston, M., and M. E. Sarty
  1978 Maternal Beliefs about Vitamin Efficacy in Four U.S. Subcultures. Journal of Cross-Cultural Psychology 9:327–37.
Jones, Elise F., Jacqueline Darroch Forrest, Noreen Goldman, Stanley Henshaw, Richard Lincoln, Jeanie I. Rosoff, Charles F. Westoff, and Deirdre Wulf
  1986 Teenage Pregnancy in Industrialized Countries. New Haven: Yale University Press.

Jong, J. T. V. M. de
  1987 A Descent into African Psychiatry. Amsterdam: Royal Tropical Institute.
Joralemon, Donald
  1985 Altar Symbolism in Peruvian Ritual Healing. Journal of Latin American Lore 11:3–29.
Jordan, Brigitte
  1977 The Self-Diagnosis of Early Pregnancy: An Investigation of Competence. Medical Anthropology, 1(2):1–38.
  1978 Birth in Four Cultures. Montreal: Eden Press Women's Publications.
  1989 Cosmopolitan Obstetrics: Insights on the Training of Traditional Midwives. Social Science and Medicine 28(9):937–945.
Jordan, Peter
  1985 Schistosomiasis: The St. Lucia Project. Cambridge: Cambridge University Press.
Joyce, C. R. B., and R. M. C. Welldon
  1965 The Objective Efficacy of Prayer: A Double-Blind Clinical Trial. Journal of Chronic Diseases 18:367–77.
Justice, Judithanne
  1983 The Invisible Worker: The Role of the Peon in Nepal's Health Service. Social Science and Medicine 17:967–70.
  1984 Can Socio-Cultural Information Improve Health Planning? A Case Study of Nepal's Assistant Nurse-Midwife. Social Science and Medicine 19:193–98.
  1986 Policies, Plans, and People: Culture and Health Development in Nepal. Berkeley: University of California Press.
  1987 The Bureaucratic Context of International Health: A Social Scientist's View. Social Science and Medicine 25:1301–06.
Kakar, Sudhir
  1982 Shamans, Mystics, and Doctors: A Psychological Inquiry into India and its Healing Traditions. New York: Alfred A. Knopf.
Kanner, Allen D., James C. Coyne, Catherine Schaefer, and Richard S. Lazarus
  1980 Comparison of Two Modes of Stress Measurement: Daily Hassles and Uplifts versus Major Life Events. Journal of Behavioral Medicine 4:1–39.
Kao, F. F., and J. J. Kao, eds.
  1979 Recent Advances in Acupuncture Research. Garden City, N.Y.: Institute for Advanced Research on Asian Science and Medicine.
Kapferer, Bruce
  1979a Emotion and Feeling in Sinhalese Exorcism. Social Analysis 1:177–98.
  1979b Entertaining Demons: Comedy, Interaction, and Meaning in a Sinhalese Healing Rite. Social Analysis 1:108–76.
  1983 A Celebration of Demons: Exorcism and the Aesthetics of Healing in Sri Lanka. Bloomington: University of Indiana Press.
Kaplan, Bert, ed.
  1961 Studying Personality Cross-Culturally. Evanston, Ill.: Row Peterson.
Kaplan, David, and Robert A. Manners
  1972 Culture and Theory. Englewood Cliffs, N. J.: Prentice-Hall.
Kaplan, R. M.
  1985 Behavioral Epidemiology, Health Promotion, and Health Services. Medical Care 23(5):564–83.
Kapur, R. L.
  1987 Commentary on Culture Bound Syndromes and International Disease Classifications. Culture, Medicine, and Psychiatry 11:43–48.
Kardiner, A.
  1939 The Individual and His Society. New York: Columbia University Press.
Kasl, S. V.
  1979 Mortality and the Business Cycle: Some Questions about Research Strategies When Utilizing, Macrosocial and Ecological Data. American Journal of Public Health 69:784.
Katon, Wayne, and Arthur Kleinman
  1980 Clinical Social Science Interventions in Primary Care: A Review of Doctor-Patient Negotiation and Other Relevant Social Science Concepts and Strategies. In The Relevance of Social Science for Medicine. L. Eisenberg and A. Kleinman, eds. Dordrecht: D. Reidel, 253–78.
Katz, M., D. Despommier, and R. Gwadz
  1982 Parasitic Diseases. New York: Springer-Verlag.
Katz, Richard
  1982 Boiling Energy. Cambridge: Harvard University Press.
Katz, Solomon H.
  1987 Food and Biocultural Evolution: A Model for the Investigation of Modern Nutritional Problems. In Nutritional Anthropology. F. E. Johnston, ed. New York: Alan R. Liss, 41–63.
Katz, S. H., and J. Schall
  1979 Fava Bean Consumption and Biocultural Evolution. Medical Anthropology 3:459–76.

References

Kaufert, Patricia A.
1982 Myth and the Menopause. Sociology Health Illness 4(2):141–66.
1985 Midlife in the Midwest: Canadian Women in Manitoba. In In Her Prime: A New View of Middle-Aged Women. Judith K. Brown and Virginia Kerns, eds. South Hadley, Mass.: Bergin and Garvey, 181–97.
1988 Inuit and Obstetricians: Analysis of a Dialogue on Risks in Childbirth. Paper prepared in advance for participants in conference on Analysis in Medical Anthropology. Sponsored by the Wenner-Gren Foundation for Anthropological Research. Lisbon, March 5–13.

Kaufman, Lorraine
1980 Thoughts on Clinical Anthropology. Medical Anthropology Newsletter 12(1):17–18.

Kaufman, Sharon R.
1988 Toward a Phenomenology of Boundaries in Medicine: Chronic Illness Experience in the Case of Stroke. Medical Anthropology Quarterly 2:338–45.

Kawashiri, N., et al.
1986 Effects of Traditional Crude Drugs on Fibrinolysis by Plasmin: Antiplasmin Principles in Eupolyphaga. Chemical Pharmaceutical Bulletin 34:2512–17.

Kay, Margarita A.
1977a Health and Illness in a Mexican American Barrio. In Ethnic Medicine in the Southwest. Edward H. Spicer, ed. Tucson: University of Arizona Press, 99–166.
1977b The Florilegio Medicinal: Source of Southwest Ethnomedicine. Ethnohistory 24:251–59.
1979 Lexemic Change and Semantic Shift in Disease Names. Culture Medicine and Psychiatry 3:73–94.

Kay, Margarita A. ed.
1982 Anthropology of Human Birth. Philadelphia: F. A. Davis Co.

Kayser-Jones, J. S.
1979 Care of the Institutionalized Aged in Scotland and the United States: A Comparative Study. Western Journal of Nursing Research 1:190–200.
1982 Institutional Structures: Catalysts of or Barriers to Quality Care for the Institutionalized Aged in Scotland and the U.S. Social Science and Medicine 16:935–44.

Kearney, Michael
1986 From the Invisible Hand to Visible Feet. Annual Review of Anthropology 15:331–61.

Keesing, Roger
1978 Review of Meaning in Anthropology, by K. H. Basso and H. A. Selby. American Anthropologist 80:132–33.
1981 Cultural Anthropology: A Contemporary Perspective. New York: Holt, Rinehart and Winston.

Kendall, Carl
1988 The Implementation of a Diarrheal Disease Control Program in Honduras: Is It "Selective Primary Health Care" or "Integrated Primary Health Care?" In J. Coreil and J. D. Mull, Anthropological Studies of Diarrheal Illness. Special Issue of Social Science and Medicine 27(1):17–24.

Kendall, Carl, et al.
1988 Dengue Control: The Challenge to The Social Sciences. Unpublished manuscript. Agenda and Readings for Workshop, Johns Hopkins University, School of Hygiene and Public Health.

Kendall, Carl, Dennis Foote, and Reynaldo Martorel
1983 Anthropology, Communications, and Health: The Mass Media and Health Practices Program in Honduras. Human Organization 42:353–60.
1984 Ethnomedicine and Oral Rehydration Therapy: A Case Study of Ethnomedical Investigation and Program Planning. Social Science and Medicine 19:253–60.

Kennedy, John
1967 Nubian Zar Ceremonies as Psychotherapy. Human Organization 26:185–94.

Kennedy, John G.
1973 Cultural Psychiatry. In Handbook of Social and Cultural Anthropology. John J. Honigmann, ed. Chicago: Rand McNally Publishing, 119–98.
1987 The Flower of Paradise: The Institutionalized Use of the Drug Qat in North Yemen. Dordrecht: D. Reidel.

Kennedy, Mark
1988 An Inquiry into the Role of the Nation State in Development: Rethinking Dependency. Paper prepared for the Tenth International Colloquium on the World Economy. Cairo, February 11–13.

Kenny, Michael
1978 Latah: The Symbolism of a Putative Mental Disorder. Culture, Medicine, and Psychiatry 2:209–23.

Kepel, Gilles
1985 The Prophet and the Pharaoh: Muslim Extremism in Egypt. London: Al Saqi Books.

Kernberg, Otto
1975 Borderline Conditions and Pathological Narcissism. New York: Jason Aronson.

Kessler, Ronald C., and Paul D. Cleary
1980 Social Class and Psychological Distress. American Sociological Review 45:463–78.

Kessler, Ronald C., and Marilyn Essex
1982 Marital Status and Depression: The Importance of Coping Resources. Social Forces 61:484–507.

Keyes, C., and E. Daniel, eds.
1983 Karma: An Anthropological Inquiry. Berkeley and Los Angeles: University of California Press.

Keyfitz, Nathan
  1972 Population Theory and Doctrine: An Historical Survey. In Readings in Population. William Petersen, ed. New York: Macmillan.
  1977 An Introduction to the Mathematics of Population, with revisions. Reading, Mass.: Addison-Wesley.
Kiefer, Christie W.
  1976 Review of Morita Psychotherapy. Medical Anthropology Newsletter 7(4):11–12.
Kiev, Ari, ed.
  1964 Magic, Faith, and Healing: Studies in Primitive Psychiatry Today. London: Free Press of Glencoe, Collier-Macmillan.
Kilborne, Benjamin
  1988 George Devereux: In Memoriam. The Psychoanalytic Study of Society, vol. 12. L. Bryce Boyer and Simon Grolnick, eds. Hillsdale, N.J.: Analytic Press, xi-xxxix.
Kirmayer, Laurence
  1988 Mind and Body as Metaphors: Hidden Values in Biomedicine. In Biomedicine Examined. M. Lock and D. R. Gordon, eds. Dordrecht: Kluwer Academic, 57–93.
Kitzinger, Sheila
  1978 Women as Mothers. New York: Random House.
Klee, Linnea, and Genevieve Ames
  1987 Reevaluating Risk Factors for Women's Drinking: A Study of Blue-Collar Wives. American Journal of Preventive Medicine 3(1):31–41.
Klein, H. E., M. M. Mosberger, T. B. Person and R. E. Vandivort
  1978 Transcultural Nursing Research with Schizophrenics. International Journal for Nursing Studies 15:135–42.
Klein, Melanie
  1955 On Identification. In New Directions in Psychoanalysis. M. Klein, P. Heimann, and R. Money-Kyrle, eds. New York: Basic Books, 309–45.
Klein, Melanie, Paula Heimann, Roger Money-Kyrle, eds.
  1955 New Directions in Psychoanalysis. New York: Basic Books.
Kleinman, Arthur M.
  1973 Medicine's Symbolic Reality. Inquiry 16:206–13.
  1980 Patients and Healers in the Context of Culture. Berkeley: University of California Press.
  1982a Clinically Applied Anthropology on a Psychiatric Consultation-Liaison Service. In Clinically Applied Anthropology: Anthropologists in Health Science Settings. N. Chrisman and T. Maretzki, eds. Boston: Reidel, 83–115.
  1982b Neurasthenia and Depression: A Study of Somatization and Culture in China. Culture, Medicine and Psychiatry 6:117–90.
  1983 Editor's Note. Culture, Medicine and Psychiatry 7:97–99.
  1985 Interpreting Illness Experience and Clinical Meanings: How I See Clinically Applied Anthropology. Medical Anthropology Quarterly 16(3):69–71.
  1986 Social Origins of Distress and Disease: Depression and Neurasthenia in Modern China. New Haven, Conn.: Yale University Press.
  1987 Anthropology and Psychiatry: The Role of Culture in Cross-cultural Research on Illness. British Journal of Psychiatry 151:447–54.
  1988a Rethinking Psychiatry. New York: Free Press.
  1988b The Illness Narratives. New York: Basic Books.
Kleinman, Arthur M., et al.
  1975 Medicine in Chinese Cultures: Comparative Studies of Health Care in Chinese and Other Societies. DHEW Publication (NIH) 75–653. Washington, D.C.: Government Printing Office.
Kleinman, Arthur M., L. Eisenberg, and B. J. Good
  1978 Culture, Illness and Care: Clinical Lessons from Anthropologic and Cross-Cultural Research. Annals of Internal Medicine 99:25–58.
Kleinman, Arthur M., and J. Gale
  1982 Patients Treated by Physicians and Folk Healers: A Comparative Outcome Study in Taiwan. Culture, Medicine, and Psychiatry 6:405–23.
Kleinman, Arthur M., and Byron Good, eds.
  1985 Culture and Depression: Studies in the Anthroplogy and Cross-Cultural Psychiatry of Affect and Disorder. Berkeley: University of California Press.
Kleinman, Arthur M., and Joan Kleinman
  1985 Somatization: The Interconnections in Chinese Society among Culture, Depressive Experiences, and Meanings of Pain. In Culture and Depression: Studies in the Anthroplogy and Cross- Cultural Psychiatry of Affect and Disorder. Arthur Kleinman and Byron Good, eds. Berkeley: University of California Press, 429–90.
Kleinman, Arthur M., and L. Sung
  1979 Why Do Indigenous Practitioners Successfully Heal? Social Science and Medicine 138:7–26.
Kloos, H.
  1977 Schistosomiasis and Irrigation in the Awash Valley of Ethiopia. Ph.D. dissertation, University of California, Davis.

References

Kloos, H.
    1985   Water Resources Development and Schistosomiasis Ecology in the Awash Valley, Ethiopia. Social Science and Medicine 20:609–25.

Kloos, H., G. I. Higashi, J. A. Cattani, V. D. Schinski, N. S. Mansour, and K. D. Murrell
    1983   Water Contact Behavior and Schistosomiasis in an Upper Egyptian Village. Social Science and Medicine 17:545–562.

Kloos, H., G. I. Higashi, V. D. Schinski, N. S. Mansour, A. M. Polderman, A. Lemma, and K. D. Murrell
    1980–1981   Human Behavior and Schistosomiasis in an Ethiopian Town and an Egyptian Village: Tensae Berhan and El Ayaisha. Rural Africana 8–9:35–65.

Kloos, H., and A. Lemma
    1977   Schistosomiasis in Irrigation Schemes in the Awash Valley, Ethiopia. American Journal of Tropical Medicine and Hygiene 26:899–908.

Kloos, H., A. Lemma, and G. De Sole
    1978   Schistosoma mansoni Distribution in Ethiopia: A Study in Medical Geography. Annals of Tropical Medicine and Parasitology 72:461–70.

Kloos, H., and F. S. McCullough
    1982   Plant Molluscicides. Planta Medica 46:195–209.

Kloos, H., A. M. Polderman, G. De Sole, and A. Lemma
    1977   Haematobium Schistosomiasis among Seminomadic and Agricultural Afar in Ethiopia. Tropical and Geographical Medicine 29:399–406.

Kloos, H., and K. Thompson
    1979   Schistosomiasis in Africa: An Ecological Perspective. Journal of Tropical Geography 48:31–46.

Kluckhohn, Clyde
    1944   The Influence of Psychiatry on Anthropology in America during the Last 100 Years. In One Hundred Years of American Psychiatry. J. K. Hall, G. Zilboorg, and H. A. Bunker, eds. New York, Columbia University Press.

Knauft, B. M.
    1987   Divergence between Cultural Success and Reproductive Fitness in Preindustrial Societies. Cultural Anthropology 2:94–114.

Knodel, John
    1983   Natural Fertility. In The Determinants of Fertility in Developing Countries. R. A. Bulatao and R. D. Lee, eds. New York: Academic Press, 1:61–102.

Koenigsberg, Richard A.
    1975   Hitler's Ideology: A Study in Psychoanalytic Sociology. New York: Library of Social Science.

Kohut, Heinz
    1971   The Analysis of the Self. New York: International Universities Press.
    1977   Restoration of the Self. New York: International Universities Press.

Konrad, G., and I. Szelenyi
    1979   The Intellectuals on the Road to Class Power. Brighton: Harvester Press.

Koptiuch, Kristin
    1985   Fieldwork in the Postmodern World: Notes on Ethnography in an Expanded Field. Paper presented at the 84th Annual Meeting of the American Anthropological Association, Washington, D.C.

Koshi, P. T.
    1972   Role of Prejudice in Rejection of Health Care. Nursing Research 21:53–58.

Koshi, P. T., ed.
    1977   Forward. Nursing Clinics of North America 12(1):1–3.

Koss, Joan
    1975   Therapeutic Aspects of Puerto Rican Cult Practices. Psychiatry 28:160–71.

Kracke, Waud H.
    1978   Force and Persuasion: Leadership in an Amazonian Society. Chicago: University of Chicago Press.

Krech, III, S.
    1978   Disease, Starvation and Northern Athapaskan Social Organization. American Ethnologist 5:710–32.

Kreier, R., and R. Baron
    1987   Health Consequences of War in Nicaragua, 1985–86. New York: National Central American Health Rights Network.

Krieger, N., and M. Bassett
    1986   The Health of Blackfolk: Disease, Class and Ideology in Science. Monthly Review 38(3):74–85.

Kris, Ernst
    1956   The Personal Myth—A Problem in Psychoanalytic Technique. Journal of the American Psychoanalytic Association 4:653–81.

Kroeber, Alfred L.
    1917   The Superorganic. American Anthropologist 19:163–213.
    1947   Cultural and Natural Areas of Native North America. Berkeley and Los Angeles: University of California Press.
    1948   Anthropology. New York: Harcourt, Brace and World.

Kuhn, Thomas
    1970   The Structure of Scientific Revolutions. Chicago: University of Chicago Press.

Kundera, Milan
  1984 The Novel and Europe. New York Review of Books 31:15–19.
Kunitz, Stephen J., and Jerrold Levy
  1981 Navajos. In Alan Harwood, ed., Ethnicity and Medical Care. Cambridge: Harvard University Press.
  1986 The Prevalence of Hypertension among Elderly Navajos: A Test of the Acculturative Stress Hypothesis. Culture, Medicine, and Psychiatry 10:97–121.
Kunstadter, Peter
  1975 Do Cultural Differences Make Any Difference? Choice Points in Medical Systems Available in North-Western Thailand. In Medicine in Chinese Cultures. A. Kleinman et al., eds. Washington, D.C.: U.S. Government Printing Office for Fogarty International Center, National Institute of Health.
  1980 Medical Ethics in Cross-Cultural and Multi-Cultural Perspectives. Social Science and Medicine 14B:289–96.
  1986 Ethnicity, Ecology, and Mortality Transitions in Northwestern Thailand. In C. Janes, et al., eds. Anthropology and Epidemiology. Dordrecht: Reidel, 125–156.
Kunzle, David
  1981 Fashion and Fetishism: A Social History of the Corset, Tight-Lacing, and Other Forms of Body-Sculpture in the West. London: Rowan and Littlefield.
Kuo, Wen
  1976 Theories of Migration and Mental Health: An Empirical Testing on Chinese Americans. Social Science and Medicine 10:297–306.
Kurtz, E.
  1979 Not-God: A History of Alcoholics Anonymous. Center City, Minnesota: Hazelden Educational Services.
Kyerematen, G. A., and E. O. Ogunlana
  1987 An Integrated Approach to the Pharmacological Evaluation of Traditional Materia Medica. La Barre, Weston, eds. Journal of Ethnopharmacology 20:191–20.
  1954 The Human Animal. Chicago: University Press, 1968.
  1956 Social Cynosure and Social Structure. In Personal Character and Cultural Milieu. Douglas G. Haring, ed. New York: Syracuse University Press, 535–46.
  1958 The Influence of Freud on Anthropology. American Imago 15:275–328.
  1962 Transference Cures in Religious Cults and Social Groups. Journal of Psychoanalysis in Groups 1(1):66–75.
  1968 Personality from a Psychoanalytic Viewpoint. In The Study of Personality. Edward Norbeck, ed. New York: Holt, Rinehart and Winston, 65–87.
  1969 They Shall Take Up Serpents: Psychology of the Southern Snake-Handling Cult. New York: Schocken.
  1970 The Peyote Cult. New York: Shocken Books.
  1971a Anthropological Perspectives on Sexuality. In Sexuality: A Search for Perspective. D. Grumman and A. M. Barclay, eds. New York: Van Nostrand Reinhold Co., 38–53.
  1971b Materials for a History of Studies of Crisis Cults: A Bibliographic Essay. Current Anthropology 12:3–44.
  1972 The Ghost Dance: The Origins of Religion. New York: Dell.
  1978 The Clinic and the Field. In The Making of Psychological Anthropology. G. D. Spindler, ed. Berkeley and Los Angeles: University of California Press, 258–99.
  1980 Culture in Context. Durham, N.C.: Duke University Press.
  1984 Muelos: A Stone Age Superstition About New York: Columbia University Press
Labov, William, and D. Fanshel
  1977 Therapeutic Discourse. New York: Academic Press.
Laderman, Carol
  1983 Wives and Midwives: Childbirth and Nutrition in Rural Malaysia. Berkeley: University of California Press.
  1984 Food Ideology and Eating Behavior. Social Science and Medicine 19(5):547–60.
  1987a The Ambiguity of Symbols in the Structure of Healing. Social Science and Medicine 24(4):293–301
  1987b Destructive Heat and Cooling Prayer: Malay Humoralism in Pregnancy, Childbirth and the Postpartum Period. Social Science and Medicine 25(4):357–67.
LaFarque, J. R.
  1972 Role of Prejudice in Rejection of Health Care. Nursing Research 21:53–58.
LaFontaine, J. S.
  1985 Person and Individual. In The Category of the Person: Anthropology, Philosophy, History. M. Carrithers, S. Collins and S. Lukes, eds. Cambridge: Cambridge University Press, 123–40.
Lagache, Daniel
  1973 Introduction. In The Language of Psycho-Analysis. J. Laplanche and J. B. Pontalis, Donald Nicholson-Smith, trans. New York: Norton, vii-ix.
Laing, R.D.
  1965 The Divided Self. Harmondsworth: Penguin.
Lancaster, Roger Nelson
  1983 What AIDS Is Doing to Us. Christopher Street 73:48–52.
Landy, David
  1977 Anthropological Approaches to the Study of Human Adaptation to Health and Disease. In Culture, Disease, and Healing: Studies in Medical Anthropology. D. Landy, ed. New York: Macmillan, 11–13.

References

1983a Medical Anthropology: a Critical Appraisal. In Advances in Medical Science. Julio Ruffini, ed. New York: Gordon and Breach 1:184–314.
1983b Pibloktoq (Hysteria) and Inuit Nutrition: Possible Implication of Hypervitaminosis A. New Approaches to Culture-Bound Syndromes Symposium at the International Congress of Anthropological and Ethnological Sciences and at the Society for the Study of Psychiatry and Culture, August 1983 and October 1983, Vancouver B. C., and Newport, R. I.

Landy, David, ed.
1977 Culture, Disease, and Healing: Studies in Medical Anthropology. New York: MacMillan

Lane, Sandra D.
1985 Health Care in Damanhour, Egypt. University of California, San Francisco, Program on Medical Anthropology.
1987 A Biocultural Study of Trachoma in an Egyptian Hamlet. Ph.D. dissertation, University of California, San Francisco.
1988 A Bitter Smile: The Political Epidemiology of Neonatal Tetanus in Egypt. Paper presented at the Annual Meeting of the American Anthropological Association, Phoenix, Arizona, November 16–20.
1989 Unpublished Research Report.

Lane, S.D. and M.I. Millar
1987 The "Hierarchy of Resort" Reexamined: Status and Class Differentials as Determinants of Therapy for Eye Disease in the Egyptian Delta. Urban Anthropology 16:151–182.

Lang, Gretchen
1974 Adaptive Strategies of Urban Indian Drinkers: Chippewa in Minneapolis. Ph.D. dissertation, University of Minnesota.

Langer, Suzanne K.
1957 Philosophy in a New Key. Cambridge: Harvard University Press.

Langner, Thomas S., and Stanley T. Michael
1963 Life Stress and Mental Health. New York: Free Press.

Lanoix, J. N.
1958 Relation between Irrigation Engineering and Bilharziasis. Bulletin of the World Health Organization 18:1011–35.

Laplanche, J., and J. -B. Pontalis
1973 The Language of Psycho-Analysis. Donald Nicholson-Smith, trans. New York: Norton.

Laquer, Thomas
1986 Orgasm, Generation, and the Politics of Reproductive Biology. Representations 14:1–41.

Larkin, G.
1983 Occupational Monopoly and Modern Medicine. London: Tavistock.

LaRocco, James M., James S. House, and John R. P. French,Jr.
1980 Social Support, Occupational Stress, and Health. Journal of Health and Social Behavior 21:202–18.

LaRoche, C., et al.
1984 Grief Reactions to Perinatal Death: A Follow-up Study. Canadian Journal of Psychiatry 29(1):14–19.

Larson, M. S.
1977 The Rise of Professionalism. Berkeley: University of California Press.

Lasker, Judith
1977 The Role of Health Services in Colonial Rule: The Case of the Ivory Coast. Culture, Medicine and Psychiatry 1: 277–97.

Last, M., and G. L. Chavunduka, eds.
1986 The Professionalisation of African Medicine. Manchester: Manchester University Press for the International African Institute.

Laughlin, Charles, Jr., and Ivan Brady, eds.
1978 Extinction and Survival in Human Populations. New York: Columbia University Press.

Laurell, Asa Cristina
1989 Social Analysis of Collective Health in Latin America. Social Science and Medicine 11:1183–91.

Laurell, Asa Cristina, J. B. Gil, T. Machetoo, J. Palomo, C. P. Rulfo, M. R. de Chavez, M. Urbina, and N. Velazquez
1977 Disease and Rural Development: A Sociological Analysis of Morbidity in Two Mexican Villages. International Journal of Health Services 7(3):401–23.

Lawler, Ronald O.
1988 Moral Reflections on the New Technologies: A Catholic Analysis. Women and Health 13(1):167–77.

Lazarus, Ellen S.
1987 What Women Want: Women and Obstetricians. Paper prepared for presentation at the 86th Annual Meeting of the American Anthropological Association. Chicago, November 18–22.
1988a Theoretical Considerations for the Study of the Doctor-Patient Relationship: Implications of a Perinatal Study. Medical Anthropology Quarterly, n.s. 2:1:34–59.
1988b Poor Women, Poor Outcomes: Social Class and Reproductive Health. In Childbirth in America: Anthropological Perspectives. Karel L. Michaelson and Contributors. South Hadley, Mass.: Bergin and Garvey.
1988c "I'm Just a Clerk": Medical Workers and Prenatal Care (Some Thoughts on Critical Medical Perspectives in Childbirth Studies). Paper prepared for presentation at the 87th Annual Meeting of the American Anthropological Association, Phoenix, November 16–20.

Lazarus, Ellen, and Gregory Pappas
　1986　Categories of Thought and Critical Theory: Anthropology and the Social Science of Medicine. Medical Anthropology Quarterly 17(5):136–37.
Lazarus, Richard S.
　1966　Psychological Stress and the Coping Process. New York: McGraw-Hill.
Lazarus, Richard S., and Susan Folkman
　1986　Cognitive Theories of Stress and the Issue of Circularity. In Dynamics of Stress: Physiological, Psychological, and Social Perspectives. Mortimer H. Appley and Richard Trumbull, eds. New York: Plenum Press.
Leacock, Eleanor
　1972　Introduction to The Origin of the Family, Private Property and the State. New York: International Publishers.
　1982　Marxism and Anthropology. In The Left Academy: Scholarship on American Campuses. New York: McGraw-Hill.
Leader, Arthus, Patrick J. Taylor, and Judith C. Daniluk
　1984　Infertility: Clinical and Psychological Aspects. Psychiatric Annals 14(6):461–62, 465–67.
Leatherman, Thomas, J. Susan Luerssen, Lisa Marowitz, and R. Brooke Thomas
　1986　Illness and Political Economy: The Andean Dialectic. Cultural Survival Quarterly 10(3):19–22.
Leavitt, Judith Walzer
　1986　Brought to Bed: Childbearing in America 1750–1950. New York: Oxford University Press.
　1987　The Growth of Medical Authority: Technology and Morals in Turn-of-the-Century Obstetrics. Medical Anthropology Quarterly (n.s.) 1(3):230–55.
Lebra, Takie Sugiyama
　1976　Japanese Patterns of Behavior. Honolulu: University Press of Hawaii.
Lederer, Wolfgang
　1959　Primitive Psychotherapy. Psychiatry 22:255–65
Lee, Nancy
　1964　The Search for an Abortionist. Chicago: University of Chicago Press.
Lee, Richard
　1978　Towards a Marxist Methodology for Anthropology. Paper presented at the symposium Ways of Knowing in Anthropology, American Anthropological Association Annual Meetings, Los Angeles, November 16.
Lee, Ronald
　1982　From Rome to Manila: How Demography Has Changed in Three Decades. Program in Population Research Working Paper no. 4, University of California, Berkeley.
　1984　Malthus and Boserup: A Dynamic Synthesis. Program in Population Research Working Paper no. 15, University of California, Berkeley.
Leeman, Larry
　1986　Pueblo Models of Communal Sickness and Wellbeing. Paper read at the Kroeber Anthropological Society Meetings, Berkeley, March 8.
Leeson, Joyce
　1974　Social Science and Health Policy in Preindustrial Society. International Journal of Health Services 4(3):429–40.
Leff, J.
　1981　Psychiatry around the Globe. New York: M. Dekker.
Leighton, Alexander H., T. Adeoye Lambo, Charles C. Hughes, Dorothea C. Leighton, Jane M. Murphy, and David B. Macklin
　1963　Psychiatric Disorder among the Yoruba. Ithaca: Cornell University Press
Leighton, Dorothea C.
　1983　Anthropology in Medicine—A Personal History: How Can the Health Professionals Use Anthropology? In Clinical Anthropology. Demetri Shimkin and Peggy Golde, eds. Lanham, Md: University Press of America, 229–38.
Leighton, Dorothea C., J. S. Harding, D. B. Macklin, A. M. Macmillan, and Alexander H. Leighton
　1963　The Character of Danger. New York: Basic Books.
Leininger, M.
　1970　Nursing and Anthropology: Two Worlds to Blend. New York: Wiley.
　1977　Transcultural Nursing and a Proposed Conceptual Framework. In Transcultural Nursing Care of Infants and Children: Proceedings of the First Transcultural Nursing Conference. M. Leininger ed. Salt Lake City: University of Utah, College of Nursing, 1–18.
　1978　Culturalogical Assessment Domains for Nursing Practices. In Transcultural Nursing: Concepts, Theories and Practices. M. Leininger, ed. New York:Wiley, 85–106.
　1981　The Phenomenon of Caring: Importance, Research Questions and Theoretical Considerations. In Caring: An Essential Human Need. Proceedings of Three National Caring Conferences. M. Leininger, ed. pp. 3–15. Thorofare, N.J.: Slack, 3–15.
Leininger, M., ed.
1978b Transcultural Nursing: Concepts, Theories and Practices. New York: Wiley.
Leland, Joy
　1976　Firewater Myths. New Brunswick, N.J.: Rutgers Center of Alcohol Studies.

References

Lemert, Edwin M.
1964 Forms and Pathology of Drinking in Three Polynesian Societies. American Anthropologist 66 (2):361–75

Leng, Chee Heng
1982 Health Status and the Development of Health Services in a Colonial State: The Case of British Malaya. International Journal of Health Services 12:397–416.

Leridon, Henri
1977 Human Fertility. Chicago: University of Chicago Press.

Leridon, Henri, and Jane Menken, eds.
1979 Natural Fertility. Liege: Ordina.

Leslie, Charles M.
1972 The Professionalization of Ayurvedic and Unani Medicine. In Medical Men and Their Work: A Sociological Reader. E. Freidson and E. J. Lorber, eds. Chicago: Aldine, 39–54.
1975 Pluralism and Integration in the Indian and Chinese Medical Systems. In E. Alexander, A. Kleinman, and P. Kunstadter, eds. Medicine in Chinese Cultures. Washington D.C.: John E. Fogerty International Center, National Institutes of Health.
1976 Introduction. In Asian Medical Systems: A Comparative Study. C. Leslie, ed. Berkeley and Los Angeles: University of California Press, 133–58.

Leslie, Charles M., ed.
1980 Medical Pluralism. Social Science and Medicine 14B.

Leslie, Charles M., and E. Taylor
1973 Asian Medical Systems: A Symposium on the Role of Comparative Sociology in Improving Health Care. Social Science and Medicine 7:307–18.

Lett, James
1987 The Human Enterprise: A Critical Introduction to Anthropological Theory. Boulder, Colo.: Westview Press.

Levi-Strauss, Claude
1963a The Effectiveness of Symbols. In Structural Anthropology. New York: Basic Books.
1963b The Sorcerer and His Magic. In Structural Anthropology. New York: Basic Books.
1963c Structural Anthropology. New York: Basic Books.

Levin, Jeffrey, and H. Vanderpool
1987 Is Frequent Religious Attendance Really Conducive to Better Health? Toward an Epidemiology of Religion. Social Science and Medicine 24:589–600.

Levine, J. D., N. C. Gordon, and H. L. Fields
1978 The Mechanism of Placebo Analgesia. Lancet 2:656–57.

LeVine, Robert A.
1973 Culture, Behavior, and Personality. Chicago: Aldine.

Levy, Jerrold E.
1984 Commentary on "Alcohol and Ethnography." Current Anthropology 25(2) 182–183.

Levy, Jerrold E., and Steven J. Kunitz
1974 Indian Drinking: Navajo Practices and Anglo-American Theories. New York: Wiley.
1981 Economic and Political Factors Inhibiting the Use of Basic Research Findings in Indian Alcoholism Programs. In Cultural Factors in Alcohol Research and Treatment of Drinking Problems. Dwight Heath et al., eds. Journal of Studies on Alcohol Supplement No. 9.

Levy, Robert, and Michelle Rosaldo, eds.
1983 Self and Emotion. Ethos 113.

Lewin, Ellen
1974 Mothers and Children: Latin American Immigrants in San Francisco. New York: Arno Press.
1985 By Design: Reproductive Strategies and the Meaning of Motherhood. In The Sexual Politics of Reproduction, Hilary Homans, ed. London: Gower, 123–380.

Lewis, Gilbert
1975 Knowledge of Illness in a Sepik Society. London: Athlone.
1977 Fear of Sorcery and the Problem of Death by Suggestion. In J. Blacking, ed., The Anthropology of the Body. ASA Monograph 15. London: Academic Press, 111–43.

Lewis, I. M.
1971 Ecstatic Religion: An Anthropological Study of Spirit Possession and Shamanism. London: Penguin.
1983 Spirit Possession and Biological Reductionism: A Rejoinder to Kehoe and Giletti. American Anthropologist 85:412–13.

Lewis, Walter H., and Memory P. F. Elvin-Lewis
1977 Medical Botany. New York: Wiley.

Lewontin, R. C.
1978 Adaptation. Scientific American 239:212–30.
1984 Adaptation. In E. Sober, ed., Conceptual Issues in Evolutionary Biology. Cambridge, Mass.: M. I. T. Press, 234–51.

Lex, Barbara
1974 Voodoo Death: New Thoughts on an Old Explanation. American Anthropologist 76:818–23.

Lex, Barbara, Margaret L. Griffin, Nancy K. Mello, and Jack H. Mendelson
  1986 Concordant Alcohol and Marihuana Use in Women. Alcohol 3: 193–200.
Lex, Barbara W., Jack H. Mendelson, Samuel Bavli, Kathy Harvey, and Nancy K. Mello
  1984 Effects of Acute Marijuana Smoking on Pulse Rate and Mood States in Women. Psychopharmacology 84:178–87.
Lex, Barbara W., Susan L. Palmieri, Nancy K. Mello, and Jack H. Mendelson
  1988 Alcohol Use, Marihuana Smoking, and Sexual Activity in Women. Alcohol 5:21–25.
Lieban, Richard W.
  1967 Cebuano Sorcery. Berkeley and Los Angeles: University of California Press.
  1973 Medical Anthropology. In Handbook of Social and Cultural Anthropology. J. Honigmann, ed. Pp. 1031–1073. Chicago: Rand-McNally.
Liebow, Elliot
  1967 Tally's Corner. Boston: Little, Brown.
Light, Donald, and Sol Levine
  1989 The Changing Character of the Medical Profession. Unpublished manuscript.
Like, Robert C., and J. Ellison
  1981 Sleeping Blood, Tremor and Paralysis: A Trans-cultural Approach to an Unusual Conversion Reaction. Culture, Medicine and Psychiatry 5:49–63.
Like, Robert C., and R. Prasaad Steiner
  1986 Medical Anthropology and the Family Physician. Family Medicine 18(2):87–92.
Lilienfeld, A. M.
  1976 Foundations of Epidemiology. New York: Oxford University Press.
Lindenbaum, Shirley
  1979 Kuru Sorcery: Disease and Danger in the New Guinea Highland. Palo Alto: Mayfield.
Lindstrom, Lamont
  1987 Drunkenness and Gender on Tanna, Vanuatu. In Drugs in Western Pacific Societies. Lamont Lindstrom, ed. Lanham Md.: University Press of America.
Lindstrom, Lamont, ed.
  1987 Drugs in Western Pacific Societies: Relations of Substance. ASAO Monograph No. 11. Lanham, Md.: University Press of America.
Linke, Uli
  1986 Where Blood Flows, a Tree Grows: A Study of Root Metaphors and German Culture. Ph.D. dissertation, University of California, Berkeley.
Little, Kenneth
  1973 African Women in Towns. Cambridge: Cambridge University Press.
Littlewood, Roland and Maurice Lipsedge
  1985 Culture-bound Syndromes. In Recent Advances in Clinical Psychiatry, No. 5, Kenneth Granville-Grossman, ed., Edinburgh: Churchill Livingstone, 105–42.
Livingstone, F. B.
  1958 Anthropological Implications of Sickle Cell Gene Distribution in West Africa. American Anthropologist 60:533–62.
  1971 Malaria and Human Polymorphisms. Annual Review of Genetics 5:33–64.
  1976 Hemoglobin History in West Africa. Human Biology 48:487– 500.
  1985 Frequencies of Hemoglobin Variants: Thalassemia, the Glucose-6-Phosphate Dehydrogenase Deficiency, G6Pd Variants and Ovalocytosis in Human Populations. New York: Oxford University Press.
Llewellyn-Jones, Derek, ed.
  1986 Abortion. In Fundamentals of Obstetrics and Gynaecology Vol. 1: Obstetrics. London: Faber and Faber, 191–201.
Lloyd, J. W.
  1971 Long-Term Mortality Study of Steelworkers: V. Respiratory Cancer in Coke Plant Workers. Journal of Occupational Medicine 13:53–58.
Lloyd, J. W., F. E. Lundin, Jr., C. K. Redmond, and P. B. Geiser
  1970 Long-Term Mortality Study of Steelworkers. IV. Mortality by Work Area. Journal of Occupational Medicine 12:151–57.
Lock, Margaret
  1980 East Asian Medicine in Urban Japan: Varieties of Medical Experience. Berkeley: University of California Press.
  1982 On Revealing the Hidden Curriculum. Medical Anthropology Quarterly 14(1):19–21.
  1986a Plea for Acceptance: School Refusal Syndrome in Japan. Social Science and Medicine 23:99–112.
  1986b The Anthropological Study of the American Medical System: Center and Periphery Social Science and Medicine 22(9): 931–32.
  1987 DSM-III As a Culture-Bound Construct: Co Culture-Bound Syndromes and International Disease Classifications. Culture, Medicine, and Psychiatry 11(1):35–42.
  1988a Introduction. In Biomedicine Examined. M. Lock and D. Gordon, eds. Dordrecht: Kluwer Academic Publishers.
  1988b New Japanese Mythologies: Faltering Discipline and the Ailing Housewife. American Ethnologist 15:43–61.

1988c The Making of a Nation: Interpretations of School Refusal in Japan. In Biomedicine Examined. M. Lock and D.R. Gordon, eds. Dordrecht: Kluwer Academic Publishers.
In press On Being Ethnic: The Politics of Identity Breaking and Making in Canada, or *Nevra* on Sunday. Culture, Medicine and Society.
Lock, Margaret, and Pamela Dunk
   1987 My Nerves Are Broken: The Communication of Suffering in a Greek-Canadian Community. In Health in Canadian Society: Sociological Perspectives. D. Coburn, C. D'Arcy, P. New, and G. Torrence, eds. Toronto: Fitzhenry and Whiteside, 295–313.
Lock, Margaret, and Deborah R. Gordon, eds.
   1988 Biomedicine Examined. Dordrecht: Kluwer Academic Publishers.
Logan, Michael H.
   1977 Anthropological Research on the Hot-Cold Theory of Disease: Some Methodological Suggestions. Medical Anthropology 1:87–108.
   1979 Variations Regarding Susto Causality among the Cakchiquel of Guatemala. Culture, Medicine and Psychiatry 3:153–66.
   1983 The Role of Pharmacists and Over-the-Counter Medications in the Health Care System of a Mexican City. Medical Anthropology 7(3):69–87.
   1988 Plant Attributes, Selection, and the Discovery of Medical Knowledge. Presented at the 87th Annual Meetings of the American Anthropological Association, Phoenix, November.
Logan, Michael, and Edward E. Hunt
   1988 Health and the Human Condition. North Scituate, Mass.: Duxbury Press.
Lopez Austin, A.
   1967 Cuarenta Clases de Magos del Mundo Nahuatl. Estudios de Cultura Nahuatl 7:87–117.
   1975 Textos de Medicina Nahuatl. Mexico City: Universidad Nacional Autonoma de Mexico.
   1980 Cuerpo Humano e Ideologica. Las Concepciones de los Antiguous Nahuas. Mexico City: Universidad Nacional Autonoma de Mexico.
Lorimer, Frank
   1958 Culture and Human Fertility: A Study of the Relation of Cultural Conditions to Fertility in Nonindustrial and Transitional Societies. Paris: UNESCO.
Louie, Kem B.
   1985 Providing Health Care to Chinese Clients. Topics in Clinical Nursing 7(3):18–26.
Lovejoy, Owen
   1981 The Origin of Man. Science 211:341–50.
Low, Setha
   1985a Culturally Interpreted Symptoms or Culture-Bound Syndromes. Social Science and Medicine 21:187–97.
   1985b Culture, Politics and Medicine in Costa Rica. Bedford Hills, N.Y.: Redgrave Publishing.
   1988 Medical Practice in Response to a Folk Illness: The Diagnosis and Treatment of Nervios in Costa Rica. In Biomedicine Examined. M. Lock and D.R. Gordon, eds. Dordrecht: Kluwer Academic Publishers, 415–38.
Lozoff, B. K. R. Kamath, and R. A. Feldman
   1975 Infection and Disease in South Indian Families: Beliefs about Childhood Diarrhea. Human Organization 34: 353–58.
Luborsky, Lester
   1986 Do Therapists Vary Much in Their Success: Findings from Four Outcome Studies. American Journal of Orthopsychiatry 56:501–12.
Luborsky, Lester, et al.
   1985 Therapeutic Success and Its Determinants. Archives of General Psychiatry 42:602–11.
   1986 Do Therapists Vary Much in Their Success: Findings from Four Outcome Studies. American Journal of Orthopsychiatry 56: 501–12.
Ludwig, Emil
   1937 The Nile: The Life Story of a River. New York: Viking Press.
Luker, Christine
   1975 Taking Chances: Abortion and the Decision Not to Contracept. Berkeley: University of California Press.
Luria, A. R.
   1972 The Man with a Shattered Sword. New York: Basic Books.
Lutz, Catherine
   1982 The Domain of Emotion Words on Ifaluk. American Ethnologist 9:113–28.
   1985 Depression and the Translation of Emotional Worlds. In Culture and Depression. Arthur Kleinman and Byron Good, eds. Berkeley: University of California Press.
MacAndrew, Craig, and Robert B. Edgerton
   1969 Drunken Comportment: A Social Explanation. New York: Aldine.
McClain, Carol
   1975 Ethno-obstetrics in Ajijic. Anthropological Quarterly 48(1):38–56.
   1982 Toward a Comparative Framework for the Study of Childbirth: A Review of the Literature. In Anthropology of Human Birth, Margarita Artschwager Kay, ed. Philadelphia: F. A. Davis Co., 25–59.

1985 Why Women Choose Trial of Labor or Repeat Cesarean Section. Journal of Family Practice 21(3):210–16.

McClain, Carol, ed.
1989 Women Healers. New Brunswick, N.J.: Rutgers University Press.

MacCormack, C. P.
1984 Human Ecology and Behaviour in Malaria Control in Tropical Africa. Bulletin of the World Health Organization (Supplement) 62:81–87.
1985 Anthropology and the Control of Tropical Disease. Anthropology Today 1(3):14–16.

McDonald, Catherine
1981 Political-Economic Structures: Approaches to Traditional and Modern Medical Systems. Social Science and Medicine 15A: 101–8.

McElroy, A., and P. K. Townsend
1989 Medical Anthropology in Ecological Perspective. 2d ed. Boulder, Colo.: Westview Press.

McEvoy, Frederick D.
1971 History, Tradition and Kinship as Factors in Modern Sabo Labor Migration. Ann Arbor: University Microfilms.

McFarlane, Allan H., Geoffrey R. Norman, David L. Streiner, Ranjan Roy, and Deborah J. Scott
1980 A Longitudinal Study of the Influence of the Psychosocial Environment on Health Status: a Preliminary Report. Journal of Health and Social Behavior 21:124–33.

McGarvey, Stephen T., and Diana E. Schendel
1986 Blood Pressure of Samoans. In The Changing Samoans: Behavior and Health in Transition. Paul T. Baker, Joel M. Hanna, and Thelma S. Baker eds. New York: Oxford University Press

McGuire, Meredith
1988 Ritual Healing in Suburban America. New Brunswick: Rutgers University Press.

Macintyre, Sally
1986 The Patterning of Health by Social Position in Contemporary Britain. Social Science and Medicine 23:393–415

McKeown, T.
1976a The Modern Rise of Population. New York: Academic Press.
1976b The Role of Medicine: Dream, Mirage, or Nemesis? Princeton: Princeton University Press, and London: Nuffield Provincial Hospitals Trust.

McKinlay, John B.
1981 Social Network Influences on Morbid Episodes and the Career of Help Seeking. In The Relevance of Social Science for Medicine. Leon Eisenberg and Arthur Kleinman, eds. Dordrecht, Holland: D. Reidel Publishing Company, 77–107.

McLaren, Angus
1984 Reproductive Rituals: The Perception of Fertility in England from the Sixteenth to the Nineteenth Century. London: Methuen.

MacLennan, Carol A.
1988 From Accident to Crash: The Auto Industry and the Politics of Injury. MAQ (n.s.) 2(3): 233–50.

Macleod, R., and M. Lewis, eds.
1988 Disease, Medicine, and Empire: Perspectives on Western Medicine and Experience of European Expansion. London: Routledge.

MacLeod, Robert B.
1969 Phenomenology and Crosscultural Research. In Interdisciplinary Relationships in the Social Sciences. Muzafer Sherif and Carolyn W. Sherif, eds. Chicago: Aldine Publishing Company, 177–96.

McLuhan, Marshall
1964 Understanding Media: The Extensions of Man. New York:McGraw-Hill.

McMillen, Marilyn M.
1979 Differential Mortality by Sex in Fetal and Neonatal Deaths. Science 204:89.

McNeill, W.H.
1976 Plagues and Peoples. Garden City, N.Y.: Doubleday.
1980 Migration Patterns and Infection in Traditional Societies. In Changing Disease Patterns and Human Behavior. London: Academic Press, 27–360.

MacNab, E.
1970 A Legal History of Health Professions in Ontario. Toronto: Committee on the Healing Arts.

McQuestion, Michael, ed.
1983 Oral Rehydration Therapy: An Annotated Bibliography. Scientific Publication no. 445. Washington, D.C.: World Health Organization.

Macrae, W. D., J. B. Hudson, and G. H. N. Towers
1988 Studies on the Pharmacological Activity of Amazonian Euphorbiaceae. Journal of Ethnopharmacology 22:143–72.

McSpadden, Lucia Ann
1987 Ethiopian Refugee Resettlement in the Western United States: Social Context and Psychological Well-being. International Migration Review 21:796–819.

Mafeje, Archie
1976 The Problem of Anthropology in Historical Perspective: An Inquiry into the Growth of the Social Sciences. Revue canadienne des etudes africaines/Canadian Journal of African Studies 10(2): 307–33.

References

Magubane, B.
1971 A Critical Look on the Indices Used in the Study of Social Change in Modern Africa. Current Anthropology 12:153-70.
1979 The Political Economy of Race and Class in South Africa. New York: Monthly Press.
Mahler, Halfdan
1981. The Meaning of "Health for All by the Year 2000." World Health Forum 3(1):5-22.
Maida, Carl A.
1984 Social-Network Considerations in the Alcohol Field. In Recent Developments in Alcoholism, vol. 2. Marc Galanter, ed. New York: Plenum.
Mail, Patricia D., and David R. McDonald
1980 Tulapi to Tokay: A Bibliography of Alcohol Use and Abuse among Native Americans of North America. New Haven: HRAF Press.
Malinowski, Bronislaw
1932 The Sexual Life of Savages in Northwestern Melanesia. London: Routledge and Kegan Paul.
Mandelbaum, David G.
1965 Alcohol and Culture. Current Anthropology 6: 281-94.
1966 Edward Sapir: Culture, Language and Personality. Berkeley and Los Angeles: University of California Press (orig. 1949).
Mandell, G. L., R. G. Douglas, Jr., and J. E. Bennett
1985 Principles and Practice of Infectious Diseases, 2d ed. New York: John Wiley.
Mandl, P. E.
1983. Growth Charts, Oral Rehydration Therapy, Breast-feeding, and Immunization on a Wider Scale. Assignment Children 61/62:11-18.
Manning, Peter, and Horatio Fabrega
1973 The Experience of Self and Body: Health and Illness in the Chiapas Highlands. In Phenomenological Sociology. George Psathas, ed. New York: Wiley, 59-73.
Mapother, E. D.
1968 The Medical Profession and Its Educational and Liscensing Bodies. Dublin: Fannin & Co.
Marchione, T.
1981 Ethnographic Study: Phase I. Field Manual. Infant Feeding Practices Study. Population Council, Columbia University, Cornell University.
Marcus, George
1986 Contemporary Problems of Ethnography in the Modern World System. In Writing Culture. J. Clifford and G. Marcus, eds. Berkeley: University of California Press.
Marcus, George, and Michael Fischer
1986 Anthropology as Cultural Critique: An Experimental Moment in the Human Sciences. Chicago: University of Chicago Press.
Maretzki, Thomas W.
1980 Reflections on Clinical Anthropology. Medical Anthropology Newsletter 12(1):19-21.
1982 A Postdoctoral Training Program for Anthropologists in Clinical Research. Medical Anthropology Quarterly 14(1):21-23.
Marino, Anthony
1970 Family, Fertility, and Sex Ratios in the British Caribbean. Population Studies 24:159-72.
Marmot, M. G., and S. L. Syme
1976 Acculturation and Coronary Heart Disease in Japanese-Americans. American Journal of Epidemiology 104:225-47.
Marmot, M. G. and J. N. Morris
1984 The Social Environment. In Oxford Textbook of Public Health. Vol. 1: History, Determinants, Scope, and Strategies. Walter W. Holland, Roger Detels, and George Knox, eds. Oxford: Oxford University Press, 97-118.
Marmot, Michael, and Tores Theorell
1988 Social Class and Cardiovascular Disease: The Contribution of Work. International Journal of Health Services 18:659-74.
Mars, Gerald
1987 Longshore Drinking, Economic Security, and Union Politics in Newfoundland. In Constructive Drinking. Mary Douglas, ed. Cambridge: Cambridge University Press, 91-101.
Marsalla, Anthony J.
1982 Culture and Mental Health: An Overview. In Cultural Conceptions of Mental Health and Therapy. Anthony J. Marsalla and Geoffrey M. White, eds. Dordrecht: D. Reidel, 359-88.
Marshall, John F.
1977 Acceptability of Fertility Regulating Methods: Designing Technology to Fit People. Preventive Medicine 6(1): 65-73.
Marshall, Lorna
1965 The Kung Bushman of the Kalahari Desert. In Peoples of Africa. J. L. Gibbs, ed. New York: Rinehart & Winston.
Marshall, Mac
1976 A Review and Appraisal of Alcohol and Kava Studies in Oceania. In Cross-Cultural Approaches to the Study of Alcohol. Michael W. Everett et al. eds. The Hague: Mouton.

1979 Weekend Warriors: Alcohol in a Micronesian Culture. Palo Alto: Mayfield.
1982 Through a Glass Darkly: Beer and Modernization in Papua New Guinea. Monograph 18. Boroko, Papua New Guinea: Institute for Applied Social and Economic Research.
1983 Alcohol and Drug Studies in Anthropology: Where Do We Go from Here? Newsletter of the Alcohol and Drug Studies Group Newsletter, American Anthropological Association 9:6–13.
1985 Social Thought, Cultural Belief and Alcohol. Journal of Drug Issues (Winter): 63–71.
1987 An Overview of Drugs in Oceania. In Drugs in Western Pacific Societies. Lamont Lindstrom, ed. Lanham, Md.: University Press of America.
1988 Alcohol Consumption as a Public Health Problem in Papua New Guinea. International Journal of the Addictions 23 (6): 573–89.

Marshall, Mac, ed.
1979 Beliefs, Behaviors, and Alcoholic Beverages: A Cross-Cultural Survey. Ann Arbor: University of Michigan Press.

Marshall, Patricia Loomis
1982 Rural and Urban Factors in Alcohol Use in an Appalachian Setting. Ph.D. dissertation, University of Kentucky.

Martin, Emily
1987 The Woman in the Body: A Cultural Analysis of Reproduction. Boston: Beacon Press.
1988 The Cultural Construction of Gendered Bodies: Biology Metaphors of Production and Destruction. Paper presented at the Meeting of the American Anthropological Association, Phoenix, Arizona, November 16–20.

Martinez, H., et al.
1988 Uso de Alimentos y Bebidas en El Hogar en El Manejo de La Diarrea Aguda del Nino. Mexico City: Instituto Nacional de La Nutricion Salvador Zubiran.

Marwick, Max G.
1964 Witchcraft as a Social Strain Gauge. Australian Journal of Science 26: 263–68.
1965 Some Problems in the Sociology of Sorcery and Witchcraft. In African Systems of Thought. M. Fortes and G. Dieterlen, eds. London: Oxford University Press for the International African Institute, 171–91.

Marx, Karl, and Frederick Engels
1970 The German Ideology. New York: International Publishers.

Mascolo, N., R. Sharma, S. C. Jain, and F. Capasso
1988 Ethnopharmacology of Calotropis procera flowers. Journal of Ethnopharmacology 22:211–21.

Mason, Douglas
1988 Licensed to Live. London: Adam Smith Institute.

Mason, John W.
1975 A Historical View of the Stress Field. Journal of Human Stress 1:6–12, 22–36.

Massey, Douglas S., and Felipe Garcia España
1987 The Social Process of International Migration. Science 237:733–38.

Masson, Jeffrey M.
1984 The Assault on Truth: Freud's Suppression of the Seduction Theory. New York: Farrar, Strauss and Giroux.

Matthews, Mervyn
1978 Privilege in the Soviet Union. London: Allan & Unwin.

Matossian, R. M., M. D. Rickard, and J. D. Smyth
1977 Hydatidosis: A Global Problem of Increasing Importance. Bulletin of the World Health Organization 55:499–507.

Mausner, J. S., and S. Kramer
1985 Mausner and Bahn Epidemiology—An Introductory Text. Philadelphia: W. B. Saunders.

Mauss, Marcel
1979 (1950) Sociology and Psychology: Essays. London: Routledge & Kegan Paul.
1985 (1938) A Category of the Human Mind: The Notion of the Person, the Notion of the Self. In The Category of the Person: Anthropology, Philosophy, History. M. Carrithers, S. Collins, and S. Lukes, eds. Cambridge: Cambridge University Press, 1–25.

May, J. M.
1958 The Ecology of Human Disease. New York: MD Publications.
1960 The Ecology of Human Disease. Annals of the New York Academy of Science 84: 789–94.
1961 Studies in Disease Ecology. New York: Hafner.

Maybury-Lewis, David H. P.
1967 Akwe-Shavante Society. Oxford: Clarendon Press.

Mburu, F. M.
1981 Implications of the Ideology and Implementation of Health Policy in a Developing Country. Social Science and Medicine 15:17–24.

Mead, Margaret
1947 The Concept of Culture and the Psychosomatic Approach. Psychiatry 10:57–76.

Mead, Margaret, and Niles Newton
1967 Cultural Patterning of Perinatal Behavior. In Childbearing—Its Social and Psychological Aspects, S. Richardson and A. Guttmacher, eds. Baltimore: Williams and Wilkins, 142–244.

Mechanic, D. M.
  1978 Medical Sociology. New York: Free Press.
Mejia, Alfonso
  1980 World Physician Migration. Paper presented at the Seminar on the Arab Brain Drain, U.N. Economic and Social Council, Economic Commission for Western Asia. Beirut, Lebanon, February 4–8.
Mellor, John W., and Sarah Gavian
  1987 Famine: Causes, Prevention, and Relief. Science 235:539–45.
Melman, Seymour
  1965 Our Depleted Society. New York: Delta.
  1988 The Demilitarized Society: Disarmament and Conversion. Montreal: Harvest House.
Menken, Jane, James Trussell, and Ulla Carsen
  1986 Age and Infertility. Science 233:1389–94.
Merchant, Carolyn
  1980 The Death of Nature: Women, Ecology, and the Scientific Revolution. New York: Harper & Row.
Merchant, James
  1980 Coal Workers, Pneumoconiosis, In Maxcy-Rosenau Public Health and Preventive Medicine. 11th ed. John M. Last, ed. New York: Appleton-Century-Crofts, 610–29.
Messerschmidt, D. A., ed.
  1981 Anthropologists at Home in North America: Methods and Issues in the Study of One's Own Society. Cambridge: Cambridge University Press.
Messing, Simon
  1958 Group Therapy and Social Status in the Zar Cult of Ethiopia. In M. Opler, ed., Culture and Mental Health. New York: Macmillan.
Metzger, D., and Gerlad Williams
  1963 Tenejapa Medicine I: The Curer. Southwestern Journal of Anthropology 19:216–34.
Michaels, David
  1988 Waiting for the Body Count: Corporate Decision Making and Bladder Cancer in the U.S. Dye Industry. MAQ (n.s.) 2(3): 215–32.
Michaelson, K., et al.
  1988 Childbirth in America: Anthropological Perspectives. South Hadley, Mass.: Bergin and Garvey.
Milingo, E.
  1984 The World Is Between: Christian Healing and the Struggle for Spiritual Survival. London: C. Hurst & Co.
Millar, M. I., and S. D. Lane
  1988 Ethno-Ophthalmology in the Egyptian Delta: An Historical Systems Approach to Ethnomedicine in the Middle East. Social Science and Medicine 26:651–57.
Miller, Jonathan
  1978 The Body in Question. New York: Vintage.
Minkowski, Eugene
  1958 Findings in a Case of Schizophrenic Depression. In Existence: A New Dimension in Psychiatry and Psychology. Rollo May, Ernest Angel, and Henri Ellenberger, eds. New York: Simon & Schuster, 127–38.
Mitchell, J. Clyde
  1961 Wage Labour and African Population Movements in Central Africa. In Essays on African Populations. K. Barbour and R. L. Prothero, eds. London: Routledge and Kegan Paul.
Moerman, Daniel E.
  1979a Symbols and Selectivity. Journal of Ethnopharmacology 1:111–19.
  1979b Anthropology of Symbolic Healing. Current Anthropology 20:59–80.
  1983a Physiology and Symbols: The Anthropological Implications of the Placebo Effect. In The Anthropology of Medicine: From Culture to Method. Lola Romanucci-Ross, Daniel E. Moerman, and Laurence R. Tancredi, eds. New York: Praeger Publishers, 156–67.
  1983b General Medical Effectiveness and Human Biology: Placebo Effects in the Treatment of Ulcer Disease. Medical Anthropology Quarterly 14: 3–16.
  1986 Medicinal Plants of Native America. Ann Arbor: University of Michigan Museum of Anthropology.
  1989 Poisoned Apples and Honeysuckles: The Medicinal Plants of Native America. Medical Anthropology Quarterly 3(1):52–61.
Moghissi, K. S., and T. N. Evans, eds.
  1977 Nutritional Impacts on Women. New York: Harper & Row.
Molgaard, C. A., and E. L. Byerly
  1981 Applied Ethnoscience in Rural America: New Age Health and Healing. In Anthropologists at Home in America: Methods and Issues in the Study of One's Own Culture. D. Messerschmidt ed. Cambridge, England: Cambridge University Press, 153–66.
Molina-Guzman, Gustavo
  1979 Third World Experiences in Health Planning. International Journal of Health Services 9:139–50.
Monod, Théodore, ed.
  1975 Pastoralism in Tropical Africa. London: Oxford University Press.

Monroe, Scott M., Donald F. Imhoff, Beverly D. Wise, and Joyce E. Harris
   1983   Prediction of Psychological Symptoms under High Risk Psychosocial Circumstances: Life Events, Social Support, and Symptom Specificity. Journal of Abnormal Psychology 92:338–50.

Montagu, M. F. Ashley
   1949   Embryology from Antiquity to the End of the 18th Century. Ciba Symposia 10(4): 994–1008.

Montague, J., and J. Lamstein
   1988   Private Sector and Family Planning: Hitting Full Stride. Family Planning Enterprise 1(1):1–3.

Montgomery, Edward
   1976   Systems and the Medical Practitioners of a Tamil Town. In Asian Medical Systems: A Comparative Study. C. Leslie, ed. Berkeley and Los Angeles: University of California Press, 272–84.

Morgan, Lynn M.
   1987   Dependency Theory in the Political Economy of Health: An Anthropological Critique. Medical Anthropology Quarterly 1(2):131–55.
   1989   When Does Life Begin? In Abortion Rights and "Fetal Personhood." Edd Doerr and James W. Prescott, eds. Long Beach, Calif.: Centerline Press, 97-114.

Morgan, W. R. W.
   1981   Ethnobotany of the Turkana: Use of Plants by a Pastoral People and Their Livestock in Kenya. Economic Botany 35(1):96–130.

Morgen, Sandra
   1986   The Dynamics of Co-optation in a Feminist Health Clinic. Social Science and Medicine 23(2): 201–10.

Morgenstern, H.
   1980   The Changing Association between Social Status and Coronary Heart Disease in a Rural Population. Social Science and Medicine 14A:191–201.

Morley, Peter
   1988   Review of Special Journal Issues. Transcultural Psychiatric Research Review 25(2):112–18.

Morningstar, Patricia Cleckner and Dale E. Chitwood
   1984   Cocaine Users' View of Themselves: Implicit Behavior Theory in Context. Human Organization 43(4): 307–318.

Morsy, Soheir A.
   1978   Sex Roles, Power, and Illness in an Egyptian village. American Ethnologist 5:137–50.
   1979   The Missing Link in Medical Anthropology: The Political Economy of Health. Reviews in Anthropology 6: 349–63.
   1980   Reorientation in Capitalist Development: A Note on Sadat's Infitah. Paper presented at the Central States Meeting of the American Anthropological Association, Ann Arbor, April 9–11.
   1981   Towards a Political Economy of Health: A Critical Note on the Medical Anthropology of the Middle East. Social Science and Medicine 15(b):159–63.
   1982   Childbirth in an Egyptian Village. In An Anthropology of Human Birth. M. Kay, ed. Philadelphia: F. A. Davis, 147–74.
   1986a   "Indigenous" Anthropology in the Context of Intellectual Dependency. Paper presented at the Annual Central States Meeting of the American Anthropological Association, Chicago, March 27–29.
   1986b   Reflections on the Politics of Health. Al-Talica, (February): 49–59 (Arabic).
   1986c   U.S. Aid to Egypt: An Illustration and Account of U.S. Foreign Assistance Policy. Arab Studies Quarterly 8(4): 358–89.
   1986d   Subdermal Implant Contraception, Women and Power in Egypt: How is a Woman to Know: What is the Anthropologist to Tell? Paper Presented at the Society for Medical Anthropology Invited Session on Knowledge and Power in the Management of Reproduction. AES Annual Spring Meeting, Wrightsville, N.C., April 24–27.
   1988a   Discussant's Commentary on "Reproductive Technology, Medical Practice, Public Expectations and New Representations of the Human Body." Invited session, Society for Medical Anthropology, Annual Meeting of the American Anthropological Association, Phoenix, November 16–20.
   1988b   Islamic Clinics in Egypt: The Cultural Elaboration of Biomedical Hegemony. Medical Anthropology Quarterly (n.s.) 2(4): 355–67.
   1988c   Spirit Possession in Egyptian Ethnomedicine: Origins, Comparison, and Historical Specificity. Paper presented at the Workshop on Contributions of the Zar Cult in African Traditional Medicine. Institute of African and Asian Studies, Khartoum, Sudan, January 11–13.
   1988d   Field Work in My Egyptian Homeland: Towards the Demise of Anthropology's Distinctive-Other Hegemonic Tradition. In Arab Women in the Field: Studying Your Own Society. Soraya Altorki and Camillia Fawzi el-Solh, eds. Syracuse: Syracuse University Press.
   1989a   Drop the Label: An "Emic" View of Critical Medical Anthropology. Anthropology Newsletter 30(2):13, 16.
   1989b   Biotechnology and the International Politics of Population Control: Long-term Contraception in Egypt. Manuscript.

Morsy, Soheir A., Cynthia Nelson, Reem Saad Luka, and Hania Shokamy
   1986   Anthropology and the Call for Indigenization of Social Science in the Arab World. Paper presented at the International Conference on Contemporary Arab Studies, American University in Cairo, October 15–17. (Forthcoming in The State of the Art in Contemporary Arab Studies. Tarek Ismail, ed. Alberta: University of Alberta Press).

References

Moses, Yolanda T.
  1977 Female Status, the Family, and Male Dominance in a West Indian Community. Signs: Journal of Women in Culture and Society 3(1): 142–53.
Mosley, W. Henry
  1983 Will Primary Health Care Reduce Infant and Child Mortality? A Critique of Some Current Strategies, with Special Reference to Africa and Asia. Paper presented at the IUSSP Seminar on Social Policy, Health Policy and Mortality Prospects, Paris: February 28 - March 4.
Mosley, W. Henry, ed.
  1978 Nutrition and Human Reproduction. New York: Plenum.
Mosley, W. Henry, and Lincoln Chen, eds.
  1984 Child Survival: Strategies for Research. Population and Development Review, Supplement to vol. 10.
Muecke, M. A.
  1979 An Exploration of "Wind Illness" in Northern Thailand. Culture, Medicine and Psychiatry 3:267–300.
Muensterberger, Werner, ed.
  1969 Man and His Culture. New York: Taplinger.
Mulkay, Michael
  1979 Science and the Sociology of Knowledge London: George Allen and Unwin.
Mullings, Leith
  1984 Therapy, Ideology and Social Change: Mental Healing in Urban Ghana. Berkeley: University of California Press.
Murphy, Henry B. M.
  1961 Social Change and Mental Health. Milbank Memorial Quarterly 39:385–434.
  1977 Transcultural Psychiatry Should Begin at Home. Psychological Medicine 7: 369–71.
  1982a Blood Pressure and Culture: The Contribution of Cross-cultural Comparisons to Psychosomatics. Psychotherapeutics and Psychosomatics 38:244–55.
  1982b Comparative Psychiatry: The International and Intercultural Distribution of Mental Illness. New York: Springer-Verlag
Murphy, Jane
  1964 Psychotherapeutic Aspects of Shamanism on St. Lawrence Island, Alaska. In Ari Kiev, ed. Magic, Faith, and Healing. New York: Macmillan.
Myers, L.
  1982 The Socialization of Neophyte Nurses. Ann Arbor: University Microfilms International.
Myntti, Cynthia
  1988 Hegemony and Healing in Rural North Yemen. Social Science and Medicine 27(5):515–20.
Nadel, S. F.
  1952 Witchcraft in Four African Societies: An Essay in Comparison. American Anthropologist 54:18–29.
Nader, Laura
  1969 Up the Anthropologist—Perspectives Gained from Studying Up. In Reinventing Anthropology, Dell Hymes, ed. New York: Random House.
Nag, Moni
  1966 Factors Affecting Human Fertility in Non-Industrial Societies. Yale University Publications in Anthropology 66. New Haven: Yale University Press.
Nag, Moni, Benjamin F. White, and R. Creighton Peet
  1978 An Anthropological Approach to the Study of the Economic Value of Children in Java and Nepal. Current Anthropology 19(2): 293–306.
Nagel, Thomas
  1972. War and Massacre. Philosophy and Public Affairs 1:19–36.
Naim, Samir
  1978 Towards a Demystification of Arab Social Reality: A Critique of Anthropological and Political Writings on Arab Society. Review of Middle East Studies 3:48–62.
Namboodiri, Krishnan, and C. M. Suchindran
  1987 Life Table Techniques and Their Applications. New York: Academic Press.
Nardi, Bonnie
  1983 Goals in Reproductive Decision Making. American Ethnologist 10(4):697–714.
Naroll, Raoul
  1983 The Moral Order: An Introduction to the Human Situation. Beverly Hills, Calif.: Sage.
Nash, June
  1979 We Eat the Mines and the Mines Eat Us: Dependency and Exploitation in Bolivian Tin Mines. New York: Columbia University Press.
  1981 Ethnographic Aspects of the World Capitalist System. Annual Review of Anthropology 10:393–423.
Nash, June, and Max Kirsch
  1986 Polychlorinated Biphenyls in the Electrical Machinery Industry: An Ethnological Study of Community Action and Corporate Responsibility. Social Science and Medicine 23(2): 131–38.
  1988 The Discourse of Medical Science in the Construction of Consensus between Corporation and Community. Medical Anthropology Quarterly (n.s.) 2(2):158–71.
Nations, Marilyn K.
  1982 Illness of the Child: The Cultural Context of Child Diarrhea. Ann Arbor: University Microfilms International.

1986 Epidemiological Research on Infectious Disease: Quantitative Rigor or Rigormortis? Insights from Ethnomedicine. In Anthropology and Epidemiology: Interdisciplinary Approaches to the Study of Health and Disease. C. R. Janes, R. Stall, and S. M. Gifford, eds. Dordrecht: D. Reidel, 97–1230.

Nations, Marilyn K., and L. A. Rebhun
1988 Angels with Wet Wings Won't Fly: Maternal Sentiment in Brazil and the Image of Neglect. Culture, Medicine and Psychiatry 12(2):141–200.

Navarro, Vicente
1974 The Underdevelopment of Health or the Health of Underdevelopment: An Analysis of the Distribution of Human Health Resources in Latin America. International Journal of Health Services 4(1): 5–27.
1976 Medicine under Capitalism. New York: Prodist.
1977 Social Class, Political Power, and the State and Their Implications in Medicine. International Journal of Health Services 7(2): 255–92.
1984 A Critique of the Ideological and Political Position of the Brandt Report and the Alma Ata Declaration. International Journal of Health Services 14:159–72.
1985 U.S. Marxist Scholarship in the Analysis of Health and Medicine. International Journal of Health Services 15(4):525–44.
1986 Crisis, Health and Medicine: A Social Critique. London: Tavistock.

Navarro, Vicente, ed.
1981 Imperialism, Health and Medicine. Farmingdale, N.Y.: Baywood Publishing Co.

Needham, Rodney, ed.
1973 Right and Left: Essays on Dual Symbolic Classification. Chicago: University of Chicago Press.

Ness, Robert C.
1980 The Impact of Indigenous Healing Activity: An Empirical study of Two fundamentalist churches. Social Science and Medicine 14B:167–80
1982 Medical Anthropology in a Preclinical Curriculum. In Noel J. Chrisman and Thomas W. Maretzki, eds. Clinically Applied Anthropology: Anthropologists in Health Science Settings. Dordrecht: D. Reidel, 35–61.

Netting, R. M.
1965 Trial Model of Cultural Ecology. Anthropological Quarterly 38:81–96.
1985 Population Pressure and Intensification: Some Anthropological Reflections on Malthus, Marx, and Boserup. Paper prepared for the symposium on Anthropological Demography, annual meetings of the American Anthropological Association.

Neu, Jerome
1977 Emotion, Thought, and Therapy. London: Routledge and Kegan Paul.

New, Peter K., and M. L. New
1975 The Links between Health and the Political Structure in New China. Human Organization 34.

Newman, Lucille, ed.
1985 Women's Medicine. New Brunswick, N.J.: Rutgers University Press.

Newton, Niles, and Michael Newton
1972 Childbirth in Crosscultural Perspective. In Modern Perspectives in Psycho-Obstetrics. J. Howells, ed. Edinburgh: Oliver and Boyd, 150–72.

Ngubane, Harriet
1977 Body and Mind in Zulu Medicine: An Ethnography of Health and Disease in Nyuswa-Zulu Thought and Practice. New York: Academic Press.

Ngokwe, Ndolamb
1987 Varieties of Palm Wine among the Lele of the Kasai. In Constructive Drinking. Mary Douglas, ed. Cambridge: Cambridge University Press.

Nichols, Philip
1988 Homeopathy and the Medical Profession. London: Routledge.

Nichter, Mark
1981 Idioms of Distress. Culture, Medicine and Psychiatry 5:379–408.
1988 From Aralu to ORS: Sinhalese Perceptions of Digestion, Diarrhea, and Dehydration. Social Science and Medicine 27 (1):39–52.

Nichter, Mark, and M. Nichter
1983 The Ethnophysiology and Folk Dietetics of Pregnancy: A Case Study from South India. Human Organization 42(3) 235–46.

Nichter, Mark, Gordon Trockman, and Jean Grippen
1985 Clinical Anthropologist as Therapy Facilitator: Role Development and Clinician Evaluation in a Psychiatric Training Program. Human Organization 44(1):72–80.

Niederland, William G.
1974 The Schreiber Case: Psychoanalytic Profile of a Paranoid Personality. New York: Quadrangle/New York Times Book Co.

Nietschmann, Bernard.
1987 Militarization and Indigenous People. Cultural Survival Quarterly 11(3):1–16.

Nogami, M., T. Moriura, M. Kubo, and T. Tani
1986 Studies on the Origin, Processing and Quality of Crude Drugs. Chemical and Pharmaceutical Bulletin 34:3854–860.

References

Noguchi, M.
   1978 Studies on the Pharmaceutical Quality Evaluation of Crude Drug Preparations used in the Oriental Medicine "Kampoo." II. Precipitation Reaction of Berberine and Glycyrrhizin in Aqueous Solution. Chemical and Pharmaceutical Bulletin 26:2624–29.

Noll, Richard
   1983 Shamanism and Schizophrenia: A State-Specific Approach to the "Schizophrenic Metaphor" of Shamanic States. American Ethnologist 10:443–59.

Notes and Queries
   1951 Notes and Queries on Anthropology. 6th Ed. Committee of the Royal Anthropological Institute of Great Britain and Ireland. London: Routledge and Kegan Paul.

Nunberg, Herman
   1955 Principles of Psychoanalysis. New York: International Universities Press.

Nzimiro, Ikenna
   1977 The Crisis in the Social Sciences: The Nigerian Situation. Third World Forum Occasional Paper 2. Mexico: Third World Forum Coordinating Secretariat.

Oakley, Ann
   1972 Sex, Gender and Society. London: Maurice Temple Smith.
   1976 Wisewoman and Medicine Man: Changes in the Management of Childbirth. In The Rights and Wrongs of Women. J. Mitchell and A. Oakley, eds. Harmondsworth: Penguin Books, 17–58.
   1977 Cross-cultural Practices. In Benefits and Hazards of the New Obstetrics. Tim Chard and Richards, eds. London: William Heinemann Medical Books. Philadelphia: J. B. Lippincott Co. Lavenham, Suffolk: Lavenham Press Ltd.
   1979a A Case of Maternity: Paradigms of Women as Maternity Cases. Signs: Journal of Women in Culture and Society 7:607–32.
   1979b Becoming a Mother. London: Martin Robertson and Co.
   1980 Women Confined. Towards a Sociology of Childbirth. New York: Schocken Books.
   1986 The Captured Womb: A History of the Medical Care of Pregnant Women. Oxford: Basil Bernstein.

Obeyesekere, Gananath
   1978 The Impact of Ayurvedic Ideas on the Culture and the Individual in Sri Lanka. In C. Leslie, ed. Asian Medical Systems: A Comparative Study. Pp. Berkeley: University of California Press, 201–270.
   1981 Medusa's Hair: An Essay on Personal Symbols and Religious Experience. Chicago: University of Chicago Press.

O'Brien, Bernie
   1984 Patterns of European Diagnoses and Prescribing. London: Office of Health Economics.

Odell, Mary E.
   1986 Price or Production? Domestic Economies, Household Structure, and Fertility in a Guatemalan Village. In Culture and Reproduction. W. Penn Handwerker, ed. Boulder, Colo.: Westview, 125–43.

Odum, E. P.
   1971 Fundamentals of Ecology 3d ed. Philadelphia: Saunders.

Okuyama, T., et al.
   1986 Effect of Oriental Plant Drugs on Platelet Aggregation. III. Planta Medica 52:171–75.

O'Laughlin, Bridget
   1975 Marxist Approaches in Anthropology. Annual Review of Anthropology 5: 341–70.

Olesen, V., and E. Whittaker
   1968 The Silent Dialogue: A Study in the Psychology of Professional Socialization. San Francisco: Jossey-Bass.

Omery, A.
   1983 Phenomenology: A Method for Nursing Research. Advances in Nursing Science 5(2):49–63.

Omvedt, Gail
   1975 The Political Economy of Starvation. Race and Class 17(2): 111–30.

O'Neill, John
   1985 Five Bodies: The Human Shape of Modern Society. Ithaca: Cornell University Press.

O'Nell, Carl W., and Henry A. Selby
   1968 Sex Differences in the Incidence of Susto in Two Zapotec Pueblos: An Analysis of the Relationships between Sex Role Expectations and a Folk Illness. Ethnology 7:95–105.

Ong, Aihwa
   1988 The Production of Possession: Spirits and the Multinational Corporation in Malaysia. American Ethnologist 15:28–42.

Onoge, Omafume
   1975 Capitalism and Public Health: A Neglected Theme in the Medical Anthropology of Africa. In Topias and Utopias of Health. S. R. Ingman and A. E. Thomas, eds. The Hague: Mouton, 219–32.

Ooms, Theodora, ed.
   1981 Teenage Pregnancy in a Family Context. Philadelphia: Temple University Press.

Opler, Marvin K.
   1957 Schizophrenia and Culture. Scientific American 197:103–10.

Opler, Morris E.
   1936 Some Points of Comparison and Contrast between the Treatment of Functional Disorders by Apache Shamans and Modern Psychiatric Practice. American Journal of Psychiatry 92: 1371–87

Orlove, B. S.
   1980   Ecological Anthropology. Annual Review of Anthropology 9:235–338.
Ornstein, R. E.
   1973   Right and Left Thinking. Psychology Today (May):87–92.
Orth-Gomer, Kristina, and Anna-Lena Unden
   1987   The Measurement of Social Support in Population Surveys. Social Science and Medicine 24:83–94.
Ortner, Sherry B.
   1974   Is Female to Male as Nature Is to Culture? In Woman, Culture, and Society. Michelle Zimbalist Rosaldo and Louise Lamphere, eds. Stanford: Stanford University Press, 67–89.
Ortner, Sherry B., and Harriet Whitehead, eds.
   1981   Sexual Meanings. Cambridge: Cambridge University Press.
Ortiz de Montellano, Bernard
   1987   "Caida de Mollera" Aztec Sources for a Mesoamerican Disease of Alleged Spanish Origin. Ethnohistory 34:381–99.
Osborne, O.
   1972   Social Structure and Health Care Systems: A Yoruba Example. Rural Africana 17:80–86.
Osherson, Samuel, and Lorna Amarasingham
   1981   The Machine Metaphor in Medicine. In E. Mishler, ed. Social Contexts of Health, Illness and Patient Care, 218– 49. Cambridge: Cambridge University Press.
Overall, Christine
   1987   Ethics and Human Reproduction. Boston: Allen and Unwin.
Owen, Roger.
   1969   Cotton and the Egyptian Economy, 1820–1914: A Study in Trade and Development. Oxford: Oxford University Press.
Owusu, Maxwell
   1979   Ethnography of Africa: The Usefulness of the Useless. American Anthropologist 80(2):310–335.
Oyebola, D. D. O.
   1981   Professional Associations, Ethics, and Discipline among Yoruba Traditional Healers of Nigeria. Social Science and Medicine 15B:87–92.
   1986   National Medical Politics in Nigeria. In M. Last and G. L. Chavunduka, eds. The Professionalization of African Medicine. Manchester: Manchester University Press for the International African Institute, 221–360.
Oyeneye, O. Y.
   1985   Mobilizing Indigenous Resources for Primary Health Care in Nigeria: A Note on the Place of Traditional Medicine. Social Science and Medicine 20:67–69.
Pacey, Arnold.
   1982   Taking Soundings for Development and Health. World Health Forum 3:40–44.
   1983   The Culture of Technology. Cambridge: MIT Press.
Padgett, Deborah, and Thomas Johnson
   1987   Patients and Physicians in Distress: The Role of Critical Perspectives in Clinically Applied Medical Anthropology. Paper presented at the American Anthropological Association Meeting, November, Chicago.
Page, J. Bryan
   1977   The Study of San Jose, Costa Rica, Street Culture: Codes and Communication in Lower-Class Society. In Drugs, Rituals and Altered States of Consciousness. Brian M. du Toit, ed. Rotterdam: A. A. Balkema.
   1987   Prevention of Alcohol and Drug Abuse: What Anthropologists Can Learn and What We Can Teach. Newsletter of the Alcohol and Drug Study Group, American Anthropological Association, no. 19.
Page, J. Bryan, Jack Fletcher, and William R. True
   1988   Psychosociocultural Perspectives on Chronic Cannabis Use: the Costa Rican Follow-up. Journal of Psychoactive Drugs 20: 57–65.
Panos Institute
   1988   AIDS and the Third World. London: Panos Publications
Parin, Paul
   1988   The Ego and the Mechanism of Adaptation. In The Psychoanalytic Study of Society, vol. 12. L. B. Boyer and S. A. Grolnick, eds. Hillsdale, N.J.: Analytic Press, 97–130.
Parin, Paul, and Goldy Parin-Matthey
   1978   The Swiss and Southern German Lower-Middle Class: An Ethnopsychoanalytic Study. Journal of Psychological Anthropology 1(1):101–19.
Parker, Seymour
   1988   Rituals of Gender: A Study of Etiquette Symbols and Cognition. American Anthropologist 90:372–84.
Parkes, Colin Murray
   1988   Bereavement as a Psychosocial Transition: Processes of Adaptation to Change. Journal of Social Issues 44:53–65.
Parry, N., and J. Parry
   1976   The Rise of the Medical Profession. London: Croom Helm.
Parsons, Talcott
   1951   The Social System. Glencoe: Free Press.

References

Partridge, William L.
  1977 Transformation and Redundancy in Ritual: A Case from Colombia. In Drugs, Rituals and Altered States of Consciousness. Brian M. du Toit, ed. Rotterdam: A. A. Balkema.
Patterson, C. H.
  1985 What Is the Placebo in Psychotherapy? Psychotherapy 22: 163–69.
Pattison, E. Mansell, N. Lapins, and F. Doerr
  1973 Faith Healing: A Study of Personality and Function. Journal of Nervous and Mental Disorders 157:397–409.
Paul, Benjamin, ed.
  1955 Health, Culture, and Community. New York: Russell Sage Foundation.
Paul, Lois
  1975 Recruitment to a Ritual Role. The Midwife in a Maya Community. Ethos 3(3): 449–67.
  1978 Careers of midwives in a Mayan community. In Women in Ritual and Symbolic Roles. J. Hoch-Smith, A. Spring eds. pp. 129–49. New York: Plenum.
Paul, Robert A.
  1976 The Sherpa Temple as a Model of the Psyche. American Ethnologist 3:131–46.
  1978 Instinctive Aggression in Man: The Semai Case. Journal of Psychological Anthropology 1(1):65–79.
  1985 Freud and the Seduction Theory: A Critical Examination of Masson's The Assault on Truth. Journal of Psychoanalytic Anthropology 8(3):161–87.
  1988 Commentary Response to Robarchek and Dentan. American Anthropologist 90(2):418–20.
Paulme, Denise, ed.
  1960 Women of Tropical Africa. Berkeley and Los Angeles: University of California Press.
Payer, Lynn
  1988 Medicine and Culture: Varieties of Treatment in the United States, England, West Germany, and France. New York: Henry Holt.
Payne, D., B. Grab, R. E. Fontaine, and J. Hempel
  1976 Impact of Control Measures on Malaria Transmission and General Mortality. Bulletin of the World Health Organization 54:369–77.
Pearce, Tola O.
  1980 Political and Economic Changes in Nigeria and the Organization of Medical Care. Social Science and Medicine 14B:91–98.
  1986 Professional Interests and the Creation of Medical Knowledge in Nigeria. In M. Last and G. L. Chavunduka, eds. The Professionalization of African Medicine. Manchester: Manchester University Press for the International African Institute, 237–58.
Pearlin, Leonard I.
  1982 The Social Contexts of Stress. In Leo Goldberger and Shlomo Breznitz, eds. Handbook of Stress: Theoretical and Clinical Aspects. New York: Free Press.
Pearlin, Leonard I., and Carmi Schooler
  1978 The Structure of Coping. Journal of Health and Social Behavior 19:2–21.
Pearson, Maggie
  1982 Social Factors and Leprosy in Lamjung, West Central Nepal: Implications for Disease Control. Ecology of Disease 1: 229–36.
Peattie, Lisa
  1968 The View from the Barrio. Ann Arbor: University of Michigan Press.
Peel, Sir John, ed.
  1985 Test Tube Babies: A Christian View. Oxford: Becket Publications.
Peiris, Ralph
  1969 The Implantation of Sociology in Asia. International Social Science Journal 21(3).
Pelaez, U., and F. Uribe
  1986 La Gran Ilusion de la Objectividad. Boletin Antropologico 6:163–78.
Pelto, G. H.
  1984 Ethnographic Studies of the Effects of Food Availability and Feeding Practices. Food and Nutrition Bulletin. 6(1) 33–43. (Based on field guide prepared for the Project on Infant and Young Child Feeding Practices in Cameroon. Educational Development Council. Newton, Mass.)
Petchesky, Rosalind Pollack
  1984 Abortion and Woman's Choice: The State, Sexuality, and Reproductive Freedom. New York: Longman.
Peters, Edward
  1985 Torture. London: Basil Blackwell.
Peters, Larry
  1981 Ecstasy and Healing in Nepal: An Ethnopsychiatric Study of Tamang Shamanism. Malibu: Undena Publications.
Peters, Larry, and D. Price-Williams
  1980 Towards an Experiential Analysis of Shamanism. American Ethnologist 7:398–418.
Petrovic, Gajo
  1988 Philosophy and Revolution: Twenty Sheaves of Questions. In Marxism and the Interpretation of Culture. C. Nelson and L. Grossberg, eds. Chicago: University of Illinois Press, 235–48.

Philips, J.
1955 The Hookworm Campaign in Ceylon. In H. M. Teaf, Jr., and P. G. Franck, eds., Hands across Frontiers: Case Studies in Technical Cooperation. Ithaca: Cornell University Press, 265–305.

Phillips, Michael R.
1985 Can "Clinically Applied Anthropology" Survive in Medical Care Settings? Medical Anthropology Quarterly 16(2):31–36.

Phillipson, J. David, and Linda A. Anderson
1989 Ethnopharmacology and Western Medicine. Journal of Ethnopharmacology 25:61–72.

Phipps-Yonas, Susan
1980 Teenage Pregnancy and Motherhood: A Review of the Literature. American Journal of Orthopsychiatry 50(3):403–31.

Physicians for Human Rights
1988 The Casualties of Conflict: Medical Care and Human Rights in the West Bank and Gaza Strip. Somerville, Mass.: Physicians for Human Rights.
1989 Winds of Death: Iraq's Use of Poison Gas against Its Kurdish Population. Somerville, Mass.: Physicians for Human Rights.

Piault, C., ed.
1975 Prophetisme et Therapeutique: Albert Atcho et la Communaute Bregbo. Paris: Hermann.

Pinxten, Rik.
1986 The Developmental Dynamics of Peace. In Peace and War: Cross-Cultural Perspectives. Mary LeCron Foster and Robert A. Rubinstein, eds. New Brunswick, N.J.: Transaction Books.

Pirie, Peter
1972 The Effects of Treponematosis and Gonorrhaea on the Populations of the Pacific Islands. Human Biology in Oceania 1:187–206.

Plattner, S., et al.
1989 Ethnographic Method. Anthropology Newsletter 30:32.

Plorde, James J.
1980 Schistosomaisis (Bilharziasis). In Harrison's Principles of Internal Medicine. K. Isselbacher, R. Adams, E. Braunwald, R. Petersdorf, and Jean Wilson, eds. New York: McGraw-Hill, 909–110.

Plowman, Timothy
1986 Coca Chewing and the Botanical Origins of Coca (Erythroxylum spp.) in South America. In Coca and Cocaine. D. Pacini and C. Franquemont, eds. Cambridge, Mass.: Cultural Survival, 5–330.

Poland, Marilyn L.
1985 Importance of Cross-Training and Research Strategies in Clinical Medicine. Medical Anthropology Quarterly 16(3):61–63.

Polderman, A. M.
1979 Transmission Dynamics of Endemic Schistosomiasis. Tropical and Geographical Medicine 31:465–75.

Polgar, Steven
1962 Health and Human Behavior: Areas of Interest Common to the Social and Medical Sciences. Current Anthropology 3:159–205.

Polgar, Steven, ed.
1971 Culture and Population: A Collection of Current Studies. Cambridge, Mass.: Schenkmann Publishing Company

Polgar, Steven, and John Marshall
1976 The Search for Culturally Acceptable Fertility Regulating Methods. In Culture, Natality and Family Planning. John Marshall and Steven Polgar, eds. Chapel Hill: Carolina Population Center, 204–18.

Pollitt, K.
1982 The Politically Correct Body. Mother Jones (May):66–67.

Powell, Dorian
1982 Network Analysis: A Suggested Model for the Study of Women and the Family in the Caribbean. In Women and the Family, Jocelyn Massiah, ed. Cave Hill, Barbados: ISER, University of the West Indies, 131–620.

Powers, Marla N.
1980 Menstruation and Reproduction: An Oglala Case. Signs 6(1):54–65.

Pratt, Mary Louise
1986 Fieldwork in Common Places. In J. Clifford and G. E. Marcus, eds. Writing Culture: The Poetics and Politics of Ethnography. Berkeley: University of California Press, 27–50.

Preble, E. and J.J. Casey, Jr.
1969 Taking Care of Business: The Heroin User's Life on the Street. International Journal of the Addictions 4: 1–24.

Press, Irwin
1985 Speaking Hospital Administration's Language: Strategies for Anthropological Entree in the Clinical Setting. Medical Anthropology Quarterly 16(3):67–69.

Pressat, R.
1972 Demographic Analysis. Chicago: Aldine.

Price, Max
1988 The Consequences of Health Service Privatisation for Equality and Equity in Health Care in South Africa. Social Science and Medicine 27(7):703–16.

References

Prince, Raymond
- 1964 Indigenous Yoruba Psychiatry. In Magic, Faith, and Healing. Ari Kiev, ed. New York: Free Press, 84–120.
- 1969 Psychotherapy and the Chronically Poor. In Culture Change, Mental Health and Poverty. Joseph C. Finney, ed. Lexington: University of Kentucky Press, 20–41.
- 1976 Psychotherapy as the Manipulation of Endogenous Healing Mechanisms: A Transcultural Survey. Transcultural Psychiatric Research Review 13:115–33.
- 1977 Foreword to Case Studies in Spirit Possession. Vincent Crapanzano and Vivian Garrison, eds. New York: Wiley, xi–xvi.
- 1980 Variations in Psychotherapeutic Procedures. In Handbook of Cross-Cultural Psychology: Psychopathology vol. 6. Harry C. Triandis and Juris G. Draguns, eds. Boston: Allyn and Bacon, 291–309.
- 1982 Shamans and Endorphins: Hypothesis for a Synthesis. Ethos 10:409–23.

Prince, Raymond, ed.
- 1968 Trance and Possession States. Montreal: R. M. Bucke Memorial Society.

Prince, Raymond, and Francoise Tcheng-Laroche
- 1987 Culture-Bound Syndromes and International Disease Classifications. Culture, Medicine, and Psychiatry 11:3–19.

Pugh, R. N. H., and H. M. Gilles
- 1978 Malumfashi Endemic Diseases Research Project. III. Urinary Schistosomiasis: A Longitudinal Study. Annals of Tropical Medicine and Parasitology 72:471–82.

Rabinow, Paul
- 1986 Representations Are Social Facts: Modernity and Post-Modernity in Anthropology. In Writing Culture: The Poetics and Politics of Ethnography. J. Clifford and G. E. Marcus, eds. Berkeley: University of California Press.

Rabkin, Judith G., and Elmer L. Struening
- 1976 Life Events, Stress, and Illness. Science 144:1013–20.

Ragucci, A. T.
- 1981 Italian Americans. In Ethnicity and Medical Care. Alan Harwood, ed. Cambridge: Harvard University Press, 211–63.

Rahe, Richard H., and Ransom J. Arthur
- 1978 Life Change and Illness Studies: Past History and Future Directions. Journal of Human Stress 4:3–15.

Rahnema, Majid
- 1986 Under the Banner of Development. Development 3:47–67.
- 1988 A New Variety of AIDS and Its Pathogens: Homo Economicus, Development and Aid. Alternatives 13:117–36.

Rajasekaran, M., J. S. Bapna, S. Lakshmanan, A. G. R. Nair, A. J. Veliath, and M. Panchanadam
- 1988 Antifertility Effect in Male Rats of Oleanolic Acid, A Triterpene from Eugenia Jambolana Flowers. Journal of Ethnopharmacology 24:115–21.

Ramsey, Mathew
- 1984 The Politics of Medical Monopoly in Nineteenth-Century Medicine: The French Model and Its Rivals. In, G. L. Geison, ed. Professions and the French State, 1700–1900. Philadelphia: University of Pennsylvania Press, 225–305.
- 1988 Professionalisation and Popular Medicine in France: The Social World of Medical Practice. Cambridge: Cambridge University Press.

Rapp, Rayna
- 1987 Reproduction and Gender Hierarchy: Amniocentesis in Contemporary America. Paper presented at Wenner-Gren Conference 103, Mijas, Spain.
- 1988a Chromosomes and Communication: The discourse of Genetic Counselling. Medical Anthropology Quarterly 2(2) 143–57.
- 1988b The Power of "Positive" Diagnosis: Medical and Maternal Discourses on Amniocentesis. In Childbirth in America: Anthropological Perspectives. Karen Michaelson, ed. 103–16. New York: Bergin and Garvey.
- n.d. Constructing Amniocentesis. Unpublished.

Rappaport, R. A.
- 1976 Adaptations and Maladaptations in Social Systems. In I. Hill, ed., The Ethical Basis of Economic Freedom. I. Chapel Hill: American Viewpoint;39-79.
- 1979 Ecology, Meaning, and Religion. Richmond, California: North Atlantic.

Ratcliffe, John
- 1978 Social Justice and the Demographic Transition: Lessons from India's Kerala State. International Journal of Health Services 8:123–44.
- 1985 The Influence of Funding Agencies on International Health Policy, Research and Programs. Mobius 5:93–115.

Ratcliffe, John and Amalia Gonzalez-del-Valle
- 1988 Rigor in Health-Related Research. Toward an Expanded Conceptualization. International Journal of Health Services 18(3): 361–392.

Raup, David M.
- 1986 Biological Extinction in Earth History. Science 231:1528–33.

Rayner, Mary
   1987   Turning a Blind Eye? Medical Accountability and the Prevention of Torture in South Africa. Washington, D.C.: American Association for the Advancement of Science.
Read, Kenneth E.
   1955   Morality and the Concept of the Person among the Gahuka-Gama. Oceania 25:253–82.
Redfield, Robert, Ralph Linton, and Melville J. Herskovits
   1936   Memorandum on the Study of Acculturation. American Anthropologist 38:149–52.
Reed, D., D. McGee, J. Cohen, K. Yano, S. L. Syme, and M. Feinleib
   1982   Acculturation and Coronary Heart Disease among Japanese Men in Hawaii. American Journal of Epidemiology 115:894–905.
Reichel-Dolmatoff, G.
   1971   Amazonian Cosmos: The Sexual and Religious Symbolism of the Tukanao Indians. Chicago: University of Chicago Press.
Reischauer, Edwin O.
   1977   The Japanese. Cambridge: Harvard University Press.
Reiter, Rayna
   1981   Toward an Anthropology of Women. New York: Monthly Review Press.
Rey, Joseph M., Gavin W. Steward, Jon M. Plapp, Marie R. Bashir, and Ian N. Richards
   1988   DSM-III Axis IV Revisited. American Journal of Psychiatry 145 (3): 286–92.
Richardson, Bonham
   1985   Panama Money in Barbados, 1900–1920. Knoxville: University of Tennessee Press.
Richman, Judith A., Moises Gavira, Joseph A. Flaherty, Susan Birz, and Ronald M. Wintrob
   1987   The Process of Acculturation: Theoretical Perspectives and an Empirical Investigation in Peru. Social Science and Medicine 25:839–47.
Rios, J. L., M. C. Recio, and A. Villar
   1988   Screening Methods for Natural Products with Antimicrobial Activity: A Review of the Literaure. Journal of Ethnopharmacology 23:127–49.
Ripp, Joseph L.
   1984   Revolutionary Nicaragua: An Arena for Research in Medical Anthropology. Medical Anthropology Quarterly 15(3): 68–69.
Ritenbaugh, Cheryl
   1982   Obesity as a Culture-Bound Syndrome. Culture, Medicine, and Psychiatry 6:347–61
Rivers, W. H. R.
   1924   Medicine, Magic, and Religion. London: Kegan, Paul, Trench, Trubner & Co., Ltd.
Robarchek, Clayton A., and Robert K. Dentan
   1987   Blood Drunkenness and the Bloodthirsty Semai. American Anthropologist 89(2):356–65.
Robbins, Michael C., and Annette M. Kline
   1988   To Smoke or Not to Smoke: A Decision Theory Perspective. Paper presented at the meetings of the American Anthropological Association.
Roberts, George, and S. Sinclair
   1978   Women in Jamaica. New York: KTO Press.
Rodenbeck, Max
   1988   The Success and Failures of US aid to Egypt. MEI (September): 17–18.
Rodriguez, E., et al.
   1985   Thiarubrine A, a Bioactive Constituent of Aspilia (Asteraceae) Consumed by Wild Chimpanzees. Experientia 41:419–20.
Rogers, Carl, et al.
   1967   The Therapeutic Relationship and Its Impact: A Study of Psychotherapy with Schizophrenics. Madison: University of Wisconsin Press.
Rohde, Jon E.
   1983   Why the Other Half Dies: The Science and Politics of Child Mortality in the Third World. Assignment Children 61/62:35–67.
Rohde, Jon, and Robert Northrup
   1976   Taking Science Where the Diarrhea Is. In Acute Diarrhea in Childhood. New York: North-Holland, 341.
Roheim, Geza
   1943   The Origin and Function of Culture. Nervous Mental Disease Monographs no. 69. New York: Nervous and Mental Disease Pub.
Romalis, Coleman
   1981   Taking Care of the Little Woman: Father-Physician Relations during Pregnancy and Childbirth. In Childbirth: Alternatives to Medical Control. Shelly Romalis, ed. Austin: University of Texas Press, 3–32.
Romalis, Shelly
   1981a   An Overview. In Childbirth: Alternatives to Medical Control, Shelly Romalis, ed. pp. 3–32. Austin: University of Texas Press.
Romalis, Shelly, ed.
   1981b   Childbirth: Alternatives to Medical Control. Austin: University of Texas Press.

References

Romanucci-Ross, Lola
  1969 The Hierarchy of Resort in Curative Practices: The Admiralty Islands, Melanesia. Journal of Health and Social Behavior 10:201–9.
Romanucci-Ross, Lola, Daniel E. Moerman, and Laurence R. Tancredi, eds.
  1983 The Anthropology of Medicine: From Culture to Method. New York: Praeger.
Romney, A. K.
  1972 Categories of Disease in American-English and Mexican-Spanish. In Multidimensional Scaling: Theory and Applications in the Behavioral Sciences. A. K. Romney, R. N. Shepard, and S. B. Nerlove, eds. New York: Seminar Press, 9–54.
Romney, A. K., S. C. Weller, and W. H. Batchelder
  1986 Culture as Consensus: A Theory of Culture and Informant Accuracy. American Anthropologist 88:313–38.
Room, Robin
  1983 Sociological Aspects of the Disease Concept of Alcoholism. In Recent Advances in Alcohol and Drug Problems vol 7. Reginald Smart et al., eds. New York: Plenum.
  1984 Alcohol and Ethnography: A Case of Problem Deflation? Current Anthropology 25 (2):169–91.
Rosaldo, Michelle Z.
  1974 Woman, Culture, and Society: A Theoretical Overview. In Woman, Culture, and Society. Michelle Zimbalist Rosaldo and Louise Lamphere, eds. Stanford: Stanford University Press, 67–89.
  1980 The Use and Abuse of Anthropology: Reflections on Feminism and Cross-Cultural Understanding. Signs: Journal of Woman in Culture and Society 5(3):389–417.
  1980 Knowledge and Passion: Ilongot Notions of Self and Social Life. Cambridge: Cambridge University Press.
  1984 Toward an Anthropology of Self and Feeling. In Culture Theory. Richard Shweder and Robert LeVine, eds. Cambridge: Cambridge University Press.
Rosaldo, Michelle Zimbalist, and Louise Lamphere, eds.
  1974 Woman, Culture, and Society. Stanford: Stanford University Press.
Rosaldo, Renato
  1984 Grief and the Headhunter's Rage: On the Cultural Force of Emotions. In Text, Play and Story. Edward Bruner, ed. Washington, D.C.: American Ethnological Society, 178–95.
Rose, Geoffrey, and D. J. P. Barker
  1978 What Is a case? Dichotomy or Continuum? British Medical Journal 23(2):873–74.
Rose, G., and M. G. Marmot
  1981 Social Class and Coronary Heart Disease. British Heart Journal 45:13–19.
Rosenfield, Patricia L.
  n.d. The Contribution of Social and Political Factors to Good Health. Unpublished manuscript.
Rosenthal, M. M.
  1987 Dealing with Medical Malpractice: The British and Swedish Experience. London: Tavistock.
Ross, Eric B.
  1986 Potatoes, Population, and the Irish Famine: The Political Economy of Demographic Change. In Culture and Reproduction. W. Penn Handwerker, ed. Boulder, Colo.: Westview, 196–220.
Roth, Julius
  1957 Ritual and Magic in the Control of Contagion. American Sociology Review 22:310–14.
  1972 Some Contingencies of the Moral Evaluation and Control of Clientele: The Case of the Hospital Emergency Service. American Journal of Sociology 77:840–55.
Rothman, Barbara K.
  1986 The Tentative Pregnancy. New York: Viking/Penguin.
  1988 The Decision to Have or Not to Have Amniocentesis for Prenatal Diagnosis. In Childbirth in America: Anthropological Perspectives, Karen L. Michaelson, ed. South Hadley, Mass.: Bergin and Garvey, 90–102.
Rothman, K. J.
  1986 Modern Epidemiology. Boston, Mass.: Little, Brown.
  1988 Causal Inference. Chestnut Hill, Mass.: Epidemiology Resources Inc.
Royal College of Physicians
  1948 The Nomenclature of Disease. 7th ed. London: His Majesty's Stationery Office.
Rubel, Arthur J.
  1960 Concepts of Disease in Mexican-American Culture. American Anthropologist 62:795–814.
  1964 The Epidemiology of a Folk Illness: Susto in Hispanic America, Ethnology 3:268–83.
  1966a Across the Tracks: Mexican-Americans in a Texas City. Austin and London: University of Texas Press.
  1966b The Role of Social Science Research in Recent Health Programs in Latin America. Latin American Research Review 2:37–56.
  1983a Mexican American Folk Healing. Reviews in Anthropology 65–71.
  1983b Review of Robert T. Trotter II and Juan Antonio Chavira, Curanderismo: Mexican American Folk Healing. Reviews in Anthropology 65–71.
Rubel, Arthur J., Carl W. O'Nell, and Rolando Collado Ardon
  1984 Susto, A Folk Illness. Berkeley and Los Angeles: University of California Press.

Rubel, Arthur J., Karen Weller-Fahey, and Mimi Trosdal
  1975 Conception, Gestation, and Delivery According to Some Mananabang of Cebu. Philippine Quarterly of Culture and Society 3:131–45.
Rubenstein, R. A.
  1984 Epidemiology and Anthropology: Notes on Science and Scientism. Communication and Cognition 17 (2/3):163–85.
Rubenstein, R. A., and J. D. Perloff
  1986 Identifying Psychosocial Disorders in Children: On Integrating Epidemiological and Anthropological Understandings. In Anthropology and Epidemiology: Interdisciplinary Approaches to the Study of Health and Disease. Craig R. Janes, Ron Stall and Sandra M. Gifford, eds. Dordrecht: D. Reidel, 303–32.
Rubin, Vera, ed.
  1975a Cannabis and Culture. The Hague: Mouton.
  1975b The "Ganja" Vision in Jamaica. In Cannabis and Culture. Vera Rubin, ed. The Hague: Mouton.
Rubin, Vera, and Lambros Comitas
  1975 Ganja in Jamaica. The Hague: Mouton.
Rubinstein, Robert A.
  1984 Epidemiology and Anthropology: Notes on Science and Scientism. Communication and Cognition 17:163–85.
  1988 Anthropology and International Security. In The Social Dynamics of Peace and Conflict: Culture in International Security. R. A. Rubinstein and M. L. Foster, eds. Boulder, Colo.: Westview Press, 17–34.
Rubinstein, Robert A., and Ronald T. Brown
  1984 An Evaluation of the Validity of the Diagnostic Category of Attention Deficit Disorder. American Journal of Orthopsychiatry 543:398–414.
Ruiz, M. C.
  1981 Open-Closed Mindedness, Intolerance of Ambiguity and Nursing Faculty Attitudes toward Culturally Different Patients. Nursing Research 30:177–81.
Ryan, Michael
  1978 The Organisation of Soviet Medical Care. Oxford: B. Blackwell.
Rycroft, Charles
  1968 A Critical Dictionary of Psychoanalysis. England: Penguin.
Saa, Louis
  1986 Anthropology's Native Problem. Harper's Magazine. (May): 49–57.
Sacks, Oliver
  1973 (1970) Migraine: The Evolution of a Common Disorder. Berkeley: University of California Press.
  1985 The Man Who Mistook His Wife for a Hat and Other Clinical Tales. New York: Summit Books.
Sahlins, M. D., and E. Service
  1960 Evolution and Culture. Ann Arbor: University of Michigan Press.
Said, Edward W.
  1979 The Question of Palestine. New York: Random House. Saleh, Saneya A. W.
  1979 The Brain Drain in Egypt. Cairo Papers in Social Science, vol. 2. Monograph 3. Cairo: American University in Cairo.
Salmon, J. W., ed.
  1984 Alternative Medicines: Popular and Policy Perspectives. London: Tavistock.
Salmond, Clare E., Jill G.Joseph, I. M. Prior, D. G. Stanley, and Albert F. Wessen
  1985 Longitudinal Analysis of the Relationship between Blood Pressure and Migration: The Tokelau Island Migrant Study. American Journal of Epidemiology 122:291–301.
Sander, Fred
  1979 Individual and Family Therapy: Toward an Integration. New York: Jason Aronson.
Sanders, David
  1982 Nutrition and the Use of Food as a Weapon in Zimbabwe and Southern Africa. International Journal of Health Services 12:201–13.
  1985 The Struggle for Health: Medicine and the Politics of Underdevelopment. London: Macmillan.
Sandner, Donald
  1979 Navajo Symbols of Healing. New York: Harcourt Brace Jovanovich.
Sandoval, Mercedes
  1979 Santeria as a Mental Health Care System: An Historical Overview. Social Science and Medicine 13B:137–51.
Santos, Jose Luis dos
  1981 Homeopathy in Campinas (Brazil): a Study of a Socio-Symbolic Field. Ph.D thesis: University of London.
Sapir, Edward
  1917 Do We Need a Superorganic? American Anthropologist 19:441–47.
  1949 Cultural Anthropology and Psychiatry. In Selected Writings of Edward Sapir in Language, Culture and Personality. David G. Mandelbaum, ed. Berkeley: University of California Press, 507–21.
Sargent, Carolyn
  1982 The Cultural Context of Therapeutic Choice: Obstetrical Decisions among the Bariba of Benin. Dordrecht: D. Reidel

References

- 1986 Prospects for the Professionalization of Indigenous Midwifery in Benin. In M. Last and G. L. Chavunduka, eds. The Professionalization of African Medicine. Manchester: Manchester University Press for the International African Institute, 137–50.
- 1988 Khmer Prenatal Health Practices and the American Clinical Experience. In K. Michaelson, et al, eds. Childbirth in America: Anthropological Perspectives. South Hadley, Mass.: Bergin and Garvey, 79–89.
- 1989 Maternity, Medicine and Power: Reproductive Decisions in Urban Benin. Berekely: University of California Press.

Scarry, Elaine
- 1985 The Body in Pain: The Making and Unmaking of the World. Oxford: Oxford University Press.

Schaefer, James M.
- 1976 Drunkenness and Culture Stress: A Holocultural Test. In Cross-cultural Approaches to the Study of Alcohol. M. Everett et al., eds. The Hague: Mouton.
- 1981 Firewater Myths Revisited: Review of Findings and Some New Directions. In Cultural Factors in Alcohol Research and Treatment of Drinking Problems. Dwight Heath et al., eds. Journal of Studies on Alcohol Supplement no. 9.

Schafer, Roy
- 1983 The Analytic Attitude. New York: Basic Books.

Schantz, P. M.
- 1983 Human Behavior and Parasitic Zoonoses in North America. In: N. A. Croll and J. H. Cross, eds. Human Ecology and Infectious Disease. New York: Academic, 21–48.

Schatzman, Morton
- 1973 Paranoia or Persecution: Case of Schreber. The Journal of Psychohistory 1(1):62–88.

Scheder, J.
- 1988 A Sickly-Sweet Harvest: Farmworker Diabetes and Social Equality. MAQ (N.S.) 2(3):251–77.

Scheff, Thomas
- 1979 Catharsis In Healing, Ritual, and Drama. Berkeley: University of California Press.

Schensul, S., and M. G. Borrero, eds.
- 1982 Action Research and Health Systems Change in an Inner City Puerto Rican Community. Special Issue of Urban Anthropology.

Scheper-Hughes, Nancy
- 1979 Saints, Scholars, and Schizophrenics: Mental Illness in Rural Ireland. Berkeley: University of California Press.
- 1984a Maternal Detachment and Infant Survival in a Brazilian Shantytown. Social Science and Medicine 19:535–46.
- 1984b Infant Mortality and Infant Care: Cultural and Economic Constraints on Nurturing in Northeast Brazil. Social Science and Medicine 19(5): 535–546.
- 1988a The Madness of Hunger: Sickness, Delirium and Human Needs. Culture, Medicine and Psychiatry 12: 429–58
- 1988b The Madness of Hunger: Sickness, Delirium and Human Needs. Paper Prepared for Wenner-Gren Conference no. 106, Analysis in Medical Anthropology.

Scheper-Hughes, Nancy, ed.
- 1984 Demographic Transition in a Sicilian Rural Town. Journal of Family History 9:245–72.
- 1987 Child Survival: Anthropological Perspectives on the Treatment and Maltreatment of Children. Boston: D.Reidel.

Scheper-Hughes, Nancy, and Margaret Lock
- 1986 Speaking "Truth" to Illness: Metaphors, Reification, and a Pedagogy for Patients. Medical Anthropology Quarterly 17(5): 137–40.
- 1987 The Mindful Body: A Prolegomenon to Future Work in Medical Anthropology. Medical Anthropology Quarterly 1:6–41.

Scheper-Hughes, Nancy, and Anne M. Lovell
- 1986 Breaking the Circuit of Social Control: Lessons in Public Psychiatry from Italy and Franco Basaglia. Social Science and Medicine 23(2): 159–78.

Scheper-Hughes, Nancy, and Howard Stein
- 1987 Child-Abuse and the Unconscious. In Child Survival: Anthropological Approaches to the Treatment and Maltreatment of Children. Nancy Scheper-Hughes, ed. Dordrecht: D. Reidel.

Scheper-Hughes, Nancy, and D. Stewart
- 1983 Curanderismo in Taos County, New Mexico: A Possible Case of Anthropological Romanticism? Western Journal of Medicine 139(6):71–80.

Schertz, Lyle
- 1972 The Success of Agriculture in Meeting World Food Needs. Ecology of Food and Nutrition 1:207–12.

Schieffelin, Edward L.
- 1976 The Sorrow of the Lonely and the Burning of the Dancers. New York: St. Martin's Press.
- 1979 Mediatros as Metaphors: Moving a Man to Tears on Papua New Guinea. In The Imagination of Reality: Essays in Southeast Asian Communication Systems. A. L. Becker and A. Yengoyan, eds. Norwood, N.J.: Ablex Publishing.
- 1985 Performance and the Cultural Construction of Reality. American Ethnologist 12:707–24.

Schiffer, R. L.
    1988   The Exploding City. Populi 15(2): 49–54.
Schilder, Paul
    1970   (1950) The Image and Appearance of the Human Body. New York: International Universities Press.
Schlesselman, J. J.
    1982   Case-Control Studies: Design, Conduct, Analysis. New York: Oxford University Press.
Schneider, Jane
    1978   Peacocks and Penguins: The Political Economy of European Cloth and Colors. American Anthropologist 5.
Schneider, Jane and Peter Schneider
    1984   Demographic Transition in a Sicilian Rural Town. Journal of Family History 9:245–272.
Schoepf, Brooke
    1975   Breaking through the Looking Glass: The View from Below In G. Huizer and B. Mannheim, eds. The Politics of Anthropology. The Hague: Mouton.
Scholte, B.
    1983   Cultural Anthropology and the Paradigm Concept: A Brief History of their Recent Convergence. In Functions and Uses of Disciplinary Histories. Loren Graham et al, eds. Dordrecht: D. Reidel.
Schram, Ralph
    1971   A History of the Nigerian Health Services. Ibadan: Ibadan University Press.
Schreiber, Janet M., and John P. Homiak
    1981   Mexican Americans. In Ethnicity and Medical Care. A. Harwood, ed. Cambridge: Harvard University Press, 264–336.
Schroyer, Trent
    1970   Marx and Habermas. Continuum 8(1).
Schueler, Elizabeth, and George Armelagos
    1989   Biological Consequences of a Nuclear War. In The Anthropology of War and Peace: Perspectives on the Nuclear Age. Paul Turner and David Pitt, eds. Granby, Mass.: Bergin and Garvey, 103–13.
Schuftan, Claudio
    1985   The Role of Health and Nutrition in Development. Dossier 49:41–56.
Schulman, S.
    1958   Basic Functional Roles in Nursing: Mother Surrogate and Healer. In Patients, Physicians and Illness, E. G. Jaco ed. Glencoe: Free Press, 528–37.
Schumann, Debra A.
    1986   Fertility and Historical Variation in Economic Strategy among Migrants to the Lacandon Forest, Mexico. In Culture and Reproduction. W. Penn Handwerker, ed. Boulder, Colo.: Westview, 144–58.
Schwartz, Theodore, and Lola Romanucci-Ross
    1974   Drinking and Inebriate Behavior in the Admiralty Islands, Melanesia. Ethos 2: 213–31.
Scotch, Norman A.
    1963   Medical Anthropology. In Biennial Review of Anthropology, 1963. Bernard J. Siegel, ed. Stanford: Stanford University Press, 30–68.
Scott, Clarissa
    1975   The Relationship between Beliefs about the Menstrual Cycle and Choice of Fertility Regulating Methods within Five Ethnic Groups. International Journal of Gynecology and Obstetrics 13:105–9.
Scott, James
    1985   Weapons of the Weak: Everyday Forms of Peasant Resistance. New Haven: Yale University Press.
Scott, Robert, and Alan Howard
    1970   Models of Stress. In Social Stress. Sol Levine and Norman A. Scotch, eds. Chicago: Aldine.
Scrimshaw, N. S., C. E. Taylor, and J. E. Gordon
    1968   Interactions of Nutrition and Infection. Geneva: World Health Organization Monograph Series, no. 57
Scrimshaw, Nevin.
    1974   Myths and Realities in International Health Planning. American Journal of Public Health 64:792–98.
Scrimshaw, Susan C. M.
    1978   Infant Mortality and Behavior in the Regulation of Family Size. Population and Development Review 4: 383–404.
    1980   Acceptability of New Contraceptive Technology. In Research Frontiers in Fertility Regulation. Gerald I. Zatuchni, Mariam H. Labbok, and John J. Sciarra, eds. New York: Harper & Row, 72–82.
    1985   Bringing the Period Down: Government and Squatter Settlement Confront Induced Abortion in Ecuador. In B. R. DeWalt and P. J. Pelto, eds. Micro and Macro Levels of Analysis in Anthropology: Issues in Theory and Research. Boulder, Colo.: Westview Press.
Scrimshaw, S. C. M. and E. Hurtado
    1987   Rapid Assessment Procedures: For Nutrition and Primary Health Care: Anthropological Approaches to Improving Programme Effectiveness. Tokyo: United Nations University, UNICEF, and UCLA Latin American Center.
    1988   Anthropological Involvement in the Central American Diarrheal Disease Control Program. In Anthropological Studies of Diarrheal Illness. J. Coreil and J. D. Mull, eds. Social Science and Medicine Special Issue 27(1):97–106.

Scudder, Thayer
1973 The Human Ecology of Big Projects: River Basin Development and Resettlement. Annual Review of Anthropology 2:45–67.
1975 Resettlement. In Man-made Lakes and Health. N. F. Stanley and M. P. Alpers, eds. New York: Academic Press, 453–710.
Scudder, Thayer, and Elizabeth Colson
1982 From Welfare to Development: A Conceptual Framework for the Analysis of Dislocated People. In Involuntary Migration and Resettlement: The Problems and Responses of Dislocated People. Art Hansen and Anthony Oliver-Smith, eds. Boulder, Colo.: Westview Press, 267–87.
Scull, Andrew
1977 Decarceration: Community Treatment and the Deviant. Englewood Cliffs, N.J.: Prentice-Hall.
1979 Museums of Madness: The Social Organization of Insanity in Nineteenth-Century England. London: Allen Lane.
Secunda, Victoria
1984 By Youth Possessed: The Denial of Age in America. Indianapolis: Bobbs-Merrill.
Segall, M. E.
1965 Blood Pressure and Culture Change. Nursing Science 3:373–82.
Seligmann, C. G.
1911 The Melanesians of British New Guinea. Cambridge: Cambridge University Press.
Selikoff, I. J., and J. Churg.
1968 Asbestos Exposure, Smoking, and Neoplasia. Journal of the American Medical Association 204:106–12.
Sell, Ralph, and Stephen Kunitz
1986 Debt, Dependency and Death in the 1970's: The Political Economy of Mortality in the Capitalist World System. Paper prepared for presentation at the Annual Meeting of the International Sociological Association, New Delhi, August.
Selye, Hans
1956 The Stress of Life. New York: McGraw-Hill.
1975 Confusion and Controversy in the Stress Field. Journal of Human Stress 1:37–44
Sen, Amartya K.
1979 Rational Fools: A Critique of the Behavioral Foundations of Economic Theory. In Philosophy and Economic Theory, 87 Frank Hahn and Martin Hollis, eds. Oxford: Oxford University Press, 87–109.
Shahid, N. S., A. S. M. Rahman, K. M. A. Azia, A. S. G. Faruque, and M. A. Bari
1983 Beliefs and Treatment Related to Diarrhoeal Episodes Reported in Association with Measles. Tropical and Geographical Medicine 35:151–56.
Shariati, Ali
1979 On the Sociology of Islam. Hamid Algar, trans. Berkeley, Calif.: Mixan Press.
Sharpe, Ella Freeman
1948 An Examination of Metaphor. In The Psychoanalytic Reader. Robert Fliess, ed. New York: International Universities Press (orig. 1940), 273–860.
Shedlin, Michelle, and Paula Hollerbach
1981 Modern and Traditional Fertility Regulation in a Mexican Community: The Process of Decision Making. Studies in Family Planning 12(6/7): 278–96.
Sheldon, H.
1984 Boyd's Introduction to the Study of Disease, 9th ed. Philadelphia: Lea & Febiger.
Sheps, M. C. and Jane A. Menken
1973 Mathematical Models of Conception and Birth. Chicago: University of Chicago Press.
Sheridan, Allan
1980 Michel Foucault: The Will to Truth. London: Tavistock.
Shiloh, Ailon
1968 The Interaction between the Middle Eastern and Western Systems of Medicine. Social Science and Medicine 2:235–48.
1977 Therapeutic Anthropology: The Anthropologist as Private Practitioner. American Anthropologist 79:443–45.
1980 Therapeutic Anthropology. Medical Anthropology Newsletter 12(1):14.
Shimkin, Demitri B., et al.
1983 The Social Sciences and Medicine in Community Health: The Community Control of Hypertension in Central Mississippi. In Clinical Anthropology. Demitri Shimkin and Peggy Golde, eds. Lanham, Md.: University Press of America, 155–221.
Shimkin, Demitri, and Peggy Golde
1983 Clinical Anthropology: A New Approach to American Health Problems? Lanham, Md.: University Press of America.
Shryock, H. S., and Seigel, J. S.
1973 The Methods and Materials of Demography. Washington, D.C.: Bureau of the Census.
Shrylock, R. H.
1967 Medical Licensing in America, 1650–1965. Baltimore: Johns Hopkins University Press.

Shukri, Ghali
   1985   Conceptual Problems on the Arab Road towards a Sociology of Knowledge. Al-Mustaqbal Al-Arabi 77(7): 126–36. (in Arabic).
Shutler, Mary Elizabeth
   1979   Disease and Curing in a Yaqui Community. In Ethnic Medicine in the Southwest. E. Spicer, ed. Tucson: University of Arizona Press.
Shweder, Richard A.
   1965   Aspects of Cognition in Zinacanteco Shamans: Experimental Results. In Reader in Comparative Religion: An Anthropological Approach. W. A. Lessa and E. Z. Vogt, eds. New York: Harper & Row, 407–12.
Shweder, Richard, and Edmund J. Bourne
   1982   Does the Concept of the Person Vary Cross-Culturally? In Cultural Conceptions of Mental Health and Therapy. Anthony J. Marsella and Geoffrey M. White eds. Dordrecht: Kluwer Academic Publishers, 97–137.
Sibisi, Harriet
   1981   Aspects of Clinical Practice and Traditional Organisation of Indigenous Healers in South Africa. Social Science and Medicine 15B:3.
Sider, Gerald
   1974   The Shaping of American Anthropology, 1883–1911 A Franz Boas Reader. New York: Basic Books.
Siegel, D., R. Baron, and J. Eitel
   1985   Health Consequences of War in Nicaragua. San Francisco: San Francisco Bay Area Committee for Health Rights in Central America.
Siegel, D., R. Baron, and F. Epstein
   1985   The Epidemiology of Aggression. Lancet 1:1492–93.
Sigerist, Henry E.
   1951   A History of Medicine: (I) Primitive and Archaic Medicine. New York: Oxford University Press
Silva, M., and D. Rothbart
   1984   An Analysis of Changing Trends in Philosophies of Science on Nursing Theory Development and Testing. Advances in Nursing Science 6(2):1–13.
Silverberg, James
   1986   The Anthropology of Global Integration: Some Grounds for Optimism about World Peace. In The Social Dynamics of Peace and Conflict: Culture in International Security, R. A. Rubinstein and M. L. Foster, eds. Boulder, Colo.: Westview Press, 281–91.
Silverman, M., P. Lee, and M. Lydecker
   1982   Prescriptions for Death: The Drugging of the Third World. Berkeley: University of California Press.
Simmons, Ozzie G.
   1968   The Sociocultural Integration of Alcohol Use. Quarterly Journal of Studies on Alcohol 29:152–71.
Simon, Julian L.
   1977   The Economics of Population Growth. Princeton: Princeton University Press.
   1986   Theory of Population and Economic Growth. Oxford: Basil Blackwell.
Simons, Ronald C.
   1985a   The Resolution of the Latah Paradox. In R. Simons and C. Hughes, eds., The Culture-Bound Syndromes. Dordrecht: D. Reidel.
   1985b   Sorting the Culture-Bound Syndromes. In The Culture-Bound Syndromes: Folk Illnesses of Psychiatric and Anthropological Interest. Ronald C. Simons and Charles C. Hughes, eds. Dordrecht: D. Reidel, 25–38.
Simons, Ronald C., and Charles C. Hughes
   in press The Culture-Bound Syndromes. In Culture, Ethnicity, and Mental Illness, Albert C. Gaw, ed. American Psychiatric Press.
Simons, Ronald C., and Charles C. Hughes eds.
   1985   The Culture-Bound Syndromes: Folk Illnesses of Psychiatric and Anthropological Interest. Dordrecht: D. Reidel.
Singer, Merrill
   1986a   Developing a Critical Perspective in Medical Anthropology. Medical Anthropology Quarterly 17(5):128–29.
   1986b   Toward a Political Economy of Alcoholism: The Missing Link in the Anthropology of Drinking. Social Science and Medicine 23(2):113–30.
   1987   Cure, Care, and Control: An Ectopic Encounter with Biomedical Obstetrics. In Case Studies in Medical Anthropology. H. Baer, ed. New York: Bordon and Breach.
   1989a   The Coming of Age of Critical Medical Anthropology. Social Science and Medicine 28(11):1193–1203.
   1989b   The Limitations of Medical Ecology: The Concept of Adaptation in the Context of Social Statification and Social Transformation. Medical Anthropology 10(4): 218–29.
Singer, Merrill, C. Arnold, M. Fitzgerald, L. Madden, and C. von Legat
   1984   Hypoglycemia: A Controversial Illness in U.S. Society. Medical Anthropology 8:1–35.
Singer, Merrill, and Hans Baer
   n.d. Why Not Have a Critical Medical Anthropology? Unpublished manuscript.
Singer, Merrill, Lani Davison, and Gina Gerdes
   1988   Culture, Critical Theory, and Reproductive Illness Behavior in Haiti. Medical Anthropology Quarterly 4:370–85.

References

Singer, Merrill, Lani Davison, and Fuat Yalin, eds.
  1988 Alcohol Use and Abuse among Hispanic Adolescents. Hartford, Conn.: Hispanic Health Council.
Singer, Phillip
  1977 Introduction. In Traditional Healing: New Science or New Colonialism? Essays in Critique of Medical Anthropology. Buffalo, N.Y.: Conch Magazine.
Siskind, Janet
  1988 An Axe to Grind: Class Relations and Silicosis in a 19th Century Factory. Medical Anthropology Quarterly (n.s.) 2(3):199–214.
Skinner, Elliott P.
  1960 Labour Migration and Its Relationship to Socio-Cultural Change in Mossi Society. Africa 30:375–401.
Skocpol, Theda
  1979 States and Social Revolutions. Cambridge: Cambridge University Press.
Slome, C., D. R. Brogan, S. J. Eyres, and W. Lednar
  1986 Basic Epidemiological Methods and Biostatistics: A Workbook. Boston/Portola Valley: Jones and Bartlett Publishers.
Smith, Carol
  1983 Regional Analysis in World System Perspective: A Critique of Three Structural Theories of Uneven Development. In Economic Anthropology: Topics and Theories. S. Ortiz, ed. New York University Press of America, 307–60.
Smith, Robert V.
  1983 Japanese Society: Tradition, Self and the Social Order. Cambridge: Cambridge University Press.
Smits, Leo
  1980 Getting Off: An Anthropological Analysis of Heroin Users. Papers on European and Mediterranean Societies. University of Amsterdam: Antropologisch-Socilogisch Centrum, No. 12.
Snow, Loudell F.
  1974 Folk Medical Beliefs and Their Implications for Care of Patients. Annals of Internal Medicine 81:82–96.
Sofowora, Abayomi
  1982 Medicinal Plants and Traditional Medicine in Africa. Chichester: J. Wiley.
Sofowora, Abayomi, ed.
  1979 African Medical Plants: Proceedings of a Conference. Ile-Ife: University of Ife Press.
Sohoni, Neera Kuckreja
  1988 Parava Seva Sanstha. New Delhi: Ford Foundation.
Sontag, Susan
  1978 Illness as Metaphor. New York: Farrar, Strauss and Giroux.
Sotiroff-Junker, J.
  1978 A Bibliography on the Behavioural, Social and Economic Aspects of Malaria and Its Control. Geneva: World Health Organization.
Southall, Aidan
  1961 Population Movements in East Africa. In Essays on African Populations, K. Barbour and R. L. Prothero, eds. London: Routledge & Kegan Paul.
Spallone, Patricia, and Deborah Lynn, eds.
  1987 Made to Order: The Myth of Reproductive and Genetic Progress. Oxford: Pergamon Press.
Spector, Rachel
  1975 Cultural Diversity in Health and Illness. New York: Appleton-Century-Crofts.
  1985 Cultural Diversity in Health and Illness. 2d ed. Norwalk, Conn.: Appleton-Century-Crofts.
Spencer, Robert
  1949–1950 Introduction to Primitive Obstetrics. CIBA Symposium 11(3):1158–88.
Spindler, George, ed.
  1978 The Making of Psychological Anthropology. Berkeley and Los Angeles: University of California Press.
Spiro, Melford E.
  1965 Context and Meaning in Cultural Anthropology. New York: Free Press.
  1978 Culture and Human Nature. In The Making of Psychological Anthropology. George D. Spindler, ed. Berkeley and Los Angeles: University of California Press, 331–60.
  1982a Buddhism and Society. 2d exp. ed. Berkeley and Los Angeles: University of California Press.
  1982b Oedipus in the Trobriands. Chicago: University of Chicago Press.
  1986 Cultural Relativism and the Future of Anthropology. Cultural Anthropology 1(3):259–86
Spitzer, Robert L., and Janet B. Williams
  1983 International Perspectives: Summary and Commentary. In Robert L. Spitzer, Janet B. Williams, and Andrew E. Sokol, eds. International Perspectives on DSM-III. Washington, D.C.: American Psychiatric Press, 339–53.
Spree, Reinhard
  1988 Health and Social Class in Imperial Germany. Oxford: Berg. (German ed. 1971).
Staiano, Kathryn V.
  1981 Alternative Therapeutic Systems in Belize: A Semiotic Framework. Social Science and Medicine 15B:317–32.

Stall, Ron
  1988 The Prevention of HIV Infection Associated with Drug and Alcohol Use during Sexual Activity. Advances in Alcohol and Substance Abuse 7(2):773–88.
  1989 Alcohol, Drug Use and AIDS: An Anthropological Research Agenda. Newsletter of the Alcohol and Drug Study Group, American Anthropological Association, no. 23.
Stall, Ron, ed.
  1985 Anthropology, Epidemiology, and Substance Use. Drinking and Drug Practices Surveyor 20:54–59.
Stamm, L., and A. Ong Tsui
  1986 Cultural Constraints on Fertility Transmission in Tunisia: A Case Analysis from the City of Ksar-Hellal. In Culture and Reproduction: An Anthropological Critique of Demographic Transition Theory. W. P. Handwerker, ed. Boulder, Colo.: Westview.
Stanworth, Michelle
  1987 Reproductive Technologies: Gender, Motherhood and Medicine. Minneapolis: University of Minnesota Press.
Stark, Evan
  1982 What Is Medicine? Radical Science Journal 12:46–87.
Starr, P.
  1982 The Social Transformation of American Medicine. New York: Basic Books.
Stavenhagen, R.
  1971 Decolonizing Applied Anthropology. Human Organization 30(4).
Stebbins, Kenyon R.
  1986 Curative Medicine, Preventative Medicine, and Health Status: The Influence of Politics on Health Status in a Rural Mexican Village. Social Science and Medicine 23(2):139–48.
  1987 Tobacco or Health in the Third World: A Political Economy Perspective with Emphasis on Mexico. International Journal of Health Services 17 (3): 521–36.
Steedly, Mary Margaret
  1988 Severing the Bonds of Love: A Case Study in Soul Loss. Social Science and Medicine 27:841–56.
Stein, Howard F.
  1973 Cultural Specificity in Patterns of Mental Illness and Health: A Slovak-American Case Study. Family Process 12(1):69–82.
  1974 Envy and the Evil Eye among Slovak-Americans: An Exploration into the Psychological Ontogeny of Belief and Ritual. Ethos 2(1):15–46.
  1978 The Slovak-American "Swaddling Ethos": Homeostat for Family Dynamics and Cultural Continuity. Family Process 17:31–45.
  1980a Medical Anthropology and Western Medicine. Journal of Psychological Anthropology 3(2):185–95.
  1980b Clinical Anthropology and Medical Anthropology. Medical Anthropology Newsletter 12(1):18–19.
  1982a Adversary Symbiosis and Complementary Group Dissociation: An Analysis of the U.S./U.S.S.R. Conflict. International Journal of Intercultural Relations 6:55–83.
  1982b Ethanol and Its Discontents: Paradoxes of Inebriation and Sobriety in American Culture. Journal of Psychoanalytic Anthropology 5(4):355–77.
  1982c The Ethnographic Mode of Teaching Clinical Behavioral Science. In Noel J. Chrisman and Thomas W. Maretzki, eds., Clinically Applied Anthropology: Anthropologists in Health Science Settings. Dordrecht: D. Reidel, 61–83.
  1984 The Scope of Psycho-Geography: The Psychoanalytic Study of Spatial Representation. Journal of Psychoanalytic Anthropology 7(1):23–73.
  1985a Principles of Style: A Medical Anthropologist as Clinical Teacher. Medical Anthropology Quarterly 16(3):64–67.
  1985b The Psychodynamics of Medical Practice: Unconscious Factors in Patient Care. Berkeley and Los Angeles: University of California Press.
  1985c The Culture of the Patient as a Red Herring in Clinical Decision Making: A Case Study. Medical Anthropology Quarterly 17(1):2–5.
  1985d Therapist and Family Values in Cultural Context. Counseling and Values 30(1):35–46.
  1985e What the Patient Wants; What the Patient Needs: A Dilemma in Clinical Communication. Continuing Education for the Family Physician 20(2):126–135.
  1985f Whatever Happened to Counter-Transference? The Subjective in Medicine. In Context and Dynamics in Clinical Knowledge. Monograph Series in Ethnicity, Medicine, and Psychoanalysis vol. 1. H. F. Stein and M. Apprey, eds. Charlottesville: University Press of Virginia, 1–55.
  1986a Cultural Relativism as the Central Organizing Resistance in Cultural Anthropology. Journal of Psychoanalytic Anthropology 9(2):157–75.
  1986b Social Role and Unconscious Complementarity. Journal of Psychoanalytic Anthropology 9(3):235–68.
  1987a Culture and Ethnicity as Group-Fantasies: A Psychohistoric Paradigm of Group Identity. In From Metaphor to Meaning: Papers in Psychoanalytic Anthropology. Monograph Series in Ethnicity, Medicine and Psychoanalysis vol. 2. H. F. Stein and Maurice Apprey, eds. Charlottesville: University Press of Virginia, 122–55.
  1987b Developmental Time, Cultural Space: Studies in Psychogeography. Norman: University of Oklahoma Press.
  1988a AIDS as Lethal Metaphor. Transcultural Research Review 25(3):231–36.

1988b The Influence of the American Group-Fantasy upon Contemporary American Biomedical Education and Practice. Journal of Psychohistory 15(3):281–93.
Stein, Howard F., and Robert F. Hill
1988 The Dogma of Technology. In Psychoanalytic Study of Society, vol. 13. L. B. Boyer and S. Grolnick, eds. Hillsdale, N.J.: Analytic Press, 149–79.
Stein, Howard F., and S. Kayzakian-Rowe
1978 Hypertension, Biofeedback, and the Myth of the Machine: A Psychoanalytic-Cultural Study. Psychoanalysis and Contemporary Thought 1(1):119–56.
Stein, Howard F., and William G. Niederland
1989. Maps from the Mind: Readings in Psychogeography. Norman: University of Oklahoma Press.
Stein, L.
1967 The Doctor-Nurse Game. Archives of General Psychiatry 16:699–703.
Steiner, Richard P., ed.
1986 Folk Medicine: The Art and the Science. Washington,D.C.: American Chemical Society.
Stenning, Derrick J.
1957 Transhumance, Migratory Drift, Migration: Patterns of Pastoral Fulani Nomadism. Journal of the Royal Anthropological Institute 87:57–73.
Stepan, J.
1985 Traditional and Alternative Systems of Medicine: A Comparative View of Legislation. International Digest of Health Legislation. 36(2):283–341.
Stephen, Lynn
1988 Zapotec Gender Politics: The Creation of Political Arenas by and for Peasant Women. Paper presented at Annual Meeting of the American Anthropological Association, Phoenix.
Stern, J.
1981 Unemployment and Its Impact on Morbidity and Mortality. Discussion Paper 93. London: Centre for Labour Economics, London School of Economics.
Sternberg, Robert J.
1985 Human Intelligence: The Model Is the Message. Science 230:1111–25.
Stevens, R., L. W. Goodman, and S. S. Mick
1978 The Alien Doctors: Foreign Medical Graduates in American Hospitals. New York: Wiley.
Stierlin, Helm
1973 Group Fantasies and Family Myths: Some Theoretical and Practical Aspects. Family Process 12:111–25.
Stock, Robert
1980 Health Care Behavior in a Rural Nigerian Setting. Ph.D. dissertation, University of Liverpool.
1987 Drugs and Underdevelopment: A Case Study of Kano State, Nigeria. Studies in Third World Societies 34:115–40.
Stocking, George W
1982 Afterword: A View from the Center. In The Shaping of National Anthropologies. Tomas Gerholm and Ulf Hanerz, eds. Special Issue, Ethos. Stockholm: Etnografiska Museet, 172–186.
Stover, Eric
1987 The Open Secret: Torture and the Medical Profession in Chile. Washington, D.C.: American Association for the Advancement of Science.
Strathern, Andrew, and Marilyn Strathern
1971 Self-Decoration in Mount Hagen. London: Gerald Duckworth.
Stratmeyer, Dennis, and Jean Stratmeyer
1977 The Jacaltec Nawal and the Soul Bearer in Concepcion Huista. In Cognitive Studies of Southern Mesoamerica. H. L. Neuenswander and D. E. Arnold, eds. Dallas: S. I. L. Museum of Anthropology, 126–59.
Straus, Robert
1982 "From the Ground Up": Medical Behavioral Sciences at the University of Kentucky. Medical Anthropology Quarterly 14(1):23–25.
Strug, David L., Dana E. Hunt, Douglas S. Goldsmith, Douglas S. Lipton, and Barry Spunt 1985 Patterns of Cocaine Use among Methadone Clients. International Journal of the Addictions 20(8):1163–75.
Sullivan, Earl L., ed.
1984 Impact of Development Assistance on Egypt. Cairo Papers in Social Science, vo. 7, monograph 3. Cairo: American University in Cairo.
Susser, Ida
1985 Union Carbide and the Community Surrounding It: The Case of a Community in Puerto Rico. International Journal of Health Services 15(4): 561–83.
1988 Directions in Research on Health and Industry. Medical Anthropology Quarterly (n.s.) 2(3): 195–98.
Susser, M.
1988 Falsification, Verification and Causal Inference in Epidemiology: Reconsideration in the Light of Sir Karl Popper's Philosophy. In Causal Inference. Kenneth J. Rothman, ed. Chestnut Hill, Mass.: Epidemiology Resources, 33–57.
Suzuki, D. T.
1960 Lectures on Zen Buddhism. In Zen Buddhism. D.T. Suzuki, E. From, and R. Demartino, eds. New York: Grove Press.

Swagman, Charles F.
    1989 Fija: Fright and Illness in Highland Yemen. Social Science and Medicine 28: 381–88.
Swartz, Harold M.
    1983 The Future Development and Role of Clinical Anthropology: The Perspectives of a Medical Educator. In Clinical Anthropology. Demitri Shimkin and Peggy Golde, eds. Lanham, Md.: University Press of America, 15–25.
Symposium
    1955 Projective Testing in Ethnography (Jules Henry, S.F. Nadel, William Caudill, John J. Honigmann, Melford E. Spiro, Donald W. Fiske, and A. I. Hallowell). American Anthropologist 57:245–70.
SYSTAT
    1988 SYSTAT Manual. Evanston, Ill.: Systat.
Talbot, Lee M.
    1986 Demographic Factors in Resource Depletion and Environmental Degradation in East African Rangeland. Population and Development Review 12:441–51.
Tambiah, Stanley
    1977 The Cosmological and Performative Significance of a Thai Cult of Healing. Culture, Medicine, and Psychiatry 1:97–132.
    1985 (1981) A Performative Approach to Ritual. In Culture, Thought, and Social Action. Cambridge: Harvard University Press.
Taussig, Mark
    1982 Measuring Life Events. Journal of Health and Social Behavior 23:52–64.
Taussig, Michael T.
    1978 Nutrition, Development, and Foreign Aid: A Case Study of U.S. Directed Health Care in a Colombian Plantation Zone. International Journal of Health Services 8(1): 101–21.
    1979 Food and Development Policy: Some Tough Questions for Anthropologists. Anthropology Resource Center Newsletter 2(2).
    1980a Reification and the Consciousness of the Patient. Social Science and Medicine 14B:3–13.
    1980b The Devil and Commodity Fetishism. Chapel Hill: University of North Carolina Press.
    1984 Culture of Terror—Space of Death: Roger Casement's, Putumayo Report and the Explanation of Torture. Comparative Studies in Society and History 26(3):467–97.
    1987 Shamanism, Colonialism, and the Wild Man: A Study in Terror and Healing. Chicago: University of Chicago Press.
Taylor, C.
    1970 In Horizontal Orbit. New York: Holt, Rinehart & Winston.
Taylor, Rex, and Annelie Rieger
    1985 Medicine as Social Science: Rudolph Virchow on the Typhus Epidemic in Upper Silesia. International Journal of Health Service 15(4): 547–59.
Tedlock, B.
    1987 An Interpretive Solution to the Problem of Humoral Medicine in Latin America. Social Science and Medicine 24:1069–83.
Teicher, M. I.
    1960 Windigo Psychosis. Seattle: University of Washington Press.
Temkin, Oswei
    1963 The Scientific Approach to Disease: Specific Entity and Individual Sickness. In Scientific Change: Historical Studies in the Intellectual, Social, and Technical Conditions for Scientific Discovery and Technical Invention, from Antiquity to the Present, A. C. Crombie, ed. New York: Basic Books, 629–58.
Therborn, Göran
    1987 Migration and Western Europe: The Old World Turning New. Science 237:1183–88.
Thoits, Peggy A.
    1981 Undesirable Life Events and Psychophysiological Distress: A Problem of Operational Confounding. American Sociological Review 46:97–109.
Thompson, D.
    1939 Report on an Expedition to Arnhem Land, 1936–39. Canberra, Australia: Government Printer.
Thompson, E. P.
    1967 Time, Work, Discipline, and Industrial Capitalism. Past and Present 38:56–97.
Thompson, J. A.
    1981 Translation: The Impact of Reactionary Perspectives in Transcultural Nursing. In Developing, Teaching and Practicing Transcultural Nursing: The Proceedings of the Sixth Transcultural Nursing Conference. P. Morely, ed. Salt Lake City: University of Utah, College of Nursing and Transcultural Nursing Society, 34–36.
Tiglao, T. V.
    1982 Health Knowledge, Attitudes and Practices Related to Schistosomiasis. Hygie 1:31–38.
Todd, Harry F., and M. Margaret Clark
    1985 Medical Anthropology and the Challenge of Medical Education. In Training Manual in Medical Anthropology. C.E. Hill, ed. Washington D.C.: American Anthropological Association, 40–58.
Topley, Marjorie
    1976 Chinese Traditional Etiology and Methods of Cure in Hong Kong. In Asian Medical Systems: A Comparative Study. Charles Leslie, ed. Berkeley and Los Angeles: University of California Press, 243–72.

References

Torrey, E. Fuller
 1973 The Mind Game: Witchdoctors and Psychiatrists. New York: Bantam Books.
Toulmin, Stephen
 1982 The Return to Cosmology: Postmodern Science and the Theology of Nature. Berkeley: University of California Press.
Tran, Thanh Van
 1987 Ethnic Community Supports and Psychological Well-being of Vietnamese Refugees. International Migration Review 21:833–44.
Trevathan, W.
 1988 Childbirth in a Bicultural Community: Attitudinal and Behavioral Variation. In K. Michaelson, et al., Childbirth in America: Anthropological Perspectives, South Hadley, Mass.: Bergin and Garvey, 216–27.
Tripp-Reimer, Toni
 1980 Clinical Anthropology: Perspectives from a Nurse-Anthropologist. Medical Anthropology Newsletter 12(1):21–22.
 1983a Retention of a Folk Healing Practice (Matiasma) among Four Generations of Urban Greek Immigrants. Nursing Research 32:97–101.
 1983b Human Variability and Nursing: A Neglected Aspect of Clinical Anthropology. In Clinical Anthropology. Demitri Shimkin and Peggy Golde, eds. Lanham, Md.: University Press of America, 245–59.
 1984a Cultural Assessment. In Nursing Assessment: A Multi-dimensional Approach. J. Bellack and P. Bamford, eds. Monterey: Wadsworth Health Sciences, 226–46.
 1984b Reconceptualizing the Construct of Health: Integrating Emic and Etic Perspectives. Research in Nursing and Health 7(2):101–9.
 1984c Research in Cultural Diversity. Western Journal of Nursing Research 6(3):353–55.
Tripp-Reimer, T., and P. J. Brink
 1985 Culture Brokerage. In Nursing Interventions: Treatments for Nursing Diagnoses. G. M. Bulechek and J. C. McCloskey eds., Philadelphia: Saunders, 352–64.
Tripp-Reimer, T., P. J. Brink, and J. Saunders
 1984 Cultural Assessment: Content and Process. Nursing Outlook 32:78–82.
Tripp-Reimer, T., and M. M. Schrock
 1982 Residential Patterns and Preferences of Ethnic Aged: Implications for Transcultural Nursing. In Focus on Transcultural Nursing: Arching the Domains of Practice. Proceedings of the Seventh Transcultural Nursing Conference. J. Uhl, ed. Salt Lake City: Transcultural Nursing Society, 144–57.
Trostle, J.
 1986 Anthropology and Epidemiology in the Twentieth Century: A Selective History of Collaborative Projects and Theoretical Affinities, 1920 to 1970. In Craig Janes et al. Anthropology and Epidemiology. Dordrecht: Reidel, 59–94.
Trostle, J. et al.
 1989 Fostering Research Capacity in The Developing World: Problems and Prospects for Medical Anthropology. Symposium at AAA Annual Meeting, Washington, D.C.
Trotter II, R. T.
 1987 The Case of Lead Poisoning from Folk Remedies in Mexican American Communities. In R. M. Wulff and S. J. Fiske, eds. Anthropological Praxis: Translating Knowledge into Action. Boulder, Colo.: Westview Press, 146–159.
 n.d. Personal Communication.
Trotter II, Robert T., and Juan Antonio Chavira
 1978 Discovering New Models for Alcohol Counseling in Minority Groups. In Modern Medicine and Medical Anthropology in the United States/Mexican Border Population. Boris Velimirovic, ed. Washington D.C.: Pan American Health Organization.
Trowell, H. C., and D. P. Burkitt eds.
 1981 Western Diseases: Their Emergence and Prevention. Cambridge: Harvard University Press.
True, William R.
 1984 Perspectives on Postdoctoral Public Health Training for Medical Anthropology. Medical Anthropology Quarterly 15 (4): 95–96.
True, William R., Mary Anna Hovey, John Bryan Page, and Paul L. Doughty
 1980 Marijuana and User Lifestyles. In Cannabis in Costa Rica. William E. Carter, ed. Philadelphia: Institute for the Study of Human Issues.
Trussell, T. James
 1979 Natural Fertility: Measurement and Use in Fertility Models. In Natural Fertility. Henri Leridon and Jane Menken, eds. Liege: Ordina, 29–64.
Tsing, Anna Lowenhaupt
 n.d. Premature Mothers: Cultural Meanings of Infanticide. Unpublished manuscript.
Tuchman, Barbara W.
 1984 The March of Folly. New York: Knopf.
Tucker, Gisele Maynard
 1986 Barriers to Modern Contraceptive Use in Rural Peru. Studies in Family Planning 17(6, pt. 1):308–16.

Turnbull, Colin
    1962   The Forest People. New York: Simon & Schuster.
Turner, Bryan
    1984   The Body and Society: Explorations in Social Theory. Oxford: Basil Blackwell.
    1986   Personhood and Citizenship. Theory, Culture and Society 3:1–16.
Turner, Terrence
    1980   The Social Skin. In Not Work Alone. J. Cherfas and R. Lewin, eds. London: Temple Smith, 112–40.
Turner, Victor
    1964   An Ndembu Doctor in Practice. In A. Kiev, ed. Magic, Faith, and Healing. New York: Free Press.
    1967   The Forest of Symbols. Ithaca: Cornell University Press.
    1968   The Drums of Affliction: A Study of Religious Processes among the Ndembu of Zambia. Oxford: Clarendon.
    1969   The Ritual Process: Structure and Anti-Structure. Chicago: Aldine.
Turshen, Meredith
    1977   The Impact of Colonialism on Health and Health Services in Tanzania. International Journal of Health Services 7(1): 7–35.
    1984   The Political Ecology of Disease in Tanzania. New Brunswick: Rutgers University Press.
    1986   Health and Human Rights in a South African Bantustan. Social Science and Medicine 22(9): 887–92.
Twumasi, P. A.
    1975   Medical Systems in Ghana. Tema: Ghana Publishing Corporation.
Twumasi, P. A. and D. M. Warren
    1986   The Professionalisation of Indigenous Medicine: A Comparative Study of Ghana and Zambia. In M. Last and G. L. Chavunduka, eds. The Professionalisation of African Medicine. Manchester: Manchester University Press for the International African Institute, 117–36.
Tylor, Edward B.
    1871   Primitive Culture. Boston: Estes & Lauriat.
Underhill, Ruth M.
    1965   Red Man's Religion. Chicago: University of Chicago Press.
Unschuld, P. U.
    1975   Medico-Cultural Conflicts in Asian Settings. Social Science and Medicine 9:303 312.
    1980   The Issue of Structured Co-Existence of Scientific and Alternative Medical Systems. Social Science and Medicine 14B:15–24.
    1985   Medicine in China: A History of Ideas. Berkeley: University of California Press.
Urdaneta, M. L.
    1975   Fertility and the "Pill" in a Texas barrio. In Topia and Utopias in Health: Policy Studies. S. Ingman and A. Thomas, eds. The Hague: Mouton, 69–83.
U.S. Institute of Medicine.
    1979.   Health in Egypt: Recommendations for U.S. Assistance. Washington, D.C.: National Academy of Sciences.
Van der Geest, Sjaak
    1987a   Unequal Access to Pharmaceuticals in Southern Cameroon: The Context of a Problem. Studies in Third World Societies 34:141–68.
    1987b   Pharmaceuticals in the Third World: The Local Perspective. Social Science and Medicine 25(3):273–76.
Van der Geest, Sjaak, and Susan R. Whyte, eds.
    1988   The Context of Medicines in Developing Countries: Studies in Pharmaceutical Anthropology. Dordrecht: Kluwer.
Van der Kuyp, E.
    1961   Schistosomiasis in the Surinam District of Surinam. Tropical and Geographical Medicine 13:357–73.
Van Schaik, Eileen
    1989   Paradigms Underlying the Study of Nerves as a Popular Illness Term in Eastern Kentucky. Medical Anthropology 11(1):15–28.
Vaskilampi, Tuula, and C. P. MacCormack, eds.
    1982   Folk Medicine and Health Culture: Role of Folk Medicine in Modern Health Care. Kuopio, Finland: University of Kuopio.
Vega, William A., Bohdan Kolody, and Juan Ramon Valle
    1987   Migration and Mental Health: An Empirical Test of Depression Risk Factors among Immigrant Mexican Women. International Migration Review 21:512–30.
Velimirovic, R.
    1984   Traditional Medicine Is Not Primary Health Care. Curare 7:61–79, 85–93.
Verpoorte, R.
    1989   Some Phytochemical Aspects of Medicinal Plant Research. Journal of Ethnopharmacology. 25:43–59.
Veterans Administration Study Group on Anti-Hypertension Agents
    1970   Effect of Treatment on Morbidity in Hypertension: II. Results in Patients with Diastolic Blood Pressure Averaging 90 through 114 mm Hg. Journal of the American Medical Association 213(7):1143–52.
Vieille, Paul
    1978   Iranian Women in Family Alliance and Sexual Politics. In Women in the Muslim World. Lois Beck and Nikki Keddie, eds. Cambridge: Harvard University Press, 451–72.

References

Villa Rojas, Alfonso
 1947 Kinship and Nagualism in a Tzeltal Community, Southeastern Mexico. American Anthropologist 49: 578–87.
Vingerhoets, A. J. J. M., and F. H. G. Marcelissen
 1988 Stress Research: Its Present Status and Issues for Future Developments. Social Science and Medicine 26:279–91
Vogel, Virgil J.
 1973 American Indian Medicine. New York: Ballantine Books.
Vogt, Evon Z.
 1969 Zinacantan: A Mayan Community in the Highlands of Chiapas. Cambridge: Belknap Press of Harvard University Press.
 1970 The Zinacantecos of Mexico: A Modern Mayan Way of Life. New York: Holt, Rinehart & Winston.
Volkan, Vamik D.
 1976 Primitive Internalized Object Relations. New York: International Universities Press.
 1988 The Need to Have Enemies and Allies. New York: Jason Aronson.
Von Mering, Otto
 1985 On Doing Anthropology in Clinical Settings: A Commentary. Medical Anthropology Quarterly 16(3):71–73.
Vries, M. W. de, R. L. Berg, and M. Lipkin et al., eds.
 1982 Use and Abuse of Medicine. New York: Praeger.
Waddell, Jack O.
 1988 Playing the Paradox: Papago Indian Management of Reservation/Off Reservation Prohibition Policies. Paper Presented at the International Union of Anthropological and Ethnological Sciences Congress, Zagreb, Yugoslavia.
Waddell, Jack O., and Michael W. Everett, eds.
 1980 Drinking Behaviors among Southwestern Indians: An Anthropological Perspective. Tucson: University of Arizona Press.
 1984 Alcoholism-Treatment-Center-Based Projects. In Recent Developments in Alcoholism, vol. 2. Marc Galanter, ed. New York: Plenum.
Waitzkin, Howard
 1979 The Marxist Paradigm in Medicine. International Journal of Health Services 9(4): 683–99.
 1983 The Second Sickness: Contradictions of Capitalist Health Care. New York: Free Press.
 1986 Micropolitics of Medicine: Theoretical Issues. Medical Anthropology Quarterly 17(5):134–36.
 1989 Introduction. Marxist Perspectives in Social Medicine. Social Science and Medicine 11:1099–1101.
Wallace, A. F. C.
 1956 Tornado in Worcester: An Exploratory Study of Individual and Community Behavior in Extreme Situations. Washington, D.C.: National Academy of Sciences/National Research Council.
 1959 Cultural Determinants of Response to Hallucinatory Experience. Archives of General Psychiatry 1:58–69.
 1960 An Interdisciplinary Approach to Mental Disorder among the Polar Eskimo of Northwest Greenland. Anthropologica 11:1–12.
Wallerstein, Immanuel
 1979 The Capitalist World Economy: Essays. New York: Cambridge University Press.
Walsh, Anthony, and Patricia Ann Walsh
 1987 Social Support, Assimilation, and Biological Effective Blood Pressure Levels. International Migration Review 21:577–91.
Warner, W. L.
 1958 A Black Civilization: A Social Study of an Australian Tribe. New York: Harper & Row.
Warwick, R., ed.
 1977 Nomina Anatomica. 4th ed. Amsterdam: Elsevier, Excerpta Medica for the International Anatomical Nomenclature Committee.
Waterman, P. G.
 1984 Food Acquisition and Processing as a Function of Plant Chemistry. In Food Acquisition and Processing in Primates. D. J. Chivers, B. A. Wood, and A. Bilsborough, eds. New York: Plenum Press, 177–211.
Watson, J. D.
 1986 The Double Helix. New York: Signet Books.
Webel, Charles P.
 1983 Self: An Overview. International Encyclopedia of Psychiatry, Psychoanalysis, Psychobiology, and Neurology. Benjamin Wolman, ed. New York: Aesculepius Press, 398–403.
Weber, M.
 1946 Class, Status, Party. In From Max Weber: Essays in Sociology. H. H. Gerth and C. Wright Mills, eds. New York: Oxford University Press.
 1947 Theory of Social and Economic Organization. New York: Free Press.
Wegrocki, Henry J.
 1953 A Critique of Cultural and Statistical Concepts of Abnormality. In Personality in Nature, Society, and Culture, Clyde Kluckhohn and Henry A. Murray, eds., New York: Alfred A. Knopf, 691–701.

Weibel-Orlando, Joan
- 1984 Substance Abuse among American Indian Youth: A Continuing Crisis. Journal of Drug Issues (Spring): 313–335.
- 1987 Culture-Specific Treatment Modalities: Assessing Client-to-Treatment Fit in Indian Alcoholism Programs. Treatment and Prevention of Alcohol Problems: A Resource Manual. New York: Academic Press.
- 1988 Hooked on Healing: The Anthropologist's Role in Substance Abuse Intervention. Newsletter of the Alcohol and Drug Study Group, American Anthropological Association, no. 21.

Weidman, Hazel H.
- 1980 Comments on "Clinical Anthropology." Medical Anthropology Newsletter 12(1):16–17.
- 1982a Introducing Transcultural Perspectives in Medical Training. Medical Anthropology Quarterly 14(1):25–26.
- 1982b Research Strategies, Structural Alterations, and Clinically Relevant Anthropology. In Noel J. Chrisman and Thomas W. Maretzki, eds. Clinically Applied Anthropology: Anthropologists in Health Science Settings. Dordrecht: D. Reidel, 201–43.
- 1983 Research, Service and Training Aspects of Clinical Anthropology: An Institutional Overview. In Clinical Anthropology. Demitri Shimkin and Peggy Golde, eds. Lanham, Md.: University Press of America, 119–55.
- 1985 Stylistic Aspects of Clinical Anthropology: A Mirrored Description. Medical Anthropology Quarterly 16(3):63–64

Weil, Peter M.
- 1986 Agricultural Intensification and Fertility in the Gambia (West Africa). In Culture and Reproduction. W. Penn Handwerker, ed. Boulder, Colo.: Westview, 294–320.

Weiss, M. G.
- 1988 Cultural Models of Diarrheal Illness: Conceptual Framework and Review. In J. Coreil and J. D. Mull, Anthropological Studies of Diarrheal Illness. Special Issue of Social Science and Medicine 27(1):5–16.

Welch, M. L.
- 1989 Trauma Recovery: An Ethnography. Ph.D. dissertation, University of Connecticut.

Weller, Susan C.
- 1983 New Data on Intracultural Variability: The Hot-Cold Concept of Medicine and Illness. Human Organization 42:249–57.

Wellin, Edward
- 1977 Theoretical Orientations in Medical Anthropology. In Culture, Disease, and Healing. D. Landy, ed. New York: Macmillan, 47–54.

Werner, David
- 1977 The Village Health Worker—Lackey or Liberator? Paper presented at the International Hospital Federation Congress, Tokyo: May 22–27.
- 1983 Health Care in Cuba: A Model Service or a Means of Social Control—or Both? In Practicing Health for All. David Morley, Jon Rohde, and Glen Williams, eds. Oxford: Oxford University Press, 17–38.
- 1988 Empowerment and Health. Talk by David Werner. Christian Medical Commission/CCPD Joint Commission Meeting, Manila, Philippines, January 12–19.

Westermeyer, Joseph
- 1982 Poppies, Pipes and People: Opium and Its Use in Laos. Berkeley: University of California Press.
- 1985 Hmong Drinking Practices in the United States: The Influence of Migration. In The American Experience with Alcohol. L. Bennett and G. Ames, eds. New York: Plenum.

Westermeyer, Joseph, J. Neider, and T. F. Vang
- 1984 Acculturation and Mental Health: A Study of Hwang Refugees at 1.5 and 3.5 Years Postmigration. Social Science and Medicine 18:87–94.

Wethington, Ethel, and Ronald C. Kessler
- 1986 Perceived Support, Received Support, and Adjustment to Stressful Life Events. Journal of Health and Social Behavior 27:78–89

Wheaton, Blair
- 1983 Stress, Personal Resources, and Psychiatric Symptoms: An Investigation of Interactive Models. Journal of Health and Social Behavior 24:208–29.

White, Kerr L.
- 1988 The Task of Medicine: Dialogue at Wickenburg. Menlo Park, Calif.: The Henry J. Kaiser Family Foundation.

Whiteford, Linda
- 1986 Economic Diversity, Family Strategy, and Fertility in a Mexican-American Community. In Culture and Reproduction, W. Penn Handwerker, ed. Boulder, Colo.: Westview, 237–48.

Whiteford, Linda M., and Michael Sharinus
- 1988 Delayed Accomplishments: Family Formation among Older First-Time Parents. In Childbirth in America. Karen Michaelson, ed. South Hadley, Massachusetts: Bergin and Garvey. 239–53.

Whiteford, Scott, and Laura Montgomery
- 1985 The Political Economy of Rural Transformation: A Mexican Case. In Micro and Macro Levels of Analysis in Anthropology. Billie R. DeWalt and Pertti J. Pelto, eds. Boulder, Colo.: Westview Press, 147–64.

Whiting, Beatrice B.
- 1950 Paiute Sorcery. Publications in Anthropology, no. 15. New York: Viking.

References

Whiting, John W. M.
- 1961 Socialization Process and Personality. In Psychological Anthropology: Approaches to Culture and Personality. F. L. K. Hsu, ed. Homewood, Ill.: Dorsey Press, 355–80.

Wiesenfeld, S. L.
- 1967 Sickle-Cell Trait in Human Biological and Cultural Evolution. Science 157:1134–40.

Wilcox, L.
- 1981 Social Support, Life Stress, and Psychological Adjustment: A Test of the Buffering Hypothesis. American Journal of Community Psychology 9:371–86.

Williams, M. A.
- 1972 A Comparative Study of Post-surgical Convalescence among Women of Two Ethnic Groups: Anglo and Mexican American. In Communicating Nursing Research. The Many Sources of Nursing Knowledge. M. Batey, ed. Boulder, Colo: Western Interstate Commission on Higher Education, 5:59–73.

Williams, T. R., and M. Williams
- 1959 The Socialization of the Student Nurse. Nursing Research 8:18–25.

Wilmsen, Edwin
- 1986 Biological Determinants of Fecundity and Fecundability: An Application of Bongaarts' Model to Forager Fertility. In Culture and Reproduction, W. Penn Handwerker, ed. Boulder, Colo.: Westview, 59–89.

Wilson, Monica
- 1977 For Men and Elders: Change in the Relations of Generations and of Men and Women among the Nyakyusa-Ngonde People, 1875–1971. New York: Africana.

Windom, R. E.
- 1987 Seeking Answers to the Slowing Progress in Lowering Infant Mortality. Public Health Reports 102(2):121–22.

Winnicot, David
- 1971 Le Corps et le self. Nouvelle revue de psychanalyse 3:37–51.

Winslow, C-E. A.
- 1951 The Cost of Sickness and the Price of Health. World Health Monograph Series, no. 7. Geneva.

Wolf, Eric
- 1956 Aspects of Group Relations in a Complex Society: Mexico. American Anthropologist 58:1065–78.
- 1982 Europe and the People without History. Berkeley: University of California Press.

Wood, James W., and Maxine Weinstein
- 1988 A Model of Age-Specific Fecundability. Population Studies 42:85–114.

World Agricultural Research Project
- 1980 The Political Economy of Food and Agriculture. International Journal of Health Services 10:161–70.

World Health Organization
- 1973 The International Pilot Study of Schizophrenia. Geneva: WHO.
- 1974 Glossary of Mental Disorders and Guide to their Classification. Geneva: WHO.
- 1976 African Traditional Medicine: A Report of an Expert Group. AFRO Technical Report Series, no.11. Brazzaville: WHO Regional Office for Africa.
- 1978a The Alma-Ata Conference on Primary Health Care. WHO Chronicle 32(11):431–38.
- 1978b The Promotion and Development of Traditional Medicine: Report of a WHO Meeting. WHO Technical Report Series, no. 622. Geneva: WHO.
- 1979 Workshop on the Role of Human/Water Contact in Schistosomiasis Transmission. WHO Technical Report Series, No. 79.3. Geneva: World Health Organization.
- 1980 Expert Committee Report on Problems Related to Alcohol Consumption. WHO Technical Report Series 650. Geneva: World Health Organization.

Worsley, Peter
- 1966 The End of Anthropology? Paper prepared for the Sociology and Social Anthropology Working Group, Sixth World Congress of Sociology.
- 1981 Social Class and Development. In Social Inequality: Comparative and Developmental Approaches. Gerald D. Berreman, ed. New York: Academic Press.
- 1982 Non-Western Medical Systems. Annual Review of Anthropology 11:315–48.
- 1984 The Three Worlds: Culture and World Development. London: George Weidenfeld and Nicolson.

Wrangham, R. W., and T. Nishida
- 1983 Aspilia spp. Leaves: A Puzzle in the Feeding Behavior of Wild Chimpanzees. Primates 24:276–82.

Wright, Anne
- 1982 Attitudes toward Childbearing and Menstruation among the Navaho. In Anthropology of Human Birth, Margarita Artschwager Kay, ed. Philadelphia: F. A. Davis Co., 377–94.

Wrigley, E. A., and R. S. Schofield
- 1981 The Population History of England, 1541–1871. Cambridge: Harvard University Press.

Wulf, Robert M. and Shirley J. Fisk, eds.
- 1987 Anthropological Praxis: Translating Knowledge Into Action. Boulder: Westview Press.

Wunsch, G. J., and M. G. Termote
- 1978 Introduction to Demographic Analysis. New York: Plenum.

Yamahara, J., S. Miki, H. Murakami, T. Sawada, and H. Fujimura
- 1985 Screening Test for Calcium Antagonists in Natural Products and the Active Principles of Cnidii monnieri. Yakugaku Zasshi 105:449–58.

Yap, P. M.
- 1974 Comparative Psychiatry: A Theoretical Framework. Toronto: University of Toronto Press.
- 1977 The Culture-Bound Reactive Syndromes. In D. Landy, ed., Culture, Disease and Healing: Studies in Medical Anthropology. New York: Macmillan, 340–49.

Young, Allan
- 1978 Rethinking the Western Health Enterprise. Medical Anthropology (Spring):1–10, 34.
- 1980 The Discourse on Stress and the Reproduction of Conventional Knowledge. Social Science and Medicine, 14B:133–46.
- 1982 The Anthropologies of Illness and Sickness. In Annual Review of Anthropology 11:257–85.
- 1983 Relevance of Traditional Medical Cultures to Modern Primary Health Care. Social Science and Medicine 17(16):1205–11.
- 1988 A Description of How Ideology Shapes Knowledge of a Mental Disorder. In Analysis in Medical Anthropology. S. Lindenbaum and M. Lock, eds. Dordrecht: Kluwer Academic Publishers.

Young, J. C.
- 1980 A Model of Illness Treatment Decisions in a Tarascan Town. American Ethnologist 7:81–97.
- 1981 Medical Choice in a Mexican Village. New Brunswick, N.J.: Rutgers University Press.

Young, J. C. and Linda Garro
- 1982 Variation in the Choice of Treatment in Two Mexican Communities. Social Science and Medicine 16:1453–65.

Yu, M. C., J. H. C. Ho, S. H. Lai, and B. E. Henderson
- 1986 Cantonese-style Salted Fish as a Cause of Nasopharyngeal Carcinoma: Report of a Case-Control Study in Hong Kong. Cancer Research 46:956–61.

Zahan, Dominique
- 1979 The Religion, Spirituality, and Thought of Traditional Africa. Chicago: University of Chicago Press.

Zatuchni, G. I., J. J. Sciarra, and J. J. Speidel, eds.
- 1979 Pregnancy Termination. New York: Harper & Row.

Zola, I.K.
- 1972 Medicine as an Institution of Social Control. Sociological Review 20(4):487–504.

Zumstein, A.
- 1983 A Study of Some Factors Influencing the Epidemiology of Urinary Schistosomiasis at Ifakara (Kilombero District, Morogoro Region, Tanzania). Acta Tropica 40:187–204.

INDEX

Abnormality, definition of, 306–8
Abortion, 13, 228, 333, 371
Acculturation: and cardiovascular disease, 262; as stress predictor, 262, 266
Ackernecht, Erwin, 116
Adaptation, 188, 191, 195–96
Adolescent pregnancy, 314–16
Advocacy, 7, 166. *See also* Medical anthropology
Africa, schistosomiasis in, 209–12
Age structure, 325–26, 328, 331
Aggression, 84, 89
Agriculture, health implications of, 194, 377
AIDS, 60, 213, 306–7, 350–52
Alcohol: biocultural approach to, 235; functional use of, 233; studies of, 230–32, 239. *See also* Drinking patterns
Alcoholism: biocultural approach to, 244, 246; causes of, 246; disease concept of, 242; and firewater myth, 244; moral model of, 242–43; social construction of, 170; treatment of, 245
Alexander, Linda, 102
Algeria, 63–64
Alland, Alexander, 191
Allison, A. C., 199
Allopathy, 118
Alma Ata, 371, 386

Alubo, Ogoh, 39
American Indians, and substance abuse, 235–36, 240–41, 244–46
Amniocentesis, 228
Amok, 141
Anthropology, male bias in, 184
Apache, 144–46
Applied anthropology: in clinical settings, 94; in medical anthropology, 94; in public health, 96
Archoses, definition of, 87
Asbestos, and disease, 201
Asylums, 168
Australia, myxomatosis in, 192–93
Ayurvedic medicine, 155, 164, 354

Baer, Hans, 42–43, 98
Barefoot doctors, 359
Bariba (Benin), 220–23, 227
Barnett, Elyse, 221
Bastien, J., 62
Bedouins (Egypt), 151
Belief, concept of, 108
Benedict, Ruth, 116
Bentley, M. E., 287–89, 293
Berry, J. W., 262
Bibeau, Gilles, 123
Biocultural approach, 3–6; to alcoholism, 246–47; in drug studies, 234–35; in

epidemiology, 191; in ethnopharmacology, 150; in nursing, 184, 212, 215, 235
Biological reductionism, 4. *See also* Biomedicine
Biomedicine: and capitalism, 45; critical analyses of, 167; cultural construction of, 4, 48, 159, 161, 164, 190; cultural variation in, 351; decision making in, 78; definition of, 159, 189; diagnosis in, 51–52; as a dominative system, 43; as ethnomedicine, 86, 118–19, 160; hegemony of, 35, 39, 42, 169; model of disease in, 36; professional dominance of, 350; and psychiatry, 136; reductionism in, 4, 53, 70, 101, 136, 161; relation to midwifery of, 170; role of physician in, 163; and standards of illness, 150; symbolic dimension of, 23
Biostatistics, 307
Birth attendants, training of, 389
Birth control, 226, 321, 333, 387
Blake, Judith, 219
Bock, Philip K., 78
Body: representations of, 47, 49–51; body politic, 65; in Buddhist thought, 55; control of, 163; in cosmology, 62; cultural constructions of, 61; imagery of, 59–60, 66–67; machine metaphors of, 64; in medical texts, 161; as metaphor of distress, 70; psychoanalytic perspectives on, 75; as symbol, 60, 63
Bolivia, 62
Bourdieu, Pierre, 63–64, 68
Brazil, 258, 286–88, 300; medical treatment in, 168–69
Brown, George, 259–60
Brown, Peter, 196–97, 377
Browner, Carole, 150, 219, 280
Bruhn, John, 260
Bulemia, 13
Bunzel, Ruth, 238–39

Canada, 239–40
Cannabis research, 232, 236, 238. *See also* Ganja
Cannon, W. B., 23

Capitalism, medicine under, 28, 167; and health, 33, 40, 43, 169
Care providers: gender of, 184; status of, 183
Caring, concept of, 181
Cartesian dualism, 51–53, 136, 161, 163, 166
Case control studies: definition of, 306; use of, 311–12
Cassel, John, 248
Catharsis, 24
Caudill, William, 93–94, 252
Cesarean section, 227
Cheesmond, Ann, 210
Child socialization, 81
Child survival, 376, 387–88
Childbearing trajectories, 341
Childbirth, 13, 168–70, 217; in Africa, 222–23; and cesarean section, 227; cultural patterning of, 221–22; and gender roles, 225; incantations for, 221; in Malaysia, 223–24, 226; medicalization of, 221; modesty in, 224; as physiological event, 221; ritual during, 224; and status, 222; and witchcraft, 222. *See also* Birth attendants; Pregnancy
China: depression and neurasthenia in, 260; dietary habits in, 200–201; medical professionalism in, 359–60
Chinese medicine, 12, 17, 55, 57, 60, 166. *See also* Medical systems
Chrisman, Noel, 93, 165
Chronic illness, 112, 166, 195, 299
Churches, as healing centers, 365. *See also* Faith healing
Class, and health, 49, 253, 262, 264
Clements, Forrest E., 116
Clinical ideology, 78
Clinical relationships, transference in, 76
Clinically applied anthropology, 3; advocacy in, 178; critical approaches to, 97; definition of, 95, 97, 159–60; and ethnography, 104, 182; methods in, 99, 277–78; systems perspective for, 102; theory in, 104; therapy in, 95. *See also* Therapeutic anthropology
Coca, 152

Cocaine, 232
Cognitive restructuring, 256
Cohort designs, 312–13, 333
Colby, Benjamin, 266
Collier, Jane, 219
Colombia, 219, 237
Colonialism: medicine under, 39, 368; political torture during, 67
Contraception, 226, 333, 387
Coping style, 259, 266
Coreil, J., 289
Cosmopolitan medicine, 118
Costa Rica, 238
Council on Nursing and Anthropology, 175
Countertransference, in medical anthropology, 85
Crawford, Robert, 66–67
Critical medical anthropology, 27, 33, 35, 45, 48; in clinically applied anthropology, 98–99; definition of, 159–60
Critical-interpretive medical anthropology, 49, 69, 97
Cross-cultural research, in nursing, 181–84
Crude birth rate, 335
Crude death rate, 335
Cultural evolution: and disease, 194; and selective pressures, 324
Cultural psychiatry, survey of, 147
Cultural relativism, 27, 86, 90; in clinical settings, 108–9, 111–12, 116
Culture, 183; in biological matrix, 132; concept in drug research, 233; concept in medical anthropology, 274–75; definitions for clinical settings, 106–7; definition of system, 160; as fantasy, 74, 82, 86–87; and patient care, 100; of patients, 103; and patterns of disease, 187; and personality organization, 82; psychopathology in, 87
Culture and personality, school of, 79, 81; and psychoanalysis, 80, 132
Culture broker, 181
Culture-bound syndromes, 36, 89, 133, 140–43; *amok* as, 141; *latah* as, 141; *piblogtok* as, 141

Culture-sensitive care, 111–12
Custom, concept of, 107

Darwin, Charles, 322
Darwin, population theory of, 322
de Mause, Lloyd, 66, 83
Decision models, 285
Decision-making, biomedical, 78; and reproduction, 226–27; role of unconscious in, 85
Demography, 7; contributions to medical anthropology, 320; policy issues in, 319; sampling in, 332
Demoralization hypothesis (in psychotherapy), 24
Dependency theory, 34–35, 39
Depression, 254, 259–60
Depth psychology, 78
Descartes, Rene, 52. See also Cartesian dualism
Development, and disease risks, 211, 264, 369; health consequences of, 383–84. See also International health
Development policy, 40, 44, 383
Devereux, George, 88–89
Deviance, and social responsibility, 137; and sick role, 137–39
Diagnosis, definition of, 12; unconscious significance of, 88
Diarrheal disease, 287–90, 368, 378, 388
Discourse, medical, 37–38, 43
Disease: biomedical standards of, 150; causation of, 58, 115–16, 130, 136, 169, 188, 198, 299, 305; cultural adaptations to, 196; cultural categories of, 71, 187, 213; definition of, 12, 110, 140, 165, 174, 190, 213, 251, 267; distribution of, 187, 197; and environment, 201; epidemic, 192; factors in transmission of, 207–8, 212–13; in human context, 187; interaction with culture, 214; macrostructural context of, 209; as metaphor, 190; methods in study of, 188; natural history of, 314; psychogenic causes of, 201; risk factors for, 197–98, 306–8; social production of, 43–44. See also Sickness
Disease ecology, definition of, 191

Dobkin de Rios, Marlene, 235
Dogon (Sudan), 62
Doll, R., 312–13
Donahue, John, 43–44
Douglas, Mary, 65
Dow, James, 19
Dreher, Melanie, 236–37
Dressler, William, 253–54, 257–58, 260, 263, 286–87
Drinking patterns, 238; and acculturation, 240–41; and culture change, 239; gender differences in, 239; occupational differences in, 239. *See also* Alcohol
Drug dumping, 383
Drug research: clinical perspectives on, 232; culture concept in, 233; history of, 231; methodology in, 238; policy issues in, 232, 238, 241, 246; relevance to medical anthropology, 230; trends in, 234
Drunken comportment, 241–42. *See also* Alcohol
DSM-IIIR, 13, 140, 313, 317; concept of culture in, 143
Dunn, Frederick, 210
Durkheim, Emile, 53, 256

Echinococcosis, 207–8
Ecology, 36–37; definition of, 188, 190
Ecosystem, 190–91
Ecuador, 152, 154, 200, 281–82
Edgerton, Robert, 241–42
Efficacy: of healing, 16–18, 20; of Yoruba medicine, 20
Egypt: childbearing in, 219; health services in, 40–41; population growth in, 386; schistosomiasis in, 210–12; social support in, 257; trachoma in, 202
Eisenberg, Leon, 165
Eliot, Charles, 368
Emic analysis, 43, 134
Emotion, theory of, 69
Empacho, 202
Endemic disease, 192–93
Engels, Friedrich, 33
Environment: definition of, 180; and disease, 201; exploitation of, 188; pollution of, 201

Epidemic disease, 192–93, 205–6
Epidemiology, 7, 187–88; causation in, 308–9; of complex society, 195; contribution to medical anthropology, 299; definition of, 299; definition of abnormality in, 308; history of, 299–300; and holistic approach, 302, 316; interdisciplinary research in, 302; methodology in, 300, 302, 304, 310–13; research design in, 310
Epstein-Barr virus, 12–13
Erikson, Erik, 85
Escobar, Arturo, 369
Ethiopia: echinococcosis in, 208; schistosomiasis in, 211
Ethnic cookbook, 100–101, 105
Ethnic stereotypes, 176; in clinical settings, 106
Ethnicity, and patient care, 104–5
Ethnoanatomy, 60
Ethnocentrism, 8, 111
Ethnography, 36; in clinical settings, 104; in nursing, 182; and rapid assessment, 292–93; and studies of reproduction, 217, 267
Ethnomedicine, 43, 196; biomedicine as, 86, 115; and concepts of self, 58; definition of, 118; history of, 118; language of, 122; methodology for, 124
Ethnoophthalmology, 202
Ethnopharmacology, 3–4; definition of, 149; methodology in, 150. *See also* Medicinal plants
Ethnophysiology, 225
Ethnopsychiatry, 3–4; semantic analysis of, 133
Ethnoscience, 183
Etic analysis, 134
Explanatory model, 110–11, 123, 165, 177, 276, 285; of diarrheal disease, 288

Fabrega, Horacio, 63–64, 275
Faith healing, 24, 365
Family planning, 321, 387
Fava bean, 197
Fecundability, definition of, 333
Feminism, 217

Ferguson, Anne, 35
Ferreira, Antonio, 83
Fertility, 218; correlation with fertility, 386; intermediate variables, 333; theories of, 322; value of, 219
Fertility rate, general, 330–31; age-specific, 331–32; total, 331
Finkler, Kaja, 278
"Firewater myth," 244, 246. *See also* Alcoholism
Folk illnesses, 119, 130, 179
Fontanel, 124
Foragers, mortality among, 194
Foucault, Michael, 67, 162–63, 169
France, 230, 299, 355–56
Frank, Jerome, 21
Frankenberg, Ronald, 41
Freud, Sigmund, 54, 74, 77–78
Functionalism, 116

Gahuku-Gama (New Guinea), 58
Ganja, 236–37. *See also* Cannabis
Gaze, medical, 68, 166
Geertz, Clifford, 160
Gender: and child survival, 376; and curing, 127; and genetic counseling, 162; and health, 33, 35, 42, 45, 97; and reproduction, 215, 221, 225
Genece, E., 289
General fertility rate, 330–31
Genetic counseling, 162
Genetic diseases, 197–99, 228
Gittelsohn, J., 284–85
Goiter, 200
Golde, Peggy, 95–96
Graves, Nancy, 254, 258
Graves, Theodore, 240–41, 254, 258
Great Britain, 357–58
Green revolution, 377
Greene, L., 200
Grief, as disease, 140
Gross reproductive rate, 343. *See also* Demography
Gruenberg, Ellen, 39–40
Guatemala, 116, 118; alcohol use in, 239; health in, 380–82

Hahn, Robert, 163–64
Haiti, 289

Haldane, J.B.S., 192
Hallowell, A. Irving, 138
Hallucinogens, 234
Hausa, 152–54, 156, 158, 197
Healers: apprenticeship of, 126; categories of, 143; empirical knowledge of, 127; and professional knowledge, 362–63; recruitment of, 115, 126; training of, 128
Healing: clinical analyses of, 19–20; definition of, 11; hegemony in, 41; medical, 13; nonmedical, 13, 15; persuasive emphasis in, 21; procedures, 129–30; religious, 14–15, 22; social relations of, 29; social support in, 20; structural analyses of, 19; symbolic, 11, 19, 23
Health: biobehavioral aspects of, 157; and capitalism, 33, 39, 40, 43, 49, 169; and cash cropping, 377; commodification of, 33; concept in nursing, 181; definition of, 189; and political repression, 379; and power relations, 37–38, 167; and social body, 62; and social class, 384
Health care practitioners: categories of, 143, 183; encounters with, 277
Health care system, 112
Health education, 207
Health policy, state role in, 40–41, 377
Health science setting, role of anthropologist in, 102, 107–8
Health-seeking behavior, 125
Heath, Dwight B., 239, 243
Hemoglobin system, 195, 199
Herbal pharmacopoeias, 151
Herbal remedies, 226. *See also* Medicinal plants
Herd immunity, definition of, 205
Hill, A., 312–13
Hippocrates, 51–52
Hispanic Americans, 20
Ho, H. C., 200
Hoben, Alan, 369
Holism, 28–29, 45, 55–56, 90, 93, 102; in epidemiology, 316–17; in nursing, 176
Homeopathic medicine, 12
Homeopathy, 353, 358–59

Homology, in analysis of healing, 19–21, 22
Honigman, John, 139
Hospital, social organization of, 103
Hot-cold theory, 226
Household, as demographic unit, 320
Howard, Alan, 250–51
Human evolution, 5, 132, 192; role of disease in, 188
Human nature, 86, 88, 180
Humoral medicine, 120–22, 226. *See also* Hot-cold
Hurtado, E., 292–93
Hypertension, 253, 263, 286, 307
Hypoglycemia, 12
Hypothesis, definition of, 273

Iatrogenesis, 169, 202
Illness: definition of, 12, 110; and social body, 62; somatization, 67; supernatural forces in, 115
Illness beliefs, 112, 125, 179; intracultural diversity in, 276
Illness-disease distinction, 109–10; 165–66, 174, 181, 189, 275
Immune system, 190, 195
India, 287–89; medical professionalism in, 359–60
Infant formula, 382–83
Infant mortality, 316, 334–35, 372
Infanticide, 340
Infectious disease, 188, 195, 203, 205–6, 299; and infant mortality, 372
Infertility, 228, 332
Institute of Applied Social and Economic Research (ISAER) Alcohol Project (Papua New Guinea), 241
International health agencies: categories of, 371; organization of, 370
International health: definition of, 368; history of, 368, 385; issues in Third World, 372; policy, 8; and political economy, 369; population programs in, 385; primary health care programs in, 386–87
Iran, 123
Ireland, 66

Islamic cosmology, 55
Ivory Coast, 39

Jamaica, 291; cannabis use in, 236–37
Janes, Craig, 281
Janzen, David, 17
Japan, 57–58, 218; Morita therapy in, 78–79
Jaundice, treatment of, 152
Jellinek, E. M., 243
Johnson, Thomas, 95

Katz, S. V., 197
Kaufman, Sharon, 277
Kenya: echinococcosis in, 208; malaria control in, 194
Kernberg, Otto, 74
Kirsch, Max, 38, 43
Kitzinger, Sheila, 218
Kleinman, Arthur, 18, 112, 123, 164–65, 260, 267, 275–77
Kloos, H., 211–12
Koch, Robert, 300
Kohut, Heinz, 74
Kramer, S., 308–9
Kris, Ernst, 83
Kroeber, A. L., 82
!Kung (Botswana), 58
Kunstadter, Peter, 280–81
Kuru, 108

LaBarre, Weston, 75, 82, 87–89, 235–36
Laderman, Carol, 224, 226
Landy, David, 191
Langer, Suzanne, 22
Lasker, Judith, 39
Latah, 13, 141
Lazarus, Emily, 99, 258
Lead poisoning, 202
Leland, Joy, 244
Levi-Strauss, Claude, 19, 21
Lexis diagrams, 334
Life events, 253–54, 264
Life expectancy, 335, 338
Life stress hypothesis, 254
Life tables, 335, 338–40
Life-style index, 286
Like, Robert, 111

Literacy, 373–75
Livingstone, F. B., 199
Lock, Margaret, 36
Locke, John, 56–57
Logan, Michael, 279–80

MacAndrew, Craig, 241–42
McClain, Carol, 225, 227
MacCormack, C. P., 197
McNeill, W. H., 193
Macroscopic analyses, 29–30, 38, 45
Madagascar, 151
MADD (Mothers Against Drunk Driving), 240. *See also* Alcohol
Magic, properties of plants, 152
Mal de ojo, 130
Malaria, 193, 196–97
Malaysia, childbirth in, 223–24, 226
Malinowski, Bronislaw, 217
Malnutrition, 40, 199–200, 376
Mandelbaum, David, 233
Manning, Peter, 63–64
Maretzki, Thomas, 93, 165
Mars, Gerald, 239–40
Marshall, Mac, 241
Martin, Emily, 169
Martinez, H., 288
Marx, Karl, 54
Marxism in anthropology, 33, 37
Mason, John, 250
Materialist perspective, 27. *See also* World system
Maternal roles, 217, 220; and gender ideology, 218
Maternal/child health, 217, 376, 389
Maternity, paradigms of, 217, 219–21, 227
Mausner, J. S., 308–9
Mauss, Marcel, 53
May, Jacques, 190, 196
Maya: childbirth among, 227; training of midwives, 169
Mead, Margaret, 225
Meaning-centered approach, 29, 165
Medical anthropology: advocacy in, 7, 166; as applied discipline, 269; in clinical curriculum, 100; clinical practice in, 96; in clinical settings, 93, 101–2, 105, 107; countertransference in, 85; definition of, 93; diversity in, 8; and epidemiology, 299; funding for, 269–70; history of, 1, 47; interdisciplinary research in, 269, 296; materialist perspective in, 28; methods in, 213, 270; policy issues in, 7, 269–70, 345, 367–70; socioculturalism in, 29; study of specific diseases in, 290; theory in, 2, 8, 36, 176, 270, 272; use of statistical programs in, 295
Medical choice, 226
Medical culture: and American model, 356; and Chinese model, 359–60; and French model, 355; and German model, 358; and Indian model, 359–60; market examples of, 357; national and international, 351–53; and Soviet model, 355; and state monopoly model, 355; and Third World model, 360
Medical ecology, limitations of, 36–37
Medical knowledge, production of, 4, 33, 49–50, 67, 162, 166–67, 171, 176, 362
Medical monopolies, 355
Medical pluralism, 41
Medical systems, 3; ayurvedic, 164; under capitalism, 169; under colonialism, 39; non-Western, 14; professional, 14
Medical technology, 41, 167, 228
Medicalization, 53; of everyday life, 140; of social problems, 68, 166
Medications, 149. *See also* Ethnopharmacology
Medicinal plants, 149–51; antimalarial, 197; contextualization of, 156; efficacy of, 152–55; as food, 152, 156; for reproductive health, 225–26. *See also* Ethnopharmacology
Medicines, compound, 155
Menopause, 161, 167–68, 220; and women's status, 221
Menstrual taboos, 220
Menstruation, 220
Mental disorders, 138; role of life events in, 252–54
Mesothelioma, 201

Methodology, 6, 31, 47, 184, 213, 290–91; in clinic setting, 277–78; in community setting, 279; control group in 273; definition of, 273; in demography, 332; in drug research, 238; for ethnomedicine, 124; in ethnopharmacology, 150, 157; and household unit of analysis, 282; in medical anthropology, 97; and political economy, 36–37; in psychoanalytic anthropology, 81; qualitative, 283; and quantitative techniques, 289; and rapid ethnographic assessment, 291–93; and sampling, 280–83; and statistical programs, 295; and structured interviewing, 285; and use of census, 283; and use of microcomputers, 294; variables in, 271, 272–73
Mexican-Americans, 262
Mexico, 58–59, 116–18; alcohol use in, 239; childbearing in, 225–26; diarrheal disease in, 288; health care alternatives in, 285–86; health-seeking behavior in, 125–26; social support in, 257; spiritualist healers, 278
Michaels, David, 37–38
Micro-macro articulation, 45
Microcomputers, 294–95, 296
Middle East, 218
Midwifery, 169, 221
Migration: adjustment to, 261, 166; as demographic process, 340; health effects of, 379; Samoan, 281
Mind-body distinction, 54, 57, 63, 69, 163, 166. See also Cartesian dualism
Mississippi Project, 96
Model, definition of, 273
Modes of production, 28
Moerman, Daniel, 22–23
Montagu, M. F. Ashley, 217, 225
Morsy, Soheir, 129, 257
Mortality, among foragers, 194
Motherhood, 219. See also Maternity
Mullings, Leith, 65–66
Multinational business, 382–83
Myntti, Cynthia, 41–42
Myth: family, 83; personal, 83. See also Culture, as fantasy
Myxomatosis, 193

Nardi, Bonnie, 227
Nash, June, 38, 43
Nasopharyngeal carcinoma, 200
National League of Nursing, 175
National Science Foundation, 270
Nations, Marilyn, 287–88, 300
Natural fertility, 341
Natural selection, 188, 192, 194–95
Nature-culture distinction, 54, 69, 150, 164, 166
Navaho medicine, 12, 22
Navaho, 14
Navarro, Vincente, 44
Ndembu (Zambia), 18, 20
Needham, Rodney, 61
Nepal, 284
Nerves, 70
Net reproduction rate, 344
Nettles, 154
Neu, Jerome, 22
Neurosis, 87
New Guinea, 198; medicinal plants of, 154, 156
New Zealand, 151, 254, 258
Ngokwey, Ndolamb, 239
Nicaragua, 43–44, 380
Nigeria, 39, 136, 212; Yoruba healers, 363
Nonhuman primates, feeding ecology of, 151
Normality, concept of, 305
North Yemen, 41–42
Nuclear war, 382
Nursing, anthropologist's role in, 178, 185; concept of caring in, 181–82, 184; cross-cultural courses in, 177; cultural assessment models in, 180; cultural content in, 175, 179–80; definition of, 175; explanatory models in, 177; and gender, 183–84; methodology in, 175–76, 182–83; orientations in, 175; socialization in, 178; theory in, 180; use of ethnographic research in, 182; vocabulary in, 184. See also Professional socialization
Nursing organizations, 175
Nursing research, funding for, 185
Nutrition, 40; and disease, 200, 376

Oakley, Ann, 218
Object relations, 77
Occupational health, 29, 37–38, 201
Oceania, 233
Oedipus complex, 77
Ojibway (Canada), 123
Onoge, Omafume, 30–31, 43
Opler, Morris, 144–47
Oral rehydration therapy, 280, 287, 368, 387–88
Ornstein, R. E., 54
Osteopathy, 166
"Other," 31, 34, 42

Paiute, 117
Paleopathology, 194
Pandemic, definition of, 206
Papua New Guinea, 241
Parasitism, 194, 372, 383–84
Partridge, William, 237
Patient culture, 103
Patient-practitioner relationship, 130
Patterson, C. H., 23
Paul, Benjamin, 96
Pearlin, Leonard, 254
Personality organization, and culture, 82
Personhood, 56–58, 70
Peru, 221; alcohol use in, 231, 239
Petchesky, Rosalind, 220
Pharmaceuticals, 35, 41; drug interactions with indigenous medicines, 158; introduction to Third World, 158
Pharmacology, and indigenous healers, 352
Phenomenology, 46, 48–50, 134–35
Philippine Republic, 117
Physician, symbolic world of, 163
Physiology, 184
Pibloqtok, 141
Placebo effect, 23, 148
Plant taxonomy, 149–50. *See also* Ethnopharmacology
Plants, sacred, 235–38. *See also* Hallucinogens; Medicinal plants
Political economy: history in anthropology, 26; and ideology, 28; methodology in, 27–28, 37
Political repression, health effects of, 379

Pollution, 201
Polynesia, 258
Population: Boserupian view of, 320; Darwinian theory of, 322, 346; definition of, 325; growth of, 319, 342, 385–86; Malthusian view of, 320; and mortality, 194; policy, 345
Population events, 328–29, 334
Positivism, 47
Posttraumatic stress disorder, 166, 170, 261
Power relations, 26–27; and sickness, 30, 37, 167
Praxis, in medical anthropology, 33, 45, 98
Pregnancy: among adolescents, 314–16; conjugal relations during, 219; cultural construction of, 219; medicalization of, 13, 168, 221; social support in, 219, 222. *See also* Childbirth
Premenstrual syndrome (PMS), 12, 67, 168–69
Prescriptive theory, 104–5; in nursing, 176–77
Primary health care, 40, 44; maldistribution of, 167; medicinal plants in, 157; programs in, 386–87
Prince, Raymond, 20–21
Profession, definition of, 8, 349–50
Professional associations: of African healers, 356; in Anglophone countries, 350; Third World examples of, 364; in Zimbabwe, 362
Professional knowledge, 362–63
Professional socialization, 178
Professionalization: and associations, 356; of healers, 7, 350–53, 389; in medicine, 7, 349; and pharmacology, 352; and regulations, 354; of Yoruba healers, 363
Projective techniques, 81, 127
Pronatalism, 218–19
Psychiatry, domain of, 135, 140; history of, 168
Psychoanalysis, 22, 52, 132; factions in, 74
Psychoanalytic anthropology, 3, 74; history of, 74; methodology in, 81

Psychoanalytic drive theory, 84
Psychological anthropology, literature in, 78
Psychological defenses, 84
Psychopathology, 90
Psychosis, 87
Psychosomatic illness, 201
Psychosomatic medicine, 52. *See also* Psychoanalysis; Psychotherapy
Psychotherapy, 16–17; and religious healing, 24. *See also* Psychoanalysis
Public health programs, and ecology, 188
Public health service, 93
Pulse, in diagnosis, 12

Qollahuaya (Bolivia), 62

Rapid Assessment Procedures manual (Scrimshaw and Hurtado), 294
Rapid ethnographic assessment, 291–93
Rapp, Rayna, 228, 277
Read, Kenneth, 58
Reflexivity, 75
Refugees: and disease, 378; and mental health, 261
Reproduction: control of, 68; cultural patterning of, 215; and decision models, 225–26; definitions of, 216; ethnography in, 217; and images of women, 162, 168; and menopause, 161, 167; physiology of, 216; theories of, 61
Reproductive goals, 220
Reproductive health, 36, 215, 221. *See also* Gender
Reproductive technology, 162, 228
Resistance resources, 250, 255, 258, 265. *See also* Stressors
Resource access hypothesis, 323, 326, 333
Rockefeller Foundation, 371, 385
Rorschach inkblots, 81
Rosaldo, Michelle, 219
Rothman, Barbara, 228
Russia, 355

Sacks, Oliver, 159
Saffron, 154–55
Sampling, 280–82

Sander, Fred, 84
Sanders, David, 378
Sapir, Edward, 82
Sardinia, 196–97, 377
Sargent, Carolyn, 220, 279–80
Schaefer, James, 246
Schall, J., 197
Scheff, Thomas, 24
Scheper-Hughes, Nancy, 36, 169
Schistosomiasis, 208, 210–11, 383
School phobias, 67, 168
Science, culture of, 48
Scotch, Norman, 94
Scott, Robert, 250–51
Scrimshaw, Susan, 281–82, 292–93
Scull, Andrew, 168
Self-medication, 354
Selye, Hans, 23, 250
Semantic illness networks, 165
Sex ratio, 326
Shamanism, 15, 18, 84, 127, 133, 144–48, 277
Shiloh, Ailon, 97–98
Sick role, 112, 137
Sickle-cell trait, 199
Sickness: etiology of, 58, 115–16, 130, 136; as punishment, 117; structural determinants of, 30, 32, 36, 38, 44, 167–69. *See also* Disease
Sierra Leone, 197
Singer, Merrill, 36, 42, 45, 243
Social action therapy, 99. *See also* Clinically applied anthropology
Social class: and health, 384; in medical anthropology, 29. *See also* Health, and capitalism
Social disorganization hypothesis, 254
Social organization, 256
Social structure, 256
Social support, 6, 256–57; crosscultural variability in, 265; and hypertension, 258; perceptions of, 260; in relationship to disease, 258
Sociobiology, 86
Socioculturalism, 29–30, 36
Sorcery, 117
Soybeans, 152
Spindler, George, 78

Spirit possession, 36, 59
Sri Lanka, 194
Stationary populations, 344. *See also* Demography
Stein, Howard, 85–86, 100, 102–3
Steiner, R., 111
Stress, 6, 38, 82, 248; and acculturation, 261–62; biopsychosocial model of, 249; and coping style, 259; and culture change, 248; definition of, 249–50; and depression, 254; and life-style incongruity, 254–55, 264; materialist understanding of, 265; and social support, 255, 258; and schizophrenia, 253; theoretical approach to, 267; theories of, 251
Stressors: chronic, 260, 264; content of, 249, 250, 252; cultural variation in, 249; life events as, 254; migration as, 261, 266, 379
Strug, David, 243
Substance use, 230–31
Sudan, 39–40, 212; cash cropping in, 378; effects of war on health, 380
Support groups, 129
Surgery, metaphoric meaning in, 23
Susto, 130
Suzuki, D. T., 56
Symbols: cultural variation in, 89; in dreams, 77; healing, 11; of human body, 62; psychopathological expression in, 89

Taiwan, 277
Tanzania, 39–40, 197
Taussig, Michael, 40, 42, 97–98, 167–68
Technolgy, and healing, 13
Thailand, 128, 245, 280–81
Theory: in medical anthropology, 36, 184; functionalist, 116; in nursing, 176–77
Therapeutic anthropology, 97
Therapeutic efficacy, 16–17; and discursive-presentational form 21–22. *See also* Efficacy
Therapeutic encounter, 277. *See also* Health care practitioners
Therapeutic narratives, 124

Therapeutic process: definition of, 11–12, 17; and outcome, 15–16, 18; as political, 18
Therapy, definition of, 12
Therapy management group, 17–19, 124
Third World: definition of, 369–70; health problems in, 372, 376; medical professionalism in, 360–61, 364–65. *See also* Development
Thompson, E. P., 63
Thyroid cancer, 202
Tobacco, 232–33, 309–10
Total fertility rate, 331
Trachoma, 202
Transcultural Nursing Society, 175
Transference, 76–77
Trevthan, W., 277
Tuberculosis, 300
Turner, Victor, 18, 20
Turshen, Meredith, 39
Type A behavior, 263, 266

Unconscious, 75, 82
Underdevelopment, 27–29; and health, 34, 38, 211, 369. *See also* International health
UNICEF, 351, 387–89
United States of America: childbearing in, 228, 277–78; drug research in, 233, 238; drug use in, 235–36; medical professionalism in, 356–57; studies of stress in, 253–54, 260
Urbanization, health effects of, 379
USAID (U.S. Agency for International Development), 269, 367–68, 371, 387
USSR, 355

Van der Geest, Sjaak, 41
Variable, definition of, 273
Vignettes, in nursing research, 182
Villerme, Louis, 299–300
Violence, health effects of, 379
Virchow, Rudolf, 32, 300
Voodoo death, 23, 201

Waitzkin, Howard, 167
Waorani (Ecuador), 152
War, health effects of, 379–81

Water supplies, 378
Water-borne diseases, 378
Wegrocki, Henry, 139
Weibel-Orlando, Joan, 245
Weidman, Hazel, 96
Welch, M. C., 280
Wenner-Gren Foundation, 270
Werner, David, 387
West Africa, 199, 202
West Indies, 253
Westermeyer, Joseph, 245
Western Samoa, 227
Whorfian hypothesis, 88
Wiesenfeld, S. L., 199
Winnicot, David, 57

Wolf, S., 260
Women, and health care, 45, 127, 162, 215, 221. *See also* Gender
World Health Organization (WHO), 244, 269, 360–61, 364–65, 367–68, 371, 387
World system, 27, 32, 34, 39, 41–42

Yoruba (Nigeria), 363. *See also* Medicinal plants
Young, Alan, 32, 38, 41, 165
Young, James, 285–86

Zaire, 123–24, 239
Zimbabwe, 365, 380

THE CONTRIBUTORS

LINDA A. BENNETT is professor of anthropology at Memphis State University; she received her Ph.D. in anthropology from American University. As a research faculty member in the Department of Psychiatry and Behavioral Sciences, George Washington University Medical Center, she conducted more than a decade of research on family culture and the intergenerational transmission of alcoholism and other pathology. She has carried out a series of alcohol studies in Yugoslavia in the areas of treatment, alcoholism and depression, and the temperance movement.

PETER J. BROWN is associate professor and chair of the Department of Anthropology, Emory University, Atlanta. He holds a joint appointment with the Division of Public Health in the Emory University School of Medicine. His doctoral research, completed at the State University of New York at Stony Brook, concerned the impact of malaria and its eradication in Sardinia, Italy. His research interests include the impact of diseases on cultural and genetic evolution, theory in medical anthropology, and the social history of obesity.

CAROLE H. BROWNER is associate professor in the Departments of Psychiatry and Biobehavioral Sciences, and Anthropology at the University of California, Los Angeles. She received a Ph.D. in anthropology from the University of California, Berkeley, and an M.P.H. in health administration and planning from the same institution. She has conducted fieldwork in Colombia and Mexico on the relationship between socioeconomic development and women's roles and their health. She is currently engaged in research on prenatal diagnostic testing and the considerations Mexican-American and non-Hispanic white pregnant women in California take into account when making decisions about its use.

NOEL J. CHRISMAN is professor in the Department of Community Health Care Systems, School of Nursing, University of Washington, with adjunct appointments in anthropology and family medicine. He received his Ph.D. in anthropology and an M.P.H. from the

University of California, Berkeley. His research interests include ethnicity, social networks, and voluntary associations as elements in urban adaptation; the relationships of health beliefs and social networks with health care seeking; American health beliefs; the role of community organization interventions in cancer prevention; and application of anthropological knowledge in clinical settings.

PAUL W. COOK, JR., received his M.A. in anthropology in 1989 from Memphis State University. He studied medical anthropology, with an emphasis on drug research and mental health. During his graduate work, he conducted research at Northeast Community Mental Health Center, the Memphis city school system, and the Veterans Administration in Memphis.

THOMAS J. CSORDAS received his B.A. in anthropology from the Ohio State University and his Ph.D. from Duke University. He is associate professor of anthropology at Case Western Reserve University. Dr. Csordas has conducted research among Catholic charismatics and Navaho Indians, and his interests include psychological and psychiatric anthropology, comparative religion, phenomenology of bodily experience, and rhetorical dimensions of language use.

MOLLY DOUGHERTY, professor and research coordinator in the College of Nursing at the University of Florida, is also an adjunct professor in the Department of Anthropology. She received her nursing degrees and Ph.D. in anthropology from the University of Florida. While she maintains an interest in the interface between nursing and anthropology, her research and clinical activities are in women's health, and her National Institutes of Health–funded research is on the behavioral management of urinary dysfunctions in aging women.

WILLIAM W. DRESSLER is associate professor of behavioral and community medicine, University of Alabama School of Medicine-Tuscaloosa Program, and adjunct associate professor of anthropology, the University of Alabama. He received his Ph.D. in the medical anthropology program at the University of Connecticut. He has conducted research on social factors and cardiovascular disease in the Caribbean, Mexico, Brazil, and the southern United States and on mental health and health behavior in the Puerto Rican community in the northeastern United States, and in the rural South. Currently he is developing a study of cardiovascular disease risk factors comparing Brazil and the United States and is beginning a study of social class and cardiovascular disease in Great Britain.

NINA L. ETKIN is associate professor of anthropology at the University of Hawaii, Manoa. She received the B.A. in zoology from Indiana University and the M.A. and Ph.D. in biological anthropology from Washington University, St. Louis. Her research interests include indigenous medicine, ethnopharmacology, nutrition, and human variation and adaptations to infectious diseases.

W. PENN HANDWERKER is professor of anthropology at Humboldt State University on California's north coast. He received his Ph.D. from the University of Oregon and has conducted field research in West Africa and the West Indies on various aspects of human population ecology, especially the political economy of development. Currently he is in the midst of a comparative study of economic development, social change, and fertility decline on the Caribbean islands of Barbados, Antigua, and St. Lucia.

The Contributors

MICHAEL R. HASS has an M.A. in psychology from California State University, Northridge, and is a candidate for the doctorate in social science at the University of California, Irvine. In addition to coordinating a program for disturbed adolescents, he is conducting research on the social and cultural dimensions of tuberculosis among Mexican immigrants in southern California.

CHARLES C. HUGHES is professor, Department of Family and Community Medicine, and professor, Department of Anthropology at the University of Utah; he is also director of the M.S.P.H. program at the University of Utah Medical School. He received his Ph.D. from Cornell University. His research interests include psychiatric issues in medical anthropology. He is currently involved in an analysis of the life history of an Eskimo shaman.

MARCIA C. INHORN is a Ph.D. candidate in the Department of Anthropology at the University of California, Berkeley. She is a graduate of the University of Wisconsin and holds an M.P.H. degree from the University of California, Berkeley. Her field research in Egypt concerns the biocultural causes and consequences of infertility in Egyptian women. Her previous publications have dealt with genital chlamydia infections and the ethno-ophthalmology of trachoma in the Middle East.

ARTHUR KLEINMAN is professor of anthropology and psychiatry at Harvard Medical School and the Faculty of Arts and Sciences, Harvard University. Educated at Stanford and Harvard Universities, he has conducted medical anthropological research in Taiwan, China, and the United States. He received the Wellcome Medal for Medical Anthropology from the Royal Anthropological Institute of Great Britain and Ireland and is a member of the Institute of Medicine, National Academy of Sciences. He is the author of numerous books and articles.

SANDRA D. LANE is program officer for reproductive health in the Middle East, Ford Foundation, Cairo office. She received the Ph.D. from the joint program in medical anthropology, University of California at San Francisco and Berkeley. She also earned a M.P.H. degree from the School of Public Health of the University of California, Berkeley, and has been a registered nurse with a specialty in pediatrics since 1972. Her research and teaching interests are in nutrition, infectious disease, maternal and child health, and the Middle East. She has conducted fieldwork in Liberia, Egypt, and the Middle East.

MURRAY LAST teaches medical anthropology and the ethnography of West Africa at University College London. He received his M.A. degree from Yale University and his Ph.D. from the University of Ibadan, in history. He is the editor of the International African Institute's journal *Africa*. He has conducted twelve years of fieldwork in Nigeria and is completing research on non-Muslim Hausa medicine and culture.

MARGARET LOCK, professor of medical anthropology at McGill University, received her Ph.D. in anthropology from the University of California, Berkeley. Together with Allan Young she coedits the Kluwer book series Culture, Illness and Healing and is a Sigma Xi national lecturer. Her research interests are in the anthropology of the body, life-cycle transitions, and culture and technomedicine. She is the author and editor of numerous articles and books.

SOHEIR MORSY is visiting Associate professor of anthropology at the University of California, Berkeley. She received her B.S. in bacteriology from Florida State University and her Ph.D. in anthropology from Michigan State University. She has taught anthropology at Michigan State University and at the American University in Cairo. Her research interests include health, women and work, and women's reproductive health. She is currently participating on a national study of women and work in Egypt.

GRETEL H. PELTO received her Ph.D. in anthropology from the University of Minnesota. She is currently professor of nutritional sciences and anthropology at the University of Connecticut. Dr. Pelto has conducted research in Mexico, the United States, and Finland, and her research interests include infant and maternal nutrition, dietary change, and research methods in primary care.

PERTTI J. PELTO received his Ph.D. in anthropology from the University of California, Berkeley. He is currently professor of anthropology and community medicine at the University of Connecticut. He has conducted research in Finnish Lapland, rural Mexico, and in rural and urban United States. His interests include research methodology, primary health care in underserved areas, and the impact of technological change and modernization.

LORNA AMARASINGHAM RHODES obtained her Ph.D. in anthropology from Cornell University. She has done research in South Asia and in the United States, where she is interested in psychiatric institutions and practice. She teaches at the University of Washington, Seattle.

ROBERT A. RUBINSTEIN is associate researcher at the Francis I. Proctor Foundation for Research in Ophthalmology, University of California, San Francisco. He received his Ph.D. in anthropology from the State University of New York at Binghamton. He also earned a master's degree in public health from the School of Public Health, University of Illinois. His research and teaching interests are in the area of medical anthropology and the anthropology of peace and international security. He has conducted fieldwork in Central America, urban United States, and Cairo, Egypt. He is currently researching trachoma control in Egypt.

ARTHUR J. RUBEL is professor, Department of Family Medicine and professor, Department of Anthropology, at the University of California, Irvine. He received his Ph.D. from the University of North Carolina, Chapel Hill. His research interests include ethnomedicine, social organization, and the epidemiology of folk illness. He has done research in Mexico, along the U.S.-Mexico border, and in the Republic of the Philippines. He is currently involved in a study of tuberculosis in Mexico and southern California.

NANCY SCHEPER-HUGHES is professor of anthropology, University of California, Berkeley, and received her Ph.D. in anthropology from the same institution. She is the author of numerous publications and was awarded the Margaret Mead Award for her book, *Saints, Scholars and Schizophrenics: Mental Illness in Rural Ireland*. Her research interests include critical perspectives on medicine and psychiatry, the social production of illness, and problems in child survival worldwide. She is currently engaged in research on survival strategies of women in a shantytown of northeastern Brazil.

The Contributors

HOWARD F. STEIN, a medical anthropologist, psychoanalytic anthropologist, and psychohistorian, is Professor of family medicine at the University of Oklahoma Health Sciences Center. He received his Ph.D. from the University of Pittsburgh. He also serves as Balint group coordinator with the Oklahoma City program and is director of behavioral science teaching at the Enid Family Medicine Clinic. From 1980 to 1988, he edited the *Journal of Psychoanalytic Anthropology*, and he has authored 130 scholarly and clinical papers.

TONI TRIPP-REIMER, R.N., F.A.A.N., is professor and director of the Office for Nursing Research Development and Utilization at the University of Iowa. She received a Ph.D. in anthropology from Ohio State University. Her focal area of research is the relationship among ethnicity, health behaviors, and aging.

WILLIAM R. TRUE is associate professor of community health at the Center for Health Services Education and Research at St. Louis University Medical Center and associate professor of anthropology in psychiatry in the School of Medicine. He is also research anthropologist in the research service of the St. Louis Veterans Administration Medical Center. He has a Ph.D. in anthropology from the University of Florida and an M.P.H. in epidemiology from the University of North Carolina in Chapel Hill. He is particularly interested in posttraumatic stress disorder. He is just beginning to participate in a study of the genetics of drug abuse with colleagues from Harvard University, Boston University, the University of Illinois, the Medical College of Virginia, and Washington University.

THE EDITORS

THOMAS M. JOHNSON is clinical associate professor of family practice and psychiatry at the University of Texas Health Sciences Center–Dallas. He received his Ph.D. in anthropology from the University of Florida and an M.A. in clinical psychology from Southern Methodist University. As an applied medical anthropologist who has worked for the past fifteen years in community mental health and medical school settings, he has emphasized teaching in clinical settings, including supervision of medical students and residents in obstetrics and gynecology, internal medicine, psychiatry, and family medicine.

CAROLYN F. SARGENT is associate professor of anthropology at Southern Methodist University. She received an M.A. from the University of Manchester, England, where she studied as a Marshall Scholar, and a Ph.D. in anthropology from Michigan State University. She has conducted fieldwork in West Africa, Jamaica, and Dallas, Texas, and her research interests include women's reproductive health, gender and child health, and the Khmer refugee experience in Dallas.

GN
296
M4.23
1990

Medical anthropology:
a handbook of theory
and method.

**NORMANDALE
COMMUNITY COLLEGE**
9700 France Avenue South
Bloomington, Minnesota 55431